S

POLITICAL PARTIES OF THE AMERICAS

The Greenwood Historical Encyclopedia of the World's Political Parties

A five-volume reference guide to the world's significant political parties from the beginnings of the party system in eighteenth-century England to the present. Each volume provides concise histories of the political parties of a region and attempts to detail the evolution of ideology, changes in organization, membership, and leadership, and each party's impact upon society.

The Greenwood Historical Encyclopedia of the World's Political Parties

POLITICAL PARTIES OF THE AMERICAS

Canada, Latin America, and the West Indies

Anguilla–Grenada

Edited by Robert J. Alexander

GREENWOOD PRESS
Westport, Connecticut · London, England

Library of Congress Cataloging in Publication Data
Main entry under title:

Political parties of the Americas.

(The Greenwood historical encyclopedia of the world's
political parties)
Bibliography: p.
Includes index.
Contents: [1] Anguilla-Grenada—[2] Guadeloupe-
Virgin Islands of the United States.
1. Political parties—Canada. 2. Political parties—
Latin America. 3. Political parties—West Indies.
I. Alexander, Robert Jackson, 1918-   . II. Series.
JL195.P64   324.2'098   81-6952
ISBN 0-313-21474-3 (lib. bdg. : set)
ISBN 0-313-23753-0 (lib. bdg. v. 1)
ISBN 0-313-23754-9 (lib. bdg. v. 2)

Library of Congress Catalog Card Number: 81-6952
ISBN: 0-313-21474-3 (set)
ISBN: 0-313-23753-0 (vol. 1)
ISBN: 0-313-23754-9 (vol. 2)

First published in 1982

Greenwood Press
A division of Congressional Information Service, Inc.
88 Post Road West, Westport, Connecticut 06881

Printed in the United States of America

10 9 8 7 6 5 4 3 2 1

To Jay Lovestone

CONTENTS

PREFACE

When Marilyn Brownstein wrote me two years or so ago to inquire whether I could recommend someone to edit a volume on political parties of the Americas, I had the temerity to recommend myself. At least from my point of view, that recommendation—which was accepted—has been a happy one. Choosing a group of contributors, working out problems of style and pattern for the contributions, trying to make sure that every nation and territory and every party of any significance within each of these was dealt with, have been challenges which I have found enjoyable to meet.

I have learned much in putting together this volume. First of all, of course, I have gotten to know a great deal more than I knew before about the subject matter with which we have been dealing. But in addition, I have learned considerably more about the contributors than I knew when I started. I have become conscious of the great differences which are possible in the interpretation of a deadline for submission of material. I have learned, sometimes with some difficulty, how to compromise the rather different views of some of the contributors—and of the publisher's editors—as to how to deal with the material at hand.

The contributors have been chosen on the basis of their familiarity with the political parties of their respective countries, rather than because of their formal affiliation with one or another intellectual discipline. Thus, although most of the writers are either historians or political scientists, we also have economists, geographers, anthropologists, and even students of literature among their number. Also, although all of them are residents of the United States, they include a Peruvian, a Guyanese, a Haitian, and two Cubans, as well as natives of this country.

The volume which our contributors have produced is one, I trust, of which they and the publisher can be proud. It is certainly unique in the breadth of its coverage, dealing as it does with every party of any importance in every nation and territory in the Western Hemisphere except the United States. Much of the work is original, being the first overall presentation for many of the countries of the parties of past and present, to appear in any language. Even in countries about whose parties a good deal has been written, there has seldom if ever been such detailed and complete treatment as can be found in these pages.

The work has been organized along broad lines of similarity insofar as each country entry is concerned. In each case, the discussion of the individual parties is preceded by a more general essay giving the reader basic facts on the area, including enough political history to make the discussion of the individual parties meaningful.

However, the reader will find considerable diversity in the various contributions in the manner in which the nations and territories are treated, and the emphasis that is given to one or another aspect of political life and the political parties. Some contributors have given more attention than others to party programs, some to the nature of the electorate and political actors, some to individual leaders, some to groups represented by the parties. To some degree, these differences are determined by the nature of the political systems and parties dealt with; in some instances, they reflect the proclivities of the writers. The editor's theory in this regard has been that (within the broad outlines agreed upon) the contributors knew best how to organize and present the material that was their responsibility.

There have been certain general rules that have governed the development of this volume. However, since it is my firm belief that rules exist (among other reasons) to have exceptions made to them, some exceptions occur. For example, although in almost all cases, discussions of individual parties are to be found under the English-language version of their names, this is not the case with two parties in French Canada, which are discussed under their French names, since this is the way they are universally known in Canada and everywhere else. Similarly, although coalitions are generally not dealt with as political parties (since they consist of several parties) there are a few cases in which coalitions are separately listed because for a longer or shorter period of time they function virtually as political parties.

It has generally been left up to the contributors to determine how to translate the names of individual parties into English. Again, they know best. In addition, there are some instances in which generally recognized translations exist which may not be the same as those used for those names (in Spanish) in some other country.

For the sake of a certain uniformity in the volume, the Spanish and Portuguese words "Democrata" and "Democratico" have usually been translated "Democratic." This rule originates, perhaps, in the editor's revulsion against the propensity of Senator Joseph McCarthy to talk about "the Democrat party" as a means of disparaging his opponents. However, even here, an exception is made in the Mexican entry, where the use of both "Democrat" and "Democratic" is required by the material itself.

Each of the contributions includes a bibliography. These listings generally include books, articles, and other material dealing specifically with the country involved. In addition to these, there have been various publications which have been used by all or most of the contributors for at least parts of their entries, and rather than repeat these in each entry, it seems better to give them a separate listing here. The publications involved are:

Facts on File, New York, N.Y.

Keesing's Contemporary Archives, Longman Group, London

Latin America Political Report, Latin American Newsletters, London
Political Handbook of the World, Council on Foreign Relations, New York, N.Y.
Statesman's Yearbook, Macmillan & Co., London; St. Martin's Press, New York,
N.Y.
Yearbook of International Communist Affairs, Hoover Institution, Stanford, Calif.

In some instances, there is little printed data available, and the contributors have relied principally, or at least in part, on their personal knowledge of the country or territory involved. In those cases, there is an entry in the bibliography, "Personal contacts of the writer."

This volume owes much to many. Only a few of the debts can be acknowledged. First, I must mention the contributors, who put up without much complaint to my many suggestions and my badgering them to meet deadlines, and for whom the work embodied herein was much more a labor of love than one for remuneration.

Second, I must thank both Marilyn Brownstein, Acquisitions Editor, and Cynthia Harris, Reference Books Editor, of Greenwood Press, who, although by no means always agreeing with me upon all issues that arose, were patient, tolerant, and encouraging throughout. Also, thanks must go to Janet Brown, copy editor, and Louise Hatem, production editor, of Greenwood Press, who were in charge of the in-house editing, once the manuscript arrived at the publisher.

Finally, I must as always thank my wife Joan for putting up with all of the typing and other distractions which were part of putting together this work. Her tolerance and encouragement have been essential.

Rutgers University
New Brunswick, N.J.
December 1981

ABOUT THE EDITOR AND CONTRIBUTORS

Robert J. Alexander received his B.A., M.A., and Ph.D. degrees from Columbia University, and has been teaching economics, political science, and history at Rutgers University since 1947. He is the author of several books on Latin America, including an earlier monograph on the political parties of the area, and studies of Communism and Trotskyism in the region.

Marvin Alisky, Professor of Political Science at Arizona State University, founded the ASU Center for Latin-American Studies and directed it for seven years. He is the author of *Latin American Media, Peruvian Political Perspective, Historical Dictionary of Mexico, The Foreign Press, Uruguay, Governors of Mexico, Who's Who in Mexican Government,* and author or coauthor of nine other books and monographs and two hundred magazine articles. He was Fulbright professor in Peru and in Nicaragua, and the U.S. delegate to UNESCO in Ecuador. He has taught at Indiana University and the University of California at Irvine, and was a research scholar at Princeton and Stanford. He has lectured for the International Communications Agency and been an NBC network news correspondent throughout Latin America.

Charles D. Ameringer received his Ph.D. degree from the Fletcher School of Law and Diplomacy. He is the author of *The Democratic Left in Exile: The Antidictatorial Struggle in the Caribbean, 1945–1959* and *Don Pepe: A Political Biography of Jose Figueres of Costa Rica,* and has contributed to numerous professional journals. He was the founder and first president of the Middle Atlantic Council on Latin American Studies. Dr. Ameringer is Professor of Latin American History at the Pennsylvania State University.

David Eugene Blank, Professor of Political Science at the University of Louisville, has published several books and monographs on Venezuela. His interest in Ecuador dates from 1976, when he led a sister-city mission from Louisville to Quito. He is presently working on several monographs for the Hoover Institution on Venezuela and on U.S.-Latin-American Relations in the 1980s. He maintains an interest in Ecuador's politics as part of his continuing research on the democratic projection of the Andean Pact.

Eugenio Chang-Rodríguez is Professor of Romance Languages at Queens College of the City University of New York and Professor *honoris causa* at the National University of San Marcos of his native Peru. He formerly taught at the University of Pennsylvania. He is editor of the *Boletín* of the North American Academy of the Spanish Language, editorial board member of *Bilingual Review, Caribe,* and *Revista Hispanica Moderna,* Chairman of the Steering Committee of the Consortium of Latin-American Studies Programs, Director of the International League for Human Rights, and member of the New York Academy of Sciences. He was President of the International Linguistics Association, Chairman of the Columbia University Seminar on Latin America, Associate Editor of *Hispania,* and member of the Joint Committee on Latin-American Studies of the Social Science Research Council and Council of Learned Societies. He has a Ph.D. from the University of Washington and an honorary doctorate from the National University Federico Villareal of Lima, Peru. He has authored, coauthored and edited twelve books, including *La literatura politica de Haya y Mariategui, The Hemisphere's Present Crisis, Frequency Dictionary of Spanish Words, Continuing Spanish, The Lingering Crisis,* and *Collins Spanish Dictionary.*

Harold D. Clarke received his Ph.D. from Duke University in 1970 and is Professor of Political Science and Head of Department at Virginia Polytechnic Institute and State University. He is the author (with Jane Jenson, Lawrence LeDuc, and Jon Pammett) of *Political Choice in Canada,* coauthor of *Citizen Politicians—Canada;* and coauthor and editor of *Parliament, Policy and Representation.* Articles by him have appeared in the *Journal of Politics, American Journal of Political Science,* the *British Journal of Political Science, Comparative Political Studies, Canadian Journal of Political Science, Canadian Review of Sociology and Anthropology,* and other professional journals.

John T. Deiner is Associate Professor of Political Science and Coordinator of the Latin-American Studies Program at the University of Delaware. He has traveled widely in Latin America, and has published a number of articles on Argentine politics, Eva Peron, the politics of the Catholic Church in Latin America, and guerrillas. Dr. Deiner is the author of a manual, *Politics in Developing Nations.* He has also written about the use of simulations in teaching, and has created and directed several simulations of the politics of Latin-American nations.

The late Vera Green, ex-Director of the Rutgers University Latin-American Institute, was an Associate Professor of Anthropology at Livingston College, Rutgers University. She is the author of *Migrants in Aruba: Interethnic Integration,* coeditor of *International Human Rights: Contemporary Perspectives,* with Jack Nelson, and author of various articles, including "The Black Extended Family in the United States: Some Research Suggestions," "Racial vs. Ethnic Factors in Afro-American and Afro-Caribbean Migration," "Methodological Problems Involved in the Study of the Aruban Family," which have appeared in several journals. Dr. Green was a member of the Executive Committee of the American Anthropological Association. She served on the Executive Board of the Society for Applied Anthropology and was the first president of the Association of Black Anthropologists. In addition to the Ph.D. degree from Arizona in Anthropology and the M.A. degree in Anthropology from Columbia University, Dr. Green held a UNESCO/OAS title of Fundamental Educator. Dr. Green died in February 1982.

C. Michael Henry was born in Guyana. He received his higher education in the United States, obtaining a Ph.D. degree in economics from Rutgers University. He has taught at the State University College at Brockport, N.Y., and is currently at Atlanta University. He has a forthcoming book on innovation in peasant agriculture in developing countries.

Allan Kornberg received his Ph.D. from the University of Michigan and is Professor of Political Science at Duke University. He is a member of the Political Science Committee of the National Science Foundation, Chairman of the Legislative Specialists Committee of the International Political Science Association, and former Chairman of the Executive Committee of the Consortium for Comparative Legislative Studies. He is the author of *Canadian Legislative Behavior;* coauthor and editor of *Legislatures in Developmental Perspective* and of *Legislatures in Comparative Perspective;* author (with William Mishler) of *Influence in Parliament: Canada;* and author (with Joel Smith and Harold Clarke) of *Citizen Politicians— Canada.* Articles by him have appeared in the *American Political Science Review,* the *British Journal of Political Science, Canadian Review of Sociology and Anthropology, Comparative Political Studies,* the *Journal of Politics, Canadian Journal of Political Science, Sociology, Social Forces, Simulation and Games,* the *Western Political Quarterly, Parliamentary Affairs, American Journal of Political Science,* and other professional journals.

Sheldon B. Liss, Professor of Latin-American History and Government at the University of Akron, specializes in Inter-American relations and Latin-American political and social thought. His published works include: *Diplomacy and Dependency: Venezuela, The United States and the Americas; Man, State and Society in Latin-American History* (with P. K. Liss); *The Canal: Aspects of United States– Panamanian Relations;* and *A Century of Disagreement: The Chamizal Conflict,* 1864–1964. He is currently writing a history of socialist thought in Latin America.

Ronald H. McDonald is Professor of Political Science at the Maxwell School, Syracuse University. His specialization is political parties, electoral behavior, and public opinion in Latin America. He is author of *Party Systems and Elections in Latin America,* and has contributed chapters to *Faction Politics, Latin-American Legislatures, Latin-American Politics and Development,* and other books. He has published articles in the *American Journal of Political Science,* the *Journal of Politics,* the *Western Political Quarterly, Inter-American Economic Affairs,* and other journals. He was awarded a Fulbright Lectureship in 1980 for the National University, Montevideo, Uruguay.

Christopher Mitchell is Associate Professor of Politics and Director of the

Center for Latin-American and Caribbean Studies at New York University. Educated at Harvard University (B.A. 1966, Ph.D. 1971), Dr. Mitchell specializes in Andean and Caribbean politics, and in Western Hemispheric international relations. He is the author of *The Legacy of Populism in Bolivia: From the MNR to Military Rule*, and a number of articles on Latin-American and inter-American themes. Dr. Mitchell has received research grants from the Foreign Area Fellowship Program, the National Science Foundation, and the Council on Foreign Relations.

James A. Morris served as a Peace Corps Volunteer in the Dominican Republic from 1962 to 1964, and was a Latin-American Teaching Fellow in Colombia, Uruguay, and Honduras from 1971 to 1973. He received his degree in political science from the University of New Mexico in 1974, and has taught at several universities in the southwestern United States. His publications include "Corporatism and Dependent Development: A Honduras Case Study," *Latin American Research Review* (coauthored with Steve C. Ropp); and "Honduras: A Unique Case?" in *Latin American Politics and Development*, edited by Howard Wiarda and Harvey Kline. Dr. Morris has lectured at the Foreign Service Institute and consulted for the U.S. Department of State. He is currently writing a book on Honduran politics.

Leslie Péan studied economics in France, and received his M.A. degree in economics at Rutgers University in the United States. His articles have appeared in *Collectif Paroles*, a bimonthly published in Canada. He writes on topics pertaining to Haitian emigration, and his current research is on institutional underdevelopment and party politics in Haiti.

Neale J. Pearson is Associate Professor of Political Science at Texas Tech University, Lubbock, Texas. He has published articles on peasant groups and agrarian reform in Brazil, Guatemala, and Honduras as well as an article on "Peasant and Worker Sindicatos and Democracy," which is part of *The Continuing Struggle for Democracy in Latin America*, edited by Howard Wiarda. He is a long-term student of Democratic and Marxist parties in Honduras, Costa Rica, Nicaragua, Chile, and Peru, and his "Nicaragua in Crisis," published in the February 1979 issue of *Current History*, reviewed the development of the opposition to the Somoza dynasty. He has been active in the Democratic party and in Lubbock community affairs, has been an officer of several professional political science and Latin-American Studies associations, and is in charge of legislative liaison for the Tech chapters of the American Association of University Professors and the Texas Association of College Teachers.

Bonham C. Richardson received his Ph.D. degree in geography at the University of Wisconsin at Madison in 1970. He has conducted field and archival research in Guyana, Trinidad, Grenada, Carriacou, Saint-Kitts-Nevis, and Barbados. Dr. Richardson has published a number of journal articles concerning historical and contemporary peasant livelihood behavior in the Caribbean in the *Geographical Review*, *Journal of Developing Areas*, *Journal of Historical Geography*, *Inter-American Economic Affairs*, and others. He has taught at California State College at San

Bernardino, Miami University of Ohio, Rutgers University, and is currently Associate Professor of Geography at Virginia Polytechnic Institute and State University.

Sergio Roca is Associate Professor of Economics at Adelphi University, Garden City, New York. He is the author of *Cuban Economic Policy and Ideology: The Ten Million Ton Sugar Harvest*, "Economic Aspects of Cuban Involvement in Africa," in *Cuban Studies/Estudios Cubanos*, and "Ideology and Development Policy: A Comparison of Mexico and Cuba," in *Interamerican Review/Revista*. Dr. Roca has also written articles on economic planning, housing, and income redistribution in socialist Cuba. His most recent visit to the island was in August 1980.

José M. Sánchez received his Ph.D. from Columbia University, and is at present Associate Professor of Political Studies at Adelphi University in Garden City, New York. He is a Cuban-American scholar. His principal fields of publication and research are United States foreign policy in the Caribbean and political socialization. His current projects include *Hollywood Politics*, a book on the American political system as depicted on film, and an article, "Straining at the Leash," on Cuba's role in the nonaligned movement.

Richard E. Sharpless is an Associate Professor at Lafayette College in Easton, Pennsylvania, where he teaches Latin-American history and American economic and labor history. He is the author of *Gaitan of Colombia*, a biography of the Colombian populist leader, and various articles on Latin-American and United States politics, immigration, and labor. Dr. Sharpless resided in Colombia and Puerto Rico for several years, and has travelled widely throughout Latin America and the Caribbean. He is a member of the Latin-American Studies Association, the Conference on Latin-American History, and other professional organizations.

Jordan Young is Professor of History at Pace University, having been there since 1957. He has also been visiting professor at Columbia University, New York University, and the College of the City of New York. He was first in Brazil during World War II, from 1941 to 1944, originally as a student, then working for the Office of Inter-American Affairs. For two years in the 1950s, he worked for the Chase Manhattan Bank in Brazil; subsequently he has visited the country virtually every year, on one occasion as a Fulbright scholar. He has lectured in various Brazilian universities as well as in the Rio Branco Institute of the Brazilian Foreign Office. His many publications include *The Brazilian Revolution of 1930 and the Aftermath*.

POLITICAL PARTIES
OF THE
AMERICAS

INTRODUCTION

The political parties of the Americas are an extremely varied lot. They reflect the diversity of the nearly four dozen countries and territories that make up the Western Hemisphere. The political units—sovereign nations and dependent territories—whose parties are discussed in this book differ greatly from one another in geography, climate, race, religion, language, and historical experience. The only thing that unites them is that they are in America, and even in that context, the largest unit of all, the United States, is not covered here, since it has been dealt with in *Political Parties and Civic Action Groups* by Edward L. Schapsmeier and Frederick H. Schapsmeier, a part of the Greenwood Encyclopedia of American Institutions. In this introductory essay, we shall try to indicate some of the differences and similarities among the various parts of the hemisphere about which generalizations can be made, and which may serve as a background for the more detailed discussion of the parties of the individual states and territories.

What Is a Political Party?

The starting point is obviously the definition of what a political party really is, at least for our purposes. When is a "party" not a party? There are many political organizations in the countries of the Americas which are not parties as we define them. On the other hand, there are also groups that do not use the word "party" which are included.

Sir Randol Fawkes, leader of one of the organizations dealt with in this book, has suggested a definition for a political party which has a good deal to recommend it. According to Fawkes, "A political party consists of a group of persons united in opinion or action, more or less permanently organized, which attempts to bring about the election of its candidates to public offices and by this means to control or influence the actions and policy of government. Its long-range goal is to put into effect its political, social and economic philosophy." (*Sir Randol Fawkes* [Nassau, 1979], p. 211).

Obviously, not all of the parties of the Americas have operated all the time under circumstances in which elections were the normal or expedient way of influencing or changing governments. To that degree, some modification must be made in Sir Randol's definition. We are also faced with the problem of the

3

ephemeral nature of many organizations which have called themselves parties in these countries. There are many groups which have not lasted long enough to be able to carry out the objectives which Sir Randol's definition would assign to them.

In soliciting contributions for this volume, the editor dealt with the problem of defining a party for inclusion within the book. He wrote contributors that "No hard and fast definition can be made. The decision must be yours for your country, but certain factors should be kept in mind, such as the existence of a formal structure, longevity, size, influence within the political system, external influence, whether it was a precursor of later significant parties, and the prominence of its leaders. Obviously not every group that has called itself a 'party' needs to be covered by this survey." Within this context, we have sought to present at least some discussion of all parties which have had any real significance in the countries and territories of the Western Hemisphere.

Obviously, political parties are a development of the last three centuries. Throughout history there have been political factions: as in ancient Greece and Rome, or in the dynastic struggles of the Middle Ages. However, only with the emergence of some form of parliamentary institution with real power, did the formally organized political party come into existence. The first more or less modern parties emerged in Great Britain in the decades following the Glorious Revolution of 1688. In America, parties emerged first in the United States, during the beginning decade of government under the Constitution.

Insofar as the Western Hemisphere countries dealt with in the present volume are concerned, the appearance of parties was directly related to the struggle for independence. In Ibero-America, sharp differences of opinion and of interest developed among the leaders of the independence movement, differences which shortly afterwards gave rise to the formation of the first parties in almost all of the countries involved. In the territories around and in the Caribbean Sea which were parts of the British and Dutch Empires, and where colonialism has only recently been disappearing, the formation of parties was a function of the development of greater local autonomy (in most cases culminating in independence) and of the struggle of people of color against the privileged position of the more or less white descendants of people from the metropolitan countries. In Canada, too, the growth of the first parties came as a direct result of the granting of internal self-government to the Dominion.

Only in the territories of the French Republic, where psychological, political, and economic association with the metropolitan power has been peculiarly close and the drive for separate nationhood has been relatively weak, is there no observable connection between the emergence of self-government and the growth of political parties. Indeed, in the French territories, most parties are still branches of or are associated with parties in metropolitan France.

Functions of Political Parties in the Americas

In countries and at times when more or less democratic procedures have been the rule, and in which more or less competitive elections played a significant part in determining who would rule and who would sit in legislative bodies, the parties have played a corresponding role. They have agitated and propagandized to present their points of view and their personalities to the voters. They have sought to mobilize their followers to go to the polls. Their elected legislators have functioned more or less cohesively in congresses and parliaments. Their elected chief executives have more or less faithfully carried out the programs which the parties have enunciated.

However, in some countries at some times, parties have had a very different function. In a number of instances, they have had as their principal role that of being instruments of control of a dictatorship. In this capacity, they have sought to mobilize real or fancied support of the populace for the regime in power, while at the same time serving as a coercive tool of that regime. Many examples of parties of this kind could be cited. Certainly, those were the functions of the Partido Dominicano in the Dominican Republic during the tyranny of Generalissimo Rafael Leónidas Trujillo Molina. They are no less the function of the Communist Party of Cuba under Castro, and the New Jewel Movement in Grenada gives indications that it will have these same functions under the revolutionary regime which seized power in that island early in 1979.

In such cases as these, in which a clear dictatorship is in power, the parties involved have had no legal opposition. However, a somewhat different role and function has characterized the party which has been in power in Mexico since 1929. Although governments controlled by that party have not allowed other parties to win any elections on a significant scale, the Mexican system has allowed a variety of other parties to take part in the electoral process, and share ever so modestly in the crumbs of patronage and prestige associated with government in that country. At the same time, the dominant Mexican party has sought to coopt within it virtually all of the most important interest groups in the economy and society, and to serve as an instrument for developing a consensus on public policies and programs.

Other parties have had still different functions. Numerous parties in the Ibero-American countries have been principally instruments for serving the personal political interests of one or another politician. The Unión Nacional Odriísta, composed of the personal supporters of General Manuel Odría in Peru; the various "Velazquista" parties in Ecuador, having as their only purpose to back the aspirations of the many-times President José María Velasco Ibarra; parties organized by Fulgencio Batista in Cuba, are a few examples of this kind of "personalist" party.

Other parties, some of which have existed for long periods of time, have had little real prospect of coming to power in the foreseeable future, but have existed for the purpose of supporting particular political philosophies or particular interest groups. The fascist parties of Chile and Brazil of the 1930s are perhaps such ideological parties. Numerous others, with or without chances of coming to power, have mainly defended the interests of particular classes, religious groups, ethnic elements, or even regions of a country.

Heterogeneity of the Americas

Certainly to begin to understand the political parties of the Americas, one must be aware of the vast differences among the political entities in which these parties have functioned and are functioning. The more than a quarter of a billion people in these nations and territories live under the greatest variety of different geographical, cultural, economic, and social situations.

Climatic contrasts are dramatic in the Americas. Most of the states and countries of the hemisphere lie in the tropics or subtropics. Other things being equal, that means that the temperatures are high throughout the year, the sun is intense, and until recent decades it has meant that devastating and debilitating diseases were indigenous to the region.

However, in important parts of tropical and subtropical America, the climate is not as we have described it. This is because the great range of mountains, with its high valleys and plateaus, which stretches down the western edge of the hemisphere from Alaska to Tierra del Fuego, has created a temperate climate, or in some cases even a quite frigid one, even in areas located in the tropical zone. There are of course also other temperate regions, in southern Brazil, Uruguay, and Argentina, as well as in Chile and in southern Canada. Then there are the forbidding sub-Arctic climates of the larger part of Canada at one extreme of the hemisphere and southern Argentina and Chile at the other, where summers are very short, and winters are very long and rugged.

These geographical and climatic differences in America have had a great influence in determining what kind of people live where. The plateaus and high valleys of the mountain chains in South America and in Mexico and Guatemala in North America, provided a temperate climate propitious to the development of high Indian civilizations and relatively large populations in pre-Columbian times. As a consequence, in spite of the havoc subsequently wreaked by the European conquerors on the Indian populations, it is in those areas—Bolivia, Peru, Ecuador in South America, and Mexico and Guatemala—that the population even today is to a very large degree Indian, with the rest being principally Indian-European mixture, that is, mestizo.

On the other hand, in the lowland tropical areas of South and Central America, and in the Caribbean Sea, the less advanced and less numerous Indians were quickly exterminated or (in much of South America) driven far into the interior. Since the Europeans had not come to America to work but to have someone work for them, the conquerors soon replaced the Indians with people from Africa. As a consequence, in the West Indies and along the coasts of tropical South, Central, and North America, people of African descent, or of mixed African-European ancestry predominate.

Finally, in the relatively flat temperate regions of southern South America the Indians remained dominant until the nineteenth century, but subsequently were helpless to prevent the mass incursion of Europeans, who either exterminated the indigenous population, absorbed a few of them into their own number, or penned the survivors up in "reservation" areas, and occupied the lands which had formerly been theirs. As a consequence, Uruguay and Argentina are today populated by people who are predominantly of European ancestry. Much the same sequence occurred at the other end of the hemisphere, in Canada.

Geographic and climatic factors were also influential in determining the nature of the economies of the various parts of the hemisphere, at least for the first three hundred years following the discovery and conquest by Europeans. The temperate areas produced crops which for the most part competed with those of Europe, and so they were either left largely untouched by the Europeans, as in the southern third of South America and most of Canada, or their economic nexus with the world market was created by the export of precious metals, as in highland Mexico, the Andean countries, and to a less degree the temperate parts of Central America. However, the hot tropical areas produced crops which were in increasing demand in Europe, most notably sugar, and so quickly came to develop economies which were of major importance in international trade.

These different kinds of economies engendered different kinds of social systems. Although wherever the Europeans became firmly dominant, they and their descendants came to control most of the arable land, they organized the use of that land in different ways in the mountainous temperate areas and the lowland tropical regions. In the former there was instituted a kind of re-creation of the manorial system of feudal Europe, where Indians lived on and worked the land without owning it, were largely tied to the land, and owed labor service of various kinds to the landlords. In the hot tropical areas, on the other hand, the commercial plantation system and outright slave labor were dominant.

All of the countries were relatively late entrants in the race for industrialization. To some degree, at least in the Ibero-American part of the hemisphere, this was due to the fact, following the first turbulent decades after independence, that political parties, the Liberals, believers to some degree in the principles of free trade and noninterference by the government in the economy became dominant. Therefore, instead of seeking to foster through action of the state the transformation of the fairly extensive handicraft industries which then existed into a modern manufacturing sector, they threw their countries open to importation of cheap, machine-made goods from Europe, and organized their national economies on the basis of exporting some major mineral or agricultural product in demand in Europe or the United States in return for imports of manufactured consumers goods and construction materials. The economic history of the region might have been vastly different had the Conservatives, many of whom believed in protectionism, won the great political struggles of the mid and later nineteenth century.

Of course, in the Caribbean countries that have moved toward independence only since the 1930s, little if any industrialization was possible so long as the territories remained colonies. It was only when they began to achieve internal self-government that their regimes started to think in terms of creating a manufacturing sector of any consequence.

Today, there is great variety among the nearly four dozen states and territories in the degree to which their economies have become industrialized. Canada is certainly now a major industrial power. Brazil, Mexico, and Argentina have very extensive and highly integrated industries, but still are "developing" rather than "developed" countries. A substantial number of the rest have a major manufacturing sector in their economies, but many others, particularly in the Caribbean area, have little more than a rudimentary beginning of an industrial revolution.

The Impact of History

Many of the states and territories were frequently fought over during the three hundred years before the independence movement began. Only six years after Columbus "discovered" America, the Spanish and Portuguese monarchies undertook to divide not only America but most of the world between themselves. In America, this division would have given Spain all but the most easterly part of present-day Brazil, which fell to the Portuguese. However, this agreement was easier to reach than to enforce.

On the one hand, the Portuguese and their Brazilian descendants were not content to control only that bit of South America allotted to them. Particularly during the sixteenth and seventeenth centuries, enterprising Brazilian *bandeirantes* (banner carriers) organized expeditions to penetrate far inland on the South American continent. They established the basis for the Portuguese and subsequently the Brazilians to lay claim, on the grounds of effective possession, to the third of the South American continent which is now included within the boundaries of Brazil.

Other expanding European powers that had not been parties to the agreement between the Iberian states were even less willing to accept that accord than were the Portuguese. Particularly, the British, French, and Dutch made frequent incursions in the Caribbean areas that were first controlled by the Spaniards. Starting in the seventeenth century, they first raided and then conquered and settled most of the islands in the Caribbean Sea. They likewise established the colonies of British, Dutch, and French Guiana on the South American mainland, and British Honduras in Central America. Elsewhere in South and Central America, the British frequently raided Spanish colonies, although unable to establish permanent settlements; while the French and Dutch established colonies in present-day Brazil which lasted for a generation before they were overrun by the Portuguese Brazilians.

But the French, Dutch, and British not only fought the Spaniards for control of much of America. They also fought one another. Many of the Caribbean islands changed hands several times between the British and the French. The Dutch laid claim, which was effective for a while, to Trinidad. In North America, the British and French (and for a short while the Dutch and even the Swedes) fought several wars over possession of what was to become the United States and Canada, before both territories finally came under British control. At that, the tiny territory of Saint Pierre and Miquelon, nestled between Nova Scotia and Newfoundland, remained and remains today, a French possession. The Danes were also able to obtain a foothold in the Caribbean, which they held until 1917, when they sold their part of the Virgin Islands to the United States.

Nor were the Virgin Islands the only area acquired by the United States. Aside from the constant usurpation of Indian lands across the continent, the United States also seized as a result of the annexation of Texas and the so-called Mexican War of 1846–1848 about one-third of the territory of their southern neighbor. Half a century later, they acquired control of the remains of the Spanish Empire— Puerto Rico and Cuba—in the three-month-long Spanish American War of 1898. Although the United States ultimately permitted the establishment of the Republic of Cuba, for more than three decades it maintained the right to oust the Cuban government if it wished to do so, and even after formally giving up that right, continued to exercise an immense impact on Cuban affairs until the Castro revolution of 1959 resulted in substituting Soviet influence for that of the U.S.A. in the island. Puerto Rico remains under the United States (and Puerto Rican) flag, and the fundamental division among the parties of that island continues to be over the status of Puerto Rico vis-à-vis the United States.

All of this carving and recarving of an empire in America left its impact on the languages, religions, political experiences, and hence political parties of the states and territories of the hemisphere. Spanish became the official language of almost two-thirds of South America, almost all of Central America, and of Mexico, Cuba, the Dominican Republic, and Puerto Rico (where that status is today shared with English). As a result of Portugal's success in the scramble for empire, Brazil, the second largest country (in terms of population) in the hemisphere is today the only Portuguese-speaking country in America. In those territories which remained under the British flag, by the early decades of the nineteenth century English had become the official language, although in some of the West Indian islands a French-based patois is the second language. In Canada more than one-quarter of the population has French as its native language. Dutch remains officially the language of the Netherlands Antilles and Surinam. French prevails in Martinique, Guadeloupe, French Guiana, and Haiti, the first and only French colony in America to win independence by armed insurrection (in 1804). However, in all of these territories except French Guiana another tongue, creole, is spoken by most of the people.

The impact of history is seen also in the religions of the countries and territories of America. Most of the people of Ibero-America are at least formally Roman Catholics, although in fact indigenous American Indian and African religions are widely practiced, with more or less syncretism with Christianity. In those islands of the Caribbean which were longest in British hands, the majority of the people are Protestants, particularly Anglicans; in those which the British acquired finally only at the time of the Napoleonic Wars, Roman Catholicism is still predominant. Similarly, in Canada, in those areas where the descendants of the early French colonists predominate, Catholicism is the majority religion. Where the British settled early (as in the Maritime Provinces) or where they or their descendants increased after taking Canada away from the French, Protestantism is predominant.

One thing which all the American states and territories share is the experience of once having been someone else's colony. The various colonial systems which once operated in America differed in major ways from one another and had great impact on the political system, and hence the political parties, which emerged in the various nations. The countries dealt with fall into five clearly differentiable groups: Ibero-America, the English-speaking West Indies, the French Republic in America, the Dutch-speaking territories, and the United States territories. Haiti and Canada have had their own particular experiences. Before turning to a study of each individual country, we shall survey the common elements which the states and territories with Iberian, British, French, United States, and Dutch colonial backgrounds share, such as their historical experience and political institutions.

Ibero-America

The Ibero-American countries include the eighteen Spanish-speaking republics and Portuguese-speaking Brazil. The Spanish-American countries shared the experience of being part of Spain's vast colonial empire for at least three centuries, while Brazil was governed during most of the same period by a Portuguese colonial system in large degree patterned after that of Spain, although with a few significant differences. All but two of these countries—Panama and Cuba—became independent at about the same time, in the first quarter of the nineteenth century as the result of the same chain of events in Europe and America. Although the economic, social, and even political development of this score of nations has diversified greatly since independence, the colonial heritage and the similarity of many of the problems with which these countries have had to cope, give them enough in common to justify our analyzing them generally as a single group.

The Colonial System

The Spanish Crown was faced, during the two generations following Columbus' fateful first voyage to America, with the need to establish a workable system to govern a vast overseas empire. In setting up this system, the Crown drew extensively on the historical experience of Spain itself during the centuries preceding the discovery and to a large degree adopted institutions patterned after those that were being used to govern European Spain.

At the time that America was "discovered" under Spanish auspices, Spain in fact consisted of two kingdoms, those of Castille and Aragón. They had been brought together under the joint sovereignty of Isabel, Queen of Castille, and Ferdinand, King of Aragón, only a few years before Columbus's trip in 1492. However, they remained then, and for more than a century thereafter, two separate kingdoms, joined (after Ferdinand and Isabel) under a single monarch.

In each kingdom, Castille and Aragón, councils existed through which the monarch ruled the two parts of Spain. This system was adapted to rule Spanish America, with the establishment of a Council of the Indies. It was this body which controlled the political and ecclesiastic affairs of the Spanish New World.

Under the Council of the Indies, viceroyalties ("vice-kingships") were established. At first, Christopher Columbus was the single "Viceroy of the Indies and Admiral of the Ocean Sea." Although Columbus soon quarreled with his patrons and was removed as viceroy, there continued for a generation to be but one viceroyalty, with its seat in Santo Domingo in what is now the Dominican Republic.

However, after the vast conquests by Spanish forces on the mainland, the system was reorganized, with the suppression of the Santo Domingo–based "vice-kingship," and establishment of two new viceroyalties, that of New Spain, with its seat in Mexico City, and Peru, with its capital in the Spanish-built city of Lima. Very late in the colonial period, in 1776, the Viceroyalty of Peru was subdivided, with two new units being established: the Viceroyalty of the Rio de la Plata, based in Buenos Aires and including present-day Argentina, Uruguay, Paraguay, and part of southern Brazil; and the Viceroyalty of New Granada, with its capital in Bogotá, and including the present republics of Venezuela, Colombia, Panama, and Ecuador.

Each of the viceroyalties was subdivided for administrative purposes. In most cases, the subordinate officials to the viceroy were captains-general. In a number of instances, it was the captaincies-general which emerged as independent countries in the early nineteenth century: Venezuela, Chile, Central America.

The Spanish Crown was faced, from the early decades of the colonial period, with the problem of preventing the viceroys, thousands of miles away from Europe in a period when it took a month or more to make the voyage from Spain to the New World, from converting themselves from deputies of the Spanish Crown into sovereigns in their own right. Indeed, in the years following the conquest of Peru such attempts were made. So a complicated system of checks and balances was established to prevent any such usurpation.

In the first place, viceroys were usually appointed for relatively short periods of time. One who stayed at his post more than half-a-dozen years was an exception. When he was relieved of his post, the viceroy was subject to an extensive fiscal and administrative inspection. Furthermore even while he was on the job, he was sometimes "visited" by people from Spain to whom he was supposed to explain his conduct of the viceroyalty's affairs.

On the spot, in his capital, an institution known as an *audiencia* existed. This was a semijudicial and semiadministrative organization which was free at any time to question the policies and procedures of the viceroy. In addition, in between the exit of one viceroy and the arrival of his successor, the audiencia was usually in charge of administering the government.

Another very important counterweight to the viceroy was the Roman Catholic Church. In 1492 in celebration of the fall of the last of the Moorish kingdoms in

Spain, Granada, to Spanish arms, the pope, Alexander VI (a Spaniard himself), had granted the Spanish Kings the *patronato*. According to this arrangement, it was the Spanish monarch who, in effect, named all members of the church hierarchy in his domains; the Crown could prevent distribution within the realm of any bulls or other documents of the Vatican to which it took exception. In return for this, the Crown collected a tithe from all Christians on behalf of the church, which it was supposed to (and usually did) turn over to the church hierarchy.

Thus, the Catholic Church in Spanish America was virtually an arm of administration of the Crown. The archbishop of the viceregal city was a man of great power, with access through church channels to the court in Madrid and could be a strong counterweight to the viceroy if he chose. As a last resort, he had the ability to excommunicate the viceroy or other lay officials, thus at least symbolically removing the subjects from the obligation of obeying that official, a power which was not used very often but was always in reserve.

The church's role was significant in two other ways. On the one hand, the church came to be exceedingly richly endowed, in many parts of Spanish America being the largest landowner, and in some cases being also the most important money-lender of a region. On the other hand, the church had at its command the Inquisition. On various occasions during the colonial period the Inquisition in Spain sent out delegations to look into affairs in the American lands, and although most of those haled before its fearful tribunals were in fact clergymen its power could also be used against the secular authorities, as it was upon occasion.

Alongside this political and ecclesiastical power structure, there existed another bureaucracy which controlled economic matters. This was the House of Trade (*Casa de Contratación*). It administered the mercantilist policy under which the parts of the Spanish Empire were only allowed to trade with Spain. It also organized the great convoys which throughout most of the colonial period went back and forth between Seville and Cádiz in Spain and Panama and Mexico in the New World, carrying European goods to the Spanish-American territories, and the gold and silver of the Andes and Mexico (and some other products) back to Spain.

Two other institutions, both of which had developed in Spain during the centuries'-long *Reconquista*, (the reconquest of Moorish Spain by the Christians) were widely applied in the New World. These were the *encomienda* and the *mita*.

The encomienda was a system in Spain by which, as the Christians overran Moslem parts of the peninsula, large numbers of villages and the lands on which they were located and which were cultivated by their residents, were turned over to a Christian nobleman. He had the obligation to "protect" the villagers, and most of all to see to it that they were converted to the Christian religion; and they had the obligation to pay various kinds of tribute to their "protector." In America, too, leaders of the conquering Spanish armies were given large grants under similar conditions. At first these were for limited periods of time, but they soon became life tenures, and inheritable, and finally in the early eighteenth century were converted into outright land grants. Under this system, much of the arable land of the Spanish territories came into the hands of the descendants of the Spanish conquerors or of others from the peninsula who were given grants subsequently.

The mita was a medieval institution under which people of a given area of Spain were mobilized periodically to do work on behalf of the community as a whole: road construction and similar projects. In America, the mita soon degenerated into a system by which Indians were rounded up to be sent to work in the gold and silver mines as little more than slaves. The mita was undoubtedly a major contributor to the decimation of the Indian population which proceeded in the first couple centuries of the colonial period.

The one thing which clearly did not exist in the Spanish-American colonies was a system of self-government. There was nothing comparable to the colonial legislatures, elected by freeholders, in the English colonies in North America. The nearest thing to a self-governing institution was the *cabildo* (municipal council). Although it began in many cases as an institution whose members were elected by the Spaniards resident within its boundaries, in time it degenerated so that the posts in the cabildo were bought and sold or were inherited. In any case, its jurisdiction was municipal rather than provincewide, and its powers were very sharply limited.

The system of colonial administration in Brazil was closely modeled on that of Spanish America, particularly after the king of Spain, Phillip II, became king of Portugal in 1580. There was a Council of the Indies, which controlled political and ecclesiastical affairs, and a House of Trade which governed economic relations between Brazil and other Portuguese colonies and the metropolis. After some experimentation with establishing proprietary colonies, somewhat similar to Pennsylvania or Maryland in North America, the Portuguese Crown established a Viceroyalty of Brazil, with governors of various provinces subordinate to the viceroy.

There were three differences of some significance between the Brazilian system and that in the Spanish colonies. One was that local *senates* existed in Brazil, somewhat akin to the cabildos in Spanish America, but with control over some revenues of their own. They were much more subject to control by the local gentry and merchants than were the cabildos. Upon occasion, these senates defied royal and viceregal orders and there were occasions in which they forced the superior authorities to compromise with them. A second difference was that individual Brazilians were able to rise much higher in the Portuguese colonial administration than was the case in Spanish America, where this was virtually impossible. There were instances of Brazilians being chosen as governors and other high officials as in Portugal's African colonies.

Finally, the Roman Catholic Church was not as important an element in public administration in Brazil as in Spanish America. There emerged in Brazil a plantation system in which the landowner was not only the owner of most of the people who worked for him—his slaves—but also was virtually sovereign in his locality.

In this plantation system, the local church became part of his administration rather than part of the viceroy's administration. Not infrequently, the priest was a close relative of the landowner and depended as much as any other family member for his sustenance on the beneficence of the plantation lord. This undoubtedly helps to explain why the church did not emerge after the colonial period as anywhere near as strong an influence in Brazil as it did in the Spanish-American countries.

The Independence Struggle

By the late eighteenth century separatist sentiments had developed in both Spanish and Portuguese America. Over the centuries the feeling had grown in both areas that the American Spanish and Portuguese were somehow different from those of Europe, which was indeed the case. These notions were greatly intensified by the successful revolt of the thirteen British colonies in North America after 1775. They were also reinforced by the events and slogans of the French Revolution.

During the last generation before the general movement for independence began, there were abortive attempts to gain freedom from European control in both Brazil and several Spanish-American territories. However, what finally precipitated the drive for independence throughout Ibero-America were events occurring in the Iberian peninsula itself.

In 1808 the emperor Napoleon decided to take over control of both Spain and Portugal. His armies marched into the Iberian peninsula and captured both the reigning Spanish monarch, Charles IV, and his son Ferdinand VII. However, the Portuguese regent, soon afterwards to be King João VI, succeeded in getting out of Lisbon with most of his court (on British warships) only a few hours before Napoleon's troops marched into his capital.

In much of Spanish America the independence movement began as an effort to assert the Spanish Americans' loyalty to their legitimate Bourbon monarchs, against the claims of Napoleon's brother Joseph, whom the emperor had placed upon the Spanish throne. In other instances, the breakdown of Spanish authority was seen as an opportunity to launch a movement straightaway for separation from the Spanish Crown. In any case, the situation was soon converted into one of revolt throughout Spanish America.

The struggle for independence in the Spanish colonies went on for about fifteen years, in contrast to the six years of severe struggle in the British North American colonies (and eight years between the outbreak of rebellion and the final peace). It was much more destructive of both lives and property in the Spanish areas than in British North America, at least in part because the populace was much more divided on the issue of independence than was true in the British colonies. In Venezuela, the Spaniards were able to arouse a virtual race war, by appealing to the slaves for support against their rebellious white masters. In Peru and Bolivia there was little real support for independence until Simón

Bolívar's forces came down from the north to rout the Spaniards. In Mexico, the revolt, which was at first an insurrection of the Indians and mestizos against their white masters as much as against Spanish authorities, was suppressed and then renewed, with elements of the local white aristocracy joining in the final struggle and carrying it to a victorious conclusion. In Cuba and Puerto Rico there was virtually no revolt at all.

In Brazil, the struggle for independence came a little later and was much easier. The difference is to be found in the fact that it was the prince regent himself, Dom Pedro I, who assumed the leadership of the independence movement after his father returned to Portugal and after the Portuguese parliament (in 1822) moved to reduce Brazil once more to the status of a colony instead of a coequal kingdom with Portugal, which status had been granted to Brazil by João VI. The few Portuguese troops stationed in Brazil were no match for the bulk of the Brazilian troops fighting for their own legitimate monarch.

The Problems of the Spanish Heritage

Once independence had been achieved, the Spanish-American countries were faced with two major problems which were the result of their heritage as former colonies of Spain. These were the difficulty in establishing a basis of legitimacy for the new republics and lack of a strong tradition of civilian control over the military.

To understand the problem of lack of legitimacy, a comparison of the situation of the Spanish-American republics and the United States may be useful. Whereas there had been no elective bodies owing their mandate to even a small part of the populace of the Spanish colonies, such institutions did exist in the British colonies in North America. In each of the thirteen colonies or provinces there was a legislature, duly authorized by the king, which had extensive control over local affairs, at least until the beginning of the crisis that led to the revolutionary movement. From this point of view, the American Revolution can be seen as being the decision of those provincial legislative bodies to substitute a continental congress for the British king and parliament which until then had been the supreme authority. This move was taken by legislatures which themselves had legitimacy, and therefore their action could be seen as itself being legitimate.

However, since no such legislative bodies elected by the Spanish Americans but with royal authorization existed in Spanish America, there was no clear line of legitimacy extending from the governmental system which had existed before the independence movement to the republican institutions which emerged thereafter. The history of most of these countries during the nineteenth century and for some time thereafter may be seen as a search for such legitimacy.

The only institution which emerged from the independence struggle that had some aura of legitimacy was the army which had brought victory in that struggle and thereby derived its claims to authority. This peculiar position of the armed forces of the new nations was reinforced by the fact that there was no tradition in

Spanish America of civilian supremacy over the military. The Spanish garrisons and the local militia enjoyed peculiar privileges which exempted them from civilian justice and from taxation. In other ways, too, the line between military and civilian authority was vague. From the early years of the independence struggle, therefore, the military leaders tended to seize control of the civilian government.

In most of the Spanish-American countries this primacy of the military degenerated into the *caudillo* system. The caudillo was usually a local landholder, who could mobilize his dependents to fight on his behalf against other caudillos. If he was lucky, a caudillo would overcome his rivals or absorb their supporters, and ultimately would be able to mobilize a sufficient force to march upon the capital and overthrow the caudillo who had preceded him in power.

The caudillo system established the tradition that governments were normally overthrown by armed force, not by elections. Even when the armed forces began, in the latter decades of the nineteenth century, to be officered by people trained in military academies and often by foreign instructors (usually from Germany or France, or some other Latin American country which had already had foreigners instructing their officer candidates), the tradition of interference in the political process by the armed forces did not die. It merely took a different form. With a professional military, coups came to be carried out by those in the top echelons of the professional armed forces. This tradition persists in most of the Spanish-American countries to the present day.

The problem of militarism came later to Portuguese America than to Spanish America. There was not the kind of vaccuum of legitimacy in Brazil right after its independence that there was in its neighbors. In fact, the entry of the military into active participation in politics did not come until the overthrow of the empire. It was the armed forces which overthrew the monarchy, and it was generally accepted thereafter that in doing so they had inherited the moderating power, the ability to act above day-to-day politics in the best interests of the nation, which the imperial constitution had conferred upon the emperor. Henceforward, until 1964, the military stepped in to change governments when the military chiefs (for whatever reason) thought the nation required it. However, except in the 1889–1894 period and after 1964 the military did not themselves assume power, but rather passed it on to the civilian next in line to exercise it.

The Emergence of Political Parties

Although the tradition of military interference in politics emerged in Spanish-American countries during the first generation or so of independence, political parties also were formed in this same period. Those leading the movement for independence soon split into rival camps, and by the fourth decade of the nineteenth century these competing groups began to take shape as political parties.

During the nineteenth century these parties were generally either Conservative or Liberal, although they did not always use those names. They were separated by fairly clear differences on major issues which were facing the recently independent countries. The Conservatives—whatever they were called in a particular country—were generally supporters of the rights and privileges of the Roman Catholic Church. They also were in favor of a strong central government, as opposed to any approach to federalism. Finally, the Conservatives were supporters of more or less extensive intervention of the government in the national economy.

The Liberals, on the other hand, were antagonists of the church. They also supported decentralization of governmental authority, and in some cases were advocates of the federal system. They also opposed intervention of the national government in the process of their nation's economic development.

Throughout most of the nineteenth century, and well into the twentieth, the Conservatives and Liberals were the major parties in most of the Spanish-American countries. However, near the end of the century other kinds of parties began to appear. In Brazil, also, the Conservatives and Liberals were the major parties during the existence of the empire. They alternated in power throughout the life of the monarchy.

The Nature of Twentieth-Century Ibero-American Parties

During the twentieth century the parties of the Ibero-American countries have become much more diversified than they were in the first hundred years of independence. This change has been the result of an alteration in the social and economic situation of the various countries. The diversification of the economies, particularly the rise of a manufacturing sector, and the rapid urbanization of the region in recent decades have brought about great social changes. Modern urban working classes have arisen, and in at least a few countries, the middle class has become predominant. In the last few decades economic change has weakened or totally destroyed the hold of the traditional landed aristocracy on the rural parts of the various nations, with the result that the peasants have begun to emerge as an important factor in political affairs in some countries.

As a result of all this, the issues which divided parties in the nineteenth century became largely irrelevant. The secular privileges of the Catholic Church, for instance, have largely disappeared and the church-state quarrel of the past is at best a dormant source of controversy. No political party in Ibero-America stands today for the kind of free enterprise—free trade policies which the Liberals advocated during much of the nineteenth century. Nor is the old issue between centralized and federal forms of government of much consequence today.

The issues between parties during most of the twentieth century have centered on the one hand on economic questions—the degree and kind of protection and assistance to be given to industrialization, the best way to get national control over the national economy and other similar problems. On the other hand, social issues have also been of major consequence—expansion and diversification of the education system, the provision of health care and adequate housing, labor and social legislation, and land redistribution. It has been around these issues that most of the parties of the twentieth century have arisen.

In a few cases, the nineteenth century parties have been able to survive, when they adapted themselves to the changed circumstances of individual countries. However, in most of the nations of Ibero-America, they have disappeared. In their place have appeared a variety of different parties.

Some of the twentieth century parties have their counterparts outside of the region. Socialist parties, more or less along the lines of the Socialist parties of Europe, have appeared from time to time, although except in Chile they are no longer organizations of major importance. Communist parties have been established in every one of the Ibero-American republics and in one of them, Cuba, have been able to establish their dictatorship. In a number of countries, too, dissident Communist parties, Maoist and Trotskyist, have also emerged.

There have been several other kinds of parties in Ibero-America which have had European counterparts. One has been the Christian Democrats. They exist in most of the Ibero-American countries, and in two of them, Chile and Venezuela, they have come to power for occasional periods. The Radical Party of Chile has had certain similarities with the French Radical Socialists, and both the Chilean and Argentine Radical parties were for many decades the principal spokesmen for the middle classes. Finally, in the 1930s fascist parties also were established, although they generally did not survive World War II.

However, in quite a few countries indigenous parties, with little connection with any organizations outside of the hemisphere, have played the major role in party politics. One distinctive group of this kind has been the National Revolutionary parties, multiclass organizations characterized by programs calling for basic social reforms—land redistribution, extensive labor and social legislation, emphasis on education, advocacy of economic nationalism and economic development, and belief in political democracy. Members of this group of parties have included the Peruvian Aprista Party, Democratic Action Party of Venezuela, the National Liberation Party of Costa Rica, the Nationalist Revolutionary Movement of Bolivia, the Febrerista Party of Paraguay, the Authentic Revolutionary Party of Cuba, the Dominican Revolutionary Party of the Dominican Republic, and the Popular Democratic Party of Puerto Rico.

Some of the indigenous parties of the area defy categorization. They have grown out of the particular political history of their respective countries, and don't have counterparts elsewhere. This is true of the Peronist Party of Argentina, brought into existence by Juan Perón in the late 1940s and still one of the major forces in national politics in that country. Another is the Brazilian Labor Party, with special appeal to the urban working class and loyalty first to the person and then to the memory of Getulio Vargas, which was of rising importance through the democratic period of 1945–1964, and has revived with the relaxation of the military dictatorship in 1979-1980. Also peculiar to its country of origin is the party which has governed Mexico since 1929, and which is currently known as the Institutional Revolutionary Party.

Do Parties Matter?

It has been fashionable among some writers about Ibero-America to argue that parties are at best of secondary importance in the political systems of the area. It is claimed that the proclivity for government to be changed by force rather than by elections has meant that the parties have not been a basic element in the political life of these countries. Such an argument was particularly popular in the late 1960s and early 1970s, when the great majority of the Ibero-American countries were under the rule of military regimes.

Another school of thought which has become increasingly popular in recent years has stressed the supposed "corporativist" nature of Ibero-American political life. According to this point of view, the Iberian medieval tradition of special rights for recognized elements within the national community has persisted in Spanish and Portuguese America. Although the number of groups with such rights has expanded from the traditional landowning elite-military-church trilogy of the nineteenth century, to include middle-class, working-class, and perhaps in some cases even peasant groups, there is little room in such a corporativist system for political parties to play a major role in national decision-making and the determination of policy.

There is something, but only something, to be said for both of these points of view. Certainly to talk about the politics of Ibero-America only in terms of its political parties would lead to complete misunderstanding of the nature of both politics and government. No one can question the major role played by the military for more than a century and a half, and indeed some have argued that the armed forces are the most important "party" of all. To ignore the fact that groups such as landlords, industrialists, the church, the labor movement and even the peasant movement are something more than the pressure groups with which the student and practitioner of politics in the United States is acquainted, and that these groups do possess certain specific rights—albeit largely unwritten ones—would be to overlook an important element in the political life of the Ibero-American countries.

However, when all of this has been said, there still remains a substantial role which the political parties have played, and continue to play in the political process in Ibero-America. Their persistence in spite of repeated persecution by regimes of force in country after country, and their ability to reorganize and rebuild after such periods of repression, bear witness to the fact that they are of great significance to substantial parts of the population of the region. Their capacity to express, and often to bring together, the interests and points of view of important segments of the community certainly indicates their importance in the past and at the present time. Their participation in the electoral process is of key significance in those countries and in those periods in which the ballot rather than the bullet is used to determine who should govern. On another plane, the role of parties as elements of control of political life and society in general in such diverse cases as postrevolutionary Mexico, Trujillo's Dominican Republic, and Castro's Cuba, indicates another way in which knowledge of the political parties of Ibero-America is important to an understanding of the general political life of the countries of the region.

The parties of Ibero-America have played a varying role in different countries at different times, depending upon the degree to which they have been able to function more or less legitimately. It seems likely that in the next few decades, at least, this will continue to be the case. They will participate in elections when those are permitted by the government in power, they will fight against military and personalist dictatorships when those are in power, or they will be instruments of one or another kind of regime to mobilize support and/or to regiment the population of countries in which the regime in power doesn't care to submit itself to the free choice of the populace. In any case, they will continue to be an important part of the political system in the Ibero-American countries.

The English-speaking West Indies

In the struggle among the British, French, and Dutch to seize parts of the empire which the Spanish Crown originally established in, around, and near the Caribbean Sea, the British ultimately ended up with the lion's share. They always occupied Bermuda and Barbados, at the northern and southern extremes of the region. They early drove the Spaniards out of the Bahamas.

British control of the other territories came later. Oliver Cromwell's government seized and maintained control over Jamaica in the mid-seventeenth century. Britain fought with France for control of the Leeward and Windward Islands throughout much of the seventeenth and eighteenth centuries, and many of the islands only became definitively British at the end of the Napoleonic Wars, as was also the case with British Guiana (now Guyana). British Honduras (or Belize, as it is now known) became securely British only in the first half of the nineteenth century.

Political Evolution of British West Indies

The islands and continental territories of the British West Indies generally went through a common process of political evolution. In the seventeenth and eighteenth centuries the British established in their dependencies colonial legislatures, similar to those set up in the thirteen original colonies on the North American mainland which ultimately became the United States of America. As in the continental mainland, the qualifications to vote for and hold office in the colonial legislatures limited the franchise to people who either owned considerable amounts of real property or had a prescribed amount of annual income. For all practical purposes, this meant that only the white landlords and merchants were able to vote or be members of the legislatures.

However, after the emancipation of the slaves by act of the British Parliament in 1837, the white aristocracy rapidly came to fear that their control of local parliamentary bodies would be endangered by their former slaves, as these became eligible to be voters. As a result, in most of the territories the landowners became absentees, returning to Britain. At the same time, in most of the British colonies of the area, the elective assemblies were abolished, on the initiative of the aristocratic voters themselves. The only exceptions to this were the Houses of Assembly of Bermuda, the Bahamas and Barbados, where there continued to exist small but powerful white minorities of landlords and merchants. These assemblies continued to be elected by the literate and propertied classes, which for the most part meant the white landowners and merchants.

British Crown Colony Government

The British imperial government supplanted the elected assemblies with legislative councils. These generally contained people chosen by the British-appointed governor to represent various interests in the respective colony. These "nominated" members were free to vote as they wished on measures submitted to the legislature. The legislatures also generally included certain ex-officio members, usually the colonial secretary (in effect, the deputy governor), the financial secretary and the attorney general. Usually these ex-officio legislators were Britishers, members of the colonial civil service, who were constitutionally bound to vote in conformity with the governor's wishes.

Sometimes there were two houses in the new colonial legislatures. The members of the upper houses, where they existed, were even more narrowly chosen. There were also usually bodies known as the executive council, a kind of cabinet, which was dependent completely on the British-appointed governor, without any reference to the legislature. This body, too, generally consisted of colonial civil servants and a smattering of local people, chosen from the landowners and merchants of the colony involved by the governor.

The third branch of government, the judiciary, was generally manned by people dispatched from the metropolis. Local magistrates constituted the courts of first instance; there were also appeals courts on various levels, and the final level of the judicial system was the British privy council in London, to which it was possible to submit only a very narrow range of cases.

This organization of Crown Colony government continued without any substantial modification until the 1920s. In the years following World War I there began to be some changes in the system, with provision for election of some of the nonofficial members of the legislative bodies of some of the colonies. However, it was not until the latter half of the 1930s that the Crown Colony system generally began to be undermined. This occurred as a result of the awakening of the mulatto and black majority of the population of the British West Indian colonies, and their unwillingness to submit any longer either to the white minorities of their particular colonies, or to the rule of appointed white rulers sent out from Great Britain itself.

Beginning of the Struggle for Black Supremacy and National Sovereignty

Inevitably the struggle for abolition of the Crown Colony system in the British Caribbean involved two aspects. On the one hand, it was a fight to end the domination of the local economic, political, and social system by the tiny white minority. On the other, it involved a struggle for the national sovereignty of the various colonies and their ultimate independence from British colonial rule. These two movements were inextricably intertwined and were in fact part of the same movement for national self-determination. This movement began right after World War I. From the beginning it bore a democratic-socialist orientation that was to remain with it during the next two or three decades, until autonomy or outright independence had been achieved throughout the area.

Three men were particularly outstanding in the earliest phase of this struggle against colonialism and aristocratic white rule. One of these was a white Trinidadian, Captain Arthur Cipriani, founder of the Trinidad Labor Party, who began the struggle for ending aristocratic rule and colonial domination in that southern Caribbean island. Another was Hubert Critchlow, founder of the British Guiana Labor Union, which was established during World War I and served as both a trade union organization and a labor party in the only British colony in South America. It was the first group to undertake the anticolonial struggle in that part of the hemisphere. The third was Albert Marryshow of Grenada, who began the struggle for constitutional reform and social change there in the 1920s. Critchlow and Marryshow were both men of mixed African and European ancestry.

However, these preliminary efforts of Cipriani, Critchlow, and Marryshow had relatively little effect on the governmental structure or the politics of the rest of the British West Indian territories. It was not until the latter half of the 1930s that the major effort to change the traditional society of the area really got under way.

The Revolution of the 1930s

One of the first indications of what was to become a generalized revolt throughout the British West Indies was an effort to organize the sugar workers of the island of Saint Kitts in January 1935. This attempt, which was balked by the economic and political powers in charge of the island, degenerated into a riot in which three people were killed and several wounded.

Two and a half years more were to pass before the spark lit in Saint Kitts spread throughout the area. In June 1937 a general strike broke out in Trinidad, and this was soon followed by strikes and widespread demonstrations in British Guiana, Saint Lucia, Jamaica, and Barbados. Subsequently, there were similar movements in the other British territories.

The British imperial government took heed of these events. After first reestablishing law and order, the British authorities decided to try to ascertain what were the underlying causes of the discontent which had obviously spread throughout the Caribbean part of the empire. A commission headed by Lord Moyne was established to investigate the situation, and in the months before the outbreak of World War II it widely interviewed participants in the events of 1937–1938 and other people who were cognizant of the conditions existing in the West Indies.

Far from being the whitewash that many people had expected, the report of the Moyne Commission frankly recognized the fact that the people of the West Indies had legitimate grounds for grievance, and Lord Moyne and his associates indicated what they thought could be done about the situation. Their two most basic recommendations were that legislation be enacted to legalize the organized labor movement, and that steps be taken to extend the franchise and give the people of the area a greater degree of self-government.

The fact was that the West Indian uprising of 1937–1938 had brought into existence in many of the territories two different kinds of organizations: trade unions and political parties. In some cases, the two were almost indistinguishable, the same organization for some time serving as the negotiating instrument for workers with their employers and also as the organization which mobilized voters for electoral purposes and carried on the struggle for a more democratic form of government.

It was in this period, too, that there appeared what was for a generation to be the archetypical kind of popular leader in the regions: a combination trade union official and political party chief. Among the earliest figures of this kind were Norman Manley and William Alexander Bustamante in Jamaica, Grantley Adams in Barbados, Lionel Luckhoo in British Guiana. In the years that followed, similar figures appeared elsewhere, including Vere Bird in Antigua, Robert Bradshaw in St. Kitts, Ebenezer Joshua in St. Vincent and Cheddi Jagan and Linden Forbes Burnham in British Guiana. Only in the 1960s did a clear distinction between the party politician and the full-time trade union leader become clear in most of the territories.

The Growth of Organized Labor

As a result of the events of the late 1930s, trade unionism became firmly established throughout the British West Indian area. The typical form of organization came to be the general union. Although having some similarities with such British organizations as the Transport and General Workers Union, the general union in the West Indies was essentially an indigenous form. It arose from the facts that there were relatively small numbers of workers to be unionized, generally in a few clearly defined categories and that the available supply of skilled union negotiators was short. Furthermore, the general union device made it possible for the labor movement to maintain the kind of full-time bureaucratic apparatus required for negotiating and administering collective agreements.

The general union in the West Indies is a centralized labor group, with divisions or branches serving particular groups of workers. Dues are paid to the general union and not to the branch; collective bargaining is done by the leaders of the general union not by officials of a branch.

Typical is the Barbados Workers Union (BWU). It represents the island's sugar workers, bus drivers, electricity employees, hotel and restaurant workers, those employed in factories, and some commercial employees. All of these different kinds of workers are members directly of the Barbados Workers Union, although for administrative purposes, they are broken down into separate sections. The BWU directly negotiates and administers collective agreements covering most of these categories. Dues, amounting to about 1 percent or less of the average worker's wages are paid directly to the BWU, which has a headquarters in the capital city of Bridgetown, with a substantial staff, including paid officers of the union as well as a considerable number of clerical workers and other specialized employees. General policy is determined by an annual conference which brings together representatives from all over the island, from all categories of workers represented by the union.

There are a few territories in which the general union has not become the pattern. These include the Bahamas, where the labor law of 1959 requires separate unions for specific groups of workers; in Trinidad, where beginning in the late 1930s specific groups — oil workers, sugar workers, government employees — established their own separate unions; and Guyana where, although there have been some general unions, most groups have their separate organizations, united in the Trades Union Congress, a federal body which concentrates largely on public relations and political activities and does not engage directly in collective bargaining.

As early as 1926 Captain Cipriani and Hubert Critchlow established the British Guiana and West Indies Labor Congress, which subsequently took the name Caribbean Labor Congress. This organization went out of existence in the early 1950s at the time of the split in the World Federation of Trade Unions and the emergence of the International Confederation of Free Trade Unions (ICFTU). At that time, most Caribbean labor groups joined the ICFTU and its American regional grouping, the ORIT (*Organizacion Regional Interamericana de Trabajadores*). A Caribbean division of the ORIT (CADORIT) was established soon afterwards. It is now known as the Caribbean Congress of Labor and still has the affiliation of most of the more important trade union groups of the region. However, a few are affiliated with the World Federation of Labor, a Catholic-oriented international group, and a handful still belong to the World Federation of Trade Unions, the pro-Moscow Communist-controlled organization.

The organized labor movement in the English-speaking Caribbean territories still tends to be associated with one or another of these territories' political parties. Thus, the Barbados Workers Union generally supports the Democratic Labor Party; the Antigua Trades and Labor Union backs the Antigua Labor Party, while its rival, the Antigua Workers Union supports the other major party, the Progressive Labour Movement. In Jamaica, the Bustamante Industrial Trade Union is closely aligned with the Jamaica Labour Party, while its rival, the National Workers Union, is a strong backer of the Peoples National Party. The same could be said about most of the other English-speaking territories.

Constitutional Developments

Starting a few years after the report of the Moyne Commission, the territories of the Commonwealth Caribbean began a process of rapid constitutional evolution. This centered basically on two types of change. One was the development of a more representative type of government, and the other was the granting of greater powers to the elected representatives of the people in the various territories, a process which in most of them finally resulted in the granting of complete independence, and in the others will sooner or later have the same outcome.

The typical Crown Colony government had few if any elected representatives in its legislature, which consisted only of nominated or unofficial people named by the governor and ex-officio members who were British civil servants. Even in those territories such as Bermuda, the Bahamas, and Barbados, where an elected House of Assembly persisted, it was checked by an upper house consisting of nominated and ex-officio members more or less subject to the governor's will.

Thus, one of the early moves to modify the system was to add a handful of elected representatives to the lower house of the colonial legislature. In some cases this move antedated the uprising of 1937–1938, having taken place in the 1920s. However, even the elected members were chosen by a very narrow property franchise which largely excluded the mulattoes and blacks who made up the great majority of the population in the various territories.

After the Moyne Commission's report the process began of increasing the number of elected members of the lower house, and having them chosen by a broadened electorate. Jamaica was the first territory, in 1944, to acquire universal adult franchise for the election of the lower house. In the Leeward and Windward Islands, universal suffrage was introduced in 1951–1952 and in the following decade was generalized throughout the area.

The adoption of the right to vote for all adult citizens is a very important aspect of the history of political parties in the region. In many cases, political parties began to appear only in the last phases of the struggle for the universal right to vote and hold office or even after universal suffrage had been achieved. Previous to that, the elected members of the legislature were all chosen as independents, their selection being made to a large degree in the local planters' associations, chambers of commerce, or other centers where the landed and commercial aristocracy gathered.

Along with extension of the right to vote and hold office, there was an evolution after World War II in the direction of "responsible" government. In some cases, a preliminary step was adoption of what came to be known as "the committee system." This was an aarrangement whereby committees consisting of civil servants and a few of the elected members of the legislature would supervise particular functions of colonial administration, such as education, agriculture, or public works. Usually, the elected member would be chairman of the committee.

A next step would often be the naming of ministers from among the elected legislators to be in charge of specific portfolios, but still serving at the pleasure of the colonial governor. But a much more decisive move was the establishment of a cabinet responsible to the majority in the lower house of the legislature. Under this system of responsible cabinet government, the governor would no longer be free to choose his ministers, but would be required to name someone from the legislature most likely to enjoy the support of the majority to serve as head of the cabinet, and then to accept his "advice" concerning whom the other ministers should be.

There were sometimes disputes over what the name of the head of the cabinet should be. When the post was first established it usually was called chief minister. The changing of this title to premier was considered a symbolic movement toward more control by the parliamentary majority. "Prime minister" was usually reserved as the title for the head of the cabinet once a former colony became independent—although in 1965 Forbes Burnham in Guyana began using the title without anyone's permission several months before the independence of Guyana had been proclaimed.

One other issue of symbolic, and sometimes substantive, importance was that of who should preside over the cabinet. Sometimes, as to this day in the British Virgin Islands, for instance, the cabinet continued to be chaired by the British-appointed governor, rather than by the chief minister.

In any case, establishment of responsible cabinet government was not the final step toward the people of a British territory running their own affairs. Short of the full proclamation of independence, certain powers were generally reserved for the governor. For instance, when in the late 1960s the islands of Saint Kitts, Antigua, Saint Vincent, Saint Lucia, Dominica, and Grenada were proclaimed Associated States with Great Britain, the British still reserved to the governor appointed by London control over foreign affairs, internal security, national defense, and the civil service.

The proclamation of full independence has been the final step in the constitutional evolution of the British territories. With independence, total sovereignty was passed by the government of the United Kingdom to the people and government of the territory involved. Although so far all of the territories except Guyana, Dominica, and Trinidad have chosen to remain monarchies, with the British sovereign as also the sovereign of those territories, the status of Her Majesty's representative in the territory changes significantly with independence. Instead of being named on the advice of the British government in London, the new representative, with the title of governor general, is in effect chosen by the newly independent government and appointed on its advice. In the cases of Guyana, Dominica, and Trinidad, the president of the republic is chosen directly by the government or parliament, and the nation's only allegiance to the queen is in her capacity as Head of the Commonwealth.

The Federation of the West Indies

Although after 1962 one after another of the British West Indian territories sought and obtained independence as a separate nation from the United Kingdom, this only occurred after the failure of an attempt to establish a single nation in the form of the federation of the West Indies. For four years, between 1958 and 1962, there existed a single state which included most of the British Caribbean territories, but it failed to result in establishment of a permanent Dominion, as its supporters originally hoped it would.

Although the initiative for formation of a single West Indian nation came from the labor and political groups of the area, it received support of the British Labour government in the years following World War II. A conference, presided over by British Colonial Minister Arthur Creech Jones, was held in Montego Bay, Jamaica, in 1947, at which representatives of the various West Indian territories agreed on the ultimate formation of a West Indian federation. In the following years, negotiations continued, and a final decision to establish the federation was taken at a conference of West Indian delegates and the Colonial Office in London in 1956.

The Federation of the West Indies, when it was finally established, included only the British insular possessions in the Caribbean. British Guiana, then led by Cheddi Jagan, and British Honduras, on the east coast of Central America, opted not to participate in the new state. The Bahamas, Bermuda, British Virgin Islands, and the Cayman Islands also opted out of the federation.

In preparation for the elections for the federal parliament, two political parties were organized. One was the Federal Labour Party, which included the Barbados Labour Party, the People's National Movement of Trinidad, the People's National Party of Jamaica, and the ruling parties in the smaller islands. The other was the Federal Democratic Labour Party, which included the opposition parties in Trinidad, Barbados, Jamaica, and the smaller islands.

However, when elections for the federal parliament were finally held in March 1958, the governing parties of Trinidad and Jamaica did very poorly. Only in Barbados, among the larger islands, did the government party, the Barbados Labour Party, win overwhelmingly, receiving four of the five Barbadian seats in the federal parliament. As a result, although the West Indian Federal Labour Party received a majority, it depended largely on its supporters in the small islands, rather than in the larger ones, a fact which proved to be one of the fatal weaknesses of the new federation.

The founding congress of the Federal Labour Party chose Norman Manley, premier of Jamaica, as party leader. However, Manley decided not to take an active part in the affairs of the federal parliament, and as a result, Grantley Adams, Barbadian premier and deputy chairman of the Federal Labour Party, was finally chosen as prime minister of the West Indian federation. He presided over it during the four years in which the federation existed.

Although Grantley Adams had been one of the early advocates of a West Indian nation, he was unable to bring it to fruition. The principal stumbling blocks to West Indian unity came from the two largest territories of the area, Jamaica and Trinidad. Each had objections to the West Indian federation as it existed after 1958.

The Jamaicans were considerably underrepresented in the parliament of the federation. Furthermore, Jamaica was more advanced in terms of industrial development than was the rest of the federation, and its leaders wanted assurance that its advanced position would be protected in the new nation. For its part, Trinidad was opposed to free migration of people from the smaller islands (which was a fundamental principle of the federation), since it did not suffer from the degree of unemployment which was characteristic of the smaller islands.

Negotiations went on after formation of the federation, to reach agreement on the basic issues which were imperilling the united West Indian nation. However, it proved impossible to reach agreement on the issues which were splitting the embryonic nation.

William Alexander Bustamante and the Jamaica Labour Party were opposed to the West Indian Federation from the beginning. Their opposition finally convinced Premier Norman Manley, of the People's National Party, to call a referendum on whether Jamaica should continue to be a member of the federation. Unfortunately for the federation, this referendum was won by those opposed to federation. As a result of his defeat in this vote, Premier Manley called a general election in Jamaica, which he also lost. As a result, the new premier of Jamaica, Bustamante, immediately negotiated with the British government the separate independence of Jamaica. Soon thereafter, Premier Eric Williams of Trinidad and Tobago also negotiated independence for that British colony.

Subsequently, there were negotiations among the eight remaining territories concerning the possibility of establishing a more limited West Indian federation. However, these failed, and as a result in 1966 the Barbadian government of Premier Errol Barrow also reached an agreement with the British government for Barbadian independence.

The Drift Toward Independence

With the collapse of the West Indian federation, the other British Caribbean territories also moved toward independence as separate members of the Commonwealth. British Guiana achieved independence in 1965, and subsequently became the Cooperative Republic of Guyana in 1970. In 1974 the government of Grenada, under the leadership of Sir Eric Gairy, also negotiated independence. Subsequently, the Dominican government of Patrick John achieved independence in November 1978, and Premier John Compton of Saint Lucia gained independence for his island in April 1979. Saint Vincent, led by Premier Milton Cato, won independence in October 1979.

Meanwhile, the government of the Commonwealth of the Bahamas, which had not been part of the federation of the West Indies, also achieved independence in 1973. By the end of the 1970s, therefore, the only British territories of the West

Indies which had not yet achieved independence were Bermuda, Saint Kitts-Nevis, Anguilla, Antigua, Montserrat, British Virgin Islands, the Cayman Islands and Belize (the former British Honduras). However, in 1981 Belize and Antigua both achieved independence and the remaining territories seemed to be on their way to separate nation status. The British Foreign and Commonwealth Office (successor to the Colonial Office) had made it clear to all of them that it wanted to get rid of the remnants of empire which it still possessed in the region as soon as possible.

Secessionist Movements

A complicating factor in the movement of the countries of the Commonwealth Caribbean toward independence has been the problem of the smallest islands. There are at least four cases in which the original British colony consisted of one main island and one or more much smaller ones, and as independence became a real possibility, these "dependencies" have indicated varying degrees of reluctance about remaining associated with their larger neighbors.

The most spectacular instance of this kind arose in Anguilla in 1969. The British had grouped the islands of Saint Christopher (Saint Kitts), Nevis, and Anguilla in one administrative unit. When the associated state system was adopted in the late 1960s, Saint Kitts-Nevis-Anguilla was established as one of these. However, the residents of Anguilla expelled the policemen representing the associated state government and proclaimed their own independence. The British government finally intervened, dispatching a company of the Royal Engineering Corps and a group of London policemen to reestablish control over Anguilla. The net result of this episode was that the British finally recognized Anguilla as a separate colony, although the Associated State continued to call itself Saint Kitts-Nevis-Anguilla.

The secession of Anguilla did not completely settle the problems of the government based in Saint Kitts. As independence approached, a movement developed in the island of Nevis in favor of its acquiring a separate identity, and as this is being written it is not clear whether Saint Kitts-Nevis will emerge as a single nation or as two.

There was a similar problem in the case of Antigua and the neighboring island of Barbuda. The latter has about 1200 people and has traditionally had one member in the legislature of Antigua. Until the mid-1970s the Antiguan government did very little to provide the Barbudians with adequate roads, water supply, health facilities, and schools. However, as independence began to appear likely, the Antiguan government launched a modest development program for the neighboring island, hoping to head off growing sentiment in favor of Barbuda's obtaining a separate political identity. When Antigua received independence in October 1981, Barbuda was part of the new nation.

Still farther to the south, the Associated State of Saint Vincent and the Grenadines, established in 1969, included both the relatively large island of Saint

Vincent and the string of smaller islands known as the Grenadines, running to the south, between Saint Vincent and Grenada. On the eve of independence in 1979, the legislative representative of the Grenadines, James Mitchell, sought to organize a secessionist movement there. However, his efforts proved fruitless, and the Grenadines remained part of the Saint Vincent state when it acquired independence in October 1979.

Finally, a somewhat similar situation exists in Trinidad and Tobago. Although there was little secessionist sentiment in Tobago before the two islands received independence together in 1962, many inhabitants of Tobago did develop a feeling subsequently that their interests were being ignored by the government in Trinidad and some sentiment for secession developed.

Territorial Problems of Guyana and Belize

The two continental territories of the Commonwealth Caribbean, Guyana in South America and Belize in Central America, have long been faced with territorial claims by their neighbors, Venezuela and Guatemala respectively. For a while, the claims of Venezuela seemed to threaten Guyana's achievement of independence, and there is no doubt about the fact that Guatemala's claims constituted for more than a decade the principal block to Belize's becoming independent.

At the time that Venezuela achieved its independence early in the nineteenth century, its eastern frontiers were vague at best. Originally, Spain had claimed the whole north coast of South America, but in the last two centuries of colonial rule, she had lost effective control of the area which came to make up the three Guianas—French, Dutch, and British. Until the end of the Napoleonic Wars, the Dutch held more or less control over what are today Surinam and Guyana but at the end of that conflict she ceded Guyana to the British.

The question of defining the border between what was then British Guiana and Venezuela remained an open one throughout the rest of the nineteenth century. However, in 1899 the issue was submitted to arbitration. Although Venezuela was awarded the mouth of the Orinoco River, most of the area from there east to the Essequibo River was given to Great Britain. The Venezuelans at that time protested the verdict of the arbitrators but were not then in a position to do anything about it.

It was not until the early 1960s, when it became obvious that British Guiana would soon become independent that the Venezuelan government of President Rómulo Betancourt again raised the border issue. Discussions between the Venezuelans and the British had borne no fruit by the time Guyana received its independence at the end of 1965. The area claimed by the Venezuelans constituted about one-third of the total territory of Guyana, and so discussions continued between Guyana and Venezuela. In 1970, although neither side relinquished its claims, it was agreed that the whole issue would be suspended for a period of fifteen years.

Meanwhile, as a result of the veto of Venezuela, Guyana is not admitted to the Organization of American States. In addition, it is clear that any circumstances that might threaten the internal unity and sovereignty of Guyana might well result in Venezuela's annexation of the part of Guyana which it claims.

In the case of Belize, Guatemala long asserted that the whole territory constituted a department of the Republic of Guatemala. The coastal strip which became British Honduras and in the early 1970s was rechristened Belize, was first occupied by British freebooters. Spain never recognized British sovereignty over the area, and when Guatemala established its independence, it reasserted the Spanish claim over the territory. In the 1850s an agreement was reached between the British and the Guatemalans, whereby the latter would formally cede British Honduras to the British Crown, in return for which the British would build a railroad from that territory to the Guatemalan capital. However, that railroad was never built, and so the Guatemalans consequently maintained that their cession of the territory was null and void.

The people of Belize had no desire to become Guatemalans. They have little in common with the Guatemalans culturally or in any other way. The people of Belize aspired to become an independent nation in their own right.

However, both the British and the government and people of Belize hesitated on the independence issue until there was some resolution of the Guatemalan claims. Negotiations began in the middle 1960s and dragged on interminably. The leaders of Belize attempted to win the backing of other Central American governments as well as that of some of the South American countries for their claims to be a separate people and nation. The issue had not been finally resolved when Belize became independent late in 1981, and consequently the British agreed to continue to keep a small contingent of troops in the country as a guarantor of the sovereignty of the new nation.

Race and Politics

As we have noted, the struggles for popular sovereignty and national independence in most of the Commonwealth territories since the late 1930s have to a considerable degree been a struggle for transfer of political power from British colonial officials and/or the local white plantocracy to the black and mulatto majorities. In most cases, the first political parties were organized with that objective in view; with the achievement of universal adult suffrage the blacks and mulattoes came to constitute the overwhelming majority of most of the legislatures; with the attainment of self-government, and then increasingly of independence, it was the blacks and mulattoes who made up the cabinets, and served as prime ministers, and even governors-general.

In most of the territories, as popular election of the legislature and the transfer of executive power to elected officials proceeded, race ceased to be a political issue of any great significance. Political philosophies, differing approaches to economic development, inequalities of wealth and income, even a growing tradition of personal and family loyalty to one party or another, succeeded race as the determinants of party affiliation and voting patterns.

However, by 1980 there were still three territories in which race remained a very important factor in national politics and in party differentiation. One of these was Bermuda, the other two were Trinidad and Guyana.

In Bermuda, the two major parties continued to be divided along racial lines. The Progressive Labour Party was still an overwhelmingly black party, while its rival, the United Bermuda Party, was mainly led by white men, drew the mass of its support from the white minority, but also received the backing of enough middle- and upper-class blacks to provide it with an electoral majority.

In Trinidad and Guyana racial politics was very different from the situation in Bermuda. The whites are all but nonexistent in those two countries, and the politically significant racial division is between people of African descent and those whose forebears came from the Indian subcontinent.

When emancipation from slavery came in Trinidad and Guyana in the late 1830s, there was a marked tendency on the part of the liberated slaves to abandon plantation agriculture, and either to become subsistence farmers or to migrate to the towns. The plantation owners and governments of those territories then sought to find substitutes for the ex-slaves. A system of indentured servitude—virtual slavery for a fixed period of time, usually seven years—was resorted to. Some Chinese and Portuguese were brought in under these circumstances, but the great majority of the indentured servants came from India. As a result, the great majority of the plantation laborers of Trinidad and Guyana even in the late 1970s consisted of people of Indian descent, although Indians had also entered into virtually every other kind of economic activity as well.

One effect of this situation has been to make the rivalry between the Africans and Indians a major if not the predominant ingredient of politics. This rivalry was intensified by the fact that the rate of population increase of the Indians has for long been significantly larger than that of the Africans, with the result that by the late 1960s they constituted a majority of the population of Guyana, and seemed likely to become the majority in Trinidad before the end of the twentieth century.

Since World War II political parties in the two nations have tended to be either predominantly black or predominantly Indian. Although most national political leaders in both countries have ostensibly deplored this situation, they have also known how to profit by it. Indian and African racial rivalry seems destined to play a major role in Trinidadian and Guyanese politics for a long time to come.

Economic Quandary of the Commonwealth Countries

During the struggles for popular sovereignty and national autonomy, there was a tendency on the part of many of the leaders in these struggles to argue that once their political objectives had been achieved, it would be comparatively easy to build prosperous national economies. However, it was also true that one of the major factors which impelled many of the leaders of the 1940s and 1950s to support the idea of a federation of the West Indies was fear that the various territories individually would not be able to establish viable economies.

It was certainly true that the countries of the area, virtually all of which were by 1980 either independent or approaching that status, were still faced with what in some cases seemed almost insurmountable economic problems. These originated from their size, their relative lack of resources, and their history.

Until well into the twentieth century the great majority of the Commonwealth territories of America had one-crop economies. Indeed, most of them depended almost entirely on the cultivation and export of sugar. It was the sugar industry that the African slaves were brought in to man in the seventeenth and eighteenth centuries. It was the sugar industry which generated huge fortunes for a small aristocracy and substantial income for the British treasury during the same period.

However, the sugar industry entered into a crisis with the emancipation of the slaves, if not before. During the twentieth century this crisis has been intensified, and sugar has entirely disappeared from some of the islands and only survives precariously in some of the others. It constitutes a major source of income only in Guyana, Trinidad, Barbados, Saint Kitts and Jamaica.

With the decline of sugar, one major economic problem has obviously been that of finding some other major export to take its place. However, there has been the additional problem of trying to develop a broader-based economy, not so disastrously dependent as the region has historically been on one particular source of income.

For attainment of both these objectives, the governments and people of the Commonwealth Caribbean have been faced with two major handicaps: the size of their populations and their paucity of resources. The populations of these countries range from perhaps 6,000 in Anguilla to 3 million in Jamaica, and the majority of the islands have been 100,000 and 200,000 people. These do not constitute a sufficient market upon which to base a broad range of economic activities. Furthermore, with the exception of Guyana's and Jamaica's bauxite and Trinidad's petroleum, none of the territories possesses any significant mineral deposits. Their resources are essentially their tropical soil, of varying quality, and their people.

The governments of different countries have sought different solutions to these problems since achievement of control over their countries' economies. In the islands of Dominica, Saint Lucia, Saint Vincent, and Grenada bananas were developed in the 1960s and 1970s as the alternative to sugar as the major export product. However, export of bananas came to be monopolized by one company, the Anglo-Dutch Geest firm. Saint Vincent has also sought to stimulate the growth and export of arrowroot, and Grenada the growing and shipping of nutmeg as supplements to banana production.

Throughout the islands of the area, tourism has become a major element of the national economy since World War II. Tax concessions and other benefits have been given to firms that build hotels or guest houses, and extensive advertising campaigns have been conducted in both the United States and Europe. However, it has been widely recognized that tourism is a precarious source of national income, depending as it does on economic trends and other influences in the countries from which the tourists come.

In the 1970s, international finance has tended to supplement tourism in Bermuda, the Bahamas, Cayman Islands, and the British Virgin Islands, as a major source of national income. Conditions have been created in those territories which make it profitable for companies in the United States and Western Europe to establish offshore branches which enable them to avoid taxes in their countries of origin.

Both Jamaica and Trinidad began programs in the 1950s for the establishment of manufacturing industries, some of which produced goods for the local market and neighboring countries, and others which had their principal markets in the United States and Europe. Subsequently, Barbados and several of the smaller islands began similar industrialization programs.

Finally, in the 1970s several of the governments of the territories of the area began programs designed to make the countries more self-sufficient in food supplies. As a result of population growth, the increase in tourism, and the general decline in agriculture, the territories had come to import a growing percentage of their food requirements. The governments' programs were designed to deal with this problem.

Efforts were also made by most of the territories of the area during the late 1960s and 1970s to work together to establish a broader economic base through setting up a common market. The Caribbean Free Trade Area was first organized, and then was converted into the Caribbean Common Market. At the same time, the Caribbean Development Bank was established, financed by the members of the Common Market and other countries, including the United States, Canada, Great Britain, and Venezuela.

Decline of British Influence

As the British withdrew politically from the Commonwealth area in the Western Hemisphere, their influence in other ways also declined drastically. They had never had the degree of association with their colonies in America which the French possessed in Martinique, Guadeloupe, and other French American territories. The British areas were never regarded as integral parts of Great Britain. They never had representation in the British parliament, as the French possessions in America did in the French parliament.

The psycho-political effects of this situation have been considerable. The British West Indians have always accepted the idea that they are blacks and the British are not, that they are West Indians first, Third-Worlders second, and people with a British tradition third.

Other influences than the British have tended to grow as the British political control over the area has relaxed. The influence of the United States, in music and education has increased, particularly as a growing number of young people have received their university training in the United States instead of Great Britain.

Developments in other areas of the Caribbean have also had their impact on the Commonwealth Caribbean. The economic influence of Venezuela has been felt in the 1970s. The political impact of the Cuban revolution has also had its effect in the English-speaking areas of the Caribbean.

The Second Revolution

The decline of British influence in the Commonwealth area became increasingly obvious by the late 1970s. A new revolutionary wave began in the region in 1979. A group of twenty-six men overthrew the government of the highly unpopular prime minister, Eric Gairy, of Grenada in April 1979. A month later, the regime of Prime Minister Patrick John of Dominica was also ousted after a series of popular demonstrations, although most of those who participated in the succeeding regime were people who had also been members of John's government.

Even the constitutional succession of the government of Prime Minister Alan Luisy of Saint Lucia Labour Party in June 1979, as a result of an election lost by the fifteen-year prime minister John Compton had revolutionary overtones. The Luisy government joined with those of Grenada and Dominica in forming a new coalition of radical regimes in the English-speaking Caribbean.

Political Parties of the Commonwealth Caribbean

In conclusion, there is no question about the fact that the political parties of the Commonwealth Caribbean are indigenous, coming into existence as the result of the changing political situation in the area itself. Although the Conservative Party of Barbados may have patterned itself for a while on the British Tories, and several of the Socialist-oriented parties of the area received help from time to time from the British Labour Party, no party of the Commonwealth Caribbean has ever officially been part of a British political party. In this, they have differed fundamentally from the parties of the French Caribbean and even from some of those of Puerto Rico and the Virgin Islands of the United States.

The political parties of the Commonwealth Caribbean have emerged from the struggle for black supremacy and national sovereignty. They have changed as the conditions in the British West Indies have altered. The newer parties have reflected generational struggles and changing ideologies in the area. They have tended increasingly to move away from the British pattern. It remains to be seen whether future developments in the English-speaking Caribbean area will make the politics and parties there conform increasingly to those of their Ibero-American neighbors.

The French Republic in America

The territories in America which are part of the French Republic are remnants of the struggles for empire among France, Great Britain, Spain, and the Netherlands during the seventeenth and eighteenth centuries. In the Caribbean area there are the relatively large islands of Guadeloupe and Martinique and the smaller ones of Saint Barthelemy and Saint Martin, as well as the South American territory of French Guiana. However, until the end of the Napoleonic Wars, Dominica and Saint Lucia had also been controlled by the French for long periods of time, and the creole patois is still spoken in those two islands — along with English. In the far north, the tiny islands of Saint Pierre and Miquelon, located between Nova Scotia and Newfoundland, are the last remaining outposts of the French Empire in North America.

The French Territories' Relationship to France

The peculiarity in the relations between these territories and France is that they have gone through the same national experiences as France itself and feel that they were part of those experiences. They, like France in Europe, went through the Revolution, the Napoleonic Empire, the Restoration, the 1848 Revolution, the Third Republic, the collapse of World War II, the de Gaulle phenomenon, to mention but the most important experiences.

This feeling of association with France has been strengthened by the fact that for a short while during the First French Republic, and continuously since the Second French Revolution, that of 1848, the French territories in America have been represented in the French legislature. At first, the representatives in the French parliament from the West Indian territories were mainly white colonists, but even in the nineteenth century there were some distinguished mulattoes and blacks who were members of the French Chamber of Deputies. Furthermore, there have been important Americans who have played roles in the history of France itself. Napoleon's first empress, Josephine, came from the French West Indies, and is still remembered and memorialized in Martinique. Félix Eboué, from French Guiana, as the governor of French Equatorial Africa, was one of the first officials to rally the territories under his control to the cause of General de Gaulle during World War II. Today, Victor Sable, from Martinique, is the only non-European sitting in the European Parliament, as a representative of France.

On another plane, too, this association with France persists. Aimé Césaire, the most important political leader of Martinique since World War II, is a distinguished French intellectual, as well as an outstanding Caribbean one. The great majority of French West Indians seeking a higher education go to France to acquire it. Reciprocally, there are substantial numbers of Frenchmen from Europe in the West Indian territories as civil servants and businessmen, although there are only tiny indigenous white communities.

Finally, the association with France is reinforced in the governmental forms of the French territories in America. They were originally regarded as colonies, in spite of their representation in the French parliament. However, in 1946 the constitution writers of the Fourth Republic decided to regard Guadeloupe, Martinique, and French Guiana as integral parts of France. The result is that for thirty-five years those territories have been "departments" of France, juridically and constitutionally in virtually the same relationship to the French government as the Department of the Seine. Thus, a foreigner who visits French Guiana, for instance, will have his passport stamped "Cayenne, France." In the late 1970s, Saint Pierre and Miquelon also became a French department.

The result of this long, close association with European France is that the people of the French West Indies — unlike their neighbors in the English-speaking West Indies — have a kind of schizophrenic attitude concerning who they really are. This is particularly the case with the better-educated people and the economic and political elites. It is perhaps less notable, although not entirely absent, among the lower classes, who speak creole as their first language, although also learning French and speaking it when that seems appropriate to them.

The French West Indians know that they are not European Frenchmen. However, to a certain degree they do consider themselves Frenchmen of some kind. They are West Indians and Americans, but they have had very little contact and interchange even with the non-French West Indian islands closest to them. The people of these French territories are not quite sure what they are, and this has had a significant impact on politics in the territories and on the political parties which have functioned there.

The psychological and political relationships between the French territories in America and European France have been complicated still more by economic factors, particularly since World War II. Traditionally, economic relations have been between each of the American territories and France itself — they have sent virtually all their exports to France and have imported almost exclusively from France. There has been little commerce even among the French territories in America and virtually none between them and their immediate neighbors.

In these regards, the French American territories have not traditionally been much different from those of the British West Indies. However, since World War II another factor has intervened in the France–French America relationship which has been markedly different from that between Great Britain and its American territories.

Since World War II the Republic of France has poured very large sums of money into the French territories. All members of the French civil service, whether coming from France or being natives of Guadeloupe, Martinique, French Guiana, have received 40 percent additional "overseas pay" for service in French America. The French social security system has been extended to French America. The French Republic has laid out substantial amounts in building up the infrastructure of the economies of these territories. Furthermore, it has subsidized a number of manufacturing enterprises and some aspects of the agriculture of these departments.

These substantial financial expenditures have tended to reinforce the inclination of the people of these territories to maintain their association with the French Republic, in one form or another. They have also had another important impact on politics, reinforcing the significance of patronage. The ability of a local mayor or a member of the general council to get public works and other expenditures from the French authorities for the community he represents, or to get favors from those authorities for his political followers, has been a matter of key importance for the survival of those French West Indian politicians.

Parties in the French Territories

One obvious impact of this importance of patronage has been the tendency for the fashions in parties in the French West Indies to follow the fashions of parties in European France. The parties which are strongest in metropolitan France have tended, with some notable exceptions, to be the strongest ones in Guadeloupe, Martinique, and French Guiana. When a party lost force in European France, it tended to do likewise in these overseas departments of the republic.

Most political parties in the French Caribbean have been the parties which existed in metropolitan France. They have been federations or local branches of those European parties. Or they have been local parties associated with one or another of the parties in the metropolis, such as the Parti Schoelcheriste of Guadeloupe in its relationship to the French Radical Party. In a few cases, such as the Communist parties of Guadeloupe and Martinique, parties which began as federations of a French party officially established themselves as separate groups, although by no means breaking all association with their counterparts in France.

The only parties which do not have French associations have been those which have advocated autonomy. Particularly notable are the Martinican Progressive Party and the Guyanese Socialist Party of French Guiana. These parties are good examples of the political schizophrenia which we have mentioned. Although seeking a greater degree of self-government for their respective territories, they have been somewhat vague in spelling out the nature of the autonomy they advocate. Significantly, they have strongly rejected the idea of complete independence from France.

Indeed, advocates of independence have been fringe parties in the area. They have had little popular support and very small electoral strength. Whether this will change as a result of all of the neighboring English-speaking territories becoming independent, and of the radicalization of politics in some of the nearby Commonwealth territories, remains to be seen.

Gaullism

Special mention must be made of the Gaulliste phenomenon during and after World War II. Although this was a feature of European French politics, it was even more significant in the French territories in America. With the fall of France in

May/June 1940, control of the French territories in the Caribbean was put in the hands of Admiral Georges Robert by the government of Vichy. Ruling from Martinique, he was governor-general of all of the French West Indian colonies. He also was custodian of a large part of the gold supply of France, which had been shipped there some time earlier, and in spite of urgent demands from Vichy to ship the gold back to Europe, he found reasons for not doing so. One reason, undoubtedly, was that the United States Navy was keeping a very close eye on everything which went into and left the French territories.

Meanwhile, the sympathies of the people of the French Caribbean territories were clearly with General Charles de Gaulle, who had raised the standard of resistance to the Vichy government. Large numbers of young men fled from Guadeloupe and Martinique to neighboring British islands, to join the de Gaulle forces. In the islands themselves a civil movement of Resistance was organized. The end of the Robert regime finally came soon after the Allied landings in North Africa in November 1942. General de Gaulle then named authorities to run the French territories in the West Indies. Almost a year before, the Gaullist flag had been raised in Saint Pierre and Miquelon, which had become one of the first parts of the French Empire to join the cause of the Free French.

With the return of peace, with de Gaulle as provisional president of France, the former Resistance leader had very strong support in the French territories in America. This backing rallied to him with his return to power in 1958, and during his ten years of administration the Gaullistes were undoubtedly the largest political element in the West Indian French departments. For his part, de Gaulle reinforced his following by directing large funds to the American departments, both as transfer payments and as contributions to economic development.

However, with the retirement of the general from active politics, the strength of his followers declined. Although the American departments overwhelmingly backed his choice as his successor, Georges Pompidou, in the 1969 presidential elections, the Gaullistes subsequently divided in those territories as they did in metropolitan France. By the end of the 1970s, the former supporters of the general were split between the neo-Gaullist movement of Jacques Chirac and the party organized by President Valery Giscard d'Estaing.

Conclusion

Party politics in the American parts of the French Republic have been played out within the context of the politico-administrative structure of the republic. As reorganized by the constitution of the Fifth Republic, Guadeloupe, Martinique, and French Guiana were made overseas departments, while Saint Pierre and Miquelon was until 1976 one of the overseas territories, also becoming a department in that year. Guadeloupe and Martinique have each had two senators and three deputies in the French National Assembly, while French Guiana and Saint Pierre and Miquelon have each had one senator and one deputy. Each of the four territories has since 1946 had a general council (*conseil general*) elected by universal adult suffrage. Each of the four, also, is divided into municipalities.

It is for this variety of legislative posts that the various political parties have contended. The only elected administrative officials have been the mayors of the municipalities. The executives of the departments have been in the hands of the prefects—as in the metropolitan departments—appointed by the government in Paris. The general councils have had no say in the appointment of the executives serving under the prefects.

Dutch-speaking America

In the scramble for colonies in the Caribbean, the Netherlands was left by the end of the Napoleonic Wars with the Netherlands Antilles, consisting of five-and-a-half islands in the Windward-Leeward group and off the South American coast, and the South American continental territory of Surinam or Dutch Guiana. Of these, Surinam has become independent and the Netherlands Antilles has acquired complete internal self-government and is on the way to full independence.

The economies of the two parts of Dutch-speaking America are very different. Surinam was originally an agriculturally based colony. It was to cultivate sugar, rice, and other such products that African slaves were first brought there and that, subsequent to emancipation, indentured servants from the Indian subcontinent and Indonesia were induced to immigrate. Although agriculture still employs a large percentage of the population of Surinam, by far the most important source of foreign exchange since World War II has been bauxite and its products, alumina and aluminum.

In contrast, the economy of the Dutch islands of Curaçao and Aruba remained very primitive until the 1920s. In that decade the oil companies which were beginning the exploitation of the petroleum reserves of neighboring Venezuela began to construct their refineries in the Dutch islands, as a precaution against possible political upheaval in Venezuela. As a result, oil refining continues to be the principal source of income for those two islands. However, since World War II tourism has also become an important economic activity there and has become the main source of income in the other islands of the Netherlands Antilles.

The Dutch were rather slow about expanding the franchise and granting self-government to their American colonies. Although legislative bodies did exist in both areas, the right to vote for their members was extremely limited, and the powers of the legislatures were minimal until after World War II.

During the war the exiled government of Queen Wilhelmina promised that after the conflict the Dutch kingdom would be reorganized, and all parts of it—the Netherlands, Indonesia, the Netherlands Antilles, and Surinam—would be placed on an equal constitutional footing. However, the fulfillment of this promise was held up very considerably by the ultimately vain attempt of the Dutch to resist the Indonesian independence movement, which culminated in 1949 with the final separation of Indonesia from the Dutch empire.

Subsequently, there were extended negotiations among the Dutch, the spokesmen for Surinam, and those for the Netherlands Antilles. These reached a conclusion in 1954, when it was agreed that the three remaining parts of the Dutch kingdom would be considered coequal members. In practice, this meant that the Netherlands Antilles and Surinam would have full internal self-government, with the Netherlands continuing to control only defense and foreign affairs. Both the Netherlands Antilles and Surinam governments would have representatives in the Netherlands cabinet in The Hague. Furthermore, in any international negotiations involving any two of the three parts of the Netherlands kingdom, all parts so involved would be represented in the Netherlands delegation. As a result of this arrangement, for instance, the Netherlands delegation to a meeting of the Economic Commission for Latin America in the winter of 1958 consisted of four members, two from the Netherlands and one each from Netherlands Antilles and Surinam, with the representative from Surinam chairing the delegation.

For many years this arrangement seemed to be satisfactory to the political leaders of both Surinam and Netherlands Antilles. However, in 1975 the government of Surinam formally requested full independence, which was granted. Subsequently, the government of the Netherlands Antilles announced its intention of also seeking complete independence in the not-too-distant future. So far, however, it has not formally begun such negotiations with the Dutch. Late in 1981, Aruba indicated that it would seek independence separate from the rest of the Netherlands Antilles.

With the emergence of self-government and popular sovereignty the political systems of both Netherlands Antilles and Surinam tended to follow the Dutch parliamentary model. The government in power in both territories needed to have the support of a majority of the members of the elected parliament. This usually required some kind of party coalition in both countries.

So long as both Netherlands Antilles and Surinam remained parts of the Dutch kingdom, the queen was represented in each case by a governor, appointed by the Netherlands government. In the case of the Netherlands Antilles there were also lieutenant governors appointed for Curaçao, Aruba, Bonaire, and the Windward Islands group. Each of these parts of the Netherlands Antilles also had an elected island council.

Political parties emerged in both Surinam and Netherlands Antilles during and after World War II—although at least one party had existed in Curaçao even earlier than that. The basis of party conflict has been quite different in the two countries, however. Because of the complex racial mixture in Surinam, the parties there have tended to be established along racial lines, although within most of the racial groups there is more than one party. In contrast, in the Netherlands Antilles, where the population is considerably more homogeneous, parties have tended to divide over economic, social, and political issues rather than along racial lines.

An event in Surinam in 1979 tended to cast a shadow over the future of parties in that country. This was a military coup, led by noncommissioned officers of the armed forces. It remains to be seen whether, in the wake of that coup, it will be possible to continue parliamentary government based on competing political parties.

The United States Territories

Two West Indian territories associated with the United States are dealt with in the present volume. These are Puerto Rico and the Virgin Islands of the United States. The Panama Canal Zone, which was also under United States jurisdiction during most of the twentieth century, is a special case, in which parties did not develop for reasons which we shall note.

These territories all came under United States control during that period, beginning with the annexation of Hawaii in 1897, in which the United States acquired substantial possessions beyond the confines of continental North America. The United States took over the Philippines, Guam, and Puerto Rico as a result of the Spanish-American War of 1898, which also resulted in the United States having a virtual protectorate over Cuba for more than thirty years. Five years after the Spanish-American War, the United States signed a treaty with the new Republic of Panama, which it had helped bring into existence, giving the United States jurisdiction over the Zone. Finally, in 1917, under the pressures of World War I, the United States purchased the Virgin Islands from Denmark.

Coming late into the practice of colonialism, the United States had no fixed patterns for handling dependent territories. It dealt with each of them in a somewhat different manner. After some hesitation, Cuba was declared an independent republic in 1902, and finally achieved full juridical sovereignty in 1934, when President Franklin Roosevelt abrogated the Platt Amendment, which had given the United States the right to remove the Cuban government when it saw fit.

The other United States territories in the Caribbean area have had a different evolution. After being dealt with quite frankly as colonies, Puerto Rico and the Virgin Islands—along with Guam in the central Pacific—evolved in a somewhat different direction after World War II. They have all come to have commonwealth status—or as it is called in Puerto Rico, the position of an *Estado Libre Asociado* (Free Associated State). Under this system, the people of these territories are United States citizens, they elect their own governors and legislatures, and their governments have considerable autonomy in internal affairs. However, the Congress of the United States remains the supreme legislative authority, the last level of appeal from the local courts is the United States Supreme Court, and these territories do not elect voting members of the United States Congress or participate in the election of the president of the United States. They also pay no federal income taxes.

In both Puerto Rico and the Virgin Islands, there has been established under United States patronage the United States system of division of powers—legislative, executive and judiciary—rather than the parliamentary system which had prevailed before the United States annexed them. The British legal and judicial system characteristic of the United States has also been established in both areas.

The linguistic problem has been of considerable consequence in Puerto Rico, although not in the Virgin Islands, where English was spoken by virtually everyone even before the territory came under United States control. In Puerto Rico, Spanish is the native language, and many political controversies in the island have centered on this issue since 1898. Since the establishment of the Commonwealth in 1952, however, Spanish has been the language of instruction in the public schools, although all students also take English as a second language throughout most of their educational careers; in governmental relations, too, Spanish is the official language, as is also the case in the local courts.

The issue of the status of the island has been the overriding political question in Puerto Rico since even before its acquisition by the United States, with competing groups favoring assimilation to the metropolitan power, independence, or autonomy with continued association with the metropolis. In contrast, in the Virgin Islands, although there has been a strong desire for more local participation in the government of the territory, neither complete assimilation nor independence has been seen as a viable alternative by any substantial portion of the citizenry.

The situation in the Panama Canal Zone, which was under United States jurisdiction "as if it were sovereign" there between 1903 and 1979, was quite a different one. Most of the residents of the Zone were people from the United States working for either the Canal Company, the military, or other U.S. government installations. Juridically, they were never regarded as constituting a separate body of citizenry. The affairs of the Zone were administered by its governor — usually also the local United States military commander — and officials appointed by him. There was never created in the Zone a legislative body to participate in the administration of its affairs. Consequently, there never developed any local political parties. "Zonians" might be registered Democrats or Republicans in the United States, but there was no occasion even to be affiliated with one of the U.S. political parties if the Zone residents had completely cut their ties with "back home."

With the new Panama Canal treaties between the United States and Panama signed and ratified in 1978, this situation changed. The Zone as such was abolished, coming for all governmental purposes under the jurisdiction of the Republic of Panama. Henceforward, if they want to be active in a partisan sense in local politics — rather than in those of the United States — people resident in the former Zone will now have to participate in the parties of the Republic of Panama.

ANGUILLA

Anguilla, a long-time British colony, is a tiny, low-lying, drought-prone island three miles wide and sixteen miles long located 150 miles east of Puerto Rico. Despite its small size, Anguilla achieved international political attention in the late 1960s when its 6,000 residents "rebelled" against continuing associated statehood with Saint Kitts, preferring direct association with the United Kingdom.

Unlike most of the other inhabitants of the Commonwealth Caribbean, individual Anguillians have traditionally worked their own lands or have been engaged in fishing or seafaring. The majority on Anguilla are black or mixed-blood descendants of imported African slaves, although a rigid planter-slave, owner-worker polarity was never as intense on Anguilla as on other West Indian islands. Mindful of their background, many Anguillians describe themselves as "middle class" in obvious contrast to the plantation, proletarian backgrounds of people from larger nearby island states.

A small group of Englishmen, led by Abraham Howell who immediately appointed himself deputy governor of Anguilla, first settled the island in 1650. For the next one and one-half centuries the English settlers and some slaves coped with hurricanes, recurring drought, and raids from the Caribs and French. The resident deputy governor ruled the island with only informal advice from local councilmen until the 1830s when a twelve-man local council was established with eleven members elected by property holders on the island. The council, however, performed only minor duties as Anguilla was governed by a lieutenant governor on Saint Kitts. Anguilla was part of the Leeward Islands federation during the 1870s, but from 1883 the island's administration was once again directly combined with that for Saint Kitts-Nevis.

Even during these early years when Anguilla and neighboring islands were governed by a white ruling class, interisland rivalries and differences frustrated Anguillians. These differences were intensified as the Leeward Caribbean began to approach political autonomy in the mid-twentieth century. Politically fused with Saint Kitts for colonial administrative purposes, Anguilla was still attached politically to larger Saint Kitts, as well as Nevis, when associated statehood was granted to the three islands together in February 1967. This only heightened antagonisms between Anguillians and Kittitians. On Saint Kitts, Robert Bradshaw had led his Labour Party, supported by a sugarcane worker constituency, and he attempted to elicit a similar following on Anguilla. Anguillian fishermen and peasant producers were however unmoved by Kittitian political strategies that appealed to the larger island's plantation workers. So during the local elections in the 1950s and 1960s Anguillians persistently elected independent candidates to represent them in Saint Kitts. Bradshaw was further angered by Anguillians often ignoring both Kittitian politicians and the policemen from Saint Kitts assigned to Anguilla.

For the two years following associated statehood with Saint Kitts and Nevis, individual Anguillians, including Ronald Webster, traveled abroad seeking support for Anguilla's secession from Saint Kitts. Two plebiscites, in 1967, then again in 1969, were also held on Anguilla, confirming that almost every Anguillian favored autonomy from Saint Kitts.

In the second of these plebiscites, on 6 February 1969, the vote was 1739 to 4 in favor of separation from the Associated State of Saint Kitts-Nevis-Anguilla. On the following day, the independence of Anguilla was proclaimed under President Peter Adams, who was soon succeeded by Ronald Webster. The resident Saint Kitts policemen were deported back home. A new constitution was written which would have welcomed all kinds of foreign business interests to the island.

Finally, in March 1969, amid rumors of international intrigue and Mafia control of Anguilla, British military and police forces landed on the island in their bloodless but now-famous operation "Calypso." The net result of the invasion was to establish a direct British presence on Anguilla which confirmed Anguilla's de facto secession from Saint Kitts. On a wider scale, the Anguilla incident earned Britain considerable international embarrassment inspired by members of the news media, who were intrigued by what they considered a zany political furor. Acrimonious charges of "recolonization" moreover came from throughout the Commonwealth Caribbean.

In February 1976, the British government put forth a new constitution for Anguilla, reestablishing it formally as a British dependency. The island is currently governed by a resident British commissioner who consults with the local twelve-member legislative assembly on almost all matters. The legislative assembly is composed of seven elected members, three ex-officio administrative specialists, and two members nominated by the commissioner in consultation with the elected chief minister who at the end of 1980 was Emile Gumbs, a political independent. The local legislature, although guided by the 1976 constitution, is an extension in spirit of the local governance that followed the expulsion of Saint Kitts police from Anguilla in 1969. At that time, a loosely organized peacekeeping committee of fifteen local leaders maintained order until a provisional council was established. The provisional council was in turn replaced by an elected pro tem council of seven members before the 1976 constitution was handed down from Britain.

Political party development and political organization in general on Anguilla have never been strong, probably owing to the island's small scale and the independence and mobility of its inhabitants. There is also an inherent solidarity among most Anguillians (which is interpreted as clannishness by most other West Indians). Within their home island society, Anguillians recognize social differences on the basis of religion or differences in wealth, distinctions that until now have had little political expression. Nevertheless, a recently developed Progressive People's Party stood in the 1976 elections, challenged by unorganized independent candidates. Earlier elections were contested by candidates from Saint Kitts-based parties, but any identification with Saint Kitts has always proved burdensome for Anguillian candidates seeking elected offices. The *Beacon* a weekly newspaper, provides a rallying point for most Anguillians. The *Beacon* is passed from one person to another on Anguilla and is sent abroad to those working overseas.

Bibliography

William J. Brisk. *The Dilemma of a Ministate: Anguilla.* Studies in International Affairs, no. 7. Institute of International Studies, University of South Carolina, 1969.

Colin G. Clarke. "Political Fragmentation in the Caribbean: The Case of Anguilla." *Canadian Geographer,* vol. 15, no. 1, 1971, pp. 13–29.

Donald E. Wastlake. *Under an English Heaven.* Simon and Schuster, New York, 1972.

Political Parties

PEOPLE'S ACTION MOVEMENT. Peter Adams, an Anguillian leader, who was the island's representative at statehood talks and its sole delegate to the Saint Kitts-Nevis-Anguilla state legislature in 1967, was a nominal member of the People's Action Movement. His party "affiliation" was more in opposition to the Saint Kitts-Nevis-Anguilla Labour Party than anything else, and there has never been any real organization of the party on Anguilla (see entry for Saint Kitts-Nevis).

PROGRESSIVE PEOPLE'S PARTY. The Progressive People's Party, formed in time for the assembly elections of 1976, is led by Ronald Webster who was an acknowledged leader in the uprising against Saint Kitts in the late 1960s. Webster sees Anguilla's status as that of partnership with Britain, but he seeks contact with other international interests who may be attracted to Anguilla in return for lenient taxation. Independent leaders who oppose Webster's point of view assert that Anguilla's relationship with Britain need not be that of a dependency.

SAINT KITTS-NEVIS-ANGUILLA LABOUR PARTY. Although the Saint Kitts-Nevis-Anguilla Labour Party was never popular in Anguilla, one Anguillian businessman-politician, David Lloyd was elected by that party to and served in the federal parliament during the short-lived West Indian Federation between 1958 and 1962.

Bonham C. Richardson

ANTIGUA

Antigua is one of the Leeward Islands, 171 square miles in area and with a 1979 estimated population of 75,000. It was discovered in 1493 by Columbus, who supposedly named it after the Santa Maria la Antigua church in Seville. However, it was not occupied by Europeans until 1632, when English colonists settled there. It was seized by the French in 1666 for a short while, but was soon returned to Great Britain and remained thereafter a British colony. Associated with it has been the nearby island of Barbuda, with sixty-two square miles and a population of 1200 people.

Party politics arose originally from the labor movement, and the major parties are still closely associated with organized labor. The first trade union group, the Antigua Trades and Labour Union (ATLU), was established in 1939, and Vere C. Bird soon emerged as its principal leader. However, the new labor movement ran into very considerable opposition from the entrenched interests in the island. Its efforts to gain some political influence were considerably hampered at the time by the fact that the franchise was severely limited by property and income requirements. Nevertheless, a few of the labor leaders were elected to the legislature, among them Vere Bird in 1945 and Ernest Williams in 1947.

However, when universal adult suffrage was adopted for elections for the legislative council in 1952, the political activities of the ATLU were much more successful. The union established a Political Committee, which named candidates, and conducted election campaigns for more than a decade and one-half, electing most of the members of the legislative council during that period. For election purposes, the political committee of the ATLU campaigned under the name Antigua Labour Party (ALP).

In 1956 ministerial government was introduced, with a cabinet presided over by a chief minister. All members of the legislative council were by then elected, except the attorney general, who had an ex-officio post in that body. Vere Bird became the first, and only, chief minister.

In 1967 two important political events occurred. First, Antigua was officially transformed from a colony into an Associated State. This meant that it had a totally elected legislature and a cabinet responsible to the majority in the lower house of Parliament, rechristened the House of Representatives, which had control over all matters except foreign affairs, internal security, and defense. The chief minister became premier. The governor was named by the British

Crown, on the recommendation of the Antigua government.

The second important event of 1967 was a split in the Antigua Trades and Labour Union led by its general secretary, George Walter, which resulted in most of the secondary leaders and members quitting the union to form the rival Antigua Workers Union (AWU). This split came about because of dissatisfaction with the situation in which most of the top officials of the ATLU were also ministers in the government, involving them in a serious conflict of interest. The dissidents had insisted that Vere Bird give up either his position as president of the union or the premiership, but he refused to do so.

The division of the ATLU gave rise directly to the formation of political parties. Each faction of the labor movement organized it's own political party. An attempt, begun in 1968, to organize a third party without connections with organized labor failed when that party was unable to elect any member of the House of Representatives in 1970. However, subsequently a third party, more radical than the two major ones, was established.

Neither of the two major parties of Antigua, the Antigua Labour Party (ALP) and the Progressive Labour Movement (PLM), has a very clearly defined ideology. The PLM has tended to put more emphasis on social and labor programs than the ALP, which draws considerably more support than its rival from the business community.

In the satellite island of Barbuda, there developed some sentiment for separation from Antigua, as the prospect of eventual independence grew. The people of that island have a feeling that they have been neglected by the government of Antigua. However, the grievances of Barbuda have not given rise to the establishment there of any separatist party, the voters continuing to elect a member from one or the other of the two major parties to the House of Representatives.

Bibliography

Personal contacts of the writer.

Antigua Trades and Labour Union. *AT&LU 40th Anniversary 1939–1979.* Saint Johns, 1979.

Novelle H. Richards. *The Struggle and the Conquest: Twenty-five Years of Social Democracy in Antigua.* Workers Voice Printery, Saint Johns, n.d.

Political Parties

ANTIGUA BARBUDA DEMOCRATIC MOVEMENT. *See* PROGRESSIVE LABOUR MOVEMENT.

ANTIGUA CARIBBEAN LIBERATION MOVEMENT (ACLM). This group originated as a "black consciousness" organization in the early 1970s, under the name Afro Caribbean Liberation Movement. However, in 1977 it was officially registered as a political party as the Antigua Caribbean Liberation Movement. It is led by Tim Hector, a graduate of McGill University, and it proclaims itself to be a "socialist" party, advocating a program of economic development, based on full revival of agriculture, so that the island can provide the food it needs, supplemented by agro-industries. It would maintain the tourist industry under private ownership as the country's principal source of foreign exchange. It advocates decentralization of the economy on the basis of voluntary farmers' cooperatives and a Farmers' Council which would participate in economic planning. It professes to believe in plural party democracy. In its first try at the polls in 1980, the ACLM did not win any seats.

ANTIGUA LABOUR PARTY (ALP). From 1951 and the introduction of universal adult suffrage, the Political Committee of the Antigua Trades and Labour Union conducted election campaigns under the name Antigua Labour Party, but a separate party organization did not exist. Finally, in 1969, faced with the challenge of the Progressive Labour Movement, the party organized by leaders of the dissident Antigua Workers Union, the Antigua Labour Party was formally separated from the ATLU. Thereafter, the two organizations had separate, although closely linked, structures. The ALP was based on organizations in each constituency, and a national committee on an island-wide level. With formation of the ALP as clearly a party organization, Vere Bird and other ministers resigned their positions as officials of the Antigua Trades and Labour Union.

In its first electoral contest in 1970, the ALP won only four of the seventeen legislative seats. For five years it constituted the official opposition. Then in 1976 it won the election, gaining eleven seats. Vere Bird again became premier. Four years later the ALP won thirteen of the seventeen seats in the House of Representatives.

Elements of the Antigua Labour Party thus directed the island's affairs from 1956, when ministerial government was established, until 1970, and again after 1976. During the earlier period it guided the country toward responsible internal self-government. In the economic field, it fought a losing battle to try to maintain the sugar industry, even having the government take over the island's last surviving sugar mill when it was threatened with bankruptcy. At the same time, the earlier ALP government encouraged the growth of tourism. In its later period in power, the ALP sought to bring about a partial revival of the sugar industry, while also seeking to diversify the economy through establishment of light industries which would prove another source of export income.

In its 1980 campaign, the Antigua Labour Party promised to lead the country into full independence during its next period in office. It achieved this objective in October 1981.

ANTIGUA PEOPLE'S PARTY. This party was formed in 1969 by J. Rowan Henry, a leading lawyer and Queen's Counsel. It was an avowed attempt to break the tie between the labor movement and the political parties. In its 1970 Election

Manifesto it proclaimed that its appearance "now offers the people . . . for the first time, opportunity to vote for a properly constituted political party." That manifesto, published in a glossy pamphlet, carried a detailed business-oriented economic and social program. However, the party failed to get any seats in the House of Representatives in the 1970 election and soon after disappeared.

ANTIGUA PROGRESSIVE MOVEMENT. *See* PROGRESSIVE LABOUR MOVEMENT.

PROGRESSIVE LABOUR MOVEMENT (PLM). Chronologically, the PLM was the first of the country's real parties. It was formed soon after establishment of the Antigua Workers Union by dissident members of the Antigua Trades and Labour Union in 1967. The principal leaders of the Antigua Workers Union joined in the following year with two small groups which had attempted to organize parties but had not succeeded in electing any legislators (the Antigua Barbuda Democratic Movement and the Antigua Progressive Movement) to form the PLM. It was formally set up in April 1968, with George Walters as its leader. Upon assuming this political post, Walters resigned as head of the AWU, becoming a simple rank-and-file member of the union.

In its first electoral contest in 1970, the Progressive Labour Movement won a sweeping victory, getting thirteen of the seventeen seats in the House of Representatives. George Walters became premier, and the PLM controlled the government until 1976. During their years in office, the PLM government closed down the last sugar mill, saving the government considerable money, and started a program for agricultural development. Grazing expanded, and served the purposes of both internal meat consumption and modest exports, sea island cotton was revived; and the production of truck-gardening crops was stimulated by the government assuring the farmers a market for those products by being willing to purchase at a reasonable price any fruits and vegetables of good quality the farmers could deliver. The PLM regime also established a social security system and consolidated the island's labor legislation into a labor code, with help from an expert from the International Labor Organization.

However, in spite of its accomplishments in office, the Progressive Labour Movement was defeated in the 1976 election. This came about in spite of the fact that the party won a majority of the popular vote, since the PLM won with very strong majorities in the constituencies in which it was victorious, and the rival ALP carried a number of the constituencies by very small margins. The PLM elected only five members of the House of Representatives, out of seventeen.

The Vere Bird government of the ALP which assumed office in 1976, brought criminal charges against George Walters for alleged corruption while in office. Although he was convicted of corrupt conspiracy, Walters's supposed coconspirator was declared innocent, which raised doubts about the validity of Walters's conviction. He appealed to the Associated States Appeal Court.

The Progressive Labour Movement won only three seats in the general election of 1980, which was called in preparation for the movement of Antigua toward full independence.

Robert J. Alexander

ARGENTINA

Argentina is the second largest of the Spanish-American republics, in area (1,072,067 square miles) and population (26,725,000 according to the 1979 estimate). It occupies most of the southern third of the South American continent. The country is located principally in the temperate zone, although the northern-most provinces are subtropical.

During the colonial period, present-day Argentina was an outpost of the Spanish Empire. Most of its territory continued to be occupied by Indians. At about the same time that the Spaniards were beginning to establish their settlements, Araucanian Indians from Chile were moving across the Andes and conquering the more peaceful Indians in the great plains of Argentina.

Present-day Argentina was originally settled by Spaniards from the Viceroyalty of Peru, with its headquarters in Lima. They established towns in the northern part of the country, including Córdoba, Tucumán, and Salta. However, the port city of Buenos Aires was not finally established until 1580.

During most of the colonial period, Argentina remained part of the Viceroyalty of Peru. However, in the 1770s the Bourbon monarch of Spain broke up that viceroyalty. One of these subdivisions was the Viceroyalty of Buenos Aires, which controlled present-day Argentina, as well as Paraguay, Uruguay, and the southernmost part of Brazil.

However, the city of Buenos Aires had characteristics which tended to separate it from most of Argentina. It tended to look outward to Europe and the rest of the world, instead of inward to the rest of America. It also tended to be settled to some degree by non-Spaniards, including Frenchmen, Britishers and others. This differentiation continued through the middle of the twentieth century.

Shortly before the beginning of the struggle for independence, the residents of Buenos Aires and nearby areas repulsed extensive efforts by the British to seize control of the colony in 1806 and 1807. This incident stimulated the feeling of national identification of the Argentines. However, the actual struggle for independence began as a movement to assert the rights of the Spanish Bourbon monarch against those of Joseph Bonaparte, whom Napoleon had placed on the Spanish throne. A *cabildo abierto*, or open meeting, was held in Buenos Aires on 25 May 1810 to proclaim this loyalty. Independence was not formally declared until 9 July 1816; as a result Argentina is one of the few countries that celebrates two independence days—May 25 and July 9.

During its early years of independence the nation lacked unity, its leaders being divided between those who wanted a unitary government and those who wanted a federal one. The first of Argentina's three great caudillos, Juan Manuel de Rosas, came to power in 1829 and stayed in control until 1852. He ruled through force, imposing unity on the country by eliminating or coopting regional caudillos. Following the ouster of Rosas, the country suffered a short period of civil warfare, during which the federal versus the unitary issue was again prominent.

With the ascension to power of General Bartolomé Mitre in 1862, there began a half-century period during which rule by the Liberal Party (established by Domingo F. Sarmiento, Mitre and other opponents of the Rosas dictatorship) and its various offshoots gave way to rule by a rural oligarchy, which largely came into existence because of the economic policies of the Liberal presidents, Mitre, Sarmiento, and Avellaneda (1862–1880). With the inauguration of President Julio A. Roca in 1880, all pretense of party government disappeared. From then on, parties supporting the succeeding administrations existed at most on a provincial level. A very strong presidency, together with a largely hand-picked Congress character-ized the government from Roca's first administration until the ascension of the Radicals to power for the first time in 1916. During that period, the government was largely a political expression of the rural landlords, who dominated the nation both economically and politically. This elite used fraudulent election practices in successfully denying their opponents any real chance of coming to power via the electoral route. The whole period from 1862 to 1916 is often referred to as the conservative epoch.

During this period, the Argentine economy was transformed. As a result of the invention of barbed wire, it became possible to fence off the pampas, which in turn made it feasible to selectively breed cattle appropriate for European—particularly British—markets. At the same time, the advent of refrigerated ships brought about establishment of packing houses in Buenos Aires and Rosario, and the shipping of meat instead of cattle on the hoof to Europe. Those parts of the pampas not given over to cattle growing were opened up as grain-producing areas. By the time this was all taking place, most of the pampas had already been divided among a relatively small number of very large landholders.

Other parts of the country were also transformed. In the south, in Patagonia, sheep growing instead of cattle breeding became the pattern of economic activity. Various areas around the periphery of the country came to specialize in other kinds of agricultural production, chiefly for the domestic market—vineyards in the foothills of the Andes, sugar in Tucumán, Salta, and Jujuy in the north.

By the advent of World War I, Argentina was one of the great grain-growing and meat-producing nations of the world. At the same time, the beginning of indus-trialization had taken place, particularly in the Greater Buenos Aires region. However, successive governments, until the advent of Peron in the early 1940s, did not encourage industrialization, because of fears of British retaliation by cutting purchases of grain and meat if the Argentines bought less British manu-factured goods.

However, in spite of government policy, the growth of manufacturing was rapid, particularly during the 1930s, when Argentine industries enjoyed de facto protection, resulting from a fall in demand for Argentine grazing and agricultural products during the Great Depression, resulting in the country's not earning sufficient foreign exchange to buy all of the consumers goods and construction materials that it needed. Subsequently, the policies of some of the governments, particularly those of Juan Perón and Arturo Frondizi, positively encouraged industrialization. As a result, by the 1970s, Argentina had an integrated industrial structure, its factories not only producing most of the consumer goods and construction materials needed by the domestic market, but also turning out iron and steel, petrochemicals and other products of heavy industry.

By this time, the patterns of Argentine trade had changed substantially. Although grazing and agricultural products still constituted most of the country's exports, it was shipping substantial quantities of manufactured goods to its Latin-American neighbors. In addition, however, the growth of the European Common Market, and the British entry into the ECC, which came to be close to self-sufficient in meat and grain, meant that Great Britain was no longer Argentina's largest trading partner. By the late 1970s, the Soviet Union occupied that position.

The Role of Argentine Political Parties

Argentina's political parties began to take modern form in the latter part of the nineteenth century. During the twentieth century, the Radical Civic Union (UCR) and the Peronist Party have vied with the military for control of the country. Since a March 1976 coup, the military has been in power and the nation's political parties, which were in disarray at the time, have ceased to function openly, although they continue to exist.

In 1916, after half a century of conservative control, the political party situation changed dramatically. The Sáenz Peña Law of 1912 provided for honest, secret elections, as a result of which the Radicals ended their longstanding boycott of the vote to participate in the presidential elections for the first time. The results were a triumph for the UCR and its leader, Hipólito Irigoyen, in the first national elections contested by that party. Irigoyen, Argentina's second great national caudillo, was president from 1916–1922 and again from 1928 to his overthrow in 1930. Another Radical, Marcelo T. de Alvear, held the presidency in the 1922–1928 period. The UCR appealed to middle-class, somewhat nationalistic interests, but did little in power to change the basic nature of Argentina's political system.

Following a year-and-a-half period of military rule after the 1930 coup, the Conservative forces again returned to power in Argentina. The Conservatives ruled under increasing pressure from the military until the armed forces openly seized power in a 4 June 1943 coup. That coup ultimately brought Colonel Juan D. Perón to power in 1946, following a three year period of internal struggle among the military leaders. Perón, the third of Argentina's great caudillo leaders, dominated Argentina's politics from 1945 until his death in 1974. Peronism has been the single largest political force in the nation since its inception, and a central question for non-Peronists, both military and civilians, has been how to interact with the Peronists.

In addition to questions relating to Peronism, three other interrelated issues have dominated Argentine politics in the years since 1943. These are economic development, the role of the military, and political violence.

Economic development issues have a long history in Argentina, with disagreements occurring over the question of agricultural versus industrial emphasis, the proper amount and method of governmental intervention in the economy, and the proper balance between national versus foreign investment and economic control. The rise of multinational enterprises has raised acute questions in Argentina. Political parties have been deeply divided in their responses to economic issues, causing economic policy to fluctuate widely under various governments.

The parties have also differed in their attitudes toward military intervention. Naturally, no party favors military rule in principle, but there have been numerous occasions when one or more parties have actively supported coups and military intervention as solutions to particular political situations or problems. (For example, there was active civilian support for the coups of 1966 and 1976). In addition to their attitudes toward coups, parties have also differed widely in respect to cooperation with military governments once those governments were in power. In some cases, the same party has taken different stances toward the military at different times.

Civil violence is a relatively new political issue in Argentina, with politics becoming extremely violent since 1955. Some political movements such as the Montoneros, Ejercito Revolucionario del Pueblo (ERP) and sections of the Peronist movement, openly espouse violent methods as being both legitimate and necessary in today's Argentina. The majority of Argentina's political parties oppose the use of violence, but the issue will remain a central one in the coming years should military government and guerrilla activities continue.

By mid-1980, almost all of Argentina's political parties had been drastically weakened by events since 1966. The military has ruled for most of that period, and has made political activity illegal during its years in power. Political meetings have been banned, and mere speeches by politicians have sometimes brought jailing for the speaker. Even when parties could operate legally, as during the period preceding the 1973 election, and during the 1973–1976 period of rule by Juan and then Isabelita Perón, the parties did not really function normally. The primary goal for many was to replace the military government, not to implement specific policies.

The dominance of the military has been the preeminent feature of Argentine politics since 1966, but other factors have also emerged which have reduced the role of the political parties. Nonparty civilian groups have come to the political forefront, particularly labor, guerrillas, the Church, and right-wing vigilantes. It is not surprising that the military's ban on elections and party activity should give rise to groups that are willing to use confrontation and violence rather than negotiation and compromise.

Trade unionists have been feuding with governments and between themselves since before the 1966 coup. The main fighting has been among factions of the Peronist trade union movement, resulting in the assassination of many Peronist leaders and rank and file. The workers have also acted directly by staging strikes and seizing factories in defiance of government orders. Guerrillas have proliferated, especially since 1969, and have killed and wounded large numbers of the military and police. They have also kidnapped and killed industrialists, government officials, financiers, foreign diplomatic personnel, and even an ex-president. These acts of violence have been answered with violence on the part of the police and military, and have also contributed to the creation of extremely right-wing vigilante-type groups, such as the Argentine Anti-Communist Alliance (AAA). Such groups have harassed, tortured, and killed suspected leftists, guerrilla activists, and sympathizers, as well as centrist and center-Left political figures. The Catholic Church has not escaped the direct action type of political activity sweeping Argentina. Lay Catholics and activist priests have worked at organizing the poor and demanding changes for the benefit of the downtrodden. The clergy's statements have been condemned as subversive and revolutionary by the military and some sectors of the Right. Churches and priests have been bombed, and some priests have been machine-gunned to death because of their political activities.

The wide variety of groups advocating direct political action, coupled with prolonged bans against party politics, have eclipsed political party activity since 1966. The decrease in party strength is abetted by internal conditions within the parties. Opportunism, personalism, regionalism, ideological cleavages, proliferation, and corruption have all served to discredit Argentina's political parties. Continuing splits and fragmentation have weakened the parties, particularly the Peronists and the Radical Party. Although the fragmentation has often been attributed to ideological or policy differences, in reality personality clashes and internal struggles for leadership have often been more important causes.

The Range of Argentine Political Parties

Argentina's most important political parties fall into several categories or families. These include the Conservatives, Radicals, Socialists, Communists, Christian Democrats, and Peronists. There are other parties which do not conveniently fall into any of these groups.

Argentina's Conservative parties held power from the time of Rosas until the 1916 election won by Irigoyen and the Radicals, and again from 1931 to 1943. The Conservative parties generally represented the interests of the large landowners and their allies, and supported free trade. They have opposed state intervention in the economy. Since 1943, the Conservatives have been out of power, but have exercised a great deal of influence through their connections with agricultural interests (the Sociedad Rural), and the banking and financial sectors. *La Nación* and *La Prensa*, two of the country's oldest newspapers, usually present a Conservative point of view.

Argentine Conservatives were not united under a single party during most of the nineteenth century, but were more a collection of local and regional parties. As the Radical Civic Union (UCR) gained strength, the Conservatives did make several attempts to form a single party to support their interests (Unión Nacional, 1912; Concentración Nacional, 1922; and Partido Demócrata Nacional, 1931–1958). None of these attempts at unification was a success, as local issues continually impeded true national unity.

The Unión Cívica Radical (UCR) was Argentina's largest party almost from its inception in the 1890s to the emergence of Peronism in 1946. During that period, it had more members and gained more votes than any other Argentine party. The Radicals and their off-shoots—the Unión Cívica Radical Intransigente (UCRI), Unión Cívica Radical del Pueblo (UCRP), and the Movimiento de Integración y Desarrollo (MID) have had their candidates in and out of the presidency a number of times since their first presidential victory in 1916. In addition, the Radicals have provided the principal civilian opposition to the Peronists. The Radicals represent a central position in Argentina, and their appeal transcends any narrow class basis of support. The Radical party has been affected by the strong personalities of several of its leaders, and personal differences have led to splits and fragmentation in the party. Splits have also developed over ideological and tactical questions. The Radicals are today deeply divided, and face severe problems due to the age of the leaders of the various factions. In addition, of course, the Radicals have been severely damaged by the policies and prohibitions of Argentina's military governments since 1966.

Socialist political activity began in Argentina in the nineteenth century. From their earliest years, the Socialists had strong ties to the labor movement, a movement in which anarchists and syndicalists also struggled for supremacy. In the first part of the twentieth century the Socialists also had to compete with the UCR, a national alternative to Conservative rule in Argentina. Subsequently, the Communists became major competitors with the Socialists in the labor movement, and the rise of Peronism in the 1940s virtually destroyed the position of the Socialists in organized labor.

Argentina's Socialists have produced a number of exceptional political leaders, but they have never been able to become the dominant leftist alternative in the country. Over the decades they have suffered a number of severe internal splits, and since 1958 these divisions have been so severe as to reduce the Socialists to a minor position in national politics.

Argentina had one of the earliest Communist movements in Latin America, a dissident Socialist group becoming the Communist Party soon after the formation of the Communist International. Until the late 1930s they remained a relatively minor force in the organized labor movement and a tiny influence in the country's general politics. The rise in their trade union strength thereafter was cut short by the phenomenon of Perón in the mid-1940s. Over the decades, the Communist movement has undergone a number of splits. These have given rise to dissident Communist groups including Trotskyists and Maoist parties.

Christian Democratic parties are latecomers to the Argentine political scene.

These parties have achieved some moderate electoral successes, but they have been weakened by the splintering and fragmentation phenomena so common in the nation's politics.

The Peronist Movement

Peronism is a movement unique to Argentina. Peronists are supporters of Juan D. Perón, a colonel who came to power after the 1943 military coup, was elected president in 1946, ruled for nine years, and was overthrown and exiled in 1955. In 1973, Perón returned from exile to again become president. He died in 1974, but was succeeded in the presidency and as head of the Peronist movement by his wife María Estela de Perón (Isabelita), who ruled until overthrown by a military coup in 1976. Perón and Peronists have dominated Argentina's politics since he first became prominent in 1943. The Peronists comprise a diverse group of people and ideologies.

The major basis of Peronist strength is the organized trade union movement, a movement which Perón strongly promoted and soon controlled. Just as with other political groups in Argentina, the Peronists are divided, and the divisions reach into the trade unions as well as among Peronist politicians. The movement is very complex, its policies are somewhat vague, and its program and strategies have changed and attracted differing sets of adherents at various points in time. Argentina's politics of the last thirty-five years can be understood only with reference to Peronism. Major political events were directed by Peronists, or were attempts by military or civilian opponents of Peronism to discredit or destroy the movement.

Perón rose to power on the basis of trade union support. The post he used for this purpose was the Secretariat of Labor, of which he was made head in 1943, and which he soon got raised to the equivalent of a ministry. From that position he aided workers both in organizational campaigns and in efforts to attain benefits to which they were entitled by law. He also began to take an active role in collective bargaining negotiations. Perón was aided by his efforts by his mistress, and later wife, Eva Duarte (Evita). She was a charismatic person, and promoted Perón's efforts in a radio program and in her personal contacts with workers, particularly after she became the president's wife. She identified with the new wave of unorganized workers who had come to urban centers from the interior in search of work in industry. She herself was a woman from a poor and socially outcast background in the provinces.

Two years after the 1943 coup, Perón had become the most powerful man in the government. Some of his colleagues, disliking his contacts with the lower classes, ousted him from office early in October 1945. Workers swarmed into Buenos Aires, demanding his return, and he was brought back to a dramatic welcome before hundreds of thousands in the Plaza de Mayo. He linked his future to the workers in a speech of gratitude, and set about running for the presidency in the 1946 elections.

Perón needed a party, and the Partido Laborista (Labor Party) was organized as one vehicle for his candidacy. The party was organized by union leaders impressed by Perón's policies as secretary of labor. Perón was also supported by a group of dissident Radical party members who supplied his vice-presidential running mate, J. Hortensio Quijano. Perón won the presidency with 56 percent of the vote against the candidate of the Democratic Union, a coalition of the Radicals, Socialists, Progressive Democrats, and Communists. Perón's electoral triumph signaled a new era in Argentine politics and represented a victory for his assorted group of supporters: workers, some members of the lower middle class, nationalists, and sectors of the new industrialist elite. These groups were generally nationalistic, desired Argentine development to be based on industrialization rather than agriculture, and felt neglected by the existing political parties and party system.

In 1955 Perón was overthrown and the Peronist party was outlawed. The military government of General Pedro Aramburu was extremely anti-Peronist and spent its nearly three years in office trying to destroy Peronism, barring former Peronist leaders from holding any political or trade union leadership posts. The Peronists struggled to regroup, but were hindered by military opposition, and by the fragmentation which affected all Argentine political parties. This 1955–1958 period set the tone for the nation's political life for the next quarter century. To a large extent, Argentine politics after Perón's fall in 1955 was a struggle by anti-Peronists to keep the movement out of power, and by the pro-Peronists to get the movement back into power. Political parties played a major role in this struggle until the late 1960s, but in the 1970's, the military and violence-prone activists became dominant. A central fact of Argentine politics is that the group of people Perón organized and brought into politics during his presidency has been unwilling to disappear in the years since his overthrow.

Although Peronist parties existed after 1955, the real strength of the Peronist movement was in the trade unions, and particularly in the General Confederation of Labor (Confederación General del Trabajo—CGT). Perón had taken a divided CGT of less than half a million members in 1943 and built it into a powerful force of perhaps three million members during his presidency. These workers and their families realized that their advances had come about because of Perón. Although both military and civilian governments tried to destroy Peronist trade union strength after 1955, their efforts were unsuccessful. Peronist trade union leaders in fact became the most powerful Peronist leaders in the country.

The general divisions which appeared in the Peronist movement were, of course, also evident in the trade union sector. The workers most personally loyal to Perón were led by José Alonso, head of the textile workers. This group called itself Peronistas de pie (at the feet of Perón) and placed itself under their exiled leader's direct control. They were opposed to any compromise solutions with either the military or civilians and sought to use the trade union movement as the spearhead of the struggle against non-Peronists. They believed in the use of violent tactics, such as confrontations, strikes, and plant takeovers.

The more moderate wing of Peronism was led by Augusto Vandor of the metalworkers union. This group included most of the largest and most powerful of Argentina's unions. They believed it was possible to work with other political groups, although they emphasized that their major concern was to improve the situation of the workers. The Vandorist faction even gave support to the 1966 coup which ended President Arturo Illia's rule. This faction increasingly took positions which differed from those advocated by Perón in exile. They pushed for Peronist goals, but without the direct leadership and control of the exiled former president. They demanded more control over the Peronist movement.

In the years following the 1966 coup, the rivalry between different Peronist trade union factions became increasingly violent, paralleling the general trend in Argentine society. Matters came to a head in 1969 when both Vandor and Alonso were assassinated, despite the fact that each was protected by elaborate security precautions as well as personal armed bodyguards. Excessive violence has remained a part of Argentina's trade union picture since that time, with several succeeding secretaries-general of the CGT being assassinated also. Hundreds, perhaps thousands, of workers have been killed in the turbulent years since 1969 in what amounted to a mini-civil war between rival Peronist trade union sectors and between militant trade unionists and the military.

The dominant division in the Peronist trade union sector has come to be between conservative Peronists, represented by the larger trade unions and the union bureaucracy centered in Buenos Aires, and the more radical unionists with their centers of strength in the provinces, and particularly among the auto workers in Córdoba. When Perón returned to the country in 1973, he sided strongly with the conservative groups. Upon his death in 1974, his wife Isabelita succeeded him to the presidency and she and her advisor José López Rega proved to be even more conservative. Their policies led to increased fighting and violence among Peronist factions, and increased violence and militancy by the far-left groups. The military has tried to take advantage of the splits among Peronist workers, but so far has been unable to reduce Peronism's dominance of labor. Similar military efforts in the 1966–1969 period had also failed.

The period following the 1966 military coup was a difficult one for Peronism, as evidenced by the internecine warfare between collaborationist and hardliner trade unionists. The 1969 assassination of Vandor deprived the collaborationists of their principal leader, giving Perón an opportunity to push for unity in the Peronist labor sector. However, Perón's ability to exert increasingly unified control over labor was offset by the emergence of new Peronist groups calling for direct action. These nonunion radical Peronists formed small guerrilla groups such as the FAP (Fuerzas Armadas Peronistas) and FAR (Fuerzas Armadas Revolucionarias), or joined with other groups of vaguely Christian and Marxist orientation to form larger guerrilla groups such as the Montoneros. Newly formed youth groups, such as the Juventud Peronista, became important elements in the campaign of violence and terrorism against the military government. These new groups in the Left incorporated a wide range of styles and thinking. They claimed to represent the true spirit of Peronism, and engaged in violence in attempts to bring down the military government and bring about Perón's return. Probably realizing that he could not control their actions, the exiled Perón skillfully avoided any confrontation with this new left-wing Peronism. He capitalized on their activities where possible, did not disavow their efforts, but never really gave any direct indication that he shared their particular goals.

In 1971 political activity was again legalized by a military regime which was by then seeking a way to get out of government. Use of Perón's name was barred, but Peronists formed a Justicialist Party to work for his goals and return. The wide range of outlooks and tactics which Peronists encompassed made it seem unlikely that any long-range unity could be attained, but the possibility of Perón's return and a Peronist victory did bring about an agreement for loose cooperation among the numerous Peronist groups. Such unity would prove impossible to maintain once Perón was actually back in power.

In the 10 March 1973 presidential election the FREJULI coalition (Frente Justicialista de Liberación—Justicialist Liberation Front) was declared the winner by the military. Perón's surrogate, Héctor Cámpora, was elected president amid speculation as to what Perón's role in the government would be. The Peronists' policy of socialistic nationalism called for state control of bank credit, the oil industry, petrochemicals and steel, and other basic industries, in addition to the already controlled utilities and public services.

When Cámpora took power on 25 May, he made a strong attack on the former military government, while praising those Peronists who had used violence to fight violence. He took a very nationalistic, anti-foreign-influence position. Five hundred political prisoners were amnestied and the Communist Party was made legal. Nevertheless, the ERP, one of Argentina's two largest guerrilla groups, vowed to continue to use violence in their efforts to achieve "social justice." Perón himself returned to Argentina in mid-June, ending eighteen years of exile. Within a month, on 13 July, Cámpora resigned the presidency to allow for new elections in which Perón could run. Cámpora's resignation reflected the deep split between the Peronist youth and other leftist Peronists on one side, and the more conservative Peronists, centered in the trade unions, on the other. Leftists charged that the Peronist Right, led by José Rucci and José López Rega, had forced Cámpora's resignation. Each side bombed the headquarters of the other.

Perón won the 23 September election with 61.8 percent of the vote. His wife was elected vice-president. Only three other parties contested the election, with Ricardo Balbin's UCRP getting 24.3 percent of the vote, Francisco Manrique's Popular Federal Alliance getting 12.1 percent, and the Socialist Workers Party getting 1.6 percent under Juan Carlos del Coral. Two days after the election, CGT Secretary-General José Rucci was assassinated. Kidnappings, assassinations, and violence against political and labor leaders continued despite Perón's appeals for calm. Perón's policies clearly favored the right wing of his supporters, turning increasingly against the Montoneros and others whose use of violence he felt was subversive and harmful to the government. On 1 May 1974, some 60,000 of Perón's leftist supporters walked out of a mass rally Perón was addressing after he had characterized them as imbeciles. Fighting among leaders of opposing Peronist labor factions increased, along with guerrilla violence, as Perón's health worsened. Finally, on 1 July 1974, Perón died of heart failure. His third wife and vice-president, María Estela de Perón, (Isabelita) took office.

Following Mrs. Perón's succession, the right wing of the Peronist movement assumed more power, especially in the CGT, and in the person of José López Rega. By September 1974 the Montoneros announced they were taking up arms against Mrs. Perón's government. The ERP also stepped up their attacks on police and the military. In addition, the Peronist Left formed parties of its own such as the Partido Auténtico and the Partido Descamisado, in order to challenge Mrs. Perón in provincial elections. Following the bombing of the federal police chief on 1 November, Mrs. Perón placed the country under a state of siege.

During her two years in office, Mrs. Perón was under constant pressure from the military, labor, and guerrillas. José López Rega, her closest advisor, was despised by many Argentines, and she was finally forced to dismiss him. He represented the extreme right-wing of Peronism, and was thought responsible for the formation of the AAA and the persecution of leftists both in and out of the Peronist movement. Mrs. Perón proved unable to balance or control the forces battling against her. She could not end guerrilla activity and was forced to grant trade unionists wage increases of as much as 100 percent despite her statements about controlling inflation. In the end, her inability to end guerrilla violence, her lack of control of the labor movement and of her own party, her personal and emotional problems, and her failure to control Argentina's staggering inflation proved to be too much. Despite frantic cabinet reshuffles, and bringing forward the date for scheduled elections, she was overthrown by a military coup on 24 March 1976.

The new military government of General Jorge Videla brought an end to virtually all legal civilian political activity, at least for the time being. It declared all political party activity to be illegal, and set no date for new elections and a return to civilian rule.

At the same time, General Videla placed the Peronist-controlled General Confederation of Labor under military control. In November 1979 the government promulgated a new law "of professional association," designed to further weaken the trade union movement, and hence Peronism. The law officially dissolved the CGT and barred union political activities. It also prohibited strikes, called for secret and direct elections of union leaders, and barred individual local unions from federating. Most importantly, it ended union control of dues checked off by employers. Instead of the deductions going directly into union coffers, they now were to be deposited in banks.

The two main informal trade union organizations, the CNT and the Orthodox Peronist Committee of 25, merged on 10 September 1979 into the Only Leadership of the Argentine Workers (Conducción Unica de los Trabajadores Argentinos – CUTA), in order to fight the government's regulations. Both merging organizations had been tolerated despite the government's ban on political activity. The

CUTA's goals were to protect the existing trade union structure, to get release of jailed union leaders, and to remove military intervenors from the unions.

In December 1979 the Videla government issued a statement of its "political bases" for a return to elected governments. This document called for the beginning of a dialogue with political and social leaders, but set no definite dates for elections or any specific rules for renewal of political party activities. The statement put clear limitations on the kinds of parties that would be acceptable to the military, barring "demagogic and anarchist parties and those based on totalitarian ideology, class struggle or personality cults." This indicated the military's intention to prohibit Peronism and the Marxist Left, and seemed to suggest that the military would remain adamant in its policies which denied representation to approximately half of Argentina's population. Early in 1981 President Videla was succeeded by General Roberto Viola, who six months later was forced by his military colleagues to resign in favor of General Leopoldo Galtieri.

The future for Argentina's political parties is cloudy. The ruling military is divided on the issue of return to party rule, with different leaders making vague and conflicting statements regarding timetables for possible elections. In any case, the military seems determined to remain a prominent force in government even should elections be held. Clearly, they intend to participate in, and set limits for, any future civilian government. Guerrillas also show no signs of disappearing in Argentina, although their ranks have been weakened by the military's drive against them since 1976. In a similar way, the trade unions continue to operate despite almost constant internal warfare and efforts to weaken them by military and civilian governments. The unions today, despite their problems, remain a more potent political force than any of Argentina's political parties. It appears certain that any political party government will have to exist in an environment containing at least three challengers to party dominance: the military, guerrillas, and the unions.

Argentina in 1981 is a paradox. The country possesses many attributes thought favorable for development, growth, and stability: linguistic, racial and religious homogeneity, a well-educated population, a highly trained work force, and good communications and transportation. Yet the country is in deep political trouble. Given the current state of disarray among political parties combined with the trend towards the use of force in politics, it is difficult to predict a bright future for Argentina's political parties.

Bibliography

Robert J. Alexander. *Communism in Latin America.* Rutgers University Press, New Brunswick, 1957.

———. *Juan Domingo Perón: A History.* Westview Press, Boulder, 1979.

———. *Latin American Political Parties,* Praeger, New York, 1973.

———. *The Peron Era.* Columbia University Press, New York, 1951.

Ramón Andino and Eduardo J. Paredes. *Breve Historia de los Partidos Políticos Argentinos.* Alzamor, Buenos Aires, 1974.

Samuel L. Baily. *Labor, Nationalism, and Politics in Argentina*. Rutgers University Press, New Brunswick, 1967.

George Blanksten. *Peron's Argentina*. University of Chicago Press, Chicago, 1953.

Héctor J. Cámpora. *La Revolución Peronista*, EUDEBA, Buenos Aires, 1973.

Gonzalo Cárdenas, Angel Cairo, Pedro Geltman, and Ernesto Goldar. *El Peronismo*. 2nd ed. Cepe, Buenos Aires, 1973.

Alberto Ciria. *Partidos y Poder en la Argentina Moderna 1930-46*. Alvarez, Buenos Aires, 1964.

John T. Deiner. "Radicalism in the Argentine Catholic Church." *Government and Opposition*, vol. 10, no. 1, Winter 1974, pp. 70-89.

Gabriel del Mazo. *El Radicalismo: El Movimiento de Intransigencia y Renovación 1945-1957*. Editora Gure, Buenos Aires, 1958.

Arturo Frondizi: *Petroleo y Política*. Editorial Raigal, Buenos Aires, 1954.

Ezequiel Gallo and Silvia Sigal. "La formación de los partidos politicos contemporaneos. la UCR (1890-1916)." *Argentina, Sociedad de Masas*, EUDEBA, 1965, pp. 124-176.

Manuel Gálvez. *Vida de Hipólito Yrigoyen: el hombre del misterio*. 2nd ed. Kraft, Buenos Aires, 1939.

Andrew Graham-Yooll. *Tiempo de Violencia: Cronología del Gran Acuerdo Nacional*. Granica, Buenos Aires, 1973.

Helene Graillot. "Argentina." *Guide to the Political Parties of South America*, Richard Gott, general editor, Pelican, Baltimore, 1973, pp. 32-106.

Donald C. Hodges. *Argentina 1943-1976: The National Revolution and Resistance*. University of New Mexico Press, Albuquerque, 1976.

Jeane Kirkpatrick. *Leader and Vanguard in Mass Society: A Study of Peronist Argentina*. MIT Press, Cambridge, 1971.

Alejandro Magnet. *Nuestros Vecinos Justicialistas*. Editorial Pacifico, Santiago, 1955.

Julio Meinvielle. *Concepción Católica de la Política*. Ed. Theoria, Buenos Aires, 1961.

Partido Communista de la Argentina. *Esbozo de historia del partido communista de la Argentina*, Anteo, Buenos Aires, 1964.

Miliades Pena. *Masas, caudillos y elites: la dependencia de Yrigoyen a Perón*. Fichas, Buenos Aires, 1971.

Rodolfo Puiggros. *El Peronismo: Sus Causas*, 3d ed. Cepe, Buenos Aires, 1972.

———. *Las Izquierdas y el Problema Nacional*. Cepe, Buenos Aires, 1973.

Jorge Abelardo Ramos. *El partido comunista en la política Argentina: su historia y su crítica*. Coyoacán, Buenos Aires, 1962.

Jorge Abelardo Ramos. *Perón: Historia de su Triunfo y su Derrota*. Ed. Amerindia, Buenos Aires, 1959.

David Rocke. *Politics in Argentina, 1890-1930: The Rise and Fall of Radicalism*. Cambridge University Press, London, 1975.

José Luis Romero. *A History of Argentine Political Thought*. Stanford University Press, Stanford, 1963.

Rubén Rotondaro. *Realidad y cambio en el sindicalismo*. Pleamar, Buenos Aires, 1971.

Alain Rouquie. *Radicales y Desarrollistas en la Argentina*. Schapire, Buenos Aires, 1975.

Charles A. Russell, James F. Schenkel, and James A. Miller. "Urban Guerrillas in Argentina: A Select Bibliography" *Latin American Research Review*, Fall, 1974, pp. 53-89.

Raul Scalabrini Ortiz. *De Yrigoyen A Perón*. Plus Ultra, Buenos Aires, 1973.

Peter H. Smith. *Argentina and the Failure of Democracy: Conflict Among Political Elites, 1904-1955*. University of Wisconsin Press, Madison, 1974.

Peter G. Snow. *Argentine Radicalism.* University of Iowa Press, Iowa City, 1965.

————. *Political Forces in Argentina.* rev. ed. Praeger, New York, 1979.

Lester A. Sobel, (ed.) *Argentina and Peron: 1970–1975.* Facts on File, New York, 1975.

Oscar A. Troncoso. *Los Nacionalistas Argentinos: Antecedentes y Trayectoria.* S.A.G.A., Buenos Aires, 1957.

Richard J. Walter. *The Socialist Party of Argentina: 1890–1930.* University of Texas Press, Austin, 1977.

Thomas E. West et al. *Area Handbook for Argentina.* Government Printing Office, Washington, D.C., 1974.

Arthur Whitaker. *Argentina,* Prentice-Hall, Englewood Cliffs, N.J., 1964.

————. *The United States and Argentina.* Harvard University Press, Cambridge, 1954.

Ricardo Zinn. *Argentina: A Nation at the Crossroads of Myth and Reality.* Robert Speller, New York, 1979.

Political Parties

ANTIPERSONALIST RADICAL CIVIC UNION (UNIÓN CÍVICA RADI-CAL ANTIPERSONALISTA). During the second Radical Party government of President Marcelo T. de Alvear (1922–1928), the party split between the followers of de Alvear and ex-President Hipólito Irigoyen. The former took the name Unión Cívica Radical Antipersonalista. The Antipersonalists opposed the reelection of Hipólito Irigoyen in 1928.

The Antipersonalist Radicals supported the military movement which overthrew Irigoyen in September 1930. When elections were finally held in 1932, the government's candidate was General Agustín Justo, who was a member of the Antipersonalist Radical Party, and the party formed part of the National Concentration coalition which controlled the country until the military coup of 4 June 1943. The second president of the period was also a leader of the Antipersonalist Radicals, Dr. Roberto Ortíz. However, he was forced to resign after about two years, because of ill health, and was succeeded by Vice-President Ramón Castillo, a Conservative.

Meanwhile, the Radical ranks were reunited a few months before the 1943 coup. Antipersonalist Radical Presidents de Alvear and Justo were recognized as the leaders of the newly reconstituted Unión Cívica Radical.

ARGENTINE REPUBLICAN PARTY (PARTIDO REPUBLICANO ARGENTINO —PRA). The Partido Republicano Argentino was brought into being in 1964 by a group of Conservatives who objected to the cooperation of the National Federation of Conservative Parties with the Radical government of President Arturo Illia. The PRA, led by Julio Cueto Rua, withdrew from the National Federation. Their main goal was to increase the role of private enterprise in all phases of national development. It had little voter support, but some influence among industrialists.

ARGENTINE SOCIALIST PARTY (PARTIDO SOCIALISTA ARGENTINO—

PSA) (1915). The PSA was established under the lead of Alfredo Palacios, and broke away from the Socialist Party in 1915. Although the excuse for the break was the disciplining of Palacios by the Socialist Party for engaging in a duel, the real reason was Palacios's militant Argentine nationalism, which conflicted with the "internationalist" ideas held by most of the party's leaders. This first PSA lasted only a few years and never was a serious competitor with the Socialist Party. Palacios rejoined the Socialist Party after the military coup of September 1930.

ARGENTINE SOCIALIST PARTY (PARTIDO SOCIALISTA ARGENTINO —PSA) (1958).

The second Partido Socialista Argentino resulted from a split in the Socialist Party in 1958. The root cause of this division involved the attitude the party should adopt toward the Peronists after the overthrow of Perón in September 1955. Those forming the PSA felt that overtures should be made toward rank-and-file Peronists and secondary Peronist leaders, and they were willing largely to forget the past enmity between Peronists and Socialists. Among the leaders of this PSA were Alicia Moreau de Justo, Alfredo Palacios, and Roberto Muñiz, the party's secretary-general.

Alfredo Palacios was named the PSA's candidate for president in 1958. In that election, the party placed a handful of members in the Chamber of Deputies, and subsequently Palacios was elected to the Senate. The PSA was in opposition to all the regimes of the 1960s.

However, the PSA suffered many splits. The first gave rise to the Vanguard Argentine Socialist Party (Partido Socialista Argentino de Vanguardia) which took a strongly pro-Castro position. Subsequently one faction of the PSA supported Peron's reelection in 1973, and another joined with a Trotskyite faction to form the Socialist Workers' Party (Partido Socialista de los Trabajadores).

CHRISTIAN DEMOCRATIC PARTY (PARTIDO DEMÓCRATA CRISTIANO —PDC).

The Christian Democratic Party was organized in 1954 and followed the pattern of contemporary European Christian Democratic parties. It was the fifth largest party in the first national election it contested (1957). Under Horacio Sueldo, the party adopted a policy of working with the Peronists, and tried to cooperate with them and others to form a popular front in the 1963 election. Such attempts in the 1960s moved the party from its original centrist position.

The PDC adopted nationalist positions regarding the oil industry, agrarian reform, and state direction of the economy. Many of its supporters were women, despite its relatively leftist policy stance. The party, however, has not been able to attract Peronist votes nor has it gotten the support of the Catholic hierarchy.

Christian Democrats have been affected by fragmentation and the presence of Peronism, as have all of Argentina's parties. In the 1973 election, a faction of the PDC split off to form the Popular Christian Party, which joined the FREJULI coalition that supported Peronist Héctor Cámpora's victorious campaign. Another sector of the Christian Democrats led by Horacio Sueldo, became the Christian Revolutionary Party (PRC). The PRC joined Oscar Alende's Center-Left Popular Alliance, with Sueldo as the Alliance's vice-presidential candidate.

CHRISTIAN REVOLUTIONARY PARTY (PARTIDO REVOLUCIONARIO CRISTIANO—PRC). *See* CHRISTIAN DEMOCRATIC PARTY.

CIVIC LEGION (LEGIÓN CÍVICA). *See* CONSERVATIVE NATIONALISTS.

CIVIC UNION (UNIÓN CÍVICA). *See* RADICAL CIVIC UNION.

CIVIC UNION OF YOUTH (UNIÓN CÍVICA DE LA JUVENTUD). *See* RADICAL CIVIC UNION.

COMMUNIST PARTY (PARTIDO COMUNISTA—PC). The Communist Party was established early in 1918 as the Internationalist Socialist Party (Partido Socialista Internacionalista—PSI), which objected to the pro-Allied position of the Socialist Party in World War I. With the emergence of the Communist International, the PSI was accepted as a member and changed its name to Communist Party.

During the 1920s the PC sought influence in the syndicalist-dominated section of the labor movement. Failing in this, it launched its own trade union group, as ordered by the Comintern. It was not until 1936 that Communist-controlled unions joined forces with those under Socialist control in the General Confederation of Labor (Confederación General del Trabajo—CGT).

The PC consistently followed the changes in Soviet and Comintern policy. This led in 1928 to the first major division in its ranks, when the Communist member of the Buenos Aires City Council, José Penelón, broke away to form Workers Concentration (Concentración Obrera). Although this proved to be a small party, it continued in existence until the early 1970s, when its remnants joined the Democratic Socialist Party (Partido Socialista Democrático—PSD).

In the late 1930s and early 1940s, the Communists gained substantial influence in the labor movement. They organized several new national unions, among metal workers, construction workers and others in the industrial belt of Greater Buenos Aires. However, with the advent of Perón as secretary of labor, Communist influence was largely destroyed, when the rank and file deserted to support Perón.

The Communists supported the Democratic Union, the alliance which opposed Peron in the 1946 election. They continued to oppose the Peron regime, more or less intensely, so long as it existed. This attitude led to another split in the party in 1945, led by Rodolfo Puiggrós, who soon became a close adviser of Perón.

During the 1955–1973 period, the Communists tried to work with the Peronists, but they had little success in winning over the followers of the exiled president.

They had a small organization which functioned in the trade union movement but were not able to become a major force in organized labor.

The Communist Party has been banned several times but never drastically persecuted. Today it is tolerated by the military government, perhaps because of the Soviet Union's soft stand on the issue of human rights violations in Argentina. The party has consistently placed its primary focus on supporting the international position of the Soviet Union. Its international orientation has hurt it in Argentina, where Peronists have been viewed as nationalists and have preempted much of the Communist Party's potential appeal. The Communist Party is hierarchically organized and has both an extensive publications network and a group of controlled functional organizations among youth, women, and others.

As a result of the Communist Party's loyalty to the Soviet Union, groups that have not favored this have broken away from the party from time to time. In the 1960s, several Maoist groups emerged, supporting the position of the Chinese. The most important of these was the Revolutionary Communist Party (Partido Comunista Revolucionario).

CONSERVATIVE NATIONALISTS. In addition to the more orthodox Conservative parties, Argentina has had a large number of nationalist groups on the far Right. In a sense, the current AAA is an extremist example of these groups. In general, the groups have been small, and have had little voter support for their programs. The Nationalist Alliance (Alianza Nacionalista), Civic Legion (Legión Cívica), Legion of May (Legión de Mayo), Republican League (Liga Republicana), Party of Nationalist Action (Partido de Acción Nacionalista), and Federal Union (Unión Federal) are examples of such rightest groups.

DEMOCRATIC SOCIALIST PARTY (PARTIDO SOCIALISTA DEMOCRÁTICO —PSD). The PSD emerged from the 1958 split in the Socialist Party. It was made up of those who were most obdurate in their opposition to Peronism and most unforgiving toward the Peronists, whether workers or middle-class people. The principal figures in the PSD included Nicolás Repetto, Américo Ghioldi, Juan Antonio Solari. The PSD participated in the 1958 presidential election, running Repetto as its presidential nominee. Then and in subsequent elections in the 1960s, it was able to place a handful of its people in the Chamber of Deputies, although it did not elect any senator. The PSD had some strength on a local level in the Province of Buenos Aires, and during periods in the 1960s and 1970s it controlled the municipality of Mar del Plata.

The PSD was more solidly organized and more unified in its point of view than was its rival, the Argentine Socialist Party (PSA). It therefore did not suffer the splits which the PSA underwent.

The political philosophy of the PSD became increasingly conservative. Its violent opposition to all aspects of Peronism and its very hard-line anti-Communism left it relatively isolated during the 1960s and 1970s. Although the PSD acknowledged kinship with the democratic Socialist parties of Europe, it was very skeptical of the virtues of wide nationalization of the economy. Its position led it to lend support to the military regime of General Jorge Videla after 1976, and Américo Ghioldi was named by that government to be ambassador to Portugal.

By the end of the 1970s, however, the PSD remained almost the only remnant of the once strong Socialist Party which had anything approaching a national following and an effective organization. It continued to publish on a weekly basis *La Vanguardia*, the newspaper which had first been established in 1894 by Juan B. Justo, even before the Socialist Party itself had been organized.

FEDERACIÓN NACIONAL DE PARTIDOS CONSERVADORES. *See* NATIONAL FEDERATION OF CONSERVATIVE PARTIES.

FEDERAL POPULAR ALLIANCE (ALIANZA POPULAR FEDERAL–APF). The March 1973 election saw the emergence of a number of new conservative parties and coalitions. The largest of these parties, gaining 15 percent of the vote, was the Federal Popular Alliance, led by Francisco Manrique. Manrique was a populist leader and former military man, holding government positions in the Lanusse government (1971–1973). His APF consisted of a number of new provincial parties, plus the already existing conservative Popular Democratic Party (Partido Demócrata Popular–PDP). In December 1974 about a dozen of these provincial parties which had supported Manrique created a new organization, the Popular Federal Forces (Fuerzas Federales Populares–FFP), which consisted of conservatives and some former supporters of Arturo Frondizi.

FEDERAL REPUBLICAN ALLIANCE (ALIANZA REPUBLICANA FEDERAL –ARF). The Federal Republican Alliance was another conservative coalition which came into being for the 1973 election. It was a grouping of provincial Conservative parties, similar to the APF, but less populist in its appeal. The ARF gained 3 percent of the March 1973 presidential vote.

FEDERAL UNION (UNIÓN FEDERAL). *See* CONSERVATIVE NATIONALISTS.

FUERZAS FEDERALES POPULARES. *See* FEDERAL POPULAR ALLIANCE.

INDEPENDENT PARTY (PARTIDO INDEPENDIENTE). The Independent Party was one of the three parties organized at the end of 1945 to support Juan Perón's first campaign for the presidency. It was intended to gather in the votes of those supporters of Perón who were neither trade unionists nor dissident pro-Perón Radicals. Although the Independent Party contributed a modest share of the votes which elected Perón, it was clearly the smallest of the three pro-Perón groups. In the middle of 1946 it was merged with the Labor Party (Partido Laborista) and the Renovating Radical Civic Union (Unión Cívica Radical Renovadora) to form what ultimately became the Peronist Party.

INDEPENDENT CIVIC PARTY (PARTIDO CÍVICO INDEPENDIENTE). The Partido Cívico Independiente, established in the early 1960s, had little electoral support, but exercised some influence on economic policy after the 1966 coup (which it supported). The party pushed for private enterprise control of the economy. Its leaders were the economist Alvaro Alsogaray and his brother, General Julio Alsogaray. In the 1973 election, this group of conservatives and business people supported the Nueva Fuerza coalition, whose presidential candidate, Julio Chamizo, gained only 2 percent of the vote, despite the huge funds spent on his campaign.

INDEPENDENT SOCIALIST PARTY (PARTIDO SOCIALISTA INDEPEN-DIENTE—PSI). The PSI resulted from a split in the Socialist Party in 1928. It represented the Socialists' right wing at that time, although personal leadership disputes between the Socialist Party's Secretary-General Antonio de Tomasso and his supporters on the one hand, and Juan B. Justo, the party's founder and his backers on the other, were a key element in the split. Also, those who became Independent Socialists were strongly opposed to the Socialist Party's somewhat sympathetic attitude towards the Irigoyen faction among the Radicals.

In the 1928 election the Independent Socialists received more votes than the Socialist Party. Two years later, their leaders participated in the plot with military leaders which resulted in the overthrow of President Hipólito Irigoyen in September 1930, as did the Conservatives and Antipersonalist Radicals. In 1932 the PSI supported the presidential candidacy of General Agustín Justo, and throughout much of the 1930s, Federico Pinedo, one of the leaders of the PSI, served as minister of finance in the National Concentration governments. By the end of the 1930s the Independent Socialist Party had disappeared.

INTERNATIONALIST SOCIALIST PARTY (PARTIDO SOCIALISTA INTERNACIONALISTA). *See* COMMUNIST PARTY.

INTRANSIGENT RADICAL CIVIC UNION (UNIÓN CÍVICA RADICAL INTRANSIGENTE—UCRI). The UCRI came into existence as a result of a split in the Unión Cívica Radical (UCR) early in 1957. It was immediately provoked by a special congress of the UCR in December 1956 which had named party president Arturo Frondizi as the UCR candidate for president—although the election was not finally held until February 1958. Those opposed to the Frondizi candidacy established the rival Radical Civic Union of the People (Unión Cívica Radical del Pueblo—UCRP).

The 1958 election campaign was basically a struggle between the nominees of the two rival Radical factions. The strength of Frondizi and the UCRI lay in the fact that during the Perón regime, Frondizi had been virtually the only major opponent of Perón who, although opposing the dictatorial aspects of his regime, had supported much of the social legislation and nationalistic emphasis of Perón. Also, in the September 1955–February 1958 period, people closely associated with Frondizi had extended help to Perónists, particularly in the labor movement, who were being persecuted by the military government. Perón's final decision to endorse Frondizi—when faced with the prospect that a large part of his followers intended to vote for him anyway—assured that Frondizi would receive a sufficiently large majority that military men opposed to his taking office would be immobilized.

Frondizi had two basic objectives upon taking the presidency. One was to get the development of the economy going again, after a decade of stagnation. The other was to reintegrate the Perónists in the legal political process.

The UCRI's economic program stressed national control of natural resources (especially oil) and industrialization which combined private enterprise with some state direction and planning. Once elected, Frondizi was soon forced to alter some of his plans. He quickly changed his nationalistic stance by signing oil development contracts—but not traditional concessions—with several foreign oil companies. He also had to give high priority to control of inflation, which called for a considerable degree of austerity. These policies alienated many of the Perónists. However, he did succeed in getting important new major parts added to the industrial sector—notably the automobile and heavy chemical industries.

Nevertheless, it was Frondizi's efforts to reintegrate the Peronists in the political process which ultimately brought his downfall. He allowed organization of "neo-Peronista" parties in the various provinces, and allowed the Peronists to regain control of the labor movement. When the Peronists defeated the UCRI in gubernatorial and Chamber of Deputy elections in March 1962, the military stepped in to oust Frondizi.

Following the ouster of Frondizi, the UCRI split into two factions, one led by Arturo Frondizi, the other by Oscar Alende. The Alende group opposed Frondizi's plans to build a national front with the Peronists for the 1963 election. In 1964, Frondizi and his faction left the UCRI to form the Movement of Integration and Development (Movimiento de Integración y Desarrollo—MID). The UCRI, with Alende as its presidential candidate, ran second in the 1963 election to the UCRP and Arturo Illia. By 1965, however, the UCRI's vote dropped significantly. In 1972 the party changed its name to Partido Intransigente, when the UCRP was granted the traditional title Unión Cívica Radical by the electoral authorities. In that same year, the Partido Intransigente joined the Popular Revolutionary Alliance (Alianza Popular Revolucionaria) coalition, along with a sector of the Union of the Argentine People (UDELPA), the Communist Party, and the Revolutionary Christian Party. As presidential candidate of the Alianza, Dr. Alende gained 8 percent of the popular vote in March 1973.

INTRANSIGENT PARTY (PARTIDO INTRANSIGENTE). *See* INTRANSIGENT RADICAL CIVIC UNION.

JUSTICIALIST PARTY (PARTIDO JUSTICIALISTA). The Partido Justicialista was the reincarnation of the Peronist Party (Partido Peronista) which appeared shortly before the March 1973 election. Since the military government of President Alejandro Lanusse forbade the use of the word "Peronista," the followers of Peron chose "Justicialista" as the name for their organization.

For the purposes of the March 1973 election, the Partido Justicialista took the lead in forming a coalition, the Justicialist Front of Liberation (Frente Justicialista de Liberación—FREJULI). This coalition was joined by a number of smaller parties, notably the MID of ex-President Arturo Frondizi.

The candidate of FREJULI was Héctor Cámpora, one-time president of the Chamber of Deputies during the first Perón administration. He was chosen because Juan Perón did not qualify to run for office under the conditions established by the Lanusse government.

Cámpora was elected in March 1973, took office 4 June and resigned a few months later, to give way to the election of Juan Perón. As in the earlier election, the FREJULI joined together the forces supporting the Peronist candidate, including the Partido Justicialista, and this time elected Juan Perón as president and Isabelita Perón as vice-president. Juan Perón died in June 1974, and Isabelita, who succeeded him in the presidency and the leadership of the Justicialist Party, was overthrown by the military in March 1976.

With the advent of the military regime of General Jorge Videla in March 1976, the Justicialist Party was outlawed along with all of the other Argentine parties. However, unlike some of them, it did not continue to exist in the underground. As had been true in the 1955–1973 period, the main leadership and support for the Peronist movement came from the trade union movement, rather than from a nationally organized political party. There is no indication that the Partido Justicialista as such continues to exist.

LABOR PARTY (PARTIDO LABORISTA). The Partido Laborista was established late in 1945 by trade union leaders to support the presidential candidacy of Colonel Juan D. Perón. The president of the party was Luis Gay, head of the telephone workers, and its vice-president was Cipriano Reyes, a major figure in the Packinghouse Workers Federation. In the February 1946 election, the party won a majority in both houses of Congress.

Shortly after his inauguration on 4 June 1946, President Juan Perón announced that all of the parties which had supported him in the February election were going to be merged into a single organization. He apparently did so without consulting the leaders of the respective parties.

Although most of the leaders and members of the Partido Laborista went along with Perón's decision, Cipriano Reyes, who had been elected to the Chamber of Deputies by the Partido Laborista, did not do so. He denounced Perón's action and announced that he would continue the Partido Laborista in existence. He was joined in this move by only one other deputy of the party.

Although Reyes and his colleague held their seats in the Chamber for two years, Reyes was arrested the day that his parliamentary immunity ended in 1948. He spent the rest of the Perón regime in jail. The Labor Party was driven underground and for practical purposes disappeared. Reyes was released from jail after the fall of Perón, but his efforts to revive the Partido Laborista completely failed.

LABOR PARTY (TROTSKYIST) (PARTIDO LABORISTA (TROTSKISTA)). *See* TROTSKYITES.

LEGIÓN DE MAYO. *See* CONSERVATIVE NATIONALISTS.

LEGION OF MAY (LEGIÓN DE MAYO). *See* CONSERVATIVE NATIONALISTS.

LIBERAL PARTY (PARTIDO LIBERAL). The Liberal Party was established immediately after the overthrow of the dictatorship of Juan Manuel de Rosas in 1852. Among its leaders were Domingo F. Sarmiento, Adolfo Alsina, and Bartolomé Mitre. According to Arturo Frondizi the Liberals "proposed to organize the Nation on a new basis, demanding the overthrow of the provincial governments which had been allied to Rosas, the constitution of new provincial political forces, and the adoption of a constitution for the whole republic" (*Petroleo y Politica* [Editorial Raigal, Buenos Aires, 1954], p. 30). The Liberals supported the separation of Buenos Aires from the Argentine Confederation between 1852–1859, but with the reintegration of the province into the Argentine Republic and the ultimate triumph of the forces led by Mitre in the battle of Pavón, which led to Mitre's assuming the presidency, the Liberal Party had its ultimate victory. However, during Mitre's constitutional presidency (1862–1868), the Liberals split over the issue of establishing the city of Buenos Aires as a federal district. Those favoring this, led by President Mitre, formed the Nationalist Liberal Party (Partido Liberal Nacionalista), while its opponents formed the Autonomist Liberal Party (Partido Liberal Autonomista), under the leadership of Adolfo Alsina.

In the election of 1868, the Autonomist Liberals supported the candidacy of Domingo F. Sarmiento, who was elected. Six years later, they triumphed once again, with the election of Nicolás Avellaneda as Sarmiento's successor; Mitre failing in an armed effort to prevent Avellaneda's taking office. Both factions of Liberalism ceased to exist as organized parties during the Avellaneda administration.

LIGA REPUBLICANA. *See* CONSERVATIVE NATIONALISTS.

MOVEMENT OF INTEGRATION AND DEVELOPMENT (MOVIMIENTO DE INTEGRACIÓN Y DESARROLLO – MID). When Arturo Frondizi left the Intransigent Radical Civic Union (Unión Cívica Radical Intransigente – UCRI), to form the MID in 1964, he took with him those supporters who favored his developmentalist ideas. The new party continued to promote Frondizi's developmentalist positions, as well as his policy of rapprochement with the Peronists. In the first election in which MID and UCRI both participated, MID outpolled the UCRI by 600,000 votes to 400,000. The MID became more of a personalist party centered on Frondizi than a continuer of the Radical tradition. Frondizi sometimes supported military government and at other times was critical (as with his opposition to Onganía after 1969). When political party activity was again legalized in 1971, the MID became part of the Frente Justicialista de Liberación (FREJULI) coalition, which elected Héctor Cámpora. The MID elected several senators and deputies on the FREJULI list. Frondizi and MID continued as part of FREJULI when Perón was elected president in September 1973, but later dropped out of the coalition and by March 1975 was strongly critical of Mrs. Perón's government's economic policies which MID felt were against the national interest. Subsequent to the overthrow of Mrs. Perón, Frondizi and the MID supported the government of General Jorge Videla but were very critical of its near laissez-faire economic policies.

MOVIMIENTO DE INTEGRACIÓN Y DESARROLLO. See MOVEMENT OF INTEGRATION AND DEVELOPMENT.

MOVIMIENTO REVOLUCIONARIO PERONISTA. See POPULAR UNION.

NATIONAL AUTONOMIST PARTY (PARTIDO AUTONOMISTA NACIONAL). The National Autonomist Party had its origins in the Autonomist Party of Buenos Aires (Partido Autonomista de Buenos Aires), which was established on 16 September 1878. Its leaders included Domingo F. Sarmiento, Bernardo de Irigoyen, Luis Sáenz Peña, Roque Sáenz Peña, Leandro Alem, and Hipólito Irigoyen. In the following year, the provincial party joined forces with the opponents of the presidential candidacy of General Julio A. Roca, who had the support of outgoing President Nicolás Avellaneda, to form the National Autonomist Party. Those participating in this movement included the remnants of the Republican Party, as well as Governor Tejedor of Buenos Aires Province (who had defeated the Republicans in 1874), and ex-President Bartolomé Mitre.

The National Autonomist Party was of short duration. Its efforts to block the candidacy of Roca failed when an attempted insurrection by Governor Tejedor on 3 June 1880 was suppressed by the national government. As a result of the failure of this uprising, the City of Buenos Aires was finally separated from the Province of Buenos Aires and was established as a Federal territory and capital of the republic.

With the ascension to power of President Julio Roca at the end of 1880 a very personalistic regime was established. One result of this was the disappearance of the National Autonomist Party, thus ending the process of national party organization begun thirty years before with the establishment of the Liberal Party.

NATIONAL CIVIC UNION (UNIÓN CÍVICA NACIONAL. See RADICAL CIVIC UNION.

NATIONAL DEMOCRATIC PARTY (PARTIDO DEMÓCRATA NACIONAL
—PDN). The PDN was one of the major efforts to organize the conservative
forces on a national level. It was established soon after the military coup of
September 1930 which overthrew the Radical government of President Hipólito
Irigoyen. From then until the coup of 4 June 1943, the PDN constituted the single
largest party in the National Concentration (Concentración Nacional) coalition,
which elected both President Agustín P. Justo in 1932 and President Roberto
Ortíz in 1938.

The National Democratic Party was the principal spokesman for the landed
interests which had controlled the country until the first Radical victory in 1916.
Its influence was obviously very great with the governments of the 1930s, which
followed a free-trade policy and opposed industrialization, both positions favored
by the large landholders and serving the interests of Great Britain.

The National Democratic Party did not have a president until the resignation
of President Roberto Ortíz, in spite of its predominant position in the government
coalition of the 1930s. With Ortiz's resignation, Vice-President Ramón S. Castillo,
a member of the Partido Demócrata Nacional, succeeded him. During his in-
cumbency, Castillo followed a policy during World War II which was "neutral in
favor of the Axis." However, he aroused the opposition of the quite pro-Nazi
elements in the Argentine Army when he endorsed the candidacy of a conservative, pro-British, large landowner, Robustiano Patrón Costas, as his successor.
This directly led to his overthrow on 4 June 1943.

The last electoral appearance of the PDN was in the 1946 presidential race.
Officially, the party was not a member of the Unión Democrática coalition, which
opposed Juan Domingo Perón. However, the PDN gave instructions to its followers to support the anti-Perón candidate.

During the first Perón administration, the Partido Demócrata Nacional continued to oppose the regime. After Perón's ouster in 1955, the Conservatives were
considerably dispersed. The PDN was succeeded as the principal national Conservative organization in 1958 by the National Federation of Conservative Parties.

NATIONAL FEDERATION OF CONSERVATIVE PARTIES (FEDERACIÓN
NACIONAL DE PARTIDOS CONSERVADORES—FNPC). The FNPC suc-
ceeded the Partido Demócrata Nacional as the principal conservative party in
1958. Like its predecessor, the FNPC represented a collection of local interest
groups, without a strong central national structure. The FNPC continued the
conservative policy of supporting free enterprise and opposing state intervention
in the economy. It particularly opposed agrarian reform and the regulation of
agricultural exports. Argentina's future was seen by it to be in agriculture, not
industry. The FNPC opposed Peronists in general, and trade union activities in
particular.

The Conservatives remained the largest non-Peronist, non-Radical group until
the 1966 coup. They have suffered some internal splits, particularly over the issue
of how to deal with Peronism. In 1956, one sector of the party split away over that

issue, and formed the Popular Conservative Democratic Party (Partido Demócrata Conservador Popular).

PARTIDO AUTONOMISTA NACIONAL. *See* NATIONAL AUTONOMIST PARTY.

PARTIDO CÍVICO INDEPENDIENTE. *See* INDEPENDENT CIVIC PARTY.

PARTIDO COMUNISTA. *See* COMMUNIST PARTY.

PARTIDO COMUNISTA REVOLUCIONARIO. *See* COMMUNIST PARTY.

PARTIDO DE ACCIÓN NACIONALISTA. *See* CONSERVATIVE NATIONALISTS.

PARTIDO DEMÓCRATA CRISTIANO. *See* CHRISTIAN DEMOCRATIC PARTY.

PARTIDO DEMÓCRATA CONSERVADOR POPULAR. *See* POPULAR CONSERVATIVE DEMOCRATIC PARTY.

PARTIDO DEMÓCRATA NACIONAL. *See* NATIONAL DEMOCRATIC PARTY.

PARTIDO DEMÓCRATA PROGRESISTA. *See* PROGRESSIVE DEMOCRATIC PARTY.

PARTIDO INDEPENDIENTE. *See* INDEPENDENT PARTY.

PARTIDO INTRANSIGENTE. *See* INTRANSIGENT RADICAL CIVIC UNION.

PARTIDO JUSTICIALISTA. *See* JUSTICIALIST PARTY.

PARTIDO LABORISTA. *See* LABOR PARTY.

PARTIDO LIBERAL. *See* LIBERAL PARTY.

PARTIDO OBRERO (TROTSKISTA). *See* TROTSKYITES.

PARTIDO PERONISTA. *See* PERONIST PARTY.

PARTIDO PERONISTA FEMININO. *See* PERONIST PARTY.

PARTIDO POPULAR CRISTIANO. *See* POPULAR CHRISTIAN PARTY.

PARTIDO REPUBLICANO. *See* REPUBLICAN PARTY.

PARTIDO REPUBLICANO ARGENTINO. *See* ARGENTINE REPUBLICAN PARTY.

PARTIDO REVOLUCIONARIO CRISTIANO. *See* CHRISTIAN DEMOCRATIC PARTY.

PARTIDO SOCIALISTA. *See* SOCIALIST PARTY.

PARTIDO SOCIALISTA ARGENTINO. *See* ARGENTINE SOCIALIST PARTY.

PARTIDO SOCIALISTA DE LA IZQUIERDA NACIONAL. *See* TROTSKYITES.

PARTIDO SOCIALISTA DE LA REVOLUCIÓN NACIONAL. *See* SOCIALIST PARTY.

PARTIDO SOCIALISTA DE LOS TRABAJADORES. *See* TROTSKYITES.

PARTIDO SOCIALISTA DEMOCRÁTICO. *See* DEMOCRATIC SOCIALIST PARTY.

PARTIDO SOCIALISTA INDEPENDIENTE. *See* INDEPENDENT SOCIALIST PARTY.

PARTIDO SOCIALISTA INTERNACIONALISTA. *See* COMMUNIST PARTY.

PARTIDO SOCIALISTA OBRERO. *See* SOCIALIST PARTY.

PARTIDO UNICO DE LA REVOLUCIÓN ARGENTINA. *See* PERONIST PARTY.

PARTIDOS POPULARES PROVINCIALES. *See* PROVINCIAL POPULAR PARTIES.

PARTY OF NATIONALIST ACTION (PARTIDO DE ACCIÓN NACIONALISTA). *See* CONSERVATIVE NATIONALISTS.

PERONIST PARTY (PARTIDO PERONISTA—PP). The Partido Peronista had its origins in the move in mid-1946 to merge the three parties which had supported Juan D. Perón in the February 1946 election — the Partido Laborista, Unión Cívica Radical Renovada, and Partido Independiente. President Juan Perón announced this move soon after becoming president on 4 June 1946, when he said that they would be united to form the Single Party of the Argentine Revolution (Partido Unico de la Revolución Argentina).

However, both many Peronists and their opponents objected to the name adopted for the government party, pointing out that it sounded too much like the "single parties" organized by the fascists who had recently been defeated in World War II. As a result, by the end of 1946 the name was changed to Peronist Party (Partido Peronista).

At the time of the establishment of the Partido Peronista only men had the right to vote in Argentina. When the campaign of Perón's wife, Evita, to gain women's suffrage was successful, and the new 1949 constitution established universal adult suffrage, the Feminine Peronist Party was established as the ally of the Partido Peronista. It was virtually completely controlled by the president's wife, María Eva Duarte de Perón, so long as she lived.

For the rest of the first Perón administration, the Partido Peronista and Partido Peronista Feminino were the country's dominant parties. They were organized in a hierarchical fashion, with Perón, and particularly his wife, determining party policies, which, of course, were in conformity with the government's policies.

These two organizations were the political party manifestation of Perón's movement. The parties' strengths came from the myriad trade union, student, women, and other groups which were controlled from above and gave fanatic support to the president. Women gained the right to vote under Perón, and many of them were enthusiastic supporters of the regime. Evita was especially active as a leader of women's groups. The movement was personalistic in nature, and Perón was far more powerful than the Peronista parties.

Perón's stated policy goal was to achieve social justice, economic independence, and political sovereignty for Argentina. In practice, this meant emphasis on social policies favorable to the workers and the poor, nationalization of key sectors of the economy (such as the railroads), and a foreign policy intended to make Argentina a leader of the developing nations. Peronists were particularly opposed to United States economic and political influence in the country and in the hemisphere. Perón pushed industrialization as the basis for a more powerful Argentina. A state organization was created to sell Argentina's agricultural and grazing products abroad, and to channel the profits into industrial expansion and other programs of the administration. Five Year Plans for the development of the nation were formulated and implemented, although with limited success. Political freedom was not a high priority for Perón, and his opponents found themselves harassed by the government. After Evita's death in 1952, Perón's economic and political fortunes declined. He was forced to compromise his extremely anti-United States stand, and ran into internal opposition from the military and the church.

In September 1955 Perón was overthrown and the Peronist parties were outlawed. The military government of General Pedro Eugenio Aramburu was extremely anti-Peronist and spent its nearly three years in office trying to destroy Peronism, barring former Peronist leaders from holding any political or trade union leadership posts. However, the Peronists continued to have an underground General Command, which kept in touch with Perón and tried to maintain contacts with his rank-and-file supporters. During most of the eighteen years that Perón was in exile, the burden of organizing support for him fell largely on the Peronist trade union leaders, rather than on a political party. It was not until a short time before the 1973 election that the Peronist Party, in a modified form, reappeared on the Argentine political scene as the Justicialist Party.

PERSONALIST RADICAL CIVIC UNION (UNIÓN CÍVICA RADICAL PERSONALISTA). Formed when the leaders and members of the Radical Party split between the followers of ex-President Hipólito Irigoyen and those of the incumbent President Marcelo T. de Alvear in the mid-1920s, the Personalist Radical Civic Union consisted of the supporters of Irigoyen.

The Unión Civica Radical Personalista represented the more left-wing elements among the Radicals, although their ideological differences with the Anti-Personalistas were relatively modest. In 1928 ex-President Irigoyen ran for reelection on the ticket of the Unión Cívica Radical Personalista and won with a substantial majority. However, he was overthrown by the military coup of 6 September 1930.

In the 1932 presidential election, the Personalista Radicals were not allowed to participate. However, subsequently they were again legalized and in the latter part of the 1930s and early 1940s, the Personalista Radicals usually had the largest membership in Congress. They also captured control of a number of the provinces, although on several occasions the Conservative-dominated national government ousted Personalist Radical governors.

Shortly before the 1943 military coup, the Personalist and Antipersonalist Radicals joined forces again in a single Radical Civic Union (Unión Cívica Radical). However, the issues which had separated the groups which split the party between the mid-1920s and the early 1940s continued and contributed to the splits in the Radical ranks which took place in the 1950s and 1960s.

POPULAR CHRISTIAN PARTY (PARTIDO POPULAR CRISTIANO – PPC). See CHRISTIAN DEMOCRATIC PARTY.

POPULAR CONSERVATIVE DEMOCRATIC PARTY (PARTIDO DEMÓ-CRATA CONSERVADOR POPULAR – PDCP). The Partido Demócrata Conservador Popular split from the Partido Demócrata Nacional in 1956, two years before that party was succeeded by the National Federation of Conservative Parties (Federación Nacional de Partidos Conservadores) as the principal national organization of Conservative forces. The PDCP differed from the Federación Nacional principally in its attitude towards the Peronists. Under its leader, Vicente Solano Lima, the PDCP argued in favor of the Peronists' right to participate openly in national politics, attempting (unsuccessfully) to form an alliance with them in 1963. In 1970 Solano Lima brought the Popular Conservatives into the Hora del Pueblo coalition, which called for a return to civilian rule, and subsequently they entered the Justicialist Front for Liberation (FREJULI). Solano Lima was elected vice-president of the republic as running mate of the Peronist, Héctor Cámpora, in March 1973. He resigned at the same time that Cámpora did, to pave the way for the reelection of Juan Perón.

As can be imagined, the PDCP underwent a number of internal splits in its journey toward cooperating with the Peronists. None of these divisions gave rise to any party of lasting significance, however.

POPULAR FEDERAL FORCES (FUERZAS FEDERALES POPULARES— FFP). *See* FEDERAL POPULAR ALLIANCE.

POPULAR UNION (UNIÓN POPULAR—UP). The Unión Popular was formed in 1955, shortly after the overthrow of President Perón, under the leadership of Juan Bramuglia, onetime foreign minister of Perón. The party was barred from presenting candidates for Congress or the presidency in 1958.

Unión Popular was completely loyal to Perón, calling for his policy of social justice, political sovereignty, and economic independence. It saw the military and the foreign capitalists as its enemies. There was some disagreement over tactics and a few hardliners, including Textile Workers Union leader Andrés Framini, deserted the UP to form a party favoring a more revolutionary plan of action—the Peronist Revolutionary Movement (Movimiento Revolucionario Peronista— MRP). Both parties were dissolved by the military government of General Ongañía in 1966.

PROGRESSIVE DEMOCRATIC PARTY (PARTIDO DEMÓCRATA PRO- GRESISTA—PDP). The Partido Demócrata Progresista is a party which had its origins in the Radical movement. Lisandro de la Torre founded the PDP in 1916 in the hope of creating a rival to the Radicals. He had been one of the earliest leaders of the Unión Cívica Radical, but he left it in 1897 in opposition to some of the policies of Radical Party leader Hipólito Irigoyen. He joined a regional party in the Province of Santa Fé, the Liga del Sur, and formed the PDP by combining this group with other small provincial parties. The PDP opposed entry of foreign economic interests into Argentina, wanted nationalization of public services, and called for land reform. It represented the interests of the middle class and small landholders of the interior against the big landowners and British meat exporting interests of the capital.

During much of the 1920s, the PDP controlled the provincial government of Santa Fé. In 1932, when the Personalist Radical Party was not allowed to run candidates, the major opponent of the dominant progovernment coalition candidate General Agustín Justo was Lisandro de la Torre. He ran as nominee of a coalition of his party and the Socialist Party, whose leader Nicolas Repetto was the vice-presidential candidate.

With the death of Lisandro de la Torre in 1939, the PDP deteriorated. De la Torre had been a strong leader, with considerable intellectual prestige, and constantly had opposed what he felt were abuses of power. Horacio Thedy emerged as the PDP's principal leader after the party founder's death. He formed an alliance in 1963 with the Union of the Argentine People (Unión del Pueblo Argentino – UDELPA), and was General Pedro Aramburu's vice-presidential running mate. He was later unsuccessful in efforts to forestall the 1966 military coup. Thedy was active in efforts which culminated in the decision to return to civilian rule in 1973, but by that time several leading Progressive Democratic leaders had defected, and the party was greatly weakened by internal splits.

PROVINCIAL POPULAR PARTIES (PARTIDOS POPULARES PROVIN-CIALES – PPP). There were various Peronist parties organized on a provincial basis in the years following Peron's overthrow which supported the policies he had advocated. They rejected violence as a path of action, and supported neo-Peronist candidates in the elections of the late 1950s and early 1960s, rather than casting blank votes. The bloc called Partidos Populares Provinciales was the main representative of these parties. They were at first not nearly as strong as the Unión Popular and represented the right wing of the Peronist movement following Perón's overthrow in 1955. However, it was their victories in ten provinces in the 1962 elections which provoked the military to overthrow President Arturo Frondizi.

RADICAL CIVIC UNION (UNIÓN CÍVICA RADICAL – UCR). The Radical Civic Union, or Radical Party, had its origins in a meeting in Buenos Aires on 1 September 1889, which established the Civic Union of Youth (Unión Cívica de la Juventud). In the following year, the young people who had established that party joined forces with a group, including ex-President Bartolomé Mitre, Leandro Alem, and others, to establish, on 13 April 1890, the Civic Union (Unión Cívica). The new party quickly gained wide support both in Buenos Aires and the provinces. It had contacts in the military, which led to the uprising of part of the army on 26 July 1890 which, although defeated, resulted in the resignation of President Juárez Celman.

About a year after this insurrection, the Unión Cívica divided, one group, led by Bartolomé Mitre, establishing the National Civic Union (Unión Cívica Nacional) and the other, headed by Leandro Alem, organizing the Radical Civic Union (Unión Cívica Radical). The two parties were distinguished by the willingness of Mitre and his followers to seek to reach compromises with the government in power, and the "intransigence" of the Unión Cívica Radical in its attitude towards the incumbent regime. The Unión Cívica Nacional soon disappeared.

The UCR, first under Leandro Alem and then under Hipólito Irigoyen, boycotted elections in protest against the existing situation. They sought unsuccessfully to organize armed insurrections, most notably in 1893 and 1905. The Unión Cívica Radical promised honest elections and administration, and offered the possibility of political participation to the growing middle and lower classes. The party's exact program was vague, based mainly on the general goal of greater democracy.

The Sáenz Peña Law of 1912 gave the Radicals their chance. The new law ensured a secret ballot and honest counting of votes. The UCR entered provincial and congressional elections in 1914, and Irigoyen ran for the presidency in the 1916 election, which he won. The Unión Cívica Radical became Argentina's largest political party in the first presidential election it contested, emerging with 46 percent of the vote. Although the majority of party members were middle and working class, the leaders' inclinations paralleled many of the economic and political ideas of Argentina's ruling conservative elites. Under Irigoyen, the Radicals did not bring about any major reforms. Indeed, Irigoyen actually increased the political control of the central government, with numerous interventions in the provinces. On the labor front, the UCR government sometimes supported the efforts of workers to organize, and on other occasions employed force against demonstrators, as during the infamous Semana Trágica (Tragic Week) of January 1919.

The UCR in power rather quickly showed evidence of the problem of fragmentation which was to plague Radicals in the future. In 1922 Marcelo T. de Alvear was elected as the second Radical president. He was head of a UCR faction which opposed Irigoyen's domination of the party. These Antipersonalist Radicals also favored some degree of cooperation with the Conservatives. The Antipersonalist faction ruled from 1922 to 1928, when Irigoyen again was elected president, only to be overthrown by the military coup of September 1930. This split in the UCR between Personalists and Antipersonalists continued until the early 1940s, when a unified Unión Cívica Radical was again established.

The type of split which had occurred after 1922 surfaced again in 1945, this time over the attitude to be assumed towards the Peronists. An "intransigent" group within the party, which formed the Movement of Intransigence and Renovation (Movimiento de Intransigencia y Renovación—MIR), led by Arturo Frondizi, Ricardo Balbín, and Gabriel del Mazo, was unwilling to form an alliance with conservative groups to oppose Perón. In fact, the program they put forth in their 1947 *Bases of Political Action* went beyond some of the reforms proposed by Perón. This MIR group became larger than the more conservative "Unionist" faction of the UCR. However, they were divided into three different subgroups. One consisted of the UCR organization in the province of Córdoba, the second was headed by Ricardo Balbín and had its principal strength in Buenos Aires Province, and the third element was headed by Arturo Frondizi, who had support among both Radical intellectuals and union people in various parts of the country.

By the last years of the first Perón administration, the Intransigents controlled the UCR organization. In the 1951 election, the UCR candidate for president was Ricardo Balbín, and his vice-presidential running mate was Arturo Frondizi. A couple years later Frondizi was chosen as president of the Radical Party.

UCR fragmentation intensified following Perón's overthrow in 1955. The Intransigents sought support from Peronists, while the Unionists favored cooperation with General Pedro Aramburu's provisional government. The situation came to a head in 1956 when the majority Intransigent group named Arturo Frondizi as the UCR's candidate for president. Ricardo Balbín, apparently upset both by the selection of Frondizi over himself, and because of the courting of the Peronists, led a group of followers out of the UCR to form the Radical Civic Union of the People (Unión Cívica Radical del Pueblo—UCRP), which included not only his Intransigent faction but those of Córdoba and the "Unionists" as well. Frondizi's majority group became the Intransigent Radical Civic Union (Unión Cívica Radical Intransigente—UCRI). Both the UCRI (Frondizi, 1958) and the UCRP (Illia, 1963) were later able to elect presidents of Argentina, although neither man was able to complete his elective term of office due to military coups. Both parties continued to be plagued by the kind of fragmentation which split the original UCR into factions.

In preparation for the 1973 election, the Radical Civic Union of the People was officially recognized by the party's traditional name of Radical Civic Union (Unión Cívica Radical—UCR), without any qualifying adjective, by the electoral authorities. It has continued to use the title ever since.

RADICAL CIVIC UNION OF THE PEOPLE (UNIÓN CÍVICA RADICAL DEL PUEBLO—UCRP). The UCRP was established as a result of the split in the UCR at the beginning of 1957 by three of the four factions then existing in the party: the Unionists, the Córdoba Intransigents, and the Buenos Aires Province Intransigents led by Ricardo Balbín. The elements which united these three groups were opposition to the presidential candidacy of Arturo Frondizi and reservations about making overtures to the Peronists.

In the 1958 presidential election, the UCRP candidate, Ricardo Balbín, was one of the two major nominees but lost to Arturo Frondizi of the UCRI. Thereafter, the UCRP constituted the largest segment of the parliamentary and civilian opposition to the Frondizi government.

President Arturo Frondizi was overthrown in March 1962 by the armed forces. However, it was almost a year and a half before new elections of president, congress, and the provincial legislatures were held. In this contest, Arturo Illia, the candidate of the Unión Cívica Radical del Pueblo was victorious. He governed for thirty-three months, after which he, in turn, was ousted by the military, who were fearful of a Peronist triumph in congressional and provincial elections scheduled for March 1967.

The UCRP has been divided into factions. The Unionist group was the most conservative. It was the successor of Antipersonalism. The Intransigent faction is the largest, and, headed by Ricardo Balbín, it has carried on the Irigoyenist tradition of strong personal leadership with pragmatic as opposed to ideological policy-making. Still another faction produced the party's victorious presidential candidate, Arturo Illia, in 1963.

When the Illia government was overthrown and political parties were proscribed in 1966, Ricardo Balbín became the leading UCRP spokesman. He led the Radicals in the March 1973 presidential election. Running without any alliances, the party finished second to the Peronists, with 21 percent of the vote. Under Balbín's leadership, the Radicals at first worked with the Perón government. They later became severe critics of Mrs. Perón. Since the 1976 banning of political parties, Balbín has remained the principal spokesman for the Radicals, and his remarks have at times led to brief jailings. His long tenure as party leader is remarkable, but also signals one of the UCRP weaknesses—lack of youthful leadership. This paucity of young leaders, combined with the Illia experience and with Balbín's later opportunism in flirting with the 1973–1974 Perón government, has somewhat discredited the party and led to further fragmentation.

Since the 1973 elections, the UCRP has had the official right to use the party's traditional title, Unión Cívica Radical.

RENOVATING RADICAL CIVIC UNION (UNÍON CÍVICA RADICAL RENOVADORA). The Renovating Radical Civic Union consisted of a small minority of Radical leaders and members who decided in 1945 to support Juan D. Perón in his aspirations to become president. It was headed by Hortensio Quijano and Juan Guillermo Cooke. Quijano became Perón's vice-presidential candidate. This dissident Radical group was the second largest of the groups supporting Perón for president but was a very weak competitor with the Labor Party (Partido Laborista). The Renovating Radical Civic Union went out of existence in the middle of 1946, when all three groups which had backed Perón in the election were merged in what was to become the Peronist Party.

REPUBLICAN LEAGUE (LIGA REPUBLICANA). See CONSERVATIVE NATIONALISTS.

REPUBLICAN PARTY (PARTIDO REPBULICANO). The Republican Party was formed during the administration of Domingo F. Sarmiento (1868–1874), as the result of an alliance between ex-President Bartolomé Mitre and Adolfo Alsina, former leaders of the Nationalist Liberals and Autonomist Liberals, respectively. Arturo Frondizi has commented, that "The movement of the republicans is essentially democratic; it found support in the suburbs of the city, in the country stores, among small agriculturalists; it defended all popular causes" (Petroles y Politica [Editorial Raigal, Buenos Aires, 1954], p. 31). The party suffered a serious blow in losing the election for governorship of the province of Buenos Aires in December 1874. However, it continued to exist until it merged with other groups to form the National Autonomist Party in 1878.

REVOLUTIONARY COMMUNIST PARTY (PARTIDO COMUNISTA REVO-LUCIONARIO). See COMMUNIST PARTY.

REVOLUTIONARY PARTY OF THE WORKERS (PARTIDO REVOLU-CIONARIO DE LOS TRABAJADORES – PRT). See TROTSKYITES.

SINGLE PARTY OF THE ARGENTINE REVOLUTION (PARTIDO UNICO DE LA REVOLUCIÓN ARGENTINA). *See* PERONIST PARTY.

SOCIALIST PARTY (PARTIDO SOCIALISTA). The Socialist Party was one of the oldest parties of Argentina. It was established in 1896, principally by a group of German, French, and Italian immigrants, but headed by an Argentine doctor, Juan B. Justo, who until then had been a member of the Unión Cívica Radical. The party was first called Socialist Labor Party (Partido Socialista Obrero), but the word "labor" was soon dropped from its title.

The Socialists were active in the labor movement which was beginning to develop in the last years of the nineteenth century. They took the lead in forming the first central labor group, the Labor Federation of the Argentine Republic (Federación Obrera de la República Argentina — FORA). However, at the turn of the century they lost control of the FORA to the anarchists who rechristened it Argentine Regional Labor Federation (Federación Obrera Regional Argentina). The Socialists then organized the General Union of Workers (Unión General de Trabajadores — UGT) but when it merged in 1906 with a group of syndicalist trade unions to form the Argentine Regional Labor Confederation (Confederación Obrera Regional Argentina) they lost most of their influence in organized labor and were not to regain it until the early 1920s.

Meanwhile, the Socialists had been making modest headway in the political field. Alfredo Palacios was elected in 1904 as their first member of the Chamber of Deputies. Half a dozen years later, they elected their first senator, Enrique Iberlucea Valle. Thereafter, they continued to be represented in both houses of the national legislature until the advent of Peronism in the 1940s.

The highpoint of Socialist influence was in the interwar period. In the early 1920s, they won control over the two railroad unions, Unión Ferroviaria and La Fraternidad, and soon afterwards built up a strong white-collar workers organization, the General Confederation of Commercial Employees (Confederación General de Empleados de Comercio) and the Union of Municipal Employees. These remained for two decades the country's most important unions. The Socialists also organized a central labor body, the Argentine Labor Confederation (Confederación Obrera Argentina) in 1926, and when this merged with a syndicalist union in 1930, the Socialists also controlled the resulting General Confederation of Labor (Confederación General del Trabajo — CGT).

They also made electoral progress. In the 1920s, they were able for the first time to elect deputies from several of the provinces in the interior instead of only in Greater Buenos Aires. In the election of 1932, because of the banning of the Personalist Radical Party from participation, the Socialists came to constitute for two years the principal opposition party in both houses of Congress. In that election they formed a coalition with the Progressive Democratic Party (Partido Demócrata Progresista — PDP), which named Lisandro de la Torre of the PDP for president and Nicolás Repetto of the Socialists for vice-president.

Meanwhile, the Socialists had undergone several splits. In 1915 a small group broke away to form the Partido Socialista Argentino, under the leadership of Alfredo Palacios. In 1918 elements which opposed the Socialist Party's pro-Allied position in World War I broke away to form the Internationalist Socialist Party (Partido Socialista Internacionalista) which ultimately became the Communist Party. A decade later, a much more serious division occurred, when Antonio de Tomasso, the party's secretary-general led a split of more conservative-minded members to form the Independent Socialist Party (Partido Socialista Independiente), which ended up supporting the military coup of 1930 and the governments which resulted from it, but had disappeared by the end of the 1930s.

In the mid-1930s there was another serious division of the Socialist Party's ranks. A group of left-wing leaders and members, attracted by the then current Popular Front strategy which the Communists were advocating, and which was strongly opposed by most Socialist leaders and the rank and file, broke away to form the Socialist Labor Party (Partido Socialista Obrero — PSO). It lasted for only a few years, most of its leaders and members ultimately joining the Communist Party, although some of them returned to the Socialist Party.

The downfall of the Socialists as a significant influence in Argentine politics was the result of the rise of Peronism. As secretary of labor, between 1943–1945, Juan Perón won away from the Socialists the loyalty of most of their trade unionists, including leaders of the CGT and of most of its major unions. Also in the 1943–1945 period the Socialist Party was severely persecuted by the military government. As a result the Socialists became perhaps the most strongly anti-Peronist party in Argentina.

The Socialists joined forces with the Radicals, Progressive Democrats, and Communists in the Democratic Union (Unión Democrática) to oppose Perón in the election of February 1946. However, they failed to elect any members of Congress in that poll, for the first time since 1904.

During Perón's first presidency the Socialist Party was severely persecuted by the regime. Many of its leaders went into exile, and others were jailed. Party publications had to be printed in Uruguay and smuggled into Argentina.

One minor split occurred in the Socialist Party's ranks during the first Perón administration. A tiny group, led by Enrique Dickmann, one of the party's founders, and Carlos María Bravo, son of a long-time Socialist deputy and senator, broke away to form the Socialist Party of the National Revolution (Partido Socialista de la Revolución Nacional), which supported the Perón government. However, it never won any significant popular support and disappeared with the end of the Perón regime.

With the overthrow of Perón, the Socialists were represented in the Consultative Assembly, which was established as a kind of pseudo parliament by the military regime. The Socialists' official representatives there adopted a particularly severe stand in opposition to Perón and his followers. However, they did succeed in regaining some influence in a few unions — notably the Commercial Workers, Tobacco Workers, and a handful of others. They also received the fourth largest vote in the constitutional assembly elections of 1957.

The particularly hard-line attitude of the Socialist Party toward the Peronists finally provoked a new split in the party's ranks in 1957. As a result, the party was divided into the Democratic Socialist Party (Partido Socialista Democrático—PSD), which continued the hard-line attitude toward Peronism, and the Argentine Socialist Party (Partido Socialista Argentino—PSA), which sought to find ways of joining forces with at least some elements in the Peronist movement.

This split brought about the end of the Socialist Party as a significant element in Argentine political life.

SOCIALIST PARTY OF THE NATIONAL LEFT (PARTIDO SOCIALISTA DE LA IZQUIERDA NACIONAL. See TROTSKYITES.

SOCIALIST PARTY OF THE NATIONAL REVOLUTION (PARTIDO SOCIALISTA DE LA REVOLUCIÓN NACIONAL. See SOCIALIST PARTY.

SOCIALIST LABOR PARTY (PARTIDO SOCIALISTA OBRERO). See SOCIALIST PARTY.

TROTSKYITES. The Trotskyist dissidence in the International Communist Movement was represented in Argentina from 1929 on. During the early 1930s several small groups broke away from the Communist Party, and maintained several generally short-lived organizations. For a short while they tried to operate within the Socialist Party and the Socialist Labor Party, but were not successful in recruiting any significant following in either of those.

The advent of Peronism split the Trotskyites, as it did most other political groups. One faction, led by Jorge Abelardo Ramos, associated itself with the Perón movement, and its members joined the Socialist Party of the National Revolution (Partido Socialista de la Revolución Nacional) established by dissident pro-Perón Socialists. However, it was not until 1962 that the Ramos group established their own party, the Socialist Party of the National Left (Partido Socialista de la Izquierda Nacional—PSIN). The PSIN continued to oppose all of the anti-Perón governments of the 1962-1973 period. In the March 1973 election, the PSIN organized a coalition, the Leftist Popular Front (Frente de Izquierda Popular), which ran Jorge Abelardo Ramos for president. He received about 1 percent of the vote. They supported Juan Perón in the later election in September 1973. By that time, although still sometimes publishing material by Trotsky, the PSIN no longer considered itself a Trotskyist organization.

Another Trotskyite group, which consistently opposed the Peronists, and was led by Nahuel Moreno, used several names during the 1940s and 1950s. It was not until January 1965 that this group established the Revolutionary Party of the Workers (Partido Revolucionario de los Trabajadores—PRT). After the uprising in the city of Córdoba by workers and students in mid-1969, popularly known as the "Cordobazo," one part of the PRT leadership decided to organize a paramilitary group. This "guerrilla" organization, the Revolutionary Army of the People (Ejercito Revolucionario del Pueblo—ERP), was by 1973 one of the two major left-wing paramilitary groups, together with the pro-Peronist Montoneros.

The establishment of the ERP split the PRT, and for a while the two factions both used the name of the Partido Revolucionario de los Trabajadores. However, shortly before the 1973 elections the antiguerrilla faction of the PRT, still led by Nahuel Moreno, merged with one of the splinters of the Argentine Socialist Party (Partido Socialista Argentino) to establish the Partido Socialista de los Trabajadores — PST (Socialist Party of the Workers). The PST ran Juan Carlos del Corral, one of its principal leaders, for president in the March 1973 election, and again in the September poll.

The PST was affiliated with the so-called United Secretariat of the Fourth International, as the PRT had been before it. However, in 1979 the PST participated in a dissident movement within the United Secretariat.

Meanwhile, the violent wing of the PRT continued to channel its activities to the Ejercito Revolucionario del Pueblo. However, in 1976–1977, after the over-throw of the second Peronist government, the military regime of General Jorge Videla largely destroyed the ERP, although the Trotskyite guerrilla remained a nuisance.

Still another Trotskyite party is the Labor Party (Trotskyist) or Partido Obrero (Trotskyista), headed by a one-time soccer player, Homero Cristali, who uses the "party name" J. Posadas. It emerged in the early 1950s. A decade later, amid confusion in the world Trotskyist movement, Posadas established his own faction of the Fourth International. The PO(T) is the smallest and least consequential of the Argentine Trotskyite factions.

UNIÓN CÍVICA. *See* RADICAL CIVIC UNION.

UNIÓN CÍVICA DE LA JUVENTUD. *See* RADICAL CIVIC UNION.

UNIÓN CÍVICA NACIONAL. *See* RADICAL CIVIC UNION.

UNIÓN CÍVICA RADICAL. *See* RADICAL CIVIC UNION.

UNIÓN CÍVICA RADICAL ANTIPERSONALISTA. *See* ANTIPERSONALIST RADICAL CIVIC UNION.

UNIÓN CÍVICA RADICAL INTRANSIGENTE. *See* INTRANSIGENT RADICAL CIVIC UNION.

UNIÓN CÍVICA RADICAL PERSONALISTA. *See* PERSONALIST RADICAL CIVIC UNION.

UNIÓN CÍVICA RADICAL RENOVADORA. *See* RENOVATING RADICAL CIVIC UNION.

UNIÓN DEL PUEBLO ARGENTINO – UDELPA. *See* UNION OF THE ARGENTINE PEOPLE.

UNIÓN FEDERAL. *See* CONSERVATIVE NATIONALISTS.

UNION OF THE ARGENTINE PEOPLE (UNIÓN DEL PUEBLO ARGENTINO – UDELPA). The Unión del Pueblo Argentino was created in January 1963 with the purpose of supporting General Pedro Eugenio Aramburu's presidential candidacy. Aramburu had been president during the 1955–1958 government which had attempted to purge Peronists from national life. He was viewed as anti-Peronist, conservative, and a personalist leader. Aramburu's vague program was mainly based on opposition to Peronism and on the maintenance of order. The emphasis was on agricultural rather than industrial development. The party called for the state to end nationalization and to return control of the railroads and the oil industry to private hands. UDELPA was designed primarily as a vehicle to support Aramburu as the leader of conservative anti-Peronism. In 1963 his candidacy brought the party third place in the presidential elections, with 7 percent of the vote, but it lost ground after that. In 1966 the party was barred by the leaders of the coup of that year, and the UDELPA effectively came to an end with the assassination of Aramburu in May 1970.

UNIÓN POPULAR. *See* POPULAR UNION.

VANGUARD ARGENTINE SOCIALIST PARTY (PARTIDO SOCIALISTA ARGENTINO DE VANGUARDIA). *See* ARGENTINE SOCIALIST PARTY (1958).

WORKERS CONCENTRATION (CONCENTRACIÓN OBRERA). *See* COMMUNIST PARTY.

John T. Deiner

THE BAHAMAS

The Commonwealth of the Bahamas, which received its independence from Great Britain in 1973, consists of about 700 islands and 2,000 reefs, cays, and rocks, stretching from just off the coast of Cuba and Haiti to a point 50 miles from Florida. The approximately quarter million inhabitants are 85 percent black and mulattoes and 15 percent whites.

Some decades after Columbus discovered the islands in 1492, the Spanish abandoned permanent occupation of the Bahamas, after having totally depopulated them of the Arawak Indians. In 1629 the British laid claim to the islands and brought in some settlers from Bermuda, but for almost a century the British Crown was unable to control the pirates and other disreputable characters who inhabited them.

During the seventeenth century, the British kings granted title to the Bahamas to a series of proprietors, none of whom succeeded in effectively controlling the pirates who operated in the islands. In 1718 King George I sent Captain Woodes Rogers, reputedly an ex-pirate himself, to be Royal Governor, and he succeeded finally in bringing the pirates under control.

Governor Rogers also established the colonial legislature, the House of Assembly, elected by white colonials. A century was to pass before any free black men were to win election to the assembly, and the blacks remained a small minority until the late 1960s because of high property and income requirements for the franchise and membership in the assembly.

A Royal Council gave the governor advice and aided him in administration. In 1841 a second house of the legislature, known then as the Legislative Council, but later christened the Senate, was established when the Royal Council was divided into the Executive Council (a kind of cabinet) and the Legislative Council. Members of the second house were appointed by the governor.

Until 1964 the pattern of government in the Bahamas continued to include a two-house legislature consisting of a Senate appointed by the governor and a House of Assembly, chosen by a limited, largely white, electorate; and an executive council. The members of the executive council were also chosen by the governor and were his principal advisors.

Until the 1950s, members of the assembly were chosen on an individual basis. Party politics in the Bahamas arose out of the black majority's struggle against the small white group that dominated both the economy and political life. Both the labor movement and the women's rights movement played key roles in that struggle.

The first union group was organized in 1936, but remained quite small for several years. However, it was a protest—which degenerated on 1 June 1942 into rioting and some casualties—by employees of the Pleasantville Company, which was building United States military installations on New Providence, the most heavily populated island, which was the beginning of what Bahamians call their "quiet revolution." It was over black Bahamians' wages, which were about half those of their United States counterparts working on the same project, due to an agreement between the United States and British governments.

Another decade passed before the black revolution took solid organizational form. In 1953 a group of black business and professional men, as well as leaders of the nascent labor movement, established the Progressive Liberal Party (PLP). As a result, a few years later the white establishment formed the United Bahamian Party.

Meanwhile, black agitation grew for reform of the voting system. Not only were there property and/or income qualifications for voting and holding office, but companies had the right to vote. Thus, if a lawyer had 100 companies with official headquarters in his office, he could cast a vote for each of his companies. Then as a property owner, if he owned property in each constituency, he could go and cast a vote in each. To facilitate his doing so, the election was not held on a single day, but was spread out over two weeks, the voting in each constituency taking place on a different day.

Not only did the United Bahamian Party, the party of the white establishment (known popularly as the Bay Street Boys), resist abolishing this system, the party also opposed the idea of allowing women to vote. A young black woman, Doris L. Johnson, a United States university graduate, who had organized a movement for women's suffrage, received permission in January 1959 to address the assembly on the issue.

The movement for change was stimulated in January 1958 by a nineteen-day general strike, called by the Bahamas Federation of Labour and led by Randol Fawkes, one of the first six PLP members elected to the assembly in 1956. More liberal labor legislation, making it easier for unions to gain legal recognition and fostering collective bargaining, was adopted as a result of the strike.

The walkout also brought the British government to insist on changes in the voting system. In 1961 women were given the right to vote. In the following year, universal adult suffrage was adopted, and the company franchise was abolished, although property owners still had one additional vote. In the 1964 election, the property franchise was finally eliminated, and a system of ministerial government, with a cabinet dependent on a parliamentary majority, was introduced. Thereafter, although the normal term of the assembly was five years, elections could be called whenever the government lost its majority in the assembly or whenever the government wished to appeal to the electorate.

With the first victory of the Progressive Liberal Party in 1967, the "quiet revolution" finally triumphed. Lynden Pindling, leader of the PLP virtually from its inception, became the first black premier. His victory led to a substantial reshuffling of political parties. The United Bahamian Party soon disappeared, and new alignments were formed by its former leaders and PLP dissidents. The PLP remained the majority party.

Generally, Bahamian parties have local organizations in all constituencies. These local groups meet regularly, are active between elections, and play a major role in nominating and campaigning for candidates. However, radio and television have become more important in elections, greatly increasing the cost of campaigns, and the parties' national headquarters now tend to finance campaigns.

Bibliography

Sir Randol Fawkes. *The Faith That Moved the Mountain.* Nassau Guardian, Nassau, 1979.
Doris L. Johnson. *The Quiet Revolution in the Bahamas.* Family Islands Press, Nassau, 1972.

Political Parties

BAHAMIAN DEMOCRATIC PARTY (BDP). The Bahamian Democratic Party (BDP) was formed in 1976 by those withdrawing from the Free National Movement. In the 1977 election, it won six seats and became the official opposition in the assembly.

The Bahamian Democratic Party primarily won seats held formerly by the United Bahamian Party, including the "white" seats, or seats for constituencies where the whites are a majority of the voters. However, the party members strongly reject the idea that they are merely a continuation of the old white establishment party. The BDP is led by J. Henry Bostwick, a mulatto lawyer.

COMMONWEALTH PEOPLE'S PARTY. Formed under the leadership of Holland Smith, who had been expelled from the Progressive Liberal Party in 1965, the Commonwealth People's Party expressed opposition to Bahamian independence. It did not survive long enough to contest any elections, however.

FREE NATIONAL MOVEMENT (FNM). In 1970 a group of eight assembly members, led by Cecil Wallace Whitfield, former Progressive Liberal Party chairman and minister in Premier Pindling's cabinet, withdrew from the Progressive Liberal Party. They set themselves apart as the Free Progressive Liberal Party, arguing that the PLP had abandoned its original principles. Then, in 1971, they merged with the remains of the United Bahamian Party, to form the Free National Movement, under the leadership of Whitfield.

In the 1972 election, the Free National Movement was severely defeated. Several of the FNM members of the House lost their seats, including Cecil

Wallace Whitfield. As a result of his defeat, Whitfield gave up the leadership of the party. However, when his successor became ill and could no longer serve, Whitfield returned to the party leadership, although he was still not in the assembly.

In 1976 the FNM members of the assembly revolted against Whitfield's leadership, and withdrew from the party to form the Bahamian Democratic Party. Those remaining in the FNM participated in the 1977 election, but only Whitfield and one other member were seated in the assembly. Both victors won seats that until then had been held by the PLP.

FREE PROGRESSIVE LIBERAL PARTY. *See* FREE NATIONAL MOVEMENT.

LABOUR PARTY. The Labour Party was organized in 1957 by Randol Fawkes, an early labor leader and head of the Bahamas Federation of Labour, who had been elected to the assembly in 1956 as one of the first six Progressive Liberal Party members. The Labour Party was largely his personal vehicle. In the 1967 election, the party ran only three candidates in addition to him, and he was the only Labour candidate elected. He helped the PLP to form a government and became minister of labor. Although he was reelected on the Labour ticket, without PLP opposition, in the election that the PLP government called in 1968, he was not invited to continue in the cabinet. He later largely retired from politics, and the Labour Party became defunct.

NATIONAL DEMOCRATIC PARTY (NDP). The National Democratic Party was formed by three Progressive Liberal Party members of the House of Assembly, Paul Adderley, Spurgeon Bethel, and Orville Turnquist. In April 1965, these three refused to boycott the assembly sessions as ordered by the PLP during a bitter dispute over constituency boundaries, and they were suspended from the PLP. Later that year they founded the NDP. As members of the PLP, they had been part of the opposition to the United Bahamian Party government, and the new party continued to constitute part of the opposition.

In the 1967 election, which saw the PLP come to power, the National Democratic Party ran eleven candidates for the House of Assembly, all but two of them in constituencies in New Providence. None of them was elected, and four of them received so few votes that they lost their deposits; that is, they did not get the minimum number of votes required by law to recoup the deposit all nominees are required to leave with election authorities. The party did no better in the 1968 election, and it did not long survive these defeats.

By 1972 Paul Adderly returned to the PLP, and in that same year he was named attorney general, a post he held for many years. Orville Turnquist joined the Free National Movement, and in 1972 he became the leader of the opposition in the Senate.

PROGRESSIVE LIBERAL PARTY (PLP). Founded in 1953, the Progressive Liberal Party was the principal party leading the "quiet revolution." Its principal founder was William Cartwright, a progressive mulatto businessman and member of the assembly. Virtually bankrupted as a result of reprisals by the Bay Street Boys, or members of the white establishment, he soon retired from politics.

Shortly after the founding of the PLP, Lynden Pindling, who had been studying law in Great Britain, returned to the Bahamas, and quickly emerged as the party's principal leader. He remained so more than twenty-five years later.

The PLP's organization spread quickly throughout New Providence, as well as in the Outer Islands (later rechristened the Family Islands). It aroused considerable enthusiasm not only among the black and mulatto elite, who had first launched it, but also among the lower-class blacks and mulattos.

In 1956 the PLP entered its first election. It won six of the twenty-nine seats in the assembly. This was a good showing, since most blacks could not vote due to property and income qualifications for the franchise, but some of the party's leaders were disappointed at the results. In 1960 the PLP won a bye-election, taking another seat from its opponents.

In the general election of 1962, the year universal adult suffrage was granted, the PLP won only eight of the then thirty-five seats, although the party polled a majority of the popular votes. The press attributed the party's relatively poor showing to the female vote and to blacks who backed opponents of the PLP, but it was most likely due to gerrymandering of legislative seats.

Subsequent to the 1962 election, the PLP fought hard to abolish the additional vote which property holders still had, and to bring about a redistricting of the constituencies. At one point, it ordered its members of the assembly to boycott its sessions in protest against the United Bahamian Party's refusal to make these changes, a move which led to a split in the party and establishment of the National Democratic Party. However, in the end, the PLP campaign for electoral changes was successful.

In the election of 1967, the PLP won eighteen seats, the same number as the United Bahamian Party. With the support of Randol Fawkes of the Labour Party and one independent member of the assembly, the PLP was able to form a government, with Lynden Pindling as premier. The following year the government called a new election, and the PLP won with a clear majority of twenty-eight seats out of thirty-eight. In 1972 it repeated its success.

In 1973, when the Bahamas were granted independence, Lynden Pindling became the first prime minister of the Commonwealth of the Bahamas, and the PLP has remained in power ever since.

The PLP's ideology can best be described as pragmatic. It has fostered the country's economic development, based principally on tourism and international finance, which was started by its predecessors. It has been friendly to organized labor, which in its considerable majority has supported the PLP. In international policy, it has been friendly to all, but has been particularly careful of the country's relations with the United States.

UNITED BAHAMIAN PARTY (UBP). The United Bahamian Party was organized soon after the election of 1956, as the establishment's answer to the

Progressive Liberal Party. In its early years, the UBP received the support of virtually all the white voters, as well as that of a considerable number of blacks. Its leader, Sir Roland Symonette, became the first premier of the Bahamas in 1964. The UBP won the 1962 election, won the same number of seats in the House of Assembly as the PLP in 1967, then suffered an overwhelming defeat in 1968, when it elected only eight members. That defeat was the signal that a party of the old white establishment no longer had a viable place in Bahamian politics. In 1971 it merged with a group of rebels from the PLP to form the Free National Movement.

VANGUARD NATIONALIST AND SOCIALIST PARTY. The Vanguard Nationalist and Socialist Party was established in 1971 by a group of young men and women, most of them university graduates. As its name indicates, the party constitutes the far Left of Bahamian politics. However, its program and policy are somewhat vague, and it is not a Marxist-Leninist party. Its principal leader is John McCartney, for some years a faculty member of Purdue University in the United States. By mid-1979 it had named a number of candidates for the next general election, scheduled for 1981 at the latest.

Robert J. Alexander

BARBADOS

In 1605 the British first landed in Barbados, and it was continuously held by the British until it achieved independence in 1966. Barbados soon became one of the most important sugar cane-producing territories of the West Indies. It was to cultivate sugar that the African slaves, the ancestors of the great majority of the country's present inhabitants, were originally brought to the island. However, unlike virtually all of the other British territories in the Caribbean, Barbados continued to have a substantial resident white planter and merchant population, and as a result, it did not give up the old-style colonial legislature after emancipation, as did most of the rest of those British possessions. In fact, the Barbados House of Assembly is said to be the second oldest parliament in the Commonwealth, only the British one having precedence.

Traditionally, the Governor of Barbados did not have the "reserved powers" over finances and other matters which were the prerogative of the governor in other nearby British territories. The House of Assembly had power to legislate on all matters of internal concern in the island.

With an area of 166 square miles and an estimated population of about a quarter of a million people, Barbados has the highest population density of any nation or territory in the Caribbean, and Central and South America.

Since World War II the economy of Barbados has become considerably more diversified. Tourism took its place as the second most important source of income after sugar. In the 1960s a modest industrialization program was launched, providing in part consumer products for home consumption and export to neighboring territories, in part components for industries in the United States and other highly industrialized countries. Although natural gas is known to exist offshore and has been exploited, and there has been considerable exploration for oil, neither of these as yet provides a substantial part of the national income.

The "Badjians," as they are known to their neighbors, are famous for being "Black Englishmen." Perhaps because of the continued presence of an appreciable white minority of British origin, and the relative ease of the transfer to black rule, British cultural and political influences upon the people of the island are substantially greater than in most of the other Commonwealth Caribbean countries.

Race relations between blacks and whites are relatively equable. Although the two groups intermix in economic and workaday affairs, social contacts are more limited, and there is little intermarriage between them. Barbadians of both races are noted for their friendliness and courtesy. However, it was found necessary in 1955 to pass legislation against race discrimination.

Although Barbados never lost its old-style legislature, like most of the other British West Indian territories the right to vote for and to be elected to the House of Assembly was limited until the post–World War II period to males with income or property qualifications which in practice meant that only plantation owners, merchants, and professional men (most of them white) could vote for or serve as members of the lower house of the Barbados parliament.

The upper house of the Barbados legislature, the legislative council, consisted entirely of members named by the British governor, and its members, once named, were seldom replaced. Finally, there was an executive committee whose members were also appointed by the governor.

The first protest against the colonial status quo was launched by the *Herald*, a newspaper established in 1919 and edited by Clenell Wickham. It became the mouthpiece for the Democratic League, formed by Charles Duncan O'Neale during World War I.

The Democratic League did not at first gain the support of the young black man who was ultimately to be responsible for bringing black control and independence to Barbados. This was Grantley Adams, who returned home in 1925 from Oxford University, where he had obtained a law degree and had been admitted to the bar. During his university career he had come to regard himself as a British-type Liberal, and opposed the Socialist cast of the ideas of the Democratic League.

However, Grantley Adams became increasingly convinced that the Democratic League was right in its fight for broadening the franchise and seeking to help to improve the status of the black and mulatto majority of the population. He also reached the conclusion that in fact the League was not "socialist," but agreed basically with his Liberal philosophy. As a result, when he announced his candidacy for the House of Assembly late in 1934, he had the support of the Democratic League.

The revolt in the British West Indies, which began with a riot of sugar workers in Saint Kitts in 1935, finally spread to Barbados early in 1937. A young labor-political agitator from Trinidad, Clement Payne, came to the island, and quickly gained backing among the poorer populace. Efforts were made to deport the Trinidadian and, Adams his attorney, was unable to prevent his deportation. However, the incident provoked a major riot by the supporters of Payne, which resulted in the death of fourteen, the wounding of forty-seven, and the imprisonment of five hundred.

As the result of the growing crisis in the island, Grantley Adams was commissioned late in 1937 by the elements working for change in Barbados to go to Britain to try to convince the British government to support these reforms. Although he was not successful in convincing the Conservative government of the time to undertake any drastic changes, he did get it to agree to undertake a general study of conditions in the island. Also, Adams made contact with the Fabian Society and the British Labour Party, who supported the movement for reform in Barbados and elsewhere in the British West Indies. As a result of this trip to Great Britain, which lasted for several months, Grantley Adams was converted to Socialism, and as a result, whatever conflicts which had existed between Adams and other leaders of the movement for greater popular political participation in Barbadian affairs disappeared.

Meanwhile, the Democratic League had been dissolved, and in October 1938 a new organization fighting for political and social reform was established. This was the Progressive League, of which Grantley Adams was at first vice-president. After a crisis with some of the other leaders of the organization a few months later, Adams emerged as president and undisputed leader of the league.

Although in the 1940 general election the Progressive League offered candidates, and won five of the twenty-four seats in the assembly, it soon became a kind of "umbrella" organization. Under the aegis of the league, four other groups were established. One of these was the Barbados Workers Union, which became the country's principal trade union organization, enlisting in its ranks the island's sugar workers as well as the dockers, transportation workers, and various other groups. Another was the Barbados Labour Party, which was in effect the political arm of the League. The third was the Peasants Association, which undertook to organize the small farmers. Finally, there was the Barbados Progressive League Friendly Society, a cooperative organization.

In 1942, the governor, Sir Gratten Bushe, for the first time named the leader of the Progressive League to be a member of the executive committee, the advisory body to the governor. Subsequently, on the governor's initiative, the legislature reduced substantially the property qualifications for voting, which resulted in the Barbados Labour Party winning eight seats in the House of Assembly in 1944 and the somewhat similar Congress Party winning the same number. Thereafter, Hugh Springer, also of the Barbados Labour Party, joined Grantley Adams in the executive committee.

A further step towards responsible self-government was taken by the governor just before the 1946 general election. He announced that when the new House of Assembly met, he would call upon the person most likely to command a majority in the House to nominate the members of the executive committee. When that election resulted in there being nine Barbados Labour Party members, eight from the Conservative Electors Association and seven from the Congress Party, Grantley Adams was asked to choose the members of the executive committee. He named himself and Springer for the Labour Party, and W. A. Crawford and H. D. Blackman of the Congress Party. This was the first time that Barbados had, in effect, a cabinet responsible to the House of Assembly.

In 1951 the first election under universal adult suffrage was held. It brought a resounding victory to the Barbados Labour Party and the introduction into the House of Assembly of a number of younger figures who were to play an important role subsequently. Three years later, the full ministerial system was established with the executive committee becoming the cabinet, and its members becoming ministers, presided over by the premier.

During the next decade the political picture of the island changed significantly. A secessionist movement in the Barbados Labour Party resulted in 1955 in the establishment of the Democratic Labour Party (DLP), which quickly took its place as the second major party in the country. The Congress Party disappeared immediately, and the Conservative Electors Association (by then called the National Party) disappeared by the early 1970s.

By the late 1960s, the membership of the House of Assembly consisted completely of black and mulatto members. As late as 1961 there were still four white members, three from the Progressive Conservative Party and one from the Democratic Labour Party. However, all of these had either retired, died, or been defeated by the end of the decade.

Meanwhile, Barbados participated between 1958 and 1962 in the West Indian Federation. Grantley Adams served as premier of the federation, abandoning his active role in Barbadian politics. In part because of his absence, the Barbados Labour Party was defeated for the first time in the general election of 1961. For the next fifteen years, the Democratic Labour Party was in control of the government, and in 1966 Prime Minister Errol Barrow led the country to full independence.

Barbados continued as an independent country to have a two-house legislature. The House of Assembly, since 1951 elected on the basis of universal adult suffrage, was the lower house, and the one with the real power. The Senate (the former Legislative Council) continued to be an appointive body, but with twelve of its twenty-one members named on the recommendation of the prime minister, two on the advice of the Leader of the Opposition, and seven at the discretion of the governor-general. It could hold up but not prevent the passage of legislation.

The long period of Democratic Labour rule was ended in the election of 1976, when a rejuvenated Barbados Labour Party, led by Grantley Adams's son J. M. G. (popularly, "Tom") Adams soundly defeated the DLP. However, the political life of the country continued to be dominated by the two major parties. Five years later the BLP was victorious once again.

Several attempts have been made to establish parties to the Left of the dominant Barbados Labour Party and Democratic Labour Party. In 1974, the People's Liberation Movement, which proclaimed itself Marxist-Leninist, was established by Robert Clarke; in 1975 Frank Allyne led the establishment of the People's Democratic Movement, as a party of the moderate Left. Finally, the Movement for National Liberation, also Marxist-Leninist in philosophy, was established under the leadership of Francis Hall. However, none of these was able to elect any members of the House of Assembly.

In 1981 Barbados appeared to have the stablest political system in the English-speaking Caribbean. However, it remained to be seen whether revolutionary developments in Grenada and more radical regimes in some of the other nearby countries, as well as economic strains caused by escalating oil prices and international recession, would disturb the relatively equable state of Barbadian affairs.

Bibliography

Personal contacts of the writer.

F. A. Hoyos. *Grantley Adams and the Social Revolution.* Macmillan & Co. , London, 1974.

————. *The Rise of West Indian Democracy.* Advocate Press, Bridgetown, 1963.

Political Parties

BARBADOS LABOUR PARTY (BLP). The Barbados Labour Party, the first real party to be established in Barbados, began as the electoral wing of the Progressive League, first organized under the leadership of Grantley Adams in October 1938. The Progressive League had its first experience at the polls in 1940, when it won five of the twenty-four seats in the House of Assembly. Two years later, however, it elected only four members of the House. Nevertheless, for the first time the Progressive League leader, Grantley Adams, became a member of the executive committee, the governor's advisory body.

By 1944 the political wing of the Progressive League had taken the name Barbados Labour Party, and it won a major victory, placing eight of its members in the assembly, the same number as the Congress Party and the Electors Association. As a result, a second BLP member, Hugh Springer, also joined the executive committee.

After the 1946 election, in which the BLP won nine seats, the Electors Association eight, and the Congress Party seven, the governor introduced the system of having membership in the executive committee depend upon support of a majority in the House of Assembly. As a result, Grantley Adams undertook to organize the House majority, forming a coalition of the BLP with the Congress Party.

However, this coalition continued for only a bit more than a year. When three members of the Congress Party in the assembly joined the BLP, giving it twelve of the twenty-four House members, Adams reorganized the executive committee. For the first time it came to consist only of BLP members: Grantley Adams, H. D. Blackman, H. G. Cummins and C. E. Talma. Shortly afterwards, the BLP suffered a defeat in a bye-election for the seat formerly held by Hugh Springer, who had resigned to become the executive officer of the new University of the West Indies in Jamaica. Nevertheless, the BLP was able to continue to control the executive committee.

Under leadership of the BLP, the government undertook a number of programs. It expanded and diversified the island's educational system, established workmen's compensation, expanded old-age pensions, and undertook prison reform among other measures.

In the general election of December 1948 the BLP won a resounding victory, electing twelve members of the House. However, since the Speaker was a member of the BLP, and could only vote in case of a tie, the situation of the Labour Party government at first seemed precarious. The situation was soon remedied when House member D. D. Garner resigned from the Congress Party and joined the BLP, giving it a majority. The new executive committee consisted of Grantley Adams, H. G. Cummins, M. E. Cox, and Frank Walcott, the secretary-general of the Barbados Workers Union.

Under Adams's leadership, the BLP government passed a measure to nationalize the country's natural gas reserves, and to set up a firm to distribute natural gas throughout the island. At the same time, the government set up a board to regulate other public utilities, announcing that as finances permitted, these enterprises would also be nationalized. In 1951 the first island-wide collective agreement in the sugar industry was signed between the Barbados Workers Union and the Sugar Producers Federation.

A high water mark in the history of the Barbados Labour Party was reached in the election of 1951. The party fought this election on a platform calling for the establishment of the ministerial form of government, limitation on the power of the legislative council, and a new system of local government. The BLP had a smashing victory, electing fifteen of the twenty-four members of the House of Assembly. The election was notable, too, for the introduction into the assembly on the BLP side of a number of younger men, notably James Cameron Tudor and Errol Barrow, both of whom had recently returned home after completing university studies in Great Britain.

Soon after the 1951 election, serious dissension began to become obvious in the ranks of the BLP. On the one hand, some of the young, newly elected assembly members became increasingly critical of what they conceived to be the too conservative attitude of Grantley Adams and the older generation of party leaders. Controversy particularly developed around a proposal to put aside some of the government's budget surplus for a revenue equalization fund, as a reserve against possible bad times.

Another source of difficulty for the BLP arose with the introduction of the ministerial system, by which the executive committee was converted into the cabinet, presided over by a premier, with each member responsible for some branch of public administration. This took place, in pursuance of the BLP's electoral promises, in 1954.

This change in governmental form presented problems for both Grantley Adams and Frank Walcott. Adams had been president of both the Barbados Labour Party and the Barbados Workers Union up until that time. Frank Walcott had been secretary-general of the union. Adams felt that both he and Walcott had to decide between continuing as members of the new cabinet and remaining officers of the union. If they continued to play both roles, they might find themselves in the incongruous situation of representing both the government and the union in a labor dispute.

Adams decided to resign as president of the Barbados Workers Union and to continue as premier and president of the Barbados Labour Party. He also insisted that Walcott make the same decision, and when Walcott refused Adams dropped him from the cabinet. This began a process of alienation of the leadership of the Barbados Workers Union from the Barbados Labour Party which was to continue for almost three decades.

Dissidence within the Barbados Labour Party culminated in 1955 in the formation of the Democratic Labour Party, led by the younger BLP back-benchers and joined by the remnants of the Congress Party. Frank Walcott and the Barbados Workers Union soon formed a tacit alliance with the new DLP.

The new Labour Government pushed an extensive program of public works. It also considerably expanded the island's public health facilities, and put into effect a program to expand tourism, and to encourage the fishing industry.

In 1956 the Barbados Labour Party won its last victory for twenty years. It elected fifteen of the twenty-four members of the House. Grantley Adams continued to serve as premier.

The formation in 1958 of the West Indian Federation, which the Barbados Labour Party had strongly supported, had a serious impact on Barbadian politics, and particularly on the BLP. After extensive negotiations, Grantley Adams was chosen by the new Federal Labour Party, consisting of the BLP and kindred parties in the other islands, to be premier of the new federal government, with its headquarters in Trinidad. Since he could not remain as Barbadian premier while holding the same post in the federation, Adams first suggested to Hugh Springer that he come back to Barbados and become leader of the BLP, and premier. When Springer refused, Adams was succeeded in Barbados by Dr. H. G. Cummins. Adams also resigned from the Barbadian House of Assembly.

With Grantley Adams no longer present to lead the Barbados Labour Party, it suffered a disastrous defeat in the 1961 general election. It won only five seats in the assembly, and soon after the election, two of those five crossed the floor and joined the Democratic Labour Party. There was little consolation for the leaders and members of the BLP to be found in the fact that the party had lost several seats by very narrow majorities, and that, because it ran more candidates than did the DLP, the Barbados Labour Party actually received more votes for its nominees than did its rival.

Having lost control over the Barbados Workers Union, the leaders of the BLP decided late in 1962 to establish their own labor organization, the Progressive Workers Union. This new group won something of a victory in 1964, when it made the government and the Barbados Workers Union back down from a proposal to put into a welfare fund part of the windfall profits which the Sugar Producers Association had agreed to turn over to the workers, and to agree instead that the total amount would be paid out as a bonus to the individual workers. However, this was not sufficient to win the Progressive Workers Union a permanent foothold among the workers, and in 1965 the organization disappeared.

Grantley Adams remained out of parliament until the 1966 general election. He was severely ill in 1964 and again a year later — at which time his situation was so critical that plans were made for a state funeral for him. However, he recovered, returned to the political wars and led his party to a partial comeback in the 1966 election, when it won nine seats in the House of Assembly. Adams returned to the House as Leader of the Opposition.

During his last years in the leadership of the BLP, Grantley Adams was a vigorous critic of the government of Prime Minister Barrow. He was particularly strong in attacking the Public Order Act which the government introduced after the frustration of an attempt to overthrow by force the government of Prime Minister Eric Williams of Trinidad, in 1969.

However, increasing ill health finally forced Grantley Adams to resign from the House in October 1970. He died a little over a year later, on November 28, 1971. He was succeeded as leader of the Barbados Labour Party by H. B. St. John.

The BLP suffered another disastrous defeat in the 1971 general election. It won only six of the twenty-four seats in the assembly, and among those defeated was the party's leader, St. John. As a result, Grantley Adams's son, J. M. G. Adams ("Tom"), was elected head of the BLP and Leader of the Opposition.

Under the leadership of Tom Adams, the Barbados Labour Party won a smashing victory in the 1976 general election. It gained seventeen seats in the House of Assembly and J. M. G. Adams became prime minister.

Although in its campaign the Barbados Labour Party had taken a position somewhat to the left of the Democratic Labour Party government of Prime Minister Errol Barrow, its policies in power were not markedly different from those of its predecessor. It was faced with the crisis presented by the dramatic rise of oil prices during the later 1970s and a resulting inflation in the Barbadian economy. However, the Tom Adams government did not alter the general program of industrialization and social welfare which had been carried out by its predecessor.

BARBADOS NATIONAL PARTY. The country's second political party chronologically, the Barbados National Party arose in the early 1940s largely in response to the formation of the Barbados Labour Party. During its quarter-of-a-century of existence, this group used several names: Voters Association, Electors Association, Conservative Electors Association, Progressive Conservative Party, and finally Barbados National Party.

In the beginning, the National Party was undoubtedly the one favored by most of the island's white minority. In the 1951–1956 parliament, three of the nine assembly members of the Conservative Electors Association, as it was then known, were whites. However, by that time, leadership of the party had in fact passed to a black man, Ernest D. Mottley, who was to continue to head the organization until its demise about a decade and a half later.

Ideologically, there was a considerable difference between the National Party and the BLP. In its 1951 Election Manifesto, the party, then the Conservative Electors Association, proclaimed its "fundamental difference with the BLP on the question of Free Enterprise and nationalization." It strongly opposed the BLP government's nationalization of the country's natural gas resources and other moves to nationalize public utilities. There is no doubt that the National Party, whatever its name at any given moment, enjoyed the support of many of the more affluent members of Barbadian society, regardless of their color.

Over the years, the National Party declined in influence. Whereas in 1940 all but five of the members of the House of Assembly were more or less aligned with the Voters' Association (the group's name at that time), four years later the Conservative Electors Association elected only eight members of the Assembly. By 1956, under the name of Progressive Conservative Party and led by E. D. Mottley, it had fallen to six seats in the House, although it remained the Official Opposition.

In 1961 the National Party, by then using that name, won only five seats in the assembly. However, it still remained the Official Opposition, now to the government of Democratic Labour Party leader Errol Barrow, because of the disastrous defeat of the BLP, which soon after the election remained with only three members of the House. In the following election, the National Party placed only one member in the assembly, and in 1971 it failed to elect any.

CONGRESS PARTY. The Congress Party was the more or less personal vehicle of W. A. Crawford. He was first elected to the House of Assembly in 1940 on the ticket of the Progressive League, using the slogan Vote for Crawford. Adams needs help. However, he soon had personal difficulties with Grantley Adams and as a result established the Congress Party.

Throughout its existence, the Congress Party proclaimed itself to be democratic-socialist. It was critical of the Barbados Labour Party on the grounds that that party did not carry out with sufficient vigor its own socialist program. The Congress Party was regarded by both its own members and those of the BLP as being to the left of the Barbados Labour Party.

In its first try at the polls in 1944, the Congress Party enjoyed a considerable success. It won eight seats in the assembly, the same number as the Barbados Labour Party and the Electors Association. In the following election, at the end of 1946, it won seven seats. As the result of the reorganization of the executive committee, the governor's advisory body, on the basis of its members commanding a majority in the House of Assembly, the Congress Party formed a coalition after the election with the Labour Party. W. A. Crawford and H. D. Blackman of the Congress Party became members of the executive committee.

Three assembly members of the Congress Party soon abandoned its ranks to join the Barbados Labour Party, giving the BLP half of the membership of the House. As a result, the Congress Party withdrew from the governmental coalition.

The defection of the Congress Party members to the BLP continued. After the 1948 general election, D. D. Garner, a Congress Party assemblyman, crossed the floor, giving the BLP a majority once again.

The Congress Party declined because, although W. A. Crawford was an outstanding orator, he was not a particularly good political organizer. It finally disappeared when Crawford and other remaining figures of the party joined with dissidents of the BLP to form the Democratic Labour Party in 1955. Subsequently, Crawford was vice-premier of the DLP government in the 1960s.

CONSERVATIVE ELECTORS ASSOCIATION. See BARBADOS NATIONAL PARTY.

DEMOCRATIC LABOUR PARTY (DLP). The Democratic Labour Party was established in 1955 as the result of a revolt of young back-bench members of the Barbados Labour Party in the House of Assembly against the leadership of Grantley Adams. This was due in part to personality conflicts, but also to a different emphasis between the founding generation of the BLP and the younger men who entered its leadership with the 1951 election.

Grantley Adams and most of the older leaders were particularly concerned with the country's political evolution. Errol Barrow and other younger figures were more interested in problems of economic development and social change. They thought that the emphasis of the movement for change in the island ought to be shifted in large part to those issues.

With the establishment of the Democratic Labour Party by four of the BLP dissident members of the assembly, it was soon joined by the remnants of the Congress Party. It also had at least the friendly neutrality of the leaders of the Barbados Workers Union, headed by Secretary-General Frank Walcott.

However, the DLP did not do very well at its first outing at the polls, in the 1956 general election. Although it ran sixteen candidates at that time, only four of these were elected, and among those who were defeated was the party's leader, Errol Barrow.

In the years that followed the 1956 election the position of the Democratic Labour Party improved. Its relations with the Barbados Workers Union were strengthened. At the same time, the party's rival, the BLP, lost its principal leader, Grantley Adams, who became premier of the West Indian Federation, and for the time being abandoned political activity in Barbados. There were also continuing feuds within the BLP.

The net result of this situation was that in the next general election, in 1961, the Democratic Labour Party, although getting fewer total votes than the BLP, won fourteen of the twenty-four seats in the House of Assembly. As a result, the DLP assumed power, with Errol Barrow as premier.

The only significant crisis which faced the Democratic Labour Party government in its first term of office (1961–1966) was the widespread opposition in 1964 to the government's support of the Barbados Workers Union leaders' suggestion that a substantial part of the windfall profit which the Sugar Producers Association had agreed to give the sugar workers be put in a benefit fund, instead of being passed out as income to individual sugar workers. Although the Barbados Workers Union and the DLP government had to reverse their decision, the union continued to have the loyalty of the majority of the island's workers, in spite of efforts of the Barbados Labour Party to organize a rival labor group.

The DLP was confirmed in power in the 1966 election. It won fourteen of the twenty-four seats in the House. Five years later, in 1971, its majority was considerably increased, when it elected eighteen of the House members, the largest majority that any party had had in thirty years.

Meanwhile, the Democratic Labour Party regime had substantially altered the country's political and economic situation. With the collapse of the West Indian Federation in 1962, followed by Jamaica and Trinidad obtaining independence individually, the Barbadian government continued negotiations with the British Leeward and Windward Islands about the possibility of a "small federation." However, by 1965 Premier Errol Barrow had come to the conclusion that such a federation was not feasible, and he and the other DLP leaders decided that Barbados should obtain separate independence for the island. This was brought to fruition in 1966.

The DLP government also carried out an extensive economic and social development program. It particularly stimulated industrialization, and by the end of its period in office about one hundred manufacturing firms had been established, including electronics plants, textile enterprises, furniture factories, and food processing firms. It also established a social security system which covered virtually all social risks except unemployment; established free secondary education; and brought about the setting up of a branch of the University of the West Indies in Barbados.

In spite of this record of accomplishment, the Democratic Labour Party suffered a severe defeat in 1976. It received only seven of the twenty-four seats in the House of Assembly, compared to the eighteen which it had had before the election.

After his party's defeat, Errol Barrow left the leadership of the DLP for some time. He was appointed a part-time lecturer at Yale University, and did not feel that he could serve as Leader of the Opposition at the same time. His successor was Stephen Smith. Within a year, Smith retired from politics and resigned from the assembly. As a result, Errol Barrow was restored as Leader of the Opposition. His party lost again in 1981 to the Barbados Labour Party.

ELECTORS ASSOCIATION. See BARBADOS NATIONAL PARTY.

PROGRESSIVE CONSERVATIVE PARTY. See BARBADOS NATIONAL PARTY.

PROGRESSIVE LEAGUE. See BARBADOS LABOUR PARTY.

VOTERS ASSOCIATION. See BARBADOS NATIONAL PARTY.

Robert J. Alexander

BELIZE

Belize, until 1973 known as British Honduras, was until achieving independence in September 1981 a self-governing British colony located on the Caribbean Coast of Central America, east of Guatemala and south of Yucatan, Mexico. It has a total of 8,867 square miles, and an estimated population of about 140,000, almost a third of which lives in Belize City. The majority of the people are almost evenly divided between Maya Indians and those of African descent, but there are also significant minorities of "Caribs," people of mixed Indian-African descent who were settled from Saint Vincent in the mid-nineteenth century, as well as East Indians, Chinese, and Arabs.

Throughout the sixteenth and early seventeenth centuries, the Spaniards were unable to subdue the Mayan inhabitants of present-day Belize, although they made several efforts to do so. By the mid-seventeenth century British adventurers, who doubled as buccaneers and pirates and as loggers, began to establish themselves in the area. They brought with them African slaves from the West Indies, and the process of miscegenation between the British "baymen" and both blacks and Mayas began almost immediately. However, it was 1780 before the British government appointed a "superintendent" for the area, and 1862 before Belize was officially proclaimed a colony.

When Guatemala became independent in the early nineteenth century, it renewed the old Spanish territorial claim on British Honduras. However, in a treaty of 1859 between Great Britain and Guatemala, the latter country recognized British sovereignty in the area, in return for a British promise to build a railroad from there to Guatemala City. That railroad was never constructed, and after World War II Guatemala actively renewed its claims to sovereignty over the territory. The question of relations with Guatemala remains an overriding problem which affects both Belize's political and economic development.

From the mid-nineteenth to the mid-twentieth century the economy, and to a large degree the political life of Belize was dominated by the Belize Estate and Produce Company, a British concern. It owned half of the privately owned land in the country, was granted permission to cut timber on much of the land owned by the government, and was favored in many other ways by both the British and colonial governments.

Since World War II, sugar cultivation has become the most important economic activity, providing most of Belize's foreign exchange. It is largely controlled by a subsidiary of United Brands. Citrus fruits, bananas, and fishing have also become important sources of income and foreign exchange. Quite recently, tourism on a few of the keys off the coast has begun to assume some importance.

Until 1936 Belize was an old-style Crown Colony, in which the governor's powers were virtually absolute. Although there existed a legislative council, a majority of its members were "official," that is, were British civil servants. It was not until 1936 that a new constitution went into effect which provided for five members to be elected, on a very limited property franchise. The official and nominated members still had a majority, however, until 1945. In 1946 for the first time two members of the legislative council became members of the executive council, which until then had consisted only of British officials.

Britain generally moved more slowly in British Honduras than elsewhere in the Caribbean area in providing for elected members of both the legislature and the executive and in increasing the number of citizens eligible to vote. This, and economic problems, led to considerable discontent in the 1930s and 1940s. The "disturbances" of the West Indian territories had their modest counterpart in a series of demonstrations by unemployed and underemployed workers between March and September 1934, culminating in a riot on October 1, led by an unemployed lumber worker, Antonio Sobranis. On another level, business and professional people in Belize City, particularly the nominated members of the legislative council, conducted protests during the 1930s and 1940s against certain policies of the governor and his generally arbitrary behavior. The major figure in these protests was Harrison Courtenay.

However, neither the incipient mass movement of Sobranis nor the middle- and upper-class protests led to a permanent organization favoring fundamental change and opposing colonialism. Two political parties had fleeting careers in the period, the People's Group and the Progressive Party, but without a mass electorate, they did not establish a firm organizational structure, and disappeared entirely with the rise of the People's United Party in the early 1950s.

However, it was only a matter of time before some incident would mobilize the growing feeling of discontent. This incident was the devaluation of the British Honduras currency on 31 December 1949. Earlier in the year the British pound had been substantially devalued and the governor had announced his intention also to devalue the British Honduras dollar, which for many years had been at par with that of the United States. Although the nonofficial members of the legislature had expressed opposition to the move and there had been popular meetings of protest, the governor used his "reserve powers" to carry out devaluation.

On the same day that devaluation occurred, the People's Committee was established. It was headed by John Smith, George Price, and Nicholas Pollard, head of the General Workers Union, the country's first labor organization. It held a series of public meetings and its protests soon broadened beyond the devaluation issue to demands for fundamental political changes.

On 19 September 1950 the People's Committee became the People's United

Party (PUP), the country's first effective political party. It received strong support not only from the General Workers Union but also from the *Belize Billboard*, a weekly newspaper which had for some time been agitating against the status quo.

In the next four years the British governor campaigned strongly against the PUP. Meanwhile, an opposition party appeared, in the form of the National Party, which ran candidates against those of the PUP in the 1952, 1954, and 1957 elections. In general, it took a position against the nationalist posture of the PUP.

In 1954 the PUP was victorious in the first election held under something approaching universal adult suffrage. This victory was the more significant because it took place soon after an official investigation to determine whether George Price of the PUP had received money from Guatemala, that resulted in a somewhat equivocal verdict.

After the PUP victory, negotiations began for a constitutional change, resulting in a new system, beginning in January 1955, in which elected members from the majority group in the legislative council would sit in the executive council and have responsibility for certain aspects of the administration. Price, Leigh Richardson, Philip Goldson, and Herman Jex of the PUP received these posts.

In the following year the first serious split occurred in the PUP. Leigh Richardson and Philip Goldson broke away to form the Honduras Independence Party (HIP). This schism also seriously split the General Workers Union, which until then had been closely allied with the PUP and had had virtually the same officers.

In the 1957 election there were twenty-six candidates for the nine elective seats in the legislature: 7 of the National Party, 6 of HIP, 9 of the PUP, and 4 independents. The PUP elected six, the HIP two, and one independent was victorious.

Soon after the election a British Honduras government delegation went to London to discuss constitutional advance and money. George Price, a member of the delegation, had luncheon with the Guatemalan minister in London, which resulted in cancellation of the talks by the British. Subsequently, two PUP members of the legislative and executive councils, Enrique De Paz and Denbigh Jeffrey, left the party. The latter joined the HIP and De Paz joined the new Christian Democratic Party (CDP).

The CDP resulted from another split in the PUP, led by its veteran trade unionist, Nicholas Pollard. It was to survive only until the 1961 election. Meanwhile, the National Party and the Honduras Independence Party had joined in 1958 to form the National Independence Party (NIP).

In December 1959 a delegation of all three parties then existing went to London to negotiate again concerning constitutional changes. This resulted in an assembly of 25, of whom 18 would be elected, 2 ex-officio, and 5 nominated, and a cabinet with a first minister (the leader of the assembly majority) and five other members chosen from the assembly by the first minister.

New elections in March 1961 gave all 18 elected seats to the PUP. However, the leader of the NIP, Philip Goldson, became a nominated member and styled himself Leader of the Opposition.

Still further constitutional talks took place in London in July 1963, resulting in full internal self-government, the system which remained in place until Belize became independent in October 1981. As of 1 January 1964 the governor was responsible only for defence, foreign affairs, internal security, and the sanctity of the civil service. The cabinet was headed by the premier, who was the leader of the majority in the eighteen-member House of Representatives. A Senate of eight, five chosen by the premier, two by the Leader of the Opposition, and one by the governor, was also provided for, but it had only a suspensive veto on measures passed by the House.

Since 1964 the People's United Party has continued to win a majority in each general election, although by varying margins. The Opposition has gone through various changes. After the 1961 election, the NIP absorbed the remains of the Christian Democratic Party. In 1969 the NIP split, with the breakaway of the People's Development Movement (PDM), headed by Dean Lindo, a leader of the NIP's younger generation.

Various changes occurred in the 1970s. A new opposition group, the Liberal Party, appeared in 1972, but in that same year merged with the NIP and PDM to form the United Democratic Party (UDP). It made considerable progress in subsequent elections.

Meanwhile, on the Left two new groups appeared, the United Black Association for Development (UBAD), a Black Power–oriented group, and the Political Action Committee (PAC), led by two young men of Arab descent influenced by concepts of "Arab Socialism." The UBAD and PAC joined forces shortly in 1970 to form the Revolitical Action Movement (RAM), but it quickly broke up, with the PAC leaders joining the PUP and UBAD continuing until after the 1974 election, when its leaders also joined the PUP.

Two small regional parties existed at different times in the Corozal area in the north. One was the Corozal United Party, set up in 1956, which soon joined the PUP. The other was the Corozal United Front, formed before the 1974 election, but which disappeared soon thereafter because of the poor results of its participation in that poll.

Finally, there has existed in the Toledo area in the south the only party supporting amalgamation with Guatemala, the Toledo Progressive Party. It has been able to rally virtually no support for that idea.

All of the national parties organized to oppose the PUP were to some degree supportive of the free enterprise idea. They were also more inclined than the PUP to maintain a relationship with Great Britain and the English-speaking territories in the Caribbean. Finally, they have been more vociferously anti-Guatemalan than has the PUP.

Bibliography

BRUKDOWN, The Magazine of Belize. nos. 6–7, 1979.
Cedric Grant. The Making of Modern Belize. Cambridge University Press, London, 1976.

John Maher. *Readings in Belizean History*, vol. 1. BISRA, Belize, 1978.

People's United Party. *25 Years of Struggle and Achievement 1950–1975.* Belize, 1975.

Assad Shoman. *Birth of the Nationalist Movement in Belize.* BISRA Occasional Publication no. 7, Belize, 1979.

Political Parties

CHRISTIAN DEMOCRATIC PARTY (CDP). The CDP was formed in 1958, when Nicholas Pollard, the veteran trade union leader, was expelled from the People's United Party. Pollard formed what he first called the Democratic Agricultural Labour Party. However, its name was soon changed to Christian Democratic Party.

Denbigh Jeffrey, originally named to the executive council of the colony by the PUP, joined the Christian Democratic Party without losing his seat in the executive council. He ran for the legislative council in 1961 as CDP candidate from Fort George but did not get elected.

The CDP cooperated with the National Independence Party in elaborating proposals for constitutional change in 1959. Nicholas Pollard represented his party in talks in London soon afterwards.

The CDP ran ten candidates in the 1961 general election. However, none was elected, and the CDP disappeared through merger with the National Independence Party soon after that election.

COROZAL UNITED FRONT (CUF). A regional party established in the northern region of Corozal in 1973, the CUF was organized when Mr. Ricaldi, who had been a member of the legislative council representing the People's United Party since 1957, resigned from the PUP. The party reflected a recurring feeling by some people of that region that their interests were being ignored by the PUP. However, although it ran candidates for the two legislative seats for Corozal in the 1974 general election, neither was victorious. The party disappeared soon afterwards.

COROZAL UNITED PARTY. The Corozal United Party was formed in October 1956 by dissident PUP leaders in the Corozal area. However, it joined forces again with the PUP in the 1957 election, and did not survive as a separate party for very long thereafter.

DEMOCRATIC PARTY. The Democratic Party was the first group organized to oppose the People's United Party, soon after the PUP's establishment in 1950. The Democratic Party ran candidates in the election for members of the Belize City Council on 20 November 1950. One of these, Lionel Francis, was elected. However, the party never seems to have been established on a strong organizational basis, and apparently disappeared with the foundation of the National Party, the major opponent of the PUP in the early 1950s.

DEMOCRATIC AGRICULTURAL LABOUR PARTY. *See* CHRISTIAN DEMOCRATIC PARTY.

HONDURAS INDEPENDENCE PARTY (HIP). The Honduras Independence Party was established in 1956, when two of the leading founders of the People's United Party, Leigh Richardson and Philip Goldson, broke with George Price, who was by then the PUP's major figure. They professed suspicion about Price's relations with Guatemala and opposed his general orientation toward regarding British Honduras as a Central American country rather than as part of the British West Indies. They favored participation in the proposed West Indian Federation, which Price successfully opposed. The immediate excuse for the break in the PUP was the accusation that Nicholas Pollard had appropriated funds of the General Workers Union for his own use. Price supported Pollard, Richardson and Goldson attacked him.

The HIP ran six candidates for the nine seats contested in the 1957 general election. In some other constituencies it apparently supported the National Party candidates. However, no HIP candidates were successful. In mid-1958 the Honduras Independence Party merged with the National Party to form the National Independence Party.

LIBERAL PARTY. The Liberal Party was established in 1970 by a group of young business and professional people. These included Paul Rodriguez, an ex-Jesuit seminarian, and Manuel Esquivel, both of whom had recently returned from studying in the United States, Harry Lawrence, a journalist, Richard Lyall, an expatriate Canadian businessman, and Frank Norris, a businessman born in the United States. The Liberal Party, which had a straight-forward Manchesterian Liberal philosophy, joined with the other opposition groups (NIP, PDM, and UBAD) to contest the 1970 municipal elections in Belize City, but the coalition was badly defeated by the People's United Party. The Liberal Party merged in 1972 with the NIP and PDM to form the United Democratic Party.

NATIONAL INDEPENDENCE PARTY (NIP). The NIP was formed by a merger of the National Party and the Honduras Independence Party in mid-1958. Its first leaders were Herbert Fuller, Leigh Richardson, and Philip Goldson. However, Fuller died shortly after its establishment, and Richardson went to live abroad. Thus, during most of the existence of the NIP its principal figure was Philip Goldson.

One of the NIP's first actions was participation in a delegation to London to discuss constitutional changes at the end of 1959. These resulted in a new constitution and new elections in March 1961. Although the NIP offered candidates in seventeen of the eighteen constituencies, it did not elect anyone. However, the new constitution provided for five nominated members of the legislature, and the governor appointed Philip Goldson as one of these. As a result, he functioned more or less as Leader of the Opposition in the 1961–1965 legislature. Shortly after the 1961 election, the NIP absorbed the remnants of the Christian Democratic Party.

In 1965 the National Independence Party somewhat improved its electoral performance. It ran candidates in all eighteen constituencies, and elected two members of the legislature. One of these was Philip Goldson, who thus became the official Leader of the Opposition.

During the latter part of the 1960s a number of young professional men, recently returned from studying in the United Kingdom and the United States, joined the NIP. However, they soon became discontented with what they thought was the lack of militancy in the NIP leadership, and its lack of concern for economic development. This discontent led in 1969 to a split in the party, led by Dean Lindo, who organized the People's Development Movement (PDM). This split took place shortly before the 1969 general election, and the two opposition parties formed a coalition for that poll. The join NIP–PDM ticket put up candidates in all constituencies. They elected only Philip Goldson.

The NIP participated in a four-party coalition (NIP, PIM, UBAD, and Liberals) in the 1970 city council election in Belize City, but it elected no one. Two years later the NIP joined with the PDM and Liberals to establish the United Democratic Party.

NATIONAL PARTY (NP). The National Party was organized in 1951, with the encouragement of the British colonial authorities, to confront the rising nationalist movement represented by the People's United Party. It was headed by Herbert Fuller, and other leaders included Lionel Francis and Henry Middleton, an early defector from the PUP. It had its first test at the polls in the Belize City Council election in March 1952, when it ran seven candidates for the nine-man council, and elected four of them (in part at least because two PUP candidates were disqualified by the authorities just before the election).

In 1953 a new constitution provided for universal suffrage for literate adults. In the first serious popular general election campaign in the following year the National Party strongly denounced the PUP for being allegedly under Catholic Church domination and for having sympathies for amalgamation with Guatemala. The National Party ran candidates in seven of the nine constituencies, and urged its followers to support independents in the other two. However, the party won only one seat.

The National Party did not have any solid system of constituency organization, and even on a national level was relatively inactive between the 1954 and 1957 elections. However, it did run candidates again in the latter year. It had nominees in seven of the nine districts, but none of them was victorious.

In mid-1958 the National Party merged with the Honduras Independence Party to form the National Independence Party. Herbert Fuller of the National Party became official leader of the new party.

PEOPLE'S DEVELOPMENT MOVEMENT (PDM). The People's Development Movement was established in 1969 as a result of a split in the NIP led by several young leaders who felt that the NIP concentrated too exclusively on opposition to the PUP and Premier George Price and on hostility toward Guatemala. In their own party they sought to put forth a more positive program of economic development, stressing the construction of an adequate infrastructure for the growth of tourism, and the provision of credit and technical assistance to small- and middle-scale farmers. The party's leader was Dean Lindo.

The PDM joined forces with the NIP in the 1969 general election, but no PDM candidate was successful. They also participated in a coalition with the NIP, Liberals, and UBAD in the 1970 municipal elections in Belize City, but failed to elect anyone.

In 1972 the PDM merged with the Liberals and NIP to form a new opposition party, the United Democratic Party. Dean Lindo became the leader of the UDP.

PEOPLE'S GROUP. The People's Group was a loosely organized party, largely made up of business and professional men which functioned in the 1930s. It participated in municipal elections in Belize City, but with unknown results. It does not seem to have survived the 1930s. The People's Group was one of two parties which can be seen as precursors of the nationalist movement which developed in the 1950s.

PEOPLE'S UNITED PARTY (PUP). The People's United Party has been the dominant party in Belizean politics since its establishment in September 1950. All other parties established since 1950 have been organized as opponents of the PUP.

The first officers of the PUP were John Smith, party leader; Leigh Richardson, chairman; George Price, secretary; and Philip Goldson, assistant secretary. The only one still in the leadership thirty years later was George Price.

The PUP led the fight for self-government in the colony. In the early years it suffered the jailing of Richardson and Goldson for a year for "sedition" published in their newspaper, the *Belize Billboard*, the dissolution of the PUP-controlled Belize City Council for a year, and the removal of George Price (in 1957) from the executive council, for which he had been chosen by the PUP majority of the legislative council. Just before the 1954 general election, the governor openly campaigned over the radio against the PUP.

However, the 1954 general election was the first great triumph of the PUP. It won eight of the nine elected seats in the legislative council. As a result, Goldson, Richardson, Price, and H. H. Jex of the PUP became members of the executive council, by vote of their PUP colleagues in the legislature.

Until 1956, the PUP was very closely associated with the country's first trade union, the General Workers Union (GWU). In some outlying parts of the country where the union had local units, these virtually doubled as PUP branches. The closeness of the relationship was shown by the fact that in 1952 Richardson,

Price, and Goldson were simultaneously officers of the PUP and the GWU.

In the late 1950s, the PUP suffered two splits. In both of these, an issue which was to plague the party for many years played a part. This was the question of the relationship of George Price with certain elements in Guatemalan politics. An investigation by the government in early 1954 concluded that Price had received money from Guatemalan sources, although it was careful not to say "the Guatemalan government." Three years later, a meeting of Price in London with the Guatemalan minister was used by the governor as an excuse to remove him from the executive council.

The splits involved the exit of Leigh Richardson and Philip Goldson in 1956 to form the Honduras Independence Party, and of Nicholas Pollard, the PUP's most important trade union leader, to establish the Christian Democratic Party, in 1958. After these splits, the PUP no longer had close connections with the labor movement, which fact, however, did not reduce the party's general popular and electoral appeal.

The PUP kept up constant pressure for changes in the constitution. These culminated in 1964 with the establishment of full internal self government. Thereafter, the final move to independence was held up only by the continuing claims of Guatemala to Belize and fear of Guatemalan invasion if British troops were removed following independence. After the 1979 election, PUP leaders talked as if independence was imminent. Independence was finally achieved in September 1981, although no firm agreement had been reached with Guatemala. Great Britain agreed to keep some troops in independent Belize for an unspecified time as guarantors of the country's independence. In March 1981 an agreement was reached among the governments of Guatemala, Great Britain, and Belize, by which Guatemala gave up claim to sovereignty over Belize. Opponents of PUP expressed worry that Premier Price and the PUP government made too many concessions to Guatemala in this agreement, and protest riots brought proclamation of an official emergency.

The ideology of the PUP has never been very precise, aside from its stress on Belizean nationalism. In the 1970s, a new element was contributed by a new generation of leaders who came into the PUP after having tried to establish their own parties inspired by the Black Power ideas of the 1960s and by a somewhat imprecise "socialism."

The PUP continued to win general elections. In 1961 it won all seats in the legislative council. In 1965 it captured all but two, and in 1969 all but one. However, in the 1970s, the PUP's majorities were considerably less. In 1974 it won thirteen of eighteen seats, and in 1979 it carried the same number. Also, in 1973 the party lost control of the Belize City Council for the first time in twenty years, a loss confirmed in 1977. It lost control of five of the seven municipalities of the interior in 1978.

To many, the PUP's victory in the 1979 general election came as a surprise. The explanation of the PUP and some neutral observers was that it was due to particularly hard campaign work and to the error of the opposition in making "anti-Communism" its main battle cry. The opposition, on the other hand, professed to see government manipulation of the electoral process as the cause of the PUP's success.

POLITICAL ACTION COMMITTEE (PAC). The PAC was a party established at the end of the 1960s under the leadership of three young men recently returned from British universities: Lionel del Valle, Assad Shoman, and Said Mussa. They have been described as being influenced by the British far Left and the ideas of Arab Socialism. In October 1969 the PAC merged with the United Black Association for Development (UBAD) to form the Revolitical Action Movement (RAM). However, this group lasted only until February 1970, when Assad Shoman and Said Mussa withdrew from it. Subsequently, these two founders of the PAC joined the PUP, and by the late 1970s were members of Premier Price's cabinet. The PAC did not last long enough to participate in any elections.

PROGRESSIVE PARTY. One of the precursors in the 1930s and 1940s of the Belizean nationalist movement, the Progressive Party took a lead in the campaign in the early 1930s for introduction of elected members in the legislative council, which was successful in 1935. For a number of years it had members of the elected Belize City Council. Although most of the members of the Progressive Party were from the business and professional classes, some elements of the party reportedly participated in the demonstrations of the unemployed in 1934 which culminated in a riot on October 1. It is not clear when the Progressive Party disappeared, but it certainly did not survive after the advent of the People's United Party in 1950.

TOLEDO PROGRESSIVE PARTY (TPP). The TPP was formed in the early 1970s under the leadership of Alejandro Vernon, after his expulsion from the PUP. What influence the party has is confined to the Toledo area in the far south. Its major distinction is that it is the only party in the country advocating annexation to Guatemala. It participated in the municipal elections in Toledo in 1978 and the general election of 1979. In both cases, the candidates did so badly that they lost their deposits.

UNITED BLACK ASSOCIATION FOR DEVELOPMENT (UBAD). The UBAD group began as an expression in British Honduras of the Black Power movement which swept the English-speaking West Indies in the late 1960s. At first it had a predominantly cultural orientation but soon turned towards politics. The chief figure in UBAD was Evan Hyde, who had recently returned home from completing his studies at Dartmouth College in the United States. In October 1969 Hyde and other UBAD leaders merged the group with the Political Action Committee to form the Revolitical Action Movement (RAM). However, when four months later the ex-PAC leaders withdrew from RAM, Hyde and his colleagues reconstituted the UBAD. It participated in a coalition of the opposition in the municipal election in Belize City in 1970. It also ran Evan Hyde for the House of Representatives in 1974. He split the opposition vote in the constituency in which he ran, to give the PUP the victory by one vote. That was the last that has been heard of UBAD as a political party.

UNITED DEMOCRATIC PARTY (UDP). The United Democratic Party was the major opposition party during most of the 1970s. Formed in 1972 by a merger of the National Independence Party, the People's Development Movement, and the Liberal Party, the UDP made substantial headway for several years. It had its first victory in 1974, when it captured control of the Belize City Council, a victory repeated three years later. In 1978 the party succeeded in winning control of five of the seven town councils in the interior.

Meanwhile, the UDP had done better than any other opposition party had ever done in general elections. In 1974 it won five of the eighteen seats in the House of Representatives. It got the same number five years later, although this showing in 1979 was widely regarded as a defeat, since it was generally expected that the UDP would win the election. The UDP's explanation for the loss was that the government manipulated the registration and polling process.

Whatever the cause of its defeat, it brought a considerable shakeup in the UPD leadership. Among those defeated was Dean Lindo, leader of the party. His place was taken by Theodore Aranda, a man of Maya descent rather than a Creole like Lindo. Several other party leaders left for extended stays abroad, and Mayor Paul Rodriguez of Belize City announced his retirement from active politics in the middle of 1980.

UDP leaders pointed out, however, that after the 1979 defeat their party still had a considerable majority of the country's elected officeholders—national and municipal. The UDP remained the strongest opposition party which the PUP had had to face in its thirty years of history.

The UDP is committed to emphasis on free enterprise and encouragement of foreign investment. It opposed moving toward independence before a definitive solution to the problem of Guatemala's claim to the country has been reached.

Robert J. Alexander

BERMUDA

Bermuda never lent itself to the plantation-type economy so characteristic of the West Indies and the neighboring mainland. The land was not good for extensive cultivation. Although African slaves were brought in the seventeenth and eighteenth centuries, most of them came from Virginia, and many of them were craftsmen and fishermen rather than field hands.

Also unlike the West Indian British territories, the white settlers did not leave Bermuda either before or after slave emancipation. As a result, approximately 30 percent of the present population is white, the rest being of African or mixed white-African descent, together classified as blacks. With the development of the economy since World War II, a relatively large number of whites have come to Bermuda from the United Kingdom and continental Europe. One of the bitterest issues in local politics is over the political rights that these recent immigrants should have, the indigenous whites favoring their rapid assimilation, the blacks being opposed to this.

A much smaller number of West Indian blacks have also migrated to Bermuda, where they are particularly noticeable in the police force. Much earlier, Portuguese, particularly from the Cape Verde Islands, came to replace blacks who abandoned work in agriculture. Although the Portuguese have generally been assimilated to the white population, they constitute a recognizable group within it.

Since World War II the economy has fundamentally altered. The former predominance of agriculture and local fishing has given way to tourism and international finance as the main sources of income.

Until the 1960s rigid segregation prevailed in Bermuda between the whites and blacks, perhaps as a reflection of proximity to the southern United States. However, in the early 1960s legal segregation was ended in public places, and by the middle of the decade segregation in the schools was also formally ended.

Party politics did not arrive in Bermuda until the 1960s. Although the territory has had a parliament since 1620, members of its House of Assembly were until 1963 elected on the basis of a property franchise, which excluded not only the great majority of the blacks, but many of the whites as well. How restricted the right to vote was can be seen from the fact that as late as 1936 only 15 percent of the white men had the right to vote and only 5 percent of the black men were eligible. It was not until 1944 that women, and then only property owners, were given the right to vote.

As a result of property qualifications for the vote, the local aristocracy, until World War II principally landowners, more recently merchants and financiers, completely dominated local politics. These men, known colloquially as the Front Street Boys or the Forty Thieves, not only controlled parliament, but made up the membership of the rigidly segregationist social clubs, particularly the Royal Bermuda Yacht Club where, it was said, many of the most important political decisions were taken over a drink or a meal.

The first hint of a challenge to the rule of the aristocracy came in the late nineteenth century with the formation of political associations, consisting of local black landholders who had the right to vote, in a number of heavily black parishes. Over time, they succeeded in electing a small number of blacks to the House of Assembly, who, however, did not offer any major challenge either to the segregation system or the economic status quo.

Then, after World War II a more militant leadership, made up in large part of black professionals who had migrated from the West Indies or children of West Indians who had come to Bermuda as laborers, emerged in the political associations. This group also took the leadership in establishing a labor movement, and in demanding various democratic reforms.

The first labor movement was the Bermuda Workers Association, organized in 1944 to protest a decision by authorities of the newly established United States naval and air base to cut wages. The base had begun by paying substantially higher wages that were general in Bermuda but decided to reduce them as the result of protests by the local white oligarchy. The association has been described as being more of a movement than a strictly trade union organization.

In 1957 the association was succeeded by the Bermuda Industrial Union, which until the mid-1960s was made up principally of dock workers. Subsequently, it expanded with the formation of units among the hotel workers, street cleaners, electricians, and some white-collar groups. By the late 1970s it had some 6,000 members.

Militant anti-Establishment political activity began in 1959. A group of black students, returning from their studies in the United States, where they had been impressed by the Montgomery bus boycott movement, organized a successful boycott of a local segregated movie theater. In the following year, the Committee for Universal Adult Suffrage was established to try to bring an end to the property franchise system. Another factor which gave impetus to change was a series of strikes, including a dockers walkout in 1959 and an electrical workers strike in 1965.

The drive for universal suffrage had its first success in 1962 when parliament passed a compromise which gave all adults the vote, but gave an additional vote to property owners, and raised the minimum age for the franchise from 21 to 25 years. However, within the next six years the property qualifications were completely eliminated and the voting age was returned to 21. In 1968 the first election under straight universal suffrage was held.

In 1968, too, a new constitution was granted the colony. It provided for a two-house legislature, consisting of the House of Assembly of forty members, elected on a constituency basis, and the legislative council of eleven members, of whom the Crown-appointed governor was free to appoint five at his own discretion, while naming four others on the recommendation of the premier, and two on the recommendation of the Leader of the Opposition. The cabinet, which had to be able to command a majority in the House of Assembly, had control over all matters except foreign affairs, defense, and internal security, which were still prerogatives of the governor.

The 1968 constitution also established a rather unusual constituency system. With one exception, each of the parishes into which the country is divided was given two electoral constituencies, each of which elects two members of the House of Assembly. In each constituency, therefore, a voter can vote for two candidates. In the populous Pembroke Parish, covering the capital city of Hamilton, there were established four two-member constituencies.

Meanwhile, the drive for change had brought into existence the country's two political parties. The first of these was the Progressive Labour Party (PLP), formed in 1963 by opposition elements in the House. It was followed in the next year by the establishment of the United Bermuda Party (UBP), which became the official government party. Seventeen years later, the UBP was still in office, and the PLP continued to be the Opposition, although the difference in strength between the two parties had narrowed considerably.

The movement for political and social change had also given rise to periodic outbursts of violence. There was a near riot in connection with the 1965 electrical workers strike, and serious riots in 1968 and 1970. In 1972-1973 there was a series of politically inspired murders, including those of a governor and a police commissioner. Finally, in 1977 there was the most serious outburst of all in Hamilton.

So far, the drive for political and social change has not brought independence to Bermuda. Most Bermudans seem to have an attitude of expectation of, rather than great enthusiasm for, eventual independence from Great Britain. The general feeling is that Britain is going to insist on independence sooner or later, and so they will have to accept it.

Bibliography

Personal contacts of the writer.

Suzannah Lessard. "Profiles—A Close Gathering." New Yorker, April 16, 1979.

Frank Manning. Bermudian Politics in Transition: Race, Voting and Public Opinion. Island Press, Hamilton, 1978.

Political Parties

BERMUDA DEMOCRATIC PARTY (BDP). The Bermuda Democratic Party emerged in 1965, when three of the six PLP members in the House of Assembly broke away because of what they saw as the leftward drift of the PLP. Until the 1968 election, they represented the BDP in parliament. However, in 1968, no BDP member nor independent was returned to the House, although together BDP and independent candidates got about 9 percent of the total vote. As a result of this poor showing, the Bermuda Democratic Party soon went out of existence.

PROGRESSIVE LABOUR PARTY (PLP) The first political party to be established in Bermuda, the Progressive Labour Party was a direct outgrowth of the Committee for Universal Adult Suffrage and was set up by a majority of the black members of the House of Assembly only three months before the 1963 general election.

In its first electoral campaign, the PLP was relatively successful. Of the nine candidates whom it fielded in that contest, six were elected. In part this was due to the party's organizational efforts, and in part to its policy of convincing voters to cast only one vote in the constituencies in which PLP candidates were put up, instead of the two votes to which they were entitled. This procedure came to be known as "plumping."

However, following this first election there was considerable dissension within the Progressive Labour Party. Five of its six elected members either quit or were expelled from the PLP. At the same time, the rise of a left-wing current melding some Black Power ideas from the United States and revolutionary socialist concepts from the British West Indies, alienated many among both the middle- and lower-class black population. As a result, in the 1968 general election, the first under full universal adult suffrage, the PLP got only about one-third of the popular vote and a quarter of the seats in the House — ten out of forty.

In 1972 the Progressive Labour Party won the same ten seats which it had obtained four years earlier. Most of these were in areas in which the population was principally of West Indian origin. In constituencies with preponderantly indigenous black voters, as many as 70 percent of the voters cast their ballots against the PLP.

Subsequently, the PLP moderated its political tone. It somewhat muted its former demand for independence, largely discarded any insistence on the attainment of socialism, and began to put new emphasis on the traditional values of religion and the family. In many cases, instead of calling religious leaders "Uncle Toms," it actively sought their support. It tended particularly to stress the issues of "Bermudianization" of the economy and limitation of white immigration. At the same time, the PLP was helped by growing dissension within the rival United Bermuda Party.

The upshot was that in the 1976 election the PLP gained four additional seats in the assembly. In a bye-election a few months later, it won an additional seat, giving it fifteen to the UBP's twenty-five, and putting it for the first time within striking distance of winning control of the government.

The PLP has from its inception been an overwhelmingly black party. It has been estimated that in 1976 about 80 percent of the black voters cast their votes for the PLP, whereas only 5 percent of the whites did so. The top leadership of the party is also overwhelmingly black, with only one white holding a major position in the party.

Traditionally, the constituency organizations of the Progressive Labour Party functioned regularly only during periods of election campaigns. However, after 1976, with victory in the following election being a real possibility, the party leaders sought to strengthen the local party organizations, keeping them in activity on a regular basis. The PLP also began publication of a party paper, established a monthly television program, and appointed a public relations officer.

The Bermuda Industrial Union has been more or less closely allied with the PLP since the party was established. Some of the union's leaders are always among the party's successful candidates for the assembly, although most of the PLP candidates tend to be middle-class professional and business people. In 1976 the president and educational director of the BIU were elected as house members representing the PLP.

In 1979 Arthur D. O. Hodgson, a black professional man was Chairman of the Progressive Labour Party, and Lois M. Browne-Evans, a black lawyer, was Leader of the Opposition in the assembly.

In the 1980 general election, the PLP increased its representation in the House of Assembly to eighteen of the forty members.

UNITED BERMUDA PARTY (UBP). The United Bermuda Party was established in 1964, as a direct response to the appearance of the Progressive Labour Party, by twenty-four of the members of the House of Assembly who had been elected in 1963 as independents. It was led by Sir Henry "Jack" Tucker, and for many years his influence was so great in the party that it was popularly referred to as "the house that Jack built."

From its inception, the UBP had as its core the traditional aristocratic politicians. Sir Henry Tucker was himself an aristocrat of unimpeachable credentials. However, it also drew support from other elements of the white community, and from a significant number of blacks, particularly of the middle and upper classes. In the first election which it contested in 1968, it won thirty of the forty seats in the assembly. It repeated this performance four years later.

Under the chieftanship of Tucker, who remained premier until 1971, the UBP government very largely robbed the original platform of the Progressive Labor Party. It carried out desegregation, established free secondary education, and instituted universal adult suffrage. In a modified form, it also established extensive government social services. These measures had the effect of keeping the loyalty to the UBP of a substantial part of the black electorate, which was essential to the United Bermuda Party's success at the polls.

With his retirement from UBP party leadership and the premier's office in December 1971, Sir Henry Tucker got his party to choose Sir Edward Richards as his successor as premier. Sir Edward, the first black knight from Bermuda, was of Guyanese African ancestry. Sir Henry also succeeded in getting the UBP to name John Swan, a leading black businessman, as candidate for the seat in the assembly which he himself was vacating, a seat from a nearly all-white constituency.

However, in spite of these moves there was a growing feeling among the black leaders of the UBP that their bargaining position within the party was diminishing. As a result, they formed the Black Caucus within the UBP in 1974. It urged better educational and job-training programs for blacks, as well as government financial help for black businessmen. It also echoed a position of the PLP against further granting of citizenship to recent white immigrants from Europe.

The formation of the Black Caucus caused a reaction from certain white elements, particularly among the Portuguese supporters of the UBP, and white working class groups. They formed the right wing of the party, and became increasingly critical of the power of the Bermuda Industrial Union, of the high cost of social services, and the increased amount of crime. They professed to see the country drifting toward socialism. Most particularly, they demanded larger representation for themselves in the government.

In preparation for the 1976 election, the right-wing dissidents challenged three Front Street UBP house members in party primaries, and succeeded in ousting two of them as candidates. With the partial decline of the party's fortunes in the 1976 election (its number of assembly seats falling from thirty to twenty-six), the right-wing criticisms of the Front Street leadership of the UBP intensified.

The victim of the growing factionalization of the United Bermuda Party was John Sharpe, who had become premier shortly before the 1976 election. Early in 1977 the right wingers joined forces with the Black Caucus to force several changes in the cabinet and finally in August 1977 to force Sharpe's resignation. He was succeeded as party leader and premier by David Gibbons, a Front Street party chieftan who won a narrow victory in the party parliamentary caucus over C. V. Woolridge, a black who was supported by both dissident wings of the party. However, Gibbons, in naming his new cabinet, considerably broadened its base, bringing in people from both dissident groups, including Harry Viera, the principal Portuguese in the party leadership, who became minister without portfolio.

The UBP kept a narrow victory in the 1981 general election, getting twenty-two of the total of forty seats in the assembly.

Robert J. Alexander

BOLIVIA

Bolivia, one of only two landlocked nations in South America, lies in the center of the continent's southern portion, surrounded by Chile, Peru, Brazil, Paraguay, and Argentina. Bolivia's 424,000 square miles include some of the most disparate terrain in any nation, ranging from the eastern Andean plateau (at more than 12,000 feet above sea level) to central temperate valleys, eastern savannah, and southern desert. Colonized by Spain in the 1540s, Bolivia achieved an embattled independence in 1825 — but her boundaries were so imprecise and her political and military power so limited that much territory was lost during the succeeding century, and boundary disputes were not ended until 1939. In colonial times, Bolivia's principal sources of wealth were her enormously rich silver mines; mining was revived in the late nineteenth century, concentrating on tin and smaller quantities of wolfram and bismuth. Although Bolivia is still the poorest nation on the continent, her five million people can now count on a modest petroleum industry and a growing agribusiness complex near the eastern city of Santa Cruz.

The history of Bolivia's political parties divides itself quite logically into five principal periods. As these phases have unfolded, major parties have at times come close to commanding widespread mass support, playing crucial roles in political decision-making. But the party system has never become stable enough or strong enough to dominate Bolivian politics, giving way time and again to conflict among narrowly based groups, especially factions of the military.

Prior to 1884, Bolivia lacked organized political parties; instead, purely personal factions vied for an unstable hold on the presidency. The often cruel and frequently incompetent leadership fostered by this system culminated in the nation's humiliating defeat by Chile in the War of the Pacific (1879–1883). Following the war, new Liberal and Conservative parties emerged in Bolivia, to organize national affairs better and to rebuild Bolivia's integrity and international standing. This system of aristocratic two-party competition lasted until 1920, with the Conservatives dominant until 1899 and the Liberals ruling for the following two decades.

During these years, limits were placed both on military intervention and on interparty feuds, though it took a brief civil war in 1899 to give the Liberals the upper hand. For the most part, civilian presidents served out their full terms and were succeeded by elected successors—elected, that is to say, from among a very limited, educated, and relatively affluent electorate. (As late as 1951, only about 3 percent of the nation's population took part in presidential elections.)

By 1920, major strains were beginning to show in this two-party system's domination of society. World War I had imposed a major export depression on Bolivia, and the nation's cities were also beginning to grow. A few iconoclastic politicians began to respond to the needs of new urban groups, especially organized artisans. The power of Liberals and Conservatives was successfully challenged by President Bautista Saavedra's Republican Party (1920–1925) and by President Hernando Siles's Nationalist Party (1925–1929). But the ruling parties in these years of tentative reformist populism did not put far-reaching policy changes into effect. At the end of the 1920s, as Bolivia's tin-based economy reeled under the shock of the worldwide depression, and the drift toward war with Paraguay over the Southeastern region of the Gran Chaco speeded up, all the civilian parties united behind President Daniel Salamanca. Embodying both the best and worst of traditional aristocratic Bolivian political leadership, Salamanca helped launch Bolivia on a war with Paraguay (1932–1935) that she was unprepared to fight and unable to win—but which was pursued so blindly and incompetently that every fifth man mobilized was killed.

In 1934, the military overthrew Salamanca, both protesting and illustrating the existing party system's inability to manage the strains of war. From that year until 1952, Bolivian parties entered a period of ideological factionalism and the development of mass parties. At the level of the elites, the late 1930s were years of intense political debate, with numerous "cells," "groupings," "associations," "parties," and "movements" appearing, splitting, overlapping, uniting, often evaporating. Ideologies ranging from Trotskyism to fascism were hotly debated, and many party leaders flirted with a wide variety of political faiths. Almost all these leaders were under thirty-five, and almost all believed that—under one or another political banner or label—some form of mass political participation lay in Bolivia's future. In the aftermath of the Chaco War and the economic crisis of the 1930s, they argued, the mass of the people should be given a voice in national decisions. The parties that would dominate the politics of the 1950s and 1960s—the Nationalist Revolutionary Movement (MNR), the Bolivian Socialist Falange (FSB), and the Revolutionary Workers Party (POR)—were all founded in the intellectual ferment after Salamanca's overthrow. Both these new parties and the very idea of mass-based politics were tenaciously opposed for most of this fifteen-year period by the tin-exporting oligarchy, and by its then faithful servants in the military. These restrictive elements—known informally as *la convivencia*—formed a unified conservative party, the Partido de la Unión Republicana Socialista (PURS).

But the new mass-based parties, particularly the MNR, succeeded in making effective alliances with newly formed unions and pressure groups among the poorest (and most numerous) Bolivian classes: wage-workers, especially miners and railway workers, and key groups of discontented peasants. By 1952, the economic-military elite's policy of simple repression (most notably the cancellation of 1951 elections in which the MNR had gained a plurality even within the restricted middle-class electorate) had lost any shred of legitimacy. The "National Revolution," beginning on 9 April 1952, brought the MNR elite and its multiclass followers to power, beginning a twelve-year phase of rule by a dominant populist party.

The MNR, which absorbed a number of leaders from the POR and from other, smaller parties, achieved greater power between 1952 and 1964 than any party during any other period of Bolivia's history. The party's presidential nomination was tantamount to election during those years; party branches reached into every departmental capital, into most provinces, and into hundreds of labor and peasant unions. Under the MNR, which abolished the literacy requirements, the Bolivian electorate expanded sixfold, and the annual 9 April party parades outshone the traditional *fiestas patrias* of early August. Although many other parties survived during this period, and several new ones were created (most notably the Christian Democrats and Social Democrats), the MNR was the institutional focus of meaningful political participation.

Probably, indeed, the MNR's very dominance played an important part in its decline. Since civilian politics and the *Movimiento* were almost synonymous, competition *within* the party was automatically encouraged, as rival politicians jockeyed for power. A number of MNR factions appeared and were even encouraged by the party's leader and subleader, Víctor Paz Estenssoro and Hernán Siles Zuazo; they, however, were unwilling to yield to new generations of leaders. The result was constant and debilitating bickering, which eroded the party's hold on the masses' loyalties and led to the creation of the Authentic Revolutionary Party (PRA) and the Revolutionary Party of the Nationalist Left (PRIN). These divisions offered a tempting opening to military leaders who were both ambitious and opportunistic. In November 1964, Paz Estenssoro was overthrown after only three months of his third presidential term, by Generals René Barrientos Ortuño and Alfredo Ovando Candia.

During the succeeding seventeen years, which have seen twelve different regimes and eight military coups, the political party system has engaged in an inconclusive search for postpopulist legitimacy. In some respects, this recent period has resembled the late 1930s: most party politics has taken place among the urban elites, and a number of new parties have appeared, especially on the Left. But the military and its civilian allies—most importantly, the remaining private mining concerns and the business class in the southeastern Department of Santa Cruz—have more effectively blocked any meaningful contact between party elites and mass organizations. Nor, in contrast to the pattern which developed during the 1940s, did any party emerge during the 1970s as a clear and dominant popular voice. The MNR continued its factional splits, although they have taken different forms since 1964; a number of parties have accepted cabinet posts under the military from time to time, only to find those positions relatively empty of any real political influence; left-wing parties, both new and old, have failed to attract much voter support in the four national elections held (1966, 1978, 1979,

1980). The most effective resistance to Bolivia's succession of military governments has come, instead, either from long-established union groups or from poorly organized but massively supported civic movements. Such a spontaneous popular movement forced Colonel Alberto Natusch Busch from power after only two weeks in November 1979, and a similar inchoate wave of resistance greeted the July 1980 coup led by General Luís García Meza.

The absence in Bolivia of a stable political party system, able to dominate national politics, is explicable in terms of the nation's pattern of social and economic development, together with key political choices made in the 1950s. During the 155 years since national independence was gained, both Bolivia's previous social structure and the course of her economic modernization have worked against the emergence of a well-led, competitive party system with strong roots in mass popular support.

From 1825 until the 1890s, Bolivia was fundamentally a semifeudal agrarian society, with power monopolized by the owners of large but relatively inefficient rural estates. Deep ethnic divisions separated the white, Hispanic landowners from their indigenous Aymara- and Quechua-speaking laborers, and from the subjugated "indigenous communities" which continued to control some lands on the Andean plain around Lake Titicaca. There were virtually no independent rural small-holders, such as existed, for example, in Colombia. Almost any mobilization of the peasants into politics would have meant massive dissent against the extractive rural economic system. Thus there were strong disincentives against any move by the Liberal and Conservative party elites to broaden their base of popular support, a tactic which might have enabled Bolivia's traditional parties to survive as their Colombian counterparts have done. Bolivia's countryside thus remained, not simply throughout the nineteenth century, but until the late 1940s, politically isolated as well as socially backward and economically exploited.

The rapid rise of the tin mining sector in the 1890's set in train several basic changes in Bolivian society. It created both an industrial working class, to run the mines and railroads, and a set of new urban classes, to provide services ranging from carpentry and shoemaking to sophisticated legal advice. The tin enclave also, in the long run, stimulated the formation of mass-based political parties; bourgeois critics of the new and monopolistic economic exploitation needed popular backing as a key political resource. This dissent, as we have seen, took shape during the 1930's, when the worldwide depression and the Chaco War provided both economic and nationalistic reasons for criticizing the tin-based system of political domination.

Bolivian middle-class political dissent, at this point, might have produced two or more competing reformist parties; that was the pattern in Venezuela at a comparable stage of development. But the continued strength of Bolivia's tin oligarchy, supported into the 1950s by the bulk of the military leaders, argued strongly for the agglutination of antienclave political forces into a single coalition. Still unable to contact the bulk of the nation's population, closed off in the essentialy unchanged semifeudal countryside, urban dissidents tended to band together for maximum influence. Thus, it was a single large but very diverse city-based coalition, led by the MNR, which achieved national power in the 1952 revolution.

In many ways, the mid-1950s constituted a new day in Bolivian politics. The old foreign-linked tin establishment had lost most of its power; mass support, through elections and demonstrations, became the most powerful political weapon; union and party organizing became free for the first time in national history. Perhaps most significantly, the countryside and the cities reencountered one another, as parts of a still-to-be-defined national social system. But the underlying social structure and the leaders' choices prevented the emergence of a multi-party system capable of channeling both mass support and political dissent.

Paradoxically, Bolivia's rural sector had changed little since colonial days, and it has changed very basically and rapidly because of the sweeping 1953 agrarian reform. The remaining primitiveness was evidenced by the near-total lack of roads, schools, telephones, electrical power, and modern agricultural methods; the revolutionary alteration had to do with land tenure and improved peasant social status. Both these sides of the rural coin enabled the MNR leadership to command an almost automatic and massive rural vote plurality—it was easy to exclude opponents from campaigning in the countryside, and anyway most peasants venerated the MNR architects of the agrarian revolution.

These conditions might have done nothing to undermine party stability in a strong one-party system; they are close parallels, for example, to the pattern of Mexican rural development in relation to the ruling Institutional Revolutionary Party there. In Bolivia, however, the populist leadership had a strong tendency to split; both in 1960, with the formation of the Authentic Revolutionary Party (PRA) of Walter Guevara Arce, and in 1963 with the founding of Juan Lechín's Revolutionary Party of the Nationalist Left (PRIN), major MNR leaders defected to form splinter groups. If access to the countryside, containing two-thirds of Bolivia's voters, had been possible for these dissidents, their criticism might have been absorbed and/or deflected by a competitive electoral system. The outcomes of the 1960 and especially the 1964 elections, however, showed that even an MNR president (such as Paz Estenssoro in the latter year) who had lost almost all urban support could still enjoy an easy victory at the polls. This fact, as much as any vengeful or opportunistic motives, led Paz's civilian opponents to join military leaders in the 1964 conspiracy that ended Bolivia's most recent period of protracted rule by civilian parties.

Since 1964, the viability and political importance of all political parties have been sharply restricted by the fact that the most crucial political resource in Bolivia is the backing of the military's semicollegial high command. Civilian leaders gain or lose influence on the basis of their current popularity with the *Alto Mando*, popularity that is at least as easily, and often more easily, gained as an independent or technocratic figure than as the leader of a popularly backed party. Given repeated military nullification of national elections, an army veto on rural campaigning, and severe repression against dissident parties, party leaders are reduced to heading little more than capital cliques. Three times, to be sure, the military has permitted national elections, under pressure from the United States government. But results unwelcome to the armed forces have been set aside, and often election campaigns have simply identified troublesome critics for later suppression; this was the case, for example, with Socialist Party leader Marcelo Quiroga Santa Cruz, killed on the first day of the García Meza coup in 1980.

In this connection, it is sometimes said in error that the true dominant political party in Bolivia is the military establishment itself. This position, while superficially plausible, distorts the nature of a political party (properly so-called). In two very basic ways, Bolivia's military departs from the model of a modern political party: it is, if anything, adverse to mass political involvement (even if that mobilization were to favor conservative policies), and it is fundamentally opposed to political compromise or to the toleration of even limited political opposition. The military may be able, for relatively short periods, to provide Bolivia with a superficially stable government; as a ruling body, however, it continues to postpone the emergence of effective civilian parties, adding conscious intervention to the many inherent social obstacles that Bolivian party formation has always faced.

Bibliography

Robert J. Alexander. *The Bolivian National Revolution*. Rutgers University Press, New Brunswick, 1958.

_____. *Trotskyism in Latin America*. Hoover Institution, Stanford, 1973.

Jean-Pierre Bernard. "Bolivia," in Bernard et al., eds. *Guide to the Political Parties of South America*. Penguin, Baltimore, 1973.

Herbert S. Klein. *Parties and Political Change in Bolivia, 1880–1952*. Cambridge University Press, Cambridge, 1969.

Guillermo Lora, ed. *Documentos políticos de Bolivia*. Los Amigos del Libro, La Paz and Cochabamba, 1970.

James M. Malloy. *Bolivia: The Uncompleted Revolution*. Pittsburgh University Press, Pittsburgh, 1970.

_____ and Richard Thorn, eds. *Beyond the Revolution: Bolivia Since 1952*. University of of Pittsburgh Press, Pittsburgh, 1971.

Christopher Mitchell. "Factionalism and Political Change in Bolivia" in Frank P. Belloni and Dennis C. Beller, eds. *Faction Politics*. ABC/Clio, Santa Barbara, 1978.

_____. *The Legacy of Populism in Bolivia: From the MNR to Military Rule*. Praeger, New York, 1977.

Mario Rolon Anaya, ed. *Política y partidos en Bolivia*. Juventud, La Paz, 1966.

Political Parties

ACCIÓN DEMOCRÁTICA NACIONALISTA. *See* NATIONALIST DEMOCRATIC ACTION.

AFIN–MNR. *See* NATIONALIST REVOLUTIONARY MOVEMENT.

AUTHENTIC REVOLUTIONARY PARTY (PARTIDO REVOLUCIONARIO AUTÉNTICO – PRA). The PRA is a right-wing factional offshoot from the Nationalist Revolutionary Movement (MNR) and was established in 1959. Its leader is Walter Guevara Arce, formerly a major MNR ideologist, foreign minister, and minister of government. Subordinate leaders have included Jorge Ríos Gamarra and José Luís Jofre (the latter a principal figure in Bolivia's union of bank clerks). The PRA has adopted a reformist, nationalist position critical of what it saw as the excessive influence of left-wing labor unions in the MNR and in Bolivian politics generally. In 1960, Guevara ran for president under the new PRA banner, polling 14 percent of the votes; he had earlier hoped for the MNR nomination that year. The party ran congressional candidates in 1962, but abstained from the 1964 voting as a measure of its continued opposition to Víctor Paz Estenssoro; the PRA supported the Barrientos-Ovando coup of 4 November 1964, overthrowing Paz.

Guevara and his party formally backed General Barrientos's presidential candidacy in 1966, and the PRA served as part of the governing coalition of parties until 1969. Even after Barrientos's death, Guevara continued as Bolivia's ambassador to the United Nations under Presidents Siles Salinas and Ovando, until 1970. The PRA was in less sympathy with the Banzer government and opposed that regime's continuance after 1974. In the 1979 election, Guevara's party supported Paz Estenssoro's candidacy, and when Congress could not agree on a choice of president between the two major candidates, Guevara was chosen as interim president. He held this post for less than three months, being overthrown by Col. Alberto Natusch Busch. The two weeks which followed were perhaps Guevara's finest as a statesman; he vigorously opposed Natusch and helped rally civilian and military opposition to the colonel's ruthless rule.

Natusch was driven from office – but political compromises were necessary which prevented Guevara from reassuming the interim presidency. That post went to Lidia Gueiler Tejada, a dissident leader of the Revolutionary Party of the Nationalist Left (PRIN), who had also backed Paz Estenssoro in the 1979 voting, and who was overthrown in turn by General Luís García Meza in July 1980.

The PRA has little popular following or basis for existence beyond Guevara's personal ambitions and prestige, and it is chiefly useful for backstage maneuvering and coalition-building. When the party ran Guevara as an independent candidate in 1980, it garnered only a negligible vote.

BOLIVIAN COMMUNIST PARTY (PARTIDO COMUNISTA BOLIVIANO – PCB). The Moscow-line Bolivian Communist Party emerged following the fiasco of the Revolutionary Left Party's (PIR) cooperation with the Bolivian right-wing (1946–1952). Officially organized in 1950 out of the PIR's youth wing, it represented the recognition by pro-Soviet forces that the PIR could not be salvaged as a vehicle for communism in Bolivia. The PCB was initially led by José

Pereira, and later by Mario Monje, Jorge Kolle Cueto, and Ramíro Otero Lugones.

The PCB has generally constituted as tame a set of "revolutionaries" as one would encounter in any Latin American nation. The party endorsed Víctor Paz Estenssoro's presidential candidacy in 1951, without contributing much real strength to his campaign (and causing painful headaches later for Paz, in his dealings with the suspicious United States government). During the years of MNR government, the PCB offered limited criticism of the *Movimiento*, although the Communists did support the anti-Paz abstentionist movement among political parties in 1964. The party offered no useful backing to Ché Guevara's guerrilla effort in 1966–1967, an omission which further assured the PCB's isolation from the emerging groups of younger Left-inclined Bolivian politicians.

The PCB's next opportunity for political prominence came during the Ovando and Torrés administrations (1969–1971), to which the party gave "critical support." Kolle Cueto argued that a "popular anti-imperialist government" would be preferable to a military regime, but that the former could only arrive at a future "properly conditioned moment." The PCB was part of the group of parties and unions that gave backing to General Torres during the October 1970 crisis that brought him to power; it counted one influential mine-workers' leader, Simón Reyes, in its ranks.

In the 1978, 1979, and 1980 elections, the PCB renewed its alliance with Hermán Siles Zuazo, forming part of his Unión Democrática Popular (UDP) coalition in those years; since the party on its own never polled more than about 1.5 percent of the total votes, it is doubtful how much added backing the PCB can swing. It is also worth noting that, among the sometimes bewildering changes in Bolivian party life, the PCB's relation with Hernán Siles has remained almost constant; the party began its electoral career in a pro-MNR 1951 alliance that was largely engineered by Siles, the MNR's in-country manager for that election campaign.

BOLIVIAN NATIONALIST ACTION (ACCIÓN NACIONALISTA BOLIVIANA). *See* BOLIVIAN SOCIALIST FALANGE.

BOLIVIAN SOCIALIST FALANGE (FALANGE SOCIALISTA BOLIVIANA —FSB). The Bolivian Socialist Falange, a right-wing nationalist party, was founded in 1937, expressing one current of middle-class opinion in the aftermath of the Chaco War defeat. Its guiding spirit for twenty years was its principal founder, Oscar Unzaga de la Vega, a charismatic figure who served as mentor to a set of largely younger followers; other early leaders included Germán Aguilar Zenteno and Hugo Arias.

The Falange's "Declaration of Principles" has a clearly fascist cast: "Guided by the principles of Organization, Justice, and Solidarity, the New Bolivian State will be an integral organism based on a nation's will to be, and will subordinate personal, group, and class interests to the supreme interests of Bolivianism. . . . What distinguishes Falange is its revolutionary style. Its members prefer decisive and energetic measures. . . . Falange will awaken vital energies in the nation which currently lie dormant, and will align all the country's forces—either with Falange or against it" (Alberto Cornejos, *Programas Politicos de Bolivia* [Imprenéa Universitaria, Cochabamba, 1949], pp. 134, 137).

Falange absorbed a small group led by Gustavo Stumpf, Bolivian Nationalist Action (Acción Nacionalista Boliviana) in 1940, and it polled 11 percent nationally in the 1951 presidential voting. But the party did not play any significant national political role until after the MNR-led revolution of 1952. In the revolution's wake, Falange came to express the resentments of middle-class groups whose social and political power had been reduced or threatened by the populist MNR reforms. FSB opposed the MNR regularly at the polls, winning 15 percent of the vote in 1956, 8 percent in 1960, and 12 percent in opposing General René Barrientos in 1966. The party also led numerous abortive coup attempts and "popular" uprisings against the MNR government, including an effort in La Paz in 1957, in which Unzaga himself died. (Government sources called his death a suicide).

Following Unzaga's death, many *falangistas* seemed in practice to accept the party's inability to overthrow the MNR and rule alone; instead, the party became a leader of what was becoming a more diverse set of opposition groups, and became a vigorous exponent of the regional interests of Santa Cruz department. Led by Mario Gutiérrez and Gonzalo Romero, FSB was a logical vehicle for the concerns of the booming southeastern province, whose growth had been triggered by MNR development measures, but whose leaders preferred a laissez-faire philosophy to the MNR's bureaucratic intervention.

In 1963 and 1964, Falange vigorously opposed Paz Estenssoro's reelection for a third term as president, and encouraged Generals René Barrientos and Alfredo Ovando in their coup plotting. (This was, in addition, the only period when FSB had an extensive following among university students.) But Barrientos and Ovando, upon taking power in November 1964, wanted some of the mantle and prestige of the MNR for their own regime, and cooperation with FSB would have been perceived by the general public as the polar opposite of "revolutionary nationalism." Thus Falange was excluded from power, and it became the leading parliamentary opposition party until Congress was closed in 1969. From that point on, the party began a period of factionalism and decline.

In 1971, the FSB for the first time participated in a cabinet, joining with Paz Estenssoro's MNR (!) in the Popular Nationalist Front to support General Hugo Banzer Suarez's presidency. This unprecedented and uncomfortable alliance demonstrated just how rooted both parties were in Bolivia's middle class, and how threatened that class had felt by General Juan José Torres's "military socialist" regime in 1970–1971. But FSB's three years in office if anything deepened the personal splits in the party, as disputes arose over the division of prominence and loot.

The deepest division was between Mario Gutiérrez, who served Banzer as foreign minister for some years, and Carlos Valverde Barbery, a Santa Cruz leader and former minister of health. Their debilitating feud led the party to abstain from the 1978 and 1979 presidential elections. Valverde Barbery finally gained control of the remainder of the party and ran under Falange's traditional label, without coalition partners, in 1980, polling less than 5 percent of the vote.

BOLIVIAN SOCIALIST LABOR PARTY (PARTIDO SOCIALISTA OBRERO BOLIVIANO—PSOB). The PSOB was established under the leadership of Tristán Marof (Gustavo Navarro), after he was expelled from the Revolutionary Workers Party—POR) in 1938. For a few years it was a major element in the left wing of Bolivian politics. Marof and some other PSOB leaders served in the chamber of deputies. Also, PSOB leaders for some time were the principal political element seeking to organize the country's tin miners. The first Mine Workers Federation which was established was under the leadership of members of the PSOB. However, during the period of the government of Major Gualberto Villarroel (December 1943–July 1946), which the PSOB opposed, the Nationalist Revolutionary Movement (MNR), in alliance with the Revolutionary Workers Party, was able to acquire dominant influence in the miners' movement. Thereafter, the PSOB declined rapidly. It suffered a death blow when Tristán Marof became secretary for conservative President Enrique Hertzog during the six-year right-wing regime between 1946 and 1952.

CHRISTIAN DEMOCRATIC PARTY (PARTIDO DE LA DEMOCRACIA CHRISTIANA—PDC). Formed in 1954, the PDC remains a conventionally "tercerista" Christian Democratic Party, calling for a "third way" between capitalism and socialism—a way that would be more humane and truly democratic than either competing social-political system. Founded and led by Remo DiNatale, Benjamín Miguel, Javier Caballero, and Emanuel Andrade, the PDC (known as the Social Christian Party—Partido Social Christiano—until 1964) took part in the 1958 and 1962 congressional elections; it boycotted the 1966 presidential vote, but took part in 1978, running former Defense Minister General René Bernal. In 1980 the party took part in an electoral coalition backing former President Luis Adolfo Siles Salinas, which polled few votes.

A major misjudgment by the PDC leadership took place in 1967, when the party accepted the labor ministry under President René Barrientos. When military forces carried out bloody raids against mining camps, the PDC was forced to withdraw in anger and embarrassment, with severe internal divisions resulting. The party's youth organization had been discontented with the third-road philosophy for some time, and the mine camp invasions helped to crystallize their rebellion; they favored revolutionary socialism as a solution to Bolivia's dilemmas. In the late 1960s, the youth wing seceded to form the Revolutionary PDC (PDCR) which later became the Movement of the Revolutionary Left (MIR). Several discontented members of the party, including José Luis Roca, also left to join General Alfredo Ovando's short-lived nationalist revolutionary government in 1969–1970.

Since the early 1970s, the PDC has declined in importance and visibility, except for a brief period in 1974 when PDC leader Benjamín Miguel gained national stature by opposing General Banzer's repressive policies, a stand for which he was unceremoniously deported. In 1980, Miguel was Dr. Siles Salinas's vice-presidential running mate.

CONSERVATIVE PARTY (PARTIDO CONSERVADOR). Formed in 1884, the Conservative Party was one of Bolivia's first formal political parties. Led by Aniceto Arce and Gregorio Pacheco, the Conservatives favored Bolivian economic development, especially through the growth of silver mining and the extension of railroads. In regional terms, the party was a supporter of southern and central interests, and some modern historians believe its key points of advocacy were regional and silver mining concerns, rather than any conservative ideology in European terms. The Conservatives never sought to become a mass party, but competed within the sharply limited Bolivian electorate.

The Conservative Party held the Bolivian presidency from 1884 to 1899, when its power was broken by the Liberals in a civil war. (The Liberals had come to represent northern tin mining interests.)

The party declined after 1900; some of its former leaders and members joined the Republican Party in 1914 and subsequent years. The Conservative Party is one of the few Bolivian parties which can now be said to be extinct.

FALANGE SOCIALISTA BOLIVIANA. See BOLIVIAN SOCIALIST FALANGE.

GENUINE REPUBLICAN PARTY (PARTIDO REPUBLICANO GENUINO). See REPUBLICAN PARTY.

INDEPENDENT SOCIALIST PARTY (PARTIDO SOCIALISTA INDEPENDIENTE). See UNITED SOCIALIST PARTY.

LIBERAL PARTY (PARTIDO LIBERAL—PL). Founded in 1883, the Liberal Party is Bolivia's oldest continually existing political party. Its initial leaders were Eliodoro Camacho, Narciso Campero, and Nathaniel Aguirre; in the early twentieth century, it was dominated by President Ismael Montes. Embracing a classical nineteenth century liberalism—support for free enterprise, freedom for capital, and gradual social change through education—the PL in practice became an exponent of the burgeoning tin-mining interests in northern Bolivia and of the interests of the city of La Paz. In opposition for almost two decades after its founding, the party seized power from the Conservatives in the 1899 civil war and ruled through the presidency until 1920. These were the years when the tin oligarchy strengthened its hold on the Bolivian economy.

After it lost power in the 1920 coup of the Republican Party, the PL faded into little more than a paper organization, although it did have one period of significant activity in the late 1940s, following the "tin barons'" overthrow of Colonel

Gualberto Villarroel in 1946. The PL-backed candidate, Fernando Guachalla, almost won the 1947 election, and the party also garnered a sizable share of the 1951 presidential vote—the last election held under Bolivia's traditional system of limited suffrage (approximately 3 percent of the adult population was then eligible to vote). After the 1952 revolution, no government has been willing to accept PL support, because of the party's identification with the conservative tin interests. Nor has it had any congressional representation. However, it still continues formally to exist.

MARXIST-LENINIST COMMUNIST PARTY (PARTIDO COMUNISTA MARXISTA-LENINISTA—PCML). The PCML is the Peking-line Bolivian communist party, formally organized in 1964. Under the leadership of Alfredo Arratia, Raúl Ruíz González, and Oscar Zamora Medinacelli, the PCML naturally jousted incessantly with the Moscow-oriented PCB and was to be found almost automatically in the opposition position (on any current question) to that adopted by the PCB. The *Pekineses,* for example, harshly attacked the Ovando and Torres governments, which had the conditional backing of the *Muscovitas;* only a "people's revolutionary war," in the PCML's view, could bring about Bolivia's liberation from imperialist domination.

In the elections in 1978 and afterwards, the PCML generally cooperated with the forces headed by Juan Lechín—a leader who has himself been torn between backing Hermán Siles and Víctor Paz Estenssoro. In 1978, Lechín's PRIN, the PCML, and the Revolutionary Workers Party (POR) backed a peasant leader, Casiano Amurrio, for president; two years later, Lechín himself was the candidate, again with PCML backing—the PCB was consistently supporting Hermán Siles.

MOVEMENT OF THE REVOLUTIONARY LEFT (MOVIMIENTO DE LA IZQUIERDA REVOLUCIONARIA—MIR). Organized in the late 1960s as the Revolutionary Christian Democratic Party (Partido Demócrata Cristiano Revolucionario), this party took the name Movement of the Revolutionary Left in 1970. The MIR grew out of the Christian Democratic Party's youth movement, which became discontented with the third-road philosophy of the PDC. Led by Jorge Ríos Dalenz (who was later killed in the post-Allende terror in Chile), the MIR was a small party with its greatest strength among university students and other urban youth groups. The MIR urged following a noncapitalist route, and that a mass-based socialist government be achieved through revolution. This regime should be national, popular, and very democratic. The working class should lead and be allied with the peasants, and the petty bourgeoisie of the cities, as well as with revolutionary intellectuals and those on the margin of society.

The MIR was persecuted during the Banzer administration, but returned to active politics after 1978. In all three post-Banzer elections (1978, 1979, and 1980), the MIR formed part of the Democratic Union of the People (Unión Democrática del Pueblo) coalition headed by Hernán Siles Zuazo.

MOVIMIENTO DE LA IZQUIERDA REVOLUCIONARIA. *See* MOVEMENT OF THE REVOLUTIONARY LEFT.

MOVIMIENTO NACIONALISTA REVOLUCIONARIO. *See* NATIONALIST REVOLUTIONARY MOVEMENT.

MOVIMIENTO NACIONALISTA REVOLUCIONARIO DE IZQUIERDA. *See* NATIONALIST REVOLUTIONARY MOVEMENT.

MOVIMIENTO NACIONALISTA REVOLUCIONARIO – UNIFICADO. *See* NATIONALIST REVOLUTIONARY MOVEMENT.

MOVIMIENTO POPULAR CRISTIANO. *See* POPULAR CHRISTIAN MOVEMENT.

NATIONALIST DEMOCRATIC ACTION (ACCIÓN DEMOCRÁTICA NACIONALISTA – ADN). Formed in 1978, ADN has quickly become Bolivia's principal right-wing party, in terms of electoral support. Espousing a conservative "nationalist" position, the party has served as an organizational tool for General Hugo Banzer Suárez, who held office as president from 1971 to 1978. The ADN, like Banzer, also serves to a considerable degree as an exponent of the regional interests of the department of Santa Cruz, an agro-industrial and petroleum center, in southeast Bolivia.

ADN, while lacking both structure as an organization and independence from Banzer, has come to command much of the voting support that formerly went to the Bolivian Socialist Falange (FSB). In both the 1979 and 1980 elections, ADN ran third, polling 15 percent of the valid votes in 1979, according to the (heavily criticized) official tally. This proportion is roughly the same as that commanded by FSB in elections prior to 1964, and probably represents much of the same urban, middle-class, conservative "developmentalist" constituency.

NATIONALIST PARTY (PARTIDO NACIONALISTA). The Nationalist Party was formed in the middle 1920s by a group of young intellectuals. At its inception, it had little popular base or power. However, when President Hernando Siles, elected in 1926 with the backing of the Republican Party leader Bautista Saavedra, quarreled with his patron, the Nationalist Party became associated with his administration and finally became the official party of the Hernando Siles administration. Although the Nationalist Party lost control of the Bolivian government with the overthrow of Siles in 1930, leading figures in the party, such as Augusto Céspedes, Carlos Montenegro, and Enrique Baldivieso, continued to play important roles in national politics. Some of them were associated with the revolutionary governments of Colonels David Toro and Germán Busch, between 1936 and 1939. Some of the ex-Nationalists figured among the founders of the Nationalist Revolutionary Movement (MNR) in 1941; others were absorbed into the United Socialist Party (PSU), which was formed about the same time.

NATIONALIST REVOLUTIONARY MOVEMENT (MOVIMIENTO NACION-
ALISTA REVOLUCIONARIO—MNR). The multiclass, mass-based Nationalist
Revolutionary Movement was formed in January 1941 and became the most
influential expression of the reformist, civilian, political ideas generated by the
Chaco War. The MNR's founders were veterans of several diverse political currents. Hernán Siles Zuazo and Walter Guevara Arce had been members in the
1930s of the "Beta Gama" organization, many of whose other members became
Trotskyites; Augusto Céspedes, Carlos Montenegro, and José Cuadros Quiroga
came from a more right-wing strand of opinion which had first chrystallized
round the Nationalist Party (Partido Nacionalista) of the 1920s, and ran the
pro-Axis newspaper La Calle. Víctor Paz Estenssoro, a lawyer from the southern
town of Tarija, was not identified with any of these informal groups, and perhaps
for this reason he was chosen as jefe, with Siles (whose father had served as
president of Bolivia in the 1920s) as subjefe.

The party's ideological combination of nationalism and reformism developed
in two stages. The 1942 document Bases y princípios de acción inmediata (written
by Cuadros Quiroga) sounded a strong nationalist note, primarily against the
three dominant internationally linked tin companies. But the MNR lacked an
organizing strategy that went beyond the middle class, until Guevara in 1946
developed the doctrine of combining workers, peasants, and members of the
middle class in a revolutionary alliance. This Aprista idea sprang in part from the
party's experience of national office (1943–1946) in alliance with Colonel Gualberto
Villarroel. Even after Villarroel's fall, the party continued to gain labor backing,
including the support of Juan Lechín Oquendo of the mineworkers. Repeated
efforts at coups and popular uprisings (especially in 1949 and 1950) failed, but
the 1951 elections crystallized popular opinion in favor of the growing MNR
coalition. When the military refused to recognize Paz's electoral plurality, a worker-
bourgeois rebellion (with the aid of the police) brought the MNR to power in
April 1952.

Although the party quickly became the largest ever seen in Bolivia, regularly
polling approximately one million votes in presidential elections, from the outset
of the 1952 National Revolution it had internal splits which have grown over
time. The old right-wing sector was quickly eclipsed, with Guevara coming to
lead the party's more conservative urban elements; these favored economic
development, rebuilding of the armed forces, and a pro-United States foreign
policy. In the party's other major wing, Lechín, Nuflo Chávez Ortíz, and other
leaders of the Sector de Izquierda (Leftist Sector) successfully pressed for nationalization of the large tin mines and for a sweeping national agrarian reform. Paz
and Siles sought to mediate between and to manage this sprawling heterogeneous
alliance.

The MNR remained organizationally united until 1959, when the party's social
composition clashed with the personal ambitions of Walter Guevara Arce. Guevara
sought the presidential nomination, but the Sector de Izquierda favored a second
presidency for Paz, who took Lechín as his vice-presidential candidate. Guevara's
supporters seceded to form the Authentic Revolutionary Party (PRA), which lost

by a margin of better than four to one. Paz, in turn, had hopes for reelection in 1964, which clashed with Lechín's ambitions for himself and his viewpoint. With the president in firm control of an increasingly bureaucratized party, Lechín and the leftists withdrew in 1963, forming the Revolutionary Party of the Nationalist Left (PRIN).

Paz and the remainder of the MNR still won the 1964 elections overwhelmingly, but the administration was so weak and the party so fragmented that the military overthrew Paz less than six months later. In the succeeding decade and a half, the party has lived a strange and shadowy political life: never uniting, never dying, continuing to exert a hold over the national imagination even though it has had virtually no organizational strength and no coherent leadership. Ideologically, leaders who invoke the party's name stretch from the electoral Left (Siles) to the nationalist Right (Paz Estenssoro).

The record of MNR factionalism after 1964 indicates shifting but constant division. Neither the PRA nor the PRIN returned to the party's main body, which was divided until 1971 into four principal factions. Paz gave his blessing to the so-called *Unificado* ("Unified") faction, led by Raúl Lema Peláez; in parliament a Pazestenssorista Revolutionary Movement was led by Jaime Arellano; among university leaders, Jorge Alderete Rosales led a more Left-oriented faction; fragments of the party's prerevolutionary right wing united behind Víctor Andrade, who obtained use of the party's traditional symbols for the 1966 elections. Siles stood apart from this factional line-up.

Paz Estenssoro was anxious to return to Bolivia from exile in Peru and to cut down on party feuding. He was flexible in considering coalitions with transient military governments, and almost worked out an alliance with General Alfredo Ovando Candia's administration (1969–1970). In 1971, he supported the far-Right coup triggered by Colonel Hugo Banzer Suárez, and the MNR became officially a member of the regime, along with the party's traditional semifascist enemy, the Bolivian Socialist Falange (FSB).

Paz's entry into the pro-Banzer Popular Nationalist Front with the FSB provoked Siles's formal exit from the party, to form the Nationalist Revolutionary Movement of the Left (Movimiento Nacionalista Revolucionario de Izquierda— MNRI). Throughout Banzer's presidency, the MNRI was a rallying-point for many left-wing parties and factions, who relied on Siles's prestige and skills as a conciliator. Paz Estenssoro, meanwhile, had difficulties in maintaining discipline over his own followers. When he and the military differed so sharply over policy in 1973 that he sought to withdraw the MNR representatives from the cabinet, a faction of younger politicians (the Jaime Otero Calderón Cell, named for a respected party leader murdered in 1970) refused to leave office. The *Oterocalderonistas*, reluctant to give up perquisites or power, continued to provide the MNR label's prestige to Banzer for almost a year, before they were removed by the military high command. This episode illustrates both Paz's waning authority, and the reduction of much intra-MNR politics to a struggle over the spoils of office.

When elections were called for mid-1978, Siles was instrumental in organizing hunger strikes and other tactics which made the electoral process an open one; in the succeeding two years, Paz and Siles (and their respective factions) became repeated rivals for top national authority. In the elections of 1978, Siles's MNRI led a new left-wing electoral coalition, the Democratic Union of the People (Unión Democrática del Pueblo—UDP) including the Moscow-line Communist Party, the Movement of the Revolutionary Left (MIR), and several peasant groups. Paz's so-called Historic MNR (MNR-H) remained neutral. The announced results, showing Siles losing to government candidate General Juan Pereda were annulled, following widespread fraud. In the 1979 election, Siles and the UDP ran against an MNR coalition led by Paz, with dissident sectors of the Revolutionary Party of the Nationalist Left (PRIN) and other groups. Siles was reported as winning the popular vote by a few thousand votes, but the parliament (which must decide the presidency following close elections) chose Walter Guevara as interim president after a congressional deadlock developed between supporters of Siles and those of Paz.

In the 1980 elections, Siles apparently was the clear victor, being credited with more than twice as many votes as Paz when counting was halted and General Luis García Meza seized power to block Siles's ascent to power. It is a measure of the MNR's continuing division (and of the party name's assumed continuing electoral magic) that two additional MNR factions appeared on the 1980 ballot: the MNR-U, led by former Paz-confidant Guillermo Bedregal, and AFIN-MNR, headed by former cabinet member Roberto Jordán Pando.

Following the 1980 García Meza coup, Siles escaped from Bolivia to organize a rival government in exile. Whatever role the MNRI or other MNR factions play in Bolivia's future politics will depend far more on the individual talents and drawing power of leaders like Siles and Paz Estenssoro, than on ideological fervor, now virtually spent, or on organizational strength, now severely sapped by nearly two decades out of Bolivia's presidential palace.

NATIONALIST REVOLUTIONARY MOVEMENT OF THE LEFT (MOVIMIENTO NACIONALISTA REVOLUCIONARIO DE IZQUIERDA.) *See* NATIONALIST REVOLUTIONARY MOVEMENT.

PARTIDO COMUNISTA BOLIVIANO. *See* BOLIVIAN COMMUNIST PARTY.

PARTIDO COMUNISTA MARXISTA-LENINISTA. *See* MARXIST-LENINIST COMMUNIST PARTY.

PARTIDO CONSERVADOR. *See* CONSERVATIVE PARTY.

PARTIDO DE LA DEMOCRACIA CRISTIANA. *See* CHRISTIAN DEMOCRATIC PARTY.

PARTIDO DE LA IZQUIERDA REVOLUCIONARIA. *See* PARTY OF THE REVOLUTIONARY LEFT.

PARTIDO DE LA UNIÓN REPUBLICANA SOCIALISTA. *See* PARTY OF THE REPUBLICAN SOCIALIST UNION.

PARTIDO LIBERAL. *See* LIBERAL PARTY.

PARTIDO NACIONALISTA. *See* NATIONALIST PARTY.

PARTIDO OBRERO REVOLUCIONARIO. *See* REVOLUTIONARY WORKERS PARTY.

PARTIDO REPUBLICANO. *See* REPUBLICAN PARTY.

PARTIDO REPUBLICAN GENUINO. *See* REPUBLICAN PARTY.

PARTIDO REPUBLICANO SOCIALISTA. *See* REPUBLICAN PARTY.

PARTIDO REVOLUCIONARIO AUTÉNTICO. *See* AUTHENTIC REVOLUTIONARY PARTY.

PARTIDO REVOLUCIONARIO DE LA IZQUIERDA NACIONALISTA. *See* REVOLUTIONARY PARTY OF THE NATIONALIST LEFT.

PARTIDO SOCIAL DEMÓCRATA. *See* SOCIAL DEMOCRATIC PARTY.

PARTIDO SOCIALISTA. *See* SOCIALIST PARTY.

PARTIDO SOCIALISTA INDEPENDIENTE. *See* UNITED SOCIALIST PARTY.

PARTIDO SOCIALISTA OBRERO BOLIVIANO. *See* BOLIVIAN SOCIALIST LABOR PARTY.

PARTIDO SOCIALISTA UNIFICADO. *See* UNITED SOCIALIST PARTY.

PARTY OF THE REPUBLICAN SOCIALIST UNION (PARTIDO DE LA UNIÓN REPUBLICANA SOCIALISTA—PURS). Formed in 1946, the PURS represented a unification of the existing Republican factions—Genuine Republican Party, Socialist Republican Party, Independent Socialist Party, and United Socialist Party, as a last-ditch effort of Bolivia's traditional political establishment to oppose the forces of mass-based populism and of socialism. Led by Enrique Hertzog, Waldo Belmonte Pool, Francisco Lazcano Soruca, and Mamerto Urriolagoitia, the PURS attempted particularly to revive (in very changed circumstances) the position and popularity of the old Saavedra wing of the Republican Party. Its doctrines were conservative, favoring anticommunism, ample room for free enterprise, and antifascism, primarily interpreted as opposition to the Nationalist

Revolutionary Movement (MNR). The PURS participated in the 1947 and 1951 elections. Hertzog was elected president in 1947, with Urriolagoitia as his vice-president; and the latter succeeded to the presidency when Hertzog resigned because of ill health. In 1951, the party supported the military takeover which followed the elections, in order to prevent Víctor Paz Estenssoro from becoming president on the basis of his popular plurality. Following the 1952 revolution, the PURS became inactive, although in formal terms it continued to exist through the early 1970s.

PARTY OF THE REVOLUTIONARY LEFT (PARTIDO DE LA IZQUIERDA REVOLUCIONARIA – PIR). In the years following the Chaco War, the PIR emerged as Bolivia's classic Stalinist Communist party – but a party that was to have, ultimately, a farcical fate. Formed in July 1940 by José Antonio Arze, Ricardo Anaya, Arturo Urquidi, and Miguel Bonifaz, it made its political debut by running José Antonio Arze for president against the government's choice, General Enrique Peñaranda. Arze did very well in the country's major cities, but was soundly defeated by General Peñaranda.

The party echoed the changing Soviet Communist line, which after June 1941 called for participation in antifascist national coalitions. In Bolivia, this was interpreted to mean opposition to the military-MNR government led by Colonel Gualberto Villarroel, which took power in December 1943. But the PIR's "coalition partners" in opposing, and (in July 1946) overthrowing and killing Villarroel, turned out to be the political supporters of Bolivia's powerful private tin-mining companies. Since these concerns were the unyielding enemies of Bolivia's nascent labor unions, the PIR found that Moscow's favored strategy had virtually destroyed the party's potential domestic base. The PIR's leaders found that they could not escape the taint of association with Villarroel's overthrow, and what had been growing labor support – especially among the influential railway workers – quickly eroded after 1946.

The PIR limped along for some years as a political partner of Bolivia's right wing; in 1947, it joined the Liberal and Social Democratic parties in supporting Fernando Guachalla, who was nearly elected president. But the MNR revolution of 1952 made the party's position untenable, and in 1952 it was announced that the PIR was dissolving. This meant that the Soviets were determined to begin anew (through the new Bolivian Communist Party). This change left the PIR's original leaders without a political place of business. In 1956 they "revived" the PIR, with an ostensibly radical socialist platform, but in fact as Bolivia's quintessential "taxi-party": defined by La Paz wits as an organization primarily designed as a vehicle, so small that all members could fit within a single taxi-cab. This "new" PIR opposed the MNR, and was formally accepted as a coalition partner by General René Barrientos in 1966–1969; Ricardo Anaya and Miguel Bonifaz held several cabinet posts. In succeeding years, the party has been inactive electorally, but its members have been available for assorted political chores: as recently as 1978, Anaya served as foreign minister for the brief right-wing military government headed by General Juan Pereda Asbun.

POPULAR CHRISTIAN MOVEMENT (MOVIMIENTO POPULAR CRIS-TIANO—MPC). The Popular Christian Movement was formed by General René Barrientos after the overthrow in November 1964 of the Nationalist Revolutionary Movement (MNR) government of President Víctor Paz Estenssoro by a military coup under the leadership of Barrientos and General Alfredo Ovando. Its purpose was to support Barrientos in the election the military regime arranged in 1966. With support of the government, Barrientos and the MPC were successful. During the three years General Barrientos remained in power, the MPC was the government party. However, for all practical purposes, it died with the accidental death of General Barrientos early in 1969. The MPC differed somewhat from other transient *oficialista* parties in that it sought—and to a degree maintained— contact with peasant union organizations. This rallying of peasant support was part of Barrientos's strategy of allying the military with the conservative postreform peasantry. No subsequent military leader has been able to sustain this alliance effectively. The MPC, like other parties organized from the presidential palace, served to give some gifted politicians a start in national politics. José Ortíz Mercado, for example, who became a major figure in the Ovando administration (1970–1971), was an MPC deputy from Santa Cruz elected in 1966.

REPUBLICAN PARTY (PARTIDO REPUBLICANO). Founded in 1914, the Republican Party represented in part the interests of emerging new urban groups, especially artisans and tradesmen, which had been formed as a result of the post-1890 tin boom. Contesting the dominance of the Liberal Party, the Republicans also attracted the backing of Simón Patiño and other tin entrepreneurs, who saw the advantage of using votes of urban artisans as a weapon in their own narrower political interests. The Republicans also won backing of some former members of the Conservative Party (out of office since 1899).

During these years the Republicans were dominated by Bautista Saavedra; lesser founding leaders included Daniel Salamanca, José Manuel Pando, and Abel Iturralde. Saavedra and the party won control of the government by a coup against the Liberal regime in 1920. However, soon thereafter the party began to erode internally over personal ambitions of its leaders. A formal split soon appeared between "Saavedrista Republicans," whose organization was the Socialist Republican Party (Partido Republicano Socialista), and the "Genuine Republicans" (Partido Republicano Genuino) backing Daniel Salamanca's political ambitions. This division in the party's ranks led to Hernando Siles's insurgent victory under the Nationalist Party (Partido Nacionalista) label in 1926.

In 1931, Salamanca finally achieved his presidential ambitions, and the Genuine Republicans were the government party until his overthrow in 1935. The much splintered ranks of the Republican Party were reunited in the Party of the Republican Socialist Union (PURS) in 1946 but, by that time, the political tide had turned against the traditional parties of the established oligarchy.

REVOLUTIONARY CHRISTIAN DEMOCRATIC PARTY (PARTIDO DEMÓ-

CRATA CRISTIANO REVOLUCIONARIO). *See* MOVEMENT OF THE REVOLUTIONARY LEFT.

REVOLUTIONARY PARTY OF THE NATIONALIST LEFT (PARTIDO REVOLUCIONARIO DE LA IZQUIERDA NACIONALISTA—PRIN). The PRIN is a factional outgrowth of the Nationalist Revolutionary Movement (MNR). Before its appearance as a separate party in 1963, it existed for a decade within the MNR as the party's "Left Sector" (Sector de Izquierda). Led by Juan Lechín Oquendo as chief, and by Mario Torres Calleja and Edwin Moller in lesser roles, the party seceded from the MNR in protest against Víctor Paz Estenssoro's decision to seek a third elected term as president in 1964, rather than permit then vice-president Lechín to have the MNR's presidential nomination.

The PRIN's ideological position espouses left-wing nationalism, rather than socialism in more traditional terms. It is critical of bourgeois influence in the main body of the MNR. Electorally, the party abstained in the 1964 and 1966 presidential votes, and supported Hernán Siles Zuazo in 1978 and 1979; it ran Lechín as an independent candidate in 1980. Through almost two decades of existence, the PRIN has not been able to reach far beyond a role as the personal political vehicle of Lechín, whose status as Bolivia's most charismatic labor leader remains unchallenged nearly forty years after he first entered politics. Its very limited electoral drawing power depends on Lechín's continuance at the party's helm, and it has always needed to act as part of a coalition in order to exert any leverage.

REVOLUTIONARY WORKERS PARTY (PARTIDO OBRERO REVOLUCIONARIO—POR). The POR, now severely factionalized, represents the Trotskyite Marxist position in Bolivian politics. It was founded in 1934, under the leadership of Gustavo Navarro (known by his pen name Tristán Marof), José Aguirre Gainsborg, Lucio Mendivil, and others. Born out of an earlier discussion group known as the Group Tupac Amaru, and other small factions, the POR adopted Leon Trotsky's thesis of a worldwide and interrelated ("permanent") revolution, led in its Bolivian aspect by the industrial proletariat, and particularly the miners. Naturally, the POR was bitterly opposed to the Bolivian representatives of Stalinist Communism, especially the PIR, which was organized a few years later.

In its early years, the POR suffered both a significant split, in which Navarro was expelled from the party, and the accidental death of Aguirre Gainsborg, its major leader, in 1938. Gradually the party rebuilt itself, particularly in developing a following among Bolivia's tin miners. The party, along with the Nationalist Revolutionary Movement (MNR), was instrumental in the formation of Bolivia's most important single labor union, the Syndical Federation of Bolivian Mineworkers (FSTMB), which first established a continuing organization in 1944. Gradually coming under the leadership of Guillermo Lora, the POR was persecuted between the fall of the government of Colonel Gualberto Villarroel in 1946 and the MNR-led revolution of 1952—a revolution which opened up opportunities but also very difficult dilemmas for the Trotskyite party.

In April 1952 and for several years thereafter, the POR was the only avowedly Marxist party that was not tarred with the brush of collaboration with the Right. As a small party, stronger (as Lora put it) in agitators than in organizers, the POR was a very junior and informal "partner" of the MNR, with its massive vote and sweeping cross-class appeal. The POR was able to shape labor-union politics only when the forces of the MNR were temporarily poorly organized or preoccupied — for example, in the FSMTB's adoption of the POR-drafted "Thesis of Pulacayo" in 1946.

Between 1952 and 1956, Lora's basic position was that the POR had little chance of taking power on its own under those conditions, and should work as a force to educate the Bolivian working class for an eventual takeover, when the situation had changed. In choosing this position, he was seeking to maneuver between two other distinct positions within the party: a view even more favorable to cooperation with the MNR, which led Edwin Moller and other POR labor leaders to leave the party and enter the MNR's left wing, and a more radical oppositionist viewpoint, set forth most clearly by Hugo González Moscoso. By 1956, Lora's disagreement with this latter position had led to a formal division of the POR into two rival parties, each seeking use of the same name and party symbols.

This party division, which was from time to time exacerbated by the many internal splits of international Trotskyism, helped to keep the POR from exerting much influence in Bolivian politics after 1954. Lora moved into avowed opposition to the MNR after President Hernán Siles Zuazo adopted his hard-line economic stabilization policies in 1956. However, although the MNR's own factional splits were becoming much more severe during these years, the POR was not in a position to exploit them.

An attempt to reunite the two principal POR factions was formalized in 1966, but did not in practice lead to common political action; still a third faction, the POR (Trotskyist) appeared briefly during the 1960's. The Lora wing of the party enjoyed a short period of public attention under the Torres government (1970–1971), when party delegates participated in the "Popular Assembly" called by Torres. But greater interest focused on the personal position and incisivie ideas of Guillermo Lora than on the organization or doctrines of the party itself, which (in practice) has lived in his shadow for much of the past twenty years.

SOCIAL CHRISTIAN PARTY (PARTIDO SOCIAL CRISTIANO). *See* CHRISTIAN DEMOCRATIC PARTY.

SOCIAL DEMOCRATIC PARTY (PARTIDO SOCIAL DEMÓCRATA – PSD). Small, elitist, and conservative, the Social Democratic Party was organized in 1944 as an expression of the more technocratic elements in Bolivia's political right wing. Led by Roberto Arce, Gastón Arduz Eguía, Tomás Guillermo Elío, and Mario Estenssoro, the party embraced developmentalist, nominally Christian-Democratic principles. In the 1947 elections, the party backed Fernando Guachalla's losing cause. During the MNR regime, the PSD was a minor force, allied electorally with the Bolivian Socialist Falange. It was generally regarded as an ideological relic of the prerevolutionary period, surviving only because its leaders were relatively young.

After the MNR's overthrow in 1964, the PSD obtained a new lease on life, as a coalition partner of General René Barrientos, along with the Party of the Revolutionary Left (PIR), Authentic Revolutionary Party (PRA), and Barrientos's weak "official" party, the Popular Christian Movement (MPC). The PSD's leader, Luis Adolfo Siles Salinas (Hernán Siles Zuazo's half-brother) was chosen as Barrientos's vice-presidential running mate. This was done largely in the hope that his surname on the ticket would suggest an identification with MNR principles (an ironic circumstance, given Siles Salinas' much more conservative views). When Barrientos died in a heliocopter crash in 1969, Siles Salinas became president, serving with conspicuous dedication and honesty for five months until overthrown by General Alfredo Ovando Candia. In succeeding years, the PSD as an organization has been inactive, although Siles Salinas was a candidate for president under other coalition labels in 1978 and in 1980.

SOCIALIST PARTY (PARTIDO SOCIALISTA—PS) (1920). The first party using the name Socialist appeared in the early 1920s, founded first in La Paz in 1920 and two years later becoming a national organization. The leaders of the group came from among young intellectuals and people active in the artisan workers organizations of La Paz and a few other cities. The party succeeded in electing two members of the chamber of deputies, who introduced a number of prolabor bills, none of which was passed. However, by the middle of the decade, the party had languished. Some of those who had been active in it were among the leaders of the Nationalist Party associated with the administration of President Hernando Siles (1926–1930).

SOCIALIST PARTY (PARTIDO SOCIALISTA—PS) (1970). The second party to use the name Partido Socialista was led by Mario Miranda Pacheco and Marcelo Quiroga Santa Cruz, and was founded during the Torres government (1970–1971). It declared itself to be a Marxist party independent of Soviet or Chinese influence, favoring popular anti-imperialist unity, directed by the working class, which would end domestic injustice and foreign intervention. The party's basic ideas differed little from those of the left wing of the Nationalist Revolutionary Movement (MNR), or of the Revolutionary Party of the Nationalist Left (PRIN), except that greater stress was placed on the proletariat's "directive" role, and on the word "socialism" itself, by the PS. What the Partido Socialista sought to offer that other parties perhaps could not was responsible leadership, prepared to act on declared principles rather than in the service of personal ambitions. Quiroga, in particular, had established a deserved reputation for honesty and courage during the Barrientos years, when he had several times been arrested and imprisoned by the government's political police.

Having supported General Torres without being in the cabinet, the PS opposed the Banzer government, and returned to the political scene in Bolivia only after Banzer's fall in 1978. It contested the 1979 and 1980 elections (suffering a minor factional split in 1979 that caused the electoral authorities to list the main group supporting Quiroga as "PS-1"). Quiroga was generally regarded as Bolivia's most promising younger political leader, and he polled a respectable 7 percent in 1980, considering the short life and small size of the Partido Socialista. Apparently, some elements in the conservative military feared Quiroga's potential following as an opposition leader; he was killed during the García Meza coup of 17 July 1980. His death leaves his party — and Bolivian left-wing politics generally — in a greatly weakened condition.

STATE SOCIALIST PARTY (PARTIDO SOCIALISTA DEL ESTADO). The State Socialist Party, established originally by Enrique Baldivieso, a one-time leader of the Nationalist Party of the 1920s, was converted into the government party (and only legal one) of the regime of Colonel David Toro (1936-1937). It espoused a somewhat confused corporativist philosophy, urging extensive government intervention in the economy, compulsory unionization of all workers, and the establishment of a legislature on the basis of functional, rather than geographical, representation. Among the other leaders of the party were Armando Arce and Augusto Céspedes, who edited *La Calle*, the newspaper which was the more or less official spokesman for the Toro government. The Partido Socialista del Estado did not long survive the overthrow of Colonel Toro.

UNITED NATIONALIST REVOLUTIONARY MOVEMENT (MOVIMIENTO NACIONALISTA REVOLUCIONARIO – UNIDO – MNR-U). *See* NATIONALIST REVOLUTIONARY MOVEMENT.

UNITED SOCIALIST PARTY (PARTIDO SOCIALISTA UNIFICADO – PSU). The United Socialist Party was established in 1940 by some elements of the Saavedrista Socialist Republican Party, when the Saavedristas decided to support General Enrique Peñaranda for president. Its principal leaders were Carlos Salinas Aramayo and Francisco Lazcano Soruco. The party elected some members of parliament in 1940, and during the first two years of Peñaranda's administration they were among the government's opponents in Congress. However, in his third year in office, Peñaranda formed a so-called cabinet of concentration which the PSU joined. It was in office when the Peñaranda government was overthrown in December 1943. With the coup d'etat of December 1943 and the coming to power of Major Gualberto Villarroel, the PSU split, with a dissident group forming the Independent Socialist Party (Partido Socialista Independiente), which for some time cooperated with the Villarroel regime. With the overthrow of Villarroel, in the middle of 1946, both of these groups joined with the Genuine Republican Party and the Socialist Republican Party to establish the Party of the Republican Socialist Union (PURS).

Christopher Mitchell

BRAZIL

Portuguese-speaking Brazil is the fifth-largest country in the world, with an area of 3,285,618 square miles. Its estimated population in 1980 was 124,400,000 and it was increasing at the rate of 2.8 percent a year. Brazil is a federal republic with 23 states, 4 territories, and the Federal District of Brasilia, the capital of the country.

Brazil is governed under a constitution promulgated in January 1967. There is a president, a legislature, and a judiciary. The president serves a six-year term and is elected indirectly by an electoral college made up of members of the National Congress and delegates appointed by the 23 state legislatures. The vice-president is elected on the same slate as the president. From April 1964 until January 1979 the president had a wide range of arbitrary powers which were frequently used through the issuing of decree laws or "institutional acts." The executive used these powers to govern, often without consulting the Congress or submitting its decisions to the Supreme Court. By the end of 1979 most of the decree laws had expired and Brazil had returned to a more democratic and representative government.

The two-house Congress consists of a 69-member Senate (3 from each state) and a 420-member Chamber of Deputies. Senators are directly elected, except for the 23 members appointed in 1978 by state electoral colleges consisting of state and municipal officials. Only a part of the Senate is up for election at one time, with one-third, then two-thirds, being chosen every four years. The 420 members of the Chamber of Deputies are elected directly by voters in the states on the basis of population, for a four-year term of office.

Southeastern Brazil is the richest and most industrialized part of the nation, containing more than 60 percent of the voters. Political parties must be powerful there to have any projection in Congress and in governing the country. Most major political leaders come from those states. Population in the key states is: Rio de Janeiro, 10,704,000; São Paulo, 21,268,000; Minas Gerais, 12,768,000 and Rio Grande do Sul, 7,623,000 (1976 estimates).

Political Parties Under the Empire

Political parties in Brazil have not been tightly disciplined, philosophically inflexible groups. The pragmatic nature of the political party system has had its roots deep in the past history of the nation.

When the Portuguese discovered Brazil in 1500, there was little that they could do concerning colonizing or governing the area. Brazil was too big for tiny Portugal. It was largely abandoned and left to shift for itself. Foreign invaders, French and Dutch, were expelled by the Brazilians themselves, and a sense of Brazilian nationalism developed as early as the mid-seventeenth century. When Dom João VI, king of Portugal, fled Lisbon in 1808 and sought refuge in Brazil to escape Napoleon's troops, he was welcomed by the colonists. From 1808 to 1821 João VI lived in Brazil, and legally he raised the country to the status of a kingdom equal to Portugal.

After Napoleon's defeat in Europe in 1814, the Portuguese king apparently was not eager to return home. He remained in Brazil until the Portuguese parliament demanded that he return and assume leadership in the government of that country. Dom João in 1821 reluctantly returned to Europe, but left his son Pedro as regent of Brazil, with the advice that should an independence movement develop, the prince regent should lead it.

In 1822 Dom Pedro, the regent of Brazil for the king of Portugal, responded to a small group of politically and socially prominent citizens of São Paulo and Rio de Janeiro, and declared Brazil an independent kingdom. As there was only slight Portuguese resistance, Brazil achieved her independence with little bloodshed and no political turmoil. Dom Pedro was declared emperor of Brazil. Thus, while the other countries of the hemisphere turned to a republican form of government upon achieving independence, Brazil became a monarchy.

The reign of Pedro I, 1822–1831, was not a calm one. When a constituent assembly called by the emperor to write a constitution, fought with Dom Pedro, he arbitrarily dismissed them. The emperor then issued a constitution of his own in 1824, establishing a constitutional monarchy with extraordinary powers granted the emperor as chief of state. These took the form of the so-called moderating power, which put the monarch in a position above partisan politics, with the right to alter the composition of the government when he thought it in the nation's interest to do so. This power remained in the hands of the emperor so long as Brazil remained a monarchy.

Pedro I soon lost the support of most native-born Brazilian politicians because of his arbitrary and autocratic methods of governing. Demands that he abdicate and leave the country were broadly based and attacks on the emperor were led by Evaristo Ferreira da Veiga, editor of the *Aurora Fluminense*, a Rio de Janeiro newspaper. In April 1831 the emperor capitulated to Brazilian nationalists and resigned in favor of his five-year-old son, Pedro II. Brazil was governed by a Regency from 1831 to 1840. It was during the Regency period that the first outlines of Brazilian political parties appeared.

Oliveira Vianna stated that "after 1832 small local organizations affiliated themselves with larger organizations, first on a provincial (state) basis and later on a national level. The Conservative and Liberal parties had their headquarters in Rio de Janeiro at the court of the Emperor, while state chiefs were Presidents of the various provinces" (*Institucões Politicas Brasileiras* [Livraria José Olympio, Rio de Janeiro, 1955], 1:298).

Guerreiro Ramos wrote, "Independence having been declared in Brazil in 1822 by Dom Pedro I resulted very quickly in the appearance of the first political groups whose differing approaches demonstrated the variety of existing viewpoints. They were Liberals, Royalists, Exalted Liberals, Moderate Liberals, Federalists, Restorationists, and Conservatives. They were not properly parties but factions dominated by influential personalities of the period" (*O Crise do Poder no Brasil* [Zahar, Rio de Janeiro, 1961], p. 71). Expanding this analysis, José Murilio de Carvalho states that "Up to 1837 one cannot speak of political parties in Brazil" ("Composicão Social dos Partidos Politicos Imperiais," *Cadernos*, December 1974, p. 4).

The most clearly identified political trends in the parliament, according to Afonso Arinos de Melo Franco were the following: Moderates favoring a liberal constitutional monarchy; Conservatives; Exaltados, favoring a provisional republic, and Restorationists, supporting return of Dom Pedro I to the throne of Brazil (*Problemas Politicos Brasileiros* [Livraria José Olympio, Rio de Janeiro, 1975], p. 59).

Two political parties would form from these vague groupings. The Conservative Party, created from former Moderates, Restorationists and Exaltados, had as its first leader Bernardo Pereira de Vasconcellos. The Liberal Party would emerge as the party favoring decentralization, but also containing former members of the Moderates, Restorationists, and Exaltados. Most of those favoring restoration of Dom Pedro I went into the Conservative Party.

The turbulent political history of the period 1830–1841 was dominated by three regencies, the most important being that of Padre Diogo Feijó (1835–1837). The turning point, from a political party perspective, came when Dom Pedro I, the former monarch, died in 1834. This eliminated the group called the Restorationists, while the Exaltados and Moderates, led by Evaristo de Veiga and Padre Feijó formed the Liberal Party in an attempt to govern the country effectively. Although some Brazilian authors give 1831 as the year for the founding of the Liberal Party, it did not have an official program or clearly defined leadership at that date. The Conservative Party was founded officially in 1837.

During the Regency, despite the formation of national political parties, the country seemed to be fragmenting, as regional rebellions indicated that the central authority of Rio de Janeiro and the empire could no longer be asserted. In the national parliament, the Conservatives had begun to exercise power under the leadership of Bernardo Pereira de Vasconcellos. They won control of the Chamber in 1839, during the Araujo Lima Regency, and sponsored legislation which the Liberals opposed. The Liberals decided that the only way to block the Conservatives was to declare young Pedro II as officially of age to rule as emperor, after which the Liberal Party and the emperor would govern Brazil, excluding the Conservatives.

When a few Conservative Party senators switched sides, the Liberal majority in the Brazilian parliament on 23 July 1840 declared Dom Pedro II of age. Pedro II ruled the nation for 49 years, but three political parties shared in the governing process: the Conservatives, the Liberals, and the Republicans. For a few brief years in the decade of the 1860s another party, the Progressive Party, made up of members of the Liberal Party and dissident Conservatives, also functioned. The leadership of all the parties represented the more conservative economic and political elements of Brazilian society. Both of the major political parties of the empire period had military consultants.

One of the characteristics of Brazil has been the slow pace of political, social, and economic change. This was true in the last years of the Imperial government of Dom Pedro II. When the Republican Party appeared in 1870, all the major actors that participated in the downfall of the Empire were on the stage. But it took almost two decades before the emperor was finally overthrown.

At no point did the mass of the population participate in the political process. In 1881 a small breakthrough was made with the passage by the Brazilian parliament of the Saraiva law, named after Senator José Antônio Saraiva who introduced the legislation. It permitted more popular participation by redefining property and other qualifications for voters. Yet, in a population of approximately 15 million, only 142,000 citizens voted. Politics and political parties were still in the hands of a very small elite.

The causes of the collapse of the political structure of Dom Pedro II can easily be pinpointed. Brazil had in the last decade of the Empire moved away from a monoculture economic base. The large landowners in the southern state of São Paulo, who had turned to coffee production, did not need or approve of slavery, because it was a drain on capital resources and the new European immigrants — particularly Italians — were doing the work more cheaply and effectively than slave labor. As a result, on 13 May 1888 a bill passed parliament which freed the 700,000 slaves remaining in Brazil. The emperor lost the support of the wealthy northeastern landowners and some of the most powerful politicians in parliament as a result of emancipation of the slaves. In addition a church-state conflict in the 1870s resulted in only lukewarm support of the monarchy by the church authorities thereafter. When this was coupled with army dissatisfaction, the aging and tired government of Dom Pedro II fell easily on 15 November 1889.

Parties Under the Old Republic

From a political point of view, the major catalyst in the overthrow of the emperor had been the military. However, the fact that the Republican Party was in existence enabled that group to step into the civilian leadership vacuum created by the elimination of the emperor and his two supporting political parties, the Conservatives and the Liberals. The Republican Party fell heir to the political structure left over from the Dom Pedro II years.

The economic interests represented by the Conservative and Liberal parties were basically those of the coffee planters of southeastern Brazil. These same economic interests were also faithfully represented by the emerging Republican Party, which had its power base firmly anchored in southeastern Brazil.

In the nineteenth century, and indeed throughout the entire colonial period as well, Brazil had been an agrarian society built on slavery with the economic activity directed toward exporting primary commodities to the more industrialized nations of the world. In the mid-nineteenth century, when coffee began to develop as the single most important export crop, the new leaders of the Brazilian parliament were those from the important coffee producing sections of the country. The province of Rio de Janeiro not only produced coffee but also skillful and powerful Conservative Party politicians such as Eusebio de Queirós, Rodrigues Torres (Visconde de Itaborai), and Paulino de Souza (Visconde do Uruguai).

Control of the Brazilian political structure by the coffee planters and other agricultural exporters effectively blocked any legislation that would have helped Brazilian industrialists during the Dom Pedro period. The agricultural bloc kept the Brazilian monetary unit cheap and Brazilian raw material exports boomed. This situation would continue throughout much of the Republic period up to 1930.

All the political parties of the Empire period and in the early days of the Republic joined in passing legislation that gave special privileges to protect the export-agriculture sector of the economy. Coffee planting extracted most of the capital investment, and with the foreign exchange credits it provided, Brazil imported everything that it needed.

Military men governed Brazil for a bit more than four years, from 1889 to 1894, when the first civilian politician, Republican Party leader Prudente de Morais of São Paulo, was elected to the presidency. For the next thirty-six years, until 1930, the Federal Republican Party controlled the political structure of the country.

The success of the Federal Republican Party was closely linked to the deep regional divisions of Brazil which existed during this period. Two states dominated national politics throughout the period of the Old Republic (1889–1930)— São Paulo and Minas Gerais. Both are located in southeastern Brazil, and shared undisputed control over the national government until 1910, when a third state, Rio Grande do Sul, began to challenge this control.

Paulista President Campós Salles (1898–1902) is considered the author of the informal political system called the "governors' policy," under which Brazilian politics functioned for more than three decades. In general terms, it meant that either São Paulo or Minas Gerais would direct the executive, while control of the less important states of the north, northeast and west was turned over to the traditional oligarchies of those regions. Thus, in most states a Republican Party existed which was dominated completely by the same powerful clans which had governed during the Empire period. The only thing that the federal government demanded was that congressional delegations sent by the smaller states to Rio de Janeiro give the president complete and unqualified support for legislation that he requested from the Congress.

As a result of this situation, the Federal Republican Party controlled the country throughout this period. However, there were periodic disputes, as in 1910, 1922, 1924, and the final challenge in 1930 that led to revolution.

The Vargas Era

The final disruption of the "governors' policy" came in 1930 when the incumbent president, Washington Luis, a Paulista, violated the rule whereby he should have been succeeded by someone from Minas Gerais, and decided instead to name another Paulista, Júlio Prestes. Thereupon, Antônio Carlos, the governor of Minas Gerais, took the lead in organizing an opposition coalition, the Liberal Alliance (Aliança Liberal). It chose as its nominee Getúlio Vargas, governor of Rio Grande do Sul, and was joined by all of the established parties in that state, as well as part of the Republican Party of Minas Gerais, and that of Paraiba. In São Paulo, the Liberal Alliance was joined by the Democratic Party. Although the Liberal Alliance and Getúlio Vargas lost the election in March 1930, a civilian-military revolution in October 1930 destroyed the political framework of the Old Republic and brought in the fifteen-year Vargas dictatorship.

One of the more important groups in the civilian-military revolution of 1930 were the *tenentes*, young army officers who had led the 1922 and 1924 insurrections against the government. Their objectives were economic and political reforms which would modernize Brazil by eliminating the overwhelming influence of the São Paulo coffee planters. Some of the leading *tenentes*, who wanted dramatically to alter the Brazilian economic and political structure, were checked by Getúlio Vargas and his civilian advisers. The *tenentes*, notably Juracy Magalhães and Juárez Távora, would return to power with the advent of the 1964 revolution.

The 1930 revolution signified the end of the political party system that had existed from the downfall of the emperor in 1889. The Republican parties of São Paulo, Rio Grande do Sul, and Minas Gerias were destroyed during the Vargas period by the skillful use of executive-office power.

A Constituent Assembly was elected in 1934 and drew up a constitution, but none of the political parties of the earlier years participated. Some new parties had appeared in the meanwhile. After accepting the recommendations made by a small committee dominated by friends of Getúlio Vargas, the Constituent Assembly voted Vargas as president for the period 1934–1938.

In the closing months of 1937 some politicians made the mistake of taking seriously statements from Getúlio Vargas that presidential elections would be freely held in 1938 and began campaigning. Armando de Salles Oliveira, Interventor of the state of São Paulo, organized the Brazilian Democratic Union (União Democrática Brasileira) and launched his opposition candidacy. The government-sponsored candidate, José Américo, a prominent politician from northeastern Brazil was also supported by most state governors from that region, but he received no official political party endorsement as there was no official or government political party.

On 10 November 1937, the armed forces, acting in close collaboration with Vargas, clamped down on all political activity and turned Brazil into a formal dictatorship, the so-called New State (Estado Novo), which would last until October 1945. During most of that period, all political parties were suppressed, and few of those which had existed before 1937 were revived after the end of the dictatorship.

In 1945, the last year of the Vargas dictatorship, it was apparent that the Allied forces would defeat Nazi Germany, and the political climate began to shift in Brazil towards democracy. In February 1945 Getúlio Vargas stated that general elections would be held in December of that year, to select a new president, Chamber of Deputies, and Senate.

The Parties of the Democratic Period

A scramble began in February 1945 to form new national political parties. As the pre-1930 Federal Republican Party of Brazil had never had a strong national organization, the fifteen years that Vargas and Rio Grande do Sul politicians had been in power had been enough to destroy it completely. Even in the three largest states, São Paulo, Minas Gerais, and Rio Grande do Sul, which had contained the strongest and most efficient state Republican machines, the attrition and systematic opposition of the central government had brought about its disappearance. Also, Brazil had changed dramatically in the 1930-1945 period and the old Republican parties represented a Brazil that no longer existed.

Vargas, a shrewd politician, threw government support to two new national parties, the Social Democratic Party (Partido Social Democrático – PSD), and the Brazilian Labor Party (Partido Trabalhista Brasileiro – PTB). The major opposition party to be established was the National Democratic Union (União Democrática Nacional – UDN). These three parties were to largely dominate the 1945-1965 years, although there were also eleven other national political parties during that period.

The political party system functioned relatively well during the years 1945-1964. The parties selected candidates, presented issues, stirred controversy, and provided the Brazilian electorate with choices. As the voting population expanded, appeals began to be mainly directed to the lower-income groups, and the middle class and the popular sections of Brazilian society polarized. Brazilians had little experience in mass political mobilization and the period 1945-1964 was a learning experience that demonstrated that the fifteen years that Vargas had governed (1930-1945) had not provided the give-and-take of democratic political pluralism.

An overview of the political parties reveals that the PSD was virtually unchallenged in the early years of the post-Vargas era. They elected the president in 1945 (Eurico Dutra, 1945-1950), and Juscelino Kubitschek in 1955 (1956-1961). In the 1945-1960 period, however, control of the presidency did not automatically mean control and power over the various states as it had in the Old Republic (1889-1930) and the Vargas dictatorship period. In the most important states of Brazil, São Paulo, Minas Gerais, and Rio Grande do Sul, there were bruising struggles for power in which all manner of compromises had to be made for a candidate to win.

When Vargas was returned as a popularly elected president in 1950, supported by the PTB and the personalist party of Governor Ademar de Barros of São Paulo (Social Progressive Party—Partido Social Progresista—PSP), it meant that the narrow elitest groups would either have to adjust their appeals to the new electorate or go down to defeat in any future elections. But the Getúlio Vargas of 1950–1954 faced a different Brazil from that which he had known in the dictatorship years. A free press, a military establishment that did not completely trust him, and a freely functioning opposition all resulted in a series of events that led Vargas to take his own life on 24 August 1954. The suicide of Vargas startled most Brazilians, but the vice-president, João Café Filho, served out the remainder of the Vargas term.

Juscelino Kubitschek and a PSD–PTB combination beat the UDN candidate for the presidency in 1955. Kubitschek launched Brazil on an industrial expansion period that coupled free political expression with dynamic industrial modernization. The capital of the country was moved to the interior and Brasilia, a twenty-first-century city was born. The Kubitschek years were ones of optimism and enthusiasm. The economic consequences of the uncontrolled spending and expansion, plus the invitation to foreign capital to invest in Brazil on very favorable terms would all create problems that would have to be faced later by future presidents. But Juscelino Kubitschek gave Brazilians fifty years of progress and fifty years of inflation in the short span of five years.

The 1960 presidential election is a turning point in Brazilian political history. The UDN, a loser in so many elections, was pushed by Carlos Lacerda, a newspaper editor and party leader, into nominating Governor Jânio Quadros of São Paulo as their candidate for the presidency even though he was not formally a member of the party. The PSD, in an alliance with the PTB and the illegal Communist Party, supported the minister of war, General Henrique Lott. With the support of incumbent President Juscelino Kubitschek, two of the major parties, and Communist Party backing, it seemed impossible that General Lott could lose. However, the populist appeals of Jânio Quadros carried the election with the one inconvenience that the electoral law permitted the vice-presidential candidate on the opposition PTB ticket, João Goulart, former labor minister and vice-president to become Jânio Quadros's vice-president.

There was great rejoicing in Brazil with the victory of Quadros as it appeared that the Brazilian electorate and the Brazilian political process had come of age. An opposition candidate had won in a free and open election.

In August 1961 Jânio Quadros unexpectedly resigned as president, claiming that mysterious forces had blocked his reform programs. He left the country when he failed to receive military support to govern the country without the legislative branch. But João Goulart, one of the politicians that the military distrusted, was blocked from the presidency until the army accepted a constitutional amendment voted by Congress that theoretically transformed the country into a parliamentary form of government with a figurehead president and gave great power to the Congress. A prime minister would be the functioning chief executive. But the new political structure did not work, and President Goulart soon regained all his power and began to build the PTB party into the most powerful in the country.

The Brazilian government was in a state of continuous chaos from September 1961 until the March 1964 revolution. That revolt signified the end of the political system that had been functioning since 1945. Military officers lost confidence in the ability of President João Goulart to maintain stability or control the political structure of the country. Goulart's increased appeals to the Brazilian masses and to enlisted men of the armed services to support him personally by promising dramatic economic and social changes, often not within a constitutional framework, resulted in the armed insurrection that had the support of the majority of middle-class Brazilians. Brazil's urban middle class resented the economic and social chaos that had developed in Brazil in the final months of 1963 and early 1964.

Most citizens, however, did not expect the army to take almost complete control of the political structure. In every military move into the political arena since 1889–1922, 1930, 1945, 1955, and 1961—the army had maintained control for only a short time and then returned the political process to the civilians. But in 1964 complete control over the political decision-making process was taken by the army. They remained in control from 1964 to 1980, when most political freedoms were reestablished.

Parties Under the Military Regime

On 9 April 1964 the military chiefs issued an Institutional Act, in effect an amendment to the 1946 constitution. It gave Congress the right to elect deposed President João Goulart's successor, made it easier to amend the constitution, and gave the president the right to submit measures to Congress which it had to act upon within thirty days or they would become law. The Institutional Act also removed all tenure for government employees, and allowed the military commanders in chief to suspend the political rights of certain citizens for up to ten years, and remove members of national, state, and municipal legislatures.

In conformity with the Institutional Act, Congress chose General Humberto de Alencar Castelo Branco to fill out Goulart's term. A few months later, that term was extended by a year, to end in early 1967.

Brazil was governed by an uneasy coalition of military and civilian politicians for the next sixteen years. Many popular former leaders were banned quickly from political activity for ten years, including ex-Presidents João Goulart, Juscelino Kubitschek, and Jânio Quadros. Later, Governor Carlos Lacerda was added to the list. Forty members of Congress were forbidden to participate in politics.

Apparently feeling relatively secure in their control of the country, the military permitted the 3 October 1965 gubernatorial elections to take place, as provided for in the constitution. These elections were a disaster for the army. The eleven state elections precipitated a political crisis when the opposition Social Democratic and Labor candidates won eight of the governorships. War Minister Arthur da Costa e Silva, supported by younger military officers, mounted a campaign against President Castelo Branco, as they felt that the election had weakened the revolution. Rather than risk a split in the army, President Castelo Branco issued on October 27 Institutional Act # 2.

This new change in the constitution contained thirty articles. It outlawed all existing parties, allowed the president to add five new members to the Supreme Court, abolished direct popular election of the president and replaced it by election by Congress, and empowered the president to cancel the political rights of any citizen for up to ten years and to remove legislators from their posts.

This act was followed by another decree which established rules for setting up new parties. This made it virtually impossible for more than two legal parties to be organized. As a result of it, a government party, National Renovating Alliance (Aliança Renovadora Nacional — ARENA), and an official opposition party, Brazilian Democratic Movement (Movimento Democrático Brasileiro — MDB), were organized. The ARENA-MDB political party arrangement existed from 1965 to 1980, but it did not function in the manner that the Brazilian military had hoped.

Whenever possible, the MDB fought the government and often succeeded in embarassing and hampering the military rulers. The army could never be sure that the ARENA politicians would not join the MDB in Congress to vote measures that would defeat the political objectives of the generals. When irreconcilable confrontations took place, the military gave up on democratic procedures, closed Congress, and changed the electoral rules.

Throughout most of the period, Congress was the docile instrument of the military. On 3 October 1966, the combined Chamber of Deputies and Senate elected Artur da Costa e Silva president for the March 1967-March 1971 term, by 238 to 0, with the MDB boycotting the election.

However, despite the legislature's general willingness to cooperate and work with the military, Congress was closed three times by the army in the period 1964-1980. On 20 October 1966, when Congressional leaders opposed President Castelo Branco's suspension of six opposition congressmen charged with corruption and opposition to the revolution, he declared Congress closed from 20 October to 2 November 1966.

The second instance of suspension of Congress was more serious. When Congress refused to suspend the parliamentary immunity of MDB Congressman Márcio Moreira Alves because he had urged Brazilians not to attend army parades on Independence Day or allow their daughters to dance with cadets, President Costa e Silva not only closed Congress indefinitely, but issued Institutional Act # 5, which placed Brazil under a tight dictatorship. It authorized the president to govern by decree, declare a state of siege, remove congressmen and other legislators, and cancel citizens' political rights for ten years.

Congress was only permitted to reopen 29 October 1969, to elect a successor to President Costa e Silva who had died of a stroke. The new president, Army General Emílio Garrastazú Médici, was docilely elected by 293 votes, with 76 abstentions, for the period to run until March 1974.

Institutional Act # 5, under which General Medici governed, resulted in violent suppression of dissent. Congress became almost a merely symbolic branch of government. Sixty-six MDB congressmen were removed and lost their political rights. In addition, three pre-1964 appointees to the Supreme Court were removed. The official government party was not spared, and lost twenty-eight congressmen in the 1968–1969 purges by the military.

The third congressional closing by the army took place 1 April 1977, and lasted only a few weeks. President Ernesto Geisel (elected by Congress in January 1974) closed the legislature when the MDB blocked a judiciary reform bill which the military had requested.

On 14 April 1977 President Geisel decreed a series of political reforms which further tightened military rule and made it virtually impossible for the MDB to gain power through elections. Using powers in the Institutional Act # 5, the president ended popular election of governors, substituting choice by an electoral college of state legislators and municipal councilmen; provided for election of one-third of the Senate by electoral colleges instead of popular vote; substituted Chamber of Deputies apportionment by population for apportionment by number of registered voters, strengthened ARENA (since illiterates could not vote anyway and they were most numerous in ARENA-controlled states); provided there would be no more than fifty deputies from a single state; banned party campaigning on radio and television; and extended the presidential term to six years instead of five.

The results of congressional elections between 1964–1980 show that ARENA, with the help of the military, won most seats in Congress and controlled most state legislatures and municipal councils. ARENA, however, could not win the major cities. Whenever the MDB was given a chance by the government to compete freely with ARENA, they gained sweeping victories. The mass of the population, the lower-income groups, voted heavily for the MDB whenever possible. Often this was not because they approved of or supported the MDB, but simply to show hostility and opposition to the government.

As President Geisel's term of office approached an end in 1979, the government launched an official candidate, General João Baptista Figueiredo, four-star general and former director of the National Information Service, as the ARENA choice for the next presidential period. Another general, Euler Bentes Monteiro, was selected by the MDB. He ran a lackluster campaign, while General Figueiredo campaigned actively, ignoring the fact that he could not possibly be defeated. On 15 October 1978 the electoral college voted 355 to 266 for General Figueiredo for the period 15 March 1979–15 March 1985.

Recent Evolution of Parties

On 1 January 1979 the very restrictive Institutional Act # 5 expired. As a result, when President Figueiredo was inaugurated on 15 March 1979, he took office under conditions in which much more political freedom was permitted than had been true for more than a decade.

In October 1979 President Figueiredo submitted a party reform bill to allow greater flexibility in the party system and bring about the extinction of the ARENA–MDB structure. The key provisions of this law were that parties had to have six senators and forty-two representatives in the sitting Congress, or include a group of deputies who could win at least 5 percent of the votes in the 1982 Chamber of Deputies election. In addition, a party must get a minimum of 3 percent of the votes in at least nine states.

President Figueiredo in 1979 neutralized and broke the challenge of hard-line opposition Generals Sylvio Frota and Hugo Abreu, who opposed his democratization program. Credit for the successful liberal political strategy appears to be the result of careful planning and tactics by the chief of the civilian cabinet, retired General Golberry de Couto y Silva.

At the end of 1979 President Figueiredo granted political amnesty to all former political prisoners in exile, released virtually all political prisoners from jail, ended most of the censorship restrictions, and announced that direct elections would be held for governors and senators, but did not announce a definite date. On 30 November 1979 by official decree ARENA and MDB disappeared and the new political parties began to form. Subsequently, one of the major political parties organized was the Democratic Social Party (PDS — Partido Democrático Social), which inherited the old mantle of the ARENA. The PDS became the semiofficial voice of the government. The 1980 legislative session which opened in March showed the PDS to be the strongest party, with 221 deputies out of the 420 seats and 37 senators out of 66.

The next biggest party was the Brazilian Democratic Movement Party (PMDB— Partido do Movimento Democrático Brasileiro). This was basically the old MDB with the word *party* inserted in the old name. The PMDB had 98 deputies and 19 senators. The third party was the Popular Party (PP—Partido Popular), a conservatively oriented party with 69 deputies and 8 senators.

The Brazilian Labor Party (Partido Trabalhista Brasileiro—PTB) reappeared, but the struggle for control of its insignia and name between Leonel Brizola and Ivete Vargas, resulted in these being awarded to the Ivete Vargas group. Brizola then organized a new party, the Democratic Labor Party (Partido Democrático Trabalhista—PDT) which carried most of the former PTB members with it. The PDT representation as of June 1980 was twenty-two deputies and one senator.

Finally, one new party was the Workers Party (Partido dos Trabalhadores—PT), organized by São Paulo metallurgical union leader Luís Inácio da Silva. As of July 1980, it claimed eight deputies and one senator.

Bibliography

Robert J. Alexander. *Communism in Latin America.* Rutgers University Press, New Brunswick, 1957.

Edgard Carone. *A Primeira Republica, 1889–1930.* Difusao, São Paulo, 1969.

José Murilio de Carvalho. "Composição Social dos Partidos Politicos Imperiais." *Cadernos,* Universidade Federal de Minas Gerais, December 1974.

Ronald H. Chilcote. *The Brazilian Communist Party.* Oxford University Press, New York, 1974.

José María dos Santos. *Bernardino de Campos e o Partido Republicano Paulista.* Livraria Jose Olympio, Rio de Janeiro, 1960.

John F. W. Dulles. *Unrest in Brazil: Political-Military Crises, 1955–1965.* University of Texas Press, Austin, 1970.

Raymundo Faoro. *Os Donos do Poder.* Editora Globo, Porto Alegre, 1958.

Afonso Arinos de Melo Franco. *Problemas Politicos Brasileiros.* Livraria José Olympio, Rio de Janeiro, 1975.

Peter Flynn. *Brazil, A Political Analysis.* Westview Press, Boulder, 1978.

Alberto Guerreiro Ramos. *O Crise do Poder no Brasil.* Zahar, Rio de Janeiro, 1961.

Robert M. Levine. *The Vargas Regime.* Columbia University Press, New York, 1970.

Francisco José de Oliveira Vianna. *Institucôes Politicas Brasileiras.* Vol. 1. Livraria José Olympio, Rio de Janeiro, 1955.

Ronald Schneider. *The Political System of Brazil, 1965–1971.* Columbia University Press, New York, 1971.

Thomas E. Skidmore. *Politics in Brazil.* Oxford University Press, New York, 1967.

Alfred Stepan. *The Military in Politics.* Princeton University Press, Princeton, 1971.

Jordan Young. *The Brazilian Revolution of 1930 and the Aftermath.* Rutgers University Press, New Brunswick, 1967.

Political Parties

ACÃO INTEGRALISTA. *See* INTEGRALIST ACTION PARTY.

ALIANÇA RENOVADORA NACIONAL. *See* NATIONAL RENOVATING ALLIANCE.

BLOQUE OPERARIA E CAMPONESA. *See* BRAZILIAN COMMUNIST PARTY.

BRAZILIAN COMMUNIST PARTY (PARTIDO COMUNISTA BRASILEIRO —PCB). On 25 March 1922 in Rio de Janeiro the Brazilian Communist Party was organized by representatives of small groups from Porto Alege and Rio de Janeiro. A major figure in founding the party was Atrojildo Pereira. Unlike many of the anarchist revolutionaries of the period who had first been attracted by the Bolshevik Revolution, but had lost confidence in it by 1922, a small group led by Pereira continued to think of themselves as Bolsheviks and so established the party.

The legal existence of the Communist Party was brief. When the July 1922 *tenente* rebellion occurred in Rio de Janeiro, the government declared a state of siege and the party went underground. It resurfaced in January 1927, when the state of siege was lifted, but was again forced underground in August of that same year. The party remained underground throughout the rest of the 1920s. However, the Communists were able to organize an electoral front, the Workers and

Peasants Bloc (Bloque Operaria e Camponesa—BOC), and through it to elect members of various municipal councils, particularly in the port city of Santos and in Rio de Janeiro.

The PCB had several internal struggles in its early years. A split took place in 1929 when a group of followers of Leon Trotsky withdrew. One of their leaders was a founder of the PCB, João da Costa Pimenta. In the following year, the critical presidential election of 1930 virtually immobilized the Communist Party. One element in the party was strongly influenced by the exiled ex-*Tenente* leader Luis Carlos Prestes, and his failure for a long time to make any statements condemning or supporting either candidate caused confusion in the Communists' ranks and weakened their influence.

Prestes's final condemnation of the Liberal Alliance (running Getúlio Vargas for president, with backing of most of the ex-*Tenentes*), resulted in criticism both from his former colleagues and from the PCB. However, in 1931 Prestes announced his support for the Communist Party, and shortly afterwards left for Moscow where he was to stay more than three years, during which he was coopted into the Executive Committee of the Communist International.

When Luis Carlos Prestes returned to Brazil in 1934 he assumed the leadership of the party, which he was to continue to hold until 1980. In 1934 the PCB claimed 5,000 members. The return of Prestes coincided with adoption of the Popular Front policy by the PCB. This brought unification of the labor movement under Communist leadership and formation of a wider political coalition, the National Liberating Alliance (Aliança Nacional Libertadora—ANL). Prestes was elected honorary president of the ANL.

The Vargas government declared the ANL illegal on 12 July 1935, but it continued to function anyway. On 25 November 1935, the Communist segment of the ANL attempted a military uprising in Natal, Recife, and the Praia Vermelho barracks in Rio de Janeiro. The revolt was brutally smashed by the army. Prestes was taken into custody 5 March 1936 and was sentenced to a long prison term. The PCB was largely dismantled. Most of its leaders were jailed, went into hiding, or dropped out of political activity. This situation continued for almost a decade.

When Allied forces won the upper hand in World War II, and the Vargas regime began to move toward more democratic government, the PCB at first supported the newly organized anti-Vargas coalition, the National Democratic Union (União Democrática Nacional—UDN). On 21 April 1945 Vargas released Prestes and 147 other political prisoners. From April 1945 until the party was again declared illegal in 1947, the PCB had the longest period of legal activity in its history and took good advantage of the situation.

Vargas gave the Communists free rein to work in the labor movement. At the same time, the Communists made a sharp political about-face in mid-1945, urging that Vargas stay in power until a constitutional assembly had been elected and had written a new constitution. They quickly became the second largest political element in organized labor, outstripped only by the followers of Vargas.

They also quickly rebuilt their party organization, and it became larger and more powerful than ever before or since. By the time the party was again declared illegal, it claimed about 200,000 members, compared to the few hundred people who belonged to it at the time of Prestes's release from prison.

In the December 1945 elections, the Communists had their own candidate for president, Yeddo Fiuza, an ex-official of the Vargas regime, who received about 10 percent of the vote. At the same time, Luís Carlos Prestes was elected senator and the Communists placed fifteen members in the Chamber of Deputies. They made further gains in state and municipal elections held early in 1947.

However, the period of the cold war had begun. Soon after the 1947 elections, the Supreme Court declared the Communist Party illegal, because of its international connections. The PCB continued to function, but its membership quickly fell to 80,000.

From 1947 until the 1964 revolution, the Brazilian Communist Party did not function legally, but the Communists continued to be a force in Brazilian politics. They still had influence in the labor movement, and their votes were openly courted by politicians of other parties. Some Communists even served in Congress, elected on tickets of various dissident Trabalhista parties. In the 1950 election, the PCB supported Vargas, and subsequently they backed his Minister of Labor, João Goulart, who was willing to work with them in the unions.

The Communists also supported Juscelino Kubitschek in the 1955 election. The Kubitschek years were good ones for the PCB. The president abolished political tests for holding trade union office, and ended prosecutions which President Dutra had started against individual Communist leaders. In the 1960 election the Communists supported the official government candidate, General Henrique Lott. Although Lott lost to Jânio Quadros, the victor resigned within seven months, and in the succeeding João Goulart administration the PCB was able to make great strides in the labor movement, where they frequently worked with trade unionists aligned with the president.

The military takeover in 1964 resulted in a harsh crackdown on all dissident groups, and the PCB particularly suffered. It lost virtually all trade union influence, and during the 1964–1980 period the Brazilian Communist Party was reduced to a quite minor role in the country's political affairs.

The Communists also experienced severe factional feuding during that period. As early as 1962 a group of pro-Chinese leaders of the PCB had withdrawn to establish the Communist Party of Brazil (Partido Comunista do Brasil—PC do B). Subsequently, during the military regime, many faction groups split with the PCB, most of them to undertake urban and rural guerrilla activities.

When the Figueiredo administration began in 1979 to carry out its program of political liberalization, various leaders of the Brazilian Communist Party, including Luis Carlos Prestes, returned to Brazil. However, the Brazilian Communists' leadership was by then involved in a severe internal conflict, which came to a head in May 1980 when Prestes was removed as secretary-general, a post he had held since 1945, and Giocondo Gervasi Dias, a 67-year-old member of the

Central Committee, was chosen to succeed him. The major issue between Prestes and the majority of the Central Committee was the committee's desire to form a kind of popular front alliance with other groups opposed to the military regime, and Prestes's advocacy of a much narrower alliance with far-Left groups.

BRAZILIAN DEMOCRATIC MOVEMENT (MOVIMENTO DEMOCRÁTICO BRASILEIRO—MDB). The MDB was the official opposition party organized after the military regime of President Humberto Castelo Branco in 1965 outlawed all parties then in existence. It was made up principally of former Brazilian Labor Party (PTB) politicians and those of some of the smaller parties of the 1946–1965 period, as well as some from the Social Democratic Party (PSD). By 6 January 1966 it had succeeded in obtaining the 120 deputies and 20 senators required for it to begin functioning as a party under Institutional Act # 2.

Among the major leaders who managed to survive throughout the fourteen years that the MDB existed as a party were Senators Ulisses Guimarães (former PSD), André Franco Montoro (former PDC), Oscar Passos (former PTB), and Ernani Amaral Peixoto (former PSD). New leaders of the MDB at the end of the period were Paulo Brossard (former Partido Libertador) and Freitas Nobre (former Brazilian Socialist Party).

The program of the MDB was basically one of opposition to the government party, the National Renovating Alliance (Aliança Renovadora Nacional—ARENA), to the military, and to the administration. They challenged the government constantly, insisting that habeas corpus be reestablished and demanding a return to a free democratic political system. However, the MDB's major role was that of keeping the parliamentary system alive and being a feeble watchdog, denouncing the most flagrant abuses by the army. A somewhat heterogeneous center-Left party, they were never able to develop a clear-cut economic and social program.

The stated aims of the Movimento Democrático Brasileiro included consolidation of democratic government, direct secret ballot for all elected officials, a free and independent Congress. Others were supremacy of civilian power, nationalization of all energy sources, redistribution of income in favor of lower-income groups, agrarian reform, removal of all laws that prohibited strikes and complete revision of the wage-salary structure.

When Congress met early in 1966, for the first time after establishment of the new parties, the MDB had 144 members in the Chamber of Deputies, and 23 in the Senate, a bit more than half as many members as ARENA. Elections held in November 1966 for Congress were very difficult for the MDB as a result of the government's decree of 20 October which placed Congress in recess and dictated reforms in the electoral procedures, all designed to help ARENA. Military security officers screened candidates of both parties, and just before the election on 11 November took away the political rights of 18 congressional candidates, most of them MDB nominees. As a result, MDB representation in Congress fell to 132 in the Chamber and 18 in the Senate.

In the municipal elections of November 1968, political tensions and student unrest resulted in even tighter military control of the political system. As a result, the MDB won control of almost none of the 1500 municipal councils.

New congressional elections in November 1970, during the administration of President Médici, were held under very oppressive conditions of Institutional Act # 5. There was a great deal of apathy on the part of the voters. It is not surprising, therefore, that MDB congressional representation declined to 90 members in the Chamber of Deputies and 7 in the Senate.

Meanwhile, the MDB had abstained from having a candidate in the 1966 presidential election, the first to be completely in the hands of Congress, which chose General Artur da Costa e Silva. It did likewise in that of 1969, when Congress chose General Garriastazú Médici. However, in the 15 January 1974 presidential election, the MDB did offer a symbolic candidacy of Ulisses Guimarães for president and Barbosa Lima Sobrinho for vice-president. They got only 76 of the 497 votes in the electoral college.

A great victory was scored by the MDB in the November 1974 congressional and state elections. Twenty-two seats in the senate were contested and MDB won 16; in the Chamber of Deputies, MDB candidates won 172 seats, while ARENA won 192. The MDB after the election also controlled 6 state legislatures.

However, before the next state and federal elections, President Ernesto Geisel issued a series of decree laws in April 1977 which destroyed any future chance of major MDB victories. Thus, in the April 1978 congressional elections, although the MDB won over 16 million votes to the 12 million of ARENA, it received only 199 seats in the Chamber of Deputies, compared with 231 for ARENA and in the Senate got only 21 seats compared to the 41 of its opponents.

The MDB nominated a retired general, Euler Bentes Monteiro, as its candidate to oppose the government's nominee, General João Baptista Figueiredo, in the 1978 presidential election. However, Monteiro's campaign was unimpressive, and he had no chance to win in any case. He received 226 of the 581 votes in the electoral college.

The party reform bill introduced by President Figueiredo in October 1979 and passed by Congress shortly afterwards presaged the extinction of the two-party system established fourteen years before. As a result of that law, the MDB officially went out of existence on 30 November 1979.

BRAZILIAN DEMOCRATIC MOVEMENT PARTY (PARTIDO MOVIMENTO DEMOCRÁTICO BRASILEIRO – PMDB). With the reorganization of the political party system at the end of 1979, a new party arose out of the MDB. This was the Partido Movimento Democrático Brasileiro. Like its predecessor, it functioned as the major parliamentary opposition to the government.

The PMDB was basically the same party as the MDB, with relatively few modifications. Congressman Ulisses Guimarães of São Paulo was named president of the party, and the two vice-presidents were Senator Teotonio Vilela of Alagoas and Congressman Fernando Coelho. The executive committee contained some of the most respected politicians of Brazil, including Senator Paulo Brossard of Rio Grande do Sul, who served as PMDB Senate leader; Senator André Franco Montoro, and Senator Orestes Quercia, both of São Paulo.

In its February 1980 manifesto to the nation, the PMDB called the existing political structure of the country a farce and accused it of obstructing the desires of the general public. The PMDB also denounced the alliance of the huge state-owned corporations with the multinational firms, as one which maintained a distorted social and political structure. The party argued for free elections to be held on every level; a restoration of all of the powers which Congress formerly held; and a constituent assembly to be called to write a new constitution. Tighter control of profit remittances by foreign companies was called for, along with a more democratic educational system. The PMDB seemed to be traveling somewhat the same route as the old MDB. But it was definitely a more cohesive alliance than the former MDB.

At its inception, the PMDB had 98 deputies and 19 senators.

BRAZILIAN DEMOCRATIC UNION (UNIÃO DEMOCRÁTICA BRASILEIRA —UDB). The UDB was a middle-class party representing basically the São Paulo commercial and industrial interests, which was organized to fight the presidential and congressional elections scheduled for 1938, but aborted by the coup of President Getúlio Vargas on 10 November 1937. The party opposed the increased power of the Brazilian national government. Prominent politicians who supported the UDB were Paulo Nogueira, Octavio Mangabeira, Prado Kelly, and Artur Bernardes. All of these politicians would play important roles in the post-1945 União Democrática Nacional (UDN). The party's presidential candidate for the 1938 election was Armando de Salles Oliveira, ex-interventor of the state of São Paulo. The party disappeared with the establishment of Vargas's Estado Novo.

BRAZILIAN LABOR PARTY (PARTIDO TRABALHISTA BRASILEIRO— PTB). The Brazilian Labor Party was organized in the early months of 1945, when President Getúlio Vargas ordered his labor minister to establish a political party that would attract working class voters. Thus, the PTB was built around the government-controlled labor unions. Funding was supplied indirectly by the national government, and most of the early officials of the Partido Trabalhista Brasileiro were employees of the Labor Ministry.

From 1945 to 1961 the PTB grew very slowly and was viewed by many as simply a pragmatic vote-getting political machine aimed at the workers in the major urban centers. When Vargas ran as the PTB candidate for the presidency in 1950, he made dramatic appeals to the party, stating that it would be the political arm of the government if he was elected and would govern with him. By beating the UDN candidate General Eduardo Gomes and the PSD nominee Cristiano Machado, the PTB took on added importance during the period that Vargas governed Brazil for the second time, 1951–1954.

As President, Vargas moved slowly with regard to the PTB, at first appointing *pelegos,* or political unionists who were loyal to him and not particularly interested in the welfare of the labor unions. But in June 1953 Vargas named João Goulart as minister of labor. Goulart continued President Vargas's plans for expanding the PTB, but his activities on behalf of the labor movement and the PTB created so much fear and tension that he was forced to resign on 22 February 1954. President Vargas committed suicide on 24 August 1954.

However, the PTB was able in 1955 to recuperate from the suicide of Vargas when Juscelino Kubitschek of the Social Democratic Party (PSD) was elected president, with João Goulart of the PTB winning the vice-presidency. The PTB slowly gained strength during the Kubitschek-Goulart administration, 1956-1961.

Jânio Quadros won the presidency in 1960, with the support of the National Democratic Union (UDN), but João Goulart, who was running as vice-president with the PSD nominee General Henrique Lott, won even though Lott was defeated. Goulart was catapulted into the presidency of Brazil when Jânio Quadros resigned in August 1961. As a result, the PTB immediately gained more power and importance than it had ever had, and this was to continue until the 1964 revolution.

During the Goulart administration, several dissident elements of the PTB tried to clean out the more blatantly opportunistic elements of the party. Elements emerged which favored planned economic development, agrarian reform, and opposition to corruption and Communist infiltration in the PTB. Some of these were led by San Tiago Dantas, who served for several months in Goulart's cabinet. Another faction broke away to form the Renovating Labor Movement— MTR.

Although many PTB leaders such as Governor Leonel Brizola of Rio Grande do Sul made dramatic appeals to the working class, the party was unable to deliver or attract the majority of the urban labor vote. The PTB's attacks on foreign business, large landowners, and its call for worker participation in business profits, made the party attractive to many Brazilians. But the labor constituency was divided among groups which forced the PTB to make many state and national level alliances that were often repudiated shortly after they were created. Yet PTB strength in the Brazilian Congress kept increasing. Its members of the Chamber of Deputies rose from 22 in 1946, to 61 in 1950, 66 in 1960, and 109 in 1963. Its representation in the Senate rose from 2 in 1946 to 16 in 1954 and 17 in 1963.

However, the PTB members rarely voted as a unified bloc in Congress. Apparently many politicians used the PTB label to get elected but did not follow the national leadership or programs.

One of the biggest problems the Partido Trabalhista Brasileiro faced was their failure to attract the São Paulo working class, which was the largest in the country. In São Paulo, a master politician, Ademar de Barros, was in control of a populist party, the Social Progressive Party (PSP), which also aimed its appeals directly at the urban masses. Most of the São Paulo labor vote went to the PSP and not to the PTB during the 1946-1965 period.

The most charismatic leader of the PTB in the early 1960s was Leonel Brizola. One-time governor of Rio Grande do Sul, and brother-in-law of President João Goulart, Brizola moved his political base of operations after his term as governor from Rio Grande do Sul to the city of Rio de Janeiro and in 1962 won a landslide victory when he ran for Congress there. After the 1964 revolution, Brizola went into exile in Uruguay and the United States. He returned to Brazil in 1979 to reorganize and restructure the PTB.

Among the outstanding figures in the PTB in the 1945–1965 period were Getúlio Vargas, João Goulart, Leonel Brizola, San Tiago Dantas, and José Emirio de Morais. Others were Almino Affonso, Badger Silveira, Sergio Magalhães, Eloy Dutra, and Ivete Vargas. Most of these politicians lost their political rights after the 1964 revolution. The party was officially abolished by Institutional Act # 2 in October 1965.

However, when President João Baptista Figueiredo brought about the reorganization of the political system which had existed between 1966 and 1979, the Partido Trabalhista Brasileiro was revived. The problems of the reestablished PTB upon its rebirth in 1980 illustrate well the chaotic conditions of the Brazilian political party system with the ending of the two-party system which the military had imposed in 1965. A struggle to control the reborn PTB and its insignia developed between Leonel Brizola and former Congresswoman Ivete Vargas, neice of the late president. When the Brazilian Supreme Electoral Court (TSE) awarded the Partido Trabalhista Brasileiro symbol and name to Ivete Vargas's faction in May 1980, Brizola and his followers withdrew to form a new party, the Democratic Labor Party (Partido Democrático Trabalhista—PDT), which attracted almost all of the former PTB politicians. As of September 1980, the Ivete Vargas PTB had only one member of the Chamber of Deputies, Jorge Cury of Rio de Janeiro. The PTB had no senators. In the beginning the party also had the support of former president Jânio Quadros, who seemed to be planning to use the PTB to run for the governorship of São Paulo in 1982. However, in mid-1981 he resigned from the party.

BRAZILIAN SOCIALIST PARTY (PARTIDO SOCIALISTA BRASILEIRO— PSB) (1933). In the early decades of the twentieth century several unsuccessful attempts were made to establish a socialist party on a national basis. However, it was not until after the revolution of 1930 that such an effort succeeded. Since then, two parties of some consequence have existed which used the name Brazilian Socialist Party. One of these was organized by some of the *Tenentes* soon after the revolution of 1930; the second was one of the more important minor parties of the 1945–1965 period.

As preparations for constitutional assembly elections began early in 1933, Major Juárez Távora, the most outstanding leader of the *Tenentes*, took the lead in organizing a so-called Revolutionary Congress which established the first Partido Socialista Brasileiro. The program which it adopted was a somewhat confusing mixture of orthodox democratic socialist ideas, advocacy of a kind of corporative state, and Brazilian nationalism.

Juárez Távora and other leaders of the PSB hoped to rally the *Tenentes* who had been named interventors (appointed governors) in many of the states by Provisional President Vargas to support the party in the constituent assembly elections and subsequent elections for state governors and legislatures. However, most of the interventors were more interested in building up personal party machines in their states than in launching a national party. As a result, the PSB did quite poorly in the constituent assembly elections and did not come to control any state government, although it was one of the few national parties which were established between 1930 and the establishment of the Estado Novo.

The Partido Socialista Brasileiro merged after the constituent assembly elections with a small Labor Party (Partido Trabalhista), which had been set up in the late 1920s, and had had fraternal relations with the Labor and Socialist International. Early in 1935 the PSB became part of the short-lived popular-front-type National Liberating Alliance (ALN) coalition of various Leftist groups against the Vargas regime. A member of the PSB, Roberto Sisson, served as president of the ALN.

When, in November 1935, a Communist-led faction of the ALN attempted a military insurrection, the Vargas government took advantage of the situation to outlaw all of the parties which had belonged to the ALN, including the Partido Socialista Brasileiro. It did not survive clandestinely.

BRAZILIAN SOCIALIST PARTY (PARTIDO SOCIALISTA BRASILEIRO—PSB) (1947). The second Partido Socialista Brasileiro was established in 1947 two years after the end of the Estado Novo. It had its origins in two groups. The first of these was Esquerda Democrática (Democratic Left), organized in 1945 as the left wing of the anti-Vargas coalition, the National Democratic Union (UDN). The Esquerda Democrática had *Socialismo e Liberdade* as its slogan and won several seats in the constitutional assembly elected in December 1945. Early in 1946, Esquerda Democrática reorganized as a separate party.

The other group going to form the PSB was a number of ex-Trotskyites, led by journalist and art critic Mario Pedrosa, who had launched a weekly paper, *Vanguarda Socialista*. This group had some modest following in the labor movement in Rio de Janeiro and São Paulo.

In 1947 the two groups merged under the name Partido Socialista Brasileiro. During the next eighteen years the PSB had continuous representation in both the Senate and Chamber of Deputies, although it never won control of any state government. It had some influence in the labor movement, although it could never compete adequately with the influence of the Brazilian Labor Party (PTB) and the Communist Party.

A major reason why the PSB failed to become a major party in the 1945–1965 period was its inability to carve out for itself a clear position as an alternative to the PTB and the Communists, the principal parties of the Brazilian Left in this period. This was most notable in the early 1950s, when the prestige and influence of both the Trabalhistas and the Communists declined sharply.

In 1955, the Socialist Party was the first one to nominate Juárez Távora for the presidency. Subsequently he was also backed by several other minor parties and by the National Democratic Union (UDN). Five years later, although Socialists had served in the cabinet of Jânio Quadros when he was governor of São Paulo, they supported his opponent in the presidential race, General Henrique Teixeira Lott.

During the early 1960s the best-known Socialist leader was Francisco Julião of the northeastern state of Pernambuco, who was the principal organizer of peasant leagues, which mobilized thousands of agricultural workers and small landholders and tenants in that region. He was elected to the federal Chamber of Deputies in 1962.

The PSB was suppressed with other existing political parties in October 1965. Most of its legislators joined the Brazilian Democratic Movement (MDB), when it was organized as the opposition party to the military regime early in 1966.

Among the principal leaders of the PSB were Aurelio Viana and Domingos Velasco, senators, Hermes Lima, and João Mangabeira, the party's presidential candidate in 1950.

CHRISTIAN DEMOCRATIC PARTY (PARTIDO DEMÓCRATA CRISTÃO —PDC). The PDC was a doctrinal reformist party organized in 1945. At various times in its short career it attracted some of the most respected and prominent politicians in Brazil, including the old Tenente leader Juárez Távora, who served for many years as its secretary-general; Paulo de Tarso, minister of education under João Goulart; Governor Ney Braga of Parana, São Paulo political leader André Franco Montoro, and Paulista finance minister and governor, Carlos Alberto Carvalho Pinto. For a short period the party demonstrated spectacular growth, surging from eight deputies in 1958 to eighteen in 1962. It won control of the state government of two states. In 1964, the PDC had twenty deputies and one senator in the federal Congress.

The general political program of the PDC was left of center, but the party was characterized during the last part of its existence by at least three clear factions. The right wing was headed by Juárez Távora and Ney Braga, a center group by most of the leaders of the Parana Christian Democratic state administration and Franco Montoro, and the party's left led by Paulo de Tarso.

The PDC was affiliated with the World Christian Democratic Union.

The Partido Democrata Christão went out of existence as a result of Institutional Act # 2 of October 1965. There was no serious effort to keep the party going clandestinely. Its leaders split, some going with the government party ARENA and others joining the new opposition party, MDB.

COMMUNIST PARTY OF BRAZIL (PARTIDO COMUNISTA DO BRAZIL —PC do B). In 1961 a splinter group broke off from the Brazilian Communist Party (PCB) and organized the Partido Comunista do Brasil, which sided with the Chinese in the Soviet-Chinese controversy. The early leaders of the PC do B were a group of men who had been in charge of the Communist Party during the

1947–1957 period in which Secretary-General Luis Carlos Prestes was forced to remain in hiding. Once the Kubitschek administration had cleared Prestes of all charges levelled against him, and he was able to take over leadership of the party once again, the group who had been running the party resented Prestes's reassertion of control. They also disagreed with his unswerving loyalty to Moscow. The most outstanding leaders of the PC do B were Mauricio Grabois and João Amazonas.

The PC do B remained small and had little impact on the national scene, although in the Goulart period it did have some small influence in new agricultural workers unions which were then being organized. After 1967 the party worked to set up rural focos of armed resistance to the military regime but with little success.

By 1980 the PC do B had been alienated by the trends of Chinese policy. After the death of Mao Tse-tung, they aligned themselves internationally with the leadership of the Albanian Communist Party.

CONSERVATIVE PARTY (PARTIDO CONSERVADOR). The Conservative Party, which was founded officially in 1837, was one of the two major parties of Brazil during most of the period of the Empire. Two years after its establishment, the Conservative Party won a majority in parliament during the Araujo Lima regency, and it sponsored a number of laws designed to carry out its program. The Conservatives lost power when Dom Pedro II was declared of age, and some Conservative senators defected from the party, giving the Liberals a majority in parliament.

During the rest of the Empire period, the Conservatives alternated with the Liberals in power. They controlled the government from 1841 to 1844, from 1848 to 1853, from 1857 to 1862, from 1868 to 1878, and finally from 1885 until shortly before the overthrow of the Empire in 1889.

The Conservative Party basically favored greater centralization of power in the hands of the emperor, and specifically approved of the moderating power of the monarch. It opposed all measures in the direction of federalism, generally favored a restrictive political system with little popular participation, and favored the privileges of the Roman Catholic Church. The core of the Conservative Party's strength lay in the northeastern provinces, particularly in Bahia and Pernambuco.

In pursuance of its basic philosophy, the Conservative Party government which came to power in 1841 reversed the reforms tending to weaken the monarchy and to introduce federalist concepts which had been passed by the previous Liberal administration. It reestablished the Council of State, a kind of council of elders who advised the emperor on the use of the moderating power. It also greatly reduced the powers of the provincial legislatures, and gave the central government control of all police forces in the country. These measures remained in force throughout the rest of the monarchy.

Although the Conservatives officially favored a go-slow attitude toward abolition, it fell to Conservative Party ministries to pass the three major laws leading to the emancipation of the slaves. These were the Law of the Free Womb enacted in

1871 under the Vizconde do Rio Branco administration, which freed all children born thenceforward to slave mothers; the Saraiva-Cotegipe Law of 1885 which freed all slaves over 65 years of age, and the so-called Golden Law of 13 May 1888, which freed the 750,000 still held in bondage.

The Conservatives were opposed to unlimited free trade, and favored the industrialization of Brazil. Their last ministry had enacted in 1885 a frankly protective tariff which reduced import duties on raw materials used by domestic manufacturers and levied an import tax averaging 48 percent on products competing with Brazilian manufactured commodities.

Among the most important leaders of the Partido Conservador were Bernardo Pereira de Vasconcellos, Paulino José Soares de Souza (Vizconde Uruguai), and José Maria Silva Paranhos (Vizconde de Rio Branco).

The Conservative Party disappeared with the overthrow of the Empire.

CONSERVATIVE REPUBLICAN PARTY (PARTIDO REPUBLICANO CONSERVADOR). See REPUBLICAN PARTY.

CONVERGENCIA SOCIALISTA. See TROTSKYITE PARTIES.

DEMOCRATIC PARTY (PARTIDO DEMOCRÁTICO). In opposition to the dominant Republican Party of São Paulo, the Democratic Party was established in 1926. Although it had counterparts in a few other states, it did not develop any really national structure or any major importance outside of São Paulo.

The principal significance of the Democratic Party was as an expression of the growing revolt against the political system which had dominated Brazil during the decades of the Old Republic. It called for electoral reform, and advocated more public participation in the political process.

The Partido Democrático supported the candidacy of Getúlio Vargas in the presidential election of 1930 and also backed the military insurrection which took place five months after Vargas had been "counted out" in that contest. However, the Paulista Democrats were soon disillusioned with the Vargas regime, and as a result joined with their Republican opponents to support the so-called constitutionalist revolution of 1932, a civil war of São Paulo against the rest of the country which lasted three months. The most important leaders of the party were Antônio Prado, Paulo Nogueiro Filho, Paulo de Morais Barros, Luis Aranha, and Prudente de Morais Filho.

DEMOCRATIC LABOR PARTY (PARTIDO DEMOCRÁTICO TRABALHISTA —PDT). The Democratic Labor Party was organized by Leonel Brizola in June 1980, when the title and insignia of the Brazilian Labor Party (Partido Trabalhista Brasileiro—PTB) were awarded to the PTB faction headed by Ivete Vargas. Brizola and other PDT leaders were quickly able to establish party organizations in fourteen states, thus becoming inscribed as a recognized political party. The congressional strength of the party was estimated at twenty-three deputies and one senator, Leite Chaves.

The program of the PDT was expected to be a broad appeal to the working class and a pragmatic platform for winning elections. The PDT was in an excellent position to make trade-offs with other parties to increase their power, as the PTB did in the 1945–1964 period.

The most important political figures of the Partido Democratico Trabalhista were Leonel Brizola and Alceu Collares. However, the party was joined by an interesting cross section of the Brazilian Left, including such figures as Darci Ribeiro, Deputy José Mauricio, J. G. de Araujo Jorge, union president Francisco Delprat of the Rio de Janeiro metallurgical union, and Bayard Boiteux, former president of the Brazilian Socialist Party.

DEMOCRATIC LEFT (ESQUERDA DEMOCRÁTICA). *See* BRAZILIAN SOCIALIST PARTY (1947).

DEMOCRATIC SOCIAL PARTY (PARTIDO DEMOCRÁTICO SOCIAL– PDS). The majority of the politicians that entered the government-sponsored PDS when it was organized early in 1980, included President João Baptista Figueiredo, former President Ernesto Geisel, and almost the entire National Renovating Alliance (ARENA) organization. Many of the older ARENA politicians who joined the PDS were men who had made the transition from the 1945–1965 Social Democratic Party (PSD) to ARENA (1965–1979) and also moved to the PDS very easily.

The PDS power was similar to that of ARENA, and was located in the many smaller states of the north and northeast. The less urbanized areas were the stronghold of the PDS. Nevertheless, the 1980 Governor of São Paulo, Paulo Salim Maluf, was a valuable supporter of the government and the PDS, and commanded large blocs of voter strength in that state.

The names of most of the elected officials of the new PDS spanned a great deal of recent Brazilian history. The first president of the PDS was Senator José Sarney from the northern state of Maranhão. The general secretary, Deputy Prisco Viana, came from Bahia. Both were popular vote getters and skillful politicians. Also on the party's first executive committee were three prominent members of President Figueiredo's cabinet: Minister of Justice Ibrahim Abi-Ackel from the state of Minas Gerais; General Golbery do Couto e Silva, who was considered the principal political strategist of the president; and Antonio Delfim Neto, economic coordinator and planning minister. Other important PDS figures were Senator Jarbas Passarinho of Para, who became PDS leader and spokesman in the Senate; Deputy Nelson Marchezan of Rio Grande do Sul, leader of the party in the Chamber of Deputies, and Senator Ernani Amaral Peixoto of the city of Rio de Janeiro, who had served President João Goulart as a cabinet minister and in 1980 controlled large numbers of voters in Rio de Janeiro and would cut into the new Brazilian Democratic Movement Party (PMDB) following there. His professional style was reminiscent of former Mayor Daley of Chicago. Governor Antônio Carlos Magalhães of Bahia gave the PDS strong support in that state.

A popular and populist program issued in February 1980 by the PDS ranged from demanding protection for those who live in the favelas (slums) to the breaking up of large estates that are not in production. It also proposed government guarantees to stimulate the Brazilian businessman so that he could compete against the multinational corporations; control of state-run corporations but not in areas critical for national security, and a plea for women's rights.

As free elections had not yet been held when the present entry was written, it is difficult to assess the real popularity of the PDS in an open political contest.

DISSIDENT LABOR PARTIES. During the 1945–1965 period several groups broke away from the Brazilian Labor Party (Partido Trabalhista Brasileiro – PTB), which was one of the three major parties of the period. None of these dissident labor parties became a major factor in national politics, but some of them played roles of some significance in the political life of the time.

Probably the most important of the dissident Labor groups was the Renovating Labor Movement (Movimiento Trabalhista Renovador – MTR). This was a group organized in 1960 around the charismatic leadership of Fernando Ferrari, a PTB deputy from the state of Rio Grande do Sul. Ferrari objected to the lack of ideological definition of the PTB, and the rank opportunism which characterized that party, and sought to mold it more like the British Labour Party. Ferrari sought at first to displace João Goulart as the principal leader of the PTB, and when he failed in this endeavor, he broke away from the PTB and established the MTR.

In the election of 1960, Ferrari ran as one of the two vice-presidential running mates of Jânio Quadros. His candidacy undoubtedly split the antiestablishment vote and assured the election of João Goulart as vice-president, leading to his ultimate assumption of the presidency.

The MTR largely collapsed when Fernando Ferrari died in an accident. Its strength was largely in the working class of São Paulo and Rio Grande do Sul. In 1964, its representation in Congress included one senator and five deputies.

The National Labor Party (Partido Trabalhista Nacional – PTN) was established in the late 1940s by Hugo Borghi, who aspired to gain the PTB nomination for governor of São Paulo but was unable to do so. However, it did not long remain a personalist party. It appealed particularly to the working class of São Paulo, and could mobilize as many as 300,000 votes, gaining more support there than did the PTB. In 1962 its congressional representation reached an all time high of ten deputies and two senators.

The PTN gained temporary national fame in the election of 1958, when it successfully ran Jânio Quadros, who was ending his term as governor of São Paulo, as candidate for the Chamber of Deputies from the neighboring state of Mato Grosso, thus keeping him in the public eye for his candidacy for president. The PTN was also the first party to nominate Quadros for president.

The Republican Labor Party (Partido Republicano Trabalhista – PRT) was significant principally because in the 1950s, when the Communist Party was illegal, it made nomination on its tickets available to Communists, as candidates for the Chamber of Deputies. Through the PRT, the Communists were able to have at least a few members of the Chamber of Deputies during that decade.

The Rural Labor Party (Partido Rural Trabalhista—PRT) was a Protestant-oriented party with most of its support in São Paulo. It had four members of the Chamber of Deputies. It was the personal vehicle of Deputy Hugo Borghi after he lost control of the PTN.

The Social Labor Party (Partido Social Trabalhista—PST) was one of the earliest groups to split from the Partido Trabalhista Brasileiro. It had some support among the workers, and very modest influence in the trade union movement. In 1964 the PST had four members of the Chamber of Deputies.

ESQUERDA DEMOCRÁTICA. See BRAZILIAN SOCIALIST PARTY (1947).

FEDERAL REPUBLICAN PARTY (PARTIDO REPUBLICANO FEDERAL). See REPUBLICAN PARTY (1889).

INTEGRALIST ACTION (AÇÃO INTEGRALISTA). The Integralist Action was Brazil's fascist party in the 1930s. It grew rapidly in that period, was outlawed by the Vargas Estado Novo dictatorship, but was revived under another name after the fall of that regime.

Ação Integralista was founded in October 1932. Its principal leader was a novelist, Plinio Salgado. It adopted all of the outward attributes of a fascist party—a green-shirt uniform, a raised-arm salute, a sigma in place of a swastika as its symbol. From 1932 until 1938 its uniformed militia paraded in the streets of Brazil's cities and underwent paramilitary training. The party recruited many young people who were discontented with the status quo of the time, including many who were to change their political opinions and become important figures in later decades. These included Helder Câmara, who later gained fame in the 1960s and 1970s as the progressive Archbishop of Recife, and San Tiago Dantas, a leading figure in the Brazilian Labor Party in the 1950s and early 1960s.

Ação Integralista was ultranationalistic and antiforeign. Some of its leaders were strongly anti-Semitic, although anti-Semitism was not an official principle advocated by the party. It supported strong centralized government and rule by a self-selected elite.

President Vargas was very much worried by the threat of Ação Integralista. Nevertheless, when he was planning the coup d'etat by which he established the Estado Novo, he brought Plinio Salgado into the conspiracy, apparently promising him participation in the new regime. However, soon after the coup of November 1937, Vargas outlawed Ação Integralista as well as other parties, and had Plinio Salgado deported to Portugal.

With the end of the Estado Novo, Plinio Salgado returned from exile. He reorganized the Integralista under a new name and with a new program. His new party was the Popular Representation Party (Partido de Representação Popular). It sought to repudiate its former fascist orientation, although continuing to use the sigma as its party symbol. It made municipal autonomy its principal agitational issue. It had some support in the city of São Paulo, as well as in the states of Santa Catarina and Rio Grande do Sul. It frequently had members in the Santa

Catarina state administration in the 1946–1965 period. In 1964 it had five members of the federal Chamber of Deputies.

LABOR PARTY (PARTIDO TRABALHISTA). The Labor Party was organized in the late 1920s by Socialist-oriented elements in the organized labor movement. It became an associate member of the Labor and Socialist International. For a few years before the 1930 revolution, the Partido Trabalhista challenged the Communists and Anarcho-Syndicalists for control of the trade union movement. However, in spite of the rapid growth of organized labor after the revolution of 1930, the Partido Trabalhista did not profit from this development. It finally merged with the Brazilian Socialist Party (Partido Socialista Brasileiro—PSB), which had been organized under the leadership of ex-*Tenente* chief Juárez Távora.

LIBERAL PARTY (PARTIDO LIBERAL). The Liberal Party was one of the two major parties of the Empire period. It began to take shape in the early years of the regency of Pedro II, although the party was formally organized only in 1840. The Liberals favored the decentralization of the government, wide autonomy for the provinces, elected justices, separation of police power from the judiciary. They also favored limitation of the moderating power of the emperor.

Even before the formal establishment of the Liberal Party, those who were to form it were able in the Additional Act of 1834 to enact a number of Liberal measures. This act abolished the council of state, an advisory body to the emperor, outlawed entailing of estates, and established provincial legislatures with substantial powers. Some of these measures were reversed by Conservative administrations of the next decade.

The Liberals alternated in power with the Conservatives throughout most of the reign of Pedro II. They were in office in 1840–1841; from 1844 to 1848, from 1862 to 1868, and from 1878 to 1885. A Liberal ministry had just returned to power shortly before the overthrow of the Empire in November 1889.

During the first decade of existence of the Liberal Party, there were movements of armed resistance in several states which were led by Liberals. However, after 1850, the Liberal Party did not resort to violence to attain power on either a provincial or national level, in effect adapting itself to the moderating power of the emperor, and to the authority it gave him to place parties in and remove them from power.

However, in 1868, in the middle of the War of the Triple Alliance with Paraguay, the program of the Liberal Party was considerably radicalized as the result of a quarrel between the party's leaders and the emperor. He refused to accept Liberal Prime Minister Zacharias de Góes e Vasconcelos's suggestions for members of the cabinet, and forced the prime minister's resignation and the entry of a Conservative Party ministry. Angered by this, the Liberals adopted a program which called for an end to the moderating power, elimination of the council of state, suppression of the national guard, and abolition of slavery. It also called for expansion of the franchise, popular election of provincial chief executives, and an independent judiciary. In practice, however, later Liberal ministries took few drastic steps to put this program into practice.

The Liberal Party had its largest following in the area of the São Paulo-Rio de Janeiro-Minas Gerais triangle in the southeast. Since the electorate remained a tiny part of the total population (an estimated 142,000 out of a total population of 15 million in the early 1880s), the party was in no way a mass organization. However, it does seem to have represented the more progressive elements of the rural and commercial aristocracy in the most dynamic part of Brazil.

The Liberal Party disappeared, as such, with the proclamation of the republic.

LIBERATION PARTY (PARTIDO LIBERTADOR). The Liberation Party was established in the period of the Old Republic as the opposition to the dominant Republican Party in Rio Grande do Sul. It continued during the early 1930s, and was revived with the overthrow of the Estado Novo, when it became a national party.

The historical roots of the party stem from the alliance of dissident political groups which supported the candidacy of Assis Brasil for the governorship of Rio Grande do Sul in opposition to Borges de Medeiros, who was running in 1923 for a fifth term. The Liberation Alliance, made up of the opposition groups, lost the election, but then mounted an insurrection, which although also unsuccessful, resulted in a constitutional amendment that prohibited the governor from succeeding himself in office. In 1928 the remnants of the old Partido Federalista and the Partido Democrático of Rio Grande do Sul joined with dissident Republicans to form the Partido Libertador under the leadership of Assis Brasil.

When Getúlio Vargas became governor of the state of Rio Grande do Sul in 1928, he succeeded in bringing the Libertadores into his cabinet. He also won their support in his candidacy for president in 1930. Subsequently, they backed the military movement which brought Vargas to power in October 1930.

During the 1945–1946 period, the Partido Libertador was led principally by Raúl Pilla, a highly respected politician who served most of the period as a member of the Chamber of Deputies. It was basically a conservative party and cast most of its votes with the União Democrática Nacional and the Partido Social Democrático, rather than with the more radical Partido Trabalhista Brasileiro.

The Partido Libertador gained status as a national party during this period, although its center of strength continued to be in the state of Rio Grande do Sul. The major point in its program was its advocacy of the parliamentary form of government, by which the cabinet would hold office only so long as it held a majority in Congress. Ironically, when the adoption of a modified parliamentary system was imposed by the military after the resignation of President Jânio Quadros in 1961, the Partido Libertador voted against the measure, on the grounds that it was not genuine parliamentarianism.

When the 1964 revolution occurred, the Partido Libertador had two senators and five members of the Chamber of Deputies.

MOVIMENTO DEMOCRÁTICO BRASILEIRO. See BRAZILIAN DEMO-CRATIC MOVEMENT.

MOVIMENTO TRABALHISTA RENOVADOR. See DISSIDENT LABOR PARTIES.

NATIONAL DEMOCRATIC UNION (UNIÃO DEMOCRÁTICA NACIONAL —UDN). The National Democratic Union was organized as a political party in April 1945 by opponents of the Vargas dictatorship, having existed some months before that as a coalition of all anti-Vargas elements. Most of the UDN founding fathers were from São Paulo, Minas Gerais, and Bahia, and represented middle-class professionals. Adding power and prestige to this group were some of the former allies and officials of the Vargas period who had become disillusioned with the fifteen-year dictatorship.

Among the founders of the UDN were prominent political and business leaders such as Júlio Mesquita Filho, who controlled the powerful newspaper O Estado de São Paulo, and Julio Prestes, presidential candidate in 1930. Minas Gerais was represented by Virgilio Melo Franco and ex-President Artur Bernardes, former Vargas allies. From Bahia, Octavio Mangabeira and ex-Tenente leader Juracy Magalhães were among the founders of the party. So was Carlos Lacerda, a rising newspaperman from Rio de Janeiro.

Basically, the UDN appealed to the Brazilian middle class. During the years 1945–1965 they gradually broadened their program so that in the early 1960s the UDN was favoring the idea that workers' wages be pegged to the cost of living. Free labor unions and a reform of the social security system were also supported by the party. In foreign policy, the UDN posture was that the country must maintain an independent approach to the world, but also that Brazil was "a cordial and independent ally of the United States."

Despite the fact that the UDN lost the presidential elections of 1945, 1950, and 1955, they maintained a cohesive bloc in the legislature which was less fragmented than the Partido Social Democrático and Partido Trabalhista Brasileiro delega-tions. The party elected 115 members of the Chamber of Deputies in 1945, 72 in 1950, 74 in 1957, and 96 in 1962. In the Senate, it placed 10 members in 1945, 13 in 1950, 17 in 1957, and the same number in 1962.

The big chance for the UDN to achieve national power came in the 1960 presidential election. Under heavy pressure from the Rio de Janeiro journalist Carlos Lacerda and José Magalhães Pinto, the UDN leader in Minas Gerais, the UDN national leadership finally decided to select as their candidate ex-Governor Jânio Quadros of São Paulo, who was not a member of the UDN. When Quadros won against apparently strong odds, Brazilians justly celebrated what they felt was a major step towards more democratic and representative government—an opposition candidate had won a closely contested election.

Major UDN leaders soon split with President Quadros. Carlos Lacerda was particularly violent in his attacks on the president. Finally, in August 1961,

President Quadros unexpectedly resigned. His place was ultimately taken by Vice-President João Goulart of the Brazilian Labor Party.

Thus the UDN was thwarted in their attempt to take advantage of the UDN-sponsored victory of Jânio Quadros, and were once again thrown into the role of the major opposition party. From September 1961 to March 1964, the party constituted the core of the element in Congress and outside of it who were against the Goulart government.

Among the principal leaders of the UDN were its two-time presidential candidate, General Eduardo Gomes, Governors Carlos Lacerda of Guanabara, José Magalhães Pinto of Minas Gerais, and Juracy Magalhães of Bahia; Senators Herbert Levy of São Paulo, Afonso Arinos de Melo of Minas Gerais, João Agripino of Parahyba, and Milton Campos, the party's 1961 vice-presidential nominee.

NATIONAL LABOR PARTY (PARTIDO TRABALHISTA NACIONAL). *See* DISSIDENT LABOR PARTIES.

NATIONAL RENOVATING ALLIANCE (ALIANÇA RENOVADORA NACIONAL—ARENA). ARENA was the government party during the 1966–1979 period, established after the military regime had dissolved all then existing parties in October 1965. Its establishment was announced on 5 December 1965. It was organized primarily by former members of the National Democratic Union (UDN) as well as by a large bloc of former Social Democratic Party (PSD) politicians. As this would be the official party, there was a rush of most politicians of the smaller parties to join ARENA.

Among the leading figures of ARENA were Daniel Krieger, retired Colonel Jarbas Passarinho, Filinto Muller, and Petronio Portela. Others were Milton Campos, Ney Braga, and José Magalhães Pinto.

The political program of ARENA called for legitimacy of political representation based on liberty and honest voting procedures. The ARENA claimed to favor social democracy, abolition of all racial, religious, and class privileges, and strengthening of the congressional branch of government, as the only legitimate representative of the people, job guarantees and employment opportunities, yearly wage adjustments for workers, and encouragement of foreign capital investments subordinate to Brazilian national interests.

In reality, ARENA was created by the military so that they could claim there was some civilian input into the governing of the country and the selection of the successor to President Castelo Branco. In all subsequent presidential elections—by Congress or an electoral college—ARENA members voted for the military men's choice.

During the whole 1966–1979 period, ARENA controlled Congress. When parliament met for the first time after the party's formation, ARENA had 254 of the 398 deputies and 43 of the 66 senators. As a result of the 1966 congressional election, which was tightly controlled by the military men, ARENA got 277 deputies and 48 senators, a more than two-to-one majority. In the November 1968 municipal election, the government party won control of almost all municipalities because of the restrictions on the opposition imposed by the military.

The ARENA had its highest degree of electoral success, dubious as it may have been, in the congressional election of 1970, under President Garrastazú Médici. ARENA got 220 deputies, compared to 90 of the opposition party and 59 senators against seven of the opposition. Five years later, the ARENA again won a "victory," getting 203 deputies (against 154 for the opposition) and 44 senators (against 20), due to the rigging of the voting procedure by the military regime.

The precarious situation as the "majority" party was clearly demonstrated in the November 1978 congressional election. Although ARENA got not quite 12 million votes, against more than 16 million for the opposition, it was certified as electing 231 deputies, against 199 for the opposition, and 41 senators, compared to 21.

As a result of the party reform bill which President Figueiredo submitted to Congress in October 1979, which suppressed both ARENA and its opponent the MDB, the ARENA came to an end. It officially was dissolved by a decree of 30 November 1979.

PARTIDO COMUNISTA BRASILEIRO. See BRAZILIAN COMMUNIST PARTY.

PARTIDO COMUNISTA DO BRASIL. See COMMUNIST PARTY OF BRAZIL.

PARTIDO COMUNISTA REVOLUCIONARIO. See REVOLUTIONARY COMMUNIST PARTY.

PARTIDO CONSERVADOR. See CONSERVATIVE PARTY.

PARTIDO DEMÓCRATA CRISTÃO. See CHRISTIAN DEMOCRATIC PARTY.

PARTIDO DEMOCRÁTICO. See DEMOCRATIC PARTY.

PARTIDO DEMOCRÁTICO SOCIAL. See DEMOCRATIC SOCIAL PARTY.

PARTIDO DEMOCRÁTICO TRABALHISTA. See DEMOCRATIC LABOR PARTY.

PARTIDO DE REPRESENTAÇÃO POPULAR. See INTEGRALIST ACTION.

PARTIDO DOS TRABALHADORES. See WORKERS PARTY.

PARTIDO LIBERAL. *See* LIBERAL PARTY.

PARTIDO LIBERTADOR. *See* LIBERATION PARTY.

PARTIDO MOVIMENTO DEMOCRÁTICO BRASILEIRO. *See* BRAZILIAN DEMOCRATIC MOVEMENT PARTY.

PARTIDO OPERARIO REVOLUCIONARIO (TROTSKISTA). *See* TROT-SKYITES.

PARTIDO POPULAR. *See* POPULAR PARTY.

PARTIDO PROGRESISTA. *See* PROGRESSIVE PARTY.

PARTIDO REPUBLICANO. *See* REPUBLICAN PARTY.

PARTIDO REPUBLICANO CONSERVADOR. *See* REPUBLICAN PARTY.

PARTIDO REPUBLICANO FEDERAL. *See* REPUBLICAN PARTY.

PARTIDO REPUBLICANO TRABALHISTA. *See* DISSIDENT LABOR PARTIES.

PARTIDO RURAL TRABALHISTA. *See* DISSIDENT LABOR PARTIES.

PARTIDO SOCIAL DEMOCRÁTICO. *See* SOCIAL DEMOCRATIC PARTY.

PARTIDO SOCIAL PROGRESISTA. *See* SOCIAL PROGRESSIVE PARTY.

PARTIDO SOCIAL TRABALHISTA. *See* DISSIDENT LABOR PARTIES.

PARTIDO SOCIALISTA BRASILEIRO. *See* BRAZILIAN SOCIALIST PARTY.

PARTIDO SOCIALISTA REVOLUCIONARIO. *See* TROTSKYITES.

PARTIDO TRABALHISTA. *See* LABOR PARTY.

PARTIDO TRABALHISTA BRASILEIRO. *See* BRAZILIAN LABOR PARTY.

PARTIDO TRABALHISTA NACIONAL. *See* DISSIDENT LABOR PARTIES.

POPULAR PARTY (PARTIDO POPULAR—PP). The third largest political party established in 1980 after the ending of the two-party system which the military had imposed between 1965–1979 was the Popular Party. It was a middle-of-the-road opposition group, somewhat to the Right of the Partido Democrático Social (PDS). It had heavy support from the banking community, with a solid electoral base in Minas Gerais and São Paulo. Many of the old-time political professionals, such as Tancredo Neves (Minas Gerais), president of the party, had made the transition from the Partido Social Democrático to ARENA and then to the PP. Another powerful Minas Gerais politician, one-time presidential aspirant and former Minas Gerais governor, José Magalhães Pinto, became part of the PP executive committee. Others were Deputy Thales Ramalho of Pernambuco, secretary-general of the party; PP Senate leader Gilvan Rocha, and Chamber of Deputies PP leader Antônio Mariz from Parahyba. Powerful political support in the state of São Paulo came from former Governor Paulo Egydio and from Olavo Stubal.

The political program of the Partido Popular, published in March 1980, was considered the most populist of all the parties' statements. It demanded an immediate return to direct elections, the right of workers to strike, redistribution of wealth and income on behalf of the low-income groups, and a special appeal for women's rights.

POPULAR REPRESENTATION PARTY. *See* INTEGRALIST ACTION.

PROGRESSIVE PARTY (PARTIDO PROGRESISTA). The Progressive Party was formed by dissident Liberals during the 1860s. Its founders were dissatisfied with the way in which the Liberals were pushing to carry out the principles to which they were presumably committed.

The Progressive Party was established in 1863. Its principal leaders were Senator Zacharias de Góes e Vasconcelos and Nacubo de Araujo. It stood for decentralization of the government, and urged that ministers of state assume the power and responsibility of the moderating power of the emperor.

The party went out of existence after about five years, in 1868. Its leaders and members were reincorporated in the Liberal Party.

RENOVATING LABOR MOVEMENT (MOVIMENTO TRABALHISTA RENOVADOR—MTR). *See* DISSIDENT LABOR PARTIES.

REPUBLICAN PARTY (PARTIDO REPUBLICANO—PR) (1870). Three parties have used the name Republican during the last century. One of these was the principal challenge to the Empire during the last two decades of the monarchy. The second was a party, or group of parties, which governed Brazil during the period of the Old Republic. The third was a relatively small party which appeared during the 1945–1965 period.

The first of the Republican parties had its origins in the Radical Club established in São Paulo in 1868. Among its founders were many of the future leaders of the Republic of Brazil, such as Bernardino de Campos, Campos Sales, Prudente de Morais, and Francisco Glicerio. In 1870, the Republican Party was established as a national organization and three years later the São Paulo Radical Club became the São Paulo branch of the Republican Party.

A very cautious party, its leaders had previously served in both the traditional Liberal and Conservative parties. The principal planks in its platform were abolition of the monarchy, establishment of a republic, and the ending of slavery.

REPBULICAN PARTY (PARTIDO REPUBLICANO—PR) (1889). With the disappearance of the Liberal and Conservative parties after the fall of the Empire, the Republican Party was virtually the only surviving party with pretensions of being a nationwide organization. It took the name of Federal Republican Party. The first civilian president, and the first one who was a member of the Republican Party, was Prudente de Morais of São Paulo, who took office on 15 November 1894. For the next thirty-six years, until 1930, the Federal Republican Party controlled the political structure of the country.

Basically representing the dominant landowning and commercial oligarchy and defending the loose federal system of the Old Republic, the Federal Republican Party had a conservative political philosophy. It stood for states' rights, fiscal responsibility, freedom of education, strengthening of the military, and aid to the coffee industry.

However, in some ways similar to the national party system in the United States, the Federal Republican Party during the Old Republic barely existed on the national level except when national elections were held every four years under the provisions of the 1891 constitution. What in fact existed was a group of state Republican parties which controlled their respective federal units with little interference from the national government or the national party, so long as they supported the Federal Republican Party presidential candidates and their members of Congress backed the policies and programs of the incumbent federal chief executive. Indeed, the state parties were usually referred to as Partido Republicano, with Paulista or Mineiro, for example, added to indicate the name of the state.

During the second decade of the twentieth century there were two short-lived dissident movements from the Federal Republican Party. One of these was headed by the Rio Grande do Sul Republican leader Pinheiro Machado, who established the Conservative Republican Party (Partido Republicano Conservador) in 1910. Its program did not differ basically from that of the Federal Republican Party, although it did give more emphasis to the supposed need for financial assistance by the national government for the Rio Grande do Sul cattle industry. The Partido Republicano Conservador disappeared soon after Pinheiro Machado's murder in 1916.

The second schism in the Republican ranks had a greater national impact. Important elements within the Federal Republican Party, led by Ruy Barbosa, objected strongly to the party's choice of a military man, Marshal Hermes da Fonseca, as its presidential candidate in 1910. Ruy Barbosa launched his own candidacy in opposition to that of Fonseca, and he received the support of several of the state Republican parties. However, after the loss of the election by Ruy Barbosa, the dissident groups that had supported him, in Bahia and several of the smaller states, were reintegrated into the Federal Republican Party.

After 1894 all of the presidents of the Old Republic, with the exception of one, Marshal Hermes da Fonseca, were civilians and members of the Federal Republican Party. Most of them were either from Minas Gerais or São Paulo. Among the outstanding figures in the party during these three and a half decades were Presidents Prudente de Morais, Manoel de Campos Salles, Wenceslau Braz, Epitacio Pessoa, Artur Bernardes, and Washington Luis, as well as Minas Gerais leader Antônio Carlos and Pinheiro Machado and Borges de Medeiros, who were successive leaders of the party in Rio Grande do Sul.

After the revolution of 1930, the old Republican Party on the national level was systematically destroyed. It had owed its national existence to the support it received from the presidents of the states of São Paulo and Minas Gerais. Since Getúlio Vargas, the president and dictator of Brazil in the 1930–1945 period, represented the state of Rio Grande do Sul as well as new political and economic elements, the Federal Republican Party collapsed.

On the state level, the formerly powerful Republican parties were dismantled by agents of the Vargas government. From one state to another the process differed, depending upon the strength of the old party and the demands of the new group of politicians represented by Getúlio Vargas's Liberal Alliance. On 11 November 1930 the 1891 consitution was suspended, and traditional political party operations came to a halt.

REPUBLICAN PARTY (PARTIDO REPUBLICANO—PR) (1945). After the fall of Getúlio Vargas's Estado Novo dictatorship in 1945, the third group using the name Republican Party appeared. A conservative party, politically and economically, it had a strong and loyal following in the state of Minas Gerais, where it was led by ex-President Artur Bernardes. In that state, the PR controlled enough votes to insure victory for either the Social Democratic Party (PSD) or the National Democratic Union (UDN) in any given election.

During the years just prior to the 1964 revolution, the PR generally sided with the UDN nationally, as well as in the state of Minas Gerais. In the northern states, the party formed alliances with the more radical Brazilian Labor Party (PTB). In 1964 the Partido Republicano had one senator and five members of the Chamber of Deputies.

REPUBLICAN LABOR PARTY (PARTIDO REPUBLICANO TRABALHISTA). *See* DISSIDENT LABOR PARTIES.

REVOLUTIONARY COMMUNIST PARTY (PARTIDO COMUNISTA REVOLUCIONARIO—PCR). The PCR was a dissident Communist Party established in December 1969 by some ex-leaders of the Brazilian Communist Party including Apolonio de Carvalho, Mario Alves de Souza Vieira, Giocondo Alves

Dias, Jacob Gorendo, and Carlos Marighela. All were dissatisfied with the tactics of the original PCB. This group, which remained marginal and suffered from constant splintering, aimed at armed insurrection and direct action to overthrow the existing political system. It was largely obliterated by the military regime and does not seem to have revived with the relaxation of controls over political parties by the military government in 1979–1980.

REVOLUTIONARY LABOR PARTY (TROTSKYIST). *See* TROTSKYITES.

REVOLUTIONARY SOCIALIST PARTY (PARTIDO SOCIALISTA REVOLUCIONARIO). *See* TROTSKYITES.

RURAL LABOR PARTY (PARTIDO RURAL TRABALHISTA). *See* DISSIDENT LABOR PARTIES.

SOCIAL DEMOCRATIC PARTY (PARTIDO SOCIAL DEMOCRÁTICO – PSD). The Social Democratic Party was organized early in 1945, on orders from the Ministry of Interior, by the interventors (appointed governors) of the various states, after President Getúlio Vargas had announced that elections would be held at the end of the year. It began as the most powerful and successful party in the country, but slowly declined and lost most of its strength by the time of the 1964 revolution.

The PSD was conservative politically and socially, representing the wealthier members of Brazilian society, especially the rural landowners and entrenched political class of the northeastern states. From 1930 to 1945 these men had worked closely with Vargas and after 1945 most managed to continue their grip on the northeast and the important state of Minas Gerais.

The PSD nationally was very pragmatic and nonideological during most of its existence. It delivered political patronage, and whenever a PSD politician was president of Brazil, the party flourished. General Eurico Dutra of the PSD was president from 1945 to 1950, and Juscelino Kubitschek, also of the Social Democratic Party, was president from 1956 to 1961. Despite these two presidencies and the control over Congress, the PSD slowly declined as voter participation increased. Only after the Kubitschek administration, during which the president had placed overwhelming emphasis on economic development, did the PSD develop the rudiments of a recognizable political doctrine, that of "developmentalism."

Brazilian voters increased from 6,200,005 in 1945 to 14,747,221 in 1962, when the last elections were held before the 1964 revolution. The new voters came principally from the larger cities and wanted more from the government than the PSD could deliver. The voters changed, but the PSD did not do so sufficiently. In the 1945 congressional elections, the PSD had 42.3 percent of the national vote, whereas in 1962, the party only received 15.6 percent. During the Dutra presidency, 1945–1950, the PSD controlled every state government, but by 1960 they had lost the governorship of all but three minor states.

Social Democratic Party chiefs such as Juscelino Kubitschek and Ernani Amaral Peixoto were unable to maintain strong party discipline or control over their members. As a result, the PSD began to fragment and formed coalitions with new groups, depending upon the issues. Unable to deliver the vote, the PSD began to fall apart in the 1960s. PSD members of Congress did not vote as a bloc, individual members shifting to alignment with the Brazilian Labor Party (PTB) or with the National Democratic Union (UDN) on different issues.

When President João Goulart of the Brazilian Labor Party took power in September 1961, the Partido Social Democrático was forced into an uneasy alliance with the PTB, which seemed to dominate the alliance. As events led up to the 1964 revolution, the PSD gave the image of a party that was divided, demoralized, and ineffective, with nothing to offer the voters. There seemed to be no attempt by the PSD leaders to capture the urban mass vote or offer social programs for the middle- and lower-income groups.

SOCIAL LABOR PARTY (PARTIDO SOCIAL TRABALHISTA). See DISSI-DENT LABOR PARTIES.

SOCIAL PROGRESSIVE PARTY (PARTIDO SOCIAL PROGRESISTA— PSP). The Social Progressive Party was the personal political vehicle of Ademar de Barros throughout the period 1945–1965. The PSP was a Brazilian version of Tammany Hall on a state and national level. Ademar de Barros put together a political machine that functioned smoothly and built up a degree of party loyalty and discipline almost unknown previously in Brazil. Ademar de Barros could control and deliver two million votes in a national election.

Elected governor of São Paulo in 1947, Ademar de Barros built a strong personal following among middle- and lower-income group voters. The wealth of the state permitted the governor to extend power well beyond the São Paulo borders. An airline patterned on Rio Grande do Sul's Varig firm, and a state bank which issued loans and credits at long-term low interest rates to business and political groups all over Brazil who cooperated with the PSP, functioned smoothly.

In 1950, the PSP joined with the Brazilian Labor Party (PTB) to support Getúlio Vargas for the presidency, with the tacit understanding that at the end of the Vargas term, Ademar de Barros would in turn be backed by Vargas for the presidency. A leader of the PSP in the Northeast, João Café Filho, was Vargas's vice-presidential running mate.

The Vargas suicide in August 1954 ended this political pact and in 1955 Ademar ran for the presidency on the PSP ticket alone. He won his two million votes but came in third, behind the winner, Juscelino Kubitschek of the PSD–PTB alliance, and Juárez Távora, backed by the National Democratic Union (UDN) and several smaller parties.

Jânio Quadros, elected governor of São Paulo in 1955, brought corruption and graft charges against Ademar de Barros, who fled the country. Returning later, when the statute of limitations for such crimes expired, Ademar de Barros vindicated himself in 1962, when he ran successfully for governor of São Paulo against Jânio Quadros, who made an unsuccessful bid to return to political life after deserting the presidency in 1961.

The PSP elected four members of the Senate in 1954, one in 1957, and two in 1962. It placed 36 members in the Chamber of Deputies in 1954, 31 in 1957, and 23 in 1962. Although the party had strength in the states of Para, Ceará, and Bahia, it was basically a São Paulo-based political group, and it was from there that it elected most of its members of Congress. In São Paulo it was particularly in competition with the PTB, and the PSP's strength in the state was a major reason for the weakness of the Partido Trabalhista Brasileiro there.

Governor Ademar de Barros was a major civilian participant in the conspiracy which culminated in the revolution of 1964, and he supported the election of General Humberto Castelo Branco for president. However, the PSP was suppressed along with all of the other existing parties in October 1965, and in the following year President Castelo Branco removed Ademar de Barros as governor of São Paulo on charges of corruption.

SOCIALIST CONVERGENCE (CONVERGENCIA SOCIALISTA). See TROTSKYITE PARTIES.

TROTSKYITE PARTIES. A Troskyist movement has existed in Brazil since 1929. Although never a major factor in national politics, the Trotskyites have been a persistent and occasionally a considerable influence in the Brazilian far-Left.

The first Trotskyite group was established by Young Communists and some dissident members of the adult Communist Party. After the revolution of 1930, they played a major leadership role in the labor movement in São Paulo, while still calling themselves the Communist Party. However, during most of the 1930s, the Trotskyist group was known as the Liga Comunista Internacionalista. One of its leaders, Mario Pedrosa, attended the founding congress of the Fourth International in 1938 and was elected to its International Executive Committee. The Trotskyists were outlawed along with all other parties during the Estado Novo, although they continued to maintain some underground organization.

The Trotskyists emerged from the Estado Novo as the Revolutionary Socialist Party (Partido Socialista Revolucionario—PSR). During the 1945–1965 period, the principal center of organization of the PSR was São Paulo, where it had at least a modicum of trade union influence. The Trotskyists also had a secondary role in the development of agricultural workers unions in São Paulo and the northeast before the 1964 revolution. The party did not offer any candidates in elections.

As the result of splits in the international Trotskyist movement, and internal struggles for leadership in the Brazilian movement, the Brazilian Trotskyites also split. By the late 1970s, there were two Trotskyist parties, the Partido Operario

Revolucionario (Trotskista), affiliated with a faction of the Fourth International headed by the Argentine J. Posadas, and the Convergencia Socialista, which was affiliated with the so-called United Secretariat of the Fourth International.

UNIÃO DEMOCRÁTICA BRASILEIRA. *See* BRAZILIAN DEMOCRATIC UNION.

UNIÃO DEMOCRÁTICA NACIONAL (UDN). *See* NATIONAL DEMOCRATIC UNION.

WORKERS PARTY (PARTIDO DOS TRABALHADORES—PT). One of the most interesting and unusual developments in the 1980 Brazilian political scene was the organization of what appeared to be Brazil's first authentic labor party. The leader of the PT, Luis Inácio da Silva (Lula), president of the Metallurgical Union of São Bernardino dos Campos, had the support of most of the unions in the São Paulo area. Despite the smashing defeat of the Metallurgical Union strike early in 1980, Lula forced the Brazilian government to deal with the workers and admit that existing legislation did not meet the needs of the labor unions' situation in the Brazil of the 1980s. Although Lula was jailed for a short while, he emerged more popular than before, and the PT gained more adherents. The PT, when organized, had eight congressmen and one senator, Henrique Santillo (from the state of Goyaz). Congressman Airton Soares of São Paulo became the leader of the PT bloc in the Chamber of Deputies.

The PT manifesto to the nation issued in February 1980 explained that the PT would be a party *of* workers and not *for* workers. They did not exclude support or membership from nonworkers, and as a result many Brazilian intellectuals and university students flocked to the PT banner. The manifesto also stated that the workers have long been exploited in Brazil, and urged them to join the PT to fight against a political and economic system that cannot solve their problems and exists only to benefit a minority of privileged people. The party declared that it was fighting for better wages and better working conditions.

WORKERS AND PEASANTS BLOC (BLOQUE OPERARIA E CAMPONESA). *See* BRAZILIAN COMMUNIST PARTY.

Jordan Young

BRITISH VIRGIN ISLANDS

The British Virgin Islands, consisting of the islands of Tortola, Virgin Gorda and several smaller islands and keys, have a population of 10,000 to 11,000 people. All of the indigenous people are "colored," although there are a few foreign whites resident in the territory.

Until World War II most of the people were engaged in subsistence agriculture. However, during that conflict military construction projects in the nearby U.S. Virgin Islands attracted many younger residents of the British Virgin Islands. Subsequent to the war, the tourist industry began to develop, and it is currently the principal component of the GNP. Also important are activities of international companies which maintain offices in the British Virgin Islands for tax avoidance purposes.

Until 1967 the British Virgin Islands lacked virtually any self-government. The administrator, appointed by the British Crown, not only presided over the executive council but also over the legislature, the legislative council. In that year, a new constitution provided for a cabinet, consisting of three ministers, chosen from the majority element among the seven popularly elected members of the legislative council. Modifications in the constitution in 1977 removed the one "nominated" member of the legislative council, increased the elected members to nine, and reduced the voting age from 21 to 18. Control of finances was also shifted from the governor to the cabinet.

Political party organization remains weak in the British Virgin Islands. Parties function principally at election time. Between elections party discipline is weak, and rank-and-file party organization is scarce and largely inactive. Parties are very much identified with individual political leaders, and party allegiances tend to be volatile. No clear ideological lines or issues of principle separate the parties of the British Virgin Islands from one another.

Bibliography

Personal contacts of the writer.

Political Parties

DEMOCRATIC PARTY. The first political party to be organized in the British Virgin Islands, the Democratic Party was established by Dr. Q. William Osborne and others just before the 1967 election. It seated two members in the legislative council that year. In the 1971 election it increased its members to three, and together with an independent, Willard Wheatley, who became chief minister, it formed the government.

Just prior to the 1975 election, the Democratic Party merged with the Virgin Island Party, and this group again won three seats. However, Mr. Wheatley, who had been elected to the legislative council this time as a member of the United Party, left its ranks to again become chief minister, with VIP-Democratic backing. Subsequently, Dr. Osborne abandoned the VIP and re-formed the Democratic Party in preparation for the 1979 election.

UNITED PARTY (UP). The United Party was formed in the 1971–1975 period under the leadership of Conrad Maduro. In the 1975 election it won three seats in the legislative council. However, Willard Wheatley, who was one of the three United Party members, left the UP ranks to join the Virgin Islands Party in forming a government, under his leadership as chief minister. The other legislators of the United Party subsequently joined the reconstituted Democratic Party.

VIRGIN ISLANDS PARTY (VIP). The Virgin Islands Party was established in 1969 under the leadership of the then chief minister, Laverty Stout. It was the government party until the 1971 election, when it suffered a defeat, winning only two of the seven elected seats. Just before the 1975 election, it was joined by the Democratic Party, and the united forces gained three seats. The government of the 1975–1979 period was officially controlled by the VIP, which Chief Minister Wheatley joined after leaving the United Party. It has been more successful than the other British Virgin Islands parties in maintaining local organizations between elections and has been the most durable of the parties.

Robert J. Alexander

CANADA

Canada is a country of immense size. Its approximately 3.8 million square miles, extending from the North Pole to the Great Lakes, make it the world's second largest state. Currently it has a population of almost 24 million, the majority of whom reside in metropolitan areas located in a relatively narrow band north of the United States border.

The country was initially settled by French colonists who established two major outposts (Quebec City, 1608 and Montreal, 1642) in what is now the province of Quebec. Periodic eighteenth-century conflicts between England and France and clashes between French and British colonists in North America culminated in Canada becoming a British possession in 1763.

Representative government and a legislature were introduced in Canada by British authorities in 1791. Basic political institutions and processes such as the cabinet form of responsible government, an independent judiciary, the rule of law, political parties, competitive elections, and peaceful transitions of executive power, were firmly established and legitimized by the time the provinces of Ontario, Québec, Nova Scotia, and New Brunswick were united in a federal union in 1867 by an act of the British parliament, the British North America Act. The provinces of Manitoba and British Columbia entered the union in 1870 and 1871, respectively, and Prince Edward Island joined in 1873. The provinces of Alberta and Saskatchewan were carved out of the west in 1905, and Newfoundland, governed by a United Kingdom commission since the bankruptcy of its own government in 1934, voted in a referendum to join Canada and become the country's tenth province in 1949.

Newfoundland elites previously had not availed themselves of periodic opportunities to become a Canadian province, preferring instead to retain their 1824 status of a British Crown Colony with autonomy in domestic affairs. Although not a part of Canada until 1949, the colony's politics were dominated by parties terming themselves Liberal and Conservative.* Social cleavages, however, were as important as ideological ones, and the labels Liberal and Conservative were convenient fig leaves covering warring configurations of local notables divided by geography, occupation, and especially religion.

---

*The labels "Conservative" and "Progressive Conservative" are used interchangeably throughout this chapter.

Demography

Similar to the United States, Canada's current population is derived from a polyglot of ethnic groups, the largest of which is the Anglo-Scottish-Irish. Unlike the United States, however, about 28 percent of the population is of French descent. Approximately 80 percent of the latter reside in the province of Quebec and are francophones. The cleavage between English- and French-speaking Canadians is arguably the most important characteristic of Canadian society. It has its origins in the aforementioned British conquest of Quebec. The British authorities did not try to assimilate the local population. Instead, the French were allowed to retain their language and Catholic religion, their system of education, and their civil law code. The legitimacy of a distinctly French Canadian culture thus was recognized and the socialization opportunities inherent in its ecclesiastically dominated educational system enabled it to be sustained. Also of importance for "survivance" until recently has been a high birth rate—so high, in fact, that although immigration from France essentially ceased after 1760, the proportion of Canada's population that is French has remained relatively constant for over two hundred years.

Party Origins and Development

In their suggestive essay, Joseph LaPalombara and Myron Weiner observe that there are both "inside" and "outside" explanations of the origins and development of political parties. In some instances, parties have their origins in legislative bodies, beginning as factional groupings loosely organized around charismatic individuals. Factional lines begin to harden, internal organizations develop and cohesive group actions increase when one or more major issues, whose resolution can extend over a generation or more, arise. Concomitant with the democratization of the electorate, the losing side(s) in such extended controversies (the "outs") generally begin to develop ties with supporters in the electorate in an effort to become the "ins." They gradually expand and develop these ties into relatively formidable electoral organizations and, since organization generally stimulates counterorganization, twentieth century political parties in democratic political systems are characterized by institutionalized patterns of communication and interaction between their legislative and extralegislative components. Outside parties, in contrast, begin not as factional groupings within legislatures, but as mass social movements responding to social and economic dislocations such as those associated with industrialization and urbanization. Some of these mass social movements solidify, they develop structures, and they institutionalize procedures that enable them to recruit candidates and elect them to public offices. The inside and outside explanations account for the origins and development of Canada's current four national political parties. The two "major" parties, the Liberal and Progressive Conservative (formerly the Conservative) are inside parties. Their beginnings are rooted in early nineteenth century legislative struggles to achieve responsible government. The New Democratic Party (formerly the Cooperative Commonwealth Federation) and Social Credit are "outside" parties—products of the social and economic conditions that were engendered by the settlement of the west and the virtual collapse of that region's economy during the Great Depression.

The Party System(s)

Three points about the Canadian party system are especially noteworthy. First, it is exceedingly complex. Indeed, one could reasonably argue that the country does not really have a single-party system, but rather several. In part, this is a consequence of the important role the provinces play in the federal system. Also in part, it is a function of the strong regional feelings based upon economic and social-cultural particularisms that have characterized Canadian political life. Whatever the reasons, the reality is a party struggle in which both the identities of the contestants and the patterns of competition between and among them can vary sharply from province to province. Moreover, within individual provinces party competition at one level of government seemingly can be unrelated (in fact, almost hermetically sealed) from competition at another.

Consider some examples. An inspection of provincial election data reveals that interparty competition in the provinces of Nova Scotia, Manitoba, and British Columbia is of the classic two-party variety. The identities of the contesting parties, however, differ as one moves from east to west. In Nova Scotia, the electoral struggle is waged between the old-line Center-Left and Center-Right parties, the Liberals and Conservatives. In Manitoba the fight is between the Conservatives and social-democratic NDP and in British Columbia it is between the latter and their professed ideological foes, Social Credit. In Quebec two parties (the Union Nationale and the Parti Québecois) that do not even compete in federal elections have governed the province during 60 percent of the postwar period. Although the Liberals have been less of a force in Quebec's provincial rather than federal politics, by winning four postwar Quebec elections they have fared much better than in the neighboring province of Ontario. Millions of Ontarians were not even born when the Liberals last won a provincial election (1937). In contrast, the Conservatives have governed Ontario continuously since 1943, and also are a formidable force in federal elections in that province. However, the party is more or less a nonstarter at both the federal and provincial levels in Quebec. In short, the competitive positions of the Liberals and Conservatives in federal and provincial politics in the two provinces which contain some two-thirds of the country's population are sharply different.

Second, although Canada has four national parties, for almost a half century the political system has tended toward one-party dominance. The Liberal Party, for example has governed the country for approximately 29 of the past 35 years. (See figure 1.) The hegemony the party enjoys in federal politics rests in part on its continuing success in Quebec. In the thirteen national elections of the post-

World War II era, the party has captured, on average, over half (53.9%) of the Quebec vote, a considerably larger share than it has received in the Atlantic provinces, Ontario and, in particular, in the west. (See figure 2.) The distortion produced by the first-past-the-post electoral system also had worked in favor of the party. In ten of thirteen national elections since World War II, the Liberals' share of parliamentary seats has exceeded its share of the vote, and on five separate occasions a minority of votes has produced a majority of parliamentary seats. (See figure 3.) Also, although many Canadians do not have strong, stable psychological attachments to particular parties, opposition parties have had little success in developing electoral strategies capable of attracting the preponderance of those with flexible party ties. Rather, the normal pattern of voter movement between elections has been a crosscutting one which has had little net effect on Liberal vote totals.

The tendency toward domination by a single party also is operative at the provincial level. There are numerous examples. As noted above, in Ontario the Tory "Big Blue Machine" has governed continuously since 1943. Newfoundland was governed for 22 years (1949–1971) by a provincial Liberal party led by Joseph Smallwood. Saskatchewan has been governed for 29 of the last 36 years by the provincial New Democratic Party, and the Social Crediters were in power in Alberta and British Columbia for 36 and 20 year intervals, respectively. In Quebec, the Liberals were in power for 39 years without interruption, and between 1936 and 1960 the Union Nationale governed for 19 years.

Third—tendencies toward one-partyism notwithstanding—there is a curious periodicity to party fortunes. A party may enjoy years of electoral success and then fall from grace. When the demise comes, it is rapid and precipitous. In this regard, even the seemingly perenially governing Liberals have not been immune. For example, in the 1953 national election, the party's candidates captured 65 percent of the parliamentary seats. They took 40 percent of the seats in 1957, but only 19 percent in 1958—a decline of more than 40 percent in a five-year period. The Conservatives captured almost 80 percent of Canada's parliamentary seats in the 1958 election but won only 36 percent six years later and were out of office. The tendency has manifested itself even more strongly at the provincial level. To illustrate, after governing for a generation, the Liberal Party of Newfoundland and the Social Credit Party of Alberta virtually disappeared from their respective provincial legislatures during the 1970s.

These sharp swings in party fortunes are at least partially the result of the aforementioned fact that the psychological identifications of many Canadians with their political parties tend to be weak and unstable. Further, the pattern whereby a party within a particular province fares much better in federal than provincial electoral competition or vice versa is related to the tendency of voters to maintain "split" party identifications: to identify with party "A" at one level of the system and with party "B" at the other.

Parties in Parliament

The institution of parliament and virtually all of the procedures it initially

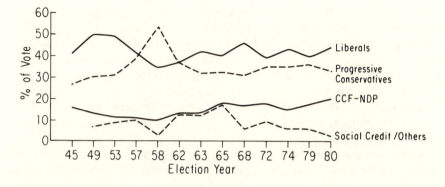

Figure 1.
Percentage of Vote for the Four National Parties in Federal Elections, 1945–1980

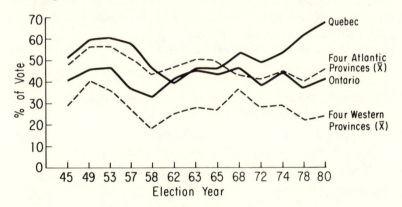

Figure 2.
Percentage of Votes Received by Liberal Party Candidates by Region, 1945–1980

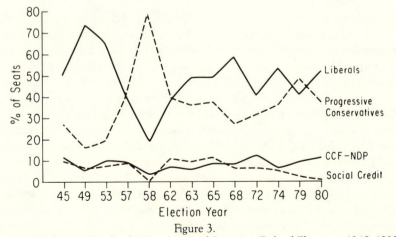

Figure 3.
Percentage of Seats Won by the Four National Parties in Federal Elections, 1945–1980

adopted were transported from Great Britain via the legislative bodies of the four provinces that united in 1867 to form a new Canadian nation. In the more than 100 years that have passed, the membership of the House of Commons has changed from loose factions into disciplined, cohesive parties carrying out their perceived function of either supporting or opposing government-initiated legislation. As has been the case in other liberal democracies with British-model parliamentary government, parliament's membership has increased significantly (in Canada from 100 to 282), while at the same time formal procedures have been generated that limit the opportunity available to private members to participate in the process of drafting and evaluating legislation. The reasons for these developments are complex. In brief, however, they may be viewed as consequences of the growth and socioeconomic development of such societies. The argument is that if their parliaments are to be representative, then their compositions must reflect both the increases and the geographic distributions of their populations. If they are also to be effective instruments for governing a modern, complex society, political parties that have won elections must have the opportunity to carry out their policies and programs.

In Canada, successive governments have tried to carry out their perceived mandates in four related ways:

1. By enlarging the cabinet, organizing it into committees, and supplying it with appropriate expert staff assistance

2. By insuring that the consideration of cabinet legislation takes calendar and time precedence over private-member legislative proposals

3. By limiting the opportunities available to private members either to initiate legislation or participate in its evaluation

4. By officially recognizing the role that opposition parties play in the policy process and providing them with the expert staff required to function effectively

The principal mechanism employed to achieve cohesive action in both governing and opposition parties in parliament is the party caucus. Each party generally caucuses weekly during a parliamentary session and the two major parties also make use of regional and subregional caucuses. A caucus performs the following functions: it provides party members with an opportunity to discuss the strategies and tactics that will be employed in evaluating current legislation in plenary and committee sessions; it enables members to hammer out party positions on policy issues; it provides party members with an opportunity to express any grievances or complaints they have and to exchange information about the distribution of grass-roots opinions in their constituencies; it socializes members to accept a division of labor in which party leaders play the principal role in legislative debates while nonleaders give their time and attention to the performance of services on behalf of individual constituents.

A recurring observation and frequent complaint of students of Canadian politics is that the Liberals and Conservatives (the only two parties that have governed at the national level) have similar values and ideological perspectives, recruit the same kinds of people as parliamentary candidates, and generate similar policies when in office. The late John Porter's version of this argument is perhaps the most widely known, but variations on this theme can be found in the work of many other political scientists and historians as well. A longitudinal analysis of the legislative outputs of Canada's first twenty-eight parliaments (1867–1972) tends to support Porter's claim regarding the relative similarity of the policy outputs of the two parties. Although Liberal governments have passed more redistributive legislation, foreign affairs bills, and expended a larger proportion of the budget on defense when in office, it can be argued that such differences between Liberals and Conservatives are time-related. The Liberals have held office for most of the twentieth century, whereas the period of Conservative hegemony was the nineteenth century, when the issues confronting parliament were less complex and the scope of desired governmental activity was more restricted.

With respect to leadership differences, an in-depth study of the distribution and correlates of influence in a reasonably typical parliament (the twenty-eighth, 1968–1972) indicates that both the parliamentary and preparliamentary careers as well as the current values and perspectives of Liberal cabinet ministers and Conservative front-benchers differ. Although the two groups are drawn largely from the same population pool, the Conservative opposition leaders tend to be older (eight years on average), are more apt to be native Canadians, are more apt to be Protestant, and more frequently derive from Anglo-Celtic and Northern European stock, whereas Liberal cabinet ministers are more frequently university and professional school graduates, especially in law.

There also is evidence that although the policy outputs of Liberal and Conservative governments have not differed greatly over the years, their parliamentary members nonetheless view themselves as occupying different ideological positions on important policy issues. This is the case, as well, with Social Credit and New Democratic M.P.s. The public also perceives differences among the four parliamentary parties' policy positions, although not as great as M.P.s believe them to be. Analysis reveals that a Left-Right ideological dimension most often underlies M.P.s' perceptions of their own and their parties' positions on policy issues, whereas, the public most often sees the parties in terms of government-opposition, major-minor, and French–non-French dimensions. Other studies have indicated that provincial legislators also take significantly different positions on Left-Right ideological scales. Although there currently is no evidence available, it seems reasonable to assume that the public probably perceives the policy positions of provincial parliamentary parties in much the same way as they view federal parties (that is, in terms of government-opposition, major-minor, and French–non-French dimensions).

Regardless of which positions the public sees parties occupying in issue space, a more important question is whether Canadian parties effectively perform the kinds of functions that we normally ascribe to them. The observation that there really is no single-party system suggests that the integrative function has been performed with less than conspicuous success over the years. In a thoughtful essay, party scholar John Meisel indicts the parties for their failure in this area and argues that their ability to perform functions such as political mobilization, interest aggregation, and policy formulation also has declined markedly since World War II. He attributes this decline to a number of long-term factors. Included are the rise of a bureaucratic state, increased interest-group activity, incipient corporatism, federal-provincial diplomacy, the rise of electronic media and investigative journalism, the dominance of economic interests, and the domination of federal politics by the Liberal Party.

A governing party's ability to formulate policy has been the area in which decline has been most severe. Concomitant with the increased scope of governmental activity in the post–World War II period there has been a vast increase in the size and power of the federal bureaucracy. Upper echelon bureaucratic officials (that is, deputy and assistant deputy ministers in traditional line departments together with central agency officials) formulate the bulk of public policy because they structure the limited number of policy alternatives from which their political masters in cabinet are supposed to choose, and they also marshall the supporting data that assist ministers in making their choices. Before any important policy decision is made, there customarily is an intense period of consultation mong cabinet ministers, their principal bureaucratic subordinates, and representatives of the interests that are likely to be affected. The consultation process has been institutionalized through the appointment of advisory committees and other bodies that insure that political officials are continuously apprised of the positions of organized group interests. However, a more recent tendency has been to carry on these consultations *without* the presence of ministers.

Another reason that parliamentary parties have become minor and segmental participants in the policy process is that many major policies are hammered out in federal-provincial ministerial conferences by the prime minister, the several provincial premiers, and their respective platoons of expert advisers. These advisors (the bulk of whom are senior-level bureaucrats) and their assistants also work out the details involved in implementing policy decisions in literally thousands of meetings of committees, task forces, and working groups which take place annually. The exercise of bureaucratic power over policy formulation and administration has been facilitated by successive Liberal governments who seem to have an affinity for bureaucrats and vice versa. Given the virtually continuous hegemony the party has exercised over federal politics, it is argued that the line between the federal bureaucracy and the Liberal party has become tenuous: so much so, in fact, that the party's entire platform in one national election supposedly was written by a group of high-level bureaucrats.

The ability of parliamentary parties to mobilize public opinion has been seriously affected by the rise of electronic media (particularly television) and the tendency of print media figures to ascribe to themselves the role of "official opposition," not only to the government of the day but also to its opposition. Legislative party leaders make statements and engage in other activities that are intended to attract the electronic media, and through them, the attention of the millions who watch television and listen to radio. In order to attract media attention, party leaders have had to accommodate themselves to media demands and needs. Their principal need, according to Meisel, is to *entertain* the widest possible audience. Consequently, with the active collaboration of party leaders, the media represent political events to the public in ways that will maximize their attractiveness. For example, an election is represented to the public as a kind of athletic contest in which the comings, goings, performance, and personality of the star player of each team (that is, the several party leaders) are the principal attractions. Although these tactics may result in short-term gains for parties, there is evidence that their long-term effect is to contribute to a cynical and negative public attitude toward parties and their leaders.

Extraparliamentary Party Organizations

In the United States one of the consequences of party officials' reliance on electronic media to publicize themselves and their messages has been a decline in party organizations generally and a diminution in the importance of their roles in electoral campaigns in particular. There is reason to assume that this also may be the case in Canada. Studies of extraparliamentary party organizations indicate that Canadian party officials are very much attuned to and make use of the latest American campaign technology. This is especially true of the Liberal and Conservative parties. The former took the lead in building extraparliamentary organizations in the nineteenth century. However, as late as 1880, only about 50 percent of the federal constituencies had even paper party associations. The Liberals did not hold their first national convention until 1893 and did not establish a national office until 1912. The Conservatives lagged behind the Liberals in both these areas (for example, their first national leadership convention was held in 1927). Not until the 1920s did either party make concerted and systematic attempts to organize their supporters into viable extraparliamentary organizations. Their efforts were spurred by the expansion of the electorate that occurred at the time and the need to deliver on at least some of their promises to newly enfranchised groups. The Social Credit and the Cooperative Commonwealth Federation (CCF)-New Democratic Party (NDP) followed the lead of the two older parties.

Historically, extraparliamentary organizations have been controlled by people whose principal goals have been to select and elect candidates for public office. This is not to say that they have not had other objectives, only that recruitment and election goals have taken precedence. The tasks associated with the performance of the recruitment-election function have been virtually monopolized by the constituency-level units of extraparliamentary party organizations. They are the most active in hierarchies that are generally skeletal, decentralized, and loosely articulated. It is true that federal parties have national and, in some provinces, provincial offices. The offices of the Liberal, Conservative, and New Democratic parties have minimum staffs that are expanded immediately before elections, but the Social Credit party lacks even this level of organization. It also is true that party offices provide financial assistance, speakers, campaign materials, and other forms of assistance to constituency organizations and their candidates. These forms of support are welcomed since under certain conditions they may provide the margin between electoral success and failure. Despite this assistance, and the periodic "parachuting" of candidates into constituencies by national or provincial organizational officials, the aforementioned tasks of candidate recruitment and electioneering are firmly in the hands of constituency party leaders.

The organizational form of most constituency parties tends to be a truncated pyramid. The more elaborately organized parties in metropolitan areas usually contain four levels of organization. From smallest to largest these are the poll, area, zone, and constituency. The less fully organized generally dispense with the two intermediate layers. In many areas party workers are paid either directly or indirectly for their services. However, in most cases these payments are very modest and are almost entirely restricted to individuals holding positions at the bottom level of a hierarchy. An overwhelming majority of a party's activists in upper-echelon positions are unpaid. Thus, constituency organizations are populated almost entirely by amateurs. Since most constituency-level party officials do not receive material rewards for their services when a conflict occurs between the demands of party work and their primary obligations the latter usually take precedence. The potential for conflict is heightened by the episodic nature of most party work, oriented as it is toward electoral competition. Since in Canada the periods between active campaigns are quite lengthy, often lasting three or four years, local parties experience considerable morale problems and the organizations are characterized by a high rate of turnover of personnel.

Democratic norms and customary practice as well as party constitutions usually require that the parties adhere to an "open-door" recruitment policy. Although they are not legally required to admit anyone, the need to maintain and broaden the base of support is a strong inducement for current leaders to accept and actively recruit or coopt representative members from a broad spectrum of social groups, including those who do not traditionally support their respective parties. Given the distinctive features of party organizational structures and functions, recruitment is by no means an easy task. Party officials proceed with the business of acquiring new members much as do other voluntary organizations. People sometimes are coopted, personal friendships are traded on, and when these do not suffice, the prospect of holding a high party position or engaging in interesting and exciting work is held out as an inducement to join. Even so, a considerable number of those recruited by these means join primarily as a convenience to current officials. If recruits of this kind rarely develop a great desire to become contenders for public offices or organizational powers, they also do not expect to devote much time or effort to party affairs, as many candidates for parliamentary or for provincial legislative seats have found to their sorrow.

Types of Party Officials

Three types of local party officials may be distinguished. The first, "Stalwarts," occupy middle-level positions of the truncated structures of constituency parties. A second group of officials, "Insiders," are holders of high-level positions in a formal party hierarchy and their principal tasks are to coordinate and supervise the work of Stalwarts. They also engage in a variety of routine record-keeping tasks and they apprise top position-holders and candidates for elected office of the distribution of partisan sentiments among voters, information collected in face-to-face canvassing and other forms of social interaction with the public. Insiders not only coordinate the work of Stalwarts, they also perform some of the same tasks. However, they generally have performed them longer and more effectively. The third category of officials, "Elites," frequently occupy the highest level of organizational positions and they, more often than others, are a party's standard-bearers in an electoral contest or its appointees to nonelective public offices. Most importantly, they are especially influential in party affairs. Although the exact proportions vary somewhat by party, approximately 60 percent of the officials of every party can be classified as Stalwarts, about 30 percent as Insiders, and the rest as Elites.

Analyses indicate Elites more frequently than Insiders or Stalwarts come from high-status backgrounds. These initial socioeconomic-status advantages are maintained and even enhanced over time. Political socialization differences also characterize the three types. Elites, more often than Insiders or Stalwarts, report that they were reared in politicized childhood and adolescent environments. In many cases their parents were politically active and, as a result, future Elites came into contact with a variety of politically involved individuals. Also, Elites tend most frequently to report steadily increasing political interest and involvement prior to joining a party.

The three types of party officials are further differentiated by varying levels of commitment to party work and by their attitudes toward their organizations and themselves. Elites report doing more work, working longer for their parties than Insiders or Stalwarts, and holding both more positions generally and more high-level positions in particular. Such objective differences also are reflected in the subjective reactions of the three types to their experiences. Elites and Insiders more frequently than Stalwarts derive a sense of accomplishment from their party activities and are more likely to view party work as leading to public-office opportunities. Finally, the three groups vary in their conceptions of self, with Elites being the most and Stalwarts the least likely to think of themselves in political terms.

Women are a minority in extraparliamentary party organizations generally and are severely underrepresented in the Insider and Elite categories. By way of illustration, the ratio of Stalwarts to Elites among male officials is approximately 3:1 but there are almost 14 times as many Stalwarts as Elites among women. Since political roles tend to be thought of as male roles in Canada, it is not surprising that women who rise in Insider or Elite status have many of the qualities and attributes that facilitate the political success of men. In fact, women who achieve Elite status manifest higher levels of commitment to party work than their male counterparts.

Since there are so few layers in a constituency party hierarchy through which officials can move upward, the pinnacle of a "Successful" party career for both men and women officials alike is (a) selection as a party candidate in a federal or provincial election, (b) appointment to a federal or provincial judgeship, or (c) appointment to one of the numerous boards, commissions, and advisory groups which are such an integral part of both federal and provincial bureaucracies. In a very real sense, these positions rather than direct monetary compensation are the principal "payoffs" to middle- and upper-middle-class individuals for their organization work in contemporary political parties.

Parties in the Electorate

Only a relatively small number of Canadians are actively involved in party organizations. For the vast majority, affiliations with parties are primarily psychological rather than behavioral. The pervasiveness of these psychological attachments to political parties is illustrated by the fact that in the four existing national election surveys (1965, 1968, 1974, 1979), the proportion of citizens expressing some sense of attachment to a federal political party varies from 86 percent to 91 percent. (See table 1.) It should be noted, however, that the strength of these attachments varies significantly, with only about one-quarter of the respondents in any survey reporting a "very strong" sense of partisanship. In each study, almost as large a proportion (approximately one person in five) indicates that their feelings are either "not very strong" or that they merely feel a "little closer" to one party than to another.

Regarding the direction of party ties, four points are noteworthy. First, consistent with their dominant position in federal politics, the Liberals have the largest number of party identifiers. In the four national surveys the Liberals, on average, have had the allegiance of 47 percent of the electorate, whereas the proportion of persons identifying with the second largest party, the Conservatives, has not exceeded 28 percent. Second, the proportions identifying with the four major federal parties have not varied greatly over time. As measured over the 1965–1979 period the number of Conservative, NDP, and Social Credit identifiers has fluctuated by 4 percent, 2 percent, and 3 percent respectively. Variance in the percentage of Liberal identifiers has been slightly larger, 9 percent. Third, the figures in table 1 mask large regional and provincial differences in patterns of party identification that are consistent with the notion that Canada has not one

TABLE 1

Distribution of Federal Party Identification in Canada in Four National Election Studies
(in percentages)

DIRECTION	INTENSITY	1965	1968	1974	1979
Liberal	Very Strong	11	13	16	13
	Fairly Strong	20	25	23	20
	Not Very Strong or Leaning	12	13	11	9
	Total	43	51	50	42
Progressive					
Conservative	Very Strong	7	7	7	7
	Fairly Strong	14	12	11	15
	Not Very Strong or Leaning	7	7	6	6
	Total	28	26	24	28
NDP	Very Strong	4	4	4	4
	Fairly Strong	6	5	5	6
	Not Very Strong or Leaning	2	2	2	3
	Total	12	11	11	13
Social Credit	Very Strong	2	2	1	1
	Fairly Strong	3	2	1	1
	Not Very Strong or Leaning	1	1	1	1
	Total	6	5	3	3
No Party					
Identification		11	8	12	14
	(N)	(2615)	(2706)	(2343)	(2624)

Figures for some years total more than 100 percent due to rounding.

but several party systems. Illustrative are findings from the 1979 national survey (conducted by H. Clarke, J. Jenson, L. LeDuc and J. Pammett) in which the percentage of identifiers with the federal Liberal party varies from a high of 60 percent in Quebec to a low of 17 percent in Saskatchewan. Conversely, only 9 percent of Quebecers but 61 percent of Albertans identify with the Conservatives. The extent of identification with the NDP also varies substantially, ranging from a low of 1 percent in Prince Edward Island to a high of 26 percent in Saskatchewan.

Finally, in a number of provinces the percentages of identifiers with parties competing at the provincial level vary sharply with the percentages identifying with the same parties when they compete in federal elections. The 1979 survey data illustrate the point: 39 percent of British Columbia residents identified with the Social Credit party in provincial politics but only 3 percent did so federally. Comparable figures for the New Democratic Party in Saskatchewan are 46 percent and 26 percent respectively. Perhaps most dramatic is the Quebec case. Here, 31 percent stated they identified with the Parti Québecois which does not even compete in federal politics. Equally striking is the fact that 38 percent of the Parti Québecois identifiers, supporters of a party dedicated to a politically sovereign Quebec, identify with the federal Liberals who long have stressed their commitment to national unity and a strong central government.

Studies of relationships between socioeconomic and demographic variables and party identification have consistently shown that in addition to region, religion and ethnicity are strong correlates of partisanship. In federal politics Roman Catholics and French Canadians tend to be Liberals. Protestants and those of Anglo-Celtic origins divide their loyalties more evenly between the Liberals and the Progressive Conservatives. Supporters of the New Democratic Party tend to be drawn from those with no formal religious affiliations and persons of other than French-Canadian origin. Over time, Social Credit partisanship has shifted so that the party's main base of support in federal politics is composed of Roman Catholic Québecois rather than Protestants residing in the western provinces.

The relationship between social class and partisan identification is considerably weaker, particularly in federal politics. Thus, although upper-middle and middle-class persons tend to be Liberal identifiers, the party's support in the working class also is very substantial. For example, at the federal level in 1979, 39 percent of the electorate labelling themselves working or lower class were Liberal identifiers. The NDP has its largest cohort of supporters among those placing themselves in the working class (18 percent) but 11 percent of middle-class identifiers also are NDP partisans. More generally, regardless of whether objective or subjective measures of social class are utilized, across the country as a whole relationships between such measures and federal partisan identification are weak. Somewhat stronger correlations can be found within particular regions or provinces. For example, in British Columbia, Martin Robin and others have pointed to the importance of class divisions in the electorate in both federal and provincial politics. Similarly, John Wilson has argued that class divisions are becoming increasingly sharp in Ontario and Manitoba. Overall, however, Robert Alford's argument that the class basis of party politics is weaker in Canada than in other Anglo-American democracies continues to receive strong empirical support.

Split and Unstable Party Attachments

It was observed above that a large number of Canadians have divided or "split" partisan attachments. Nationally, 22 percent of the 1979 electorate reported different federal and provincial party identifications, 11 percent maintained an identification at one level only, and 8 percent did not have a party identification at either level. As might be expected, levels of congruence between federal and provincial identifications differ markedly across provinces. (See table 2.) In the 1979 national election survey, in the Atlantic provinces no more than 13 percent (Newfoundland) identify with different parties at the federal and provincial levels. In sharp contrast, in Quebec 31 percent and in British Columbia fully 50 percent of the respondents report different federal and provincial party identifications. Survey data drawn from earlier studies are generally similar (for example, 18 percent of all partisans reported split identifications in 1974). Research in federal systems such as Australia and the United States has failed to reveal large numbers of split identifiers, suggesting that this aspect of the linkage between citizen and party in Canada may well be unique.

TABLE 2

Patterns of Federal and Provincial Party Identification by Province, 1979 (in percentages)

PROVINCE (N)		SAME FEDERAL & PROVIN CIAL IDENTIFI CATION	DIFFER ENT FEDERAL & PROVIN CIAL IDENTIFI CATION	FEDERAL IDENTIFI CATION ONLY	PROVIN CIAL IDENTIFI CATION ONLY	NO IDENTIFI CATION
Newfoundland	(112)	82	13	2	2	2
Prince Edward Island	(109)	80	4	2	2	13
Nova Scotia	(195)	76	6	1	7	10
New Brunswick	(144)	69	8	3	1	19
Quebec	(724)	48	31	4	10	7
Ontario	(747)	69	14	7	4	7
Manitoba	(131)	65	16	4	5	10
Saskatchewan	(108)	57	17	6	7	13
Alberta	(197)	71	15	3	4	7
British Columbia	(277)	35	50	3	8	5
Canada	(2609)	60	22	5	6	8

Figures for some provinces total more than 100 percent due to rounding.

There also is mounting evidence that ties between the electorate and parties may be less stable in Canada than in other relatively similar societies. There are two types of evidence on this point—recalled changes in party identifications and changes that are measured with the use of panel data. Regarding the former, Canadian figures are consistently higher than those of Great Britain or the United States. In the 1979 survey 32 percent of those interviewed indicated changing their federal party identifications one or more times in the past. Comparable figures for the United States are 21 percent and 26 percent in the 1976 and 1972 surveys respectively, whereas in Great Britain, data collected over the past fifteen years show that the incidence of recalled changes in party identification varies between 20 percent and 25 percent.

Perhaps a more accurate measure of changes in party identification is provided by studies in which the same respondents are interviewed at different points in time. Data from such inquiries indicate that partisan instability is greater in Canada than in other Anglo-American democracies. Over the 1974–1979 period, at the federal level 34 percent of the Canadian panel respondents either had switched their identifications, or moved between identification and nonidentification (See table 3.) The comparable figure at the provincial level is 38 percent. Similar changes are reported by 20 percent of an American (1972–1976) and 22 percent of a British panel (1970–1974). Canada also differs in having relatively large numbers of two types of people: those who change party identifications, and those who shift between identification and nonidentification. In the United States, one finds a substantial number of the latter but fewer of the former whereas the British pattern is opposite to the American.

TABLE 3

Patterns of Change in Party Identification in National Panel Studies in Canada, the United States, and Great Britain
(in percentages)

COUNTRY	SAME PARTY IDENTIFICATION	DIFFERENT PARTY IDENTIFICATION	IDENTIFIER ↑ NON IDENTIFIER*	IDENTIFIER ↓ NON IDENTIFIER*	(N)
Canada federal	60	16	18	6	(1361)
(1974–79) provincial	58	21	17	4	(1357)
United States (1972–76)	75	7	13	5	(1276)
Great Britain (1970–74)	77	16	6	1	(1077)

*Nonidentifiers are defined as persons who do not "feel closer" to a party at a specified level of government.

Two additional observations may heighten the readers' appreciation of the theoretical significance of the relatively high rates of partisan instability in Canada. The first concerns the forces which encourage persons to change their party identifications. It appears that Canadians are willing to shift their partisan allegiances in response to relatively mundane short-term forces that are part and parcel of the normal political process. When requested to specify the reasons for shifting their federal party identifications, 25 percent of the respondents in the 1974 national election study mentioned party leaders, 31 percent cited issues, 16 percent referred to the parties' performance, but 30 percent cited local or personal matters. Data from this study also reveal that 31 percent of those who had changed reported doing so during the 1974 election campaign itself, and an additional 51 percent cited the 1967–1973 period, which also was characterized by "politics as usual." Data regarding the time of changes in provincial partisan attachments are quite similar.

Second, since partisan change frequently is a function of the short-term forces of normal politics, party identification is very strongly correlated with voting behavior. Thus, in the 1979 federal election, the percentages of Liberal, Conservative, New Democratic, and Social Credit partisans casting ballots for "their" parties were 86 percent, 97 percent, 90 percent, and 77 percent, respectively. Comparable figures for 1974 were 90 percent (Liberal), 92 percent (Conservative), 86 percent (NDP), and 87 percent (Social Credit). These extremely high correlations indicate that changes in party identification and voting behavior "travel together" more frequently in Canada than in some other political systems. National panel data for Canada, Great Britain, and the United States illustrate that Canadian-American differences are particularly salient in this regard (See table 4.) In Canada 14 percent of the 1974–1979 panel respondents switched *both* their party identification and their vote, whereas 7 percent retained their partisan identification but changed their vote. Comparable percentages for the United States are 6 percent and 16 percent respectively. Great Britain occupies an intermediate position with 8 percent of British voters changing both their party identifications and votes, and 9 percent altering their vote while maintaining stable party identification.

TABLE 4

Patterns of Party Identification and Voting Behavior in National Panel Studies in Canada, the United States, and Great Britain
(in percentages)*

Voting Behavior	CANADA (1974–79)		GREAT BRITAIN (1970–74)		UNITED STATES (1972–76)	
	Party Identification Stable	Party Identification Unstable†	Party Identification Stable	Party Identification Unstable†	Party Identification Stable	Party Identification Unstable†
Vote Same Party	51	9	59	6	51	9
Vote Different Party	7	14	8	9	16	6
Vote →Non ←Vote	11	9	12	7	13	5
(N)	(1145)		(1003)		(937)	

*for each country cell percentages are calculated in terms of total panel N. Figures for some countries total more than 100 percent due to rounding.
†unstable party identification includes movement into or out of the status of nonidentifier.

Significance of Party Identification

The strong relationships between party identification and voting, coupled with substantial instability of partisanship, suggest the limited explanatory power of party identification for understanding individual voting behavior and electoral outcomes. To reiterate, the properties of party identification and their relationship to electoral choice indicate that many Canadians lack long-term, firmly rooted, psychological ties to political parties. For many persons, a particular vote decision and a current partisan allegiance *both* reflect the operation of short-term electoral forces. As a result, the outcome of any given election may be in doubt. Research suggests that in most elections the parties simply "exchange" supporters and thus leave the net balance of party strength largely undisturbed. When this is not the case and the shifts in partisan attachments are asymmetric, a governing party may be forced to leave office. The 1979 election is a case in point. Over the 1974–1979 period panel data indicate that 15 percent of those voting in both elections shifted away from the governing Liberal party while only 7 percent shifted to them. The victorious Conservatives, in contrast, gained 12 percent but lost only 5 percent.

More dramatic disturbances in the balance of partisan forces occur at the provincial level. As noted earlier, the Social Credit party dominated provincial politics in Alberta from 1935 to 1971 but less than a decade later (in 1979) only 5 percent of Albertans identified with the provincial Social Credit Party. In Quebec, the once mighty Union Nationale, the governing party as recently as 1970, now claims the partisan allegiance of only 3 percent of the electorate. In contrast, the Parti Québecoise, formed in 1967, gained power in 1976 and currently claims the loyalties of over 30 percent of the electorate.

The case of the Parti Québecois also serves to illustrate a third element of change in public support for political parties. Many studies have shown that support for the Parti Québecois is strongly age-related. In the 1979 election study, for example, the percentage of PQ identifiers decreased monotonically from 53 percent among persons in the 18–25 age bracket to 14 percent among those 56 and over. An opposite pattern obtains for the Québec Liberals who have more partisans among older-age cohorts. Patterns similar to these obtain for other parties, with the federal Conservatives and New Democrats being good examples. Such party identification-age correlations suggest that long-term demographic processes operate hand-in-hand with shorter-term forces to structure the configuration of party systems at particular points in time. Although a realignment of electoral forces may be delayed or perhaps even permanently deflected by the weak, often ephemeral qualities of partisan attachments, over time, replacement of the electorate can serve as the impetus for more enduring changes at both levels of the federal system.

Scholars have pointed to the volatility of the electorate and argued that it illustrates the failure of the parties to integrate the policy by, for example, formulating issues whose attractiveness could transcend provincial and regional cleavages and the particularities on which they rest. This and other criticisms of the performance of the parties are not without merit. On the other hand, it is doubtful, to say the least, that the parties could exercise the kind of powerful independent and transformative effects on the political system that some critics desire. Indeed, given the historic skewness in the numerical and ethnic-religious distributions of the population across the several provinces, the incompatibility of federal and parliamentary forms of government, persistent regional economic disparities, and the other centrifugal forces currently operative in Canadian society, it can be argued that what is most notable about the parties is that over the years they have been able to exercise more than a modicum of influence on the political system's operation. They are unlikely to become powerful and independent variables in the future.

Bibliography

Robert R. Alford. *Party and Society: The Anglo-American Democracies.* Rand McNally, Chicago, 1963.

Harold D. Clarke. "Partisanship and the Parti Quebecois: The Impact of the Independence Issue." *American Review of Canadian Studies,* vol. 8, 1978, pp. 28–47.

———, Jane Jenson, Lawrence LeDuc, and John Pammett. *Political Choice in Canada.* McGraw-Hill Ryerson, Toronto, 1979.

———, Richard G. Price, Marianne Stewart, and Robert Krause. "Motivational Patterns and Differential Participation in a Canadian Party: The Ontario Liberals." *American Journal of Political Science,* February 1978, pp. 135–51.

John C. Courtney. *The Selection of National Party Leaders in Canada.* Macmillan, Toronto, 1973.

Frederick C. Engelmann and Mildred A. Schwartz. *Canadian Political Parties: Origin, Character, Impact.* Prentice-Hall, Scarborough, Ontario, 1975.

J. A. Irving. *The Social Credit Movement in Alberta.* University of Toronto Press, Toronto, 1959.

Allan Kornberg, Joel Smith, and Harold D. Clarke. *Citizen Politicians—Canada: Party Officials in a Democratic Society.* Carolina Academic Press, Durham, 1979.

——— and William Mishler. *Influence in Parliament: Canada.* Duke University Press, Durham, 1976.

———, William Mishler, and Joel Smith. "Political Elite and Mass Perceptions of Party Locations in Issue Space: Some Tests of Two Positions." *British Journal of Political Science,* vol. 5, 1975, pp. 161–85.

Joseph LaPalombara and Myron Weiner, eds. *Political Parties and Political Development.* Princeton University Press, Princeton, 1966, chap. 1.

Seymour M. Lipset. *Agrarian Socialism: The Cooperative Commonwealth Federation in Saskatchewan.* Anchor Books, New York, 1968.

C. B. Macpherson. *Democracy in Alberta: Social Credit and the Party System.* University of Toronto Press, Toronto, 1962.

Kenneth McRoberts and Dale Posgate. *Quebec: Social Change and Political Crisis.* McClelland and Stewart, Toronto, 1980.

John Meisel. *Working Papers on Canadian Politics,* 2d enl. ed. McGill-Queen's University Press, Montreal, 1975.

William Morton. *The Progressive Party in Canada*. University of Toronto Press, Toronto, 1963.

Norman Penner. *The Canadian Left: A Critical Analysis*. Prentice-Hall, Scarborough, 1977.

George Perlin. *The Tory Syndrome*. McGill-Queen's University Press, Montreal, 1980.

Maurice Pinard. *The Rise of a Third Party: A Study in Crisis Politics*. Prentice-Hall, Englewood Cliffs, 1971.

John Porter. *The Vertical Mosaic: An Analysis of Social Class and Power in Canada*. University of Toronto Press, Toronto, 1965, chapts. 12–14.

Robert Presthus. *Elite Accomodation in Canadian Politics*. Macmillan, Toronto, 1973.

Herbert F. Quinn. *The Union Nationale: A Study in Quebec Nationalism*. University of Toronto Press, Toronto, 1963.

Escott M. Reid. "The Rise of National Parties in Canada." *Papers and Proceedings of the Canadian Political Science Association*, vol. 4, 1932, pp. 187–200.

Martin Robin. *Canadian Provincial Politics: The Party Systems of the Ten Provinces*, 2d ed. Prentice-Hall, Scarborough, Ontario, 1978.

Michael Stein. *The Dynamics of Right Wing Protest: Social Credit in Quebec*. University of Toronto Press, Toronto, 1973.

Hugh Thorburn, ed. *Party Politics in Canada*, 4th ed. Prentice-Hall, Toronto, 1979.

Frank Underhill. *In Search of Canadian Liberalism*. University of Toronto Press, 1960.

Reginald Whitaker. *The Government Party*. University of Toronto Press, Toronto, 1977.

John Wilson. "The Canadian Political Cultures: Toward a Redefinition of the Nature of the Canadian Political System." *Canadian Journal of Political Science*, vol. 7, 1974, pp. 438–83.

Conrad Winn and John McMenemy. *Political Parties in Canada*, McGraw-Hill Ryerson, Toronto, 1976.

Walter Young. *The Anatomy of a Party: The National C.C.F., 1932–1961*. University of Toronto Press, Toronto, 1969.

Leo Zakuta. *A Protest Movement Becalmed: A Study of Change in the C.C.F.*. University of Toronto Press, Toronto, 1964.

Political Parties

ACTION LIBERALE NATIONALE. *See* UNION NATIONALE.

BLOC POPULAIRE. *See* PARTI QUÉBECOIS.

COMMUNIST PARTY. The Communist Party of Canada was formed in 1921 shortly after the Russian Revolution by members of three small socialist parties—the Socialist Party of Canada, the Social-Democratic Party of Canada, and the Socialist Party of North America. After the expulsion of its leading theorist, Maurice Spector, in 1928 and its general secretary, Jack MacDonald, in 1929, the party became the creature of the Communist International. Under the guidance of long-time leader Tim Buck, the party faithfully tried to adapt its strategies and tactics to the prevailing Stalinist line.

Similar to its counterpart in the United States, the Communist Party of Canada has played a negligible role in electoral politics. While Communist candidates often stand for election, in only a handful of instances have they been successful. Perhaps their chief electoral impact has been to occasionally embarrass the CCF and later the NDP by endorsing their candidates. More important than its electoral efforts has been the party's involvement in trade union activities, particularly in the 1930s and 1940s when it battled the CCF for influence in the new industrial unions some of its members had helped to organize.

Early in World War II the party was declared illegal under the Defense of Canada Regulations. However, in 1943, altered international political circumstances, principally the wartime alliance with the Soviet Union, provided the party with an opportunity to renew its public activities. At this time its name was changed to the Labor Progressive Party, thus avoiding the need to force the government into the embarrassing position of having to retract its order banning the party.

Always small in numbers, the Communist Party became a very minor actor on the Canadian political stage after World War II. Postwar affluence, the cold war, and rigid adherence to an unimaginative Stalinist orthodoxy doomed the party to increasing irrelevance. Although the party continues to exist, and even to offer candidates in several of the larger urban areas, it has only the most marginal impact on Canadian political life.

CONSERVATIVE PARTY. *See* PROGRESSIVE CONSERVATIVE PARTY.

COOPERATIVE COMMONWEALTH FEDERATION (CCF). *See* NEW DEMOCRATIC PARTY.

LABOR PROGRESSIVE PARTY. *See* COMMUNIST PARTY.

LIBERAL PARTY. The ancestors of the present Liberal Party were rural and small town, nonestablished church, and moderate reform groups in Ontario, and antibusiness, anticlerical, relatively radical reform elements in Quebec. Under the leadership of Alexander Mackenzie, the "Grits," as they then were generally termed, were able to oust Macdonald and his Tory colleagues in the election of 1874. Although the Liberals benefited in this election from a financial scandal involving the Conservatives and the Canadian Pacific Railroad Company, to whom Macdonald had awarded a charter and contract to build a transcontinental railroad, the attractiveness of the proposed railroad, especially to the people of the new provinces of Manitoba and British Columbia, helped bring about a Liberal defeat in 1878.

Denied victory in three successive national elections, the party turned its attention to building grass-roots strength in the provinces. By the time it came to power in 1896, it controlled the government of every province but Quebec. Even in the latter province, however, Wilfrid Laurier had broadened the base of

Liberal support by purging it of more extreme anticlerical elements and making it palatable to the traditional doctor-lawyer elites of the small towns. So impressive was Laurier's performance that a national convention on the American model chose him party leader in 1893. A combination of his own political skills, economic prosperity, and the chauvinism generated by the inclusion of the union of the new western provinces of Saskatchewan and Alberta kept his Liberal administration in office from 1896 to 1911. His downfall is usually ascribed to the alienation of isolationist elements within Quebec (who objected to his proposal to begin building a Canadian navy) and the loss of important business support in Ontario because he had championed limited reciprocal free trade with the United States.

The party was deeply divided during World War I over the issue of conscription for overseas service. French-speaking Liberals, including Laurier himself, were opposed; their English-speaking colleagues, in contrast, generally were in favor, and a number of prominent Liberals actually joined with the governing Conservatives in a coalition Unionist government during the wartime election of 1917. Laurier retired at the end of the war and in a leadership convention held in 1919, William Lyon Mackenzie King was elected leader. By 1921 he was prime minister of a minority Liberal government.

King, who was to serve as prime minister for nearly a quarter of a century, spent his first years in office resolving differences between Liberals and members of the newly formed Progressive Party and bringing some of the Liberals-turned-Progressives back into the party fold. Apparently such a task was consistent with King's political philosophy. He viewed the party primarily as a mechanism for mediating and resolving intergroup conflicts and only secondarily as a vehicle for generating and implementing public policy. Even if King's style was to react rather than to innovate, the foundation of much of Canada's welfare program was laid during his tenure as prime minister. This program, together with other redistributive measures, as well as policies intended to broaden the industrial base of the Canadian economy, were pursued by King's successor, Louis St. Laurent, during the years 1948–1957. With regard to industrial and economic expansion policies, it was the insistence of the Liberals (particularly of King's long-time cabinet colleague, C. D. Howe) in pursuing what they regarded as a necessary and highly desirable development policy, but which the opposition parties regarded as a raid on the treasury, that led to the famous "Pipeline" debate, the invoking of cloture, and the Liberal defeat in the election of June 1957.

St. Laurent retired after the 1958 election and was succeeded by Lester B. "Mike" Pearson, an experienced diplomat and recipient of the Nobel Peace Prize. Pearson—although he enjoyed great popularity with party regulars and ordinary citizens alike—was unable during the ten years he led the party to translate his personal popularity into a majority victory at the polls. Unable to win a majority of Commons seats, he gave way in 1968 to the party's current leader, Pierre Elliot Trudeau.

Liberal fortunes have fluctuated during Trudeau's stewardship of the party. A smashing victory in the 1968 election was followed by near defeat and reduction to minority government status in 1972. Another solid victory in 1974 was followed by the progressive erosion of his own and his government's popularity and electoral defeat in 1979. The latter defeat, personal problems, and weariness after a decade in office led him to announce his resignation. However, the unexpected Commons defeat of the Conservative government's first budget, the dissolution of parliament, and the pleas of party leaders induced him to stay on as party leader. In this capacity he led his party to a majority victory in the 1980 election. How long he will continue as party leader and prime minister is highly problematic.

NEW DEMOCRATIC PARTY (NDP). Formed in 1932, the CCF (Cooperative Commonwealth Federation), the predecessor of the NDP, was at once a "party" and a "movement." This was the source of both its strength and its weakness. In the Regina Manifesto, drafted at the party's first convention in 1933, the CCF declared its adherence to the principles of democratic socialism — the ideology of those academics and intellectuals in the League for Social Reconstruction (also founded in 1932) who were instrumental in founding the party although the League as such was never affiliated with the CCF. As a vehicle of political protest, the party quickly claimed the support of many of the groups (principally farmers and workers) who had been attracted to the Progressive Party in the 1920s. Led by J. S. Woodsworth, the CCF contested elections at the federal level and in several provinces during the 1930s and 1940s. Although not able to effect dramatic electoral breakthroughs in national politics, the party established itself as a prominent feature on the political landscape. Provincially, the CCF fared considerably better, particularly in Saskatchewan, where it captured power in 1944.

After achieving its greatest federal electoral success in 1945 (capturing 28 seats), the CCF's dream of establishing a socialist commonwealth through the mechanism of parliamentary democracy slowly faded. Postwar prosperity, the cold war, and continuing frustration at the ballot box led the party to moderate its ideological pronouncements and electoral platforms, a trend culminating in the 1956 Winnipeg Declaration in which the party agreed to accept and support a "mixed" private-public economy. Ideological stagnation and the lengthy series of electoral disappointments finally produced a reconstruction of the party in 1961 as the NDP (New Democratic Party). In founding the NDP, CCF leaders attempted to broaden the political base of their old party by uniting with major labor unions in the Canadian Labor Congress. It was hoped that the party would be able to reduce its traditionally heavy reliance on rural support in the west and become a strong political force in the industrialized, urban areas of central Canada.

Under the guidance of the long-time CCF premier of Saskatchewan, Tommy Douglas, the NDP tried to present itself as a viable alternative to the two older "centrist" parties — the Liberals and the Conservatives. To build a solid mass base, the party adopted a step-by-step strategy, directing its limited resources to selected ridings where there were meaningful opportunities for electoral success. Throughout the 1960s and 1970s the NDP was able to capture an average of 23 seats in successive federal elections, but the gradualist strategy did not produce any demonstrable cumulative gains.

While remaining a third force in federal politics, the party has had some major successes at the provincial level. After a brief hiatus in the 1960s the NDP regained power in Saskatchewan—stronghold of its predecessor, the CCF. It also formed provincial governments in British Columbia (1972) and Manitoba (1969), and has become a major contender in Ontario. However, the party has been unable to effect breakthroughs in provincial politics in the Maritimes or Quebec. The same is true federally in these regions, although recently the party has finally shown meaningful electoral muscle at the federal level in Newfoundland.

Ideologically, the NDP has continued to tread a cautious path characteristic of the CCF in its declining years. This tendency has found strong support from "pragmatic" labor leaders in the CLC who occupy positions of considerable influence in the new party. At the same time, however, the NDP's ideological stance has been subjected to vigorous criticism from within by a number of academics and intellectuals (dubbed the "Waffle Movement"). The Waffle gained strength quickly during the late 1960s and early 1970s, articulating a platform which called for a return to basic socialist principles and greatly expanded emphasis on Canadian nationalism. It was the latter that seemed to have particular resonance. Essentially, the Waffle contended that nationalism, expressed through such traditional socialist programs as the nationalization of industry as well as by a vastly expanded Canadian content in the mass media and other vehicles of popular culture, was the precondition for building an independent socialist Canada. Internecine struggles between the Waffle and less radical elements in the NDP cultimated in 1973 with the defeat and expulsion of Waffle forces in the Ontario wing of the party. Although disbanded as an organizational element within the party, ex-Waffle members and sympathizers have continued to argue that neither the NDP nor Canada will achieve its potential until the present course of ideological moderation is abandoned.

At present, the NDP's future is uncertain. National party leaders Tommy Douglas (1961–1971), David Lewis (1971–1975), and Edward Broadbent (1975–present) have maintained a low ideological profile. In the 1979 and 1980 elections this approach yielded 26 and 32 seats respectively. Although the latter figure represents a new high, the party's caucus still constitutes less than 12 percent of the membership of the House of Commons.

Provincially, the party retains power in Saskatchewan, but has been displaced in British Columbia and Manitoba. In Ontario, the NDP is strong in several major urban areas, but few would argue that it is on the verge of seizing power. Prospects in other provinces remain dim. Basically, the NDP is operating in a matrix of social, economic, and political forces beyond its control and is unlikely to be able to implement its ideological goals in the foreseeable future. As a result, its ability to command a continuing commitment from party activists who have seen it as the logical vehicle for the achievement of socialism in Canada is problematic.

PARTI CRÉDITISTE. *See* SOCIAL CREDIT PARTY.

PARTI QUÉBECOIS (PQ). Formed in 1968, the Parti Québecois rallied disparate separatist elements in Quebec, including members of small parties such as the Rassemblement pour L'Independence National (RIN) and the Ralliement National (RN). The RIN and RN differed regarding the future of Quebec, with the former calling for complete independence and the latter opting for associate-state status. In addition, the RN espoused a brand of political and social conservatism quite similar to that of the Social Credit Party, whereas the RIN tended to take positions on the left of the ideological continuum. Both parties, however, manifested a demagogic and populist political style at odds with the technocratic approach of many of the ex-Liberal nationalists who rallied to René Lévesque, a former cabinet minister in the "Quiet Revolution" government of Premier Jean Lesage. Still neither ideological nor stylistic differences prevented these groups from offering enthusiastic support to the Parti Québecois. Under the dynamic leadership of Lévesque the PQ came to the forefront of Quebec politics within eight years. The party's meteoric rise to power culminated in November 1976, with the election of a majority PQ government (69 of the 110 seats, 41 percent of the popular vote). Avowedly dedicated to the establishment of a sovereign Quebec, the PQ in power plunged Canada into its present constitutional crisis.

Politically, sovereignty is viewed by the *Pequistes* as the sine qua non for the realization of Québecois economic, political, and cultural aspirations. In this respect, the party differs from early Quebec nationalist parties such as the Bloc Populaire (a short-lived nationalist party formed in Quebec during World War II to oppose conscription) or the Union Nationale, which were content, or at least resigned, to trying to *defend* the interests of Québecois within the framework of Canadian federalism. In emphasizing the positive role of the Quebec state as the vehicle for the *advancement* of nationalist goals, the PQ has carried to its logical conclusion the ideological reorientation in Quebec political thought first manifested in the Quiet Revolution of the early 1960s. In essence, this reorientation was twofold. In addition to a commitment to transform Quebec into an economically and technically advanced urban secular society, it defined the province as the true "homeland" of the Québecois "nation." *Only* within Quebec, it was argued, could French-Canadians become *maitres chez nous* that the Quiet Revolution initially had envisaged.

Beyond a strong consensus on sovereignty and the instrumental role of the state for achieving this and other goals, the Parti Québecois manifests considerable ideological heterogeneity within its ranks. Although many members of the party's elite (including Lévesque himself) have described themselves as social democrats, since coming to power the PQ has done relatively little to implement redistributive policies. In this respect, there is reason to believe that the party's record in office has disappointed many younger PQ militants who are both nationalists and socialists. To date, arguments about the need to design all government policies in such a way as to facilitate the achievement of sovereignty have succeeded in muting ideological struggles within the party. How long such arguments will prove compelling is unknown.

In striving to attain sovereignty, the PQ has consciously pursued a strategy of *étapisme,* that is, it has tried to proceed in a step-by-step fashion. This strategy frankly recognized that a majority of the Quebec population did not favor independence. However, PQ leaders calculated that over time public opinion would swing in their favor if they could allay fears regarding Quebec's ability to survive and prosper as an independent entity. To this end, the party stressed two principal themes. First, it developed the concept of sovereignty association. In brief, this concept, if implemented, would make Quebec a sovereign state, but one which would retain economic ties with Canada. Presumably, sovereignty association would assuage those concerned about the economic viability of an independent Quebec. Second, the party has tried to present an image of competence and rationality: that it has the ability to govern a modern industrial state. Indeed some Péquiste leaders have rationalized their moderation regarding social policies in terms of the need to avoid a radical image that might frighten away much-needed foreign capital and thereby throw the Quebec economy into a tailspin for which the party would be blamed.

To establish its "good government" image and propagate the wisdom of a sovereign Quebec, the PQ estimated that it had to move slowly and cautiously. Thus, the promised referendum on sovereignty association was deferred for nearly four years after the party captured power. Even this was not enough. On 20 May 1980, voters denied the PQ a mandate to negotiate sovereignty association by a decisive margin (60 percent voted no). Analyses indicate that the result was not merely a byproduct of overwhelming Anglophone opposition, but rather that even among Québecois, a majority rejected the proposition. In the aftermath of the referendum, both the *etapiste* strategy and the PQ itself were in at least temporary disarray. The party's future is not necessarily bleak. First, the PQ remains in power and public opinion polls have consistently shown it to be considerably more popular than the idea of sovereignty. Second, there is the possibility that outside of Quebec the results of the referendum will be misconstrued. While a majority of Québecois have rejected sovereignty association, only a small minority are in favor of the status quo. If the prime minister and provincial government leaders outside of Quebec should fail to negotiate a "renewed federalism" satisfactory to Quebec, Levesque may yet be able to convince a majority of Québecers of the wisdom of the PQ option.

Third, there is reason to believe that support for the party and its policies may grow both relatively and absolutely. The core of PQ support comes from young, well-educated professionals, many of whom currently occupy key positions in the mass media and various educational and cultural institutions. Others will occupy such positions in the near future. These young professionals are committed to the goal of a sovereign Quebec and can be expected to propagate their faith to the society generally and to younger Québecois in particular. In contrast, persons supporting the Liberals or other federalist parties tend to be older, less well-educated, and not in positions to mold public opinion. Over time, socialization and demographic processes may yet yield the PQ the *independentiste* majority needed to create the new state of Quebec. A straw in the wind may be indicated by the return of the PQ to power in the April 1981 election.

PROGRESSIVE PARTY. The Progressives constituted the first "third party" successfully to challenge the Liberal-Conservative duopoly. Similar to the CCF and Social Credit, the Progressive Party was largely the product of rural discontent. This party received its initial impetus in 1919 when the United Farmers of Ontario were swept into power in the provincial election of that year. This electoral breakthrough stimulated similar agrarian movements in other provinces. The Progressives contested the 1921 federal election under the leadership of former Liberal-Unionist T. A. Crerar, elected sixty-five M.P.s, and became the second largest party in Parliament.

Motivated by the accurate perception that rural interests were overshadowed by those of commerce and industry in the parliamentary caucuses of the two older parties, the Progressives reacted negatively to traditional models of party organization and emphasized grass-roots democracy. Their opposition to party discipline greatly weakened their position in Parliament. Reduced to internecine squabbling, the party quickly lost its drive for power. After a few years a number of Progressive M.P.s joined the Liberals, and by the mid-1920s the Progressives were a spent force in federal politics. Provincially, the Progressives remained important in the prairies, particularly in Alberta and Manitoba. In the former province, the party retained power until displaced by Social Credit in 1935, while in the latter it remained influential well into the 1940s.

PROGRESSIVE CONSERVATIVE PARTY. The Progressive Conservative Party grew out of an 1854 coalition of business-professional and Established Church (Anglican) elites who held sway in Ontario, and ultramontane French-Catholic and Anglo-Scottish business and financial oligarchies in Quebec. Sir John A. Macdonald, the architect of this coalition, used its support to induce a not unwilling British government to pass the British North America Act that in 1867 joined the provinces of Ontario, Quebec, Nova Scotia, and New Brunswick in a federal union that Macdonald with remarkable prescience termed a "confederation." He became the first prime minister of the new state, the Dominion of Canada, and except for a five-year hiatus, remained the head of government until 1891.

It was Macdonald who proposed a series of modernization measures termed the National Policy. The linchpin was a transcontinental railroad, completed in 1885. Other components included the creation of an industrial infrastructure in the Province of Ontario to be nurtered by protective tariffs, the exploitation of the primary resources of the maritime and western regional hinterlands, and the development of interprovincial east-west trade to be carried primarily by the new railroad. The struggle generated by the National Policy was responsible for the hardening of party lines in the House of Commons. It also induced the Conservatives and their parliamentary opponents, the Liberals, to establish contacts with groups of supporters in the electorate and to mobilize these supporters on behalf of party candidates for Parliament and for the several provincial legislatures.

The Conservative government's decision to execute Louis Riel, a Francophone Catholic Métis who was the leader of an aborted rebellion in Saskatchewan in 1885, put severe strains on the Quebec segment of the Conservative coalition. The party's support in Quebec was further eroded because of the government's waffling on the issue of provincial government financial support for Catholic schools. These issues and the death of Macdonald resulted in defeat in the election of 1896. The party remained in the electoral wilderness until 1911 when its new leader, Sir Robert Borden, utilized a combination of antifree trade and anti-American sentiments in Ontario, and isolationism in Quebec, to oust the Liberal government of Wilfrid Laurier.

This alliance dissolved during the conscription crisis of 1917. The bitterness of French Canada over Borden's insistence on conscripting men for overseas service in World War I was not dispelled when he retired and Arthur Meighen, the very symbol of conscription to many French Canadians, became prime minister in 1920. Lacking support in Quebec, the party was defeated in the election of 1921 and remained out of office until 1930. The party's new leader and prime minister, R. B. Bennett, took office at the depth of the depression, and neither his political sagacity nor his attempts to emulate Franklin Roosevelt by proposing a Canadian version of the New Deal were capable of maintaining the party in power. Soundly defeated in 1935, Bennett gave way as leader to R. J. Manion in 1938. Despite Manion's and his successors' (Arthur Meighen, John Bracken, and George Drew) efforts to broaden the base of the party support by—among other actions—changing the party's name to Progressive Conservative, they were unable to defeat the Liberals in the elections of 1945, 1949, and 1953. That task was accomplished by Drew's successor, John Diefenbaker.

Diefenbaker, a small-town Saskatchewan lawyer, was chosen leader of his party in 1956 and led them to a minority government victory in the election of 1957. The next year, largely as a result of his personal charisma ("Follow John" was the Conservatives' principal campaign slogan), the Conservatives won the greatest electoral victory in Canadian history. They suffered a sharp reversal in electoral fortunes in 1962 and were defeated in the 1963 election.

Serious intraparty divisions over the quality of Diefenbaker's leadership led to the "Chief's" replacement by Robert L. Stanfield in 1967. Stanfield, unable to oust the Liberals in 1968, 1972, and 1974, retired under pressure in 1976, and Joe Clark was elected leader in a hotly contested national leadership convention. After two years as Opposition Leader, he led the party to a narrow victory in the

May 1979 election. Clark's status as the country's political leader was short-lived, however. In December 1979 the Conservative finance minister, John Crosbie, introduced a controversial austerity budget in the House of Commons. To the surprise of many observers, the House declared its lack of confidence in the government. In the ensuing February 1980 election, the Liberals swept back into office with a majority government.

RALLIEMENT NATIONAL. See PARTI QUÉBECOIS.

RASSEMBLEMENT POUR L'INDEPENDANCE NATIONAL. See PARTI QUÉBECOIS.

RHINOCEROS PARTY. A comic interloper on the political scene, the Rhinoceros Party provides satirical commentary on Canadian elections. In 1979 the party made a substantial electoral effort, placing candidates on the ballot in approximately 60 ridings. Rhino candidates received 62,623 votes (running ahead of the NDP or Conservatives in six Quebec ridings), thereby becoming at least temporarily the fifth largest electoral force in the country.

An appreciation of the party's humorous bent can be gained from its attempts to run an eight-year-old against David Crombie (Conservative), in Toronto Rosedale. Crombie, formerly mayor of Toronto, had been labelled the "tiny, perfect mayor" by the media. In commenting on their efforts to place the youngster on the ballot, a Rhino spokesman explained to the press that the child was obviously "more tiny" and "more perfect" than Crombie. Be that as it may, the Rhinos were forced to select another candidate and Crombie won Rosedale.

SOCIAL CREDIT PARTY. Similar to the CCF, the Social Credit Party began in 1933 as part of the political protest movement of the 1930s. Unlike the CCF, however, the intellectual roots of Social Credit reside not in democratic socialism, but rather in a mixture of prairie populism and the curious economic theories of the eccentric British engineer, Major Douglas. The deceptive simplicity of Douglas's "A plus B" theorem had considerable resonance for persons hard pressed by the Great Depression. Perhaps even more appealing was Social Credit's promise to end economic woes by distributing periodic "dividends" to increase public purchasing power. More generally, Social Credit doctrine, with its emphasis on the fundamental flaws of modern capitalism and the ineptitude of parliamentary government, dovetailed nicely with the long-standing grievances of many in the western provinces who blamed eastern financial interests and their allies in the Liberal and Conservative parties in Ottawa for the plight of prairie farmers.

Although prevailing social, economic, and political conditions laid the groundwork for the development of the Social Credit movement in the west, the crucial catalyst was provided by the propagation of Social Credit doctrine by the evangelist high school principal, William "Bible Bill" Aberhart. Broadcasting from his Prophetic Bible Institute in Calgary, Aberhart's heady mixture of fundamentalist

Christianity and Social Credit theory quickly found a vast and receptive audience. Aberhart, an organizational genius, quickly converted this doctrinal appeal into a potent political force and succeeded in electing fifty-six MLAs to the sixty-three member Alberta legislature in 1935. Once in power, Aberhart, under pressure from party militants, made limited efforts to implement Social Credit economic policies. These were unsuccessful, overruled by the federal government (using its disallowance power) or declared ultra vires by the Supreme Court. After the late 1930s, the Alberta party regime evolved into a relatively orthodox conservative government—one which remained in power until 1971. Defeated by the Progressive Conservatives in the provincial election of that year, the party's strength diminished rapidly. Today it holds only four seats in the Alberta legislature and shows no signs of revitalization.

Outside of Alberta, Social Credit's major successes have been in British Columbia and Quebec. In the former province, Social Credit came to power (as a minority government) in 1952, largely as a result of a protracted series of political maneuverings by Liberal and Conservative party leaders determined to keep "the socialists" (that is, the CCF) out of office. Operating under their new leader, W. A. C. Bennett, Social Credit contested subsequent elections promising "to oppose equally as strongly the forces of monopoly and the forces of socialism." In fact, however, the party has received strong and continuing support from corporate leaders who perceive it as the only viable "free-enterprise" option in British Columbia politics. This support, and its ability to attract the votes of all those opposing the CCF-NDP, enabled the British Columbia Social Credit Party under Bennett's leadership to remain in office continuously from 1952 to 1972.

After the NDP's victory in the 1972 election, the party reorganized and selected as its new leader William Bennett, the son of the former premier. Popular dissatisfaction with the policies of the NDP government and the performance of Premier David Barrett coupled with the demise of the provincial Liberal and Conservative parties enabled Social Credit to return to office in 1975. The current premier, "Bennett the younger," has shown little regard in practice for either Social Credit or traditional conservative orthodoxies. Instead, the party continues to represent itself as the pragmatic alternative to dogmatic socialism, a tactic that has proved remarkably successful in a province where, by Canadian standards, class cleavages are relatively important. Victorious again in 1979, the party shows no signs of the political sclerosis afflicting Social Credit elsewhere in the country.

In contrast to its western counterparts, the Social Credit party in Quebec (le Parti Créditiste) has been successful primarily at the federal level. Although Social Credit had been active as a political movement in Quebec since the 1940s, it was not until 1962 that the party achieved any significant electoral breakthrough. The party's charismatic leader, Réal Caouette, publicized Social Credit among voters in small towns and rural areas by means of a popular weekly television program he hosted. So successful were his efforts, party candidates captured twenty-six seats in the federal election of that year. Essentially a vehicle of political protest for persons suffering social and economic dislocations during Quebec's Quiet Revolution, continuing Creditiste success during the last two decades must be attributed in large part to the ability of Caouette to express the frustrations of those disaffected from the dominant Liberal party. After his death, the party contested the 1979 and 1980 elections under the leadership of Fabien Roy. Despite the presumed popularity of the new leader, the *Creditiste* caucus was reduced to five M.P.s in 1979. In 1980 the party failed to elect a single member to Parliament.

Provincially, party prospects are also dim. During the mid-1960s, the Creditistes entered an abortive alliance with the right-wing nationalist party, the Ralliement National (RN). After the RN's total failure in the 1966 provincial election, the Social Crediters decided to contest the 1970 election under their own banner. Although 13 Crédiste MNAs were successful in 1970, in 1973 they won only two seats and in 1976 they failed to elect a single candidate. Presently caught between the federalist Liberals and the separatist Parti Québecois, the Creditistes have little room to maneuver and probably will be largely irrelevant in political struggles that will shape Quebec's future.

UNION NATIONALE. Formed in 1936 of Conservatives and dissident Liberals (the Action Liberale Nationale), the Union Nationale employed a combination of economic discontent and charges of corruption to sweep the Liberals from provincial government office after the latter had held power continuously for thirty-nine years. The Union Nationale quickly established itself as the dominant party in Quebec provincial politics and under the leadership of Maurice Dupléssis, the party governed for nineteen of the next twenty-four years.

Although the Union Nationale in the Dupléssis era received strong support from the farmers and the urban working class, it could not be characterized as a left-of-center party. Indeed, Dupléssis opposed state intervention in the economy and actively opposed trade union activity. Party scholars have offered a number of explanations to account for the party's attractiveness to so many Quebec voters for so long a time. It has been argued that the Union Nationale benefited from the special circumstances surrounding its formation in the economically troubled depression years. Severe economic dislocations combined with one-party dominance led disadvantaged groups to seek new political options. The Union Nationale was the only available alternative. To maintain its appeal to workers and farmers, Dupléssis was careful to cultivate the party's populist image as the defender of *les petits* against the *haute bourgeoisie*. The party's success also has been attributed to Dupléssis' persistent efforts to present it as the defender of French-Canadian cultural interests threatened by the expansionist policies of Liberal governments in Ottawa. He was able to identify Quebec provincial Liberals with the policies of their federal namesake—policies opposed by large segments of the Quebec population. Finally, Union Nationale success has been attributed to the astute way in which Dupléssis and his party colleagues used patronage and the pork barrel to build an extensive network of patron-client relationships, particularly in rural areas that were disproportionately favored by the electoral system.

The modernization of Quebec society eroded the basis of the party's appeal. To the extent that the Union Nationale's electoral strength rested on its reputation as the defender of French-Canadian culture, societal transformations attendant upon modernization set in motion a reorientation of Québecois nationalist ideology which tended to make the Union Nationale appeal irrelevant. Under Dupléssis the party had attempted to minimize state intervention in society. In contrast, first the Liberals and then the Parti Québecois relied heavily on the positive use of the instrumentalities of the state to advance both the socioeconomic and the cultural interests of Québecois. Thus, although Daniel Johnson was able to lead the party back to power in 1966, in retrospect his victory appears to have been "a last hurrah," for in the next three provincial elections (1970, 1973, 1976) the Union Nationale managed to capture only 28 of 328 seats. During the 1970s the party found itself ground between the opposing forces of federalism and separatism. As the debate over the future of Quebec unfolded, the resulting polarization of political forces obliterated most of the Union Nationale's remaining support. Electoral failures and a continuing inability to find a popular leader in tune with contemporary ideological trends provide little cause for optimism about the party's future.

UNITED FARMERS OF ONTARIO. *See* PROGRESSIVE PARTY.

Allan Kornberg
Harold D. Clarke

CAYMAN ISLANDS

The Cayman Islands, a British Crown Colony, consist of Grand Cayman (22 miles long, 4 to 8 miles broad), Little Cayman (10 miles long, 1 mile wide) and Cayman Brac (12 miles long and 1¼ miles wide). They are located 200 miles northwest of Jamaica.

The Caymans were apparently unoccupied when Columbus first discovered them, when blown off course on his way from Panama to Hispaniola, on 10 May 1503. The Spaniards did not settle them, and it was 1658 before a group of British colonists arrived from Jamaica. However, thirteen years later the British withdrew from the island, because of the impossibility of protecting them from pirates and other marauders. In the eighteenth century they continued to be a favorite haven for pirates, including Sir Henry Morgan and Blue Beard.

Effective British authority was finally established over the Caymans in the latter part of the eighteenth century. Until 1962 they were governed as a dependency of Jamaica. When Jamaica became independent in that year, the Caymans were made a separate Crown Colony at the request of their inhabitants.

The population of the Cayman Islands is estimated to be about 15,000 (1980). The majority of the indigenous population is wholly or partly of African origin. However, a substantial minority, perhaps approaching one-third, is of European origin, principally British. There are also many resident foreigners, some of them immigrants from Jamaica; others from the United States, Great Britain and Canada. Most of these last are business or professional people.

Agriculture has never particularly prospered in the Cayman Islands, with their coral base. However, at the present time there is some growing of garden crops for local consumption.

The economy of the Cayman Islands is now based on offshore banking and tourism. With absolutely no direct taxes except a $10-a-year head tax, the colony has become one of the world's most important tax havens. Over three hundred banking and allied firms are estimated to be conducting business in the islands.

Tourism began to develop substantially in the mid-1960s. It was estimated that by 1980 some 200,000 tourists were visiting the colony each year. Deep sea diving is the tourist specialty of the Caymans. In the late 1970s tourism took a different direction, with the construction of condominiums.

Universal adult suffrage was introduced in 1951. At that time, the legislative

221

assembly consisted of twelve elected members, two to three nominated members, and three officials. The executive council included only two elected members of the assembly.

Under the present constitution, introduced in 1969, there exists a legislative assembly consisting of twelve elected members chosen on a constituency basis, ten of the constituencies being on Grand Cayman, with Little Cayman and Cayman Brac having one each. There is also an executive council presided over by the governor (an appointee of the British Crown), and made up of four of the elected members of the legislative assembly, together with the attorney general, chief colonial secretary and the financial secretary, who are all British civil servants.

Although the executive council is not officially a cabinet, and its members are not ministers, it in fact functions as a cabinet. Each of the four elected members has charge of a portfolio, that is, has administrative control over a part of the government's business. Together, these four agree on policies to be pursued by the government, and the governor accepts the "advice" offered by the four elected members. However, the governor still has administrative control of the police, the courts, finances, and foreign affairs.

No sentiment has developed for independence. Elected representatives of the Cayman Islands government, along with the governor, appeared before the United Nations' Committee of 24, dealing with decolonization, in 1979, and advised the committee that the people did not desire any substantial change in their status. However, this did not deter the committee from recommending independence for the islands.

At the present time there are no political parties in the Cayman Islands. However, in the 1950s, soon after introduction of universal adult suffrage, two parties did exist, the National Democratic Party and the Christian Democratic Party. Although by the late 1960s formal party organization had disappeared, elements formerly aligned with the National Democratic Party still constituted a majority in the legislative assembly until the election of 1976.

In 1971 J. M. Bodden, a leading businessman, established a new political movement which, however, did not take the form of a political party and did not have a name. Bodden, the grandson of two former governors of the colony, had returned home in 1963 after many years in the United States during which he had been an organizer for the National Maritime Union, the United Steel Workers, and the Teamsters Union, and had also had a business career. Upon returning to the Cayman Islands, Bodden entered the real estate business and within a few years was one of the wealthiest men of the territory.

The political group established by Bodden was frankly conservative. It supported free enterprise and the development of the islands by indigenous and international business. It also strongly supported continued association of the Cayman Islands with the United Kingdom.

In its first try at the polls, in 1972, the Bodden group won five seats in the legislative assembly. Four years later, the group won all twelve seats and Bodden became the unofficial leader of the government.

In all three elections in which it participated, the political group headed by J. M. Bodden was faced in each constituency with an organized opposition. However, these opponents did not officially establish a political party. An attempt by James Brandon, an electrical engineer, to establish a labor party in the late 1970s was a failure.

Bibliography

Personal contacts of the writer.
International Investment Services. *Under All Is the Land.* Grand Cayman, 1980.

Political Parties

CHRISTIAN DEMOCRATIC PARTY. The Christian Democratic Party existed in the late 1950s and early 1960s but had disappeared by the middle 1960s. It was the smaller of the two parties of the period. It favored affiliation of the Cayman Islands with the West Indian Federation.

NATIONAL DEMOCRATIC PARTY. The majority party during the late 1950s and early 1960s, the National Democratic Party was led by Warren Connolly, a lawyer and by Norman Panton. It successfully opposed affiliation of the Cayman Islands with the West Indian Federation. Elements formerly associated with the National Democratic Party continued to control the legislative assembly until 1976, although the party itself had disappeared some years before. They held seven of the twelve seats during the 1972–1976 legislature.

Robert J. Alexander

CHILE

Chile, the "shoestring republic," clings to the western side of the Andean mountain chain for a length of 2,485 miles and an average width of only 110 miles.

The Spaniards first invaded Chile from Peru in 1536. Subsequently, they more or less effectively occupied and settled the central part of the country. During the colonial period, Chile was administered as a subdivision of the Viceroyalty of Peru. Racial intermixing between the Spanish conquerors and the Indians began virtually from the onset of the conquest, and it has continued ever since. The result is that the great majority of the population of Chile consists of mestizos, that is, people of mixed European and Indian ancestry. However, in the nineteenth and twentieth centuries there was some immigration, principally from Europe.

In spite of the peculiar geography of Chile, and the mixed elements in its population, one of the striking things about the nation is the sense of homogeniety of its people. The feeling of national identity is as strong in the far north as it is in the center or in Magallanes and is shared by the people regardless of their national or ethnic origins.

During the colonial period an oligarchical type of society developed. People of predominantly Spanish ancestry—many of them Basques, so that even today a substantial percentage of upperclass Chileans have Basque names—became the country's large landowners and merchants. They tended to dominate the economic and social life of the country, although as long as Spanish rule was maintained, political and ecclesiastical control remained in the hands of people sent over from Spain. Once the Spanish rule had been thrown off, the indigenous aristocrats added political control to the economic and social eminence which they already possessed.

During most of the country's history as an independent republic, the Chilean aristocracy showed an amazing ability to make enough concessions to rising groups challenging its control to give those groups a role in the economic, social, and political system without completely jeopardizing the position of the aristocracy. In this, they could be compared with their counterparts in Great Britain. However, in its proclivity for producing many diverse political groups, and endless political coalitions, the Chilean political system could be compared to that of the French Third and Fourth Republics.

The political history of Chile since independence falls into a number of clearly definable periods. The first of these went from the outbreak of the independence movement in 1810 until the 1830s. It was marked by bitter struggles between two predominant political currents, centering at first on two major leaders of the independence struggle, Bernardo O'Higgins and José Miguel Carrera. The first of these was broadly "liberal" in its outlook, being somewhat anticlerical and more or less associated with the notions of economic liberalism. It included some advocates of federalism. The second group was more or less closely aligned with the Roman Catholic Church, stood for a highly centralized form of government, and saw a larger role for the state in economic affairs.

Carrera, having sought refuge in Argentina, was executed there by orders of the Argentine government in 1821. Bernardo O'Higgins, after serving some time as Supreme Director of the Chilean government, was forced out in 1823, and went into exile in Peru, where he died some years later. However, the successors to these two men continued to fight for control, and the decade of the 1820s was marked by a series of coups and countercoups.

The last successful seizure of power by the more conservative group, known popularly as the *pelucones* ("the wigged ones"), took place in 1830. After some difficulties, the pelucones established what has come to be known as the Conservative Republic. This found its clearest expression in the constitution of 1833, which provided for a very strong president and a relatively weak congress. However, the congress had two important powers which limited the authority of the president. It had to approve the annual budget, and it had to give permission periodically to the president to station troops within fifty kilometres of Santiago, the capital.

The real founder of the Conservative Republic and author of the constitution of 1833, was undoubtedly Diego Portales, a man who can be compared in Chilean history with Alexander Hamilton in the history of the United States. Neither man ever became president, but both served as key policy-making members of the cabinet for extended periods—Portales holding the ministry of treasury, interior, and war at various times between 1830 and 1837. Both men believed in a strong central government and sought to harness the interests of the dominant economic forces of the time to its support. Both men were assassinated by their political enemies.

During the Conservative Republic power remained firmly in the hands of the rural-commercial oligarchy, although some new class groups were beginning to appear. Although there were several attempted armed revolts during the period, none succeeded, and the basis was laid for the tradition that the reins of government were to be passed peacefully from one president to his elected successor. Three men, each of whom served two five-year terms, were president during the Conservative Republic.

It was during this 1831–1861 period that real political parties began to emerge. Although they certainly did not clearly represent different economic interest groups or classes, they did take contrasting positions on issues of public policy, particularly with regard to the government's attitude towards the Church, and the relative strength of the president and congress.

With the election of President José Joaquín Pérez in 1861, there began the so-called Liberal Republic, which was to last for another thirty-year period. During the decades of the Liberal Republic, the power of the congress began to grow vis-à-vis the president, and the privileges of the church were substantially limited. It was during this period, too, that Chile fought the successful War of the Pacific and expanded its territory far to the north, acquiring the forbidding but mineral-rich deserts.

During the Liberal Republic, the party system further expanded. For the first time, parties representing some middle-class and artisan groups made their appearance, and a labor movement also was born. The Liberal, Conservative, and National parties of the earlier period were supplemented by the Radical and Democratic parties.

There were several bitter public controversies during the Liberal Republic. Some of these centered on church-state issues, and others around economic matters and the question of how much influence foreign enterprisers should have in the economy. However, the most violent quarrels were between the president of the republic and Congress, over whether the cabinet was responsible to the president or to a majority in Congress. It was this which provoked the revolution of 1891, although the two sides in the struggle also had different positions on a number of other public issues.

When Congress refused to pass a budget for 1891, President José Manuel Balmaceda decreed on 5 January that the budget of the previous year should continue. He also moved troops into Santiago without congressional permission. In retribution, the congressional majority, supported by the navy, rose in revolt, and established a rival government in Iquique. By early September, the congressional forces had won, and one day after the expiration of his constitutional term President Balmaceda, who had taken refuge in the Argentine legation, committed suicide, on 19 September 1891.

The revolution of 1891 and the death of President Balmaceda signaled the beginning of the Parliamentary Republic, which was to last until 1924. During this period the cabinet could not stay in office unless it had a majority in Congress, and the powers of the president were therefore severely limited. The political parties tended to subdivide, and the various segments of them to form coalitions to support or overthrow a cabinet.

During the Parliamentary Republic, the political life of the country was characterized by bossism, with political machines dominating one or another province, usually in alliance with the principal landlords and business interests of the region. These machines sought particular advantages for their provinces and sought to protect those whose economic interests were supported by the machines. A system which permitted political leaders to collect the electoral registration cards of voters and cast their votes for those voters assured the power of the machines.

Until near the end of the Parliamentary Republic, the rural-commercial aristocracy remained firmly in charge of the government. However, during those decades the political parties representing middle- and literate lower-class elements (the literacy franchise prevailed) grew in power, and became increasingly discontented with continued oligarchic domination of political life.

This discontent reached a climax in the election of 1920, in which the paladin of middle- and lower-class forces, Arturo Alessandri, faced Luis Barros Borgoño, the nominee of the oligarchy, in the presidential election. After much dispute over the election results, victory was finally conceded to Arturo Alessandri.

President Alessandri put forth a governmental program calling for an income tax, the separation of church and state, the enactment of a labor code, and various other more or less progressive measures. He was able to achieve few of these, and because of an economic and financial crisis provoked by the postwar decline of the nitrate industry, upon which the government had been almost solely dependent for its revenue, the administration found it hard to pay its bills, including the salaries of civil servants and the military.

The denouement of this crisis was the first successful military move against the government since 1891. Young officers first protested in Congress in an incident which came to be known as "The Rattle of the Sabres," and then formed a military junta. When President Alessandri conferred with them, it was agreed that sixteen laws would be rushed through Congress—including elements of the labor code and a pay increase for the military—after which the soldiers would "return to the barracks." The laws were passed, but when the young officers then refused to dissolve their junta, Alessandri resigned the presidency.

After three months of a military government of senior officers, a further coup by young officers brought the summoning back of Alessandri from exile. Between his return in March 1925 and his second resignation in September, a new constitution was adopted which provided for separation of church and state and substitution of a strong presidency for the parliamentary regime, a central bank was established, and the implementation of the new labor laws was begun.

Alessandri resigned in September 1925 because of the presidential aspirations of one of the leaders of the young officers, Colonel Carlos Ibáñez. In elections held soon afterwards, Ibáñez did not run, but in May 1927 he forced out of office President Emiliano Figueroa Larraín, and soon afterwards was elected president. He remained in office until August 1931, when economic collapse and worker and student unrest brought about his downfall. His four years in office saw the only dictatorship which Chile suffered between 1830 and 1973, but was also marked by large-scale public works during the first three years and by full application of the labor laws of September 1924, which resulted in the growth of a government-authorized labor movement, the adoption of collective bargaining, and the establishment of a social security system, one of the first in Latin America.

Free elections were not characteristic of the Ibáñez regime. When it came time for parliamentary elections in 1930, President Ibáñez called together the leaders of the various legal parties. He let them know that there would be no competitive elections for Congress, and in effect announced to them how many members of the Chamber of Deputies and the Senate each would "elect." Because this meeting took place at a hot springs spa, the Congress resulting from it was popularly dubbed the *Congreso termal*.

Various governments succeeded one another from August 1931 until December 1932. A military regime first held elections which were won by Juan Esteban Montero, who took office in December 1931. He was overthrown on 4 June 1932 by a civilian-military conspiracy which established a "Socialist Republic." During the first twelve days of the Socialist Republic, the regime led by Colonel Marmaduque Grove, one of the young officers of the 1924-1925 period, rallied widespread labor support. In the last 100 days of that regime, presided over by Carlos Dávila, a former supporter of President Ibáñez, backing came more from middle-class elements. The Socialist Republic was overthrown in September 1932 and in December new elections were held. Ex-President Arturo Alessandri, by then a slightly Left-of-Center candidate, was the victor.

The 1931-1932 period was significant because it saw the emergence of new political forces, principally on the Left, in the wake of the Ibáñez regime. A series of small "Socialist" parties, and some new middle-class groupings made their appearance, which signified that the center of gravity of Chilean politics was moving substantially to the Left.

The six years of Arturo Alessandri's administration of the 1930s saw the reestablishment of constitutional government, which was to persist until 1973. It also saw Chile recover from the Great Depression and commence a process of industrialization with some modest support from the Alessandri regime. Copper took its place definitively as the country's principal source of foreign exchange.

Although Alessandri came to power this time principally with the support of the Radical Party, he was forced by political circumstances to rely increasingly for congressional support on the traditional Liberal and Conservative parties. As a consequence, the Radicals moved to the Left, and in 1936 formed the Popular Front with the new Socialist Party, the Communists, and several smaller parties. In 1938 the Popular Front won the presidential election and Pedro Aguirre Cerda became president.

The inauguration of President Aguirre Cerda in 1938 began a period of fourteen years in which the Radical Party was the axis of the government, under three successive presidents belonging to that party, Juan Antonio Ríos and Gabriel González Videla succeeding Aguirre. During those years the government intensively pushed industrialization, including the establishment of a modern steel plant. It also saw the Radical presidents govern with the participation in their cabinets, at one time or another, of virtually every significant party in the country.

By the end of President González Videla's administration in 1952, there was widespread disenchantment in the electorate with all of the political parties, but particularly with the Radicals. As a result, General Carlos Ibáñez was elected president. He had returned from exile in the mid-1930s, run unsuccessfully for president in 1938 and 1942 and had been chosen a senator in the late 1940s. In

1952 he campaigned as a man above and divorced from the parties, and people tended to remember the "law and order" of his earlier regime, and the prosperity of its first two years rather than its dictatorial nature. General Ibáñez' election was also significant because the voting figures showed evidence that peasant voters had voted for Ibáñez in substantial numbers, instead of for the candidates of the Liberal and Conservative parties favored by their landlords, as they had traditionally done. This presaged significant shifts to come.

During the second Ibáñez regime substantial changes occurred in the Chilean political scene. The Law for the Defense of Democracy, which had been passed under González Videla to outlaw the Communist Party (after he had broken with it) was repealed. The size of the electorate was very greatly increased, with the virtual elimination of the literacy qualification for the franchise. (Literate women had been given the right to vote under González Videla). Also, a new Left electoral coalition was established, the Popular Action Front (Frente de Acción Popular—FRAP), which joined together the Socialist, Communist, and other small left-wing parties. It was to play a significant role in the 1958 and 1964 elections and to pave the way for the Popular Unity (Unidad Popular) coalition which won the 1970 election.

The FRAP candidate, Salvador Allende (who had first run for president six years earlier), was the principal opponent in the 1958 election of the nominee of the right-wing parties, Jorge Alessandri, son of the late president, Arturo Alessandri. Alessandri won by a few thousand votes, and during his administration major emphasis was placed on trying to restrain inflation (without great success) and on a public housing program. To conform to the Alliance for Progress, the Alessandri regime also passed an agrarian reform law but redistributed virtually no land.

By 1964 the presidential election campaign was clearly between Salvador Allende, again supported by the FRAP, and Eduardo Frei, the nominee of the Christian Democratic Party. The Frei campaign used the slogan Revolution in Liberty, and his program called for legal unionization of rural workers, a large-scale agrarian reform, "Chileanization" of the big mining enterprises to bring them under majority Chilean government control, and a massive drive to expand and modernize the educational system.

Although the Christian Democratic government of President Frei got under way most of the programs for which it had campaigned in 1964, it did not win the 1970 election. This was due to a number of causes, not the least of which was the presence of Jorge Alessandri, again as the candidate of the Right. The winner was Salvador Allende, this time the candidate of Popular Unity, a coalition of the old affiliates of FRAP plus the Radical Party. He won in 1970 with a smaller percentage of the vote than he had received six years earlier. Although he did not get the majority required under the constitution, his election was confirmed when the parliament was called upon to choose between him and Jorge Alessandri, the runner-up. The Christian Democrats backed Allende, after he had supported passage of legislation and constitutional amendments which presumably assured that a Popular Unity government would not undermine the democratic regime.

President Salvador Allende came to power promising to take the country on "The Chilean Road to Socialism." He pushed through total nationalization of the copper mines, as well as extensive nationalization of other parts of the economy. His regime also launched experiments with worker participation in management of state-owned firms, and completed the agrarian reform provided for in the law passed by the Frei administration. However, his regime was undermined by widespread illegal seizures of land and urban enterprises by elements among his supposed followers, and the government's failure to restrain such activities; by the government's own nationalization of many enterprises not on its original list of firms to be taken over; and by the president's efforts to substitute a Soviet-type parliament for the traditional Chilean Congress and to end the independence of the judiciary. Its position was also imperilled by the virtual disappearance of all foreign exchange reserves and a runaway inflation.

However, the thing which ultimately brought down the Allende government was fear on the part of the military that their monopoly of the instruments of force would be destroyed. There was both widespread arming of the citizenry—of both Left and Right—and open conspiring among enlisted men and junior officers of the navy and air force by elements of the Socialist Party and the far-Left Movement of the Revolutionary Left (Movimiento de la Izquierda Revolucionaria —MIR), and the United Movement of Popular Action (Movimiento de Acción Popular Unido—MAPU).

On 11 September 1973 the Chilean armed forces rose against the Allende government. In the fighting, President Allende himself died during attacks on the presidential palace. A strongly authoritarian military regime headed by Army General Augusto Pinochet was installed, and remained in power more than seven years later.

The military regime established in September 1973 sought to turn back the clock of history. It abolished all political parties, it completely vitiated the urban labor movement and destroyed that of the agricultural workers. It established an all-pervasive secret police force. It undid the agrarian reform of the Frei and Allende governments. It seriously undermined the social security system. It also adopted an economic policy of extreme laissez-faire and free trade. In conformity with this, it proclaimed that any manufacturing industry that could not stand up against competition of imported goods was "artificial" and therefore should perish. It accepted the result of this, the more or less permanent continuance of 12 to 15 percent unemployment (according to official statistics, the real figures being perhaps twice this amount). Finally, it divested the government not only of the firms nationalized by Allende, but most of those which had been built with the aid of the Chilean Development Corporation as well.

In terms of the country's political system, the Pinochet government destroyed more or less completely that which had evolved over the previous century and a half. Eight years after the 1973 coup it remained unclear what the military leaders intended to put in place of that traditional system It also was by no means clear whether the political democracy (and with it, the political parties) which had been swept aside on 11 September 1973 would ever be restored.

Bibliography

Robert J. Alexander. *The Tragedy of Chile.* Greenwood Press, Westport, Conn., 1978.
Lia Cortes and Jordi Fuentes. *Diccionario Politico de Chile.* Editorial Orbe, Santiago, 1967.
Alberto Edwards Vives. *La Fronda Aristocrática.* Editorial del Pacifico, Santiago, 1959.
Federico Gil. *The Political System of Chile.* Houghton Mifflin, Boston, 1966.
George W. Grayson, Jr. *El Partido Demócrata Cristiano Chileno.* Editorial Francisco de
    Aguirre, Buenos Aires, 1968.
Ernst Halperin. *Nationalism and Communism in Chile.* MIT Press, Cambridge, 1965.
Julio César Jobet. *El Partido Socialista de Chile.* 2 vols. Ediciones Prensa Latinoamericana,
    Santiago, 1971.

Political Parties

ACCIÓN NACIONAL. See NATIONAL PARTY.

ACCIÓN POPULAR INDEPENDIENTE. See POPULAR INDEPENDENT ACTION.

ACCIÓN REVOLUCIONARIA SOCIALISTA. See SOCIALIST PARTY.

AGRARIAN LABOR PARTY (PARTIDO AGRARIO LABORISTA). The Agrarian Labor Party was established in 1945 by a merger of the Agrarian Party (Partido Agrario) and the Popular Liberating Alliance (Alianza Popular Libertadora). It was soon afterwards joined by members of the Nationalist Movement of Chile (Movimiento Nacionalista de Chile). From its inception, the party advocated the reorganization of the Chilean government on a corporative or functional basis, a program which was spelled out in several congresses in the years following its establishment.

The Agrario Laboristas had their first electoral triumph in a bye-election for senator in 1945, when its candidate, Jaime Larraín, supported by the Conservative and Liberal parties defeated a nominee of the Left. In the following year, the party participated with the Conservatives and Liberals in a convention to choose a candidate in the election of a successor to President Juan Antonio Ríos. It put forth the name of Jaime Larraín. However, when this convention was unable to agree on a candidate, the Agrarian Labor Party finally supported Fernando Alessandri, who came in third.

The Agrarian Labor Party grew rapidly in the late 1940s. In the parliamentary election of 1949 fourteen of its candidates for deputy and four for senator were successful. Two years later it was the first party to proclaim the presidential candidacy of Carlos Ibáñez, although a minority group of party leaders broke away to back the Liberal-Conservative nominee, Arturo Matte Larraín. They called their group the Movement of Doctrinary Recuperation (Movimiento de Recuperación Doctrinaria) and it was headed by Jaime Larraín.

The Agrarian Labor Party played a major role in the second government of Carlos Ibáñez. It was the only party to continue to support his government throughout Ibáñez' administration, and had members in all of his cabinets. Its new importance was reflected in the parliamentary election of 1953, when it placed twenty-seven members in the Chamber of Deputies and six in the Senate. This proved to be the highpoint of the party's history.

During the latter part of the 1950s, the Agrarian Labor Party suffered a number of divisions. In 1954 a group broke away to join with the Movement of Doctrinary Recuperation in forming the National Agrarian Party (Partido Nacional Agrario), under the leadership of Julián Echavarrí Elorza. In 1956 the National Agrarian Party joined with still another dissident Agrarian Labor group, the Recuperationist Agrarian Labor Party (Partido Agrario Laborista Recuperacionista) and a group of independents, to form the National Party (Partido Nacional) which supported the candidacy of Jorge Alessandri in the 1958 presidential election.

Meanwhile, in the election of 1957 the Agrarian Labor Party had suffered a severe setback, winning only four seats in the Senate and thirteen in the Chamber of Deputies.

As the 1958 presidential election approached, the Agrarian Laborites split once again. The majority supported the candidacy of the Christian Democrat, Eduardo Frei, but a minority element backed Jorge Alessandri, the victor. Immediately after the election, the majority group merged with the National Party to form the Popular National Party, which lasted only two years. Just before the 1961 parliamentary election, the Agrario Laboristas split three ways. One group, the Agrarian Labor Democracy, entered the Christian Democratic Party, another joined the National Democratic Party (Partido Democrático Nacional), and a third sought to keep the Agrarian Labor Party alive. However, these efforts came to naught, and in 1965 the Agrarian Labor Party ceased to exist.

AGRARIAN LABOR DEMOCRACY (DEMOCRACIA AGRARIO LABOR-ISTA). *See* AGRARIAN LABOR PARTY.

AGRARIAN PARTY (PARTIDO AGRARIO). The Agrarian Party was formed by agriculturalists of the Temuco region in 1931. Although seeking at first merely to give expression to the farming element, it soon became an exponent of the establishment of a corporative state. Among its other proposals was one for transformation of the Senate into a body representing specific functional interests, while the Chamber of Deputies would continue to be chosen on the basis of popular election. Most of the founders of the party were ex-Radicals, and they included Braulio Sandoval, Vicente Reyes, and Manuel Bart Herrera. Subsequently, they were joined by a group of recent university graduates, including Felipe Herrera and Alejandro Hales. The party elected four deputies in 1932, and continued to have at least three members of the Chamber so long as it lasted. In 1941 it also elected a senator. In 1942 it supported the presidential candidacy of

Juan Antonio Ríos. In 1945 the Partido Agrario merged with the tiny Alianza Popular Libertadora to form the Agrarian Labor Party.

ALIANZA POPULAR LIBERTADORA. See POPULAR LIBERATING ALLIANCE.

ALLIANCE LIBERAL PARTY (PARTIDO LIBERAL ALIANCISTA). See LIBERAL PARTY.

AUTHENTIC SOCIALIST PARTY (PARTIDO SOCIALISTA AUTÉNTICO). See SOCIALIST PARTY.

CHRISTIAN DEMOCRATIC PARTY (PARTIDO DEMÓCRATA CRISTIANO – PDC). The Christian Democratic Party was established in June 1957 as the result of a merger of the National Phalanx (Falange Nacional) and the majority element of the Social Christian Conservative Party (Partido Conservador Social Cristiano). Its real antecedents are to be found in the Falange Nacional.

The Falange Nacional was founded in 1938 by the Youth Movement of the Conservative Party. The Conservative Youth refused to support the party's candidate for president that year, Gustavo Ross, and as a result were expelled from the party and reorganized as a separate political group.

Soon after its establishment, the Falange Nacional was joined by the members of the Popular Corporative Party (Partido Corporativo Popular). This small group, which never won any members of Congress, had been founded during the Socialist Republic in 1932, and advocated the "corporative" reorganization of society along lines proposed by some Social-Catholic political philosophers.

From its inception, the Falange Nacional was of Christian Democratic tendency, claiming to base its political philosophy on the Papal Encyclicals *Rerum Novarum* and *Quadragesimo Ano*. Among its principal founders were Eduardo Frei, Radomiro Tomic, and Rafael Agustín Gumucio.

During the 1940s the Falange Nacional slowly gained in importance. In 1941 it elected three deputies, in 1945 four, and in 1949 it elected three deputies and a senator. It began to win a foothold in the organized labor movement and had a considerable following among university students. In successive presidential elections, it backed the candidates of the Radical Party, Juan Antonio Ríos in 1942, Gabriel González Videla in 1946, and Pedro Enrique Alfonso in 1952. It had members for short periods in the cabinets of President Juan Antonio Ríos, Acting President Alfredo Duhalde and President Gabriel González Videla.

In 1955 the Falange Nacional joined with the Social Christian Conservative Party (Partido Conservador Social Cristiano) and a dissident group from the National Christian Party (Partido Nacional Cristiano), which had been formed in 1952 to back Carlos Ibáñez's presidential candidacy and was led by José Musalem, to form an alliance known as the Social Christian Federation (Federación Social Cristiana). In the 1957 parliamentary election, that coalition won two seats in the

Senate (one a Falange member, the other a Social Christian) and fifteen deputies (fourteen Falangistas and one Social Christian).

After the 1957 election, it was decided to merge the parties of the Social Christian Federation into the new Christian Democratic Party, although a minority of the Social Christian Conservative Party opposed this and ultimately returned to the orthodox Conservative Party ranks. In the following year, the PDC had its first electoral test, when it ran Eduardo Frei for president. He came in third, after the victor, Jorge Alessandri, and the FRAP candidate, Salvador Allende, but ahead of the Radical Party's nominee Luis Bossay.

The Partido Demócrata Cristiano scored a major triumph in the 1961 parliamentary election. It obtained four seats in the senate and twenty-three in the Chamber of Deputies and emerged as the country's single largest party, a position it was to maintain until the suppression of all political parties in 1973.

The Christian Democrats had made substantial advances in the organized labor movement, becoming, along with the Socialists and Communists, one of the three parties with major influence in the trade unions. Its members were particularly active in forming labor organizations among the agricultural workers. These organizations were not legalized until the Christian Democrats came to power, but by that time they had come to constitute a major element in the labor movement.

After the 1961 parliamentary election, it became increasingly clear that the presidential contest of 1964 would be between the PDC nominee and that of the left-wing combination, the FRAP. For this campaign the Christian Democrats again nominated Senator Eduardo Frei, and they launched a very extensive and intensive campaign under the slogan Revolution in Liberty. Their platform called for fundamental changes in the Chilean economy and society, including legalizing the unionization of rural workers, an agrarian reform; "Chileanization" of the mining industry, with majority control in the mining firms being assumed by the Chilean government; renewed economic development on the basis of the expansion of the copper-mining industry and the establishment of manufacturing firms which could produce new exports; a rewriting of the labor code, to permit legal recognition of national industrial and craft unions and central labor organizations, and the legal formation of competing unions in different parts of the economy.

At the beginning of the 1964 campaign there were three candidates: Frei, Salvador Allende of the FRAP, and Julio Durán as the nominee of the Democratic Front (Frente Democratico) consisting of the Conservative, Liberal, and Radical parties. After a victory of a FRAP candidate in a bye-election for deputy, the Frente Democratico broke up and Durán withdrew his candidacy. However, upon urging of the Christian Democrats, who were afraid that without Durán in the race, many Radicals might vote for Allende, Durán renewed his candidacy, but this time with the support only of the Radical Party. Although Frei refused to negotiate with the Conservatives and Liberals for their backing, they did in fact support him as the lesser evil.

The Christian Democrats won a very strong victory in September 1964. Eduardo Frei got a majority of the popular vote, the first time this had occurred since 1942. In subsequent congressional elections in March 1965, the Christian Democratic Party won a majority in the Chamber of Deputies (82 of 150), the first time any party had done this for a hundred years. They also elected twelve new senators, in addition to the thirteen holdovers which they already had.

Although his party lacked a majority in the Senate, President Frei proved adept at getting through Congress most of the measures which had been promised in the PDC platform. A special law for unionization of agricultural workers, embodying many of the Christian Democratic leadership's ideas about rewriting the general labor code, was passed. An agrarian reform law was enacted, calling for breaking up all estates with more than eighty hectares of land, and by the end of the Frei administration a sufficient start had been made in redistributing land so that no elected successor government could have reversed the process. A law providing for government majority ownership and reincorporation in Chile of the big mining firms was passed and by the end of the Frei period the large copper-mining firms and the nitrate companies had been reorganized under this law. A massive program for building schools and training teachers, particularly for rural areas, was carried out; and the school system was reorganized. Important new firms were established in the paper and pulp, metal, and chemical industries, and a major augmentation of the national steel plant was gotten under way.

The principal legislation promised in the PDC platform which was not enacted was a reform of the general labor code. This was not undertaken in part because of opposition of left-wing elements in the PDC itself, and because President Frei did not give the item high priority. Had the proposed legislation been pushed through Congress, it would in all likelihood have been possible for the Christian Democrats to organize a branch of the labor movement under their influence, instead of having to be a minority voice in a labor movement dominated by the party's left-wing opponents, the Socialists and Communists. This proved to be one of the major errors of the Christian Democratic regime, since the Socialists and Communists were able to mobilize the labor movement to support their candidate in the 1970 election.

The Christian Democratic regime also enacted substantial new taxation, making the general tax system considerably more progressive. This action, and the fact that inflation, after being checked in the first half of the Frei regime, had reached over 30 percent per year by the end of the Christian Democratic government, tended to alienate many middle-class voters who had supported the PDC in the 1964 and 1965 elections.

Another factor which weakened the Christian Democrats was the growth of intense factionalism within the Christian Democratic Party. By the middle of the Frei administration, the party had three distinct tendencies: the *oficialistas* who unequivocally supported the administration, the "rebels" (*rebeldes*) who were increasingly militant in their criticism of the Frei government and wanted an alliance with the Socialists and Communists in the 1970 election, and the *terceristas* who stood between the other two factions.

In mid-1969 the factional fighting within the party reached its apogee. Some of the rebeldes were expelled from the party and others left it. This somewhat further reduced the Christian Democratic strength in Congress, which had already been weakened in mid-term elections. The dissidents who left the PDC formed a new party, the United Movement of Popular Action (Movimiento de Acción Popular Unido—MAPU). The MAPU joined forces with those supporting the candidacy of Salvador Allende in the 1970 election.

As the 1970 election approached, the Christian Democrats nominated for president Radomiro Tomic, generally recognized to be second only to Eduardo Frei in the party's leadership. He proved to be a somewhat quixotic candidate. At first seeming to seek an alliance with the Leftist parties in the campaign, when this proved impossible he conducted his own campaign as if he were trying to outflank Salvador Allende from the Left. Although those on the Left were not impressed by this, many people of the Center and Right who might have voted for a Christian Democratic candidate with a different position, ended up supporting Jorge Alessandri, the nominee of the new National Party (Partido Nacional). Another aspect of Tomic's campaign was that almost until the end he seemed to seek to dissociate himself as much as possible from the government of Eduardo Frei, who without any question was at that point the most popular political figure in the republic.

Tomic faced two rivals in the campaign. One was Salvador Allende, running for the fourth time, in this case as the nominee of Popular Unity (Unidad Popular), a coalition of all of the parties of the Left plus the Radical Party. The other was ex-President Jorge Alessandri, clearly the nominee of the Right, but with personal support which cut across ideological and class lines. When the votes were counted, the Christian Democratic candidate came in third, behind the winner, Salvador Allende, and Jorge Alessandri.

Since Allende did not get a majority of the popular vote on 4 September 1970, it was necessary for Congress to decide between him and Jorge Alessandri. The Christian Democrats had the casting vote, and before they agreed to support Allende, they demanded—and received—the passage through Congress of a Statute of Constitutional Guarantees, which was designed to prevent the Popular Unity government from undermining the democratic constitutional system. With that statute passed, the Christian Democrats gave their votes in Congress to Salvador Allende.

During the Allende regime, the Christian Democrat constituted the largest element in the Opposition. In the beginning, they did not adopt a position of unlimited objection to everything Allende's government did. Indeed, on three separate occasions they negotiated with the president's representatives to seek agreement on a program, within the limits of the platform on which Allende had been elected, which both the Popular Unity and Christian Democrats could support. Although agreement was reached at least once between Christian Democratic negotiators and those of the president, Allende finally repudiated what had been agreed to because of the pressure of his own more left-wing supporters, particularly in the leadership of the Socialist Party.

Chilean politics became increasingly polarized during the Allende administration. As a result, the Christian Democrats joined forces with the other opposition parties during elections which took place during those three years. The opposition won three of four parliamentary bye-elections in 1971–1972, and in two of these, Christian Democrats were elected. In the March 1973 general congressional election, the PDC first joined forces in an electoral "federation" with the small National Democratic Party (Partido Democrático Nacional—PADENA) and Left Radical Party (Izquierda Radical), and then that federation coalesced with one formed by the National Party and Radical Democracy (Democracia Radical), to present common lists of candidates throughout the country. In that election, the Christian Democratic Party won ten senators and thirty-nine deputies, and remained the largest party, with 29 percent of the total vote.

The Christian Democratic Party had nothing to do with the military coup that overthrew Salvador Allende on 11 September 1973. Its first pronouncements after the coup adopted a wait-and-see attitude toward the new regime, urging it to get back to a constitutionally elected government as soon as possible. However, by the beginning of 1974, the Christian Democrats had frankly joined the opposition to the military government.

Meanwhile, the government of General Augusto Pinochet had outlawed all parties belonging to Popular Unity, and had "suspended" all other parties, by a decree issued about two weeks after seizing power. In March 1977 the military regime formally outlawed all of the previously "suspended" parties.

In spite of being officially suppressed, the Christian Democratic Party continued to exist. Its leading bodies continued to meet clandestinely from time to time, and to issue public statements denouncing various aspects of the policies of the military government. During the first years of the dictatorship, at least, the PDC was, along with the Communist Party, one of the two parties which were able to maintain some semblance of organization.

The regime took reprisals against the Christian Democrats. Several of the party's leaders were arrested and deported, including Renán Fuentealba and Jaime Castillo, both past-presidents of the party. Many lower ranking Christian Democrats were arrested and otherwise harrassed. Christian Democratic trade union leaders were removed from many of their posts, even before the government completely reorganized the labor movement in 1979.

Although the Christian Democratic Party generally assumed a hostile attitude toward the military dictatorship, some of its leaders did not. As a result, some of these, including Juan de Díos Carmona, José Musalem, and William Thayer, were expelled from the party.

The degree to which the Christian Democratic Party will be able to recuperate its strength once it is again possible to organize legally will depend on how long the hiatus in party activities continues, and how persistently the PDC continues from clandestiness to resist the military dictatorship.

CHRISTIAN LEFT PARTY (PARTIDO IZQUIERDA CRISTIANA). The Christian Left Party was formed in mid-1971, when the so-called *tercerista* faction of the

Christian Democratic Party decided to quit the PDC. Among its founders were six PDC members of the Chamber of Deputies. They were soon joined by some of the leading figures who had broken away from the Christian Democrats two years earlier to establish the United Movement of Popular Action (Movimiento de Acción Popular Unido—MAPU), among them Senator Alberto Jerez, Deputy Vicente Soler, and Jacques Chonchol. The Izquierda Cristiana, which held its first convention in October 1971, immediately joined the government's Popular Unity coalition, and for some months Chonchol served in President Allende's cabinet. However, the party refused to continue in the government in November 1972, when President Allende gave key posts in the cabinet to leaders of the armed forces.

The Izquierda Cristiana was one of the parties outlawed two weeks after the coup against the Allende government in September 1973. Most of its leaders were arrested, and ultimately were exiled. There is little evidence that the party was able to maintain any substantial underground organization, although its leaders continued to be active in the Chilean exile community.

COALITIONIST LIBERAL PARTY (PARTIDO LIBERAL COALICIONISTA). See LIBERAL PARTY.

COMMUNIST LEFT (IZQUIERDA COMUNISTA). See TROTSKYISTS.

COMMUNIST PARTY (PARTIDO COMUNISTA). The Chilean Communist Party had its origins in the Socialist Labor Party (Partido Obrero Socialista), founded in 1912 by Luis Emilio Recabarren. A printer by trade, Recabarren had first been active in the Democratic Party (Partido Democrático), of which he had served for a time as secretary-general. However, he felt that the Democratic Party was tending to abandon its allegiance to socialism and as a result broke away from it to form the Partido Obrero Socialista. Recabarren's influence was centered particularly in the northern nitrate *oficinas* and the cities nearby. In the Santiago area, the leadership of the party was largely in the hands of Manuel Hidalgo. From its inception the Socialist Labor Party had influence among the nitrate workers of the north and the artisans and factory workers of the Santiago-Valparaiso region. In 1917 it captured control of the country's central labor organization, the Great Labor Federation of Chile (Gran Federación Obrera de Chile). Recabarren and his followers renamed the organization Federación Obrera de Chile (FOCh), and tightened its organization and discipline.

At a Congress in Valparaiso in December 1920, the delegates decided to rename the party Partido Comunista and to affiliate with the Communist International. A few weeks later, the FOCh decided to join the Red International of Labor Unions, associated with the Comintern. In 1921 Recabarren and Luis Víctor Cruz were elected to the Chamber of Deputies by the party.

Late in 1924 Luis Emilio Recabarren committed suicide. The titular leadership of both the Communist Party and the FOCh passed to Elías Lafertte. Two-and-a-half years later, when Colonel Carlos Ibáñez established his dictatorship, Lafertte and a number of other Communist leaders were arrested and deported to Easter Island. While he was there, Lafertte was nominated by his party to run against Ibáñez for president, the only person to do so.

During the Ibáñez dictatorship, the Communist Party was officially outlawed, although its members of Congress, who included Senator Manuel Hidalgo and several members of the Chamber of Deputies, were allowed to continue to hold their seats. During this period, too, the Communists lost their predominant position in the labor movement. Legally recognized unions provided for in legislation passed in September 1924 came to constitute the majority of the country's labor organizations. Since the Communists did not allow unions under their control to seek legal recognition in that period, this meant that the Federación Obrera de Chile was reduced to a minority element in organized labor. A new National Confederation of Legal Unions (Confederación Nacional de Sindicatos Legales) emerged soon after the Ibáñez dictatorship as the majority element in the labor movement. A third group consisted of unions under anarchosyndicalist control, which formed the General Confederation of Workers of Chile (Confederación General de Trabajadores de Chile — CGTCh).

It was during the Ibáñez administration also that the Communist Party suffered its major split. This originated as a struggle for control between two groups, one headed by Senator Manuel Hidalgo, the other under Elías Lafertte and Carlos Contreras Labarca. The Comintern's South American Bureau, with its headquarters in Montevideo, sided with the Lafertte-Contreras Labarca faction in this dispute. The result was that after the fall of the Ibáñez dictatorship in 1931 two Communist parties, both using the name Partido Comunista de Chile, emerged. The one headed by Hidalgo soon changed its name to Izquierda Comunista, and joined forces with the international movement of Leon Trotsky. The Lafertte-Contreras Labarca party became the Stalinist group in Chile, continuing to be part of the Communist International.

The Stalinist Communists ran Elías Lafertte for president in the 1931 elections, held after the fall of Ibáñez. He got only a few thousand votes. In the short-lived administration of Juan Esteban Montero, the victor in the 1931 election, the most notable activities of the Communists were their efforts to capitalize on a naval mutiny in Valparaiso, and their leadership of a military uprising at Copiapó on Christmas Eve 1931. Both mutinies were quickly suppressed.

With the establishment of the Socialist Republic of Colonel Marmaduque Grove on 4 June 1932, the Lafertte-Contreras Labarca Communist Party, in conformity with the extremely sectarian position of the Communist International at that time, carried on violent opposition to the regime, although the Socialist Republic had the support of most of the country's working class. Subsequently, with the end of the Socialist Republic, and the calling of new elections at the end of 1932, the party again named Elías Lafertte as its candidate, and he received only 4,128 votes. The Communists won no seats in Congress in that election.

With the abandonment by the Communist International in 1934–1935 of its extremely sectarian "Third Period" line, which had been faithfully followed by the Chilean Communists, the founder of the Peruvian Communist Party, Eudosio Ravines, who had been working as a Comintern official, was sent to Chile to supervise the application of the new Popular Front policy. Although he met some resistance to the abrupt change of tactics, the Chilean Communists generally conformed.

The Communists ceased the bitter and violent attacks which they had been directing against other Left parties, particularly the Socialists and Radicals, and instead began to court leading figures in those parties, especially the Radicals. They put forth the idea of a Popular Front of the Left in Chile, to confront the "fascist menace" there. They also proposed unification of the three labor confederations.

There was strong resistance within both the Socialist and Radical parties to the idea of a Popular Front. However, the increasing reliance of President Arturo Alessandri upon the support of the Conservatives and Liberals in Congress, which threw the Radicals into the opposition, and Alessandri's energetic suppression of a railroad strike early in 1936, served to overcome that opposition. On 6 May 1936, the Popular Front was officially established, with the participation of the Radical, Communist, Socialist, Democratic, and Radical Socialist parties. About six months later, with the merger of the Socialist-controlled Confederación Nacional de Sindicatos Legales and the Communists' FOCh to form the new Confederation of Workers of Chile (Confederación de Trabajadores de Chile – CTCh), the CTCh also officially became part of the Popular Front.

The Communists had ideas for extending the Front even farther. At one point, they suggested that the ex-dictator Carlos Ibáñez be invited to join it with his followers. However, neither the Radicals nor the Socialists were willing to accept this idea.

Perhaps in fear of the possible results of the Popular Front, the government forces in Congress forced through Law # 6020 of 12 February 1937, entitled "Law for the Internal Security of the State," which outlawed the Communist Party. However, the Communists were able to avoid the practical application of this law by reorganizing as the National Democratic Party (Partido Nacional Democrático). In the parliamentary elections of 1937 they made substantial gains, electing six members of the Chamber of Deputies and placing Elías Lafertte in the Senate.

In preparation for the presidential election of October 1938, the Popular Front held a convention 15–17 April of that year. Although the Communists officially had only 120 of the 1030 delegates present, they also had almost half of the 60 delegates of the CTCh. They had enough votes to block the candidacy of Marmaduque Grove, backed by the Socialists, and to assure that the nominee would be a Radical. The convention finally chose Pedro Aguirre Cerda.

With the victory of the Popular Front and the inauguration of Aguirre Cerda in December 1938, the new president offered cabinet posts to the Communists. However, they refused to accept that degree of responsibility in the government, although they did obtain a number of positions as provincial governors, members of councils of public corporations, and consular posts in the foreign service.

With the advent of the Stalin-Nazi Pact of August 1939 and the outbreak of World War II two weeks later, the Chilean Communists were thrown into some confusion. However, they quickly adapted to the situation, abandoning their previous violent antifascism and support of collective security, and taking a position of pro-German neutrality in the war. This ultimately led to a vituperative break with the Socialists who, under the leadership of Oscar Schnake, Minister of Production of President Aguirre Cerda, took a strongly pro-Allied position. That began a decade of very bitter strife between the Communists and Socialists. It also brought about another short illegalization of the Communist Party which, nonetheless, continued to function as the National Progressive Party (Partido Progresista Nacional).

With the entry of the Soviet Union into World War II, the Chilean Communists again changed their position on international affairs by 180 degrees, becoming the strongest advocate of Chilean support for the Allies, and urging a policy of class collaboration within the labor movement. They supported the candidacy of Radical leader Juan Antonio Ríos in the 1942 presidential election provoked by the death of President Aguirre Cerda. In congressional elections three years later, the Communists made very substantial gains, winning fifteen seats in the Chamber of Deputies and three in the Senate, still under the name of the National Progressive Party.

The Chilean Communists got their first experience as participants in a government with the election of President Gabriel González Videla in September 1946. In that election, made necessary by the death of President Ríos, the Communists were the only group except his own Radical Party to back González Videla. However, since González Videla did not receive a popular majority, Congress had to make the ultimate electoral decision, and for this purpose, González Videla negotiated an arrangement with the Liberal Party, still led by Arturo Alessandri.

As a result of this agreement, González Videla's first cabinet consisted of members of his own Radical Party, as well as Communists and Liberals. The Communists held the three posts of public works, agriculture, and lands and colonization. They sought to use their position in the government to strengthen their party as much as possible, and particularly to destroy their enemies in the labor movement, especially the Socialists and anarchosyndicalists. They provoked wildcat strikes in industries where unions were controlled by their opponents, and got the government to deal with Communists in those unions instead of with the duly elected union representatives. They used government funds to subsidize their own work in the unions. Upon occasion, they even used violence against their opponents, some of whom were killed by Communist gangs.

In retrospect, the Communists undoubtedly concluded that they had overplayed their hand in the González Videla administration. When they returned to the government, almost a quarter of a century later, under President Salvador Allende, they went out of their way to avoid any actions which might turn the president against them.

González Videla did finally turn violently against them. He dismissed them from his government in April 1947 and, convinced that they were trying to repeat in Chile the kind of Communist seizures of power which were then under way in Eastern Europe, he sponsored passage in September 1948 of the Law for the Defense of Democracy, which outlawed the Communist Party once again and removed its registered voters from the electoral rolls. That law was to remain in effect for almost a decade.

However, although driven partially underground, the Communist Party did continue to function. After some time, it was able to publish its daily newspaper under another name than it had previously used, and after González Videla left office late in 1952, the government no longer seriously persecuted the party. However, one serious effect of this period of illegality was that it for some time greatly reduced Communist influence in the labor movement.

As the 1952 election approached, the Communists made overtures to Senator Salvador Allende, and suggested that if the Socialist Party of Chile (Partido Socialista de Chile), to which he then belonged, would nominate him for president they, the Communists, would support him. This brought about one of the most dramatic political about-faces seen in recent Chilean history, when the Socialist Party of Chile, which had until then been the most violently anti-Communist party in the country, suddenly became the Communists' closest allies. However, in spite of Communist support, Allende came in fourth among four candidates in that election.

The victor was General Carlos Ibáñez. This gave the Communists a chance to recuperate their position in the labor movement. The Socialists, who controlled the larger faction of the CTCh—which had split into two rival organizations under Socialist and Communist control respectively in early 1946—had been discussing for a considerable time the organization of a new central labor group, to include not only the CTCh unions, but also those controlled by the rival Socialist group, the Popular Socialist Party (Partido Socialista Popular), by the anarchosyndicalists, and by independents. Until the 1952 election, however, they had refused any unity with unions under Communist control.

Nevertheless, with Ibáñez's election there was great fear that he might once more try to establish a dictatorship and try to copy Perón in getting control of the labor movement. This fear lent credence to the Communists' insistence that the new central labor group should result in complete "labor unity," and therefore should include their unions. Consequently, when the new Central Union of Workers of Chile (Central Unica de Trabajadores de Chile—CUTCh) was finally established, not only were the Communist unions included, but the Communists were given major posts in its leadership. Thereafter, the Communists were able to largely dominate the CUTCh, not because they had control of a majority of the unions in it, but because they were the only party which had a large corps of functionaries who could spend full time on trade union work, without having to be paid by the labor movement itself.

Shortly before the presidential election of 1958, the Law for the Defense of Democracy was repealed over President Ibáñez' veto. As a result, the Communist Party was able to come completely out into the open once again. It officially formed part of the Front of Popular Action (Frente de Acción Popular—FRAP), which supported Salvador Allende in his second unsuccessful bid for the presidency in 1958. In parliamentary elections in 1961, the Communist Party obtained sixteen deputies and four senators.

In the early 1960s the Communists suffered a minor Maoist split. In 1963 a small group of Communist intellectuals and students established, with Chinese help, a publishing company Espártaco Editores (Spartacus Publishers), which began to put out Chinese Communist propaganda, including attacks on the pro-Soviet attitude of the Chilean Communist Party. Ultimately this group was thrown out of the Communist Party and formed the Revolutionary Communist Party (Partido Comunista Revolucionario—PCR). This party never became a significant element even on the far Left of Chilean politics. However, it survived, and by the late 1970s—after the various zigzags of the Chinese Communist policy—it was aligned with a somewhat strange international group of Communist parties which saw the Albanian Party of Labor as the only Communist party in power which "truly" represented Marxism-Leninism.

The Communists again formed part of the FRAP in the 1964 election in which Salvador Allende was defeated by Eduardo Frei, the Christian Democrat. In the March 1965 congressional election, the Communists again increased their representation, getting eighteen deputies and six senators.

By that time, the Communists clearly represented the largest element in the CUTCh. The head of the Central Unica was the Communist member of the Chamber of Deputies, Luis Figueroa. Under his leadership the Communists and their Socialist allies were able to prevent the half-hearted attempts of the Christian Democratic government to undermine the CUTCh as the principal bastion of the far Left in national politics. Indeed, President Frei reinforced the Communist-Socialist control of CUTCh by having his minister of finance negotiate with Figueroa the annual general wage increase which it was by then the custom of the government to enact by legislation.

As the 1970 election approached, the Communists advocated broadening the FRAP coalition which had three times supported Salvador Allende's presidential candidacy. They finally succeeded in overcoming Socialist opposition to inclusion of the Radicals in a new coalition, which was named Popular Unity (Unidad Popular—UP).

In the jockeying for position which preceded the naming of a UP candidate, the Communists first put forward the name of Pablo Neruda, Communist senator and world-famous poet. They announced that if the Unidad Popular could not agree on a common candidate, Neruda would continue to be the Communist nominee. However, agreement was finally reached, and Salvador Allende once again was the candidate of the Left. This time he won a plurality in the popular vote, and was finally confirmed as president-elect by Congress.

During the nearly three years of the Allende administration the Communists played the role of the most moderate element in the government coalition. They had participation in all of Allende's cabinets, and they put particular emphasis on their loyalty to the president. They urged him to reach some kind of agreement with the Christian Democratic part of the opposition, so as to assure the stability of the administration. They also urged him privately, and occasionally publicly, to discipline the more rash leaders and members of his own Socialist Party, who were carrying on a campaign of widespread illegal seizures of land and factories.

The Communists in those years seemed even willing to run the risk of losing the elections scheduled for 1976 and expressed willingness to turn over power to the winner if that should happen, an attitude not shared by the left-wing Socialists. There is no question that the Chilean Communists saw the experiment of the Allende regime as having great bearing on the ability of their French and Italian comrades to convince leaders of other parties in those countries that the advent of Communists to power did not automatically mean establishment of a dictatorship.

The Communists' counsels of moderation went unheeded. The Allende government was overthrown in a bloody coup on 11 September 1973. Soon afterwards, the Communist Party was outlawed along with all of the other affiliates of Unidad Popular. However, the Communists were better prepared than the other UP parties for carrying on underground activity. Relatively few of their top leaders were caught by the new military regime, and the Communist Party was without doubt able to maintain its party structure more or less intact. The Christian Democrats were the only other party which was able to do this to some considerable degree.

The Chilean Communist Party remains illegal and underground. Its policy since 1973 has been one of seeking to bring together all of the parties and groups opposed to the dictatorship of General Augusto Pinochet. In all likelihood, when the opportunity once again presents itself, the Communist Party will be able to reorganize publicly with at least the strength and influence which it had before 11 September 1973.

CONFEDERACIÓN REPUBLICANA DE ACCIÓN CÍVICA. *See* REPUBLICAN CONFEDERATION OF CIVIC ACTION.

CONSERVATIVE PARTY (PARTIDO CONSERVADOR). The Chilean Conservative Party of 1857 had its origins in the faction among the fighters for independence known as the *pelucones* ("wigged ones"), named after the fact that many of them wore the powdered wigs then popular among the aristocrats. The pelucones sought to maintain "the principle of authority" and were opposed to the ideas derived from the French Revolution advocated by their opponents, the *pipiolos*, ("beginners"), who had been the supporters of Bernardo O'Higgins until his fall in 1823.

The pelucones won a definitive victory over their antagonists with the overthrow of President Ramón Freire in 1830. However, the emergence of the Conservative Party as a faction of the pelucones did not take place for more than two decades.

The third president of the so-called Conservative Republic of 1831–1861, Manuel Montt, who served two terms from 1851 to 1861, adopted a somewhat more antagonistic attitude towards the Catholic Church than had his predecessors. He moved to end the church's complete control of education and opposed the reestablishment of the Jesuit order in the country. Those who were against his measures were the people who established the Conservative Party in 1857.

In that same year, the Conservatives, now as opponents of the Montt regime, joined forces with their ideological antagonists, the Liberals, who were also opposed to the Montt regime. The Conservatives supported the election in 1861 of President José Joaquín Pérez, who like his three predecessors served two five-year terms. Representatives of the party served in the cabinet throughout his administration, together with Liberals.

The Conservatives also supported the victor in the 1871 election, Federico Errázuriz Zañartu, a Liberal. However, midway through his administration, church-state issues intensified, and the president dismissed the Conservatives and formed a cabinet with Liberals and Radicals. As a result, in 1876 the Conservatives supported Benjamín Vicuña Mackenna, a dissident Liberal, who lost to the regular Liberal candidate, Aníbal Pinto.

Two years later, the Conservative Party held its first full-fledged convention. This adopted a party program that called for administrative decentralization, "church freedom," tax reform, and freedom of the church to maintain schools and license members of the learned professions. These continued to be the principal points of the Conservative platform for several decades.

In the 1881 presidential campaign, the Conservatives supported General Manuel Baquedano, one of the heroes of the War of the Pacific with Peru and Bolivia. However, convinced that he could not win, Baquedano withdrew before the election, and the Conservatives abstained from the concurrent congressional election.

During the government of Domingo Santa María, victor in the 1881 election, major anticlerical measures were passed. These included establishment of government control of vital statistics, civil marriage, and government control of cemeteries. After the passage of these laws, the Conservatives returned to participation in congressional elections in 1885, but they only were able to place five members in the Chamber of Deputies.

In the 1886 presidential campaign, the candidate whom the Conservatives first proposed to support refused to accept their conditions, and subsequently withdrew, as a result of which the Liberal, José Manuel Balmaceda, won without opposition. As the quarrel between President Balmaceda and Congress over their respective powers, as well as over economic and social issues, developed, the Conservatives threw their support behind the Congressional faction. As a result, they participated in the victorious civil war against President Balmaceda in 1891.

With the advent of the Parliamentary Republic after the 1891 civil war, the

Conservative Party was the axis of the political alliance known as "The Coalition" (*La Coalición*). The party at first participated in the cabinet of President Jorge Montt and won thirty-nine deputies in the parliamentary election at the end of 1891. However, early in 1892 it withdrew from the government. During most of the next three decades, the Conservatives played the game of all of the parties then represented in Congress during the Parliamentary Republic, being in some of the cabinets and not in others. They supported the winner in the presidential election of 1896, and the loser in 1901 and 1906. Once again it backed the winner in the next two elections, 1910 and 1915. At the time of the 1906 election, the party suffered a temporary division in its ranks over the presidential candidacy, but this was healed soon after the election of President Pedro Montt.

Although in 1901 the Conservative Party had proclaimed itself a supporter of the ideas of Christian democracy and an adherent of the social reform ideas of Pope Leo XIII's encyclical *Rerum Novarum*, the party as such did little in the next few decades to try to bring about any basic reforms. However, during the first two decades of the twentieth century some individual Conservative parliamentarians did propose an outline of a labor code, but none of the elements of this suggested code was enacted until 1924.

With the approach of the end of the Parliamentary Republic and the rise of sharp social and economic issues, the Conservative Party became the axis of the National Union (Unión Nacional) coalition, which supported the candidacy of the right-wing Liberal Luis Barros Borgoño in the 1920 presidential election, against that of Arturo Alessandri. During the Alessandri regime, the Conservatives remained in the opposition and did all that they could to thwart the president's reform program. In the March 1924 congressional election, they won seven senators and twenty-one deputies.

The Conservatives supported the military movement which overthrew President Arturo Alessandri in September 1924. Upon his restoration to power in March 1925, some members of the party participated in the commission which drew up the constitution of that year. Subsequently, they supported the candidacy of Emiliano Figueroa Larraín in the election following President Alessandri's second resignation in September 1925, along with the Liberals, Democrats, and Radicals.

During the dictatorship of Carlos Ibáñez between 1927 and 1931, the Conservative Party's ability to function freely was severely limited as was the case with all of the country's other parties. It was allotted ten senators and twenty-two deputies by President Ibáñez, when he chose the membership of the Congress which was supposed to be elected in 1930. These parliamentarians continued to serve in Congress after the fall of Ibáñez and during the short administration of President Juan Esteban Montero (1931–1932). The party was strongly opposed to the so-called Socialist Republic of June–September 1932.

The Conservative Party named its own candidate for president both in 1931 and in 1932. However, as a result of a working alliance with the major elements of the Liberal Party established during the second administration of President

Arturo Alessandri (1932–1938), the Conservatives thereafter usually supported the same presidential nominee as the Liberals. By the 1930s, the old church-state issues which had originally divided the Liberals and Conservatives had been largely dissipated—particularly after the separation of church and state in the Constitution of 1925. Since by that time these two parties were the main spokesmen for the rural and urban propertied interests, they had a good deal more in common than they had in opposition to one another.

During the Alessandri administration of the 1930s, the Conservatives and Liberals came to constitute most of the president's support in Congress. As the end of that term approached, the Conservatives joined with the Liberals to back the candidacy of Gustavo Ross Santa María, ex-Finance Minister of Alessandri. He was defeated in the election of 1938 by Pedro Aguirre Cerda, nominee of the Popular Front.

During the administrations of the first two Radical presidents, Aguirre Cerda and Juan Antonio Ríos, the Conservatives remained in the opposition. In the 1942 election they joined with the majority faction of the Liberals to support the presidential candidacy of General Carlos Ibáñez.

With the death of Juan Antonio Ríos early in 1946 and the need to elect his successor, the convention of Conservatives, Liberals, and smaller right-wing groups was unable to reach agreement on a nominee. As a result, the Conservatives named their own candidate, Senator Eduardo Cruz Coke, who came in second to the Radical Party victor, Gabriel González Videla.

Although throughout most of its history the Conservative Party had been remarkably free of the factionalism and division which plagued most of the other parties, it did suffer serious splits in the 1930s and 1940s. In 1938 the youth movement of the party, the so-called Conservative Phalanx (Falange Conservadora) refused to support the presidential candidacy of Gustavo Ross Santa María, backed by the Conservative Party, and as a result they were expelled from the Conservative ranks, and established their own party, the National Phalanx (Falange Nacional), the precursor of the Christian Democratic Party.

Although this split did not result in a major division in the adult ranks of the Conservatives, the schism in the late 1940s was more serious. It originally arose over the question of passage of the Law for the Defense of Democracy, proposed by President Gabriel González Videla, to outlaw the Communist Party. Important Conservative leaders, including the party's president, Horacio Walker Larraín, and its 1946 presidential candidate, Eduardo Cruz Coke, opposed this bill. Cruz Coke finally voted against it, and his position was upheld by the executive committee of the Conservative Party.

At about the same time, President González Videla invited the Conservatives to provide two members of his cabinet. Although the executive committee refused this invitation, two Conservatives did in fact join the González Videla government. This precipitated a split between the two factions of the party, which took the names Traditionalist Conservative Party (Partido Conservador Tradicionalista) and Social Christian Conservative Party (Partido Conservador Social Cristiano), the latter led by Walker Larraín and Cruz Coke. The electoral authorities gave the Social Christians the right to use the name Partido Conservador, their opponents officially coming to be known as the Traditionalist Conservative Party.

In the 1952 election, the two wings of the Conservatives supported different candidates. The Tradicionalistas backed the Liberal nominee, Arturo Matte Larraín, a son-in-law of the ex-president, Arturo Alessandri. The Social Christians backed the Radical candidate, Pedro Enrique Alfonso.

In spite of officially having the Conservative Party name, the Social Christian faction declined rapidly after 1952. In the parliamentary election of 1953, the Traditionalist faction won seventeen members of the Chamber of Deputies, the Social Christian element winning only two. Late in that same year, many of the Social Christians, including their two deputies and one senator (Eduardo Cruz Coke), returned to the Traditionalist ranks, and the Partido Conservador Tradicionalista changed its name to United Conservative Party (Partido Conservador Unido). Although this left the Social Christians without parliamentary representation, they did win one deputy in the 1957 congressional election, which they fought as part of the Social Christian Federation (Federación Social Cristiano), the other element of which was the National Phalanx. In June 1957, the Partido Conservador Social Cristiano merged with the Falange Nacional and another small group to form the Christian Democratic Party.

Meanwhile, the United Conservative Party backed the successful presidential candidacy of Jorge Alessandri, along with the Liberals, in 1958. During his administration, they were part of the Democratic Front (Frente Democrático), along with the Liberals and Radicals. As the presidential election of 1964 approached, the Democratic Front first named as its candidate Julio Durán, a Radical. However, after a bye-election defeat of the Front, Durán withdrew as its candidate and the Democratic Front went out of existence. The Conservative Party thereupon left its members free to support Eduardo Frei, the nominee of the Christian Democrats, which most of them did.

The Conservative Party, as well as the Liberals, suffered a disastrous electoral defeat in the congressional poll of March 1965. The Conservatives were able to elect only three members of the Chamber of Deputies and no senators. The Conservative parliamentarians came to form part of the right-wing opposition to the Frei government in Congress.

The electoral debacle of March 1965 resulted a year later in the liquidation of the Conservative Party. In June 1966 it merged with the Liberal Party and the small National Action party (Acción Nacional) to form a new National Party (Partido Nacional).

DEMOCRÁCIA AGRARIO LABORISTA. *See* AGRARIAN LABOR PARTY.

DEMOCRÁCIA RADICAL. *See* RADICAL PARTY.

DEMOCRATIC NATIONAL PARTY (PARTIDO NACIONAL DEMOCRÁT-ICO). *See* COMMUNIST PARTY.

DEMOCRATIC PARTY (PARTIDO DEMÓCRATA or PARTIDO DEMO-CRÁTICO). From its inception in 1887 the Democratic Party used interchangeably the names Partido Demócrata and Partido Democrático. Subsequently, the two names were sometimes used to differentiate conflicting factions of the group, which throughout its history suffered many schisms.

The Democratic Party was the first socialist party of Chile and of Latin America. It was established in November 1887 by a group of dissident Radicals and some of the leaders of the labor movement which was just beginning to appear in Santiago, Valparaiso, and a handfull of other cities. Among its founding members were Antonio Poupin, Artemio Gutiérrez, Angel Guarello, and Malaquías Concha.

The party held its first convention on 14 July 1889, the centenary of the French Revolution. It put forth several basic ideas: universal suffrage, end of administrative centralization, the enactment of social security legislation, and protectionism for industry.

The Partido Democrático supported President José Manuel Balmaceda in the civil war of 1891, and when he lost, it suffered severe persecution for about a year. However, in July 1892 it was able to hold its second national convention. Two years later, it had its first electoral triumph of significance, when Angel Guarello was elected a deputy from Valparaiso.

During the Parliamentary Republic, the Democratic Party participated in the various parliamentary and electoral alliances which characterized that epoch. During most of the period, it was part of the Liberal Alliance, although at times it took an independent position. In 1901, it suffered its first split, when a "Regulation" faction favored an independent position for the party, and a "Doctrinary" group supported association with the Liberal Alliance. This division was not healed until 1904.

Another split occurred in 1906, when the party decided to support the presidential candidate of the Coalition, with a dissident group headed by Luis Emilio Recabarren breaking away to support an independent Democratic candidate, Zenón Torrealba. Although this division was to presage a more serious one six years later, this time it was patched up after the presidential election. In 1912 the Democrats elected their first senator, Angel Guarello; it already had five deputies.

During the first decade of the twentieth century the Democratic Party was the principal political spokesman of the labor movement. In the north its influence was extensive among the nitrate workers, who were fighting heroic battles against both employers and government officials to establish a trade union movement. Luis Emilio Recabarren was its most notable figure there. It also had influence among the workers of the Santiago-Valparaiso region and was beginning to get a following among the coal miners just south of Concepción.

During this period, the Democratic Party had informal relations with the Socialist International. Although it was not officially affiliated with the International, it did keep that body regularly informed about its activities.

In 1912 Recabarren led a major split in the Democratic ranks, forming his own Socialist Labor Party (Partido Obrero Socialista), which ultimately became the

Communist Party of Chile. The impact of this division was particularly important in the north, somewhat less so in the Santiago-Valparaiso region. However, for another twenty-five years, the Democráticos were to continue to be the major political element among the coal miners.

In January 1916 the Democratic Party for the first time got a member of the cabinet, Angel Guarello, as minister of industry and public works. At that point, the Democrats were, along with the Radical Party and the faction of the Liberals led by Arturo Alessandri, one of the three principal components of the Liberal Alliance.

The Democratic Party strongly supported the candidacy of Arturo Alessandri in the 1920 presidential election. When there was a question for some weeks about recognizing Alessandri's election, Juan Pradenas Muñoz, Democratic leader in the Concepción area, threatened to organize a march of coal miners on Santiago to enforce Alessandri's claim of victory.

During the first Alessandri government, 1920–1924, the Democrats constituted part of his support in Congress and served on various occasions in his cabinet. In the congressional election of 1921, they won twelve seats in the Chamber of Deputies, and one in the Senate. Three years later, they elected twelve deputies and four senators.

The Democratic Party opposed the military movement which forced Alessandri out of the presidency in September 1924. Although Angel Guarello accepted a post in the cabinet organized by the military, his action was repudiated by the party. After the second military coup in January 1925, Nolasco Cárdenas of the Democratic Party signed a cable sent by the parties of the Liberal Alliance urging Alessandri to return home and to the presidency. Subsequently, it supported adoption of a new constitution written under Alessandri's influence and adopted in a popular referendum.

In the presidential election held after Alessandri's second resignation, late in 1925, the Democrats joined with the Conservatives, Liberals, and Radicals in supporting Emiliano Figueroa Larráin. In parliamentary elections in the following year, they had an alliance with the Communist Party and some smaller groups.

During the dictatorship of Carlos Ibáñez, the freedom of the Democratic Party to operate was limited, as was the case with all of the parties. However, when the dictator handpicked members of Congress in 1930, he allotted four senators and thirty-one deputies to the party.

With the overthrow of Ibáñez, the Democrats backed Arturo Alessandri, then running as a candidate of the Left in the elections of November 1931, against the victor, Juan Esteban Montero. Subsequently, when Montero's government was overthrown and the Socialist Republic was proclaimed on 4 June 1932, the Democrats supported the new regime. A Democrat, Nolasco Cárdenas, served in the second junta of the Socialist Republic.

However, when the party held a convention on 20 September 1932, there was strong criticism there of the Democrats' participation in the de facto government. This controversy resulted in a split in the party into the Partido Demócrata and the Partido Democrático. Although the latter was supposedly considerably to the Left of the Partido Demócrata, both parties supported once again the candidacy of Arturo Alessandri in the election at the end of 1932. However, the split of 1932 was to be but the first of several in the decades that followed, all of which contributed greatly to the decline and ultimately virtual disappearance of the Democratic Party.

A unity convention, presided over by the veteran Artemio Gutiérrez resulted in the formation once again of a single Democratic Party in July 1933. However, less than six months later, the split between the Partido Demócrata and Partido Democrático emerged once again, when the executive of the reunited party decided to support the government of President Alessandri, which was beginning to move to the Right. In the parliamentary elections of 1937, the Partido Demócrata won three seats in the Chamber and two in the Senate; the Democráticos got five deputies and also two senators.

The Partido Democrático became a member of the Popular Front, and as such supported the presidential candidacy of Pedro Aguirre Cerda in 1938. The Partido Demócrata, on the other hand, continued its alliance with the forces backing President Alessandri, and in function of that position, supported Gustavo Ross Santa María in the same election.

It was not until 1941 that the two factions of the Democratic Party were once again reunited, under the name Partido Democrático. In that year the party won nine deputies and three senators, but four years later, it gained only eight deputies and no senators.

The ranks of the Democratic Party were again split early in 1946, this time as a result of a division in the Confederation of Workers of Chile (Confederación de Trabajadores de Chile—CTCh). One faction of the Democrats, headed by Fidel Estay, threw its support behind the faction of the CTCh dominated by the Socialist Party; the other, led by Juan Pradenas Muñoz, backed the part of the CTCh controlled by the Communist Party. They both used the name Partido Democrático this time, with the Fidel Estay group being granted official use of that name by the electoral authorities. That faction backed Fernando Alessandri, the Liberal Party candidate, in the 1946 presidential election; while the Pradenas Muñoz group supported Gabriel González Videla.

Although unity was subsequently reestablished, it was broken once again as a result of the election of 1952. This time the two factions were known as the Partido Democrático de Chile, which supported the presidential candidacy of the Radical, Pedro Enrique Alfonso, and the Partido Democrático del Pueblo, which backed Carlos Ibáñez.

Both factions of the Democratic Party joined the Front of Popular Action (Frente de Acción Popular—FRAP), when it was formed by the two Socialist parties and the Communist Party in 1957. Soon afterwards, they were reunited in a single Partido Democrático.

Although the 1958 election again precipitated divisions within the Democratic Party ranks, with factions breaking away to support both Jorge Alessandri and

Eduardo Frei, the majority remained in the FRAP, and supported its nominee, Salvador Allende. Two years later the Partido Democrático merged with splinters of the Socialist and Radical parties to form the National Democratic Party (Partido Democrático Nacional—PADENA), which remained in the FRAP. In the 1961 parliamentary elections, the PADENA won twelve seats in the Chamber of Deputies but did not elect any senator.

In the 1964 presidential election, although a small group again broke away to back Eduardo Frei, the PADENA as a whole once more supported Salvador Allende. Six months later, in the parliamentary elections, it placed only three members in the Chamber, but also elected a senator.

The final split in the Democratic Party ranks took place soon after the 1965 election. PADENA decided to leave the FRAP, and in the latter part of the Frei government it was allied with the Christian Democrats and even had one member of the cabinet. It continued the association with the Christian Democrats during the Allende government, and formed part of an electoral "federation" in the 1973 congressional elections, of which the Christian Democrats and the Left Radical Party were also members.

Those within the party who were opposed to withdrawing from the FRAP in 1965 split with PADENA and formed the separate Social Democratic Party (Partido Social Demócrata—PSD). In 1968 it had one senator and three deputies. The PSD formed part of Popular Unity (Unidad Popular), which backed Salvador Allende in the 1970 election. However, early in 1972 the party went out of existence when it merged with the Radical Party, which was also part of Popular Unity.

There is no evidence that PADENA was able to survive intact after the military coup of 11 September 1973. It seems highly unlikely that the Democratic Party will be revived in any form when it becomes possible once again to establish legal political parties in Chile.

DEMOCRATIC PARTY OF CHILE (PARTIDO DEMOCRÁTICO DE CHILE). *See* DEMOCRATIC PARTY.

DEMOCRATIC PARTY OF THE PEOPLE (PARTIDO DEMOCRÁTICO DEL PUEBLO). *See* DEMOCRATIC PARTY.

DEMOCRATIC RADICAL PARTY (PARTIDO DEMOCRÁTICO RADICAL). *See* RADICAL PARTY.

DOCTRINAL LIBERAL PARTY (PARTIDO LIBERAL DOCTRINARIO). *See* LIBERAL PARTY.

DOCTRINAL RADICAL PARTY (PARTIDO RADICAL DOCTRINARIO). *See* RADICAL PARTY.

FEDERALIST PARTY (PARTIDO FEDERALISTA). The first party to be formally established in Chile, the Federalist Party was organized soon after the fall of Bernardo O'Higgins as supreme director in 1823. Virtually the only plank in its platform was the conversion of the highly centralized Chilean regime into a federation. In elections held early in 1826 the Federalist Party won a sweeping victory, placing fifty-six deputies in the single-house legislature of the time. Later in the year this Congress enacted a law providing for a federation of eight provinces, each of which would have a provincial assembly and an elected *intendente* (governor).

However, bitter quarrels in the election of provincial assemblies, and struggles over boundaries among the provinces discredited very rapidly the federalist idea and the party which had sponsored it. Less than a year after the establishment of federalism, it was abolished by the legislature. Efforts by Federalist-controlled assemblies in some provinces to take over collection and disbursement of all taxes were quickly suppressed by the central government in Santiago. Federalism was never revived as a serious issue, and the Federalist Party was liquidated by the end of the 1820s.

FEMININE PARTY (PARTIDO FEMININO DE CHILE). The Feminine Party was formed in 1946 as the result of efforts of a group of women to obtain the suffrage and equal civil rights. It proclaimed that the "mixed" parties (with people of both sexes) had failed in these efforts, and that it was necessary for women to establish their own party. The Partido Feminino soon came under the leadership of María de la Cruz.

In 1950 the party ran its first candidate, María de la Cruz, in a bye-election for the Senate in Santiago. She received very few votes. At the party's first convention in the same year it put forth its platform: female suffrage, the right of women to be elected, equality between the sexes in civil matters, and laws for the protection of women.

With the approach of the 1952 presidential election, the Partido Feminino threw its support behind the candidacy of General Carlos Ibáñez. There is little doubt that the party profited from both the broad upsurge of support for the general, and from the example of Eva Duarte de Perón, head of the Feminine Peronist Party in neighboring Argentina.

In a bye-election resulting from the fact that Senator Carlos Ibáñez became president in December 1952, María de la Cruz ran for the senatorship from Santiago, with support of the parties which had just elected Ibáñez president. She won a strong victory. However, in the Senate María de la Cruz caused several scandals, and the Senate finally disqualified her from membership. Soon thereafter, the Partido Feminino began a rapid decline and it had disappeared by the late 1950s.

Several factors undoubtedly help explain the rapid demise of the Feminine Party. The demagoguery of María de la Cruz, a split of a number of the party's leaders in revolt against her, to form the Progressive Feminine Party (Partido Progresista Feminino); the disclosure of the fact that President Juan Perón of

Argentina, during a visit to Chile in mid-1953, had promised the party a subsidy if it would unite its ranks; and the establishment of women's suffrage shortly before the end of the González Videla administration, are undoubtedly among these factors.

INTERNATIONAL SOCIALIST PARTY (PARTIDO SOCIALISTA INTERNACIONAL). *See* SOCIALIST PARTY.

INTERNATIONALIST WORKERS PARTY (PARTIDO OBRERO INTERNACIONALISTA). *See* TROTSKYISTS.

IZQUIERDA COMUNISTA. *See* TROTSKYISTS.

LEFT RADICAL PARTY (PARTIDO IZQUIERDA RADICAL–PIR). *See* RADICAL PARTY.

LIBERAL PARTY (PARTIDO LIBERAL). The antecedents of the Liberal Party are to be found in the *pipiolo* ("beginner") group which emerged among the fighters for independence in the second decade of the nineteenth century, that is, those favoring less centralized government and reduced privileges for the church. However, the party did not emerge until the administration of Manuel Bulnes (1841–1851).

Although the exact date of the founding of the Liberal Party is not known, it was in existence by 1846, when it offered support to Minister of Interior Manuel Camilo Vial Formas, whose opposition to the influence of the church was well known. The new party had its first test at the polls in the congressional election of 1849.

In 1851 the Liberals supported the presidential candidacy of José María de la Cruz Prieto against that of Manuel Montt, favored by outgoing President Bulnes. When Montt won, the Liberals constituted the major opposition to his administration.

When in 1857 a group of President Montt's supporters turned against him because of his moves to restrict the influence and privileges of the church, and formed the Conservative Party, there was established an ideologically peculiar but politically practical alliance. The Liberals, the strongest critics of the church, and the Conservatives, its strongest defenders, formed the Liberal-Conservative Fusion (Fusión Liberal Conservadora) to oppose the Montt government. This alliance was to persist for a decade and a half.

All three parties, President Montt's National Party, as well as the Liberals and Conservatives, supported the candidacy of José Joaquín Pérez, who was elected president in 1861. He governed principally with Liberal and Conservative ministers. During his administration laws were passed authorizing non-Catholics to practice their religion privately, and forbidding the immediate reelection of the president, both of which were planks in the Liberal platform.

In 1871 the Liberals again joined the Conservatives in supporting the victorious candidate for president, Federico Errázariz Zañartu. However, two years later, the Conservatives withdrew their support of him, and for the first time an all-Liberal cabinet was formed by President Errázuriz.

The election of 1876 brought the first of innumerable splits in the Liberal Party. The majority of the party supported the candidacy of Aníbal Pinto, but a minority withdrew to organize what they called the Democratic Liberal Party (Partido Liberal Democrático) to back the candidacy of Benjamín Vicuña Mackenna. Aníbal Pinto was elected, but the Partido Liberal Democrático continued to exist until the death of Vicuña Mackenna in 1886. Pinto's cabinet members were all Liberals.

Another Liberal was elected president in 1881, Domingo Santa María, who also had the support of the Radicals and Partido Nacional. During the Santa María government a serious struggle between church and state took place. It resulted in passage of a number of Liberal measures, including secularization of the collection of vital statistics and of cemeteries, and the establishment of compulsory civil marriages. However, the Liberals did not push forward with separation of church and state.

The Santa María administration also brought another split in the Liberal Party. A group headed by Victorino Lastarría broke away in protest against what they conceived to be high-handed methods of the president, to form the Doctrinal Liberal Party (Partido Liberal Doctrinario). It was to persist as a separate Liberal group until 1932.

The orthodox Liberals and the "doctrinarios" supported different candidates in the 1886 presidential election. The major group backed José Manuel Balmaceda, their opponents supported a Radical, José Francisco Vergara, who retired from the contest, however, when the Conservatives failed to endorse him against the government nominee.

President Balmaceda sought to unite all factions of the Liberals. However, his efforts proved fruitless. As a consequence, the proadministration and antigovernment factions ran rival lists of candidates in the 1888 parliamentary elections. The government list won seventy-six deputies and sixteen senators, and the dissidents got eight deputies and four senators.

At the time of the 1891 civil war the division of the Liberals persisted. Most members and leaders of the party supported President Balmaceda, although a minority backed his congressional opponents. As a result, the Liberal Party was in shambles after the victory of the rebels.

In 1892 two Liberal factions again emerged. The bulk of the party held a convention in 1892 which reestablished the Partido Liberal. In the same year, after intense persecution for a few months, the supporters of the late President Balmaceda formed a second Democratic Liberal Party (Partido Liberal Democrático), which was to maintain a separate existence until 1933.

The first president after the 1891 civil war, Jorge Montt, was an admiral. However, thereafter, throughout the rest of the Parliamentary Republic the president was always a member of one or another of the Liberal factions. Different Liberal factions participated in the two broad coalitions which formed and reformed during this period, the Alianza Liberal and the Coalición, but allegiances shifted frequently, insofar as the various Liberal groups were concerned.

In the crucial election of 1920, the Liberals were divided, as usual. Supporting Arturo Alessandri, candidate of the Liberal Alliance (Alianza Liberal), were the Doctrinal Liberals and part of the Partido Liberal Democrático, as well as the Radicals and the Democratic Party. Supporting Luis Barros Borgoño in the National Union (Unión Nacional) were the Unionist Liberals (Liberal Unionista), and another faction of the Partido Liberal Democrático, together with the Conservatives and the National Party.

This alignment of the Liberal factions continued during the Alessandri administration. In the parliamentary elections of March 1924, the pro-Alessandri Liberals won nineteen seats in the Chamber of Deputies and seven in the Senate. The Unionist Liberal group won eight deputies and three senators.

The Unionist Liberals supported the overthrow of Alessandri in September 1924. When he was recalled as the result of another military coup in January 1925 and undertook the writing of a new constitution which replaced the Parliamentary Republic with a presidential regime, the Doctrinal Liberals and the Partido Liberal Democrático both supported the new constitution. Insofar as the Partido Liberal Democrático was concerned, this was the fulfillment of the program which it had advocated since 1892, when it had adopted the position of favoring a strong presidency which President Balmaceda, whose supporters it mobilized, had favored.

During the dictatorship of Ibáñez from 1927 to 1931, the Liberals, like all of the other parties, had difficulties in carrying on normal activities. The Liberals virtually disintegrated. When President Ibáñez in effect appointed members of Congress in the "election" of 1930, he gave the Liberals thirty-one deputies and sixteen senators.

During the Ibáñez regime an attempt was made to unite all of the Liberal factions. Out of this emerged the United Liberal Party (Partido Liberal Unido). However, this effort merely resulted in the formation of one new Liberal faction.

With the overthrow of Ibáñez in August 1931, three Liberal groups still existed: the United Liberal Party (Partido Liberal Unido), the Doctrinal Liberal Party (Partido Liberal Doctrinario), and the Democratic Liberal Party (Partido Liberal Democrático), the old Balmacedistas. In the election of that year, the United Liberals supported the presidential candidacy of Juan Esteban Montero, while the Doctrinal and Democratic Liberals backed Arturo Alessandri, then a candidate of the moderate Left.

Meanwhile, soon after Ibáñez' overthrow a new attempt was made to unite the dispersed Liberal forces. However, the only result of the convention held for this purpose was the establishment of a fourth faction, known simply as the Liberal Party (Partido Liberal).

When Juan Esteban Montero was overthrown and the Socialist Republic was proclaimed, the Doctrinal and Democratic Liberals supported the revolutionary regime. Members of these groups served as ministers in the cabinet of Carlos Dávila, during the second phase of the Socialist Republic.

In parliamentary elections held late in 1932, the new Partido Liberal won eighteen deputies and five senators. The United Liberals got six deputies and one senator and the Doctrinary Liberals won two seats in the Chamber of Deputies. In the presidential election, the United Liberals supported the candidacy of Enrique Zañartu Prieto, the Doctrinal and Democratic Liberals supported Arturo Alessandri, while the new Partido Liberal left its members free to vote for whomsoever they wished.

After the election of Arturo Alessandri, the new president sponsored a new effort to unite the scattered Liberal forces. At a convention held in Valparaiso in October 1933 all factions were united in a single Partido Liberal. It immediately became the country's largest party, getting thirty-four deputies and eleven senators in the 1934 parliamentary election.

The Liberals and Conservatives provided President Alessandri's parliamentary majority during his 1932–1938 administration. In 1938 they joined forces to support the presidential candidacy of Gustavo Ross Santa María, who was defeated by the Popular Front candidate, Pedro Aguirre Cerda.

The Liberals were part of the opposition during the first two Radical administrations after 1938. However, the unity of the party was temporarily destroyed again at the time of the 1942 election of a successor to President Aguirre Cerda. Although the majority of the party backed the ex-dictator, Carlos Ibáñez, a minority led by Arturo Alessandri backed the Radical candidate, Juan Antonio Ríos, and their support gave Rios the margin of victory.

By the 1930s the church-state issues which had traditionally divided the Liberals from the Conservatives had been largely resolved. As a result, since both parties were representatives of the country's agrarian, commercial, and industrial elites, they had more in common than they had to separate them. Consequently, they were to be united in most presidential election campaigns from 1938 forward.

At the time of the 1946 presidential election, the Liberals participated in a convention of the Right to choose a common candidate. However, when it failed to reach agreement, the Liberals first nominated ex-President Arturo Alessandri. However, he subsequently withdrew his candidacy, and with the promise of support from a faction of the Radicals, the Liberals nominated Don Arturo's son, Fernando Alessandri. He came in third in the popular election.

Since the front-runner, the Radical Gabriel González Videla, did not have a popular majority, Congress had to decide between him and the runner-up, Conservative Eduardo Cruz Coke. Arturo Alessandri negotiated with the Radicals and reached an agreement for the formation of a cabinet composed of members of the two parties which had supported González Videla—the Radicals and Communists—and the Liberals. This tripartite cabinet continued in office from November 1946 until April 1947.

After municipal elections in the latter month, which showed that the Conservatives who were in the opposition, had gained considerable ground on the Liberals, the latter withdrew from the government. Thereupon, President González Videla reorganized his cabinet. During part of the remainder of the González Videla administration the Liberals were again represented in his administration.

In the 1952 election, the Liberals joined with the Conservatives in supporting the candidacy of Arturo Matte Larraín, a Liberal and a son-in-law of the late president, Arturo Alessandri. He was defeated by General Carlos Ibáñez, and in the six years of Ibáñez's second administration, the Liberals did not have any members of the cabinet. In the 1953 parliamentary election they won only twenty-four deputies and no senators, although four years later they gained thirty seats in the Chamber of Deputies and nine senators.

The Liberals again joined with the Conservatives to support Jorge Alessandri in the presidential election of 1958. He defeated Salvador Allende and Eduardo Frei. The Liberals had representation in several of President Alessandri's cabinets.

As the 1964 election approached, the Liberals at first formed part of the Democratic Front (Frente Democrático), with the Conservatives and Radicals, which supported the candidacy of a Radical, Julio Durán. When the Democratic Front dissolved early in 1964, the Liberals threw their support to the Christian Democratic nominee, Eduardo Frei, who was the victor.

In the congressional elections which followed, in March 1965, the Liberal Party suffered a disastrous defeat. It won only six seats in the Chamber of Deputies, and elected no senators, although it had five holdovers in that body. The Liberals in both houses formed part of the right-wing opposition to the Christian Democratic government of President Eduardo Frei.

Not only the Liberal Party but the Conservatives also had suffered a catastrophe in the 1965 congressional election. As a direct result of this, the traditional enemies, the Liberals and Conservatives, decided to join forces. Consequently, the Liberal Party went out of existence when it joined with the Conservatives, the National Action Party (Acción Nacional), and independents at a convention in June 1966, to establish the National Party (Partido Nacional).

LIBERAL DEMOCRATIC PARTY (PARTIDO LIBERAL DEMOCRÁTICO). *See* LIBERAL PARTY.

MARXIST SOCIALIST PARTY (PARTIDO SOCIALISTA MARXISTA). *See* SOCIALIST PARTY.

MOVEMENT OF THE REVOLUTIONARY LEFT (MOVIMIENTO DE LA IZQUIERDA REVOLUCIONARIA—MIR). The Movement of the Revolutionary Left was formed in 1964 by dissident members of the Socialist Party, members of the *Polémica* group, who had broken with the Trotskyists some time before, and followers of Clotario Blest, who had for many years been secretary-general of the Central Union of Workers (Central Unica de Trabajadores). The orthodox

Trotskyists also merged their organization, the Revolutionary Labor Party (Partido Obrero Revolucionario) with the MIR for some years, but broke away from it again in 1969.

In the beginning the most significant figure in the MIR was Oscar Waiss, at one time a leading member of the Popular Socialist Party (Partido Socialista Popular). However, he was soon pushed out of the leadership—and ultimately quit the MIR to return to the Socialist Party—by a group of younger people, mainly university students.

The MIR was largely inspired by the example of the Cuban Revolution, and proclaimed its belief that violence and guerrilla war were the only means to bring about the Marxist-Leninist revolution. During the administration of President Eduardo Frei (1964–1970), they carried on numerous "urban guerrilla" activities, such as robberies of banks and supermarkets. A substantial number of those involved in these activities were captured by the police.

The victory of Popular Unity (Unidad Popular) in the 1970 election was a psychological-political defeat for the MIR, which had taught that victory of the far Left by an election was impossible. However, the MIR finally decided to give "critical support" to the Allende government.

President Allende legalized the MIR and pardoned its members who had been jailed for robberies and other illegal activities. Thereafter, although it consisted mainly of middle- and upper-class youths, it established groups in the labor movement and among the peasants. These were the Front of Revolutionary Workers (Frente de Trabajadores Revolucionarios—FTR) and the Revolutionary Peasants Movement (Movimiento de Campesinos Revolucionarios—MCR). The FTR received about 3 percent of the votes in the internal elections in the Central Union of Workers in mid-1972. Through the MCR and FTR, the MIR engaged in many seizures of land and industries during the Allende regime, frequently in conjunction with left-wing members of Allende's own Socialist Party. Although the president several times exhorted them to desist from these activities, he seldom took any steps to prevent them.

The MIR did not participate with candidates of its own in any election. However, in the 1973 congressional election, it did support some of the more left-wing candidates of the Socialist Party.

Elements of the MIR conspired with enlisted men in the navy—along with Socialist Secretary-General Carlos Altamirano and leaders of the left-wing Catholic party MAPU—in the last months of the Allende regime. This was undoubtedly one of the principal factors which provoked the overthrow of the Allende government by the armed forces on 11 September 1973.

Once in power, the military turned their attention particularly to the suppression of the MIR. Its rural base in the Temuco area was completely overrun by the army, and its leaders there were executed. In the year or two following the coup there were several clashes between underground elements of the MIR and units of the armed forces. Most of its top leaders were either killed, jailed, or escaped into exile. It is still not clear whether the MIR will revive as a viable political party when it is possible once again to establish legal parties in Chile.

MOVIMIENTO DE ACCIÓN POPULAR UNIDO (MAPU). *See* UNITED MOVEMENT OF POPULAR ACTION.

MOVIMIENTO DE LA IZQUIERDA REVOLUCIONARIA (MIR). *See* MOVEMENT OF THE REVOLUTIONARY LEFT.

MOVIMIENTO NACIONAL SOCIALISTA DE CHILE. *See* NATIONAL SOCIALIST MOVEMENT OF CHILE.

NATIONAL PARTY (PARTIDO NACIONAL) (1851). Three parties have used the name "National." One of these was founded in the second third of the nineteenth century and lasted for three-quarters of a century. The other two were of more recent origin and of much shorter duration.

The first Partido Nacional originated during the presidency of Manuel Montt (1851–1861) as a result of the division which took place among the old *pelucones* ("wigged ones") group, which had been in power since 1830. When President Montt and his interior minister, Antonio Varas, took steps to limit the power of the church, those opposed to this policy turned against the president in 1857 and formed the Conservative Party (Partido Conservador). In response to this move, the president's followers formed the National Party in the same year. For many years it was also frequently referred to as the "Montt-Varista Party," after the names of its two principal founders.

At its founding meeting, the National Party issued its basic program. This laid stress on the importance of "the principle of authority," and a strong central government to maintain this. It supported maintenance of the "patronage" arrangement with the Roman Catholic Church, whereby the Chilean president in practice named the members of the church hierarchy in the country.

Throughout the remainder of President Montt's administration, the Partido Nacional provided the main parliamentary support of the president. In congressional elections held during the last year of the Montt regime, the party obtained a majority in both houses.

However, in the next administration, of President José Joaquín Pérez, after a year the Partido Nacional went into the opposition. In 1864 the Nacionales lost their majority in Congress and two years later were unsuccessful in efforts to block Pérez's election for a second term. They continued in the opposition, and in the 1867 parliamentary election joined with the new Radical Party (Partido Radical) to put up joint slates.

The National Party and the Radicals supported José Tomás Urmeneta in the 1871 campaign, and for this occasion the Nacionales presented a relatively advanced program, calling for religious freedom, strong guarantees of individual rights, noninterference by the government in elections, and strong limitations on the powers of the president. The National-Radical candidate was defeated by

Federico Errázuriz Zañartu, backed by the Liberals and Conservatives. The National Party remained in the opposition during his administration. In 1876 it elected twenty-six members to the Chamber of Deputies and thirteen senators.

In the 1876 presidential election, the Partido Nacional supported the government's candidate, Liberal Aníbal Pinto, against the dissident Liberal, Benjamín Vicuña Mackenna. As a result, the Nacionales had representation in most of President Pinto's cabinets and Antonio Varas was even minister of interior (virtually prime minister) for some time. The situation continued the same in the administration of President Domingo Santa María (1881–1886), whose election the Nacionales had also supported.

Once again, in 1886 the Nacionales supported Liberal nominee José Manuel Balmaceda and for a while had ministers in his cabinet. However, when the civil war broke out in 1891, the National Party sided with the Congressional rebels and as a result were represented in the government of President Jorge Montt, who took over at the end of the civil war. By this time, however, the strength of the Partido Nacional had diminished greatly. In 1891 it was able to elect only nine members of the Chamber of Deputies and in 1894 only five.

During the Parliamentary Republic, the Partido Nacional, although theoretically in favor of a strong presidency, played the game of shifting alliances which characterized that period. It was alternatively part of the Liberal Alliance and the Coalition, the two major blocs during that period. One president of the era, Pedro Montt (1906–1910) was a member of the National Party, elected with the support of that party, the Radicals, and one Liberal faction. On various occasions, the National Party had members of the cabinet.

In the crucial election of 1920, the National Party split. The majority backed the more conservative candidate, Luis Barros Borgoño, although a dissident group broke away to support Arturo Alessandri. During the Alessandri administration members of the National Party served several times in his cabinet. In the 1924 election, the party placed one senator and five members of the Chamber of Deputies.

During the turbulent years following the first ouster of President Arturo Alessandri in September 1924, the National Party declined rapidly. It was not able to elect any members of Congress. In 1930 when President Carlos Ibáñez in effect named the members of Congress, a few Nacionales were given seats, but as members of the United Liberal Party. In 1933 this National Party officially disappeared when it joined with various factions of the Liberals to form what from then on was known simply as the Liberal Party (Partido Liberal).

NATIONAL PARTY (PARTIDO NACIONAL) (1956). A second, very short-lived National Party was formed in August 1956 by various groups which had broken away from the Agrarian Labor Party (Partido Agrario Laborista). Its principles were at best vague. In the 1957 parliamentary election, it placed five members of the Chamber of Deputies and four senators. It officially went out of existence in October 1958.

NATIONAL PARTY (PARTIDO NACIONAL) (1966). The third National Party was officially created in June 1966. It was established as a result of the disastrous defeat of the Liberals and Conservatives in the March 1965 congressional election. This rout convinced the leaders of those parties of the need to pool their forces, and establishment of the new Partido Nacional was the result. The small National Action Party (Acción Nacional), the personalist vehicle of Jorge Prats, also joined in this merger.

The National Party brought about a very strong comeback for the traditional Right in Chilean politics. During the Frei and Allende administrations it was able to rally support among substantial middle-class elements which had not previously supported the Right. In the congressional election of March 1969 it placed thirty-four members in the Chamber of Deputies instead of the nine which it had had before the election; and got five senators in place of the three which it had previously held.

The National Party put forward ex-President Jorge Alessandri as its candidate in the 1970 election. Partly because of his personal prestige, and partly because of the ineptitude of the campaign of the Christian Democratic nominee Radomiro Tomic, Alessandri came in a close second to Salvador Allende, candidate of Popular Unity (Unidad Popular). In the negotiations in Congress made necessary by Allende's failure to get a popular majority, the Nacionales refused to go along with Allende's election, and continued to support Alessandri.

The National Party constituted the second largest element in the Opposition during the Allende regime. It strongly opposed the Christian Democrats' efforts to reach an accommodation with President Allende. However, it did join forces with the Christian Democrats in several bye-elections and in the general congressional election of March 1973. The Nacionales formed an electoral "federation" with the Radical faction known as Radical Democracy (Democracia Radical), which federation then joined with another established under Christian Democratic hegemony, to form a "confederation" which ran candidates against those put up by Popular Unity. In this election, the National Party gained three additional Senate seats and one new seat in the Chamber of Deputies.

Although the National Party was not directly involved in the coup which overthrew the Allende government on 11 September 1973, it strongly endorsed it once it had taken place. Subsequently, the National Party made no effort to keep its party structure intact once the government had "suspended" (and subsequently completely outlawed) it. Many leading members of the party accepted posts in the government of General Pinochet.

It is impossible to predict what form a party to represent the traditional Chilean Right will take once it becomes possible to establish legal parties once again.

NATIONAL ACTION PARTY (ACCIÓN NACIONAL). See NATIONAL PARTY (1966).

NATIONAL AGRARIAN PARTY (PARTIDO AGRARIO NACIONAL). See AGRARIAN LABOR PARTY.

NATIONAL CHRISTIAN PARTY (PARTIDO NACIONAL CRISTIANO). *See* CHRISTIAN DEMOCRATIC PARTY.

NATIONAL DEMOCRATIC PARTY (PARTIDO DEMOCRÁTICO NACIONAL–PADENA). *See* DEMOCRATIC PARTY.

NATIONAL PHALANX (FALANGE NACIONAL). *See* CHRISTIAN DEMOCRATIC PARTY.

NATIONAL PROGRESSIVE PARTY (PARTIDO PROGRESISTA NACIONAL). *See* COMMUNIST PARTY.

NATIONAL SOCIALIST MOVEMENT OF CHILE (MOVIMIENTO NACIONAL SOCIALISTA DE CHILE. Also known as the Nazi Party (Partido Nacista), the National Socialist Movement was a reflection in Chile of the rise of European Fascism in the 1930s. It had all of the outer trappings of a fascist party: a "leader," a paramilitary militia, the fascist salute. It also had a typically fascist program, although after 1938 it abandoned that program during its last three years of existence.

The National Socialist Movement was founded in April 1932 under the leadership and inspiration of a young lawyer, Jorge González von Mareés. Soon afterwards it adopted its Fundamental Declaration. This proclaimed that the state "had complete supervision of all national activities and the individual must be the servant of the State, submitted to strict discipline." It denounced the idea of the class struggle and advocated "the cooperation of different social groups."

Supreme authority in the party rested with the "chief" (*Jefe*), that is, Jorge González von Mareés, who was assisted by a "consultative council." Under the chief were party sections in various parts of the economy, each with its own chief. Each new member had to swear an oath of allegiance.

Soon after the organization of the Nazi Party, its uniformed paramilitary "shock troops" began to organize "demonstrations of force." There were numerous clashes between them and members of the Youth group of the new Socialist Party. A conflict in Santiago in September 1933 brought a motion of condemnation of the Nazi Party by the Chamber of Deputies.

President Arturo Alessandri was more worried about the menace of the Nazis to the Chilean political system than he was about the rise of the left-wing Popular Front. His government first banned the public marches by the Nazi storm troopers and then the wearing of the Nazi uniform at all in public. Then after a shooting incident by the Nazi storm troopers in Rancagua in November 1933, Alessandri banned further circulation of the Nazi paper *Trabajo*.

The first electoral participation by the Movimiento Nacional Socialista in March 1937 won them three seats in the Chamber of Deputies. A bit more than a year later, on 21 May 1938, the Nazis caused a major scandal when they set off a bomb in the Congress building, and a few minutes later Nazi deputy Jorge

González von Mareés shot off a gun and narrowly missed hitting President Arturo Alessandri, who was presenting his annual report to Congress.

The start of the decline of the Nacistas was the famous "massacre" in the Social Security Building on 5 September 1938. That day the Nazis launched an armed uprising against the Alessandri government; when it got no support from the Santiago garrison, the Nazi storm troopers barricaded themselves in the Social Security Building, across the street from the Presidential Palace. When the militarized police, the Carabineros, moved into the building on President Alessandri's orders, they massacred virtually all of those in the building, including some who had surrendered.

Although the "massacre" temporarily discredited President Alessandri, it also undermined the Nazis. Many of their leading militants were among those killed, and the act of insurrection itself served to turn many against Jorge González von Mareés and his followers.

The events of 5 September 1938 also greatly influenced the presidential election a few months later. The Nazis had been the main element in the Popular Liberating Alliance (Alianza Popular Libertadora) which was backing the candidacy of ex-dictator Carlos Ibáñez for president. Although after his capture Jorge González von Mareés testified that Ibáñez had had nothing to do with the Nazi insurrection, Ibáñez withdrew his candidacy and threw his support to the Popular Front candidate, Pedro Aguirre Cerda, who won the election by a narrow margin. One of Aguirre Cerda's first acts as president was to declare an amnesty for those who had participated in the September 5 insurrection. Soon thereafter, the Nacistas reorganized their party under the name Popular Socialist Vanguard (Vanguardia Popular Socialista). The Vanguardia adopted positions diametrically opposed to those they had originally held. They declared their loyalty to democracy, that they were part of the Chilean Left, that they believed in the class struggle and supported the workers in it, and that they were opposed to all racial discrimination. In the election of 1941, the Vanguardia Popular Socialista elected two deputies. However, after an incident in Congress between the Nazis and the Radicals, which resulted in the minister of interior ordering González von Mareés to be placed in a mental institution and his subsequent freeing by the Supreme Court, the Vanguardia Popular Socialista decided to dissolve. Its leaders subsequently joined a wide variety of other parties.

NATIONALIST MOVEMENT OF CHILE (MOVIMIENTO NACIONALISTA DE CHILE). Organized in 1941 by Guillermo Izquierdo Araya, the Nationalist Movement of Chile advocated the establishment of a corporative state and its members wore distinctive uniforms. When it sought legal recognition, a move was made in the courts to deny this, on the grounds that the party violated a law which prohibited groups "opposed to Democracy." However, the appeals court upheld the party's registration. The Nationalist Movement of Chile merged with other groups to establish the Agrarian Labor Party (Partido Agrario Laborista) in 1945.

NAZI PARTY (PARTIDO NACISTA). *See* NATIONAL SOCIALIST MOVEMENT OF CHILE.

NEW PUBLIC ACTION (NUEVA ACCIÓN PUBLICA). *See* SOCIALIST PARTY.

NUEVA ACCIÓN PUBLICA. *See* SOCIALIST PARTY.

ORDEN SOCIALISTA. *See* SOCIALIST PARTY.

PARTIDO AGRARIO LABORISTA. *See* AGRARIAN LABOR PARTY.

PARTIDO COMUNISTA. *See* COMMUNIST PARTY.

PARTIDO COMUNISTA REVOLUCIONARIO. *See* COMMUNIST PARTY.

PARTIDO CONSERVADOR. *See* CONSERVATIVE PARTY.

PARTIDO CONSERVADOR SOCIAL CRISTIANO. *See* CONSERVATIVE PARTY.

PARTIDO CONSERVADOR TRADICIONALISTA. *See* CONSERVATIVE PARTY.

PARTIDO CONSERVADOR UNIDO. *See* CONSERVATIVE PARTY.

PARTIDO CORPORATIVO POPULAR. *See* CHRISTIAN DEMOCRATIC PARTY.

PARTIDO DEMÓCRATA. *See* DEMOCRATIC PARTY.

PARTIDO DEMOCRÁTICO. *See* DEMOCRATIC PARTY.

PARTIDO DEMOCRÁTICO DE CHILE. *See* DEMOCRATIC PARTY.

PARTIDO DEMOCRÁTICO NACIONAL (PADENA). *See* DEMOCRATIC PARTY.

PARTIDO DEMOCRÁTICO RADICAL. *See* RADICAL PARTY.

PARTIDO FEMININO DE CHILE. *See* FEMININE PARTY.

PARTIDO IZQUIERDA CRISTIANA. *See* CHRISTIAN LEFT PARTY.

PARTIDO IZQUIERDA RADICAL. *See* RADICAL PARTY.

PARTIDO LIBERAL. *See* LIBERAL PARTY.

PARTIDO LIBERAL ALIANCISTA. *See* LIBERAL PARTY.

PARTIDO LIBERAL COALICIONISTA. *See* LIBERAL PARTY.

PARTIDO LIBERAL DEMOCRÁTICO. *See* LIBERAL PARTY.

PARTIDO LIBERAL DOCTRINARIO. *See* LIBERAL PARTY.

PARTIDO LIBERAL UNIDO. *See* LIBERAL PARTY.

PARTIDO LIBERAL UNIONISTA. *See* LIBERAL PARTY.

PARTIDO NACIONAL. *See* NATIONAL PARTY.

PARTIDO NACIONAL AGRARIO. *See* AGRARIAN LABOR PARTY.

PARTIDO NACIONAL CRISTIANO. *See* CHRISTIAN DEMOCRATIC PARTY.

PARTIDO NACIONAL DEMOCRÁTICO. *See* COMMUNIST PARTY.

PARTIDO NACIONAL POPULAR. *See* AGRARIAN LABOR PARTY.

PARTIDO NACISTA. *See* NATIONAL SOCIALIST MOVEMENT OF CHILE.

PARTIDO OBRERO INTERNACIONALISTA. *See* TROTSKYISTS.

PARTIDO OBRERO REVOLUCIONARIO. *See* TROTSKYISTS.

PARTIDO OBRERO SOCIALISTA. *See* COMMUNIST PARTY.

PARTIDO PROGRESISTA FEMININO. *See* FEMININE PARTY.

PARTIDO RADICAL. *See* RADICAL PARTY.

PARTIDO RADICAL DOCTRINARIO. *See* RADICAL PARTY.

PARTIDO RADICAL SOCIALISTA. *See* RADICAL SOCIALIST PARTY.

PARTIDO SOCIAL DEMÓCRATA. *See* DEMOCRATIC PARTY.

PARTIDO SOCIALISTA. *See* SOCIALIST PARTY.

PARTIDO SOCIALISTA AUTÉNTICO. *See* SOCIALIST PARTY.

PARTIDO SOCIALISTA DE CHILE. *See* SOCIALIST PARTY.

PARTIDO SOCIALISTA DE TRABAJADORES. *See* SOCIALIST PARTY.

PARTIDO SOCIALISTA INTERNACIONAL. *See* SOCIALIST PARTY.

PARTIDO SOCIALISTA MARXISTA. *See* SOCIALIST PARTY.

PARTIDO SOCIALISTA POPULAR. *See* SOCIALIST PARTY.

PARTIDO SOCIALISTA REVOLUCIONARIO. *See* SOCIALIST PARTY AND TROTSKYISTS.

PARTIDO SOCIALISTA UNIFICADO. *See* SOCIALIST PARTY.

POPULAR CORPORATIVE PARTY (PARTIDO CORPORATIVO POPULAR). *See* CHRISTIAN DEMOCRATIC PARTY.

POPULAR INDEPENDENT ACTION (ACCIÓN POPULAR INDEPEN-DIENTE—API). The Popular Independent Action was organized just after the election of Salvador Allende as president in late 1970. It was established by independents who had backed Allende's candidacy. Its president was Rafael Tarud, one-time leader of the Agrarian Labor Party (Partido Agrario Laborista), and one of its other leading figures was Lisandro Cruz Ponce, a leader of the Socialist Party in the 1940s and early 1950s. The API, which had its principal following among small businessmen, became part of the Popular Unity coalition backing the Allende government. There is no evidence that the API survived being outlawed by the military dictatorship of General Augusto Pinochet in September 1973.

POPULAR LIBERATING ALLIANCE (ALIANZA POPULAR LIBERTA-DORA). Popular Liberating Alliance was at first the name of the coalition formed to back Carlos Ibáñez's candidacy for president in 1938. When Ibáñez withdrew the Unión Socialista and other Ibáñez supporters established a party with this name. It remained very small, gaining no members of Congress, and in 1945 it merged with other groups to form the Agrarian Labor Party (Partido Agrario Laborista).

POPULAR NATIONAL PARTY (PARTIDO NACIONAL POPULAR). *See* AGRARIAN LABOR PARTY.

POPULAR SOCIALIST PARTY (PARTIDO SOCIALISTA POPULAR). *See* SOCIALIST PARTY.

POPULAR SOCIALIST UNION (UNIÓN SOCIALISTA POPULAR). *See* SOCIALIST PARTY.

POPULAR SOCIALIST VANGUARD (VANGUARDIA POPULAR SO-CIALISTA). *See* NATIONAL SOCIALIST MOVEMENT OF CHILE.

PROGRESSIVE FEMININE PARTY (PARTIDO PROGRESISTA FEMININO). *See* FEMININE PARTY.

RADICAL DEMOCRACY (DEMOCRÁCIA RADICAL). *See* RADICAL PARTY.

RADICAL PARTY (PARTIDO RADICAL). The Radical Party was established by those members of the Liberal Party who opposed its alliance with the Conservative Party in 1857. Subsequently, it was to become for many decades the principal political spokesman for the expanding middle class.

During the rest of the administration of Manuel Montt (1851–1861), and that of his successor, José Joaquín Pérez (1861–1871), the Radical Party formed part of the Opposition. At the end of the Pérez term the Radicals joined with the Partido Nacional to support the losing presidential candidacy of José Tomás de Urmeneta.

Meanwhile, the Radicals in 1864 were able for the first time to elect two members of the Chamber of Deputies. By 1873 the party had four members in the Chamber and one in the Senate. Two years later, as a result of a quarrel between President Federico Errázuriz Zañartu and the Conservative Party, which resulted in the retirement of the latter from the government, the Radicals were invited for the first time to have a member of the cabinet. The party was represented regularly in the cabinet of Errázuriz's successor, President Aníbal Pinto (1876–1881).

The Radical Party supported the election of President Domingo Santa María in 1881, and the party continued to have members in his government. It was during his administration that there began to be formed what became the typical local organization of the Radical Party, the Radical Assembly (Asamblea Radical). This was a kind of club, which was not only a political group but also a social center, where party members could drink beer or wine, have a meal, and converse not only about politics but anything else that interested them. The Asamblea Radical was to become one of the chief sources of strength for the party, since to break with it meant not only to split with one's political associates but also with those with whom one shared sociability and conviviality.

The Radicals split over whom to support in the 1886 election. However, the majority backed José Manuel Balmaceda and the Radicals were represented in President Balmaceda's first cabinets. In the congressional election of 1888, the party got one senator and seven deputies.

In 1888 the Radical Party held its first national convention. This meeting drew up the party's program, which among other things called for separation of church and state, establishment of elected provincial assemblies, free and lay public education, proportional representation, and strong support of individual rights.

Near the end of the Balmaceda government, the Radicals joined the opposition, and so sided with the Congressional rebels against Balmaceda in the civil war of 1891. The party participated both in the revolutionary junta and in the cabinets of President Jorge Montt, who took over after the death of Balmaceda.

During the Parliamentary Republic, the Radical Party was the only one which was consistently a member of the Liberal Alliance (Alianza Liberal), one of the two coalition groups of that period. In consequence of this, it supported the winning presidential candidates in 1901, 1906, and 1910, and the losing one in 1896 and 1915. Party members served in the cabinet on numerous occasions between 1891 and 1920.

One of the most important events in the Radical Party during the Parliamentary Republic was its third convention in 1906. In this meeting a more advanced group, headed by Valentín Letelier, sought to have the party declare itself "socialist," a move opposed by a rival faction headed by Enrique MacIver. The Letelier group won. For more than the next half century, the question of whether the Radical Party was a Socialist party would continue to divide the Radicals from time to time.

By 1920 the Radical Party had become the principal spokesman for middle-class elements in Chilean society. These included white-collar workers, teachers, small farmers, merchants, and artisans. These elements, in contrast to many of the urban manual workers and most of the peasants, were literate and so had the right to vote. Therefore, the influence of the Radical Party was larger than it would have been had there existed universal adult suffrage.

The Radical Party was the axis of the forces which supported Arturo Alessandri in the presidential election of 1920. With his inauguration, a Radical, Pedro Aguirre Cerda, was Alessandri's first minister of interior, and the Radicals were represented in virtually all of his subsequent cabinets. In the congressional election of March 1924, the Radical Party placed forty members in the Chamber of Deputies and ten in the Senate.

The Radicals strongly opposed the military junta after the resignation of President Alessandri in September 1924. They also supported Alessandri upon his restoration to power in March 1925, and participated in his government. They endorsed the new Constitution of 1925, which included the old Radical proposal, separation of church and state.

During the dictatorship of Colonel Carlos Ibáñez (1927–1931), the Radical Party had the same difficulties as other parties in functioning freely. Radical leaders were considerably divided, with one faction headed by Juan Antonio Ríos cooperating closely with Ibáñez, and other leaders being strongly opposed to such cooperation. In 1930, when President Ibáñez in effect named the new members of Congress, he put thirty-four Radicals in the Chamber of Deputies and twelve in the Senate.

With the fall of Ibáñez in August 1931, there was a purge of the Radical Party leadership. Among others, Juan Antonio Ríos was expelled from the party, and he and others who had collaborated with Ibáñez were not readmitted for three years.

The man elected president after Ibáñez fell, Juan Esteban Montero, was a Radical, the first member of the party to be elected chief executive. The Radicals were represented in Montero's cabinet during his short period in power. However, they also participated in that part of the Socialist Republic, following the overthrow of Montero, presided over by Carlos Dávila.

With the end of the Socialist Republic, new presidential elections were called, and Gabriel González Videla, president of the Radical Party, led it in throwing its backing to the successful candidate, Arturo Alessandri. At the same time, the Radicals elected thirteen senators and thirty-one deputies.

The Radicals were represented in President Alessandri's cabinet from December 1932 until April 1934. Thereafter, although Alessandri tried to maintain the association of the Radicals with his government, they moved increasingly into the opposition. In May 1936 they formally joined the new Popular Front, together with the Socialist, Communist, Democratic, and Radical Socialist parties.

When the Popular Front held a convention to choose its presidential candidate in April 1938, Pedro Aguirre Cerda of the Radical Party was chosen. He won a narrow victory in the election at the end of the year.

Aguirre Cerda was the first of three successive Radical presidents. Upon his death, he was succeeded in 1942 by Juan Antonio Ríos, and when Ríos died early in 1946, he was succeeded by Gabriel González Videla. During their fourteen years in power, the government carried out an extensive program of import substitution industrialization, and the labor movement was greatly strengthened.

During the period of Radical presidents, the Radical Party suffered two splits of some importance. After the death of President Ríos, the party divided over who should be his successor. The majority of the Radicals backed Gabriel González Videla, who also enjoyed the support of the Communist Party. Those who opposed González Videla, supported Alfredo Duhalde, who was Acting President after Ríos death, and formed the Democratic Radical Party (Partido Radical Democrático). Finally, Duhalde withdrew in favor of Liberal Party candidate Fernando Alessandri. This split was healed in 1949 when the Duhalde faction returned to the Radical Party.

However, another split had already occurred. When President Gabriel González Videla broke with the Communists, and in 1948 proposed the Law for the Defense of Democracy, which outlawed the Communist Party, some Radicals opposed this and withdrew to form the Doctrinal Radical Party (Partido Radical Doctrinario). This group supported the candidacy of Carlos Ibáñez in 1952, and in the 1953 congressional election it won three seats in the Chamber of Deputies. In 1957 it entered the Popular Action Front (Frente de Acción Popular), but was divided a year later, with one faction supporting Jorge Alessandri, the other backing Salvador Allende in the 1958 election. By the middle 1960s, the Partido Radical Doctrinario had disappeared entirely.

At the end of the González Videla administration, the Radical Party nominated Pedro Enrique Alfonso, who had been a minister several times in the Radical governments. However, he came in third, behind the winner, General Carlos Ibáñez, and the right wing candidate, Arturo Matte Larraín. In the 1953 congressional election, the Radicals elected only thirty deputies. In the next election, in 1957, the party somewhat recovered, electing nine senators and thirty-seven deputies.

During the second administration of Carlos Ibáñez, the Radicals were in the opposition. Then in the 1958 election they named their own candidate, Luis Bossay, who came in fourth, behind Jorge Alessandri of the Right, Salvador Allende of the Popular Action Front, and the Christian Democrat Eduardo Frei.

During the administration of Jorge Alessandri, the Radicals remained in the opposition for three years, but in the last half of that government had members in the cabinet. They also participated in the Democratic Front (Frente Democrático), along with the Conservatives and Liberals, in preparation for the election of 1964. The candidate of the Frente Democrático was Julio Durán, a Radical. However, he withdrew after a defeat of the Frente in a bye-election for Congress. The Radical Party finally renewed Durán's candidacy as a purely Radical nomination shortly before the end of the campaign. He came in third, behind Eduardo Frei, the Christian Democratic victor, and Salvador Allende, nominee of the leftist Popular Action Front.

During the Christian Democratic administration of President Eduardo Frei the Radicals continued in the opposition. The party also moved considerably to the Left, joining with the FRAP to establish a new combination, Popular Unity (Unidad Popular), which ended up supporting Salvador Allende in the 1970 election.

However, the Radicals suffered the first of two major splits during the Frei government. This took place in 1969, when those who opposed alignment with Popular Unity were expelled or resigned from the Radical Party to form Radical Democracy (Democrácia Radical). This party, which took with it a substantial number of those who had led the party during the previous two decades, ended up supporting Jorge Alessandri in the 1970 election.

In the late 1960s the Radical Party apparently resolved the problem which had first been presented in its 1906 convention, when it declared itself to be "socialist." It formally affiliated with the Socialist International and subsequently had delegates at various congresses and other meetings of the International.

The Partido Radical continued to support President Allende's government as long as it continued to exist. However, although they served in all of Allende's cabinets, the Radicals were distinctly junior partners in the Allende government, and their size and power continued to decline.

During the Allende administration, the Radicals suffered another major split. This arose as a result of changes in the party's constitution by its twenty-fifth convention in 1971. These changes declared the party to represent the working class, and its objective to be "the construction of a socialist society," and the Radicals' acceptance of "historical materialism and the idea of the class struggle as the means of interpreting reality." Those who opposed these changes looked upon the Radical Party as what it had in fact always been, a spokesman for the middle class. They were opposed also to the new dogmatism which was quite uncharacteristic of the traditional Radical Party. Finally, they were also strongly against the convention's decision to do away with the Radical Assembly as the local unit of the party and to replace it with a purely political cell.

The dissidents broke away to form the Left Radical Party (Partido Izquierda Radical—PIR). For some months it stayed within Popular Unity, but when President Allende refused to ratify an agreement with the Christian Democrats negotiation on his behalf by a PIR member of his cabinet, the Left Radical Party went into the opposition. In the congressional election of March 1973 it formed an electoral "federation" with the Christian Democrats and the National Democratic Party (PADENA), which then joined with a similar federation of the National Party and Radical Democracy to present united opposition slates.

All factions of the Radicals were outlawed by the military government of General Augusto Pinochet, which came to power on 11 September 1973. The Democracia Radical made no attempt to keep alive any illegal party. The Partido Radical was particularly severely persecuted as a member of Popular Unity, and most of its leaders were first arrested and then exiled. However, both it and the PIR, which suffered somewhat less severely at the hands of the military regime than did the Partido Radical, were able to maintain some semblance of underground organization.

Whether a single Radical party will emerge once again will only be determined when it once more becomes possible for parties to organize legally.

RADICAL SOCIALIST PARTY (PARTIDO RADICAL SOCIALISTA). Although the Radical Socialist Party was formed immediately after the fall of the dictatorship of Carlos Ibáñez late in 1931 by a group of ex-Radicals, it did not originate from a split in the Radical Party, and was not extinguished by merger with the Radicals, as happened with the schismatic Radical groups. Therefore, it requires an entry separate from that of the Radical Party.

From its inception, the Radical Socialist Party proclaimed itself a supporter of Socialism. At its congress in 1935 it adopted a program urging nationalization of the country's major industries and all of its banking system, recognized the class struggle "as a social fact," and expressed its opposition to imperialism and its support of political democracy and federalism.

The Radical Socialists supported Arturo Alessandri in the presidential campaign of 1931, and he was a major speaker at its first convention on May Day 1932. The party participated in the Socialist Republic, with a member in both the juntas which led the regime, as well as ministers in the cabinet.

The party again backed Alessandri in the 1932 presidential election, in which it won one seat in the Chamber of Deputies and five in the Senate. During the Alessandri regime of the 1930s, the Radical Socialists constituted part of the left-wing opposition. At the end of 1934, it became part of the Left Bloc, together with the Socialists, Left Communist Party, and Democratic Party, and in May 1936 it became part of the Popular Front.

The party suffered a crisis at the time of the 1938 election. Some of its leaders joined the Socialist Union (Unión Socialista) which supported the candidacy of Carlos Ibáñez, until he withdrew in September; others backed the Popular Front nominee, Pedro Aguirre Cerda from the beginning.

The Radical Socialist Party did not win any members of Congress in the 1937 parliamentary election. However, four years later it elected one deputy, Juan Bautista Rossetti, who by that time was the party's most outstanding figure. He was reelected in 1945. However, by that time the Partido Radical Socialista had dissolved, and its members had joined the Socialist Party, an event which took place in 1943.

RECUPERATIONIST AGRARIAN LABOR PARTY (PARTIDO AGRARIO LABORISTA RECUPERACIONISTA). See AGRARIAN LABOR PARTY.

REPUBLICAN CONFEDERATION OF CIVIC ACTION (CONFEDERACIÓN REPUBLICANA DE ACCIÓN CÍVICA—CRAC). Although the Republican Confederation of Civic Action was very short-lived, it was of significance as an attempt to organize politically the members of the legally recognized trade unions which had been established in accordance with the legislation of September 1924. This attempt took place during the dictatorship of Carlos Ibáñez (1927–1931).

The CRAC was based on the Workers Congress of Chile and the Union of White Collar Workers of Chile, two central labor organizations established with the patronage of the Ibáñez regime. It was established in 1930, and its first leader was deputy Luis Moreno Fontanés. It proclaimed its loyalty to the Ibáñez regime. In 1930, when President Ibáñez chose the members of the next Congress, he assigned fourteen deputies to the CRAC, but no senators. During the rest of the Ibáñez dictatorship, the CRAC deputies were characterized principally by their support of the administration. With the fall of the Ibáñez regime, the CRAC disappeared.

REVOLUTIONARY COMMUNIST PARTY (PARTIDO COMMUNISTA REVOLUCIONARIO). See COMMUNIST PARTY.

REVOLUTIONARY LABOR PARTY (PARTIDO OBRERO REVOLUCIONARIO—POR). See TROTSKYISTS.

REVOLUTIONARY SOCIALIST ACTION (ACCIÓN REVOLUCIONARIA SOCIALISTA). See SOCIALIST PARTY.

REVOLUTIONARY SOCIALIST PARTY (PARTIDO SOCIALISTA REVOLUCIONARIO). See SOCIALIST PARTY AND TROTSKYISTS.

REVOLUTIONARY SOCIALIST UNION (UNIÓN REVOLUCIONARIA SOCIALISTA). *See* SOCIALIST PARTY.

SOCIAL CHRISTIAN CONSERVATIVE PARTY (PARTIDO CONSERVADOR SOCIAL CRISTIANO). *See* CONSERVATIVE PARTY.

SOCIAL DEMOCRATIC PARTY (PARTIDO SOCIAL DEMÓCRATA). *See* DEMOCRATIC PARTY.

SOCIAL REPUBLICAN PARTY (PARTIDO SOCIAL REPUBLICANO). Formed shortly after the fall of the Ibáñez dictatorship in August 1931, the Social Republican Party lasted only a few years. However, in the turbulent period following the end of the Ibáñez regime, and the first years of the Arturo Alessandri government of the 1930s, it played a significant role.

At its founding convention in November 1931, the Social Republican Party proclaimed its purpose as defending public freedoms and republican institutions. Most of its founders had been Radicals, but there were also some ex-Liberals, and others who had had no previous party affiliation.

In 1932 the Social Republican Party supported the election of Arturo Alessandri. It also won one senator and four deputies in that election. During the first part of the Alessandri administration, it had ministers in his government. However, it split with the president, particularly on the issue of the Republican Militia (Milicia Republicana), a paramilitary group which Alessandri supported as a counterweight to possible subversive elements in the regular armed forces.

In 1935 the Social Republican Party went out of existence. Its leader said that the establishment once again of a constitutional regime, which was the party's major objective, made its continued existence unnecessary.

SOCIALIST PARTY (PARTIDO SOCIALISTA). The Socialist Party, which was one of the country's major political organizations in the middle decades of the twentieth century, was established in 1933, about a year and a half after the fall of the Ibáñez dictatorship in August 1931. It had its origins in two groups: a number of small, mainly middle-class led socialist parties which emerged right after Ibáñez's fall, and the new labor movement, consisting of unions legally recognized under the laws passed in September 1924, and which had become the majority element in organized labor by the end of the Ibáñez dictatorship.

Right after the fall of Ibáñez, six small Socialist parties appeared. These included Revolutionary Socialist Action (Acción Revolucionaria Socialista), organized mainly by a group of ex-anarchosyndicalists, among whom the most important were Oscar Schanke, Eugenio González, and César Godoy Urrutia; Socialist Order (Orden Socialista), in which Arturo Bianchi was the principal figure; and the Marxist Socialist Party (Partido Socialista Marxista), headed by Eleodoro Domínguez. Another such party was New Public Action (Nueva Acción Pública), the most important of the group, whose leaders included Colonel Marmaduque

Grove, founder of the Chilean Air Force, an old trade union leader Carlos Alberto Martínez, and the head of the Chilean Masons, Eugenio Matte Hurtado. It participated in the 1932 congressional election, and won three seats in the Chamber of Deputies and two in the Senate; Marmaduque Grove was also elected to the Senate a few days before formation of the Socialist Party. Finally, there were the Revolutionary Socialist Party (Partido Socialista Revolucionario), led by Albino Pezoa, and the International Socialist Party (Partido Socialista Internacional), headed by Santiago Wilson.

Before the establishment of the Socialist Party, some of these groups had already merged. The Partido Socialista Revolucionario and Partido Socialista Internacional joined to form the Partido Socialista Unificado, and it in turn merged with Acción Revolucionaria Socialista to establish the Revolutionary Socialist Union (Unión Revolucionaria Socialista).

All of these parties were in opposition to the short-lived administration of President Juan Esteban Montero. All of them also supported the uprising which established the Socialist Republic of Chile on 4 June 1932. Colonel Grove was at first the military force behind the regime, and Eugenio Matte Hurtado was a member of its ruling junta. During this first phase of the Socialist Republic which lasted about two weeks, the Socialist parties helped mobilize popular support behind the regime. However, when the first junta was ousted, and Colonel Grove was exiled to Easter Island, the Socialist parties supported him and opposed the phase of the Socialist Republic which was dominated by Carlos Dávila.

After the end of the Socialist Republic, when new elections were called, the Socialist parties united behind the presidential candidacy of Colonel Marmaduque Grove, who was still in exile. He came in second to Arturo Alessandri, but the political campaign on his behalf by all of the Socialist parties was a major element in their decision to join forces as a single organization a few months later.

In addition to these small parties, the other major element behind formation of the Socialist Party was the new labor movement. Soon after the end of the Ibáñez regime, the legally recognized unions had joined to form the National Confederation of Legal Unions (Confederación Nacional de Sindicatos Legales—CNSL). Since the Communists and anarchists, who had dominated the labor movement before the Ibáñez dictatorship, had both refused to allow unions under their control to seek legal recognition, they had no influence at all in the CNSL. Indeed, in the nature of the situation, the leaders of the CNSL, although considering themselves socialists, were strongly opposed to both the Communists—then going through their extremely sectarian "Third Period" phase—and the anarchists. Members of the unions affiliated with the CNSL were to provide much of the rank-and-file support for the new Socialist Party, and some of the union leaders also became important secondary leaders of the party.

The Socialist Party was established at a congress in April 1933. From its inception, it was one of the country's major parties, and the principal party on the far Left. It dominated the largest trade union group, the CNSL, and after 1937, when the Communist Left (Izquierda Comunista) merged with it, the party gained new adherents in organized labor, particularly in the "unlegal" unions which did not have official government recognition. In its first major electoral test, in March 1937, the party placed four members in the Senate and nineteen in the Chamber of Deputies.

The Socialist Party had strong attraction for young people in the 1930s. It had a Young Socialist group, which on appropriate occasions wore a uniform of blue, touched off with a red neckerchief. It was the members of the Socialist Youth who principally gave battle in the streets to the storm troopers of the National Socialist Movement.

There was a strong personalist strain in the Socialist Party. During the 1930s its most outstanding figure was undoubtedly Marmaduque Grove, who was rather weak on ideology, but had strong personal appeal which went beyond the ranks of the Socialist Party. Other leaders, although in many cases cultivating their own "cults of personality," sought to capitalize on that around Grove. He was declared "lifetime president" of the party. During the first five years, however, Oscar Schnake Vergara, the secretary-general, was in firm control of the party organization.

The Socialists were in strong opposition to the government of President Arturo Alessandri. They took the lead at the end of 1933 in forming the Left Bloc, inside and outside of Congress, to which the Democratic, Radical Socialist, and Left Communist parties were also affiliated. Although there was considerable resistance in the Socialist ranks to broadening this bloc into the Popular Front, by inclusion of the Radical and Communist parties, the Socialist Party finally accepted the idea in March 1936. Two months later the Popular Front was officially launched.

In preparation for the presidential election of 1938, the Socialists put forward the name of Marmaduque Grove to be the Popular Front candidate. However, in the Popular Front convention in April 1938, the Communists joined with the Radicals to block Grove's candidacy, and the Socialists were finally forced to accept that of the Radical, Pedro Aguirre Cerda.

The 1938 election brought the first of several splits which were to plague the Socialists during the next decade, and were to greatly weaken it and almost threaten its existence. In November 1937, a group headed by Ricardo Latcham, who were opposed to continuation in the Popular Front for the 1938 election, broke away to form the Socialist Union (Unión Socialista). This group became part of the Popular Liberating Alliance coalition—along with the Nazis and personal followers of Carlos Ibáñez—to support the ex-dictator's candidacy. Soon after the 1938 election the Unión Socialista joined with others who had backed Ibáñez to convert the Popular Liberating Alliance into a political party, which did not long survive, however.

Meanwhile, the Socialist Party had entered the government of President Pedro Aguirre Cerda. This was, in retrospect, a disastrous turn of events for the Socialist Party. Having within it, as it did, a number of personalist leaders who tended to form cliques around themselves, participation in the government tended to arouse ambitions among these cliques to obtain governmental positions. From then on, too, the question of whether or not the party should continue in (or join) the government became a fertile source of controversy, which was to figure in all of the divisions in the party during the next decade. The other major contentious issue within the party was the attitude it should have toward the Communists.

The two most notable Socialist cabinet members in this period were Oscar Schnake, the minister of development, and Minister of Health Salvador Allende. The former took the lead in setting up the Chilean Development Corporation, which was to be the major force in the country's industrialization during the next thirty years. Allende carried out an extensive program to improve the country's public health services.

Only a year after the entry of the Socialists into the Aguirre Cerda government, the party suffered its second, and much graver, split. The question at issue was whether or not the Socialists should continue in the government. The dissidents, led by deputy César Godoy Urrutia who argued that government participation without real control over the administration was debilitating the party, withdrew in April 1940 to form the Socialist Workers Party (Partido Socialista de Trabajadores—PST). Their exit did considerable damage to the party in the labor movement, where the dissidents had some following. In parliamentary elections in 1941, the PST placed two members in the Chamber of Deputies, César Godoy Urrutia and Natalio Berman. In June 1944, the PST officially merged with the Communist Party.

Meanwhile, relations between the Socialists and Communists had become very bitter. Within the new Confederation of Workers of Chile (Confederación de Trabajadores de Chile—CTCh), which had been formed in December 1936 by a merger of the Socialist-controlled CSNL and the Communists' Labor Federation of Chile (Federación Obrera de Chile), a conflict arose at the CTCh's second congress in 1939. The Communists refused to recognize the election of Socialist Bernardo Ibáñez as secretary-general, and for some weeks split away, forming a rival CTCh. Although this controversy was soon ended when the Communists returned to the CTCh of Ibáñez, rivalry between the two parties in the labor movement continued to be intense.

The two parties took strongly different stands towards the World War II during its first two years. The Communists followed the Comintern's policy of neutrality in favor of the Axis, while the Socialists, under the leadership of Oscar Schnake, took a strong stand in favor of the Allies. When the Socialists' demand that the Communists be expelled from the Popular Front was rejected by the Radicals, the Socialists themselves withdrew, and their ministers quit the government. The Socialists even went so far as to vote for a bill in Congress to outlaw the Communist Party. In the 1941 parliamentary elections, the Socialists ran their own slates and elected two senators and fifteen deputies.

After the 1941 election, the Socialist ministers returned to the government. In the presidential election made necessary by the death of Pedro Aguirre Cerda early in 1942, they supported the candidacy of Radical Juan Antonio Ríos. For a year, 1942–1943, they also had ministers in his cabinet.

However, in August 1943, the issue of government participation was again a factor in splitting the party. Another was the suggestion of a possible merger of the Socialist and Communist parties. Marmaduque Grove this time led the elements which supported further collaboration in the Ríos government and negotiations for merger with the Communists. When they were overruled in the party's Fourth Extraordinary Congress in August 1943, they withdrew to form the Authentic Socialist Party (Partido Socialista Auténtico — PSA). Salvador Allende was the principal spokesman for the faction opposed to that of Grove.

The PSA survived only four years. It participated with one minister in the last phase of the Juan Antonio Ríos government. In elections following Ríos's death, it supported the Liberal Party candidate, Fernando Alessandri. In May 1947 most of what remained of the PSA, led by Asdrúbal Pesoa, merged with the Communist Party. Marmaduque Grove and Eleodoro Domínguez returned to the Socialist Party.

Meanwhile, relations between the Socialist Party and the Communists became increasingly bad. In January 1946, the situation led to a split in the Confederation of Workers of Chile. In this split, a majority of unions — not only those controlled by the Communists, but also those under influence of the Radicals, the National Phalanx (Falange Nacional), and one faction of the Democratic Party — went with the Communists. A minority, still headed by Bernardo Ibáñez, consisted of unions controlled by the Socialists and a Democratic Party faction. At the same time that this split took place, the Socialists entered the government of Acting-President Alfredo Duhalde.

In the 1946 presidential election, the Socialists first supported the candidacy of Duhalde, but when he withdrew in favor of Fernando Alessandri, they nominated their own candidate, Bernardo Ibáñez. He came in a very poor fourth among the four nominees then running, and this election marked the low point in the decline of the fortunes of the Socialist Party.

During the first months of the administration of President Gabriel González Videla, when the Communists were in the cabinet, the Socialists were the victims of the attempts of the Communists to use governmental power to break the Socialist faction of the labor movement. However, this persecution, which included some violent physical attacks on Socialists, served to strengthen rather than weaken the party. This was shown in the municipal elections of April 1947, which showed a substantial improvement for the party, as compared with the presidential vote the year before.

With the exit of the Communists from the González Videla government, and their launching of a number of frankly political strikes, the Socialist faction of the CTCh rallied behind the administration. However, the party formally remained in opposition to the González Videla government.

In 1948 the Socialists suffered their last major split. As before, the principal issues were the attitude of the party toward the government on the one hand and toward the Communists on the other. The division was provoked by the fact that two Socialist deputies voted for the Law for the Defense of Democracy, which outlawed the Communist Party and removed its registered members from the voters list. Those deputies were expelled, but as a result their supporters, who included Bernardo Ibáñez and deputy Juan Bautista Rossetti, separated from the party in the XII Ordinary Congress. The Ibáñez-Rossetti faction was ultimately recognized by the electoral authorities as the Socialist Party of Chile (Partido Socialista de Chile—PSCh), and the rival group took the name Popular Socialist Party (Partido Socialista Popular—PSP).

Raúl Ampuero, the secretary-general of the Partido Socialista Popular, sought to form quite a different sort of party from that which the Socialists had traditionally been. He got the PSP to commit itself to Marxism-Leninism, and to impose on itself the kind of discipline to which the party was quite unaccustomed. Although his efforts to install rigid discipline were by no means completely successful, the party and its successor were committed from then on to Marxism-Leninism and the dictatorship of the proletariat.

The PSP remained in the opposition. However, the PSCh joined the González Videla government, one of its members becoming minister of education. In the 1949 parliamentary election, the PSP placed one member in the Senate and six in the Chamber of Deputies, while the PSCh elected five deputies.

The PSCh kept most of the Socialist faction of the Confederation of Workers of Chile under its control. However, the PSP rallied the backing of most of the Socialist workers in the copper miners' unions in the north, which they were to continue to have so long as the PSP existed as a separate party.

As the 1952 election approached, there was another realignment among the Socialists. The bulk of the PSP threw its support to General Carlos Ibáñez, arguing that he had virtually no governmental program and the Socialists would therefore be able to provide one—and that Ibáñez was going to win anyway. However, a minority group in the PSP, headed by Senator Salvador Allende, opposed this and broke away to join forces with the PSCh. However, Allende came to the PSCh with the proposal of the still-illegal Communist Party that if he were nominated for president by the PSCh, they would support him. The PSCh agreed to this proposal.

These events brought about one of the most spectacular about-faces in the twentieth-century Chilean politics. The PSCh, which had for half a decade fought the Communists more bitterly than any other party, suddenly became the Communists' closest ally. There are at least two explanations for this. First, Chilean politics during most of the twentieth century had been notoriously opportunistic, with parties suddenly switching alliances on the basis of electoral maneuvers and possibilities. Second, the Socialists were frankly exhausted by their long struggle with the Communists, in which they had had great disadvantages in terms of money and organs of publicity, and were frankly relieved to obtain immunity, at least temporarily, from Communist attacks.

A group within the PSCh opposed this switch. It was led by Juan Garafulic and Bernardo Ibáñez and formally expelled the leaders of the other faction. In the

1952 election it supported the candidacy of the Radicals, Pedro Alfonso, but did not long survive that election.

Meanwhile, with the victory of Carlos Ibáñez in the 1952 election, the Popular Socialists entered his cabinet, where they remained for about a year. In the parliamentary election following Ibáñez' election, they placed four members in the Senate and nineteen in the Chamber of Deputies. The PSCh elected only five deputies.

The election of Ibáñez stimulated fear that he might establish a new dictatorship. Previously, the faction of the Confederation of Workers of Chile controlled by the PSCh had been negotiating for a merger with independent and anarchist-dominated unions to form a new central labor organization, but had not included Communist-controlled unions in the negotiations. However, fear of the intentions of the new Ibáñez government, and their new alliance with the Communists, brought the Socialists to include the Communist unions in their plans.

The result was the formation of the Central Union of Workers of Chile (Central Unica de Trabajadores de Chile (CUTCh). The Communists gained a dominant position in the CUTCh which they were to maintain until it was suppressed by the military dictatorship of General Augusto Pinochet in September 1973. In spite of occasional revolts, the Socialists generally accepted a subordinate position in the CUTCh, in spite of the fact that until the late 1960s they had a larger rank-and-file following than the Communists.

Once the Popular Socialists abandoned the Ibáñez government and went into the opposition, the two Socialist factions moved closer together. In 1956 they both joined the Popular Action Front (Frente de Acción Popular—FRAP), which aligned most of the country's Leftist parties. They merged once again in July 1957 in what they called the 17th Ordinary Congress of the Socialist Party. The newly united group was called the Socialist Party of Chile (Partido Socialista de Chile).

The FRAP nominated Socialist Senator Salvador Allende for the election of 1958. This time Allende came in second in the presidential race, behind the victor, Jorge Alessandri, nominee of the Right. In the parliamentary election two and one-half years later, the Socialists elected four senators and twelve deputies.

Allende was again the candidate of the FRAP in the presidential election of 1964. His major opponent this time was Eduardo Frei, of the Christian Democratic Party. Allende received 39 percent of the vote, compared to the 56 percent of Frei. In the parliamentary elections six months later, the Socialists won fifteen members of the Chamber of Deputies.

After his defeat, Salvador Allende suggested the merger of the Socialists with the Radicals to form a single party capable of confronting the Christian Democrats successfully. When his suggestion was rejected by his party, Allende withdrew for some time from party leadership. The Socialists continued to be strong opponents of the Frei regime.

In 1967 the Socialist Party suffered another split, although it proved not to be a major one. Raúl Ampuero, who had been secretary-general, first of the Popular Socialist Party and then of the reunited Socialist Party, had decided not to run for reelection at the 21st Congress in June 1965. Undoubtedly one reason for this was that he was held in part responsible for the relatively poor showing of Salvador Allende in the 1964 election. He quickly became a center of opposition to the new party leadership, headed by his former right-hand man, Aniceto Rodríguez. This opposition culminated in his expulsion from the party, along with Senator Tomás Chadwick, in October 1967. Six Socialist deputies quit the party in solidarity with Ampuero.

The dissidents soon organized the Popular Socialist Union (Unión Socialista Popular). However, its following proved to be quite limited. The Popular Socialist Union supported the Popular Unity in the 1970 presidential campaign, although it did not belong to Unidad Popular. In the 1973 congressional elections, it ran its own candidates but did not elect any. There is no indication that Unión Socialista Popular was able to survive after the military coup of September 1973.

Meanwhile, the Socialists had an important conflict with their Communist partners at the time of the Soviet invasion of Czechoslovakia in August 1958. The Communists strongly supported the invasion, and the Socialists attacked them as being subservient to the Soviet Union. However, this conflict, although imperilling the FRAP, did not destroy it.

As the 1970 election approached, the Communists urged expansion of the FRAP to include the Radical Party. The Socialists resisted this idea, fearful that the Communists and Radicals would unite against them, as they felt had occurred during the Popular Front. However, they finally agreed to the formation of this wider alliance, Popular Unity (Unidad Popular – UP).

In preparation for the election, each party in UP put forward its own nominee. There was considerable opposition within the Socialist Party to naming Allende to run for a fourth time. When the first vote was taken in the party's central committee, Allende won by a very narrow majority and so refused to run; as a result, a second vote was taken, which overwhelmingly named Allende. He finally became the nominee of Unidad Popular.

Soon after the inauguration of President Allende, the Socialist Party held a convention. In this meeting, the president threw his influence against Aniceto Rodríguez, the party's secretary-General. As a result, Rodriguez was succeeded by Senator Carlos Altamirano, and the new central committee of the party included only a small minority of members who had been in the leadership since the unification of the PSP and PSCh. Most of the new central committee members were young people with little experience in leadership.

President Allende rallied wide new support for his party. This was shown in the March 1971 municipal election, when the Socialists far outstripped their Communist colleagues. This was the high point of the Unidad Popular, which got about half of the total vote.

During the Allende regime, the leadership of the Socialist Party virtually constituted a left-wing opposition to the administration. Secretary-General Carlos Altamirano and his associates joined with leaders and members of the Movement of the Revolutionary Left (Movimiento de la Izquierda Revolucionaria – MIR), to carry out hundreds of illegal seizures of landholdings, factories, and commercial enterprises. Furthermore, as Altamirano announced proudly two days before Allende was overthrown, the party leadership had thwarted all attempts by the president to reach an agreement with the Christian Democrats. In that same speech, Altamirano threatened that the Socialists would refuse to support the regime further if Allende didn't give up all attempts to reach any agreement with any part of the opposition.

The Altamirano leadership of the Socialist Party was also responsible for an action which did more than anything else to provoke the overthrow of Allende. The Socialist secretary-general himself was involved in conspiring with enlisted men in the armed forces, something which he admitted to proudly in his final speech before the downfall of the Unidad Popular regime.

After the fall of Allende, most of the top Socialist leaders were arrested. Allende himself, of course, was killed during the coup. The Socialist Party which, in spite of its extensive talk about violent revolution was not at all prepared to organize underground activities, certainly suffered more than any other party of Unidad Popular in the aftermath of the 11 September 1973 coup. In some parts of the country, the military rounded up the total leadership of provincial units of the Socialist Party and executed them.

It is not clear to what degree the Socialists were able to maintain an underground organization during the military regime. In exile, their ranks were split into three groups. One, with headquarters in East Berlin, was headed by ex-Senator Clodomiro Almeyda and was most closely associated with exiled leaders of the Communist Party. Another was led by Carlos Altamirano who, in exile, sought to present himself as a democratic Socialist, and to develop ties with European Socialist parties. The third was headed by Aniceto Rodríguez, with its base in Venezuela and with close relations with Acción Democrática and similar parties in other Latin American countries.

SOCIALIST LABOR PARTY (PARTIDO OBRERO SOCIALISTA). See COMMUNIST PARTY.

SOCIALIST ORDER (ORDEN SOCIALISTA). See SOCIALIST PARTY.

SOCIALIST PARTY OF CHILE (PARTIDO SOCIALISTA DE CHILE). See SOCIALIST PARTY.

SOCIALIST UNION (UNIÓN SOCIALISTA). See SOCIALIST PARTY.

SOCIALIST WORKERS PARTY (PARTIDO SOCIALISTA DE TRABAJADORES). See SOCIALIST PARTY.

TRADITIONALIST CONSERVATIVE PARTY (PARTIDO CONSERVADOR TRADICIONALISTA). See CONSERVATIVE PARTY.

TROTSKYISTS. A Trotskyist movement has existed in Chile since the early 1930s. Except in its first half-decade, Chilean Trotskyism has not been a substantial element even on the Chilean Left, but it has been a persistent element in national politics.

Chilean Trotskyism originated in a split in the Communist Party which took place during the Ibáñez dictatorship. The Chilean Communists emerged from the dictatorship as two parties, one enjoying the endorsement of the Communist International and headed by Elías Lafertte and the other headed by Manuel Hidalgo. For about a year and a half they both used the name Partido Comunista, but in a congress early in 1933 the Hidalgo group adopted the name Communist Left (Izquierda Comunista). By that time it had become associated with the International Left Communist Opposition of Leon Trotsky.

In the presidential election of 1931, the Left Communists ran their leader, Manuel Hidalgo, who only received 1,343 votes. In the following year, after the overthrow of President Juan Esteban Montero, they supported the Socialist Republic during the first two weeks, when Colonel Marmaduque Grove was its guiding spirit. Then at the end of 1932, they formed part of the coalition supporting Grove for president, in his race against Arturo Alessandri. However, when most of the other groups which had supported Grove's candidacy joined in April 1933 to form the Socialist Party, the Izquierda Comunista did not participate in this merger.

In those years, the Chilean Trotskyists were more influential than their Stalinist rivals in the labor movement and in general politics. They largely controlled the important Construction Workers Union and had influence in a number of other "unlegal" labor groups.

In 1935 the Izquierda Comunista became part of the Left Bloc (Bloque de Izquierda) formed by the Socialists, Radical Socialists, and Democráticos. Two years later, the majority of the Izquierda Comunista agreed to merge with the Socialist Party.

Meanwhile, elements which were still loyal to International Trotskyism had broken away from the Izquierda Comunista. This break took place late in 1935 when the party's Santiago Regional Committee split away to form what they first called the Bolshevik-Leninist Group (Grupo Bochevique-Leninista), and then the Revolutionary Labor Party (Partido Obrero Revolucionario—POR). At about the same time a small group broke away from the Socialist Youth, to form the Internationalist Labor Party (Partido Obrero Internacionalista), which also proclaimed its allegiance to Trotskyism. The two parties merged in June 1941 under the name of the POR.

In the 1940's the Trotskyists ran some electoral candidates. Humberto Valenzuela ran for president on the POR ticket in 1942, and they had several candidates for deputy in 1945, who received a total of about 1,000 votes, none of them being elected.

In the 1960s the Trotskyists again split, largely as a reflection of the divisions in the world Trotskyist movement. One faction, the POR, became affiliated with the

United Secretariat of the Fourth International. The other faction, the Partido Obrero Revolucionario (Trotskista), belonged to a schismatic Fourth International headed by an Argentine, J. Posadas.

The POR of the United Secretariat participated in the establishment of the Movement of the Revolutionary Left (Movimiento de la Izquierda Revolucionaria —MIR), and for half-a-dozen years, Luis Vitale, a Trotskyite, was one of its principal figures. However, in 1969 the Trotskyists split with the MIR, and reestablished their own party, the Revolutionary Socialist Party (Partido Socialista Revolucionario—PSR), which was also affiliated with the United Secretary of the Fourth International.

The POR(T) strongly supported the Allende government in the early 1970s, while the PSR gave it "critical" backing. Both groups have maintained a precarious underground existence since the advent of the military dictatorship in September 1973.

UNIFIED SOCIALIST PARTY (PARTIDO SOCIALISTA UNIFICADO). *See* SOCIALIST PARTY.

UNIÓN REVOLUCIONARIA SOCIALISTA. *See* SOCIALIST PARTY.

UNIÓN SOCIALISTA. *See* SOCIALIST PARTY.

UNIÓN SOCIALISTA POPULAR. *See* SOCIALIST PARTY.

UNIONIST LIBERAL PARTY (PARTIDO LIBERAL UNIONISTA). *See* LIBERAL PARTY.

UNITED CONSERVATIVE PARTY (PARTIDO CONSERVADOR UNIDO). *See* CONSERVATIVE PARTY.

UNITED LIBERAL PARTY (PARTIDO LIBERAL UNIDO). *See* LIBERAL PARTY.

UNITED MOVEMENT OF POPULAR ACTION (MOVIMIENTO DE ACCIÓN POPULAR UNIDO—MAPU). The MAPU was originally established by the *Rebelde* faction of the Christian Democratic Party, when it split from the PDC in 1969. It almost immediately joined the Popular Unity coalition which was supporting the presidential candidacy of Salvador Allende. Among its original leaders were Jacques Chonchol and Vicente Soler.

However, when the *Terceristas* of the PDC also broke with their party in 1971, and established the Christian Left (Izquierda Cristiana), most of the top leaders of the MAPU joined that party. Both dissident Christian Democratic groups were part of Unidad Popular.

The MAPU constituted one of the far-Left elements in the Allende regime.

Early in 1973 it split, with one faction, headed by Oscar Garretón, aligning itself with the Movimiento de la Izquierda Revolucionaria and the far Left of the Socialist Party; the other led by Jaime Gazmuri, was a more moderate element of Popular Unity.

Shortly before the ouster of the Allende regime on 11 September 1973, it was disclosed that Oscar Garretón was involved, along with Carlos Altamirano, secretary-general of the Socialist Party, and Miguel Henríquez of the MIR, in conspiring with enlisted men of the navy. This was one of the factors which undoubtedly provoked the military coup of 11 September 1973.

There is little indication that the MAPU has been able to survive the persecution of the military regime. Its exiled leaders continue to be divided into two antagonistic groups.

VANGUARDIA POPULAR SOCIALISTA. *See* NATIONAL SOCIALIST MOVEMENT OF CHILE.

Robert J. Alexander

COLOMBIA

The Republic of Colombia, located in the northwestern corner of the South American continent, with its northern frontier on the Atlantic Ocean and its western border on the Pacific, comprises approximately 440,000 square miles, thus making it the fifth largest country in Latin America. Its topography and climate are immensely varied.

The present population is about 27 million. Today more than half of the population is urban; this sector is growing at double the rate of the rural population. Much of this growth has occurred in ten cities, each with a population in excess of 200,000.

The ethnic mix of the population is varied. Mestizos and mulattoes account for approximately 75 percent; whites 20 percent; and blacks and Indians four and one percent respectively. Mestizos and whites are found mostly in the urban centers, in the Andean highlands, and coastal regions. Mulattoes and blacks are more numerous in the Cauca Valley, the lower Magdalena river region, and the Pacific lowlands. Small Indian communities are scattered throughout the country, including the eastern plains.

Turbulent Politics of the Nineteenth Century

Nineteenth century Colombia's history was turbulent, even by Latin American standards. Political conflicts, uprisings, and civil wars occurred with monotonous regularity. Historians have provided numerous explanations for these conflicts: regional struggles between pro-clerical Conservatives who desired a corporative social and economic structure and a centralized state, and Liberals who wanted a secular society free of church influence, a federalized state, and a laissez-faire economy; and long-term economic stagnation that provided fertile ground for elite competition for available wealth. Continuous internal order and stability did not really occur until after the end of the devastating three-year Civil War of the Thousand Days in 1902.

Although church-state relations and centralist-federalist conceptions contributed mightily to nineteenth-century Liberal-Conservative conflicts, there is no question but that economics played an important, if not fundamental, role. Independent Colombia inherited an economy dominated by large landowners and allied monopolistic commercial groups. The vast mass of the population lived in or near poverty as tenants, sharecroppers, small landholders, and in the case of the Indians, people economically marginalized on reservations. Small sectors of artisans, professionals, and bureaucrats were dependent upon policies of a treacherously unstable, elite-dominated state. Political independence had not solved the problems of a colonial economy with its seignorial social order.

Nevertheless, elements of the elite, including many who had supported independence, sought to reorient the economy, and hence society, toward directions that they considered progressive. Influenced by the more spacious and secular ideas of the Enlightenment, by the bourgeois revolutions in Europe, by the North American example, and by English notions of free trade and economic individualism, these groups became increasingly powerful by mid-century. For example, Florentino González, treasury secretary in the Cipriano de Mosquera administration, in 1847 and afterwards, pushed through policies of free trade and manufacturing, encouraged an export-oriented agriculture (based upon large estates), and eliminated state protection of artisan industries and state monopolies over such commodities as tobacco in order to encourage private capitalist enterprise. Other measures were adopted to stimulate internal transportation, such as roads, steamboat navigation, and railroads.

Eventually policies were changed to allow for the distribution, settlement, and development of the large amount of land inherited by the state after independence. These initiatives, when combined with the ideological framework of *laissez-faire*, federalism, secularism and individualism, naturally were inimical to various interests: the church, with its vast land holdings; Indians, on their communal lands; artisans, competing with advanced industrializing nations; commercial groups, previously benefitting from state-supported monopolies; large landowners, out of the mainstream of commercial agricultural development; professionals and bureaucrats, who feared for their role in a weakened, decentralized state. Herein are the roots of much of nineteenth-century conflict.

The liberal policies did not change the Colombian reality overnight. Indeed, until the 1880s there was disruption, slow growth in certain sectors, decline in others. Yet the stage was set for the country's eventual integration into the international capitalist system. The old seignorial order was partially disrupted. Entrepreneurial groups with bourgeois attitudes fostered international trade through production of such crops as tobacco, indigo, cinchona. They also controlled the gradually expanding coffee industry being developed by both large growers and thousands of small landowners in western Colombia. Eventually, too, both Conservatives and Liberals in the elite realized the necessity for internal stability and order, and the role that a strong state could play in this process.

The Emergence of Political Parties

From the 1840s to the present the Colombian political system has been characterized by the domination of two parties, the Conservatives and the Liberals.

Their monopoly over political power has never been overcome by third parties or movements, which have had, with the exception of the small Communist Party, relatively short lives. Since the nineteenth century the Conservative and Liberal parties have been controlled by the country's upper-class elite, which has direct connections with the dominant economic interests and sectors. The parties' national leaderships control their respective constituencies through a system of regional and local political groups and bosses, with their own economic connections and patronage, and in the twentieth century, with influence in such organizations as trade unions. Traditionally, the lower classes have been largely excluded from any meaningful participation in national politics. Party loyalties, usually hereditary until recent times, were cemented by the dependency of the majority of the people upon large landowning families and allied commercial interests, who mobilized their followers as partisans in their internecine struggles. Under these circumstances, villages, towns, and even parts of regions were indelibly stamped as either Conservative or Liberal. Class-based mass politics did not really appear until well into the twentieth century.

The conflicts over national versus regional or local government and state-church relations formed the background for the emergence of the Conservative and Liberal parties during the chaotic decades of the 1830s and 1840s. During most of the years between 1849 and 1880, however, the Liberals dominated the country. The constitutions of 1853 and 1863 were federalist and provided much local autonomy. The power of the church also was generally circumscribed. Still, major and minor civil conflicts persisted, and administrations changed hands frequently, often as a result of splits and realignments among and between parties and party factions. Coalitions between factions of both parties during periods of crisis became a feature of Colombian politics that persists to the present.

In 1880 Rafael Núñez, nominally a Liberal, was elected president under the slogan Regeneration by a coalition of moderate Liberals and Conservatives. Until 1894 he dominated Colombian politics as president and strong-man. During his autocratic rule the highly centralist and still-existing Constitution of 1886 was imposed, a strong presidency created, and the church restored to an official and influential role in national life. The Liberals rebelled unsuccessfully in 1884–1885 and again in 1899–1903, but the system he established provided the basis for Conservative hegemony until 1930.

The Twentieth Century Political System

The principal features of Colombian politics during the twentieth century have been periods of single-party domination, often with some collaboration from the opposite party, followed by coalition governments of both Conservatives and Liberals. The latter arrangement facilitated transfers of power, while assuring both parties continuing roles in government and their permanent domination of the political system.

During the decades of Conservative rule until 1930, Colombia began to experience economic and social transformation. The export of primary products, such as coffee, bananas, and oil accelerated; the construction of railroads, ports, roads, and communication systems increased; and industrialization began. In the growing cities new middle and working classes appeared. The old differences between Conservatives and Liberals became less important as the elite of both parties shared in the new wealth, largely to the exclusion of the lower classes.

But as a result of the new conditions agitation among workers, students, and intellectuals increased in the 1920s. The chief beneficiary was the Liberal Party, which under the leadership of Benjamín Herrera after 1922 modified its programs to attract the new social formations. The ineptitude of Conservative governments, a split in the Conservative Party's leadership, and the economic crisis of 1929 combined to set the stage for Liberal domination between 1930 and 1946.

The Liberal administrations, especially that of Alfonso López (1934–1938), carried out economic, social, educational, and governmental reforms designed to provide more benefits and greater participation for the middle and working classes. They also strengthened the state's role in economic development. But these initiatives caused increasing apprehension among the elite of both parties, who feared the potential power of the mobilizing middle and working classes. During the economic dislocations brought on by World War II, and amid intense social agitation, the reactionary Laureano Gómez captured the Conservative Party and launched vociferous attacks on the reformist Liberals.

The Liberal era ended in 1946 when the party split between the regulars' candidate, moderate Gabriel Turbay, and the populist-socialist Jorge Eliécer Gaitán, long the champion of the party's urban masses. The Gómez-picked Conservative, Mariano Ospina Pérez, won the election by a plurality of votes.

During the next seven years, under the Conservative presidents Ospina and Gómez, the country journeyed into disaster. Conservative attempts to reduce Liberal electoral majorities in certain rural departments through violence engendered reaction. Gaitán, spokesman of the country's impoverished millions, captured the Liberal Party and preached social revolution. When he was assassinated on 9 April 1948, massive uprisings occurred in cities throughout the country. Although these were repressed, savage conflict between Conservatives and Liberals increased throughout vast areas of the countryside. Known as *La Violencia*, this civil war claimed over 200,000 lives before it was finally contained in the late 1950s. Another victim was Gómez, who was ousted by a military coup in 1953, amid generalized rejoicing.

La Violencia, although it began primarily as a Liberal-Conservative conflict with aspects of intense class hatred, degenerated into a multifaceted phenomenon. While partisans of the traditional parties continued to do battle, various other groups emerged with differing motives. For example, former Gaitanistas and Liberal elements organized guerrilla bands with the intention of fostering revolution. The Communists, sometimes allied with the Liberal bands, organized peasants into "self-defense" groups that established several virtually autonomous rural "republics."

Other groups, following years of terror and counterterror, simply became bandit gangs without any other motivations than vengeance and despoilment. Still others, hired as thugs by landowners and political bosses, terrorized the countryside in order to acquire abandoned lands after the inhabitants fled, or to assure quiescence among the rural population. In many cases, a mixture of motives could be found among the guerrillas. Perhaps most tragic of all were the "children of La Violencia," who had come to adolescence amid an atmosphere of murder, rape, pillage, sadistic torture, and official repression, and who knew only the rule of machete and gun. Finally, it must be noted that La Violencia touched few members of the national elite. While the elite remained united at the top, no matter what political persuasion, the country was virtually torn apart.

The National Front and Afterwards

The military dictatorship of General Gustavo Rojas Pinilla, sanctioned by the majority of leaders in both parties, put an end to the worst of the violence. But when Rojas evidenced personal political ambitions and threatened the traditional party system, he was ousted by his own colleagues in 1957. A year later, as a result of a political pact between the Conservative and Liberal leaderships, the first National Front coalition government assumed power.

The National Front arrangement, endorsed by a national plebiscite, was unique. Liberal and Conservative presidents alternated in office every four years until 1974. Seats in the Senate, House, departmental assemblies, and municipal councils were divided equally between the two parties, as were cabinet posts. Parity also was introduced into the public bureaucracy. The purpose of the National Front was to reduce conflict between the two parties by providing political stability. All other parties were excluded.

The National Front governments achieved their primary purpose. Liberal-Conservative violence subsided, although continuing social unrest by the early 1970s assumed an urban and class basis. Successes were obtained in professionalizing the bureaucracy, and limited advances were made in the areas of social welfare, housing, agrarian reform, education, and economic development. The widespread reforms expected by the populace, however, were not accomplished. The exclusive bipartisan agreement, while reducing the intensity of political conflict, caused widespread voter apathy (less than 40 percent of the electorate voted in most National Front elections), government stalemate, and factionalism within both parties. Both the leftist Liberal Revolutionary Movement (Movimiento Revolucionario Liberal), led by Alfonso López Michelsen, son of the former president, and the populist National Popular Alliance of the former dictator Gustavo Rojas Pinilla raised temporary but serious challenges to the National Front.

In 1974 Alfonso López Michelsen, now reintegrated into the regular Liberal Party, was elected by a wide margin over the Conservative Alvaro Gómez Hurtado, son of Laureano Gómez. Although this was the first "free" election after the end of the National Front, by mutual agreement of the parties many of its features were continued.

Although the López Michelsen government began with great expectations, economic difficulties, corruption, social unrest, and continued political bickering marred its years in office. Widespread voter apathy was evident again in the election of 1978, when the Liberal, Julio César Turbay, son of the 1946 regular Liberal candidate, won by a narrow margin over the Conservative Belisario Betancur.

As the 1980s began amid increasing economic uncertainty, social tension, and official repression, the long-term viability of the traditional Colombian political system once again was being called into question.

Bibliography

Robert J. Alexander. *Communism in Latin America.* Rutgers University Press, New Brunswick, N.J., 1957.

R. Albert Berry, Ronald G. Hellman, Mauricio Solaun. *Politics of Compromise.* Transaction Books, New Brunswick, N.J., 1980.

Orlando Fals Borda. *Subversion and Social Change in Colombia.* Columbia University Press, New York, 1969.

Robert H. Dix. *Colombia: The Political Dimensions of Change.* Yale University Press, New Haven, 1967.

James Payne. *Patterns of Conflict in Colombia.* Yale University Press, New Haven, 1968.

Richard E. Sharpless. *Gaitán of Colombia.* University of Pittsburgh Press, Pittsburgh, 1978.

Political Parties

ALIANZA NACIONAL POPULAR. *See* NATIONAL POPULAR ALLIANCE.

BLOQUE SOCIALISTA. *See* FAR LEFT PARTIES.

CHRISTIAN SOCIAL DEMOCRATIC PARTY (PARTIDO SOCIAL DEMÓ-CRATA CRISTIANO—PSDC). Founded in 1959 by a group of intellectuals and professionals, the reformist PSDC had ties to other Christian Democratic movements on the continent. It regarded itself as advocating a third way between capitalism and socialism; its program called for a "just distribution of wealth," and state control in such areas as banking, transport, natural resources, and other services. Middle sector in leadership and orientation, it was fairly well organized in the larger cities, with its major strength in Antioquía and Bogota.

In 1974, Hermes Duarte, the PSDC candidate for president, received less than 10,000 votes.

COLOMBIAN BROAD MOVEMENT (MOVIMIENTO AMPLIO COLOMBI-
ANO). *See* FAR LEFT PARTIES.

COLOMBIAN POPULAR SOCIALIST PARTY (PARTIDO POPULAR SO-
CIALISTA COLOMBIANO—PPSC). In 1943 Antonio García and other left-
wing intellectuals, disenchanted with both Liberalism and its Communist allies,
formed the League of Political Action (Liga de Acción Política) and formulated a
program of nationalization of basic resources and industries, agrarian reform, and
Latin-American economic integration. The league was short-lived, but several of
its members, including García, affiliated with the Gaitanista campaign that was
organized in 1944. García, an economist, became, in fact, one of Gaitán's principal advisers and conceived important parts of the populist leader's Colón Platform, which called for sweeping economic and social reforms.

After Gaitán's assassination in 1948, García went on to organize the Colombian
Socialist Movement in 1950. Three years later this became the Colombian Popular Socialist Party. The PPSC claimed to be nationalist, democratic, and socialist,
and offered itself as the only revolutionary alternative to communism. It established ties with other socialist parties outside of Colombia, insisted upon democratic methods, and elaborated a program similar to Gaitán's and that of the
earlier league. The PPSC supported the military regime of General Gustavo
Rojas Pinilla, in the expectation that it would carry out substantial democratic
reforms. When Rojas was ousted in 1957, the PPSC went into eclipse.

The party experienced a brief revival in the late 1950s and early 1960s in
opposition to the "oligarchical" National Front and its policy of exclusion of third
parties. Elements of its leadership were influenced by the Cuban Revolution and
began to organize revolutionary activities. This caused a split over tactics and
direction, and the PPSC dissolved as a result.

García, one of the most articulate and original Colombian left-wing intellectuals, has continued to write penetrating analyses of the Colombian and Latin-
American realities and to agitate for structural change. He was for a time in the
1960s an advisor to Gloria Gaitán in her efforts to revive her father's movement.
He also was affiliated with left-wing elements of the National Popular Alliance
(Alianza Nacional Popular—ANAPO), as that movement took a more leftist
direction in the early 1970s.

COMITÉS DEMOCRÁTICOS POPULAR Y REVOLUCIONARIOS. *See* FAR
LEFT PARTIES.

COMMUNIST PARTY (PARTIDO COMUNISTA). The Colombian Commu-
nist Party had its remote origins in the mid-1920s when a Russian immigrant,
Silvestre Savitsky, organized a discussion group of young workers and students in
Bogotá that became known as the Grupo Comunista. The members soon established similar organizations in the industrial centers of Cali and Medellín, and on
the north coast among the workers in the so-called Banana Zone.

The period was one of intense intellectual debate and organizational activity among the nascent working class. Various currents, ranging from leftist Liberalism to anarchosyndicalism, were competing for influence, and the communist groups were deeply involved. Much of this activity was clandestine, owing to the repression of the ruling Conservative administrations. Eventually, following workers' congresses in 1925 and 1926, a convergence of sorts occurred, and in the latter year, the Revolutionary Socialist Party (Partido Socialista Revolucionario – PSR) was formed.

The Partido Socialista Revolucionario never became a full-fledged Communist Party. With its dissolution in 1930, the Communist Party of Colombia was founded by most of those who had remained in the PSR.

During the early 1930s, with first Guillermo Hernández Rodríguez and then Luis Vidal, as secretary-general, the Communists concentrated much of their efforts among the landless rural workers in the mountainous regions east and southwest of Bogotá. They organized peasant leagues, "self-defense" groups, and put various kinds of pressure on large landowners in the region. Several of the areas organized in those early days remain firmly under the influence of the party today. The party also opposed the "imperialistic" border war between Colombia and Peru in the Amazon region in 1933, a position which earned them severe government repression.

The period of the Communist Party's greatest influence began in the mid-1930s, during the first Alfonso López Pumarejo administration. Although initially opposed to López as a "bourgeois reformer," the party switched its attitude in 1936, after international communism began its "popular-front" strategy. The party continued to support the Liberal administrations until 1946 with the argument that they represented progressive reformist and democratic tendencies and were a bulwark against the kind of reactionary, pro-Fascist policies advocated by the Laureano Gómez brand of Conservatism. In return for its support, the party generally was allowed by the government to carry on its activities openly, and to continue in its influential role in the trade union movement.

The party had organized a labor confederation in 1929, but it had remained relatively small and localized. In 1935 Liberal-controlled unions formed the Trade Union Confederation of Colombia (Confederación Sindical de Colombia), later renamed the Confederation of Workers of Colombia (Confederación de Trabajadores de Colombia – CTC), with a broadened membership. As a result of the Liberal-Communist alliance, the latter became important within the CTC, and at times exercised effective control of its central committee. Thus, the Communists' most important influence in Colombian life was exercised through the trade union movement. Despite occasional internal conflicts that were usually the result of shifts in Moscow's international strategy, the Communists maintained their position in the CTC until 1951. In that year, the CTC split between its Liberal and Communist factions, a development facilitated by the appearance of rival trade union organizations, the Jesuit-sponsored Union of Workers of Colombia

(Unión de Trabajadores de Colombia) and the Peronist National Confederation of Labor (Confederación Nacional de Trabajo).

The party's most important political gains occurred in the 1940s. As the economy suffered from dislocations occasioned by the war, and the second López administration came under increasingly vociferous attacks from the reactionary Gómez, the Communist Party reiterated its support for reformist Liberalism. In the 1945 mid-term elections, the party achieved its most notable electoral success, when it gained over 27,000 votes and elected members to congress, departmental assemblies, and municipal councils.

The Communist Party, however, refused to support the 1946 presidential campaign of Jorge Gaitán, opting instead for the regular Liberal candidate Gabriel Turbay (party propaganda called Gaitán a demagogue and even a fascist). Although it subsequently recanted and later supported Gaitán in his take-over of the Liberal Party, it lost much of its electoral support, in addition to some of its membership, to the populist's movement. The party's equivocation caused a split, with its leader Augusto Durán and his followers being ousted, and the "official" faction being taken over by Gilberto Vieira at the Fifth Party Congress in 1947.

The Communist Party's fortunes continued to decline thereafter. It was blamed for playing a major part in the uprisings following Gaitán's assassination, but this seems unlikely. During the Ospina and Gómez administrations of the late 1940s and early 1950s, it suffered persecution along with the Liberals. Its influence in the CTC also declined, as organized labor came under attack from the Conservative administrations. During the Rojas military dictatorship, the party was officially outlawed. Its most notable achievements during these bleak years were retaining control over unions in the departments of Valle and North Santander, and in keeping its rural peasant zones free of most violence and military attacks. But it did not organize the peasants into a coherent revolutionary force, preferring instead to continue its political line of seeking alliances with the "national bourgeoisie" and other "progressive" forces.

In 1958 the Communists supported the election of Liberal Alberto Lleras Camargo, the first National Front president. Although favoring the restoration of constitutional rule, they objected to the oligarchic arrangement of the Front and the fact that it excluded third parties like their own. However, the Communists did run and elect some candidates for office on Liberal slates throughout the period. They also achieved some influence in the Liberal Revolutionary Movement (Movimiento Revolucionario Liberal) of Alfonso López Michelsen. But opposition charges that they dominated that movement were unfounded.

The most notable revival of Communist influence during the National Front period and after occurred in the trade union movement. As the CTC regained lost ground and the party itself won legal status once more, the Communists returned to positions of power, especially at local and regional levels, within the CTC. But this caused alarm in the CTC national leadership, and in 1960 several affiliates were expelled for being Communist-dominated. In 1966 the Communists organized their own Trade Union Confederation of Colombia (Confederación Sindical de Trabajadores de Colombia), which received official government recognition in the 1970s. By the end of that decade, the Communist-controlled unions represented perhaps 20 percent of all organized workers.

The party also made some headway among students, intellectuals, and the peasantry. Through its youth arm, the Union of Communist Youth of Colombia (Unión de la Juventud Comunista de Colombia), it managed to gain positions of power in the various national student federations that existed throughout the 1960s and 1970s, which were decades of intense activism and strife in the state-controlled universities. Through the party's publishing plant, which puts out a weekly newspaper, theoretical journal, and other materials, as well as in the party leadership, intellectuals gained a voice. Finally, the party has continued its organizational work among rural inhabitants, especially in the southern part of the country and, more recently, in newly settled zones in the eastern region. The party also has provided support for the guerrilla Revolutionary Armed Forces of Colombia (Fuerzas Armadas Revolucionarias de Colombia) which, despite repeated government military campaigns, continues to operate in Huila and other southern departments.

It is impossible accurately to estimate present party membership. Figures variously given run from ten to twenty thousand, with some even higher. There is no question, however, that despite its relatively minor role in Colombian electoral politics, the Communist Party is better organized now than at any other time in its history. This despite splits that occurred in 1964 and 1965, when pro-Chinese factions were expelled from the party's student organization and adult Communist ranks. The pro-Chinese group became the Communist Party of Colombia (Marxist-Leninist) (Partido Comunista de Colombia [Marxista-Leninista]) and organized its own guerrilla band.

Since its inception, the Communist Party has been dominated at its national leadership level by middle-class intellectuals, although efforts have always been made to include workers and peasants as well. The most frequent criticism of the leadership is that it has been excessively opportunistic, unimaginative, and bureaucratic, charges frequently made against Latin-American Communist parties affiliated with the Moscow branch of international communism. Yet, the party has remained, through favorable and adverse times, the longest-lived third party in Colombian history.

The Communists have long sought a "national, democratic and anti-imperialist" front, based upon collaboration of all leftists in alliance with workers and peasants. Toward that end, it joined in 1974 the two other left-wing groups, the Independent Revolutionary Workers Movement (Movimiento Obrero Independiente Revolucionario—MOIR), and the Colombian Broad Movement (Movimiento Amplio Colombian), to form an electoral alliance called the National Union of Opposition (Unión Nacional de Oposición). Their presidential candidate, Hernán Echeverri, received approximately 3 percent of the vote.

Internal differences, revolving around charges that the Communists were supporting the López Michelsen administration, and were violating collective and democratic procedures, resulted in MOIR's subsequent withdrawal from the National Union of Opposition. But differences among the various Left groups were sufficiently patched up to provide unity for the 1976 mid-term elections, in which the union increased its electoral support. In 1978 the Left again split into three main groups, and the union's presidential candidate, Julio César Pernía, received less than 2 percent of the vote, in an election marked by charges of widespread fraud, violence and official persecution.

Since 1978, the Communists have continued to seek a basis for left-wing unity. In late 1979 the party joined with the FIRMES movement organized around the novelist Gabriel García Márquez to form the Democratic Front (Frente Democrático). Although the Communists abandoned their insistence on unconditional support for Cuba and its foreign policies (a factor in previous left-wing differences), the Democratic Front has not proved to be entirely viable, owing to a lack of a coherent revolutionary program and democratic internal procedures. The Communist Party, in sum, continues to vacillate between a reformist and revolutionary strategy, and between its support for a democratic popular opposition front and its insistence upon dominating such a movement.

COMMUNIST PARTY OF COLOMBIA (MARXIST-LENINIST) (PARTIDO COMUNISTA DE COLOMBIA (MARXISTA-LENINISTA)). See COMMUNIST PARTY.

CONSERVATIVE PARTY (PARTIDO CONSERVADOR). Historically one of Colombia's two dominant parties, the Conservatives emerged, like the Liberals, in the 1840s during a period of intense political agitation over the future direction of the nation. The party had its roots in the Popular Societies, organized by the Jesuits and presided over by the astute politician and future president, Mariano Ospina Rodríguez. These groups, consisting of members of the aristocratic elite, were developed as a counterweight to the liberal, artisan-led Democratic Societies.

In this era, the Conservatives were staunch defenders of the social and economic status quo. They were members of proud, aristocratic Creole families who were large landowners and slaveholders; or powerful and influential commercial groups who benefitted from various state monopolies. Outside of the former imperial cities of Bogotá, Popayán, and Cartagena, they were often located in those regions that had not yet been developed by commercial-export agriculture or artisan industry, where they dominated a passive peasantry in almost feudal fashion. Their closest allies were found in the church hierarchy, which considered itself threatened in terms of wealth, power, and status by the subversive doctrines of liberalism.

Nineteenth-century Conservatives thus were dedicated to authority, order, and hierarchy; to a Hispanic Catholicism which was the repository and safeguard of traditional values that were rooted in the seignorial agrarian order which had evolved over centuries. In contrast to the Liberals, who were attempting to impose foreign and "artificial" ideas upon the country, the Conservatives saw themselves as defenders of the authentic Colombia. Although they were willing to defend the republicanism that had resulted from independence, for them it meant an "Athenian Democracy" ruled by an upper-class elite of family, wealth, and merit.

The Conservatives were in the forefront of the resistance to the radical Liberal upsurge of 1848–1853. Their representatives fought the artisans in the streets, as later they fought in the name of Religion on the battlefields. But what they resisted was not the liberalism of the upper-class elite, the emerging bourgeoisie, so much as the popular liberalism, which they regarded as subversive, of those beneath them in the social class system.

In the period between 1853 and 1867, a series of internal conflicts rocked the country. In retrospect, it is seen that these were not principally over economic and political issues, but over the Liberals' assaults on the church. Taking the condemnation of liberalism by Pope Pius IX in 1864 as their watchword, the Conservatives, under the ideological mentorship of Rufino Cuervo, and the political leadership of Carlos Holguín, waged war against various Liberal administrations and their constitutions, on the basis of principles of morality, religion, family, and property. Their ultimate success occurred in 1886, when the centralist constitution of that year secured a powerful place for the church in Colombian society. This was ratified two years later when the concordat with the Vatican was signed.

Yet, despite their vociferous resistance to popular liberalism, and its attacks upon the system of privilege and the church, Conservatives were quite capable of accommodating themselves to the new realities of the last third of the century. As Colombia slowly became integrated into the international capitalist system, as commercial agriculture and international trade developed, and new economic opportunities appeared, Conservatives joined with upper-class Liberals to create a national bourgeoisie. A convergence of interests, sealed through family and commercial ties, occurred, which indiscriminately cut across party lines. These brought with them new nationalistic and market orientations. The process was facilitated, as well, by the expansion of the Antioquian populations southward into the Quindio region, where a rich coffee-growing culture was developed by market-oriented middle-class farmers with strong Conservative ties. Further, with the Liberal impetus of mid-century spent, the newly prosperous upper-class members of that party found increasing advantages in order and stability. Class interest came to prevail over "subversive" ideology. The Liberal bourgeoisie was willing to make compromises with the Conservatives.

Perhaps the best example of this was Rafael Núñez. In the 1850s he had been president of the Democratic Society in his native Cartagena, editor of *La Democrácia*, which proclaimed the values of the French Revolution, a fanatical anticlerical supporter of the Liberal Constitution of 1853, who had signed decrees that eliminated church properties from mortmain. When traveling in Europe, he came under the influence of the English sociologist Herbert Spencer, who also had an impact upon other Liberals of his generation. For Núñez, Spencer showed how the gap between Conservative traditionalism and Liberal innovation might be bridged.

Gradually, Núñez abandoned his earlier radicalism. He claimed that Liberals and Conservatives were becoming more and more alike, a theme that would be heard repeatedly in the twentieth century. He also gave up his anticlerical attitudes by stating that Jacobinism did not belong in a Catholic country. Politically, Núñez called for "regeneration" of the country through reconciliation between the parties; his vehicle was the National Party, consisting of Conservatives and independent Liberals. As president, he joined with Conservatives and like-minded Liberals to crush those Liberals who rose against him in 1884–1885 because they felt he had betrayed their party. It was during this presidency that the Constitution of 1886, a thoroughly conservative charter inspired by Miguel Antonio Caro, was implemented. This marked the beginning of Conservative hegemony.

Once firmly in power, the Conservatives proved as intolerant and exclusive as their foes had been earlier. The Liberals, without other recourse, rebelled in 1895 and again in the devastating War of the Thousand Days between 1899–1902. But these conflicts served to solidify Conservative power and reduced Liberalism to a secondary role in Colombian politics until 1930.

An arrangement worked out after the War of the Thousand Days between the Conservative and Liberal elites gave the latter an assured, but minority, position. The era of the nineteenth century civil conflicts ended; it was replaced by an upper-class "Athenian Democracy" that at least took on the semblance of republican forms. The issues that divided the parties in the previous century began to recede as the upper-class leaderships of both parties participated in the benefits derived from economic expansion. Conservatives became more tolerant, at least to the extent of admitting Liberals of the same social class into government on a limited basis. Further, the social doctrines of Conservatism became influenced to some extent by the teachings of Pope Leo XIII. But the Conservative paternalistic approach to social relations had clear limits, as was amply demonstrated in the decade of the 1920s.

As the Colombian economy grew, as industrialization and urbanization began, new social classes and institutions also appeared. Sectors of the Liberal Party, seeking its revitalization, appealed to these, as did newly formed socialist and communist groups. Indeed, the 1920s was a period of intense ideological debate and organizational effort, especially among the working class. The Conservative administrations responded with repression, as in their use of the army to crush the banana workers' strike in the Santa Marta region in 1928. But the Conservative Party itself became divided over how best to proceed. Younger elements, intensely nationalistic, and alarmed by the impact of modernization, began to be influenced by the corporativist ideologies emanating from Europe.

A combination of factors resulted in the Conservatives' loss of the presidency in 1930. There were internal divisions, both ideological and personalistic, within the party; there were widespread charges of government corruption, and popular repugnance over use of the army in the interests of the United Fruit Company; and finally, there was the government's seeming inability to deal creatively with the socioeconomic crisis afflicting the country. Although factions of the Conservative Party served in the following Liberal regime of President Enrique Olaya Herrera (1930–1934), its monopoly on power had definitely ended.

As the popular reformist Liberalism of the 1930s attracted larger numbers of the electorate, Conservatism entered into a period of deep crisis. Out of this came the increasingly influential Laureano Gómez, an admirer of Franco's Spain, who denounced the whole thrust of modern liberal development, and who eventually captured the leadership of the Conservative Party. Gómez withdrew the party from any participation in presidential politics after 1934 and proceeded to vociferously attack the Liberals for subverting the social order. For him, Liberalism, and especially the Liberalism of Alfonso López, was merely the opening for godless communism. Instead, he invoked the virtues of Hispanic Catholic traditionalism which, in its modern form, took on a falangist, corporativist configuration.

It was Gómez and his brand of Conservatism that contributed, in part, to the collapse of the second López administration in 1945. And it was Gómez who shrewdly took advantage of the Liberal division of that era to put forward the successful presidential candidacy of the Conservative, Mariano Ospina Pérez in 1946.

Once again in the presidency, the Conservatives, who sought some collaboration from the upper-class Liberal leadership, moved to consolidate their power. They dealt with the Liberal voter majority by claiming that it was based upon fraud; in "swing" departments, they moved to reduce Liberal majorities through intimidation and violence. Thus began *La Violencia*. Between 1946 and 1948 intense political polarization occurred. Jorge Eliécer Gaitán captured the Liberal Party and, denouncing both the Liberal and Conservative "oligarchs," appealed to the people with a broad program of social and economic reforms and democratic politics. From the Liberal-dominated Congress, Gaitán also attacked the Ospina administration. As they lost control of their own party, even the Liberal regulars were of no help to Ospina. The latter, increasingly beleaguered, reacted with more repressive measures in the countryside and against the pro-Liberal labor movement. When, following Gaitán's assassination on 9 April 1948, massive uprisings broke out in virtually every major Colombian city, it appeared that the Conservative administration was doomed.

But with the death of their leader, the Gaitanista masses were left without direction. The Conservative-dominated army crushed the uprisings, and the regular Liberals who had been displaced by Gaitán, fearing social revolution as much as the Conservatives, rushed to collaborate with Ospina. By doing so, they legitimized the latter's administration and tacitly agreed with his policies. Thus reassured, the Conservatives continued in their established direction. When the presidential candidacy of the feared Laureano Gómez was assured for 1950, the

Liberals withdrew from further collaboration with the Conservatives and declared their abstention from the electoral process. But this empty gesture merely played into the hands of Gómez and assured his victory.

In the almost three years that Gómez presided alone or through intermediaries (when he was ill), the Conservatives virtually established a civilian dictatorship. Although there was a split in the party between Ospina moderates and the Gómez faction over the direction of the administration, the former had little influence. Gómez's intention was the establishment of a falangist, corporativist state and the destruction of modern Liberalism, which he regarded as the seedbed of communism. It was during this era that *La Violencia* reached its peak of intensity. But his policies succeeded in nothing more than mounting opposition to him, even among the relatively unscathed Liberal upper-class leadership. Finally, even the army, which was the Conservatives' ultimate repressive arm, had had enough. On 3 June 1953 Gómez was ousted by an army coup that had the blessing of many Conservatives.

Both Conservatives and Liberals supported the subsequent initiatives of the army in reducing the level of violence, but they balked when the military dictator, General Gustavo Rojas Pinilla, attempted to create a third political force as an alternative to the traditional parties. Negotiations between the exiled Laureano Gómez and the Liberal ex-President Alberto Lleras Camargo resulted in an agreement between the two parties which was a major factor in the fall of Rojas Pinilla in mid-1957. The Conservatives joined with the Liberals after the ouster of Rojas to establish the National Front arrangement, in which both parties agreed to share political power on an alternating basis between the years 1958–1974.

Since the demise of Gómez in 1965, the Conservatives have moderated much of their ideological fervor, as they have attempted to construct a modern political party adapted to contemporary realities. They have sought, for example, to gain more adherents among the urban lower classes. Some Conservatives have utilized the slogans and messages of Christian Democratic parties elsewhere. Nevertheless, the party leadership's attitude toward the lower classes remains generally paternalistic, and its permanent electoral base is still largely in the rural areas.

Organizationally, the Conservatives have a strong national directorate that provides close control over its regional and local bodies. But since the 1950s, factionalism, less ideological than personalistic, has characterized the party. The major factions, originating in the personal rivalry between former presidents Gómez and Ospina, have solidified into competing blocs, each with strong regional bases (the Ospinistas in Antioquia, for example), but also with ties to different, powerful economic interests. Following the death of Laureano Gómez, leadership of his faction passed to his son, Alvaro Gómez Hurtado, a moderate rightist who continued in opposition to the Ospinista wing of the party until 1974. As the result of an internal party agreement, Alvaro Gómez was the party's presidential candidate that year. But, although he was less authoritarian than his father, the voters gave him only 32 percent of the vote, or more than one million less than his Liberal opponent. The more moderate Ospina faction, now headed by Ospina's widow, Berta, and by Misael Pastrana, former president of the Republic during the National Front period, have pursued a policy of collaboration with the Liberals within an arrangement very similar to that of the National Front. They have urged a continuation of this understanding as a means of securing the permanent participation of the minority Conservatives in the government. To that end, they have supported moderate reform programs and a developmentalist economic approach.

The Conservatives' 1978 presidential candidate, former university professor and ex-Minister of Labor, Belisario Betancur, who campaigned as a centrist with a mildly populist style, gained 46.6 percent of the votes cast, and lost the election to his Liberal opponent, Julio César Turbay, by less than 150,000 votes. The personal attraction of Betancur, along with the popular disaffection with the previous Liberal administration of Alfonso López Michelsen, with whom Turbay was closely identified, were the principal reasons for the Conservative resurgence. It remains to be seen, however, if the Conservatives can provide candidates and programs sufficiently attractive to appeal to an increasingly sophisticated electorate in a country experiencing profound socioeconomic changes.

FAR LEFT PARTIES. During the decade of the 1970s various left-wing organizations appeared in response to the relatively exclusive Colombian political system dominated by the Liberal and Conservative parties. These groups also have presented themselves as alternatives to what they regard as the bureaucratic and opportunistic Communist Party, although some of them have been willing to enter into alliances with the Communists. It is impossible to determine accurately their true strength, either organizationally or at the polls, but they presently play no major role in national politics. The fact that they continue to exist, however, indicates the continuing crisis of the existing system, reflected in widespread voter alienation and abstention. The most important of these left-wing splinter groups have been the following:

1. Colombian Broad Movement (Movimiento Amplio Colombiano) is a small group with ties to the Venezuelan Movement To Socialism (Movimiento al Socialismo) that seeks to establish a broad-based movement incorporating various classes and leftist tendencies.

2. FIRMES was sponsored initially by the magazine *Alternativa*, and comprised left-wing intellectuals, including the novelist Gabriel García Márquez. It seeks to unify the Left around a working-class leadership with a program appealing to wide sectors of the population.

3. Independent Revolutionary Workers Movement (Movimiento Obrero Independiente Revolucionario—MOIR) is sometimes called the Labor Party of Colombia. It is the largest and most important of the leftist movements outside of the Communist Party. It is Marxist-Leninist in orientation, with a decided bias in favor of Maoism. Organized in the early 1970s, it has been an important component in various attempts to create a revolutionary united front.

4. 19th of April Movement (Movimiento 19 de Abril—M-19) achieved interna-

tional recognition during its two month takeover of the Dominican embassy in early 1980. Consisting of elements from the National Popular Alliance (Alianza Nacional Popular—ANAPO) and its splinter, ANAPO Socialista, it was organized in 1974 and became an urban guerrilla group engaged in clandestine activities. It calls itself a nationalist organization and claims to be influenced by such diverse figures as Simón Bolívar, Ernesto Guevara, and Salvador Allende. Holding largely to the *foco* theory of revolutionary war popularized by Guevara, it seeks to create conditions for a mass popular uprising rather than develop a broad-based popular movement.

5. Popular Democratic National Movement (Movimiento Nacional Democrático Popular—MNDP) is a peasant-based organization, comprised of elements of the National Association of Shifting Cultivators (Asociación Nacional de Usuarios). It formed part of the Front for the Unity of the People (Frente para la Unidad del Pueblo—FUP), an alliance of far-Left groups established for the 1978 election. The FUP's candidate, Jaime Piedrahita Cardona, got approximately 0.5 percent of the total official vote.

6. Popular and Revolutionary Democratic Committees (Comités Democráticos Popular y Revolucionarios), is an anti-imperialist and antioligarchical group led by Avelino Nino. It also participated in the FUP coalition and subsequently merged with the MOIR.

7. Socialist Bloc (Bloque Socialista) consists of three Trotskyist groups. It was organized in 1974 and at the time affiliated with the United Secretariat of the Fourth International.

FIRMES. See FAR LEFT PARTIES.

INDEPENDENT REVOLUTIONARY WORKERS MOVEMENT (MOVI-MIENTO OBRERO INDEPENDIENTE REVOLUCIONARIO). See FAR LEFT PARTIES.

LIBERAL PARTY (PARTIDO LIBERAL). Like their principal opponents, the Liberals emerged as a coherent force in the 1840s. The party grew out of the Democratic Societies, formed by artisans and farmers to discuss such ideas as progress, democracy, and equality, and to push their own economic interests. Another source for this multiclass party was the Republican School, consisting of young members of aristocratic families, such as José María Samper, Salvador Camacho Roldán, Aníbal Galindo, and others, who were influenced by the ideas of the European Revolutions of 1848, and who became enamored of liberal and utopian socialist ideologies.

Nineteenth-century Liberalism, infused with secular, individualistic, rationalist, and equalitarian attitudes, thus became the weapon at mid-century for those who desired to continue the revolutionary promise of the independence era, and assault the bastions of privilege, monopoly, and hierarchy. But it is important to note that they did not wish to sweep away existing social and economic patterns, so much as to participate in them. Those who supported Liberalism were the new international trading groups unconnected to the old system of state-granted monopolies; entrepreneurs in commercial agricultural products such as tobacco; intellectuals imbued with the social concepts of the French Revolution and the message of English political economy; upwardly mobile veterans of the independence wars who coveted the lands of the church and the labor of the Indians; and finally, the artisans, professionals and others of little means trapped by the monopoly of wealth and power.

In the early 1850s these groups gained sufficient control of the national government through both violence and electoral processes to pass legislation that restricted the powers of the church, encouraged secular education, decentralized the state by granting important powers to the departments, ended state monopolies and instituted free trade, abolished slavery, and ended the tribute as well as the reservation rights of Indians. These and similar legislative enactments eventually were codified in several Liberal-oriented constitutions.

These initiatives naturally caused a reaction among the Conservative forces, who rallied around the slogans of religion, order, and authority. As a result, the period through the late 1860s was one of political turbulence. But after that date the newly prosperous bourgeoisie within Liberalism increasingly found it worthwhile to reach accomodation with its political enemies. Fear of the artisans and other members of the lower classes aroused by Liberal slogans undoubtedly had much to do with this. The old members of the Republican School, now matured as Liberal leaders, were interested in economic and social innovations that fostered their own interests and those of their class, rather than popular aspirations. Some even returned to the Conservative fold. An example was Rafael Núñez, who repented of his youthful liberalism by becoming the architect of Conservative hegemony in the 1880s. Nineteenth-century Colombian Liberalism thus fulfilled its historical function of partially eroding the traditional seignorial order inherited from the colony, and opening the way for the emergence of modern capitalist ideas and forces. But as its moderate, elitist leadership gained control and compromised in the name of order and stability with their political foes, the stage was set for the Conservative restoration.

The eclipse of Liberalism as Colombia's most dynamic nineteenth century political force occurred in the late 1870s and 1880s, during the era of Rafael Núñez. As if in recognition of the converging interests of the country's ruling elite, he announced that "conservatives have become more liberal and the liberals have come to understand that no seed becomes productive overnight." Outraged Liberals rooted in the earlier radical tradition rose against him in 1884–1885, but much of the Liberal leadership joined the Conservatives to crush the rebellion. This was followed by the takeover of the state by the Conservatives, who carried out centralization under a strong presidency and signed a concordat with the Vatican that restored church privileges and gave it control over education. Subsequent Conservative governments, reinforced by the Constitution of 1886, ruthlessly suppressed Liberals and abrogated much of the earlier social legislation, while turning the proclerical centralist state to the support of capitalism. Liberals, without other recourse, rebelled in 1895 and again in 1899–1902, but their failed efforts decimated their ranks and reduced them to a seemingly permanent minority.

During the decades of Conservative domination until 1930, Liberalism's upper-class leadership collaborated as a junior partner in government, while participating in the benefits deriving from economic growth and expansion. The popular impulse in the party was kept alive by the old caudillos Rafael Uribe Uribe and Benjamín Herrera, who argued that Liberalism must keep pace with the times by attracting the emerging urban middle sectors and working class. In 1924, at a party convention, planks in support of the rights of labor, and other social measures, were written into the platform. At the same time, a younger generation of Liberals, including Alfonso López and Jorge Eliécer Gaitán, saw Liberalism as a mechanism for socioeconomic development and popular participation. For López, Liberalism was a means to modernization, reforming the system from above while retaining the class structure basically intact. Gaitán, on the other hand, saw Liberalism as a step in the direction of socialism.

The various currents at work in the party came together in 1930, following a split in the Conservative ranks that gave the Liberals the presidency. The Liberal administration of Enrique Olaya Herrera, in which the Conservatives participated, provided a favorable period of preparation in which the party consolidated its growing strength among the new urban masses. The election of Alfonso López Pumarejo in 1934, with the slogan Revolution on the March, inaugurated the so-called Liberal Republic, an era of almost total political domination by the party that lasted until 1946.

The first López administration (1934–1938) was a departure from the usual party "occupation of the state." Genuinely concerned with the progress of Colombia, López signaled the new direction of Liberalism by pushing through wide-ranging reforms in the areas of labor, land tenure, health, education, taxation and fiscal policy, and government. He turned the state into an agency of economic development, broadened suffrage, provided official recognition and protection for trade unions, and generally sought to expand participation of the broad mass of the people in public life. Although López' reformist impulse was, in the final analysis, only partially successful, he nevertheless demonstrated that the state could be an active and dynamic force for change and modernization. As one result, the Liberals became the majority party in Colombia, primarily through their hold on the urban classes.

López was not without opposition, however, either from the Conservatives or from within his own party. Probably most of the Liberal leadership, big businessmen and landowners, and the political bosses, opposed the direction he took. As a result, the party split in the late 1930s between the old-line leadership and the López reformers. The latter temporarily won out, and in 1938 the moderate Eduardo Santos, publisher of the prestigious newspaper of the Liberal elite, *El Tiempo*, was elected president and inaugurated a "pause" in the López "revolution." The acrimony between the factions increased. With the economy disrupted by war, and the working and middle classes increasingly frustrated in their expectations, López was elected again after a bitter inner-party fight in 1942. But his second administration was marred by scandal, intense Conservative opposition, and severe party strife which hindered his legislative programs. Further, in 1944 Gaitán launched his populist campaign for the presidency, appealing to the Liberal masses against the "oligarchs" who dominated the party. In an atmosphere of intense agitation, López resigned in 1945 and Vice-President Alberto Lleras Camargo became president.

With the party split between Gaitán, with his support strongest among the urban working and lower-middle classes, and the regulars, who wanted nothing so much as to stay in power and were led by Gabriel Turbay, the Conservatives took advantage of the situation by launching their first presidential candidate since the early 1930s. Their choice, Mariano Ospina Pérez, won against the divided Liberals in the bitter election of 1946.

With the party in disarray, Gaitán immediately began a vigorous campaign to take it over. He elaborated a progressive program of agrarian reform, state-fostered industrialization, social reform, and political democratization designed to improve the condition of the nation's poor majority while curbing the power of the traditional elite. By late 1947 he had captured the party, despite the opposition of the old leadership, who feared that he was heading in the direction of social revolution. Indeed, Gaitán's campaign was the first major threat to oligarchic rule in the nation's modern history. While the old politicos organized among themselves, Gaitán organized the people.

But following Gaitán's assassination in April 1948, probably instigated by elements of the elite, the populist impulse initiated by Gaitán was repressed and dissipated. Conservative-sponsored persecution of Liberals in the countryside already was intensifying; the massive uprising of the people immediately after Gaitán's murder was brutally crushed, and this was followed by further repression. The Liberals, especially those in the countryside, reacted, and Colombia continued its tragic journey into La Violencia. Meanwhile, the regular leadership of the Liberal Party returned and began to collaborate with the Ospina government, at least at the national level. But as the violence intensified, and as the reactionary Conservative, 1950 presidential candidate, Laureano Gómez, spoke of the need for a Falangist state, even the regular Liberals withdrew their cooperation. Although they were not willing to take on the mantle of Gaitanismo, desired by the party's popular masses, they did abstain from the charade which politics had become.

In 1953 the Liberal Party leadership, like most Colombians, supported the army coup of General Gustavo Rojas Pinilla, which overturned the Gómez administration. By this time even the Liberal elite feared the devastating impact of La Violencia on the country. But the party leadership was disappointed in their expectations that Rojas would simply return power to the civilian elite. When the general showed ambitions of creating a "Third Force" apart from the regular parties, Liberals and Conservatives joined against him, and convinced the military to go along. The result was the elaboration of the National Front, in which Liberals and Conservatives shared and alternated in power between 1958 and 1974.

Modern Liberalism, since its ascendancy as the majority political party in the 1930s, has supported national industrialization and economic development, social welfare legislation and prolabor policies, broadened political participation, and such programs as agrarian and tax reform, public control of natural resources, and a stronger directing role for the state in national life. The party's major electoral strength has always been in the urban centers; in the twentieth century it has attracted additional support among the middle and working classes. It was Alfonso López Pumarejo who first officially recognized and courted organized labor; Colombia's first major labor organization, the Confederation of Workers of Colombia (Confederación de Trabajadores de Colombia) provided him with strong support in the 1930s and 1940s, and a major part of organized labor has generally supported the Liberal Party ever since. The party also has continued to have support from small businessmen. However, its leadership also retains close ties with powerful financial and industrial groups in various parts of the country.

This diverse constituency has been the source of intense party rivalry and factionalism. Since the end of party control by López and Gaitán, the upper-class national leadership has always been more conservative than the party masses, and either reluctant or unwilling to push the party's stated programs to their logical conclusion. Their fear, of course, is of upsetting the basic class structures and relationships of capitalism by opening the road to genuinely democratic and popular government. They have no intention of moving, *à la Gaitán*, in the direction of democratic socialism. What they do want is a modern capitalist nation in which they retain basic economic and political power.

These contradictions resulted, during the National Front period, in internal challenges. The most serious was that mounted by Alfonso López Michelsen, the son of the former president, who organized the Liberal Revolutionary Movement (Movimiento Revolucionario Liberal—MRL) in 1960. The MRL picked up support from various groups: those who wanted a fundamental transformation of society, including Communists and independent Marxists; those opposed to the National Front arrangement; Liberals who wanted no collaboration with Conservatives; and political opportunists who felt closed out by the existing system. The MRL elaborated a program of widespread economic and social reform, appealing principally to rural and urban labor and the middle classes.

Although opposed to the National Front arrangement, the MRL operated within it for tactical reasons, and in the 1962 congressional elections captured 36 percent of the Liberal vote. But the movement split in 1963 between those, like López Michelson, who wanted to take the existing Liberal Party in a more progressive direction, and others, led by Alvaro Uribe, who saw the MRL as a separate, more radical alternative to Liberalism. The MRL dissolved after 1968, when López Michelsen accepted the position of foreign minister in the National Front administration of Liberal President Carlos Lleras Restrepo, with whose policies he was in accord.

Through the 1970s the party was dominated by three factions: that of Julio César Turbay, a politician of the old school with close ties to regional party bosses and their machines, who is an expert in compromise and accommodation, and generally represents the party's right wing; that of Carlos Lleras Restrepo, former president (1968–1972), who has worked closely with moderate Conservatives, has close ties to important financial groups, but who had supported progressive agrarian and social legislation; and that of López Michelsen, who retained much of his old support from the MRL. It must be noted, however, that these factions were less ideological than personalistic in nature. Despite these personal rivalries, the Liberal Party usually managed to unite during elections. As a result, it has enjoyed majorities in the national congress and most departmental and local assemblies.

In 1974 its presidential candidate, Alfonso López Michelsen, was elected with over 56 percent of the vote as the National Front arrangement ended at the presidential level. His administration, beset by economic and social problems, proved to be a disappointment, however, and the successful Liberal presidential candidate, Julio César Turbay, won a narrow victory in 1978 with 49.5 percent of the vote.

As the decade of the 1970s ended, the Liberal Party, like the Conservatives, was confronted with widespread popular dissatisfaction, as manifested in voter abstention. The party leadership, drawn from and representative of the country's upper class, maintained their exclusivity and appeared unwilling and/or unable to deal with urgent economic and social problems and the lack of popular, democratic participation.

LIBERAL REVOLUTIONARY MOVEMENT (MOVIMIENTO REVOLUCIONARIO LIBERAL). See LIBERAL PARTY.

MOVIMIENTO AMPLIO COLOMBIANO. See FAR LEFT PARTIES.

MOVIMIENTO 19 DE ABRIL. See FAR LEFT PARTIES.

MOVIMIENTO NACIONAL DEMOCRÁTICO POPULAR. See FAR LEFT PARTIES

MOVIMIENTO OBRERO INDEPENDIENTE REVOLUCIONARIO. See FAR LEFT PARTIES.

MOVIMIENTO REVOLUCIONARIO LIBERAL. See LIBERAL PARTY.

NATIONAL PARTY (PARTIDO NACIONAL). Comprised of Conservatives and independent Liberals, this party existed from 1883 to 1888 as a vehicle of

Rafael Núñez' "Regeneration" movement. It failed in its attempt to do away with the traditional parties.

NATIONAL POPULAR ALLIANCE (ALIANZA NACIONAL POPULAR— ANAPO). Founded in 1961 by the former dictator, General Gustavo Rojas Pinilla, as a movement to vindicate his reputation, ANAPO evolved by 1970 into a powerful party and the most serious threat to the exclusive Liberal-Conservative National Front system. Through a contradictory and often vague ideological position that stressed both traditional and Christian values, and nationalistic, populist social reform programs, ANAPO became, by 1970, a party that drew its most substantial electoral support from the urban lower classes and the marginalized people from the poorest neighborhoods. It also attracted support among the military and elements in the church.

Under the strong, personalistic leadership of Rojas Pinilla, ANAPO became the most highly organized and structured party in Colombia. It had all the trappings of a modern political party: mass rallies, dues, local organizations, newspapers and other media, and a centralized command capable of enforcing party discipline.

Unable to compete as an independent party during the National Front, it elected candidates at all levels, first as a dissident Conservative faction, and later on both Conservative and Liberal tickets. In 1970 Rojas Pinilla ran for president, and according to official returns, received 39 percent of the vote compared to 40.7 percent for the official National Front candidate, Misael Pastrana. Many observers, however, believe that Rojas actually won the election, which was supervised by the National Front administration of Carlos Lleras Restrepo.

ANAPO's fortunes declined during the 1970s as Rojas' health weakened. His forceful daughter, María Eugenia Rojas de Moreno, took over leadership of the party, gave it a more coherent leftist ideological orientation, and ran for president in 1974. However, she lacked the appeal of her father and faced the situation of having many ANAPO leaders return to the Liberal and Conservative parties as the National Front ended. She polled only 9.5 percent of the vote, two million less than the Liberal victor, López Michelsen. By the 1978 election, as more and more Anapista leaders defected to either the traditional parties or more radical left-wing groups, ANAPO had virtually ceased to exist as a coherent political force.

19TH OF APRIL MOVEMENT (MOVIMIENTO 19 DE ABRIL). See FAR LEFT PARTIES.

PARTIDO COMUNISTA. See COMMUNIST PARTY.

PARTIDO COMUNISTA DE COLOMBIA (MARXISTA–LENINISTA). See COMMUNIST PARTY.

PARTIDO CONSERVADOR. *See* CONSERVATIVE PARTY.

PARTIDO LIBERAL. *See* LIBERAL PARTY.

PARTIDO NACIONAL. *See* NATIONAL PARTY.

PARTIDO POPULAR SOCIALISTA COLOMBIANO. *See* COLOMBIAN POPULAR SOCIALIST PARTY.

PARTIDO SOCIAL DEMÓCRATA CRISTIANO. *See* CHRISTIAN SOCIAL DEMOCRATIC PARTY.

PARTIDO SOCIALISTA REVOLUCIONARIO. *See* REVOLUTIONARY SOCIALIST PARTY.

POPULAR DEMOCRATIC NATIONAL MOVEMENT (MOVIMIENTO NACIONAL DEMOCRÁTICO POPULAR). *See* FAR LEFT PARTIES.

POPULAR AND REVOLUTIONARY DEMOCRATIC COMMITTEES (COMITÉS DEMOCRÁTICOS POPULAR Y REVOLUCIONARIOS). *See* FAR LEFT PARTIES.

REPUBLICAN UNION (UNIÓN REPUBLICANA). Organized between 1909 and 1914 by moderates from both Liberal and Conservative parties, the Unión Republicana opposed the strong-man rule of Rafael Reyes. Subsequently, it devised a system for sharing of cabinet posts by members of both parties, and provided for a guaranteed, if subordinate representation of the Liberal Party in Congress.

REVOLUTIONARY LEFTIST NATIONAL UNION (UNIÓN NACIONAL IZQUIERDISTA REVOLUCIONARIA–UNIR). Founded by Jorge Eliécer Gaitán in 1933 as a progressive alternative to the traditional parties, UNIR stressed the need for agrarian, labor, and social reforms, a directing role for the state in fostering rapid economic development, and greater democratic participation in the national life by the masses. Its socialist message was aimed primarily at the working class and peasants. It gained some support in the larger cities and certain coffee-growing regions, but was dissolved in 1935, when Gaitán was reintegrated into the Liberal Party as the López administration coopted UNIR's programs and followers.

REVOLUTIONARY SOCIALIST PARTY (PARTIDO SOCIALISTA REVOLUCIONARIO–PSR). The PSR had its origins in the Grupo Comunista that formed around the Russian immigrant Silvestre Savitsky after 1924, among anarchosyndicalist workers, and among left-wing Liberals associated with Luis Cano, director of the Bogotá daily *El Espectador*. The party was an effort to pull together the various leftist tendencies among workers and intellectuals during a period (the late 1920s) of rapid economic expansion and intense labor organizing activity.

The party's official founding occurred in 1926, following the Third Workers Congress, at which discussions were held concerning the organization of a labor party. At the congress, three distinct tendencies emerged: one, led by Grupo Comunista member Ignacio Torres Giraldo, a trade union leader from Cali and head of the National Labor Confederation (Confederación Obrera Nacional), organized the previous year, opposed the establishment of a labor party; a second group favored the immediate founding of a communist party; the majority faction led by Francisco de Heredia, a socialist propagandist, won the day when he proposed the organization of the Partido Socialista Revolucionario, which would be procommunist, but not affiliated with the Communist International. Its purpose was to provide the ideological orientation and organizational base for the eventual establishment of a Marxist-Leninist party.

The PSR's central committee included Torres Giraldo, Tomás Uribe Márquez and Guillermo Hernández Rodríguez. Uribe later became a prominent leader of the Liberal Party, as did Hernández Rodríguez after being secretary-general of the Communist Party from 1930 to 1932. Thus, the PSR provided training for several important Liberal and trade union leaders who later contributed to the reformist Liberalism that emerged in the 1930s.

At the PSR's Second Congress in 1927, it was decided to seek affiliation with the Communist International as a fraternal party. When this was granted, several leaders journeyed to Moscow, where they played a role in international communist organizations. Torres Giraldo became a member of the Presidium of the Red International of Labor Unions; Uribe Márquez was appointed to the Executive Committee of the Communist International; Hernández Rodríguez and the trade unionists Naftali Arze and Alberto Castrillón were delegates to various international Communist conferences.

Despite continuous government persecution, the PSR achieved some success organizing workers in the emerging industrial cities of Cali, Medellín and Bogotá, among banana and port workers on the north coast, and in the oil fields around Barrancabermeja in the Department of Santander Sur. The party also succeeded in establishing half a dozen newspapers aimed at the new working class. Yet it continued to be beset by internal factionalism. For example, one group led by Torres Giraldo was primarily trade unionist in orientation. Another consisted essentially of Liberal dissidents who saw the PSR as a revolutionary mechanism for the violent overthrow of the Conservative government.

When the banana workers in the United Front concession on the north coast began to organize for a strike in 1928, the PSR's Marxist faction, led by Torres Giraldo, María Cano, and future Communist Party Secretary-General Augusto Durán, went to the banana zone to organize a solidarity committee in support of the banana workers' anarchosyndicalist leader, Raúl Mahecha. When the strike broke out, another PSR leader, Alberto Castrillón, played a prominent part in maintaining unity among the workers and strengthening their resistance in the face of severe repression.

The strike was broken by the army, which killed over eighty-five workers and wounded many more. Castrillón and other strike leaders were imprisoned. But the massacre and events surrounding it became the center of an intense national controversy, publicized in large part by the young Liberal congressman Jorge Eliécer Gaitán, which contributed significantly to the electoral defeat of the Conservative Party in the presidential election of 1930.

The PSR did not reap the benefits from this development, however. The party's 1930 presidential candidate, the imprisoned Castrillón, received only a few hundred votes; with the Liberals' victory virtually assured, many of the PSR's Liberal members deserted. Thus, the party was reduced to a minor role in the country's political life.

In 1930, the PSR's fate was sealed in Moscow, when the Latin-American Secretariat of the Communist International decided to dissolve it, and to reorganize the Comintern's Colombian followers as the Communist Party. Hernández Rodríguez and his wife, in the Soviet Union at the time, returned to Colombia for this purpose. At a party congress held in the late summer of 1930, the Marxist remnants of the PSR officially became the Communist Party of Colombia.

SOCIALIST BLOC (BLOQUE SOCIALISTA). *See* FAR LEFT PARTIES.

UNIÓN NACIONAL IZQUIERDISTA REVOLUCIONARIA. *See* REVOLUTIONARY LEFTIST NATIONAL UNION.

UNIÓN REPUBLICANA. *See* REPUBLICAN UNION.

Richard E. Sharpless

COSTA RICA

Costa Rica is a small Central American country, less than half the size of the state of Ohio. It has a population of slightly over two and a quarter million, 60 percent of which is concentrated on the Central Plateau in and around the principal cities of San José, Alajuela, Heredia and Cartago. The population is strikingly homogeneous, predominantly white and mestizo, with small Indian (8,000) and black (30,000 plus) minorities. There are no sharp class distinctions, and education occupies a central position in Costa Rican society.

In Costa Rica coffee is king. Although today the Costa Rican economy is relatively diverse, with bananas and other agricultural products, a large public sector, and an expanding industrial output, coffee remains the principal export and main source of foreign exchange. Coffee transformed Costa Rica from Central America's poorest colony to its richest republic, although the country is still poor in comparison with the industrialized nations of the world. Coffee, of course, produced the "coffee barons," but an egalitarian spirit and prevailing scarcity of labor helped reduce their impact, so that Costa Rica appeared to take its change in fortune in stride.

During the twentieth century, Costa Rica has enjoyed a reputation as the most stable country in Latin America. Its reputation for stability is further enhanced by the popular notion that its governments have been democratic, reflecting the free choice of the Costa Rican people in honest elections. Although this viewpoint may not be wholly accurate, it has existed for a long time, and the following observation by North American journalist Ernie Pyle is characteristic: "Practically none of the comic opera aspects of government in the banana republics is visible in Costa Rica. It is a genuine democracy—in fact, the finest democracy we have found outside the United States. It is almost the only one of all the Latin countries that can pretend with a straight face to be a democracy" (*Miami Herald*, 8 February 1939).

And, if this comment by the man who became the GI's correspondent in World War II was not enough to fix the image of Costa Rica, he also wrote: "For years, and in many Latin countries, I have had my neck craned for some beautiful señoritas such as you see in books. But I never saw them until I came to San José. This city is crawling with them. Really lovely ones." Looked upon as a peaceful, democratic country, with beautiful women, Costa Rica has had an identity crisis.

Its exception seemed so exceptional that it has aroused little interest, even for comparative purposes, and it has rarely been taken seriously.

Despite the myth of Costa Rican democracy, or *leyenda blanca*, the country has had its share of political turmoil. In the twentieth century alone there have been at least a dozen coups or attempted coups. A military dictator, Federico Tinoco, ran the country from January 1917 to August 1919, and Rafael Angel Calderón Guardia dominated it for eight years, 1940–1948, under a regime characterized by violence and fraudulent elections. Costa Rica had a bloody civil war in 1948, which claimed 2,000 lives, followed by a provisional government which lasted eighteen months. During this provisional rule and even after the restoration of constitutional government, there were two attempts, in 1948 and 1955, by Costa Rican exiles based in Nicaragua and enjoying the support of Anastasio Somoza to invade the country and impose a new regime by force. Since 1953, however, electoral politics have been the norm, and one would describe Costa Rica as a functioning democracy.

By law, all persons eighteen years of age and older must vote, and in recent elections at least 80 percent of them actually did. Government power is shared by the executive, a unicameral legislative assembly, and a fiercely independent judiciary. In addition, the integrity of the electoral process is maintained by the Supreme Electoral Tribunal, a virtual fourth branch of government. Under the Constitution of 1949, currently in force, the nation provides a full array of social services, and the government exercises extensive influence and control over the economy. Yet, for all Costa Rica's obvious political maturity, the development of political parties has been slow.

Before the 1950s, and going back to the beginnings of the republic, Costa Rican political parties have been little more than electoral vehicles of individual leaders. They rarely appealed to the electorate on ideological grounds or presented a specific program. Costa Rican politics were consensus politics, concentrating upon responsible leadership, with a scorn for sectarianism as alien to the national spirit. The Republican Party, which dominated Costa Rican political affairs from the end of the nineteenth century through the fourth decade of the twentieth, was comprised of a small circle of liberal (anticlerical) elites, primarily coffee planters and successful professional men, who looked upon the presidency as an exercise of citizenship—noblesse oblige—and who, according to the findings of Samuel Stone, had descended from one or two of the founding families of colonial times. It was enough for these presidents to be "builders of roads, schools, and bridges."

By the 1930s, opposition to this seemingly genial political situation developed, particularly as the limitations of the coffee-based economy became apparent. In most cases, it took the form of "parties" which were directly linked to the career and ambition of a specific individual, such as the Reformist Party of the maverick Jorge Volio, the Democratic Party of León Cortés, or the National Union Party of Otilio Ulate. In a few cases, however, an ideological content did emerge. The Communist Party, organized in 1929, obviously was ideological, although even in its case personalism persisted. Manuel Mora Valverde has led the party since its founding and is so closely identified with it that he is described by Costa Ricans as "our Red Pope." This mix of personalism and ideology was more pronounced in the National Republican Party of Rafael Angel Calderón Guardia, founded (or refounded) in 1941, which was identified as *calderonista* but which in the 1940s enacted the most progressive social legislation in the nation's history, including Social Security and a labor code. During World War II and lasting until 1948, Calderón Guardia and Mora formed an alliance, the Victory Bloc, which created a new political climate wherein issues became almost as important as personalities.

In the early 1940s, a group of young men, dissatisfied with the failure of the old "Olympians" to sense the need for economic and social change, but suspicious of the "extremist origins" of the Victory Bloc, formed the Center for the Study of National Problems. The center initially eschewed electoral politics and undertook a series of studies to discover the "national reality." However, in 1945, owing to the growing repression of the Calderón regime, the center merged with Democratic Action, a liberal wing within the Democratic Party led by José Figueres and Francisco Orlich, to form the Social Democratic Party. The Social Democrats, although maintaining a vestige of independence, were soon absorbed by the National Liberation Party (Partido Liberacion Nacional—PLN), founded in 1951.

Arising from the turmoil of "the eight years" (the Calderón rule, 1940–1948) and shaped in the crucible of the Costa Rican civil war of 1948, the National Liberation Party became the only Costa Rican party worthy of the name. Although the party is closely identified with its principal founder and leader, José Figueres, National Liberation has a clearly defined program and a functioning national organization, complete with training and educational programs and disciplinary, financial, and special-sector organs. For the last thirty years, it has been Costa Rica's dominant political party, winning the presidency five times and, with the exception of the period 1978-1982, exercising a majority in the legislative assembly. There is no other party existing in Costa Rica today which has enjoyed a similar continuity.

The PLN has transformed the Costa Rican economy, nationalizing banking, energy, transportation, and communications and allocating the nation's resources to provide for a more diversified agriculture, and, in the social sector, support for a welfare state, with a substantial bureaucracy. It has also stimulated a modest program of import substitution industrialization, as a result of which the country has become substantially self-sufficient in a number of consumers goods categories.

Virtually identified as the guardian of the new economic and social structure, Liberation's political setbacks have stemmed as much from its own internal strife as from the effectiveness of opposing groups. The PLN has maintained an amazing unity, but some elements resent the extraordinary influence exercised by Figueres and the Old Guard. The controversy surrounding the second Figueres administration (1970–1974), particularly the president's associations with Robert

Vesco, exacerbated this situation. Even so, the nation is closely divided between *liberacionistas* and anti-*liberacionistas*, so that opposition parties need to achieve unity in order to defeat the PLN.

Such unity was achieved in 1965 by ex-presidents Calderón Guardia and Ulate, who fused their Republican and National Union parties to form National Unification. This coalition elected José Joaquín Trejos in 1966, but, owing to the antagonistic elements comprising it and the appearance of new personalities, it was unable to repeat its success in the following two elections. By 1978 it had all but vanished.

The eclipse of Unification stemmed from the success of a new, more broadly based coalition in the 1978 elections. Using his own Democratic Renovation Party as a base, under which he obtained about 10 percent of the vote in 1974, Rodrigo Carazo Odio formed the Unity Party coalition and won the presidency in 1978, with over 50 percent of the vote. The Unity Party also won 27 seats in the legislative assembly to 25 for Liberation. Carazo had been a rising young leader in the PLN, but, failing in his quest for the National Liberation nomination against Figueres in 1970, became something of a pariah, and was, in effect, forced to leave the party. He then presented himself as a *"liberacionista* without Figueres," which enabled him to appeal to youth, tired of the Old Guard, and to capitalize on the corruption issue. Equally important, he gained the support of Rafael Angel Calderón Fournier, the son of Calderón Guardia, who brought many of the old calderonistas with him. These elements had always been closer philosophically to liberacionistas than to conservatives, but never joined with the PLN because of the hatred engendered by the 1948 civil war. The small Christian Democratic Party also joined the coalition, and, in the end, the nation's moneyed interests, grouped around the Popular Union Party, abandoned Unification and jumped on the bandwagon.

The future of Costa Rican democracy seems secure, but paradoxically the future of a true party system remains uncertain. The principal ideological party, National Liberation, may be in decline, particularly if internecine strife prevails in the post-Figueres era. Aside from the Figueres landslides, the PLN has won only about 43 percent of the vote in national elections (Daniel Oduber won in 1974 with a smaller percentage than Luis Alberto Monge, who lost in 1978), so that its best strategy is to keep the opposition divided and prevent the emergence of a two-party system. This strategy relies upon the fact that the principal opposition parties are essentially coalitions and exhibit the weaknesses inherent in such groupings. National Unification ceased to be a coalition in 1978 and failed to obtain even 2 percent of the vote.

The Unity Party of Carazo may present a more serious challenge, particularly if it is able to satisfy the ambitions of *calderonista* leaders. Carazo appointed "Junior" Calderón to his cabinet as foreign minister. Calderón became the coalition's standard bearer in 1982. However, the development of serious economic prob-lems midway through Carazo's term and his inept handling of the situation undermined Calderón's candidacy.

Luis Alberto Monge, given a second chance by the PLN, won the 1982 election handily, with 58.7 percent of the vote, and Liberation captured thirty-three seats in the Assembly, a clear majority. Whether this turnabout is permanent, or is merely a response to the prevailing economic crisis, remains to be seen. One thing is certain: the PLN will be the principal reference point for Costa Rican politics for years to come. Calderón's dreams are not completely shattered—he received 32.8 percent of the vote—but his future and that of Unity depends largey upon how well the PLN performs.

Bibliography

American University. *Area Handbook for Costa Rica.* Government Printing Office, Washington, D.C., 1970.

Charles D. Ameringer. *Don Pepe: A Political Biography of José Figueres of Costa Rica.* University of New Mexico Press, Albuquerque, 1979.

Carlos Araya Pochet. *Historia de los partidos políticos. Liberación Nacional.* Editorial Costa Rica, San José, 1968.

Oscar Arias Sánchez. *Quien Gobierna en Costa Rica?* Editorial Universitaria Centroamericana, San José, 1978.

John Patrick Bell. *Crisis in Costa Rica: The Revolution of 1948.* University of Texas Press, Austin, 1971.

Mavis Hiltunen de Biesanz, Richard Biesanz, and Karen Zubris de Biesanz. *Los Costarricenses.* Editorial Universidad Estatal a Distancia, San José, 1979.

Charles F. Denton. *Patterns of Costa Rican Politics.* Allyn and Bacon, Boston, 1971.

Bert H. English. *Liberación Nacional in Costa Rica: The Development of a Political Party in a Transitional Society.* University of Florida Press, Gainesville, 1971.

Samuel Stone. *La dinastía de los conquistadores: La crisis del poder en la Costa Rica contemporanea.* Editorial Universitaria Centroamericana, San José, 1975.

Political Parties

ACCIÓN DEMÓCRATA. *See* NATIONAL LIBERATION PARTY.

BLOQUE DE OBREROS Y CAMPESINOS. *See* COMMUNIST PARTY.

CALDERONIST REPUBLICAN PARTY (PARTIDO REPUBLICANO CALDERONISTA). *See* REPUBLICAN PARTY.

CHRISTIAN DEMOCRATIC PARTY (PARTIDO DEMÓCRATA CRISTIANO). Beginning in 1962 with a group of young Catholic intellectuals, the Christian Democratic Party was formally organized in 1967, with the support of the Confederation of Christian Workers and Peasants (Confederación de Obreros y Campesinos Cristianos) trade union group, and appeared on the ballot for the first time in 1970. Despite some encouraging signs, the party did not fare well then or in 1974. Although the Christian Democrats joined the winning Unity Party coalition in 1978, the future of the movement in Costa Rica is uncertain.

COMMUNIST PARTY (PARTIDO COMUNISTA). The Costa Rican Communist Party was first organized in 1929, although the formal date of founding is frequently given as 1931. For tactical reasons and also because it was outlawed from 1948 to 1974, the party has appeared under other labels or fronts. It originally used the name Workers and Peasants Bloc (Bloque de Obreros y Campesinos) for electoral purposes. It changed its name to the Popular Vanguard Party (Vanguardia Popular) in 1943, in order to make acceptable the participation of Catholics in the Victory Bloc, that is, the wartime alliance between the National Republican and Communist parties. As part of the Victory Bloc, the Popular Vanguard Party shared in the electoral triumph of 1944, but the coming of the cold war and consequent opposition to Communist influence in the government contributed to the outbreak of the 1948 civil war and the eventual outlawing of the party. The Popular Vanguard label is in use today, but during the time that it was illegal, the Communist Party contested national elections as the Popular Democratic Action Party (Partido Acción Demócrata Popular) in 1962 and the Socialist Action Party (Partido Acción Socialista) in 1970 and 1974. In the latter year, Manuel Mora himself ran as the party's candidate for president but failed to attract much support. In 1978 and 1982, the Popular Vanguard participated in a coalition with the Costa Rican Socialist Party (Partido Socialista Costarricense) known as the United People's Party (Partido Pueblo Unido).

Aside from its heyday during the 1940s, the Communist Party has not attracted wide general or electoral support. What success it has enjoyed is attributed to the influence and leadership of its founder Manuel Mora Valverde, who remains its chief today. However, since its inception, the party has had extensive influence in the trade union movement. The first national trade union confederation, the Confederation of Workers of Costa Rica (Confederación de Trabajadores de Costa Rica—CTCR) was organized in the 1940s under its leadership. The CTCR was outlawed after the revolution of 1948. However, in the 1960s a new Communist-led trade union group, the General Confederation of Workers of Costa Rica (Confederación General de Trabajadores de Costa Rica), was established, which soon became the largest of the country's several labor confederations. The Communists' influence has been particularly consistent among the banana workers, whom they first organized in the mid-1930s.

COSTA RICAN POPULAR FRONT PARTY (PARTIDO FRENTE POPULAR COSTARRICENSE). One of several minor Marxist parties in Costa Rica, separate from the Popular Vanguard Party (Communist), the Costa Rican Popular Front Party presented candidates for the legislative assembly in 1974 and 1978 and won one seat in 1978. The party demonstrates the fragmented nature of Costa Rican politics, even among the far Left.

COSTA RICAN SOCIALIST PARTY (PARTIDO SOCIALISTA COSTAR-RICENSE). The Costa Rican Socialist Party was organized originally in 1962 as a party in support of the Cuban Revolution. However, it was declared illegal and was denied a place on the ballot, touching off an acrimonious debate in the legislative assembly and causing pro-Castro PLN deputy Marcial Aguilúz to leave Liberation. Aguilúz, Honduran-born and a former Caribbean Legionnaire (the legendary band of Caribbean exiles who aided Figueres in the 1948 civil war), became its principal spokesman and Costa Rica's Cuban connection throughout most of the 1960s. Conservative elements sought to strip Aguilúz of his Costa Rican citizenship and to deport him to Honduras, without success. In 1978, after Marxist parties achieved legal recognition in Costa Rica, the Socialist Party appeared on the ballot as part of a coalition with the Popular Vanguard Party (Communist), under the name United People's Party (Partido Pueblo Unido).

DEMOCRATIC PARTY (PARTIDO DEMÓCRATA). This was principally a personalist party used by León Cortés in his unsuccessful campaign for the presidency in 1944. Following the death of Cortés in 1946, José Figueres and Fernando Castro Cervantes competed for the leadership. The party supported Otilio Ulate in 1948. Castro Cervantes, representing conservative business interests, ran as its candidate in 1953, against Figueres of the National Liberation Party. The name reappeared on the ballot in 1974, 1978, and 1982, more by the inclination of the rather bizarre personalities who used the label than by the existence of any permanent organization.

DEMOCRATIC ACTION (ACCIÓN DEMÓCRATA—AD). See NATIONAL LIBERATION PARTY.

DEMOCRATIC RENOVATION PARTY (PARTIDO RENOVACIÓN DEMÓ-CRATA). The Democratic Renovation Party is the party of Rodrigo Carazo Odio, made up essentially of disaffected elements of the National Liberation Party (Partido Liberación Nacional—PLN). Carazo had challenged José Figueres for the PLN nomination in 1970 and, unsuccessful, had been virtually driven from Liberation. He formed Democratic Renovation to support his candidacy in 1974. Although he won only a modest vote (about 10 percent), it provided him with sufficient leverage to put together and win the nomination of the Unity Party, the victorious coalition in 1978.

FRENTE NACIONAL. See NATIONAL FRONT.

INDEPENDENT PARTY (PARTIDO INDEPENDIENTE). Independent Party was the personalist party label used by Jorge Rossi in his unsuccessful bid for the presidency in 1958. The split of Rossi, who had been vice-president under Figueres (1953–1958), contributed to the defeat of the National Liberation Party in the 1958 elections. He later rejoined Liberation and served as vice-president in the second Figueres administration (1970–1974). The Independent Party label reappeared in 1978, used by Gerardo W. ("G.W.") Villalobos Garita, who had run as a Democrat in 1974. Villalobos won few votes but gained a great deal of notoriety by riding around on a white horse and spraying bullets into the home of Robert Vesco. The party received less than 1 percent of the vote in 1982.

INDEPENDENT NATIONAL PARTY (PARTIDO NACIONAL INDEPEN-DIENTE). The Independent National Party was the personalist, right-wing party of Jorge González Marten. A wealthy businessman, González Marten claimed to be a "nationalist" in opposition to the "socialistic" domestic program and "internationalist" economic policy of the National Liberation Party (PLN). In 1974 he won a surprising 11 percent of the total vote (almost enough to assure the victory of the PLN), and his party captured six seats in the legislative assembly. In 1978 he refused to join the Unity Party coalition if he could not be its candidate, but the voters abandoned him anyway, and he obtained less than 0.5 percent of the vote. The party won no seats in the congress. Having exhausted his personal fortune, González Marten fled the country and his creditors, and without him the party has disappeared.

NATIONAL FRONT (FRENTE NACIONAL). The National Front, also known as the Third Front (Tercer Frente), was an *antifiguerista* group which supported the candidacy of Virgilio Calvo Sánchez in 1970. Calvo had been elected vice-president in the National Unification coalition in 1966, and his candidacy represented dissatisfied calderonista and progressive elements, particularly younger persons. The Front ran a poor third in the election, and its principal effect was to siphon votes from the National Unification coalition. However, Rodrigo Carazo later successfully built upon these elements in forming the Unity Party (Partido Unidad) in the 1978 election.

NATIONAL LIBERATION PARTY (PARTIDO LIBERACIÓN NACIONAL—PLN). The National Liberation Party has been Costa Rica's dominant political party from its founding in 1951 until the present time. The PLN expresses a commitment to economic and social reform within the framework of a represent-ative democratic system. The ideological roots of the PLN took shape in the Social Democratic Party, founded in 1945, which in turn was created by a merger of the Center for the Study of National Problems and Democratic Action (Acción Demócrata), a liberal wing of the Democratic Party in the mid-1940s. However, its preeminence stems from the military victory of José Figueres and his followers in 1948, and his leadership of the Founding Junta of the Second Republic, the provisional government of 1948–1949.

Figueres and the PLN have reshaped the economic and social institutions of Costa Rica, creating autonomous agencies to administer the broadly nationalized sector of the economy and to provide a wide variety of social services. The PLN won the presidency in 1953, 1962, 1970, and 1974, and has had a majority in the legislative assembly throughout most of its active political life. It achieved a remarkable comeback in 1982 when Luis Alberto Monge got 58.7 percent of the presidential vote and it took 33 seats in the legislative assembly, an absolute majority.

Since the early 1960s the PLN has been affiliated with the Socialist International. It has also cooperated closely with a training school for cadres of parties ideologically associated with the PLN and the International, which was financed in its early years by a United States organization headed by Norman Thomas, and since the early 1970s by the Frederick Ebert Foundation of the German Social Democratic Party.

NATIONAL REPUBLICAN PARTY (PARTIDO REPUBLICANO NACIONAL —PRN). Rafael Angel Calderón Guardia founded (or refounded) the National Republican Party in 1941 and used it as his vehicle to dominate Costa Rican politics for "the eight years" (1940–1948). Calderón undertook significant social reforms, including Social Security, a labor code, and a constitutional amendment outlining social guarantees, that had the support of the Catholic Church, but which aroused the bitter opposition of the former ruling elites. Calderón accepted the offer of support by the Communist Party and in 1943, in the context of the wartime alliance with the Soviet Union, fashioned the Victory Bloc, a coalition of the PRN and Popular Vanguard (the rechristened Communist Party) which elected Teodoro Picado Michalski to the presidency the following year. In the long run, the participation of the Communists in the governing coalition played into the hands of Calderón's enemies and contributed to the outbreak of the civil war in 1948. Following the armed conflict, the National Republican and Communist parties were outlawed. The PRN tried to resurface in the 1960s without Calderón, but without success, and it has virtually ceased to exist.

NATIONAL UNION PARTY (PARTIDO UNIÓN NACIONAL—PUN). Although the name appeared earlier, the National Union Party was essentially the personalist electoral vehicle of Otilio Ulate. He won the disputed election of 1948 and, after the extraordinary events of 1948–1949, served as president from 1949 to 1953. Because Ulate was ineligible for reelection to the presidency, the party nominated and won with Mario Echandi in 1958. Ulate himself failed in a comeback in 1962. Four years later, he joined forces with Calderón Guardia to form the National Unification coalition, which elected José Joaquín Trejos, but he withdrew again in 1970. The party has virtually ceased to exist following Ulate's death in 1973.

NATIONAL UNIFICATION (UNIFICACIÓN NACIONAL—UN). The National Unification was a coalition formed in 1965 by Rafael Angel Calderón Guardia of the Republican Party and Otilio Ulate of the National Union Party. It elected José Joaquín Trejos in 1966 but has failed to repeat its success in subsequent elections. Its weakness is its lack of any unifying program or ideology other than its opposition to the dominant National Liberation Party. After its poor showing in 1978, it offered no candidates in 1982.

PARTIDO ACCIÓN DEMÓCRATA POPULAR. *See* COMMUNIST PARTY.

PARTIDO ACCIÓN SOCIALISTA. *See* COMMUNIST PARTY.

PARTIDO COMUNISTA. *See* COMMUNIST PARTY.

PARTIDO DEMÓCRATA. *See* DEMOCRATIC PARTY.

PARTIDO DEMÓCRATA CRISTIANO. *See* CHRISTIAN DEMOCRATIC PARTY.

PARTIDO FRENTE POPULAR COSTARRICENSE. *See* COSTA RICAN POPULAR FRONT PARTY.

PARTIDO INDEPENDIENTE. *See* INDEPENDENT PARTY.

PARTIDO LIBERACIÓN NACIONAL. *See* NATIONAL LIBERATION PARTY.

PARTIDO NACIONAL INDEPENDIENTE. *See* INDEPENDENT NATIONAL PARTY.

PARTIDO PUEBLO UNIDO. *See* UNITED PEOPLE'S PARTY.

PARTIDO REFORMISTA. *See* REFORMIST PARTY.

PARTIDO RENOVACIÓN DEMÓCRATA. *See* DEMOCRATIC RENOVATION PARTY.

PARTIDO REPUBLICANO. *See* REPUBLICAN PARTY.

PARTIDO REPUBLICANO CALDERONISTA. *See* REPUBLICAN PARTY.

PARTIDO REPUBLICANO NACIONAL. *See* NATIONAL REPUBLICAN PARTY.

PARTIDO SOCIAL DEMÓCRATA. *See* SOCIAL DEMOCRATIC PARTY.

PARTIDO SOCIALISTA COSTARRICENSE. *See* COSTA RICAN SOCIALIST PARTY.

PARTIDO UNIDAD. *See* UNITY PARTY.

PARTIDO UNION CÍVICA REVOLUCIONARIA. See REVOLUTIONARY CIVIC UNION PARTY.

PARTIDO UNIÓN NACIONAL. See NATIONAL UNION PARTY.

PARTIDO UNIÓN POPULAR. See POPULAR UNION PARTY.

PARTIDO VANGUARDIA POPULAR. See COMMUNIST PARTY.

POPULAR DEMOCRATIC ACTION PARTY (PARTIDO ACCIÓN DEMÓ-CRATA POPULAR). See COMMUNIST PARTY.

POPULAR UNION PARTY (PARTIDO UNIÓN POPULAR). The Popular Union is a small party representing the old coffee interests and marking their reemergence on the national political scene. Founded around 1974, and led by Cristian Tattembach, it has yet to present a presidential candidate or a separate slate of candidates for the legislative assembly. It is almost more a pressure group than a political party and seems content to play coalition politics (anti-Liberation). It supported Unification in 1974 and participated in the Unity Party coalition in 1978 and 1982.

POPULAR VANGUARD PARTY (PARTIDO VANGUARDIA POPULAR). See COMMUNIST PARTY.

REFORMIST PARTY (PARTIDO REFORMISTA). A short-lived party of the 1920s, the Reformist Party, although closely identified with the erratic and volatile Jorge Volio, was the first Costa Rican party to advocate social reform. Volio, a former priest, was inspired by Christian Socialist philosophy. Failing in his bid for the presidency in the disputed election of 1924, Volio gave his support to Ricardo Jiménez Oreamuno and accepted a vice-presidency as part of the deal. When Volio lost favor, owing to his quixotic behavior, the party likewise declined.

REPUBLICAN PARTY (PARTIDO REPUBLICANO). The dominant political party from the turn of the century to 1940, the Republican Party was, in turn, dominated by the "Olympians," particularly Cleto González Víquez and Ricardo Jiménez Oreamuno who, together, occupied the presidency for twenty of the thirty years between 1906 and 1936. It faced little real political opposition for four decades, only experiencing occasional challenges from personalist-style leaders who adopted meaningless party labels which quickly disappeared after the electoral campaigns. Although politically liberal (anticlerical and favoring broader suffrage and ballot reform), the party's failure to deal effectively with economic and social problems led to its disappearance in 1940. Rafael Angel Calderón Guardia revived the party label to run for president in 1962, when his own National Republican Party abandoned him, and he used it again in forming the

National Unification coalition in 1965. After his death in 1970, his followers renamed the party Calderonist Republican Party (Partido Republicano Calderonista), and participated in the Unity Party coalition in 1978 and 1982.

REVOLUTIONARY CIVIC UNION PARTY (PARTIDO UNIÓN CÍVICA REVOLUCIONARIA—PUCR). The Revolutionary Civic Union was the ultimate in personalist parties. Its leader and founder, Frank Marshall Jiménez, used it as a vehicle, not to run for the presidency, but to win a seat in the legislative assembly in 1958. It supported the National Unification coalition in 1966. Although it has an extreme rightist, anti-Communist orientation, it has failed to attract support even from this sector of society and is today virtually moribund.

SOCIAL DEMOCRATIC PARTY (PARTIDO SOCIAL DEMÓCRATA—PSD). Founded in 1945 through a merger of Democratic Action and the Center for the Study of National Problems, the Social Democratic Party supported Otilio Ulate in the 1948 elections. After the 1948 civil war, most of its members formed the nucleus of the National Liberation Party. It resurfaced momentarily in 1970 in a power play to force the nomination of José Figueres by Liberation, threatening to present an independent candidacy if Liberation rejected him.

SOCIALIST ACTION PARTY (PARTIDO ACCIÓN SOCIALISTA). See COMMUNIST PARTY.

TERCER FRENTE. See NATIONAL FRONT.

THIRD FRONT (TERCER FRENTE). See NATIONAL FRONT.

UNIFICACIÓN NACIONAL. See NATIONAL UNIFICATION.

UNITED PEOPLE'S PARTY (PARTIDO PUEBLO UNIDO). A coalition of the Costa Rican Socialist Party (Partido Socialista Costarricense) and the Popular Vanguard Party (Partido Vanguardia Popular), that is the Communists, the United People's Party supported the candidacy of Rodrigo Gutiérrez in 1978 and 1982. Pueblo Unido ran a distant third in the presidential election but won three seats in the legislative assembly. Since neither the National Liberation Party nor the Unity Party won a clear majority in the assembly, the three Marxist deputies exercised inordinate influence and raised the expectations of the left-wing coalition. It did not do well in the 1982 election, however, obtaining only 3.3 percent of the vote. Although it won four seats in the assembly, the gain is not significant in view of the clear PLN majority.

UNITY PARTY (PARTIDO UNIDAD). The Unity Party is a coalition of the Democratic Renovation, Calderonist Republican, Christian Democratic, and Popular Union parties. It supported the successful presidential candidacy of Rodrigo

Carazo in 1978 and won twenty-seven seats in the fifty-seven-seat legislative assembly. Its good beginning was damaged by the perceived ineptness of the Carazo administration and the growing economic problems after 1980, for which Carazo was blamed. "Junior" Calderón led the troubled coalition in 1982 and, although he did better than anticipated, securing 32.8 percent of the vote, the future of the coalition is in doubt. It won eighteen seats in the assembly, and some of its leaders suggest that Unity's best hope for survival is to organize as a permanent political party.

WORKERS AND PEASANTS BLOC (BLOQUE DE OBREROS Y CAMPE-SINOS). *See* COMMUNIST PARTY.

Charles D. Ameringer

CUBA

The Republic of Cuba consists of the major island of Cuba, the Isle of Pines (now renamed Isle of Youth), and some 1,600 islets and keys, covering a total area of about 45,000 square miles, roughly equivalent in size to the state of Pennsylvania. When Columbus landed in 1492, three different Indian groups coexisted but the Spanish conquest quickly decimated their numbers. Cuba's cultural values and ethnic roots are to be found in a mixture of Spanish, African, and *criollo* antecedents.

During the last half of the eighteenth century, the development of the sugar industry became the major force shaping Cuba's economy and society, which it has remained to the present time. Already by 1850, about 40 percent of Cuban sugar was sold to the United States. The economic relationship virtually preordained by proximity was to kindle the expectations and aspirations, on both sides, of political linkage.

The Cuban annexationists and their U.S. allies (mostly in New Orleans) financed several military expeditions intended to produce the desired union. The most famous incursions were led by Narciso López, a Venezuelan who attained the rank of general in the Spanish Army. López and his motley regiment of fighters (Americans, Germans, Hungarians, and some Cubans) landed in Cárdenas in 1850, and for the first time raised the national flag over Cuban soil. They were forced to retreat and embarked for the United States. The following year, a new attempt failed again and López was captured and executed.

López's failure and the outcome of the U.S. Civil War ended, at least temporarily, the clamor for annexation. But what the annexationists were unable to achieve in the 1850s, the expansionists of the 1890s accomplished by means of the Spanish-American War and later through considerable political and economic influence over the island in the republican era.

Cuba's destiny seemed inexorably tied to sugar and the United States. Sugar was king and sugar dictated the political and economic direction of the country. As the nineteenth century progressed, latifundia replaced small landholding, black slaves drove away white workers, and the United States began to cast its shadow over the future development of Cuba.

The First Emergence of Political Parties

In the 1860s, with annexation a thing of the past and the possibility of independence still remote, some Cubans turned to attempts at reform within the

Spanish empire. The *reformista* movement gathered force and in 1865 the Reformist Party (Partido Reformista) was organized. Madrid took note of unrest and disputes in the island and felt the need for some moderation and adjustment toward Cuba. The Junta de Información, a commission to study problems and propose changes, was composed of Cubans and Peninsulares (people from Spain). The junta met in Madrid in late 1866 and early 1867 with considerable success, including agreements to extend parliamentary representation to Cubans and to protect civil rights. But in the summer of 1867, the Spanish government disbanded the junta, dismissed all suggestions, imposed additional taxes, and appointed a tough new governor who prohibited public meetings and curtailed the distribution of Reformista literature. The failure of the junta in particular and of *reformismo* in general, gave new impetus to the incipient independence movement. The criollos began preparing for war.

The Cuban wars for independence spanned a period of thirty years, from 1868 to 1898. The Ten Years' War (1868–1878) started on October 10, 1868, under the leadership of Carlos Manuel de Céspedes, who issued the "Grito de Yara" from his plantation near Bayamó, Oriente province, calling for national independence at the same time that he freed his slaves to fight the common colonial enemy alongside him. The war effort was organized and directed by radical *criollo* landowners together with lawyers and other professionals. The bulk of the Cuban Army consisted of peasants, blacks, and Chinese immigrants. The major military leaders were General Máximo Gómez, born in Santo Domingo and an experienced military strategist, and General Antonio Maceo, a black Cuban, who was a daring tactician and tight disciplinarian. The war dragged on for ten years with neither side able to win a decisive victory. Finally, the Peace Treaty of Zanjon ended hostilities in 1878. Cuba remained under Spanish control.

Among the reasons contributing to the failure of Cuban arms, internal dissension, regionalism, and the lack of external support were paramount. In the 1880s, many Cubans turned to *autonomismo*, which advocated autonomous rule for the island under the Spanish flag. Many political and economic reforms were proposed but none was implemented. Madrid did not give any ground. By the 1890s, rebellion was brewing again in and outside of Cuba.

One major problem of the Cuban patriots was the lack of unity. To the old schisms based on regional, class, and racial differences one more was added: the generational gap between the old warriors of 1868 and the new fighters of 1895. It would take a very gifted man to heal the wounds and to create unity. That man was José Martí: poet, writer, politician, orator, and fund-raiser. He organized the Cuban Revolutionary Party (Partido Revolucionario Cubano—PRC) and became its political and intellectual leader. The military commanders of the new battle for freedom were again Máximo Gómez and Antonio Maceo.

The War of Independence (1895–1898) began on February 24, 1895, and the Cuban cause quickly gained momentum. But within two years both Martí and Maceo had been killed on the field of battle and the war effort had become stalemated. Then, in a decisive way, the United States entered the Cuban struggle for independence, and in a few months the Spanish-American War produced the collapse of Madrid's domination over the island. Cuba acquired freedom from Spain, but received the tutelage of the United States. To most Cubans, the latter was a bitter imposition.

United States Interventionism

The first U.S. intervention, from 1898 to 1902, under Generals John Brooke and Leonard Wood, was beneficial in some respects: it avoided famine, introduced a system of public administration, education and health were improved, many public works were built. However, Cuban lawmakers had to accept, as a prerequisite for U.S. troops leaving the island, the Platt Amendment to the Cuban Constitution of 1901 which included the provision that "the United States may exercise the right to intervene" in Cuba if and when it deemed it necessary. On 20 May 1902, the first Cuban president, Tomás Estrada Palma, was inaugurated. The Republic of Cuba started its history.

The problems and issues arising in early republican life were varied and deep-seated. The growth of large sugar plantations restrained the development of a rural middle class and created a landless agrarian proletariat of poor whites and blacks. Commercial dependence on the United States intensified due to U.S. tariff concessions on sugar in return for Cuban preferences for U.S. imports. The development of political dependence (the Platt Amendment mentality) was not conducive to responsible self-government. The new bureaucrats preserved the colonial attitude toward public service as a source of personal profit and privilege. *Personalismo,* the allegiance to the leader, became the staple of Cuban politics. Finally, the solution to political differences was commonly sought through violence. Small wars and rebellions were constant threats to social stability.

To illustrate the Cuban milieu described above, consider the following events. In 1906, President Estrada Palma called for U.S. intervention to help overcome the insurrection led by José Miguel Gómez, the president's rival who had switched from the Conservative Party to the Liberal Party to run for the highest office. The second United States intervention lasted from 1906 to 1909 and increased internal doubts about Cuba's ability for self-government. The veterans of the War of Independence rebelled in 1912, asking for the ouster of pro-Spanish elements in the government bureaucracy. In 1909, Alfredo Zayas became vice-president as a Liberal, but in 1920 he was elected president on the Conservative line. During his term of office, President Zayas had a cabinet imposed on him by the U.S. envoy Enoch Crowder who dictated policy from aboard the U.S.S. Minnesota anchored in Havana harbor.

In sum, during the first two decades of republican existence the bleak picture is one of corruption, violence, electoral fraud, dependence, and cynicism. In the words of Luis Aguilar (p. 33): "The names of the candidates or the parties do not mean very much. The real essence of politics, the interplay of programs and ideas, did not exist. Conservatives changed positions with Liberals and vice versa;

the political struggle was limited to differing slogans and the personal appeal of individuals. The real objective was to gain power in order to distribute positions and privileges among followers."

The Machado Regime and Its Aftermath

In 1924, Gerardo Machado, a Liberal, was elected president in a coalition with Conservatives and the small Popular Party. His platform stressed nationalism, honesty, and economic development, but his political methods degenerated into dictatorship. In late 1926, Machado asked for and received extraordinary powers from the legislature. Later he declared that he wanted more years in power and demanded an extension of the presidential term of office. Through coercion and trickery, Machado obtained a second term of six years, to last until May 1935.

Widespread popular opposition to the dictator coalesced around the Student Directorate (Directorio Estudiantil—DE), the Student Left Wing (Ala Izquierda Estudiantil), the ABC, and the Communist Party (Partido Comunista—PC). All opposition groups, except the Communists, waged urban guerrilla warfare against the Machado forces. Government repression was bloody and Cuba began drifting toward civil war. Under great pressure from the United States, conducted through the efforts of Ambassador Sumner Welles, Machado finally resigned and left Cuba on 12 August 1933.

Conservative Cuban army officers and Welles, supported by the ABC, named Carlos Manuel de Céspedes (son of the 1868 hero) to head a caretaker government. But Céspedes could not control a revolutionary situation heady with demands for nationalism, economic reform, and social justice. On 4 September Sergeant Fulgencio Batista staged a military coup which overthrew the Céspedes government. The Student Directorate became allied with the young armed forces rebels and imposed its candidate, Ramón Grau San Martín, a popular university professor, as president of the new Revolutionary Government. From 10 September 1933 to 15 January 1934 the unlikely and uneasy alliance among Batista, Grau, the DE, and Antonio Guiteras (a fiery leftist radical who held a cabinet post) produced remarkable political changes in Cuba. The revolutionary government abrogated the Platt Amendment, created the Department of Labor, introduced the eight-hour workday, required Cubans to replace foreigners in some jobs, and took over control of several U.S.-owned businesses. Strong opposition against the policies of the government developed from internal groups (the ABC, conservative parties, and the Communists), and of course, by the United States, which did not recognize the Grau regime.

Finally, weakened by internal dissension and several defections and by the popular mood favoring moderation, the Revolutionary Government ceased to exist. Batista, with the blessing of the United States, forced Grau to resign and sent him into exile. Ambassador Welles and later the new envoy, Jefferson Cafferey, saw in Batista the purveyor of law and order, the protector of U.S. interests. Batista ruled through puppet regimes and presidential figureheads until

1940. That year the general himself was elected to serve a term at the Palacio Presidencial, after which he relinquished power in freely held elections.

The Democratic Interlude and Second Batista Regime

The electoral campaign of 1944 was won by Grau and his Authentic Party (Partido Auténtico—PA). From the new administration, the Cuban people expected reforms and honesty but they got instead corruption and chaos. During his second turn in power, Grau was interested only in the spoils of office. Armed urban groups (grupos de acción) ruled the streets with impunity; their leaders were appointed to government positions and their members were rewarded with sinecures. According to Hugh Thomas (p. 737): "Grau turned his presidency into an orgy of theft, ill-disguised by emotional nationalistic speeches. He did more than any other single man to kill the hope of democratic practice in Cuba." Despite this record, the auténticos retained power in the elections of 1948 under the leadership of Carlos Prío Socarrás, an old DE revolutionary. Under Prío civil disorder was contained but corruption continued unabated. He was well-liked by the United States for his tough policies against the Communists, who were removed from control over organized labor.

Elections were scheduled for 1 June 1952. Carlos Hevia was the PA candidate. Roberto Agramonte and his reform-minded Cuban People's Party (Partido del Pueblo Cubano-Ortodoxo—PPC) were given a good chance of success. Fidel Castro was a candidate for the House of Representatives on the Ortodoxo ticket. Under the banner of the United Action Party (Partido de Acción Unitaria—PAU), Fulgencio Batista was running last in the presidential polls.

On 10 March 1952, Batista staged another military coup and built a coalition with business and labor groups. In 1954 Batista conducted rigged elections in an attempt to legitimize his regime, but widespread opposition had been steadily rising since the previous summer. It was on 26 July 1953 that Fidel Castro directed a group of young students and workers in an attack on the Moncada army garrison in Santiago. Castro's speech at his trial ("History Will Absolve Me") later became the ideological platform of the major anti-Batista revolutionary groups: the 26th of July Movement. The rest of the opposition, mainly students and auténticos at first but later to include virtually all socioeconomic classes, accepted Castro's leadership. Guerrilla warfare in the mountains and terrorist tactics in the cities brought down Batista's dictatorship. January first, 1959, started a new era in Cuban history.

The Castro Regime

From the beginning, the Cuban Revolution manifested strong nationalist and anti-imperialist sentiments and pursued populist economic policies. After some hesitation, all pre-1959 political parties except the Communists were banned under the new regime. Political power was concentrated in Castro; it flowed from him through a small group of trusted veterans of Moncada and the Sierra Maestra. When the time came to create a formal political structure, the old Communists provided the organizational expertise but the Castro loyalists retained control over policy-making. Many times during the 1960s the relationship between old Communists and Fidelistas was severely strained. After the failure of the utopian economic goals and policies of the late 1960s (which emphasized the new society achieved through centralization and moral incentives), and propelled by the debacle of the 1970 ten-million ton sugar harvest, Castro turned toward the Soviet model of political and economic organization.

During the 1970s the process of institutionalization produced significant changes in party structure, government decision-making, legal statutes, and even politico-administrative boundaries (there are now fourteen rather than six provinces). The aim of this process has been to reduce charismatic leadership and to increase institutional policy-making. But Fidel is still in control. He is now president of the Council of State, president of the Council of Ministers, first secretary of the Cuban Communist Party, and commander in chief of the armed forces. Fidel is the personification of the process of institutionalization.

Bibliography

Luis Aguilar. *Cuba 1933: Prologue to Revolution*. Norton, New York, 1974.

Jorge Dominguez. *Cuba: Order and Revolution*. Harvard University Press, Cambridge, 1978.

Carmelo Mesa-Lago. *Cuba in the 1970s: Pragmatism and Institutionalization*. University of New Mexico Press, Albuquerque, 1978.

Jaime Suchlicki. *Cuba: From Columbus to Castro*. Scribner's, New York, 1974.

Hugh Thomas. *Cuba: The Pursuit of Freedom*. Harper and Row, New York, 1971.

Political Parties

ABC PARTY (PARTIDO ABC). The *abecedarios*, like many political parties in Cuba, entered public life as a revolutionary movement. The ABC group was organized in October 1931 to combat the dictatorship of President Gerardo Machado, who had illegally extended his term of office. The main leaders were Joaquín Martínez Sáenz, Carlos Saladrigas, and Juan Andrés Lliteras. The ABC was a secret organization made up of small cells of cadres to prevent police infiltration into the highest levels of the group; it used terrorist tactics. Its membership consisted mainly of middle-class professionals and intellectuals who held moderate Leftist ideas. Its ideological credo was contained in the Manifesto of 1932, written by some of Cuba's most outstanding young intellectuals, including Jorge Mañach and Francisco Ichaso. The manifesto was considered the most serious study of Cuban social and economic problems to date and many of its policy suggestions were later adopted by other political parties. The document favored small rural landholdings, nationalization of public utilities, and protection of the working class. It strongly condemned both fascism and communism while advocating political liberty and social justice.

In the summer of 1933, during the last days of the Machado regime, the ABC participated in mediation efforts between the government and some opposition groups orchestrated by U.S. Ambassador Sumner Welles, who attempted to remove the politically bankrupt Machado but to install an equally friendly successor. As a consequence of this move, the integrity and independence of the ABC became tarnished. In August, the ABC was part of the ruling coalition in the post-Machado government of Carlos Manuel de Céspedes. The ABC had made another mistake. The Céspedes government lacked popular support and moved very slowly in implementing its reform program. As Jorge Domínguez put it: "The ABC participated in a government over which they did not have complete control. A minor factor in a weak government" (*Cuba: Order and Revolution* [Harvard University Press, Cambridge, 1978], pp. 154-55).

After the 4 September 1933 military coup by Batista and the installment of the student-backed Grau government, the ABC was shut off from all positions of power. By the end of October, the ABC and the Student Directorate, the two main anti-Machado groups, were fighting each other in the streets of Havana. In November, the ABC, joined by some purged army officers, lost a major battle against the Student Directorate and Batista forces at Atares Fortress, near the Havana docks. That military defeat began the ABC's long slide into political oblivion. By 1940 it had become a small and insignificant political entity. It formally dissolved in 1952.

ALA IZQUIERDA ESTUDIANTIL. *See* STUDENT LEFT WING.

AUTHENTIC ORGANIZATION. *See* AUTHENTIC PARTY.

AUTHENTIC PARTY (PARTIDO REVOLUCIONARIO CUBANO [AUTÉNTICO] or PARTIDO AUTÉNTICO – PA). The Auténticos were organized by Ramón Grau San Martín shortly after his removal as president and the collapse of the Revolutionary Government in January 1934. The party was named after Martí's organization of the 1890s in an attempt to portray itself as the current depository of the values of the Cuban fight for independence. Throughout most of the 1930s, Grau and his group did not participate in legal political activities but remained underground under the name of Authentic Organization (Organización Auténtica). In 1939, the Auténticos emerged as a full-fledged party with a strong showing in the elections for members of the constituent assembly. The party's ideological tenets stressed nationalism, anti-imperialism, and democratic socialism; its platform called for agrarian reform, industrialization, government regulation, prolabor laws, and increased public health and education services. Most of the party's views were strongly reflected in the 1940 Constitution.

In 1944, Grau was elected president in coalition with the conservative Republican Party (Partido Republicano). Under Grau there was a massive failure to achieve the long-promised reforms in Cuba's political and economic system. The revolutionary spirit of the 1930s turned instead into the corrupt venality of the 1940s. Graft was the main currency of the political game and civil disorder was commonplace. Over the issue of corruption, large numbers of party members defected in 1946 to form the Cuban People's Party (Partido del Pueblo Cubano-Ortodoxo) led by Eduardo Chibás. But the PA retained enough clout to carry its nominee, Carlos Prío Socarrás, to the presidency in 1948, again with Republican Party support.

Although corruption continued during the Prío regime, there were some significant economic reforms. A central bank was established and for the first time it began issuing Cuban currency in place of the dollars which had until then been legal tender; and an Agricultural and Industrial Development Bank was also set up.

In March 1952, Prío was finishing his term when Batista again seized power illegally. In 1954, Grau agreed to participate as a candidate in fraudulent elections called by Batista to "legitimize" his regime, but the old professor withdrew at the last moment when the general refused the Auténticos equal representation in the electoral supervisory commissions. Inexplicably, Grau was also a candidate in the meaningless 1958 elections, held just one month before Castro's victory.

However, the Prío faction within the Auténtico party fought Batista in both political and military terms. Prío returned to Cuba in August 1955 and tried to rally the opposition around himself but failed. Prío participated in an anti-Batista rally at the Havana waterfront in November 1955 and his representatives attended the meetings of the Civic Dialogue early the next year. Batista sent Prío back to exile in the United States in May 1956 after the attack on the Goicuría barracks in Matanzas in which Prío was implicated. In May 1957, Prío financed the ill-fated *Corinthia* expedition which landed in northern Oriente, in an attempt to launch an Auténtico guerrilla operation. Prío also gave financial assistance to Castro in Mexico and to the Revolutionary Student Directorate in Cuba.

During the first months of the Castro regime, the Auténticos sought to reorganize their political forces in Cuba. However, by that time, they were a small minority element. They were finally outlawed by the Castro regime on the grounds of collaboration with the Batista dictatorship.

AUTONOMIST PARTY (PARTIDO AUTONOMISTA). After the failure to achieve independence through the Ten Years' War (1868–1878), many Cubans turned to *autonomismo*, seeking some measure of self-governance under the Spanish flag. Their demands included equal rights for Cubans and Peninsulars, permanent guarantees for freedom of speech, assembly, and the press, and the abolition of slavery. The party, founded in early 1878, was the last colonial refuge of the annexationists and reformists of earlier decades. It entered the Spanish Cortés in 1879 and the utter failure of its legislative efforts paved the way for the renewal of the armed struggle against Madrid in the 1890s.

COMMUNIST PARTY (PARTIDO COMUNISTA). *See* POPULAR SOCIALIST PARTY.

COMMUNIST REVOLUTIONARY UNION PARTY (PARTIDO UNIÓN REVOLUCIONARIA COMUNISTA. *See* POPULAR SOCIALIST PARTY.

CONSERVATIVE PARTY (PARTIDO CONSERVADOR or PARTIDO MOD-ERADO). The Conservative Party took shape after independence around the remnants of assorted small colonial parties, and included several prominent Autonomistas. The party was formally organized for the congressional elections of 1904.

Tomás Estrada Palma, Cuba's first president, was elected in 1901 without party affiliation, even though he leaned toward the Conservatives. He was reelected in 1905 under the party's banner in a contest filled with fraud in voter registration and massive balloting irregularities. After the Liberal Party revolt of August 1906, which brought about the second U.S. occupation, Estrada Palma resigned his office.

The Conservatives took power again in 1912, when Mario García Menocal was elected president with the usual disregard for electoral procedures. Menocal's long tenure (he was reelected in 1916) was characterized by large-scale graft and corruption; it is estimated that the president himself stole $40 million from the public treasury. In 1920, Alfredo Zayas, a former Liberal vice-president, became president on the Conservative ticket in coalition with the Popular Party, an organization of his own making composed of disaffected Liberals. Zayas fanned the flames of nationalism for his own purposes of personal enrichment and power-grabbing. In the late 1920s, when Conservatives joined with most other parties in practicing "cooperativism" with Machado, the party gradually lost its independent hold on national affairs, and soon afterwards it disappeared from the political scene.

CONSTITUTIONAL UNION PARTY (PARTIDO UNIÓN CONSTITU-CIONAL). The Constitutional Union Party was organized in the summer of 1878 as the "Spanish party," in reaction against the gathering of many *criollos* into the Autonomist Party. The objective of the Constitutionalists was to insure that Cuba would be always an integral part of Spain. In their view, autonomist concessions would lead sooner or later to independence. Their platform called for limited civil liberties and stressed the formation of a customs union with Spain. Together with the Autonomists, the Constitutionalists elected members of the Spanish Cortes in 1879, where they succeeded in preventing the adoption of moderate policies toward the island.

CUBAN COMMUNIST PARTY (PARTIDO COMUNISTA DE CUBA—PCC). The establishment of the Cuban Communist Party as the official party of the Castro regime went through three phases. The first of these was the establishment in the latter part of 1961 of the Integrated Revolutionary Organizations (Organizaciones Revolucionarias Integradas—ORI). This was a transitional arrangement which attempted to bridge the gap between the collection of several anti-Batista revolutionary groups and the formation of the definitive party of the Cuban Revolution. The ORI was an umbrella-type organization under which the 26th of July Movement (Movimiento 26 de Julio—M-26-7), the Revolutionary Student Directorate (Directorio Estudiantil Revolucionario—DER), and the Popular Socialist Party (Partido Socialista Popular—PSP) were assembled starting in the summer of 1961.

The organizing secretary of the ORI was Aníbal Escalante, an old Stalinist leader of the PSP, who placed many of his former comrades in key positions in the new party. The membership of the National Directorate was announced in March 1962, and consisted mainly of M-26-7 leaders (15 members), and minorities from the DER and PSP (5 members each). However, a few weeks later, Escalante was charged with "sectarianism" (that is, favoritism toward PSP cadres) and was removed from his position. The PSP faction had suffered the first of its many setbacks of the 1960s.

The ORI never attained significant membership and never acquired operational importance. At best, it was an informal vehicle for general discussion among the top revolutionary leadership; it lacked policy-making powers.

Shortly after Escalante's disgrace, the ORI was transformed, without much substantive change, into the United Party of the Socialist Revolution (Partido Unido de la Revolución Socialista—PURS). The main function of the PURS, of which Fidel Castro was secretary-general, was to build up party membership among rank-and-file workers and peasants in order to proceed to the founding of the PCC.

The creation of the Cuban Communist Party was announced by the revolutionary leadership in October 1965, culminating the process of party-building. In view of its antecedents, the initial membership of the PCC was derived mostly from the M-26-7, the DER and the PSP.

The PCC came to life without the holding of a founding congress and without public debate of its goals and functions. It was under the firm control of Fidel Castro and his loyalists. The executive organs of the party (the politburo with eight members and the secretariat with six members) and its deliberative body (the central committee with one hundred members) seldom met during the 1960s. The central committee included sixty-seven military officers. Party membership in 1969 was estimated at 55,000 militants and candidates. During the late 1960s, many former PSP members were removed from leadership positions in the party and the government. At the same time, the PCC became increasingly involved with detailed administrative matters related to the economy, foreign policy, and labor unions.

In 1972, in the midst of the process of institutionalization, the politburo was holding formal meetings twice monthly and the secretariat convened weekly. The party structure consisted of 6 provincial secretariats, 60 district offices, 401 municipal directorates, and 14,360 local cells.

The First Congress of the PCC was held in December 1975, with 3,116 delegates in attendance. The politburo was enlarged to thirteen members to include three former PSP leaders (Arnaldo Milián, Blas Roca, and Carlos Rafael Rodríguez), a symbolic move which, after many years in purgatory, formalized the restitution of the old Communists to revolutionary legitimacy. Total party enrollment, including the youth section and candidates, stood at 212,000 members in 1975. The First Congress approved the draft of the new Socialist constitution, the first five-year economic plan, the new system of economic management, the politico-administrative division of the country into fourteen provinces, and the temporary party platform. The Second Congress, in December 1980, discussed and approved the definitive party program outlining the objectives and strategies for the construction of communism in Cuba.

In the late 1970s, despite attempts to clearly separate the functions of the party and the government, the PCC remained involved in operational details. Likewise, despite the introduction of decentralization in party policy-making, Fidel and his inner circle retained overwhelming clout over the conduct of PCC affairs.

CUBAN NATIONAL PARTY (PARTIDO NACIONAL CUBANO). *See* REPUBLICAN PARTY (1940s).

CUBAN PEOPLE'S PARTY (PARTIDO DEL PUEBLO CUBANO-- ORTODOXO – PPC). In protest against the wave of corruption and gangsterism engulfing the Grau administration of the 1940s, Eduardo Chibás led a large group of disaffected Auténticos to found the PPC in May 1947. Chibás had strongly supported Grau, in fact becoming his apologist during the early years of the regime. But the issue of honesty in government turned Chibás into Grau's (and later Prío's) most formidable opponent. The PPC ideology, emanating mainly from Chibás, was largely limited to the promise of clean government: no theft of public monies, no electoral frauds. The party slogan was *verguenza contra dinero* (honor against money) and the party symbol was a broom. Aside from this promise, there was no specific party program except for general statements condemning U.S. monopolies in public utilities and favoring land redistribution to the peasants.

In 1948, after rejecting pleas from other opposition parties to form a coalition, Chibás ran for president on the Ortodoxo line and received 17 percent of the votes cast, a remarkable showing for such a small and young party. During the Prío administration, Chibás, a fiery orator and unabashed demagogue, publicly accused a cabinet minister of outright theft and promised to produce convincing evidence of such an act. Unable to do so, Chibás shot himself during one of his popular Sunday afternoon radio broadcasts and subsequently died of his wounds.

In 1952 Roberto Agramonte was the PPC presidential candidate and he registered strong support in preelectoral polls. However, Batista's coup of March 10 did away with the scheduled elections. The Ortodoxos assumed a staunch anti-Batista line and refused to participate in the rigged electoral processes held in 1954 and 1958. Many Ortodoxo leaders and members joined Castro's forces in the mountains. The PPC, together with all other prerevolutionary non-Communist parties, ceased to exist legally by the end of 1959.

CUBAN REVOLUTIONARY PARTY (PARTIDO REVOLUCIONARIO CUBANO – PRC). The Cuban Revolutionary Party was organized by José Martí in 1892 while exiled in the United States. It drew its support from Cuban tobacco workers in Tampa and Latin-American intellectuals in New York. The PRC was the political instrument which produced the Second War of Independence (1895–1898). That it was more a revolutionary movement than a political party can be gauged by the fact that it disappeared after independence. Martí's essential contributions included organization, persuasion, and fund-raising. Questions about the basic ideology of the PRC, as expounded by Martí, continue to be raised even today. Martí wrote both laudatory and critical comments on multiple subjects and issues; he combined elements of romanticism, anarchism, socialism, and even capitalism. The dream was an independent, prosperous Cuba but the details were not spelled out. After his death, Martí would become all things to all people. The party's spokesman in the island was Juan Gualberto Gómez, a mulatto intellectual who later strongly opposed the Platt Amendment.

DIRECTORIO ESTUDIANTIL. See STUDENT DIRECTORATE.

DIRECTORIO ESTUDIANTIL REVOLUCIONARIO. See REVOLUTIONARY STUDENT DIRECTORATE.

INDEPENDENT PARTY OF COLORED PEOPLE (PARTIDO INDEPENDIENTE DE COLOR). In 1908, during the second United States occupation, Evaristo Estenóz, a Dominican and a veteran of the War of Independence, founded the Independent Party of Colored People for black Cubans. In marked departure from the standards of the time, the party's platform contained socioeconomic goals such as the distribution of state lands to peasants, an eight-hour workday, the abolition of the death penalty, and the end of racial discrimination. During the next few years, there was no progress on the economic demands and the racial issue became exacerbated.

In 1912, reacting against an election law which prohibited political parties or movements limited to members of any single ethnic group, a violent black rebellion broke out in Las Villas and Oriente provinces. Estenóz assumed leadership of an armed group near Guantánamo. But the revolt was put down harshly by the army and volunteers under order of President José Miguel Gómez, at a cost of 3,000 black dead, including Estenóz. It was the last time in Cuba that a movement would be organized along racial or ethnic lines.

INTEGRATED REVOLUTIONARY ORGANIZATIONS (ORGANIZACIONES REVOLUCIONARIAS INTEGRADAS – ORI). See CUBAN COMMUNIST PARTY.

LIBERAL PARTY (PARTIDO LIBERAL—PL). The Liberals broke into Cuban politics in classic fashion befitting that genre: they abstained from running candidates in the 1905 election due to allegations of fraud, and the next year they revolted against the Conservatives, precipitating the second United States occupation. The policy of agitation paid off when José Miguel Gómez was elected president in 1908 under U.S. auspices. From then on, the United States pursued a policy of "preventive intervention" which entailed close monitoring of Cuban events to avoid the need for another occupation. The Liberals took up arms again in 1917 against Conservative President Mario García Menocal, and clamored for United States support in contesting the 1920 election of Menocal's candidate, Alfredo Zayas, to the highest office. In both instances, the U.S. responded mainly by sending diplomats in warships but no troops, thus achieving its objective of stability at reduced risk.

The Liberal Party's long absence from power ended with the election of Gerardo Machado in 1924. Machado had stolen his party's nomination away from Carlos Mendieta by resorting to trickery and secret deals with opponents. Machado based his electoral campaign on the "Platform of Regeneration," a progressive document calling for limited bureaucracy and government spending, revision of the Platt Amendment to insure national independence, and tariff protection for domestic industries. In 1926 all important political parties (Conservatives, Liberals and Populars) decided to support the regime in an arrangement called "cooperative opposition" (*cooperativismo*). Afterwards, Machado's thirst for unlimited power could not be quenched and he succeeded in extending illegally his term of office to a total of ten years. The popular revolt against Machado was launched in full force in 1930 and he was ousted in August 1933.

During Batista's years of indirect rule in the 1930s, the Liberals once again briefly held the limelight of illusory power. Miguel Mariano Gómez, son of José Miguel, was installed as president in 1936 but was quickly forced to resign when he protested Batista's policy of militarizing rural education. Federico Laredo Bru, Gomez's vice-president, filled the puppet role until 1940 when Batista was properly elected to the office.

In 1948, Liberal candidate Ricardo Núñez Portuondo, with support from the National Democratic Union, gathered 30 percent of the presidential vote but lost to Carlos Prío's coalition of Auténticos and Republicans. However, Liberals later joined the Prío administration. When Batista returned himself to power with the 1952 coup, the opportunistic Liberals jumped upon his bandwagon. By the 1954 elections, the Liberal Party was reduced to being a small component in the Batista coalition of political forces.

MOVIMIENTO 26 DE JULIO. See TWENTY-SIXTH OF JULY MOVEMENT.

NATIONAL DEMOCRATIC UNION (UNIÓN NACIONAL DEMOCRÁTICA —UND). The National Democratic Union was organized in 1936 by Mario García Menocal, the former Conservative president. The UND constituted the major legislative opposition which impeached President Miguel Mariano Gómez over the issue of his refusal to accept military control over rural education. Menocal made a deal with Batista in 1940 and the UND joined the government coalition, with party leader Gustavo Cuervo Rubio becoming vice-president during Batista's term. However, in 1944 Cuervo Rubio abandoned the UND to organize the new conservative Republican Party allied with Grau. The remaining UND loyalists supported the Liberals in 1948 against Prío and the Auténticos, but lost. However, in typical fashion, during Prío's administration the UND joined him in power, occupying some minor cabinet posts. After Batista's 1952 coup, the UND also joined his coalition.

NATIONALIST UNION PARTY (UNIÓN NACIONALISTA). The Nationalist Union Party was founded in 1927 by Carlos Mendieta, a former Liberal, in an effort to join all anti-Machado politicians into a common front. The Nationalists were barred by an emergency law from participating in the 1928 elections rigged by Machado. In 1930, a party meeting in Artemisa was attacked by the police, marking the first major bloodshed in the fight against the dictator. In the summer of 1933, the Nationalists, led by Cosmé de la Torriente, participated in the mediation group (together with the ABC) which attempted to solve the governmental crisis but to no avail. After the demise of Grau's short-lived revolutionary government, Mendieta became president for two years under the aegis of Batista, and the Nationalists remained in power by their alliance with Batista through 1944. After that year, the party disbanded and most members joined Grau and his Auténticos, then in control of the government.

ORGANIZACIÓN AUTÉNTICA. See AUTHENTIC PARTY.

ORGANIZACIONES REVOLUCIONARIAS INTEGRADAS. See CUBAN COMMUNIST PARTY.

PARTIDO ABC. See ABC.

PARTIDO ACCIÓN UNITARIA. See UNITED ACTION PARTY.

PARTIDO AUTÉNTICO. See AUTHENTIC PARTY.

PARTIDO AUTONOMISTA. See AUTONOMIST PARTY.

PARTIDO COMUNISTA. See POPULAR SOCIALIST PARTY.

PARTIDO COMUNISTA DE CUBA. See CUBAN COMMUNIST PARTY.

PARTIDO CONSERVADOR. See CONSERVATIVE PARTY.

PARTIDO DE ACCIÓN PROGRESISTA. *See* PROGRESSIVE ACTION PARTY.

PARTIDO DEL PUEBLO CUBANO. *See* CUBAN PEOPLE'S PARTY.

PARTIDO INCONDICIONAL ESPAÑOL. *See* SPANISH UNCONDITIONAL PARTY.

PARTIDO INDEPENDIENTE DE COLOR. *See* INDEPENDENT PARTY OF COLORED PEOPLE.

PARTIDO LIBERAL. *See* LIBERAL PARTY.

PARTIDO MODERADO. *See* CONSERVATIVE PARTY.

PARTIDO NACIONAL CUBANO. *See* REPUBLICAN PARTY.

PARTIDO POPULAR. *See* POPULAR PARTY.

PARTIDO REFORMISTA. *See* REFORMIST PARTY.

PARTIDO REPUBLICANO. *See* REPUBLICAN PARTY.

PARTIDO REVOLUCIONARIO CUBANO. *See* CUBAN REVOLUTIONARY PARTY.

PARTIDO REVOLUCIONARIO CUBANO (AUTÉNTICO). *See* AUTHENTIC PARTY.

PARTIDO SOCIALISTA POPULAR. *See* POPULAR SOCIALIST PARTY.

PARTIDO UNIÓN CONSTITUCIONAL. *See* CONSTITUTIONAL UNION PARTY.

PARTIDO UNIÓN REVOLUCIONARIA. *See* POPULAR SOCIALIST PARTY.

PARTIDO UNIÓN REVOLUCIONARIA COMUNISTA. *See* POPULAR SOCIALIST PARTY.

POPULAR PARTY (PARTIDO POPULAR). In 1919, Alfredo Zayas left the Liberal Party because José Miguel Gómez had wrested for himself its presidential candidacy. Afterwards, Zayas founded the Popular Party, which in conjunction with Menocal and the Conservatives carried Zayas to the presidency in 1920. That the Popular Party was little more than a personal vehicle of Zayas may be gauged by the fact that after his term the party never again played an important role in national political affairs. By 1944, the party had dissolved and many members had joined Grau's Auténticos.

POPULAR SOCIALIST PARTY (PARTIDO SOCIALISTA POPULAR–PSP). Popular Socialist Party was the last name used by Cuba's orthodox Stalinist Communist Party. The Communist Party was first organized in Havana in 1925 by student leader Julio Antonio Mella, former Martí collaborator Carlos Baliño, and Polish-born Fabio Grobart. The original group of eleven founders was later joined by the poet Ruben Martínez Villena. In the early years, the party's policies strictly followed the Comintern line of opposition to anyone outside the fold, from Machado to the ABC and the Directorio Estudiantil. The Cuban Communists were staunchly antireformist and antiterrorist, while oftentimes acting on opportunistic grounds. Afraid of direct U.S. intervention, party secretary-general César Vilar attempted to make a deal with Machado during the dictator's last days in power. Concerned about the possible impact of reformism upon its ability to condemn the system, and following the Comintern's sectarian "Third Period" policy, the party bitterly opposed Grau's revolutionary administration in 1933, denouncing it as a "bourgeois-landlord imperialist government." While the early 1930s saw the party strongly opposed to Batista, by 1937 the Communists were in coalition with him in response to Moscow's directives favoring the popular-front approach. In exchange for their lavish support, Batista in 1937 legalized the Communist front party, the Revolutionary Union Party (Partido Unión Revolucionaria), and gave them control of organized labor in 1939 by allowing Lázaro Peña to become head of the newly formed Confederation of Workers of Cuba (Confederación de Trabajadores de Cuba–CTC). In 1939, also, the underground Communist Party merged with the Revolutionary Union Party to form the Communist Revolutionary Union Party, which was legalized and became part of the victorious Batista coalition in the 1940 elections. As a reward, party leaders Juan Marinello and Carlos Rafael Rodríguez served as ministers in the Batista cabinet. Later they would hold important positions in Castro's regime.

In an effort to broaden its popular base, the party's name was changed in 1944 to Popular Socialist Party (Partido Socialista Popular), the designation which lasted until the 1960s. Blas Roca was general secretary during most of those years. In the 1944 elections, the PSP backed Batista's candidate, Carlos Saladrigas, an old ABC leader. But after the victory of Ramón Grau San Martín, the PSP supported the Auténticos which, among other things, allowed Peña and his lieutenants to retain control over the CTC at least for another three years. The PSP ventured into the 1948 elections by itself, without entering into any coalition, and received only 7 percent of the national vote. Under Prío's anti-Communist administration, the PSP completely lost control of the CTC to the Auténticos and was forced to assume a passive role in domestic affairs.

After his 1952 coup, Batista, wishing to secure U.S. support for his regime, declared the PSP illegal. Some party leaders went into exile to eastern Europe and some party members were jailed. But the party continued to function largely unmolested, albeit at reduced intensity. Party publications, but not its daily paper, continued to be printed and distributed publicly. Although banned from the 1954 electoral farce, the PSP exhorted its members to support Grau's candidacy under the Auténtico banner. During the armed struggle against Batista, the PSP not only refrained from participation, but strongly condemned violence and rebellion as sterile and romantic tactics. After the attack on the Moncada barracks in July 1953, the official PSP statement "repudiated" the attack, calling it "putschist" and "adventurist." It was only in the summer of 1958, when Castro's victory seemed imminent, that the party sent Carlos Rafael Rodríguez to make a deal with him in the Sierra Maestra.

In 1959, the PSP was the only prerevolutionary political party allowed to retain legal existence. In 1961, in Castro's own words, the glorious flag of the PSP was delivered to the Revolution by Blas Roca. The PSP was merged into the Organizaciones Revolucionarias Integradas (ORI) and later into the Cuban Communist Party of Castro. During most of the 1960s, when Castro was following independent political and economic policies differing from Moscow's line, the old PSP adherents were relegated to minor posts. But at present, many former PSP leaders occupy highly prominent positions in the Cuban Communist Party (for example, Roca, Rodríguez, and Arnaldo Milián are members of the politburo and many others are members of the central committee).

PROGRESSIVE ACTION PARTY (PARTIDO DE ACCIÓN PROGRESISTA —PAP). Upon returning to Cuba from the United States in 1948, Batista organized his political forces into the United Action Party (Partido de Acción Unitaria—PAU). In 1952 Batista was running for president under the PAU banner when he staged the March coup that returned him to power. For the 1954 elections, held to attempt to legitimize his regime, Batista built a coalition around the newly formed Progressive Action Party, in fact a reorganization of the old PAU. The PAP-led coalition included Liberals and National Democrats. In 1958, the PAP candidate Andrés Rivero Aguëro won a presidential term he would never serve.

REFORMIST PARTY (PARTIDO REFORMISTA). The Reformist Party, in fact a loose coalition of diverse forces, was organized in 1865, to channel existing reformist aspirations. The party wanted economic and political concessions for the island from Madrid, including more equitable taxation, freer trade, representation in the Spanish parliament or Cortés, and equal rights for Cubans and Peninsulares. The failure of *reformismo* after the futile Junta de Información meetings in 1866~1867 led in part to the outbreak of the Ten Years War.

REPUBLICAN PARTY (PARTIDO REPUBLICANO) (1930s). The Republican Party was founded in the mid-1930s by Miguel Mariano Gómez, former Liberal mayor of Havana and son of José Miguel. With the indispensable backing of

Batista, the younger Gómez was elected president in 1935, but his first attempt at independent decision-making was also his last. Miguel Mariano Gómez was impeached and removed from office in 1936 when he differed with Batista over the issue of assigning military personnel to rural schools. After a few years of ineffectual congressional opposition, the party disbanded in 1944, with most members transferring to the Liberal and Auténtico parties.

REPUBLICAN PARTY (PARTIDO REPUBLICANO) (1940s). In the same year that the first Republican Party was dissolved, a new Republican Party was organized by Gustavo Cuervo Rubio, who had split with the National Democrats (UDN), taking many party adherents with him. The new Republicans were very conservative and held strong anti-Communist convictions. As members of the coalition with the Auténticos in 1944, the Republicans shared power during Grau's tenure in office. In 1948, the party's name was changed to Cuban National Party (Partido Nacional Cubano—PNC), under the leadership of Guillermo Alonso Pujol and Nicolás Castellanos, the Auténtico mayor of Havana. The PNC's support of the victorious Carlos Prío in 1948 won the vice-presidential slot for Alonso Pujol. After Batista's coup, the PNC disappeared from the political scene.

REVOLUTIONARY STUDENT DIRECTORATE (DIRECTORIO ESTUDI-ANTIL REVOLUCIONARIO—DER). In the pattern of the anti-Machado groups of the 1920s and 1930s, the DER was formed in December 1956 to fight against the Batista dictatorship. Although mainly drawing its strength and leadership from the University Students Federation (Federación de Estudiantes Universitarios —FEU), the DER welcomed professionals and workers into its ranks. Among the group's founders were José Antonio Echeverría, Fauré Chomón, and Carlos Gutiérrez Menoyo.

The DER ideology espoused democratic and middle-class values strongly influenced by Catholic beliefs, and it was explicitly anti-Communist. In many matters, the DER disagreed with Fidel Castro's 26th of July Movement. The most daring military action undertaken by the DER was the frontal attack on the Presidential Palace on 13 March 1957, during which Echeverría and Gutiérrez Menoyo were killed. In January 1958, a group of DER fighters under the command of Chomón opened a guerrilla front in the Escambray mountains of central Cuba.

After 1959, relations between the DER and Castro were oftentimes difficult and tense. In 1961, the Directorio was absorbed into the Organizaciones Revolucionarias Integradas (ORI). Later, with the formation of the Cuban Communist Party, some DER leaders were given membership in the central committee and the secretariat. However, with the ascendancy of old PSP cadres after 1975, the DER faction has lost considerable power in PCC affairs (for example, Chomón, formerly in the secretariat, is now a provincial first secretary).

REVOLUTIONARY UNION PARTY (PARTIDO UNIÓN REVOLUCION-ARIA—PUR). See POPULAR SOCIALIST PARTY.

SPANISH UNCONDITIONAL PARTY (PARTIDO INCONDICIONAL ESPAÑOL). The Spanish Unconditional Party was hastily organized in 1865 to respond to the perceived threat to Spanish sovereignty over Cuba represented by the demands of the *criollo*-led Reformist Party. The Unconditionals were dead set against any change in the *status-quo* and campaigned to make Cuba a full-fledged province of the mother country. The party had a formidable press vehicle for communicating its views in the *Diario de la Marina*, a daily newspaper which was a staunch defender of Cuban conservatism until its abolition by Castro in 1960.

STUDENT DIRECTORATE (DIRECTORIO ESTUDIANTIL—DE). It was students of the University of Havana banded together in the DE of 1927 who first protested against Machado's usurpation of power—the DE group organized in September 1930 which led the anti-Machado struggle. Their political views were anti-imperialist and radical and they used terrorist tactics. During the brief Céspedes government of August 1933, the DE issued a manifesto calling for agrarian reform and social welfare legislation. The document was signed, among others, by Carlos Prío Socarras, Justo Carrillo, and Manuel Antonio Varona.

On 4 September 1933, the DE supported Batista's takeover and joined him in forming the Revolutionary Government with Ramón Grau San Martín, the DE's choice, as president. Grau and the students succeeded in enacting laws and regulations fully reflective of their strongly nationalist and populist ideology, summarized in the slogan Cuba for the Cubans. Grau wanted "to liquidate the colonial structure that has survived in Cuba since independence." However, internal dissension escalated within the DE to the point that on 5 November the DE, as an organized political group, dissolved itself. This action further weakened the Revolutionary Government, already threatened by domestic Conservative and Communist opposition and by the refusal of the United States to recognize its existence. In January 1934, Batista ousted Grau and the remaining DE leaders from power. In later years, many DE leaders were to participate in key events in Cuban history (Prío became president in 1948 and Varona was involved in the Bay of Pigs landing).

STUDENT LEFT WING (ALA IZQUIERDA ESTUDIANTIL—AIE). This radical student group was organized in the spring of 1931 by splinter elements of the 1930 Directorio Estudiantil (DE), together with some former members of the 1927 and 1929 DE groups. The Ala Izquierda recruits exhibited Marxist tendencies but were less dogmatic than the Communists. Using terrorist techniques, they participated on their own in the anti-Machado struggle, without entering into any tactical alliance or political coalition. Among the AIE's most prominent members were Aureliano Sánchez Arango, Raúl Roa, and Pablo de la Torriente Brau. After 1933 the AIE disbanded but many of its members later occupied important government positions (for example, Sánchez Arango was minister of education under Prío and Roa was foreign minister under Castro).

TWENTY-SIXTH OF JULY MOVEMENT (MOVIMIENTO 26 DE JULIO — M-26-7). The attack on the Moncada garrison in Santiago by Fidel Castro and his group on 26 July 1953, started the armed struggle against Batista's second dictatorship. Brutal repression by the army cost the lives of dozens of Castro's followers after surrendering. Fidel and some close associates were captured, tried, and given long prison sentences.

After his release under a general amnesty and before leaving for Mexico, Castro organized the M-26-7 at a Havana meeting in July 1955. He returned to Cuba in December 1956 leading an expeditionary force of 82 men aboàrd the yacht *Granma* and started guerrilla operations in the Sierra Maestra. The movement also opened urban warfare fronts under the leadership of Frank Pais, Faustino Pérez, and Armando Hart. They were able thoroughly to penetrate the organized labor movement under the leadership of David Salvador. During 1957 and 1958, Castro and his delegates established contacts and signed agreements with other anti-Batista groups, always securing the dominant role for the M-26-7 and its leader.

The precise ideological position of the M-26-7 on political and economic issues remains to the present a difficult and controversial subject. According to Jorge Domínguez (p. 130): "Even at their most radical, Castro's proposals and those of the Twenty-sixth of July Movement had many points in common with the programs of the Ortodoxo party of the late 1940s and early 1950s and with intellectual Catholic proposals of the period.... The main points of all the documents were always political change, legitimacy, and purification of government. As the socioeconomic content of proposals declined, the stress on politics increased. Moderate nationalism reappeared, though with a change in emphasis from expropriation of foreign property to the prevention of United States intervention." The moderate wing of the movement was led by Raúl Chibás, Faustino Pérez and Manolo Ray, while the leftist forces were concentrated around Raúl Castro and Ernesto Guevara. As with all major decisions in recent Cuban history, the decisive voice was that of Fidel Castro.

After the revolutionary victory early in 1959, the political role of the M-26-7 organization was further diminished while that of Fidel Castro and his inner circle soared to commanding heights. The movement had served its function during the insurrectional phase, but a new organization instrument was required for the revolutionary era. The fusion of the M-26-7, the DER, and the PSP into the Organizaciones Revolucionarias Integradas started the process of party-building which culminated in the Cuban Communist Party. At present, the top leadership of the Cuban Communist Party consists largely of M-26-7 veterans, including 77 percent of the politburo, 67 percent of the secretariat, and 75 percent of the central committee.

UNITED ACTION PARTY (PARTIDO DE ACCIÓN UNITARIA—PAU). *See* PROGRESSIVE ACTION PARTY.

Sergio Roca

DOMINICA

One of the most distinctive of the English-speaking Caribbean islands, the Commonwealth of Dominica became independent from Great Britain in November 1978. The island, 29 miles long by 16 miles wide, covers approximately 305 square miles, is of volcanic formation and retains one of the largest areas of virgin rain forest while sheltering a comparatively narrow range of fauna. The mountains are among the highest in the area and the percentage of interior rainfall is among the highest in the world. Located in the Atlantic trade wind zone, the August to September sector of the hurricane season, *l'hivernage*, is a particular threat.

While the majority of the estimated population of 80,000 (1978) is of African descent, there are also families of European and Middle Eastern extraction. In addition, there are Caribs and their descendants whose numbers may vary between 500 to 1000 depending on the criteria utilized for distinguishing Carib from non-Carib residents. A Carib reserve is located on one section of the island. The population has a chief and a separate sociopolitical organization. Although the island population is predominantly Roman Catholic, Anglican and Methodist adherents also have long historical roots on the island. The island is divided into ten parishes. French culture and linguistic traditions predominate in eight out of ten people.

The economy of the island was traditionally based upon diversified agricultural production. During the period of slavery, first coffee and later coffee and sugar were major export items. Recently the major exports have been bananas, fruits and fruit products, cocoa, coconut oil, and soap. While there are large estate owners, much of the production has been in the hands of small proprietors of ten or so acres of land. This tendency is increased as large landlords find it progressively difficult to find labor due to the level of out-migration.

Assigned to the Leeward Island group, in 1940 Dominica was transferred to the Windward Islands for administrative purposes. In 1956, the island was incorporated into the territory of the Windward Islands and became part of the Federation of the West Indies in 1958. Dominica became a self-governing West Indies Associated State in March 1967. One of the more isolated and, consequently, relatively less developed Caribbean countries, Dominica is making every effort to reduce the problems related to isolation. It became the fifth English-speaking country and the twenty-sixth member of the Organization of American States in 1979 and became the 151st member of the United Nations.

During the seventeenth and eighteenth centuries, the French and English fought over control of Dominica. It was not until the early 1800s that sustained development and settlement of the island by the English got under way. However, French influence in areas such as language, legal practices, and tenant-landlord relations continued. An improved judicial structure which included the introduction of a jury system, was introduced in 1836. By 1838 it was modified to restrict jury service to those with a knowledge of English. In 1865 the general franchise was restricted. During 1871 Dominica and other Leeward Islands were organized into a Crown Colony. Political activities were subsequently curtailed. An act passed by Great Britain in 1898 abrogated the remaining elective rights of Dominicans and resulted in a legislative council composed of twelve nominated members of whom six served in an ex-officio capacity.

While Dominicans petitioned for withdrawal from the Leeward Islands Federation and restitution of representative election in 1921, it was only in 1924 that partial restoration of electoral rights occurred. Islanders were allowed to elect four of the nonofficial members of the legislative council, although there were property qualifications to vote and hold office. In 1936, the legislative council was modified to include five elected members (still chosen by a restricted franchise) and three nominated members, in addition to the administrator, the crown attorney and the colonial treasurer. The transfer of Dominica from the Leeward to the Windward Island group in 1940 resulted in fiscal independence and greater independence in other spheres.

In 1951, a new constitution was adopted which provided universal adult suffrage and the elected members of the legislative council were increased by three. In addition, three members were also elected from the legislature, and one member was appointed, to serve on the executive council. In 1956, the elected members of the executive council became administrators of departments and were titled ministers, and in 1960 the leader of the elected members became chief minister.

Until 1954 the local, village-level governing bodies scattered throughout the parishes were nominated village boards. Thereafter, the opportunity for active grass-roots participation increased as the local boards were replaced by councils consisting of eight members, five of whom were elected in comparison to the three members nominated by the government.

Dominica was an active participant and supporter of the West Indian Federation from 1958 through 1962. Phyllis S. Allfrey, founder of the Dominica Labour Party, became the federal government's minister of labor and social affairs.

In 1967 Dominica became an Associated State with Great Britain which, of course, retained responsibilities for defense and international relations. The chief minister became premier and presided over the cabinet. The former administrator became governor.

During the 1967–1978 period, the village councils, the lowest level of island government, proliferated. In the early 1970s, 23 councils, which were elected every three years, existed. At the highest level of island government were the House of Assembly and the Cabinet. The House consisted of twenty-five members—twenty-one elected and four nominated. One of the latter was nominated on the advice of the Leader of the Opposition. The Speaker of the House could be elected from among the members of the assembly or from outside. The premier presided over the cabinet which consisted of five members plus the attorney general. The governor appointed the premier from the elected members of the House of Assembly. The other cabinet members were appointed by the governor on the advice of the premier.

Although the West Indies Act of 1962 indicated that the ties between Dominica and Great Britain were voluntary and might be terminated by either party, the relationship was maintained as the Dominican government prepared for independence. While the government was in favor of independence, the opposition presented qualifications which, although clarified to varying extents during conferences in London in March and May 1977, continued as a source of underlying friction prior to independence.

E. O. LeBlanc served as premier until 1974, when he resigned from both the premiership and the House of Assembly. Patrick R. John, who had become deputy premier and minister of finance in 1973, became the new premier. Sir Louis Cools-Lartigue served as acting governor.

On 3 November 1978, Dominica became an independent member of the Commonwealth. The new constitution provided for a president to hold office for no more than two terms. He was to be jointly nominated by the Leader of the Opposition and the prime minister. In the event of lack of agreement, the president can be elected by secret vote of the House. The prime minister, an elected member of the majority party in the House, is appointed by and may be removed by the president, in the event of a no-confidence vote. Parliament is composed of the House of Assembly and the Presidency. Patrick R. John became the first prime minister, Frederick E. Degazon, former Speaker of the House, was elected president by 16 votes to 10.

In the late 1960s and early 1970s, the Black Power Movement, which had considerable influence in the English-speaking West Indies, had its impact in Dominica. It resulted in formation of a short-lived party, and some of its adherents called themselves "dreads," and adopted the "dread locks" of the Rastafarian movement of Jamaica. The government reacted by outlawing the wearing of long hair in the Dreads Act of 1974.

The Dominica Labour Party government met growing opposition. This reached a peak in May 1979, with demonstrations against bills to outlaw strikes and limit press freedom, in which three persons were killed. Five trade unions, including the powerful Civil Service Association, called for a general strike, which resulted in cessation of public services. Public gatherings were banned but took place anyway. Certain unions favored the Leader of the Opposition, Eugenia Charles, assuming responsibility for the government. By 12 June seven members of the ruling Dominica Labour Party resigned to form a new party, the Democratic Labour Party. On 15 June, President Degazon resigned, Patrick John dissolved Parliament and called for new elections on 1 December. Sir Louis Cools-Lartigue, who became the acting president, reversed the dissolution of Parliament, and then resigned on 16 June. On 21 June 1979, Patrick John was ousted by the House of Assembly, and was succeeded by interim Prime Minister James Oliver Seraphine, while Jenner Armour became acting president. Seraphine's government was made up of Dominica Labour Party leaders who had broken with John in 1978 and 1979.

During the elections in July 1980, Eugenia Charles, Leader of the Opposition, was elected prime minister by a landslide vote, when the Dominica Freedom Party won seventeen of twenty-one seats. Dominica thus became the first Caribbean country to elect a woman to such a post. In addition, a career civil servant, Marie Davis-Pierre, was appointed Speaker. The first Carib was also elected to the legislature. Both ex-Prime Minister John and the incumbent Prime Minister Seraphine, lost their seats.

Bibliography

A. S. Banks and William Overstreet. "Dominica." *Political Handbook of the World.* McGraw-Hill, New York, 1980.

Basil Crocknell. *Dominica: Aspects of Dominican History.* David and Charles, Newton Abbot, 1973.

Cecil A. Goodridge. "Dominica: The French Connexion." *Aspects of Dominican History.* Government Printing Division, Dominica, W.I., 1972.

Earl S. Huntley. "The Foreign Affairs of Independent St. Lucia, St. Vincent, St. Kitts-Nevis and Dominica." *Bulletin of Eastern Caribbean Affairs.*

C. Kunsman. *The Origins and Development of Political Parties in the British West Indies.* Part 2. University Microfilms International, Ann Arbor, Mich., 1963.

N. J. O. Liverpool. "The Politics of Independence in Dominica." *Bulletin of Eastern Caribbean Affairs,* vol. 4, no. 2, May–June, 1978.

John Paxton. "Dominica." *Statesman's Year Book: Statistical and Historical Annual of the States of the World, 1978–1979.* St. Martin's Press, New York, 1979.

Linden Smith. "Dominica: The Post-Hurricane David Period." *Bulletin of Eastern Caribbean Affairs,* vol. 5, no. 4, September–October, 1979.

————. "The Political Situation in Dominica." *Bulletin of Eastern Caribbean Affairs,* vol. 5, no. 3, July–August, 1979.

Political Parties

ASCENDANCY PARTY. The Ascendancy Party existed in the mid-nineteenth century. The group was led by the Methodist George Charles Falconer, and served principally to monitor governmental activities.

DEMOCRATIC LABOUR PARTY. The Democratic Labour Party was formed by Minister of Agriculture Oliver Seraphine, when he resigned from the government of Prime Minister Patrick John in June 1979. It took with it a majority of the Dominica Labour Party members of the House of Assembly. With John's resignation, Seraphine became Prime Minister. However, in the election of July 1980, the Democratic Labour Party won only two seats and Seraphine himself was defeated.

DOMINICA DEMOCRATIC ALLIANCE. Formed by Michael Douglas, when he was dismissed from the cabinet in January 1978 by Prime Minister Patrick John, the Dominica Democratic Alliance remained in opposition to the John government. When Prime Minister John was forced to resign in June 1979, Michael Douglas, who was also a leader of the Farmers Union, became minister of finance. He subsequently also took over the agriculture portfolio. His party did not win any seats in the July 1980 elections, however.

DOMINICA FREEDOM PARTY (DFP). Led by barrister Miss Eugenia Charles, the Dominica Freedom Party was organized in October 1968 in protest against passage of the Seditious and Undesirable Publications Act. It became the primary opposition party. The DFP, whose base was primarily urban, dominated the town council in the capital city, Roseau. In 1970 the DFP won two seats in the House of Assembly. In the 1975 election, it won three seats.

Although the DFP participated in the movement against the John government in June 1979, it did not join the new administration, but remained the official opposition party.

The July 1980 election brought the Dominica Freedom Party into office by a landslide, winning seventeen of twenty-one seats. The DFP has the reputation of being more conservative than its old rival, the Dominica Labour Party.

DOMINICA LABOUR PARTY (DLP). One of the first official political parties, the Dominica Labour Party was founded by Phyllis Shand Allfrey, a Fabian socialist of English extraction in 1952. The party which she hoped would uphold principles of "tropical socialism," was modeled on the British Labour Party. It was supposedly geared not to local and international big business, but rather toward the local middle and lower classes.

In 1956, the DLP won three of the eight seats in the legislative council. DLP members won all the Dominica seats in the West Indian Federal Parliament and Phyllis Allfrey served in the Federal Cabinet. By 1961, under the leadership of E. O. LeBlanc, the DLP ousted the Dominica United Peoples' Party by winning seven of the eleven seats. In the election of 1966, the party won ten of the eleven seats.

The DLP suffered internal problems at various times. In 1961, Phyllis Allfrey was expelled from the party. In 1970, the DLP split into the LeBlanc Labour Party and the Dominica Labour Party. Of the eleven seats in the assembly, one was won by the DLP candidates, while eight were carried by the LLP. Patrick John was one of the LLP candidates. However, the rift in the party was subsequently healed, and the Dominica Labour Party remained in power until the ouster of Prime Minister Patrick John in 1979. Subsequently, under Patrick John's continuing leadership, the Dominica Labour Party joined the Dominica Liberation Alliance in a coalition in contesting the 1980 election, but it won no seats in the assembly.

DOMINICA LIBERATION ALLIANCE. The Dominica Alliance was founded to participate in the July 1980 election. Its leadership was made up principally of young intellectuals trained in the United States and was divided into two factions. One was headed by Atherton Martin, an agronomist and deputy leader of the party, and William Riviere, a historian. The other faction was headed by Bernard Wilshire. The Alliance gained no seats in the House in those elections.

DOMINICA PEOPLE'S PARTY. The Dominica People's Party was formed under the leadership of a large landowner, Franklin Boron, in 1957 by winners of five seats in the legislature during the election that year. While three of the candidates had been independents, two (LaVille and Didier) were members of the People's National Movement, which had been formed earlier, inspired by the Trinidad and Tobago party of the same name, headed by Eric Williams.

DOMINICA UNITED PEOPLES' PARTY (DUPP). In 1958, a number of groups hostile to the Dominica Labour Party, including the Dominica Peoples' Party, Peoples' National Movement, and the Dominica Taxpayers Reform Association, joined together to form the Dominica United Peoples' Party. The DUPP, under the leadership of Franklin Boron, chief minister, won the election, and led the government until their defeat by the DLP in 1961, when they won only three seats.

MOVEMENT FOR A NEW DOMINICA (MND). The Movement for a New Dominica was the party of the Black Power Movement which emerged in Dominica in 1968. The movement first published a periodical, *Black Cry*. In 1972 the movement was converted into a political party, one of whose principal leaders was Desmond Trotter. The MND supported a general strike of agricultural workers in June 1973, and subsequently suffered considerable persecution by the government. In May 1974, Desmond Trotter was charged with the murder of two American tourists. His case became an international cause celebre. The MND does not seem to have participated in any general election.

PEASANTS AND WORKERS MOVEMENT IN DOMINICA. Headed by Stafford Lestrade, the Peasants and Workers Movement in Dominica was one of the most important third parties during the early 1960s. The platform focus was on the improvement of peasant population conditions. It did not win any seats in the House.

PEOPLES' NATIONAL MOVEMENT OF DOMINICA (PNM). The second political party of twentieth century Dominica, the Peoples' National Movement was founded in 1957 by Clifton Dupigny. It followed the format and constitution of the Trinidad party of the same name. The party won two seats in the 1957 election, compared to three of the Dominica Labour Party and three seats won by independents. Efforts by members of the organized parties to form a coalition after the election, resulted in the PNM-elected candidates, Lionel Laville and L. C. Didier, resigning from the party. However, the majority of the party joined with other groups in forming the Dominica United Peoples' Party.

Vera Green

DOMINICAN REPUBLIC

The Dominican Republic occupies the eastern two-thirds of the island of Hispaniola in the Caribbean Sea. Four mountain ranges crosscut the country and they impaired transportation and communications until the advent of modern technology. The large majority of the 5.3 million Dominicans reside either in the urban areas, with nearly one million in the capital city of Santo Domingo alone, or in the fertile lands of the valley of Cibao in the north.

Discovered during Christopher Columbus's first voyage, Hispaniola was the first colony settled by the Spaniards in the Western Hemisphere. While Spain occupied the portion of Hispaniola that is now the Dominican Republic, France settled Haiti, the western sector the island. It was in Haiti that the first stirrings of anticolonial sentiment were felt. Haitian slaves rebelled against their masters and quickly spread their revolution into Santo Domingo, in fact conquering it in 1822. Haiti occupied its larger neighbor until 1844, when the Dominicans took up arms and declared their independence from what they considered Haitian despotism. Relations between the two countries have been strained ever since the Haitian occupation; the massacre of 20,000 Haitians by the Dominican government in 1937 and numerous reported invasions have made both sides quite wary of each other.

Two of the military leaders in the war against Haiti, Generals Buenaventura Báez and Pedro Santana, ended up as bitter contenders for power. A bloody civil war ensued, culminating ironically in 1861 with Spain again re-annexing the Dominican Republic. Foreign interference became a familiar facet of Dominican politics. Local factions, unable to impose their will on the society, have resorted to collaboration with outside forces even at the cost of yielding Dominican sovereignty. The second period of Spanish rule lasted only four years; by 1865, a number of quasi-guerilla groups had successfully driven out the Spaniards and proclaimed Dominican independence anew.

The last thirty-five years of the nineteenth century witnessed the seemingly endless sequence of civil wars, corrupt governments, coups, and attempts to turn the country to a foreign state. One man who broke the cycle was General Ulises Heureaux, who ruled the country from 1882 to 1899. Heureaux became an absolute dictator, systematically eliminating whatever opposition dared to surface against him. Although numerous political organizations, parties in name only, were critical of Heureaux, their only common denominator was an antigovernment stance. Party affiliation seemed an empty semantic distinction except for its connotation of support for one individual. Two leading factions emerged at this time: the Jimenista party of Juan Isidro Jiménez and the Horacista party of Horacio Vásquez.

Heureaux was assassinated in 1899 and, as might have been expected, civil war between the Jimenistas and Horacistas followed. Unrest and more episodes of foreign interference continued until Ramón Cáceres, a cousin of Vásquez and one of the men who had killed Heureaux, became president in 1906. Cáceres's five-year term was a remarkable period of peace and prosperity, unique in Dominican annals. Unfortunately, he too was murdered by political foes, and anarchy returned to the Dominican Republic in 1911.

Until this time, the United States government had repeatedly rejected open intervention in the Dominican Republic. In 1870, President Ulysses S. Grant did complete a treaty of annexation with the Dominican government, but the U.S. Senate refused to ratify the agreement. However, the emergence of the United States as a major international power increased the strategic importance of the Caribbean area. Chaos and instability in Santo Domingo ultimately produced occupation by United States Marines in 1916. Their announced purpose was to create the conditions necessary for democracy to flourish in the Dominican Republic, although it soon became obvious that the top priority was the establishment of a stable regime supportive of the burgeoning American interests in the region.

After a number of false starts following the withdrawal of the marines, elections were finally held in 1924, with the aging Horacio Vásquez emerging victorious. The Vásquez administration was fairly uneventful until he attempted unconstitutionally to retain the presidency after the prescribed term of office. A young and energetic military officer, Rafael L. Trujillo, succeeded in uniting the armed forces against the president, and he forced Vásquez to resign in 1930. Elections were held in a few weeks and Trujillo, a candidate for the presidency, left nothing to chance. Most of his opponents died or disappeared during the campaign and the official returns later showed Trujillo with many more votes than the total number of Dominicans eligible to cast ballots. Rafael Trujillo thus became president and for the next thirty-one years the history of the Dominican Republic would be inexorably tied to his career.

Before Trujillo, regional caudillos had set up their own armies; there was no real national entity to protect the Dominican government. Once he identified the military as the most serious challenger for political power, Trujillo set out to neutralize the army. He restructured the armed forces into a truly national institution, giving them a new sense of purpose: the defense of the country which, of course, was synonymous with the backing of Trujillo. The new strongman had actually developed a caudillistic regime at the national level.

Through the army and the newly created secret police, Trujillo was able to control the entire country in a manner that no previous Dominican leader had ever envisioned. Once the support of the armed forces had been assured at the institutional level, Trujillo secured the loyalty of individual officers by arranging for what amounted to personal fiefdoms in various areas of the country. The top brass of the army could plunder what they pleased so long as they shared their loot with the generalissimo and continued to favor Trujillo. To assure his control over them, the dictator frequently shifted military commands.

Trujillo also acquired control over much of the economy. Virtually all profitable parts of the economy were apportioned among members of his family and other close associates, with the dictator himself always being a major partner in any important enterprise. The import-export trade, much of the sugar industry, all important manufacturing firms, the national airline, and even prostitution were thus brought under the ownership and control of Trujillo and his inner circle.

The population was kept under control through the reign of official terror instituted by the secret police. Often, individuals would be arbitrarily arrested, detained, tortured, or murdered without even learning of the offense that had warranted such treatment. Individuals with potential leadership qualities were accorded a different treatment. First, they were made aware of the three basic options confronting them: they could remain in the Dominican Republic as Trujillo supporters; they could attempt to leave the country, in itself a very difficult feat; or they could organize an opposition movement, possibly losing their lives in the process. It is hardly surprising that most prospective leaders accepted the first choice.

To destroy their self-respect and to assure their subservience to the dictator, all important subordinates of Trujillo were forced to humiliate themselves from time to time. The dictator arranged for them to be accused of heinous crimes and of "disloyalty to the Generalissimo," and to have to publicly deny such allegations. Another technique was to imprison a prominent figure, even have him sentenced to death, and then after a few months, to have him offered a return to favor and a high post in the administration—with torture and death the likely alternative to acceptance of such humiliating return to public office.

The regime's control over the country was all-encompassing. Every form of communication that could be regulated—the mass media, telephones, mail—was tightly censored. Infiltration by the secret police was so extensive that no exchanges could be treated confidentially, irrespective of the participants. This pervasive presence had the effect of practically eliminating politics as a topic of discussion.

Finally, Trujillo used a "cult of personality" to solidify his regime. Aside from renaming mountain peaks, provinces, and the capital city after himself or members of his family, the generalissimo had himself proclaimed the ultimate authority in all realms of human knowledge and endeavor. As a result, if one delivered a public talk or speech about virtually anything, and did not "recognize" Trujillo's primacy in that field—whether philosophy, biology, sports, literature, or anything else—one was likely to land in jail for a longer or shorter time.

In the thirty-one years during which he controlled the Dominican Republic, Rafael Trujillo was actually elected president only four times. Figureheads would serve as "presidents," although no one doubted that Trujillo was in charge, and one of these nominal presidents, Joaquín Balaguer, happened to be in office when Trujillo was assassinated in May 1961. The legacy of the Trujillo dictatorship was highly predictable. A totalitarian government entrenched in power for more than three decades had not allowed any persons, groups, or institutions to oppose Trujillo. The power vacuum left by the assassination could not be filled by political elites, pressure groups or political parties which normally produce democratic competition and orderly continuity. The population, terrorized for thirty-one years, was equally ill-equipped to assume the responsibility for making political decisions.

And yet, it was the Dominican Republic of 1961 which came to be singled out by the Kennedy administration as one of the symbols of the success of the Alliance for Progress. With the encouragement of Washington, Dominicans were now expected to endorse a liberal democratic government which would institute the social and economic reforms needed to bring progress to the country and, equally important to the United States, counteract the appeal of the alternative exemplified by Fidel Castro's Cuba. The United States even threatened military intervention in November 1961, when members of the Trujillo clan attempted to thwart the experiment by seizing power. A new constitution was adopted in 1962 and free elections in 1963 produced the seemingly ideal candidate, a liberal intellectual with a long record of anti-Trujillo activities, Juan Bosch.

Bosch's commitment to an open democratic system included the acceptance of participation by all elements of the political spectrum, including the radical Left. Such tolerance apparently extended beyond what Washington had contemplated. Bosch's insistence on free competition coupled with his weak administrative and political skills, led to a right-wing military coup only seven months after he had been inaugurated. Kennedy refused to recognize the "Triumvirate" which seized power under the aegis of the armed forces. This policy was reversed, however, under President Lyndon Johnson.

The civilian triumvirate which replaced Bosch tried in vain to settle the major differences of opinion which had gained exposure under Bosch. Now, national unity and security were invoked to justify political suppression. Dissatisfaction with the triumvirate finally exploded into open rebellion in April 1965. One faction within the armed forces, with substantial popular backing, insisted on Bosch's return as the only legitimate president. These "constitutionalists," led by Colonel Francisco Caamaño Déño, were opposed by "loyalists," under General Elías Wessin y Wessin, who defended the existing government. Before the conflict had reached a conclusion, the government of President Johnson identified the pro-Bosch forces as having fallen under the control or influence of extreme Leftists and, therefore, marines were landed to "prevent another Cuba."

The American government obtained the endorsement of the Organization of American States, converting this unilateral intervention into an act of collective security. Under OAS supervision, elections were held in 1966 and Joaquín

Balaguer, the former Trujillo associate, easily defeated Bosch, 57 percent to 39 percent. A new constitution was drafted in 1966; not nearly as radical as the earlier document promulgated by Bosch, it avoids specific issues and bypasses the commitment to extensive social and economic change which characterized the previous constitution.

As had happened to many of his predecessors, Balaguer also fell prey to the lure of power. Despite numerous efforts by the opposition to dissuade him from seeking reelection, Balaguer was returned to power in 1970 and 1974. Both campaigns featured many charges of fraud; major contenders for the presidency boycotted both elections rather than participating in what they perceived to be a thinly disguised sham to rubber-stamp Balaguer's rule. In addition, considerable political violence returned to the Dominican Republic in 1970 and 1971. A group known as *La Banda* murdered opposition spokesmen; although they were tacitly encouraged by the military and police, *La Banda* discontinued operations in 1971.

Balaguer's centrist approach did bring stability to the country and encouraged foreign investors to return after the 1965 civil war. While his critics justifiably condemned the lack of political development attained under Balaguer, it is equally accurate to praise the economic growth experienced during those years. The Dominican Republic is essentially a monocultural economy with sugar at the heart of the system. Some light and medium industry combined with tourism have helped to ease a still critical unemployment problem. But with over 60 percent of the people residing in rural areas and half of the labor force engaged in agriculture, the economy's dependence upon sugar is undeniable. The slightest fluctuations in the world sugar markets have severe repercussions in the Dominican Republic. With consumer goods, petroleum, and machinery imports vitally necessary, high sugar sales are indispensable if the foreign debt is to be reduced.

The per capita income of Dominicans is over $900 annually, but the figure is misleading since stark differences between rich and poor are evident. For example, nearly 75 percent of all Dominican children—obviously at the bottom of the socioeconomic scale—suffer from extreme malnutrition. Many Dominicans still live outside the money economy, barely scratching out a subsistence living on a day-to-day basis. By contrast, the landed oligarchy and those entrepreneurs who have established profitable contacts with transnational corporations enjoy opulent life-styles.

Balaguer gained the strong support of the armed forces through a maneuver made popular by his mentor: the use of corruption for personal profit. Balaguer himself was not implicated in any corrupt practices, but there was ample evidence of shady business transactions involving high military officers. In another tactic borrowed from Trujillo, Balaguer dispensed patronage jobs in exchange for political support. It was not uncommon for the president to spend hours receiving petitioners for assorted government favors which, when granted, ensured the receivers' loyalty to the government.

Even though an economic boom had slowed down considerably during his third administration, Balaguer was a heavy favorite to secure a fourth term in 1978. A heavy turnout of voters, however, opened the way for a stunning upset by the candidate of Bosch's old reformist party, Antonio Guzmán. When it became certain that Balaguer would lose badly, the army interrupted the counting of ballots and seized all returns. After several days of uncertainty, international protests—the strongest coming from Washington and Caracas—resulted in the armed forces announcing that Guzmán was indeed the winner.

The 1978 election was evidently perceived as a referendum on Balaguer's *continuismo* and the majority of the Dominican voters backed Guzmán as the better alternative. The results were so polarized that no party other than Balaguer's Reformist Party (Partido Reformista—PR) and Guzmán's Dominican Revolutionary Party (Partido Revolucinario Dominicano—PRD) secured any seats in the Senate. The preliminary outcomes had given the PRD a 15-12 edge over the PR in the Senate, but the army's final tally showed Guzmán's party with only eleven senators, the apparent price for military acquiescence in the results of the presidential race. This blatant form of a forced compromise ensured Balaguer's supporters of a constitutional check on Guzmán's reforms through their Senate majority.

The Guzmán administration has proved to be somewhat of a surprise for most Dominicans. Initially, it seemed as if the new president would make a concerted effort to implement the sweeping reforms long advocated by the PRD. In an attempt to reduce the endemic corruption that Balaguer had tolerated by the military, Guzmán quickly fired most of the senior pro-Balaguer officers. The government forestalled the possibility of a coup by acting swiftly and decisively and taking advantage of the support which the United States provided for Guzmán. President Carter had dispatched Lieutenant General Dennis McAuliffe, commander in chief of the U.S. Southern Command, to Guzmán's inauguration as a reminder to the Dominican army of U.S. opposition to a coup. The pro-Balaguer military faction was so weakened that Guzmán had little trouble crushing a subversive plot in September 1979.

President Guzmán has also pursued quite vigorously the Dominican case against the Gulf and Western transnational corporation over owed shares of the company's profits. Gulf and Western had agreed to use Dominican sugar in futures trading in exchange for 60 percent of the net income derived from such deals. The company turned over $19 million to the Dominican Republic, but a reviewing investigation by the Guzmán government arrived at a sum twice as large. Since the PRD has long recommended the expropriation of the huge land holdings of Gulf and Western, Guzmán's tough policy was warmly endorsed by his party.

However, it has also become evident that the Dominican president does not plan to abandon the road of moderation and compromise. The members of his cabinet are rather conservative in their political outlook, including a good number from the old Dominican oligarchy. By the end of his first year in office, Guzmán had certainly disappointed those who had anticipated dramatic changes in the Dominican system. When, as part of his economic plan, Guzmán announced a hike in the price of gasoline from $1.85 to $2.39 a gallon, public resentment produced a series of bloody demonstrations, riots, and strikes throughout the country.

The PRD won again in 1982, electing Salvador Jorge Blanco as president and getting a majority in both houses.

Political parties represent a very recent component of the Dominican system. In the first place, the country never had the traditional liberal and conservative alignments that existed elsewhere in Latin America during the nineteenth century. From the beginning of competitive political activity, organizations developed around individual leaders rather than principles. For example, the predominant movements in the 1880s called themselves "Reds" and "Blues," apparently unable to agree on any designation of ideological content. Specific programs extrapolated from broader philosophical concepts were hardly necessary in a society plagued by civil war and violence, where assassinations were more common than elections as instruments of transition. Another explanatory variable with reference to the absence of Dominican parties is Trujillo's dictatorship. Only one party—the Dominican Party (Partido Dominicano)—was really allowed to operate, although some puppet "opposition" parties were established when it served the dictator's purposes. The Dominican Party was cleverly used by Trujillo to integrate political activities into the government. All public employees were forced to "donate" 10 percent of their salaries to the party and membership in it was compulsory for anyone of consequence. The only tangible political activity for Dominicans opposed to Trujillo had to take place outside the country.

Following Trujillo's assassination, more than twenty parties contested the 1962 elections, with a field of eight presidential candidates. Once again, the tendency was to revert to personalistic and poorly organized groupings instead of parties with mass appeal. Virtually all of the parties of 1962 disappeared shortly after that election, and in the following Political Parties section only those with some lasting significance are noted.

The results of the 1978 election may suggest the emergence of a two-party system, dominated by Guzmán's Dominican Revolutionary Party and Balaguer's Reformist Party. However, it is still uncertain if these two organizations have substantive futures beyond those of their respective leaders.

Bibliography

American University. *Area Handbook for the Dominican Republic.* Government Printing Office, Washington, D.C., 1973.

F. A. Avelino. *Las Ideas Políticas en Santo Domingo.* Editorial Arte y Cine, Santo Domingo, 1966.

"Elecciones en Graficos." *Ahora,* 6 May 1974.

John Bartlow Martin. *Overtaken By Events: The Dominican Crisis From the Fall of Trujillo to the Civil War.* Doubleday, Garden City, N.Y., 1966.

German E. Ornes. *Trujillo: Little Caesar of the Caribbean*. Thomas Nelson & Sons, New York, 1958.

Howard J. Wiarda. *Dictatorship and Development: The Methods of Control in Trujillo's Dominican Republic*. University of Florida Press, Gainesville, Fla., 1968.

Political Parties

DOMINICAN COMMUNIST PARTY (PARTIDO COMUNISTA DOMINI-CANO—PCD). Marxist-Leninist organizations have existed in the Dominican Republic under an assortment of names. The PCD, established secretly in 1942, is the oldest of these and, as in other Latin-American countries, represents a more conservative, pro-Soviet line. Trujillo repeatedly used the party, which was founded in the mid-1940s as the Popular Socialist Party (Partido Socialista Popular—PSP), to further his own interests. At times, he would openly court the support of the Communists, thus raising concern in the United States, and then subsequently suppress the party as brutally as he treated any other foe.

With the death of Trujillo, the leaders of the PSP returned to the Dominican Republic. They soon took the name Dominican Communist Party, although a dissident group continued to use the old name. After some time, the PCD gained the recognition of the Soviet party and government as the Dominican member of the pro-Soviet bloc of parties.

The PCD remained underground until 1974. Its influence, even in the labor movement, remained quite marginal. However, in 1974 President Balaguer asked Congress to legalize the PCD after the party had officially rejected revolution as a means of attaining power. While the move was probably a mere electoral maneuver designed to project an image of benevolence for the Balaguer regime, it did serve to endow the PCD with some legitimacy. The secretary-general of the PCD is Narciso Isa Conde.

DOMINICAN LIBERATION PARTY (PARTIDO DE LIBERACIÓN DOMINI-CANA). The Dominican Liberation Party was founded by Juan Bosch after quitting the Dominican Revolutionary Party (Partido Revolucionario Dominicano) in 1973. However, Bosch had taken few PRD members or followers with him and his new party remained a very minor factor in national politics. It was unable in 1974 or 1978 to elect a single member of Congress.

DOMINICAN PARTY (PARTIDO DOMINICANO—PD). The Dominican Party was Rafael Trujillo's personal political machine. The legislative process was effectively controlled through the PD. An article in the party statutes actually required all officeholders to "submit, in writing, their respective resignations, without date, to the Chief of the Party." Trujillo, as the chief of the party, could simply submit these letters whenever he wished; resignations en masse were the norm for readjusting the government to suit Trujillo's preferences. For example, 143 vacancies occurred in the Chamber of Deputies between 1942 and 1947. Of these, 139 were due to resignations and four because of death. One deputy held office for all of seven days before "resigning."

In addition to manufacturing the sycophantic propaganda required by the dictator, the PD served as a means of contact between the government and the people. Local needs were often articulated through the party to Trujillo, who would then act on requests for assistance. Since all improvements made in the country were invariably credited to Trujillo, the party could rely on some genuine popular support. Membership "drives," crude campaigns to forcibly recruit new members, resulted in almost 80 percent of the population registering with the PD at one time or another. The party ceased to function after the death of Trujillo.

DOMINICAN POPULAR MOVEMENT (MOVIMIENTO POPULAR DO- MINICANO — MPD). Organized by Dominican exiles in Havana in 1956, the Dominican Popular Movement originally was a heterogeneous group, of no definite ideology, united mainly by its members' opposition to the Trujillo dictatorship. However, when its leaders and members returned home after Trujillo's death in 1961, it quickly evolved in a Marxist-Leninist direction, and those who were not of that persuasion abandoned the party.

The MPD was formally organized as a political party in August 1965. It quickly became, together with the Dominican Communist Party (Partido Comunista Dominicano) and the 14th of June Movement (Movimiento 14 de Junio), one of the three major elements in the much-splintered far-Left of Dominican politics. It was the principal representative of Maoism in the country. Although before the 1978 election it sought to gain legal recognition, it did not succeed. Subsequently, it split into two rival factions, one headed by Onelio Espaillat and Jorge Puello Soriano, and the other by Rafael Chaljub Mejía. Although in the 1960s the party had had some influence in the organized labor movement, this had largely disappeared during the 1970s.

DOMINICAN REVOLUTIONARY PARTY (PARTIDO REVOLUCIONARIO DOMINICANO — PRD). The Dominican Revolutionary Party is currently the most important political organization in the Dominican Republic. Founded in exile in 1939 by Juan Bosch, the PRD was pledged to extensive social and economic reforms which would follow Trujillo's overthrow.

After the death of Trujillo, the PRD was organized on Dominican soil in 1961. Bosch, a charismatic figure, effectively appealed to the working and lower classes with a platform that combined revolutionary change and economic development within a framework of political democracy. After attaining power for only seven months in 1963, the PRD was relegated to opposition status for the next fifteen years. Many of its leaders were victims of political violence during the Balaguer years and Bosch consistently boycotted any national or local election in which he felt that the government was planning to perpetrate fraud. In trying to attract new voters and also shake off the radical label which Balaguer repeatedly used against it, the PRD toned down its reformist rhetoric in the early 1970s.

The party's long-time secretary-general, José Francisco Peña Gómez, had endorsed the more moderate direction of the PRD. When Bosch publicly denounced such a "sell out," Peña Gómez resigned from his post in May 1973. Within a short while, however, it became evident that Bosch, not Peña Gómez, was out of touch with the members of the party. In November 1973, the former president quit the PRD and announced plans to form a new party, the Dominican Liberation Party. In a parting message, Bosch lashed out at Peña Gómez ("an old man, politically backward and ideologically weak") and his supporters ("the right wing of the PRD is now in control.") Bosch's well-known disenchantment with the electoral process—his concept of "dictatorship with popular support" does not allow for elections—stands in stark contrast with the pragmatism of Peña Gómez, a man dedicated to democratic socialism.

Even before Trujillo's death, the PRD had established close contacts with the Venezuelan Democratic Action Party (Acción Democrática) and other social, democratically oriented parties in Latin America. Under Peña Gómez' leadership, it established a close relationship with the Socialist International, with Peña Gómez becoming head of the International's Latin-American Committee. He and the party were quite effective in mobilizing support from member parties of the International against efforts of the Balaguer regime to conduct a fraudulent election in 1978.

Although the PRD regained power under Antonio Guzmán in 1978, major internal divisions persist, in part a result of a hard-fought internal campaign for the party's presidential nomination. Guzmán has not been able to generate effective responses to recent economic setbacks; the price of sugar dropped at the same time that the price of oil skyrocketed, producing massive increases in the foreign debt, an unemployment rate of 20 percent, and double-digit inflation. In 1979 even a natural disaster exacerbated the disharmony within the PRD. After two hurricanes had caused extensive damage in the country, Peña Gómez, as party secretary-general, arranged for relief aid from Cuba. President Guzmán, who had not been consulted, rebuked his colleague, asserting that the executive branch—not the legislature and not the PRD—was in charge of Dominican foreign policy.

In a surprising move to close ranks within the party, Guzmán announced the nationalization of the Rosario gold mines in December 1979. The PRD officially hailed the president's action as "a return to the sphere of our party's principles." Subsequently, President Guzmán announced that he would not be a candidate for reelection. The party nominated Salvador Jorge Blanco as its 1982 candidate.

FOURTEENTH OF JUNE MOVEMENT (MOVIMIENTO 14 DE JUNIO). Deriving its name from a Castro-supported invasion of the Dominican Republic on 14 June 1959, this organization initially appealed to young intellectuals. In the wake of Trujillo's assassination in 1961, the 14th of June movement presented an attractive third alternative to the political establishment as embodied in the National Civic Union (Unión Cívica Nacional) and the Partido Revolucionario Dominicano, an essentially exile group until Trujillo's death. As the Cuban revolution moved in the Communist direction, and as the original 14th of June leaders disappeared as a result of attempting a guerilla uprising following the overthrow of President Bosch, the party moved far .to the Left. It came to represent the "Fidelista" current within the Dominican far-Left. Its influence was reduced by several internal divisions, and it is currently an ineffectual, and illegal, force.

LABOR PARTY (PARTIDO LABORISTA). The Labor Party was one of two "opposition" parties organized by the Trujillo regime to provide a "democratic" facade for the 1947 general election. It published a list of candidates, headed by Francisco Prats Ramírez, who was also running for Congress on the Dominican Party (Partido Dominicano) ticket. Prats Ramírez forgot himself, and together with other Dominican Party deputies, signed a petition favoring Trujillo's reelection. The Partido Laborista was credited officially with receiving 29,186 votes in the 1947 election. It "elected" one deputy, Consuelo Prats Ramírez, wife of the presidential candidate. Nothing more was heard of the Labor Party after the 1947 election, by which time, apparently, Trujillo felt it unnecessary to continue the "democratic" charade.

MOVEMENT FOR DEMOCRATIC INTEGRATION AGAINST REELECTION (MOVIMIENTO DE INTEGRACIÓN DEMOCRÁTICA ANTI-REELECCION-ISTA—MIDA). Led by Vice-President Francisco Augusto Lora, MIDA was a coalition of political groups opposed to Balaguer's first reelection bid in 1970, and was revived as a party in 1974 and 1978. With only its anti-Balaguer stance as a unifying force, the party did have some strength in urban areas, but its only distinctive characteristic was that it rejected Balaguer.

In 1978, Lora was approached both by Balaguer, who allegedly offered him another term as vice-president, and by the PRD candidate Antonio Guzmán, who hoped to have the MIDA join the PRD. Instead Lora headed a coalition of the Movement for National Conciliation (Movimiento de Conciliación Nacional), the Quisqueyan Democratic Party (Partido Quisqueyano Democrático) and MIDA, but it failed to attract much support. The poor showing at the polls, coupled with Balaguer's defeat, may mean the end of the MIDA.

MOVEMENT FOR NATIONAL CONCILIATION (MOVIMIENTO DE CON-CILIACIÓN NACIONAL—MCN). A relatively minor party, the MCN was established by Héctor García Godoy, who had served as provisional president between the 1965 civil war and the 1966 election. Its center-right ideological program did not generate much enthusiasm among the voters in the 1970 election. The death of Garcia Godoy of natural causes two weeks before the election was a grave blow for the party, which received only 4.4 percent of the total vote. After initially nominating Jaime Manuel Fernández for president in the 1978 race, the MCN withdrew his name and threw its support behind the coalition supporting the candidacy of ex-Vice-President Francisco Augusto Lora, of the MIDA.

MOVIMIENTO CATORCE DE JUNIO. *See* FOURTEENTH OF JUNE MOVEMENT.

MOVIMIENTO DE CONCILIACIÓN NACIONAL. *See* MOVEMENT FOR NATIONAL CONCILIATION.

MOVIMENTO DE INTEGRACIÓN DEMOCRÁTICA ANTI-REELECCIONISTA. *See* MOVEMENT FOR DEMOCRATIC INTEGRATION AGAINST REELECTION.

MOVIMIENTO POPULAR DOMINICANO. *See* DOMINICAN POPULAR MOVEMENT.

NATIONAL ACTION PARTY (PARTIDO DE ACCIÓN NACIONAL—PAN). A moderate party founded in 1980 by retired general Neíd Rafael Nivar Seíjas, chief of the national police under Balaguer, the PAN advocates agricultural development and the creation of new jobs. However, it will rely primarily on Nivar Seíjas's popularity for whatever influence it may acquire.

NATIONAL CIVIC UNION (UNIÓN CÍVICA NACIONAL—UCN). After Trujillo's death, business and professional interests in the Dominican Republic organized themselves under the banner of the UCN, offering the most viable conservative option to Juan Bosch and the Dominican Revolutionary Party in the 1962 election. Its major leader was Viriato Fiallo, its 1962 presidential nominee. The PRD's overwhelming victory at the polls and the radicalized views of the electorate after the 1965 civil war led to a decline in the fortunes of the UCN. The emergence and success of Joaquín Balaguer's Reformist Party thereafter, appealing basically to the same natural constituency as the UCN, terminated the meaningful participation of the organization in Dominican politics.

NATIONAL DEMOCRATIC PARTY (PARTIDO NACIONAL DEMOCRÁTICO). The National Democratic Party was an "opposition" party organized by the Trujillo regime to give an appearance of "democracy" during the 1947 general election. It held its convention on 31 March 1947, and named a list of candidates for Congress and other posts, but apparently had no presidential nominee. It was credited with receiving 29,765 votes in the election. Nothing more was heard of this party, once it had served Trujillo's purpose of giving a "democratic" whitewash for a short period to the Trujillo regime.

NATIONAL PARTY (PARTIDO NACIONAL). The *Horacista* movement established by General Horacio Vásquez in the 1890s ultimately evolved into the National Party. Vásquez was elected to the presidency in 1924 under the Partido Nacional banner. However, the competition for leadership within the party badly fragmented the Nationals between backers of Vice-President José Dolores Alfonseca and Martín de Moya. To avoid the collapse of the party, Vásquez agreed to run for a second term even though his health was rapidly deteriorating. It was this attempt by Vásquez to retain the presidency in 1930 that enabled Rafael Trujillo to cleverly maneuver himself into power. An attempt to revive the Partido Nacional after the death of Trujillo failed.

NATIONAL PROGRESSIVE ALLIANCE (ALIANZA NACIONAL PROGRES-ISTAS—ANP). This was a coalition of the remnants of Horacio Vásquez's National Party and the Progressive Party of Federico Velásquez formed to oppose Trujillo's election in 1930. Torn by dissension and the well-founded suspicion that Trujillo would become president regardless of the election's outcome, the Alliance withdrew from the contest the day before the balloting. Velásquez and ex-President Vásquez left the country a few days after Trujillo's "victory," and for all practical purposes, organized political opposition in the Dominican Republic fell into desuetude.

PARTIDO COMUNISTA DOMINICANO. See DOMINICAN COMMUNIST PARTY.

PARTIDO DE ACCIÓN NACIONAL. See NATIONAL ACTION PARTY.

PARTIDO DE LIBERACIÓN DOMINICANA. See DOMINICAN LIBERATION PARTY.

PARTIDO DOMINICANO. See DOMINICAN PARTY.

PARTIDO LABORISTA. See LABOR PARTY.

PARTIDO NACIONAL. See NATIONAL PARTY.

PARTIDO NACIONAL DEMOCRÁTICO. See NATIONAL DEMOCRATIC PARTY.

PARTIDO PROGRESISTA. See PROGRESSIVE PARTY.

PARTIDO QUISQUEYANO DEMOCRÁTICO. See QUISQUEYAN DEMO-CRATIC PARTY.

PARTIDO REFORMISTA. See REFORMIST PARTY.

PARTIDO REPUBLICANO. *See* REPUBLICAN PARTY.

PARTIDO REVOLUCIONARIO DOMINICANO. *See* DOMINICAN REVOLUTIONARY PARTY.

PARTIDO REVOLUCIONARIO SOCIAL CRISTIANO. *See* SOCIAL CHRISTIAN REVOLUTIONARY PARTY.

PARTIDO SOCIALISTA POPULAR. *See* DOMINICAN COMMUNIST PARTY.

PARTIDO TRUJILLISTA. *See* TRUJILLO PARTY.

POPULAR SOCIALIST PARTY. *See* DOMINICAN COMMUNIST PARTY.

PROGRESSIVE PARTY (PARTIDO PROGRESISTA). The Progressive Party was organized in the 1920s by Federico Velázquez y Hernández, described by German Ornes (p. 56) as "a most respected elder statesman." Although it had been in opposition to the administration of Horacio Vásquez, it joined with Vásquez's National Party in an alliance which sought to prevent the election of General Rafael Trujillo, after the resignation of President Vásquez in 1930. Velásquez was the candidate of the subsequent National Progressive Alliance (Alianza Progresista Nacional), with National Party leader Angel Morales as his running mate. After the election, both Velásquez and Morales left the country.

QUISQUEYAN DEMOCRATIC PARTY (PARTIDO QUISQUEYANO DEMOCRÁTICO – PQD). The Quisqueyan Democratic Party has largely served as the vehicle for the personal ambitions of General Elías Wessin y Wessin, one of the principal actors in the 1965 civil war. A right-wing organization, the party appealed to ex-military officers and former Trujillo followers who favored the virulent anti-Communism of Wessin. The PQD reached its peak in 1970, when Wessin received 13 percent of the vote in the presidential election, most of his backing emanating from rural conservative areas. In 1971, the Balaguer government discovered that Wessin was involved in plans for a military coup and the PQD leader was sent into exile in Spain. He was allowed to return for the 1978 campaign, but the Quisqueyan Party, after nominating him, withdrew his name in order to endorse the coalition around ex-Vice-President Francisco Lora of the MIDA.

REFORMIST PARTY (PARTIDO REFORMISTA – PR). The Dominican Party of Rafael Trujillo seems to have served as the model for Joaquín Balaguer's formation of the Reformist Party in 1963. However, by paying lip service to socioeconomic reforms, the PR duplicated the general philosophy of the PRD, although it actually favored a much more gradual approach to change. Balaguer was able to retain the endorsement of business and conservative interests which viewed him as a far more reasonable candidate than Bosch, and at the same time he mobilized enough support among the masses to be elected in 1966.

Balaguer governed through the Partido Reformista from 1966 to 1978. During that period the country enjoyed considerable economic growth, although not enough to overcome the persistent unemployment problem. There was relatively little social change, although Balaguer did launch a modest agrarian reform effort.

Despite the 1978 defeat, the PR and Joaquín Balaguer remain potent political forces in the Dominican Republic. The party controls sixteen of twenty-seven Senate seats, serving as a moderating influence on appointments and appropriations of the Guzmán administration. Balaguer was again the PR presidential candidate in 1982.

REPUBLICAN PARTY (PARTIDO REPUBLICANO). The Republican Party was an opposition party organized during the Horacio Vásquez administration (1924–1930) by Rafael Estrella Ureña, described by German Ornes (p. 46) as "a belligerent, scathing local orator and firebrand politician." As the 1930 election approached, Estrella Ureña and the Republicans decided not to wait but instead launched an armed uprising against Vásquez. Largely as a result of the refusal of General Rafael Trujillo, the army commander, firmly to support President Vásquez, the Republican uprising succeeded. As a result, Estrella Ureña became president on 3 March 1930.

In the ensuing election campaign, Estrella Ureña ran as vice-presidential nominee accompanying General Trujillo as candidate for president. They were "elected" in a poll in which more people were recorded as casting ballots than there were registered voters.

However, under President Trujillo, the Republicans were no more able than any other party to function legally. The election of Trujillo signified the death of the Partido Republicano. In August 1931, Estrella Ureña went into exile.

SOCIAL CHRISTIAN REVOLUTIONARY PARTY (PARTIDO REVOLU- CIONARIO SOCIAL CRISTIANO—PRSC). Founded in 1961 by Christian Socialists in exile, the Social Christian Revolutionary Party received support from other Christian Democratic parties, particularly the Copei Party of Venezuela. It came to control one of several factions of the labor movement which developed after Trujillo's death. The PRSC initially operated in the shadow of the Partido Revolucionario Dominicano; since both parties were advocates of liberal reforms and relied on the same constituencies, the PRSC had no opportunity to succeed so long as the PRD prospered.

The Social Christian candidate in 1978, Alfonso Lockwood, received very few votes and subsequently relinquished party leadership to Delgado Bogaert, a former priest. The PRSC appeared to be receptive to ex-President Joaquín Balaguer's overtures for an anti-PRD coalition in 1982, as the only pragmatic alternative to continued status as a minor party.

TRUJILLO PARTY (PARTIDO TRUJILLISTA). The Trujillo Party was organized at the time of the 1942 presidential election by dictator Rafael Trujillo's personal dentist, José Enrique Aybar. Although it was officially recognized, it supported the candidates of the Dominican Party, including Generalissimo Trujillo. Its principal function seems to have been to conduct a purge of cabinet members and other officials on behalf of the dictator, submitting them to long interrogations by students belonging to the Trujillo Party's "University Guard." Nothing was heard of the Trujillo Party after the 1942 election.

UNIÓN CÍVICA NACIONAL. See NATIONAL CIVIC UNION.

José M. Sánchez

ECUADOR

The continuing instability and traditionalism of Ecuadorean politics seem to reflect, in large part, its rugged and varied beauty. One of Latin America's more mountainous countries, the eastern and western ranges of the Andes have effectively divided the country into three often hostile regions. Ecuador's history has been plagued with both geographic and political volatility; frequent earthquakes periodically rock its communities, and the present (1978) constitution is the seventeenth since independence. The high mountain valleys formed by these two Andean ranges constitute the *Sierra*, the home of a rigidly stratified society compromising "whites" (some of whom claim descent from the sixteenth century conquerors), the racially mixed *cholos* or *mestizos*, and below both, the Indian masses. A traditional form of tenant farming, *huasipungaje*, which kept many Indians tied to both the land and their landlords, survived until the mid 1960s. The Sierra has remained the stronghold of the conservative political forces, centered around the capital, Quito (9,500~10,000 feet above sea level).

Quite distinct from the Sierra is the more socially dynamic and politically vibrant coastal region (*La Costa*). Compared to the introspective and conservative Sierra, the people of the Coast are more outgoing and accepting of change. The ethnic and racial mixture of the Coast is more fluid, its social structure more open. While Quito preserves much of its colonial charm, the cities of the coast, particularly Guayaquil, by far Ecuador's largest city and major seaport, are more functional and modern. The politics of the Coast tends toward free-wheeling European-style liberalism and contemporary demagogic populism. While the economy of the Sierra is still largely dominated by large landed estates, that of the Coast reflects its more equalitarian society. Bananas, one of Ecuador's principal agricultural exports since the 1940s when this cash crop was introduced by the Liberal president, Galo Plaza Lasso, are largely grown on small and medium-sized farms.

Ecuador's eastern jungle region (*El Oriente*), comprises close to half the national territory but less than 5 percent of its total population of 7,800,000. The Oriente has Ecuador's limited oil reserves. The Oriente's oil has tantalized and disappointed the nation. Unless new reserves are found, Ecuador may cease its oil exports and status membership in OPEC by the mid-1980s. Ecuador's elites, however, have acquired the tastes of all oil-rich nations, causing both a 15 percent inflation rate and a four-billion-dollar foreign debt.

In 1941, Ecuador lost the bulk of the Oriente to Peru following a disastrous war. This 1941 defeat, which cost Ecuador its access to the Amazon River, has become a symbol of Ecuador's political weakness. It is now hoped that the natural resources of what remains of the Ecuadorean Oriente may hold the key to its future strength and prosperity.

Ecuador is still predominantly an agricultural country. But there is striking contrast in the agriculture in the Sierra and the Costa. Large estates, many if not most of which have their origin in the distribution of the land among the Spanish conquerors more than four centuries ago, are owned by "whites" but cultivated largely by Quechua-speaking Indians, as has been the case since colonial times. Since the high altitude creates a temperate climate in the Sierra, the region produces principally such things as corn, barley, wheat, rye and potatoes, lentils, and beans, which are almost completely grown for the domestic market.

In contrast, both the land-owning pattern and the crops grown in the coastal region are different from those of the Sierra. Although there are large plantations along the coast, small and middle-sized holdings are more prevalent there. The crops are tropical, including rice, sugar, cacao, castor beans, cotton, and bananas. There is also the toquilla palm, which provides the raw material for "Panama" hats, in the production of which Ecuador has a virtual monopoly. Most of the crops of La Costa are grown to a greater or less degree for export.

Since the Great Depression, Ecuador has experienced some industrialization. It is centered particularly in the Guayaquil area, around Quito and in one or two provincial cities. Most of the manufacturing enterprises produce consumers goods such as textiles, processed foodstuffs, pharmaceuticals, and shoes, although there are also oil refineries, cement plants and some metallurgical firms. Artisan shops are still very prevalent, particularly in Quito and other highland cities.

With independence, which was assured to Ecuador by the Battle of Pichincha on 24 May 1822, Ecuador became part of the Republic of Gran Colombia, of which Simón Bolívar was president. However, in 1830 that republic broke up, and Ecuador became a separate country under the presidency of Antonio José de Sucre, one of Bolívar's generals, and victor of the Battle of Pichincha. However, he was soon murdered, and his successor was another Venezuelan general, Juan José Flores, who dominated the country until 1845, when he was finally exiled.

It was during Flores's rule that the division of political opinion in the country between Conservatives and Liberals first took place, although actual political parties with those names were not established until several decades later. Flores was the paladin of the Conservatives, and the principal leader of the Liberal current was Vicente Rocafuerte, a native Ecuadorean, who found his major backing in the Costa area around Guayaquil. This pattern of a Conservative Sierra and the Liberal Costa was to persist for at least a century.

Between 1845 and 1860, the country suffered a period of virtual chaos in which there were three different constitutions and eleven presidents or juntas. Most of these rulers claimed to be of Liberal persuasion. The one positive accomplishment for the country in this period was the elimination of slavery for the people of African descent, although this did little to change the state of servitude of the Indian population of the Sierra, who were not technically slaves.

In 1860, Gabriel García Moreno became president, and he was to remain such until he was finally assassinated in 1875. García Moreno sought to install a kind of theocracy. He enacted two constitutions, the second of which gave citizenship only to practicing Catholics, and even before that he had given the Catholic Church more power than it had had even in the Spanish colonial days. However, his regime also stimulated some development of the nation's economy, and extended educational institutions, principally under Jesuit control.

With the death of García Moreno, Ecuador suffered through another period of near-chaos. During the next twenty years there were six different dictators, most of whom proclaimed themselves Conservatives. It was during this period that the Liberal and Conservative parties were formally established.

In a civil war in 1895–1896, Eloy Alfaro brought the Liberals to power. They were to remain in control under one or another leader during most of the next fifty years. Alfaro served as president from 1896 to 1901 and again from 1906 to 1911. The other great Liberal caudillo of this period was General Leonidas Plaza Gutiérrez, who served as president from 1901–1905 and again from 1912 to 1916. After him, several people of less fame continued the Liberal regime in power.

Under the Liberals, the powers of the church were very severely curtailed. It was deprived of its control over education and the recording of vital statistics. The Liberals also established freedom of religion, and confiscated much of the church's land. However, they did relatively little to change the economic and social system, particularly in the Sierra, which had been inherited from the Spanish conquest. By the end of the Liberal Era, by which time the church-state issues had largely receded in importance, the differences between the Liberals and Conservatives, in terms of principles, had become increasingly blurred.

During the second decade of the twentieth century, the coastal area flourished as the result of a cacao boom. This was also a period in which commercial and financial interests of Guayaquil dominated the government. The successive administrations were ruthless in putting down the beginnings of labor and other lower-class movements, particularly in suppressing a popular protest in Guayaquil in November 1922, during which hundreds of people were killed.

The rule of the Guayaquil aristocracy was finally overturned by an uprising of young military officers, mainly from the Sierra, in the Revolution of July 1925. That began a period of political turbulence which has not yet really ended. In the twenty-five years following the 1925 revolution there were twenty-two different presidents. Few of them could be said to have been democratically elected and almost none served out his full term.

The last of the clearly Liberal presidents of this period was Carlos Arroyo del Río, chosen in the election of 1940. He had the misfortune of being president when Ecuador suffered its absolute defeat by Peru in 1941–1942. Arroyo was overthrown in 1944.

A period of constitutional government lasted from 1948 to 1961. Three duly elected presidents filled out their terms of office: Galo Plaza, José María Velasco Ibarra, and Camilo Ponce Enríquez. However, this period was ended in 1961 when Velasco Ibarra, once again returned to office, was overthrown by the military. Since 1960, no president has come into office through election and turned his office over to an elected successor.

Traditional political values such as personalism, which places one's individual interest or that of one's family or clan above that of abstract collective good or impersonal institutions (such as political parties), continues to largely dominate Ecuadorean politics. The organization of politics around the personal magnetism of an individual leader is called caudillo or strong-man politics. Personalism and caudillism have thwarted the growth of a programmatic and coherent political party system. Public conflict in Ecuador is all too often coincident with a family feud.

The remarkable career of the late politician, José María Velasco Ibarra (1893–1979) illustrates the enduring strength of caudillism and the weakness of Ecuador's party institutions. Velasco combined a brilliant and demagogic electoral campaign style with a profound administrative and executive ineptness, which enabled him to occupy the presidency no fewer than five times (1933–1935; 1944–1947; 1952–1956; 1960–1961; 1968–1972) and to be forcibly removed from the presidency no less than four times. During his forty-year political career, Velasco campaigned alternatively as the candidate of conservative law and order and leftist reform. No expression better describes the apparent cynicism underlying Velasco's career than the one he enjoyed repeating, "Give me a balcony and the people are mine."

Five years of military control followed the 1963 coup which ousted Velasco's successor, Carlos Julio Arosemena and ended more than a decade of constitutional civilian rule. The election of Velasco in 1960, a time of great social ferment brought about by the example of the Cuban Revolution, was followed a year later by his next-to-last overthrow. Vice-President Carlos Arosemena ascended to the presidency, but was himself overthrown by the military in 1963. The fall of Arosemena was facilitated by both his own personality defects and CIA involvement. Despite the intention of the military, the return to electoral politics in 1968 led to the election that year of none other than the irrepressible Velasco Ibarra who, however, was again ousted by the armed forces in 1972.

The resulting military junta under General Guillermo Rodríguez Lara proclaimed itself to be both "revolutionary and nationalist." Admiral Gustavo Jarrín Ampudía, minister of natural resources, brought Ecuador into OPEC. For this and other progressive acts, the Ecuadorean Communist Party considered Jarrín Ampudía as a possible broad-based presidential candidate in the forthcoming election. A more traditional military junta seized power in 1976, and reluctantly agreed to return power to an elected civilian administration.

Two years of intense political activity, complex intrigues, violence, and one major political assassination followed before Jaime Roldós Aguilera was finally sworn in as Ecuador's elected president on 10 August 1979. The first of a series of elections during that period involved the decision as to whether to write a new constitution. The favorable vote resulted in the nation's seventeenth constitution, the most notable aspect of which was the granting of the vote for the first time to illiterates, who comprised about 27 percent of Ecuador's 1977 adult population. The new constitution also called for the election of a president by a majority, even if this necessitated a runoff election.

In the election of July 1978, the military junta moved to exclude all potential presidential candidates not to their liking. All former presidents, including José María Velasco Ibarra and Carlos Julio Arosemena, were thereby eliminated. Most significant, the apparent presidential front runner, Assad Bucarám, leader of the Concentration of Popular Forces (Concentración de Fuerzas Populares—CFP), was barred on the grounds that his parents were not native Ecuadoreans. The candidates of four political parties, including two rightist groups, the Maoist Communists, and the Popular Democracy-Christian Democratic Union (Democracia Popular-Unión Demócrata Cristiana—DP–UDC) were also disqualified from participating in the election.

Six presidential coalitions, which were often cemented by the choice of the vice-presidential candidate, finally competed in the 1978 election. The CFP named a youthful lawyer and former deputy, Jaime Roldós Aguilera, as the party's standard bearer. His wife was the niece of Assad Bucarám, and Roldós' slogan was "Roldós to the presidency, Bucarám to power." However, his choice of a vice-presidential running-mate hinted at a more institutional and programmatic political preference on his part. Roldós's vice-presidential nominee was Osvaldo Hurtado Larrea, leader of the reform-minded DP–UDC. The candidate of the traditional establishment and military high command was the mayor of Quito, Sixto Durán Ballén, of the conservative National Constitutional Front coalition.

Although the election occurred on 16 July 1978, four months passed before the results were certified. They showed Roldós with 31 percent, followed by Durán with 23 percent. One of the conservative presidential candidates, Abdón Calderón Muñoz, who received 9 percent of the vote, was assassinated in November 1978.

A runoff election was held in April 1979. This second-round election, in which over 1.6 million votes were cast, was a landslide victory for Jaime Roldós. Not only did he win 68 percent compared to Durán's 32 percent, but he was able to win the popular vote in Quito and most other Sierra cities. For the first time, a liberal and populist politician from the Coast also won an overwhelming victory in the Sierra. In his 10 August 1979 inaugural address, Roldós symbolically reached out to the marginal and exploited indigenous population by reading part of his speech in Quechua, Ecuador's principal Indian language.

The CFP victory of April 1979 brought a bitter split between Roldós and Bucarám over reform proposals of the president and Bucarám's efforts to maintain personalist control over the party to which both men belonged. Roldós was drawn close to both the DP–UDC of Vice-President Hurtado (which won five of the thirty CFP congressional seats) and the Democratic Left Party (Izquierda Democrática—ID) of Rodrigo Borja (which won fourteen seats), while Bucarám as president of Congress made a pact with the conservative congressional delegations led by Rafael Armijos.

For a year after Roldós's inauguration, a struggle took place between the president and congress, led by Bucarám. However, a threat of the president to submit a constitutional amendment allowing him to dissolve Congress and, once during his term, to call new parliamentary elections to a popular referendum, brought about a realignment of the parties in Congress, with the emergence of a majority backing the president of the republic in mid-1980. Early in 1981, President Roldós died in an aircrash but was succeeded peacefully by Vice President Osvaldo Hurtado.

Indicative of the continuing fragmented nature of Ecuador's political system is the fact that six electoral coalitions contested the July 1978 first-round election. In the April 1979 congressional elections held at the same time as the second-round presidential runoff, no fewer than eleven political parties won representation in the national congress. However, in the following section on political parties only those of some durability and national significance are dealt with.

Bibliography

Philip Agee. *Inside the Company: CIA Diary.* Stonehill, New York, 1975.

George I. Blanksten. *Ecuador: Constitutions and Caudillos.* University of California Press, Berkeley, 1951.

Albert William Bork and George Maier. *Historical Dictionary of Ecuador.* Scarecrow Press, Metuchen, N.J., 1973.

George W. Grayson. "Populism, Petroleum and Politics in Ecuador," *Current History,* January 1975.

Osvaldo Hurtado. *Political Power in Ecuador.* University of New Mexico Press, Albuquerque, 1980.

George Maier. *The Ecuadorean Elections of June 2, 1968.* Institute for the Comparative Study of Political Systems, Washington, D.C., 1970.

John D. Martz. "Ecuador: Authoritarianism, Personalism and Dependency," in Howard J. Wiarda & Harvey F. Kline, *Latin American Politics and Development.* Houghton Mifflin, Boston, 1979.

———. *Ecuador: Conflicting Political Culture and the Quest for Progress.* Allyn and Bacon, Boston, 1972.

———. "Marxism in Ecuador." *Journal of Inter-American Studies and World Affairs,* Summer 1979.

———. "The Quest for Popular Democracy in Ecuador." *Current History,* January 1980.

Martin C. Needler. *Anatomy of a Coup d'Etat: Ecuador 1963.* Institute for the Comparative Study of Political Systems, Washington, D.C., 1964.

Galo Plaza. *Problems of Democracy in Latin America.* University of North Carolina Press, Chapel Hill, 1955.

Political Parties

ACCIÓN REVOLUCIONARIA NACIONALISTA ECUATORIANA. *See* ECUADOREAN REVOLUTIONARY NATIONALIST ACTION.

COMMUNIST PARTY OF ECUADOR (PARTIDO COMUNISTA DEL ECUADOR–PCE). The present Communist Party of Ecuador was originally established in 1926 as the Socialist Party of Ecuador (Partido Socialista del Ecuador), by a group of young intellectuals under the leadership of Ricardo Paredes. After Paredes had spent about a year in Moscow, the Socialist Party was accepted as a "fraternal" member of the Communist International at the Comintern's Sixth Congress in August 1928. In 1931 it changed its name to Partido Comunista and was accepted as a full member of the Comintern. In the early 1950s Paredes was succeeded as PCE Secretary General by Pedro Saad, who still holds that position.

From its inception, the PCE had some influence in the organized labor movement in Guayaquil, Quito, and a few provincial cities. In 1944 it took the lead in establishing the Confederation of Workers of Ecuador (Confederación de Trabajadores del Ecuador–CTE), and for the first three years, Pedro Saad was secretary-general of that group. Although the Socialists were able to oust the Communists from formal control of the CTE in 1947, they continued to have the confederation affiliated to the Communist-dominated Confederation of Workers of Latin America (CTAL), fearing Communist retribution if they sought to end that association. As Socialist influence in organized labor declined in the 1960s and thereafter, the Communists gained complete dominance over the CTE.

During most of its existence, the Communist Party has been legal. However, on several occasions it was outlawed—sometimes along with all other parties, sometimes individually. It was last forced underground in 1970, but was legalized again in 1973.

The Communists have regularly participated in elections. The party first elected a deputy from Guayaquil in 1928. In 1933 it first ran a presidential candidate, Ricardo Paredes. Over the years, it has formed electoral coalitions with a variety of different groups. For many years, under the system whereby particular interest groups had members of the Senate, Pedro Saad, who comes from Guayaquil, was the representative in the Senate of the workers of La Costa. The party ran its own presidential candidate, Elías Gallegos, in 1968.

In 1977 the Communists took the lead in organizing the Broad Based Leftist Front (Frente Amplia de la Izquierda), which included the Revolutionary Socialist Party (Partido Socialista Revolucionario), a splinter group from the Christian Democrats called the Revolutionary Movement of the Christian Left (Movimiento Revolucionario de Izquierda Cristiana), and some others. In the first-round presidential election of July 1978, the candidate of the Frente Amplia, René Mauge Mosquera, a member of the PCE, came in last place, with barely 5 percent of the vote.

In the 1979 congressional election, the Communists used an electoral front called the Democratic Popular Union (Unión Democrática Popular), which they had first established in 1968. However, in that race, the Communist ticket received only 3 percent of the vote. It elected only one member of Congress.

The PCE has remained loyal to the Soviet Union in the international Communist disputes of the last two decades. However, in 1963 a pro-Peking group broke away from the PCE to form the Marxist-Leninist Communist Party of Ecuador (Partido Comunista Marxista Leninista del Ecuador).

CONCENTRACIÓN DE FUERZAS POPULARES. *See* CONCENTRATION OF POPULAR FORCES.

CONCENTRATION OF POPULAR FORCES (CONCENTRACIÓN DE FUERZAS POPULARES—CFP). The Concentration of Popular Forces was established in 1947 by Carlos Guevara Moreno, who got his start in politics as a member of the Communist Party, and subsequently was minister of interior for a short while in the government of José María Velasco Ibarra after the coup of 1944. In 1951 the party had its first major electoral triumph when Guevara Moreno was chosen mayor of Guayaquil. Under Guevara Moreno, the influence of the CFP remained largely concentrated on the Coast, and particularly around Guayaquil. In 1952 the party supported the presidential candidacy of José María Velasco Ibarra, although the two caudillos, Guevara Moreno and Velasco Ibarra, frequently quarreled. In 1960 the CFP coalesced with the Revolutionary Socialist Party and the Communist Party to back Antonio Parra, and in 1968 it supported the Liberal candidate, Andrés Fernández Córdova.

When Guevara Moreno died, and his leadership position was taken over in the 1960s by Assad Bucarám, who was also elected mayor of Guayaquil in 1962 and 1967 (when he got 70 percent of the vote), the party began to become a contender for national power. During the military dictatorship of General Rodríguez Lara, Bucarám was one of the first political leaders with national prestige to insist, in 1975, on the need for a return to elections and a constitutional regime.

However, as the 1978 elections were being prepared, the ruling military government vetoed the presidential candidacy of Assad Bucarám, ostensibly because his parents had not been born in Ecuador, but reportedly because they felt that he was a dangerous demagogue. However, in spite of this initial setback, the CFP's first bid for national power was successful. The man the party substituted for Bucarám as its candidate, Jaime Roldós Aguilera, came in first in the 1978 first-round presidential election, and won the second one in 1979 overwhelmingly. The party also received a majority in Congress.

However, even before the inauguration of President Roldós, a deep split developed between him and his erstwhile patron, Asaad Bucarám, who was elected president of Congress. It is not clear whether the Concentración de Fuerzas Populares can survive as a united party.

The Concentration of Popular Forces has never had a clear-cut ideology. It has largely been the personal vehicle of the two leaders who headed it, Carlos Guevara Moreno and Assad Bucarám. It has drawn wide support from the lower classes of the coastal area, who have looked upon the CFP chiefs as their spokesmen, but its program has remained vague and ill-defined. One of the roots of the conflict between President Roldós and Asaad Bucarám was the former's attempt to give the party (and his government) a clearer definition as belonging to the reformist democratic Left.

CONSERVATIVE PARTY (PARTIDO CONSERVADOR). Long considered the political champion of the traditional Sierra landowners, the Partido Conservador traces its roots back to the clericalist dictatorship of Gabriel García Moreno (1860–1875). However, it was not formally established as a political party until 1883, largely as a response to the organization of the Liberal Party. It continued to dominate the government until the civil war of 1895–1896, which brought the Liberals to power.

For almost forty years thereafter, no one was elected president as the candidate of the Conservative Party. It was not until 1934 that, in his first successful attempt to become president, José María Velasco Ibarra succeeded with the backing of the Partido Conservador. However, Velasco Ibarra, a Mason, was not himself a Conservative, and in any case, lasted in power that time for something less than a year.

Nevertheless, the Conservatives continued to remain one of the country's major parties. In the 1930s and early 1940s they were one of the three largest parties, along with the Liberals and Socialists. They supported the movement to overthrow President Carlos Arroyo del Río in 1944. The Conservatives participated in the succeeding government of José María Velasco Ibarra, and in the constituent assembly which wrote the country's fifteenth constitution in 1945. Furthermore, when President Velasco Ibarra declared a dictatorship and suspended that constitution a year later, the Conservatives were the only party to participate in elections for still another constitutional assembly, which wrote the sixteenth constitution, which remained in effect until 1978.

In 1948, the Conservative candidate for president was defeated by Galo Plaza, but their nominee for vice-president was elected. Four years later, the Conservatives were again defeated, this time by the perennial Velasco Ibarra, but once more a Conservative was elected vice-president.

In 1951 the Conservatives suffered a split, with the formation of the Social Christian Party (Partido Social Cristiano). However, in 1956 the Conservatives supported the victorious candidate of the Social Christians, Camilo Ponce Enríquez.

During the military dictatorships of the 1960s and 1970s, the Conservative Party leaders suffered some mild persecution. However, perhaps more damaging to the future of the Conservative Party was the establishment in the 1978 constitution of universal adult suffrage.

The Conservative Party has remained the political arm of the oligarchy of the Sierra. It has also been the most consistent supporter of the secular rights of the church, although in recent decades church–state issues have not been the subject of a great deal of debate.

In the 1978 and 1979 presidential elections, the Partido Conservador supported the unsuccessful candidacy of Sixto Durán Ballén. It elected nine members of Congress in 1979, the third largest delegation. Its congressional leader, Rafael Armijos Valdivieso, was a retired army colonel.

DEMOCRACIA POPULAR. See POPULAR DEMOCRACY AND CHRISTIAN DEMOCRATIC UNION.

DEMOCRACIA POPULAR-UNIÓN DEMOCRÁTICA CRISTIANA. See POPULAR DEMOCRACY AND CHRISTIAN DEMOCRATIC UNION.

DEMOCRATIC LEFT (IZQUIERDA DEMOCRÁTICA—ID). Izquierda Democrática was created under the leadership of Rodrigo Borja Cevallos in 1970, after he left the Radical Liberal Party. A substantial part of the remnants of the Socialist Party also joined the ID. In the municipal elections of 1970 the party received more votes than the Liberals.

The leadership of the new party came largely from middle-class elements in Quito, Guayaquil, and other cities. However, it also won considerable backing in the non-Communist and non-Catholic labor movement, the Ecuadorean Labor Confederation of Free Trade Unions (Confederación Ecuatoriana Obrera de Sindicatos Libres). The party aligned itself internationally with other democratic-Left parties of Latin America which were more or less closely associated with the Socialist International.

In the 1978 first-round presidential elections, Izquierda Democrática named Rodrigo Borja as its candidate. He came in fourth, with about 10 percent of the vote. In the following year, it threw its backing to Jaime Roldós of the Concentration of Popular Forces (Concentración de Fuerzas Populares), who was the victor. In the congressional elections held at the same time as the second-round presidential one, it placed twelve members in Congress, the second largest party delegation. In view of President Roldós's difficulties with the leader of his own party in Congress, Assad Bucarám, Roldós came increasingly to rely for support on the Izquierda Democrática's members. In mid-1980, Izquierda Democrática became part of the new congressional majority formed to support President Roldós.

ECUADOREAN REVOLUTIONARY NATIONALIST ACTION (ACCIÓN REVOLUCIONARIA NACIONALISTA ECUATORIANA—ARNE). The Ecuadorean Revolutionary Nationalist Action party was created in 1942 in the wake of Ecuador's military defeat by Peru. Its leadership comprised a number of admirers of Spain's fascist caudillo, Francisco Franco, and of traditional Spanish values and political structures, and of the concept of an "organic society." ARNE can be considered Ecuador's extreme right-wing party.

In 1952 ARNE supported the successful Velasco Ibarra presidential coalition, and for some time the party had members in Velasco's cabinet. However, it later broke with him. ARNE members helped create a widespread climate of disorder in 1963, which paved the way for the military seizure of power of that year. The field personnel of the CIA may have encouraged this antidemocratic ARNE activity. The party's 1968 presidential candidate, Jorge Crespo Toral, won only 4 percent of the vote. In early 1978, ARNE was one of the four parties which the military government eliminated from the first-round presidential elections.

FEDERACIÓN NACIONAL VELAZQUISTA. *See* NATIONAL VELAZQUISTA FEDERATION.

INSTITUTIONAL DEMOCRATIC COALITION (COALICIÓN INSTITU-CIONALISTA DEMOCRÁTICA—CID). The Institutional Democratic Coalition was created in 1965 by a right-of-center Guayaquil businessman, Otto Arosemena Gómez, a one-time Liberal Party member. In 1967, Arosemena Gómez was provisional president of Ecuador as the nation prepared for the 1968 election. The CID supported José María Velasco Ibarra in 1968. In 1979 it elected three members of Congress and subsequently supported President of Congress Assad Bucarám in his conflict with President Jaime Roldós.

MARXIST-LENINIST COMMUNIST PARTY OF ECUADOR (PARTIDO COMUNISTA MARXISTA-LENINISTA DEL ECUADOR—PCMLE). In 1963, those who formed the PCMLE broke away from the Partido Comunista del Ecuador to form a party aligned with the Chinese against the Soviet Union. The PCMLE preferred more direct action and mass mobilization activities rather than simply attracting members for action in the electoral arena. Soon after its estab-lishment, the Marxist-Leninist Communist Party attempted to mount a guerrilla action, but this was quickly suppressed.

PCMLE members were founders of the Comité del Pueblo (People's Commit-tee) which organized thousands of poor, squatter, slum families around commu-nity development and defense issues. It also has had strong influence among faculty members and students of the National University in Quito. However, the party has had relatively little support in the organized labor movement, not being able seriously to challenge the pro-Moscow Communists' control of the Confed-eration of Workers of Ecuador (Confederación de Trabajadores del Ecuador).

The PCMLE was barred by the military government from participating in the first-round presidential election in 1978. Thereafter, some of its members advo-cated abstaining completely from the electoral "charade," and some ended up supporting the pro-Moscow party's electoral coalition. However, the majority of the party organized its own coalition, the Popular Democratic Movement (Movimiento Popular Democrático) as its vehicle for the 1979 congressional election. In that contest, the PCMLE got 5 percent of the vote and elected one of its leaders, Jaime Hurtado González, to the Congress.

MOVIMIENTO POPULAR DEMOCRÁTICO. *See* MARXIST-LENINIST COMMUNIST PARTY OF ECUADOR.

NATIONAL VELAZQUIST FEDERATION (FEDERACIÓN NACIONAL VELAZQUISTA—FNV). Formed in 1952 as the vehicle for the personalist presi-dential campaign of José María Velasco Ibarra, the FNV remained his personal political instrument.

The 1952 campaign was the third time that Velasco Ibarra sought to become president of the republic. He had first been elected with Conservative support in

1933 and had been overthrown the following year; had come to power again in 1944 as a result of the revolution against President Carlos Arroyo del Río, and was ousted again in 1947. Subsequent to his 1952 election, he was elected twice more, in 1960 — being overthrown a year later — and in 1968, when he lasted four years before being ousted by the military.

Usually, Velasco Ibarra prided himself on being free of any partisan allegiance. However, in 1952 he organized the FNV to back his renewed presidential ambitions, and thereafter his personal followers continued to have the FNV as their vehicle. Following the death of Velasco Ibarra in March 1979, the FNV was converted into the Partido Nacional Venazquista (PNV), and it elected one member of Congress. It is unlikely that this party will long survive the death of its caudillo.

NATIONALIST REVOLUTIONARY PARTY (PARTIDO NACIONALISTA REVOLUCIONARIO — PNR). The PNR is the personal political vehicle of former President Carlos Julio Arosemena Monroy. Elected vice-president in 1960, Arosemena became president when President José María Velasco Ibarra was overthrown by the military. Arosemena was also overthrown, in 1963, and the fact that the CIA was involved in that event became a source of embarrassment to the United States. Subsequently, he led in the formation of the PNR. Ex-President Arosemena was banned by the military government from running in the 1978 first-round presidential election. However, in 1979 the PNR was able to elect two members to Congress. Arosemena may be considered to be the leader of the more progressive wing of the old coalition behind José María Velasco Ibarra.

PARTIDO COMUNISTA DEL ECUADOR. See COMMUNIST PARTY OF ECUADOR.

PARTIDO COMUNISTA MARXISTA-LENINISTA DEL ECUADOR. See MARXIST-LENINIST COMMUNIST PARTY OF ECUADOR.

PARTIDO CONSERVADOR. See CONSERVATIVE PARTY.

PARTIDO DEMÓCRATA CRISTIANO. See POPULAR DEMOCRACY AND CHRISTIAN DEMOCRATIC UNION.

PARTIDO LIBERAL. See RADICAL LIBERAL PARTY.

PARTIDO LIBERAL RADICAL. See RADICAL LIBERAL PARTY.

PARTIDO NACIONAL VELAZQUISTA. See NATIONAL VELAZQUIST FEDERATION.

PARTIDO NACIONALISTA REVOLUCIONARIO. See NATIONALIST REVOLUTIONARY PARTY.

PARTIDO SOCIAL CRISTIANO. *See* SOCIAL CHRISTIAN PARTY.

PARTIDO SOCIALISTA DEL ECUADOR. *See* SOCIALIST PARTY OF ECUADOR.

PARTIDO SOCIALISTA REVOLUCIONARIO. *See* SOCIALIST PARTY OF ECUADOR.

PARTIDO SOCIALISTA UNIFICADO. *See* SOCIALIST PARTY OF ECUADOR.

POPULAR DEMOCRACY (DEMOCRACIA POPULAR). *See* POPULAR DEMOCRACY AND CHRISTIAN DEMOCRATIC UNION.

POPULAR DEMOCRACY AND CHRISTIAN DEMOCRATIC UNION (DEMOCRACIA POPULAR–UNIÓN DEMOCRÁTICA CRISTIANA–DP –UDC). The Popular Democracy and Christian Democratic Union is the successor to the Christian Democratic Party (Partido Demócrata Cristiano–PDC), originally established in 1962, which was affiliated with the Christian Democratic International. The PDC did not support any presidential candidate in 1968, although it did elect one senator and one deputy at that time. The Christian Democrats had more or less close relations with the Catholic-oriented trade union group, the Ecuadorean Confederation of Christian Laborers (Confederación Ecuatoriana de Obreros Cristianos (CEDOC). Known by 1977 as the Christian Democratic Union (Unión Democrática Cristiana), the party merged in that year with the Popular Democracy (Democracia Popular), a progressive splinter group which had broken away from the Conservative Party in 1976 under the leadership of Julio César Trujillo. While the DP–UDC failed to qualify for the 1978 first-round presidential election, it won five congressional seats in 1979. Its leader, Julio César Trujillo, was elected on the list of the Concentration of Popular Forces (Concentración de Fuerzas Populares), and he led the legislative supporters of President Roldós. At the same time, Osvaldo Hurtado Larrea, another DP–UDC leader, was President Roldós's vice-president. He succeeded to the presidency when Roldós was killed in an airplane accident in early June 1981.

POPULAR DEMOCRATIC MOVEMENT (MOVIMIENTO POPULAR DEMOCRÁTICO). *See* MARXIST–LENINIST COMMUNIST PARTY OF ECUADOR.

RADICAL LIBERAL PARTY (PARTIDO LIBERAL RADICAL–PLR). The Radical Liberal Party, usually known as the Liberal Party, was the country's first organized political party and was founded in 1878. It was the Opposition from the time of its establishment until, under the leadership of Eloy Alfaro, it seized power in the civil war of 1895–1896. From 1896 until 1944 the Liberal Party remained in power. During the first twenty years, the party was dominated by

Eloy Alfaro and his successor and rival, General Leónidas Plaza, who remained an important figure in the party for a decade after he left the presidency for the second time in 1916.

With the overthrow of the last clearly Liberal president, Carlos Arroyo del Río in 1944, the Liberal Party fell upon hard times. It split into rival factions on various occasions, and no clearly Liberal candidate was again elected president. However, it remained one of the country's major parties. In 1948, Galo Plaza, the son of the late Leónidas Plaza, was elected with Liberal Party support although officially Galo Plaza was not then a member of the Liberal Party. Subsequently, he joined the party, and in 1960 again ran for the presidency as the Liberal candidate, but was defeated by José María Velasco Ibarra.

At its inception, the Radical Liberal Party was particularly the spokesman for those opposed to the temporal influence of the Roman Catholic Church. During the period of Liberal domination of the country's politics, it succeeded in depriving the church of control over education, much of its land, and other aspects of temporal society. However, by the second quarter of the twentieth century, religious issues had ceased to figure greatly in national politics. During the Eloy Alfaro regime the first impetus was also given to the development of workers' organizations, particularly mutual benefit societies. However, in the last decades of Liberal rule, the party's enthusiasm for support of the urban labor movement drastically declined, and the leadership of the workers passed largely into the hands of the new Socialist and Communist parties.

The Liberals also traditionally pledged support to the defense of the Indian peasant masses and for an agrarian reform to redistribute the land of the Sierra to the indigenous peasants. However, during the long period that it was in power, it never took any significant steps to carry out these aspects of its program. Perhaps this was the result of the fact that the Liberal Party leadership came largely from upper-class elements, or because its political base was largely in the coastal area, where the issue of land redistribution was not as pressing as it was in the Sierra.

During recent decades, the power and influence of the Radical Liberal Party has drastically declined. This was undoubtedly due in part to the numerous divisions within the party's ranks. It was also the result of the fact that the party did not keep up with the social and economic issues which increasingly became matters of controversy in national politics.

In 1978, the Liberal Party's candidate in the first-round presidential election was Raúl Clemente Huerta. He came in a very close third, behind Jaime Roldós of the Concentration of Popular Forces (Concentración de Fuerzas Populares), and Sixto Durán, the Conservative nominee. The PLR elected only four members of Congress in the 1979 parliamentary election.

SOCIAL CHRISTIAN PARTY (PARTIDO SOCIAL CRISTIANO – PSC). The PSC was founded in 1951 by Camilo Ponce Enríquez, a member of a traditional Conservative family. It was originally called the Social Christian Movement (Movimiento Social Cristiano). Ponce was elected president of Ecuador as the

PSC candidate, with Conservative Party support, in 1956. Thereafter, the party remained principally the personal political vehicle of the ex-president until his death. It backed him in an unsuccessful run for president in 1968, when he came in third. It supported Sixto Durán in the 1978 and 1979 presidential elections. In 1979 the PSC elected two members of Congress.

SOCIALIST PARTY OF ECUADOR (PARTIDO SOCIALISTA DEL ECUADOR—PSE). Two groups have used the name Socialist Party of Ecuador. The first was founded by Ricardo Paredes and a group of young intellectuals in 1926. Five years later it changed its name to Partido Comunista del Ecuador and became a full-fledged member of the Communist International.

Those Socialists in Quito opposed to converting the PSE into a Communist Party seceded and re-formed the Partido Socialista del Ecuador. At the same time, a similar dissident group in the Guayaquil area formed the Partido Social Cooperativista. In 1933 they joined forces with the Quito group under the name Partido Socialista del Ecuador.

During the 1930s, 1940s, and 1950s, the Socialist Party was one of the country's major political organizations. It had members in the government of the short-lived dictatorship of General Henríquez in the late 1930s, during which the country's labor code was written and other advanced social legislation was passed. During that period, the then current constitution provided for equal representation in parliament by the Left, Right, and Center, and so the Socialist Party had one-third of the members of Congress. The Socialists participated in the movement which overthrew President Carlos Arroyo del Río in 1944, and for a short while had members in the cabinet of President José María Velasco Ibarra. However, when he proclaimed a dictatorship, the Socialists withdrew from the Velasco regime. In the election of 1948, which followed the overthrow of Velasco, they supported the candidacy of Galo Plaza and for some time after his victory had members in his cabinet.

During this period, the Socialists played a major role in the country's labor movement. Their labor supporters participated in the establishment in 1944 of the Confederation of Workers of Ecuador (Confederación de Trabajadores del Ecuador—CTE), and in 1947 they succeeded in wresting control of the organization from the Communists. However, they continued to keep the CTE affiliated to the Communist-dominated Confederación of Workers of Latin America (CTAL).

During the 1940s and 1950s, the Socialists were divided into a pro-Communist and an anti-Communist faction, although the party did not split into two organizations in that period. Traditionally, the party considered itself to be to the left of the majority of the parties in the Socialist International, and so it did not affiliate with the International either before or after World War II.

In the 1960s, the Socialists split into three different parties, and their influence generally declined. The first division took place at the time of the 1960 elections, when the majority of the party supported the candidacy of Galo Plaza, running as the Radical Liberal Party nominee, and a minority group broke away to form the

Revolutionary Socialist Party (Partido Socialista Revolucionario—PSR), and back the candidacy of Antonio Parra, whose vice-presidential nominee was Benjamín Carrión, a PSR leader. Parra also had the support of the Communist Party and the Concentration of Popular Forces (Concentración de Fuerzas Populares). The PSR was very much influenced by the Castroite revolution in Cuba, and ultimately proclaimed itself to be Marxist-Leninist.

After the military dictatorship of 1963~1966, the Socialists emerged as three separate organizations: the Partido Socialista del Ecuador, the Partido Socialista Unificado, and the Partido Socialista Revolucionario. The first two of these merged again in 1968 under the name Partido Socialista del Ecuador. It still exists, but is a very minor factor in national politics. In 1978 it supported the Liberal Party candidate, Raúl Clemente Huerta. It failed to elect any congressmen in 1979. Many former Socialists participated in founding the Democratic Left (Izquierda Democrática) in 1970.

In the presidential election of 1978, the PSR joined forces with the pro-Moscow Communists and several other groups in forming the Broad Front of the Left (Frente Amplio de la Izquierda). A member of the PSR, Aníbal Muñoz, was the Front's candidate for vice-president, along with presidential nominee Raúl Mauge, of the Communist Party. The Front's candidates came in last in a field of six, with only about 5 percent of the total vote.

SOCIALIST REVOLUTIONARY VANGUARD (VANGUARDIA REVOLU-CIONARIA SOCIALISTA—VRS). The Socialist Revolutionary Vanguard, which was of considerable significance from the late 1930s until the early 1950s, was formed by a group of dissident Socialists in 1935. They broke from the Partido Socialista del Ecuador over what attitude the party should assume toward one of the governments of the period. The leader of the party was a military man, Luis Larrea Alba, who had been one of the leaders of the young military's revolution of 1925.

During the 1930s and 1940s, the Vanguardia was one of the three principal parties of the Left, along with the Socialists and Communists. They participated in the movement against President Carlos Arroyo del Río in 1944, and for a while had a representative in the cabinet of Arroyo's successor, President José María Velasco Ibarra. However, when Velasco established a dictatorship with Conservative support, the Vanguardia, along with the other leftist parties, withdrew from the government, and suffered some persecution at the hands of Velasco.

The Vanguardia never had much support in the organized labor movement. It was principally a party of professional and middle-class people, in spite of its "revolutionary" position. It maintained that it would never be possible for the Left to come to power peacefully, and that once the Left had seized power, it should exercise a dictatorship for some time, to carry out fundamental reforms in the economy and society. The Vanguardia disappeared in the early 1950s.

UNIÓN DEMOCRÁTICA CRISTIANA. *See* POPULAR DEMOCRACY AND CHRISTIAN DEMOCRATIC UNION.

VANGUARDIA REVOLUCIONARIA SOCIALISTA. *See* SOCIALIST REVOLUTIONARY VANGUARD.

David Eugene Blank

EL SALVADOR

El Salvador, the smallest of the continental Latin-American nations, is densely populated, with a rapid population growth rate and highly developed communications. Land, fundamental to the survival of Salvadoreans, is scarce and inequitably distributed. During the nineteenth century, El Salvador was divided by an internecine elite struggle between Liberals and Conservatives, loosely structured as parties, which paralleled similar groups elsewhere in Central America. Elections were held periodically, but few citizens were allowed to participate, and the electoral results were neither permanent nor respected by those who did participate.

A series of rural uprisings in the late nineteenth century over the distribution of land prompted that nation's oligarchy to mend its ways and reach a "gentlemen's agreement," whereby the dominant families controlling the country agreed to alternate presidential power among themselves. A period of relative political stability and economic growth followed. In the 1920s a Marxist movement emerged, as it did in many Latin American nations. In 1931 the nation experienced the first competitive election in which large numbers of Salvadoreans participated.

The election produced a president, Arturo Araújo, who was committed to national reform, but peasants and workers mobilized to organize protests and demonstrations demanding immediate changes. Araújo was unable to control the ensuing violence and was deposed by a military coup less than a year after taking office. His successor, General Maximiliano Hernández Martínez, had been his minister of war. The Hernández Martínez regime resembled numerous of its contemporaries in Latin America, a personalized, arbitrary, authoritarian dictatorship. The president was forced to resign in April 1944 by a general strike, a massive nonviolent protest known as the "Folded Arms Strike" (*Huelga de los Brazos Caídos*).

The Salvadorean military organization, by comparison with those of other Central American nations, was institutionalized fairly early, through a national academy established in the late nineteenth century. Military professionalization had many implications. It made promotion to higher ranks more dependent on ability and performance and resulted in individuals being recruited to the military from lower socioeconomic classes, mostly outside the capital city. It also imbued in the military a strong sense of national patriotism and a paternalistic commitment to the welfare and stability of the republic. Although two military officers with obvious political ambitions ruled El Salvador from 1932–1948 (Hernández Martínez and his successor, Salvador Castaneda Castro), the military as an institution first took power in the coup of 14 December 1948.

By 1950 the military leaders presented the country with a new constitution, and formed a new political party, the Revolutionary Party of Democratic Unification (Partido Revolucionario de Unificación Democrática—PRUD). Elections were held, and the PRUD candidate, Major Oscar Osorio, easily won the presidency. Osorio committed his regime to economic development, embarked on a housing program, began a social security system, legalized urban labor unions, and initiated projects to expand the nation's infrastructure to promote economic development, the most important of which was a large hydroelectric project on the Lempa River. Osorio's regime, and most of those after him, became involved in a delicate balancing act, trying to improve the living standards of the masses while at the same time maintaining the political support of the small, economic elite that controlled the wealth, resources, and skills necessary for economic development.

In 1956, Lieutenant Colonel José María Lemus, the handpicked candidate of Osorio, was elected president in an uncontested election firmly under the control of the military. Lemus was an unpopular president and resorted to harsh tactics to remain in office. He was finally deposed in a bloodless coup in October 1960, and a new civilian-military junta was established, committed to a return to the principles of the 1948 "Revolution." A few months later, in January 1961, another coup occurred, which outlawed the newly emerging leftist parties, and established a new national party, the Party of National Conciliation (Partido de Conciliación Nacional—PCN) which continued, by one means or another, to dominate national political life until the coup of October 1979.

Colonel Julio A. Rivera was nominated for the presidential elections of 1962 as the PCN candidate. New opposition parties emerged for this election, the most important of which was the Christian Democratic Party (Partido Demócrata Cristiano—PDC) which, along with a few others, finally boycotted the election in protest of suspected fraud. Rivera embraced the basic concepts of the Alliance for Progress, and encouraged electoral reforms to insure free elections. In 1964 legislative elections were held, and were remarkable both for their honesty and for the fact that opposition parties gained representation in the national legislature for the first time since 1931. Rivera's regime was one of considerable progress in economic development, liberalization in political activity, and political mobilization of the electorate, as witnessed by the rapid expansion in voter participation.

Rivera was succeeded by another military officer, Colonel Fidel Sánchez Hernández, in 1967. Beset by growing economic problems, Sánchez found himself involved in a war with Honduras in 1969, the result of lingering tensions caused by the migration of large numbers of landless Salvadorean peasants into Honduras and alleged brutality by Hondurans toward them. The war briefly united Salvadoreans around President Sánchez and the military, but pressures for major reforms were steadily building in the country.

Colonel Arturo Armando Molina defeated the PDC candidate for the presidency, José Napoleón Duarte (former mayor of the capital city, San Salvador), in the national election of 1972. Molina's victory was shrouded with charges of electoral fraud which, when combined with subsequent incidents, would ultimately discredit the legitimacy of PCN national elections. During Molina's term as president, organized violence and terrorism broke out in the country, resulting in the deaths of many political and economic leaders, and retaliation by right-wing terrorist organizations thought to be linked with the government. As terrorism and protests increased, the Molina regime became increasingly repressive.

In the presidential election of 1977, General Carlos Humberto Romero, former minister of defense, was elected in a contest with (retired) Colonel Ernesto Claramount, who was supported by a coalition of opposition parties known as the National Opposition Union (UNO), and comprised the Christian Democratic Party and two smaller political parties. The election was generally thought to be fraudulent, and afterwards thousands of Claramount's supporters gathered in the streets of the capital to protest. Several were killed by government troops, many more wounded, and Claramount was hastily shuttled off to Costa Rica by the Salvadorean air force. Violence escalated under Romero. Attacks by left-wing terrorist groups and government subsidized right-wing groups became more frequent. Not only were politicians and businessmen involved, but foreigners, educational and religious leaders, and eventually even embassies came under attack. The country seemed to be moving in the direction of civil war, and the economy began to suffer as firms closed down their operations because of the violence. International attention became focussed on El Salvador, as charges of human rights violations and brutality became increasingly common.

In October 1979, President Romero was overthrown in a military coup organized by younger military officers committed to reversing the oppressive policies of the regime and coming to terms, almost thirty years after the 1948 revolution, with the major inequalities between the rich and poor of the country. The military junta called for support from all the dissident political elements in the country, including the terrorist organizations, the Christian Democratic Party, and the Roman Catholic Church. The new junta announced major reforms, including a program of land reform, nationalization of the banking system and external commerce, and legalization of rural labor unions. The extreme Left refused to go along with the new junta, and the conservative interests in the country were equally opposed to it.

This junta resigned after about two months in office. It was succeeded by another in which the only party represented was the Christian Democrats. In March 1980, the Christian Democrats split, with the dissident group withdrawing its support of the junta. Terrorism on both sides continued. Several embassies were seized, new waves of violence broke out, and in March 1980, Archbishop Oscar A. Romero, long identified as a critic of the military-backed regimes and an advocate of human rights, was assassinated while celebrating mass.

In December 1980 the military forced changes in the ruling junta. Several Christian Democratic leaders who had endorsed the original junta disassociated themselves from the new junta, as did Guillermo Ungo and other Social Democrats who joined forces with the Democratic Revolutionary Front (FDR), which had been formed in April 1980 as a civilian political arm of the combined revolutionary forces.

On 28 March 1982 elections were held to select sixty representatives to a constituent assembly, charged with drafting a new constitution and selecting an interim government. A heavy turnout in the voting, estimated to be about 1.5 million voters, gave Duarte and the Christian Democrats a plurality of about 36 percent of the vote. All of the remaining five parties that participated were from the right; the FDR and other leftist groups boycotted the election.

International involvement in the Salvadorean conflict had escalated by 1981, as the United States substantially increased its military and economic aid to the junta and charged that the revolutionaries were being aided by Nicaragua, Cuba, and perhaps ultimately the Soviet Union. El Salvador's tenuous experiment with party politics remained as violent as it had begun thirty years before. Polarized politically, devastated by civil war and revolution, wracked by political violence and killing, and controlled ultimately by a stubborn if weakening military, the fundamental problems of the society—overpopulation, economic inequalities, and underdevelopment—were no closer to solution. The subtleties of party processes and elections seemed increasingly irrelevant to the issues at hand.

Bibliography

Thomas P. Anderson. *Matanza, El Salvador's Communist Revolt of 1932.* University of Nebraska Press, Lincoln, 1971.

Howard Blutstein, et al. *Area Handbook for El Salvador.* Government Printing Office, Washington, D.C., 1971.

David Browning. *El Salvador, Landscape and Society.* Clarendon Press, Oxford, 1971.

Roland H. Ebel. "The Decision-Making Process in San Salvador," in *Latin American Urban Research,* ed. Francine F. Rabinovitz and Felicity Trueblood. Sage Publications, Beverly Hills, 1970.

Ricardo Gallardo: *Las Constituciones de El Salvador: Volume 1, Historia de la Integración Racial, Territorial e Institucional del Pueblo Salvadoreño.* Ediciones de Cultura Hispánica, Madrid, 1961.

Paul R. Hoopes. "El Salvador," in *Political Forces in Latin America: Dimensions of the Quest for Stability,* ed. Ben G. Burnett and Kenneth F. Johnson, 2d ed. Wadsworth Publishing Co. Belmont, Calif., 1970.

David R. Raynolds. *Rapid Development in Small Economies: The Example of El Salvador.* Praeger, New York, 1967.

Stephen Weber. *José Napoleón Duarte and the Christian Democratic Party in Salvadoran Politics 1960-1972.* Louisiana State University Press, Baton Rouge, 1979.

Henry Wells, ed. *El Salvador Election Factbook, March 5, 1967.* Institute for the Comparative Study of Political Systems, Washington, D.C., 1967.

Political Parties

AUTHENTIC REVOLUTIONARY PARTY OF DEMOCRATIC UNIFICA-
TION (PARTIDO REVOLUCIONARIO DE UNIFICACIÓN DEMOCRÁTICA
AUTÉNTICO – PRUDA). The Authentic Revolutionary Party of Democratic
Unification was founded in 1959 by former president Oscar Osorio following his
break with President José María Lemus. The party did not survive after the coups
of 1960 and 1961.

CENTRAL AMERICAN UNITY PARTY (PARTIDO UNIONISTA CENTRO
AMERICANO – PUCA). The Central American Unity Party existed in the 1960s
with the purpose of advocating Central American unity. It was instrumental in
bringing about minority representation in the legislature by the adoption of an
electoral system of proportional representation. It never had more than very
limited popular support.

CHRISTIAN DEMOCRATIC PARTY (PARTIDO DEMÓCRATA CRISTIANO
– PDC). The Christian Democratic Party was founded in 1960, with a platform
calling for reform and an end to military control. It first participated in the 1964
elections, winning nearly one-third of the national legislative seats. The leadership was from the upper middle class, mostly professional persons, and the party
enjoyed the support of a small, but articulate, radical minority within the Roman
Catholic Church. Support came also from the small, but restless, middle class,
located mostly in the capital city. Its principal leader and executive secretary in
the early years was Dr. Abrahám Rodríguez, who ran unsuccessfully for the
presidency in 1967. In the 1964 elections, the PDC candidate for mayor of San
Salvador, José Napoleón Duarte, won, and he subsequently became the party's
principal leader, the highest ranking official unaffiliated with the official Party of
National Conciliation (PCN).

Duarte ran for the presidency in 1972, but lost to the PCN candidate. The
election was generally considered fraudulent, and Duarte and his supporters
claimed the victory was theirs. The same year Duarte became involved in an
unsuccessful coup and was subsequently exiled.

In 1974, the PDC supported the National Opposition Union (UNO) coalition
in the legislative elections, winning eight seats compared to the thirty-nine won
by the PCN. In 1977 the PDC, along with the other two parties in the UNO,
endorsed Colonel (Retired) Ernesto Claramount Rozeville for the presidency.
Claramount was a political moderate, son of the well-known General Antonio
Claramount, a prominent military figure who had himself run for the presidency
in 1931 and 1944.

Efforts were made by the military to enlist support of PDC leaders in the
government after the 1979 coup, and several well-known PDC leaders did
participate for a while, most notably Héctor Dada Hirezi. Dada subsequently

resigned, and following the assassination of Archbishop Romero, two more PDC ministers resigned and the party split.

After the shakeup in the junta in December 1980, José Napoleón Duarte returned to El Salvador from exile and joined the government, being named president by the military dominated junta. Duarte's decision to join forces with the military further divided the party, although it remained the strongest single political force apart from the revolutionaries. The PDC participated in the elections of 1982, receiving 36 percent of the vote and twenty-four of the sixty delegates to the constituent assembly.

COMMUNIST PARTY OF EL SALVADOR (PARTIDO COMUNISTA DE EL SALVADOR—PCS). El Salvador's Communist Party was established in 1925, with support from its Guatemalan counterpart. It supported the candidacy of Arturo Araújo in 1931. The PCS was repressed by General Maximiliano Hernández Martínez during his regime (1932–1944), but operated clandestinely in subsequent years through its efforts to create an organized labor movement. Never legalized, the party has persisted only as a secret organization without any measurable electoral importance.

CONSTITUTIONAL DEMOCRATIC PARTY (PARTIDO DEMOCRÁTICO CONSTITUCIONAL). The Constitutional Democratic Party supported the candidacy of Colonel Rafael Carranza Amaya in the 1956 presidential election, and was supported by a small army faction loyal to Carranza. It disappeared after the 1956 election.

DEMOCRATIC ACTION (ACCIÓN DEMOCRATICA—AD). The Democratic Action Party was formed in November 981 to participate in the 1982 elections. It is comprised primarily of middle-class and professional persons and owners of medium-sized farms. The party's principal leader is Rene Fortin Magana, an attorney. The AD has supported the first phase of the land reform program, but objected to converting private farms of smaller size into peasant cooperatives, part of the program advocated by the Christian Democrats. It supports free enterprise, denationalization of the banks, and a civilian regime based on democratic elections. It is generally regarded as somewhat to the right of the Christian Democrats. Democratic Action received 7 percent of the popular vote in the 1982 elections and two seats in the constituent assembly.

DEMOCRATIC INSTITUTIONAL PARTY (PARTIDO INSTITUCIONAL DEMOCRÁTICO). The Democratic Institutional Party, founded in 1930, was a regional party centered in the department of Santa Ana. It nominated José Alberto Funes for the 1956 presidential election, and was supported by a small number of army officers disenchanted with the incumbent regime. The party was declared illegal after the 1956 election.

FRENTE UNIDO DEMOCRÁTICO INDEPENDIENTE. *See* UNITED DEMOCRATIC INDEPENDENT FRONT.

LABOR PARTY (PARTIDO LABORISTA). The Labor Party, formed in the late 1920s, was the first political party in El Salvador to lay claim to a mass following. It was a personalistic party, designed and created to advance the candidacy of Arturo Araújo. Loosely organized, it served as a coalition of the disadvantaged,particularly peasants and workers. Support came from many diverse radical elements in the country, including Marxists. The party participated in the national campaign of 1931 and saw its leader elected president. Following the overthrow of President Araújo in 1932, the party was repressed and then disappeared.

MOVIMIENTO NACIONAL REVOLUCIONARIO. *See* NATIONAL REVOLUTIONARY MOVEMENT.

NATIONAL ACTION PARTY (PARTIDO DE ACCIÓN NACIONAL—PAN). The National Action Party was founded in 1956 in opposition to the candidacy of Colonel José María Lemus, the official government nominee. It was supported by some younger military officers and a few civilians disenchanted with the dominant political machine. It did not participate in any subsequent elections.

NATIONAL DEMOCRATIC UNION (UNIÓN DEMOCRÁTICA NACIONALISTA). The National Democratic Union was formed in 1970 and joined the National Opposition Union (UNO) coalition in 1972. It was led by and was a political vehicle for former vice-president Francisco Roberto Lima, and enjoyed the support of some dissident army officers who disliked the government's tactics in the war with Honduras. Lima ran for the legislature in the 1972 elections, but his victory was subsequently annulled by the Central Council of Elections on a technicality.

NATIONAL REFORMING PARTY (PARTIDO REFORMADOR NACIONAL). The National Reforming Party was established in 1963 as a successor to the outlawed Revolutionary Party of April and May (Partido Revolucionario Abril y Mayo—PRAM). It had support from students and Marxists and was itself outlawed shortly after its founding.

NATIONAL REPUBLICAN ALLIANCE (ALIANZA REPUBLICANA NACIONAL—ARENA). The National Republican Alliance was founded in 1981 by Roberto d'Aubissón, a former major in the Salvadorean army who was forced to "retire" in the face of charges that he was associated with ultra-right wing paramilitary activities in the country. He has indicated that he is opposed to a negotiated settlement of the Salvadorean war, and promised to "exterminate" the guerrillas in three months following the 1982 elections were he elected president. ARENA won 26 percent of the vote and nineteen seats in the 1982 constituent assembly elections. The party advocates free enterprise, strengthening of national security, an all-out war against the revolutionary movement, and elimination of human rights constraints from the armed forces in fighting the war. The party is very much a vehicle for the political ambitions of its leader, d'Aubissón, a vigorous and charismatic figure whom former United States Ambassador to El Salvador, Robert E. White, once described in Congressional testimony as a "pathological killer."

NATIONAL REVOLUTIONARY MOVEMENT (MOVIMIENTO NACIONAL REVOLUCIONARIO – MNR). The National Revolutionary Movement was one of three parties participating in the National Opposition Union in the 1977 election. Founded in 1965, the party was originally supported largely by university students and faculty. It advocates a moderate form of democratic socialism, and has become affiliated with the Socialist International. Its appeals are intellectual, and it has never obtained a broad popular following.

The MNR participated in the first junta which took office after the October 1979 coup, with Guillermo Manuel Ungo, the MNR's principal leader, being its representative. However, the party went into the opposition with the resignation of the first junta in January 1980. Later it helped establish and became part of the Democratic Front, which united several democratic parties, unions, and entrepreneurial groups; and of the Democratic Revolutionary Front, which joined these with mass organizations associated with major guerrilla groups. It did not participate in the 1982 election.

NATIONALIST DEMOCRATIC PARTY (PARTIDO DEMÓCRATA NACIONALISTA). The Nationalist Democratic Party was a small organization led by Major José Alvaro Díaz, who opposed President Oscar Osorio's attempt to insure the election of his choice as a successor, José María Lemus, in 1956. The party disappeared during the Lemus administration.

PARTIDO ACCIÓN RENOVADORA. See PARTY OF RENOVATING ACTION.

PARTIDO COMUNISTA DE EL SALVADOR. See COMMUNIST PARTY OF EL SALVADOR.

PARTIDO DE ACCIÓN NACIONAL. See NATIONAL ACTION PARTY.

PARTIDO DE CONCILIACIÓN NACIONAL. See PARTY OF NATIONAL CONCILIATION.

PARTIDO DEMÓCRATA CRISTIANO. See CHRISTIAN DEMOCRATIC PARTY.

PARTIDO DEMÓCRATA NACIONALISTA. *See* NATIONALIST DEMO-CRATIC PARTY.

PARTIDO DEMOCRÁTICO CONSTITUCIONAL. *See* CONSTITUTIONAL DEMOCRATIC PARTY.

PARTIDO INSTITUCIONAL DEMOCRÁTICO. *See* DEMOCRATIC INSTI-TUTIONAL PARTY.

PARTIDO LABORISTA. *See* LABOR PARTY.

PARTIDO POPULAR SALVADOREÑO. *See* SALVADOREAN POPULAR PARTY.

PARTIDO RADICAL DEMOCRÁTICO. *See* RADICAL DEMOCRATIC PARTY.

PARTIDO REFORMADOR NACIONAL. *See* NATIONAL REFORMING PARTY.

PARTIDO REPUBLICANO DE EVOLUCIÓN NACIONAL. *See* REPUBLI-CAN PARTY OF NATIONAL EVOLUTION.

PARTIDO REVOLUCIONARIO ABRIL Y MAYO. *See* REVOLUTIONARY PARTY OF APRIL AND MAY.

PARTIDO REVOLUCIONARIO DE UNIFICACIÓN DEMÓCRATA. *See* REV-OLUTIONARY PARTY OF DEMOCRATIC UNIFICATION.

PARTIDO REVOLUCIONARIO DE UNIFICACIÓN DEMOCRÁTICA AUTÉNTICO. *See* AUTHENTIC REVOLUTIONARY PARTY OF DEMO-CRATIC UNIFICATION.

PARTIDO REVOLUCIONARIO SALVADOREÑA. *See* SALVADOREAN REVOLUTIONARY PARTY.

PARTIDO UNIONISTA CENTRO AMERICANO. *See* CENTRAL AMERI-CAN UNITY PARTY.

PARTY OF NATIONAL CONCILIATION (PARTIDO DE CONCILIACIÓN NACIONAL—PCN). A government-sponsored, military civilian coalition founded in 1961, the PCN continued to dominate party activity in El Salvador until the coup of October 1979. The successor of the Revolutionary Party of Democratic Unification (Partido Revolucionario de Unificación Democráta—PRUD), it was established by the moderate-to-conservative military leaders who overthrew the more radical leaders who had brought down the regime of Colonel José María Lemus in the bloodless coup of 1960. In the interim between the coups of October 1960 and January 1961, former President Oscar Osorio had reemerged with the support of the student-backed Revolutionary Party of April and May (Partido Revolucionario Abril y Mayo—PRAM) and then founded the reformist Social Democratic Party (Partido Social Demócrata—PSD). Both the PRAM and the PSD were short-lived, being outlawed by the new regime after the second coup.

The PCN monopolized all presidential and legislative elections until 1982 although under one of its leaders, Colonel Julio A. Rivera, president from 1962 to 1967, it liberalized the electoral system and permitted other parties to win legislative seats. Like the PRUD, the PCN sought to emulate the Mexican Institutional Revolutionary Party (PRI), but while it often espoused reform, for political and economic reasons it was unable or unwilling to implement significant change in Salvadorean society.

The PCN was never well-organized, particularly outside the capital, and it functioned only during electoral campaigns. Yet most of its vote came from the more traditional areas of the country, rural and provincial, not from the capital city, which had both the most intense party activity and opposition. The phenomenon is a familiar one in Latin America, attributable to electoral fraud, traditionalism, and government control of rural areas.

President Rivera, who was the first to run for office backed by the newly formed PCN, in 1962, succeeded in imposing on the party's convention in 1967 his hand-picked successor, Colonel Fidel Sánchez Hernández; Sánchez Hernández had been minister of the interior under Rivera, a position which, as in Mexico, tends to be a proving ground for aspiring presidential candidates. Under the Sánchez Hernández regime, El Salvador became engaged in a short, but bitter, war with Honduras in July 1969, which momentarily rallied Salvadoreans around their government, and by extension, the PCN. In the next presidential election (1972), Colonel Arturo Armando Molina narrowly defeated José Napoleón Duarte, leader of the Christian Democratic Party, following which Duarte and other unsuccessful candidates attempted a coup against President Sánchez Hernández, which failed and resulted in their exile. The 1977 elections were so visibly fraudulent that they virtually destroyed the legitimacy of the process itself.

The party participated in the 1982 elections, winning 17 percent of the popular vote and receiving fourteen delegates to the constituent assembly. Although its leaders, with the notable exceptions of the presidents, were mostly civilian and its financing came largely from civilian sources, the party was generally regarded by Salvadoreans as little more than an instrument of the military rulers and the oligarchy.

PARTY OF RENOVATING ACTION (PARTIDO ACCIÓN RENOVADORA —PAR). The PAR was organized in 1944 as a consequence of the "Folded Arms

Strike." In its earliest years, it was little more than a personalistic vehicle for the ambitions of its founder, Colonel José Asencio Menéndez, who ran for the presidency in 1950. From 1950 to 1964, it was the only viable opposition in El Salvador, committed to moderate reform and change. Control was exercised by a group of more traditional military officers, known as the "old line." In a strange, if not bizarre, series of events, the party was literally taken over in 1964 by young radicals, many of them Marxists, who formally "joined" the party just before its national convention, and voted the old-line leaders out of office. At this point, the Central Council of Elections designated the party subversive, and it was outlawed.

POPULAR ORIENTATION PARTY (PARTIDO DE ORIENTACION POPULAR—POP). The Popular Orientation Party is a conservative organization founded by José Alberto Medrano to participate in the 1982 elections. Medrano, a retired general, commanded the national guard in the 1960s, and founded the clandestine ORDEN, a rural paramilitary organization generally thought to be responsible for terrorist activities against rural peasants. Medrano was dismissed by the guard in 1971, and was a candidate for the presidency in the 1972 national elections, supported by the United Democratic Independence Front. The Popular Orientation Party received less than 1 percent of the popular vote in 1982 and no seats in the constituent assembly.

RADICAL DEMOCRATIC PARTY (PARTIDO RADICAL DEMOCRÁTICO —PRD). The Radical Democratic Party was founded in 1959, and advocated an end to military control of the government and land reform. Its radical program insured its prompt demise as the government declared it illegal.

REPUBLICAN PARTY OF NATIONAL EVOLUTION (PARTIDO REPUBLICANO DE EVOLUCIÓN NACIONAL. The Republican Party of National Evolution participated in the legislative elections of 1964 and 1966, and was a personal vehicle for the candidacy of Colonel Luis Roberto Flores, a popular politician of that era. The following for the party was very small, and it disappeared after the 1967 election.

REVOLUTIONARY PARTY OF APRIL AND MAY (PARTIDO REVOLUCIONARIO ABRIL Y MAYO—PRAM). The Revolutionary Party of April and May was founded in 1959. It was a radical movement, sympathetic to the Castro revolution in Cuba, and tried to promote a Fidelista type movement in El Salvador. Its principal leader was Roberto Carlos Delgado, a student leader who was jailed for his opposition to the Lemus regime. The party played a significant role in the short-lived regime presided over by a civilian-military junta of progressive inclination between October 1960 and January 1961. PRAM was declared illegal in 1961 and thereafter disappeared.

REVOLUTIONARY PARTY OF DEMOCRATIC UNIFICATION (PARTIDO

REVOLUCIONARIO DE UNIFICACIÓN DEMÓCRATA–PRUD). The PRUD was formed in 1950 by the military leaders who had seized control in 1948. It was inspired by the example of the Mexican Institutional Revolutionary Party (PRI), which the Salvadorean leaders openly respected and admired, but it never gained the organizational complexity, sophistication, or the popular acceptance of the PRI. In the election of 1950, PRUD nominated Major Oscar Osorio, who had been head of the junta that came into power in 1948. Osorio won the election, with token opposition from another military leader, Colonel José Ascencio Menéndez. In 1956, Osorio hand-picked Lieutenant Colonel José María Lemus to succeed him, and in a controlled election, the PRUD easily won. Lemus eventually alienated most of the PRUD coalition, including his predecessor; he was overthrown in 1960 in a bloodless coup staged by more radical leaders of the army, who had taken the goals of the 1948 "revolution" seriously. They, in turn, were overthrown in early 1961 by other military leaders, more moderate, if not conservative, in their perspective. The PRUD had become so identified with Lemus that his successors decided to abolish the party and form a new one of their own design, the Party of National Conciliation.

SALVADOREAN POPULAR PARTY (PARTIDO POPULAR SALVADOREÑO –PPS). The PPS was founded in 1965 as a coalition of old-line PAR leaders and disaffected PCN members. It participated in the 1967 presidential campaign, nominating Major Alvaro Martínez, a rightist and nationalist who had no particular ideological orientation. The party was supported by business interests and wealthy Salvadoreans, allegedly for leverage over PCN leaders rather than as a serious contender for national power.

The PPS won four of the fifty-two legislative seats in the 1974 election, and four of the fifty-four seats in 1978, the only opposition party in the legislature after 1978, due to the United Opposition (UNO) boycott of the elections. Despite its persistence, the party never was able to mobilize a popular following and relied for its success almost solely on the personalities of its few candidates. The party participated in the 1982 election, receiving 3 percent of the vote and one seat in the assembly.

SALVADOREAN REVOLUTIONARY PARTY (PARTIDO REVOLUCION-ARIO SALVADOREÑO). The Salvadorean Revolutionary Party is the political wing of the Popular Revolutionary Army, an important guerrilla movement in El Salvador. It is, of course, an illegal organization, and does not participate in elections.

SOCIAL CHRISTIAN POPULAR MOVEMENT (MOVIMIENTO POPULAR SOCIAL CRISTIANO). The Social Christian Popular Movement was established in March 1980 by Christian Democrats who opposed the continuation of the Christian Democratic Party in the junta which had taken control of the government in January. Seven of the thirteen members of the executive committee of the PDC withdrew to lead the new party. They claimed that the great majority of the party's leaders and members followed them in this move.

Subsequently, the Social Christian Popular Movement joined with the National Revolutionary Movement (Movimiento Nacional Revolucionario) and four leading trade union federations, and some entrepreneurial groups, to form the Democratic Front. The Democratic Front coalesced with five mass organizations representing the major guerrilla groups opposing the incumbent government, to establish the Democratic Revolutionary Front.

SOCIAL DEMOCRATIC PARTY (PARTIDO SOCIAL DEMÓCRATA— PSD). The Social Democratic Party was founded in 1960 by supporters of former President Oscar Osorio, many of whom had been active in the original Revolutionary Party of Democratic Unification (PRUD). It favored gradual reform in the economy and redistribution of land. It was inactive after 1962.

UNIÓN DEMOCRÁTICA NACIONALISTA. See NATIONAL DEMOCRATIC UNION.

UNITED DEMOCRATIC INDEPENDENT FRONT (FRENTE UNIDO DEMOCRÁTICO INDEPENDIENTE—PUDI). The United Democratic Independent Front participated in the 1972 presidential election, nominating General José Alberto Medrano, who was the former commander of the National Guard and a hero of the Honduran War. The party campaigned on the issues of the government's restrictive policy toward coffee growers, and a "normalization" of relations with Honduras. Its funding seems to have come from the influential Salaverría family in the department of Ahuachapán, which broke with the official National Conciliation Party (PCN) in 1971 over the issue of the government's coffee policy.

Ronald H. McDonald

FALKLAND ISLANDS

The Falkland Islands (referred to by the Argentines as the Islas Malvinas), consist of a group of about 200 islands, with a total land area of 4,700 square miles, lying 480 miles northeast of Cape Horn in the South Atlantic. There are two large islands, East Falkland and West Falkland, where most of the 1,805 people (31 December 1977 estimate) live. Almost all of the population is of British descent, 80 percent were born in the islands, and most had ancestors there in the nineteenth century; some 1,000 tracing their families' residence in the territory back to at least 1850. The population reached its peak at 2,392, in 1931, and has been declining ever since. Males considerably outnumber females.

The Falkland Islands were probably first sighted in 1592 by English explorer John Davis. However, it was 1764 before a small French colony was established at Port Louis in East Falkland. Subsequently, French, British, and Spanish settlements were made and disappeared. In 1820 the Argentine government asserted sovereignty over the Falklands on the basis of earlier Spanish claims, and between 1826 and 1832 an Argentine settlement existed on East Falkland. It left with the arrival of a British force to occupy the islands. However, Argentina never gave up its claim to the Falklands, and since the early 1970s negotiations have been going on about the issue between the British and Argentine governments.

The economy of the territory is based on sheep-raising. It was estimated in 1977 that there were 683,100 sheep in the islands. The major firm in the business is the Falkland Islands Company, established in 1851, which owns about half of the land in the territory. Those working for the company live in company houses, buy in company stores and have been described as living under "semi-feudal" conditions. There is a single trade union, the Falkland Islands General Employees Union, with 500 members, and labor and social legislation provides for minimum wages, workmen's compensation, family allowances, old age pensions, and arbitration of labor disputes.

Since 1845 a legislative council has existed, which until 1951 had a majority of "official" members. In 1949 the first members elected by universal adult suffrage were chosen. Under the constitution of November 1977 there are six elected members and two ex-officio ones in the legislative council. The capital city, Stanley (estimated population in 1975, 1,050) has three elected members, East and West Falkland one each and one member is elected at large in the country districts. The executive council, or cabinet, consists of two ex-officio members, two unofficial ones appointed by the governor, and two elected members of the legislative council chosen by the legislature's own elected members.

Elections are held on the basis of independent individual candidacies. The Falkland Islands are the one nation or territory of America which does not have and never has had any political parties.

In April 1982 Argentine troops occupied the islands, provoking an armed conflict with Great Britain.

Bibliography

British Information Services. *Fact Sheet: The Falkland Islands and Dependencies*, May 1978.

Robert J. Alexander

FRENCH GUIANA

French Guiana, located on the northeast coast of South America, consists of a narrow coastal plain where 90 percent of the people live and an interior area which is largely uninhabited. There are an estimated 57,600 people (December 1976 estimate) in the territory, of whom 30,500 live in the capital city, Cayenne.

The Spanish were the first Europeans to try to settle in French Guiana, establishing a colony at Cayenne in 1503. However, they did not stay. Throughout the first half of the seventeenth century, there was a series of ephemeral French companies based on Rouen and Paris which sought to colonize the area. The French definitively established themselves in Cayenne in 1643. Louis XIV's great minister Colbert established a company for the systematic colonization of the territory in 1663. During this period there were several Dutch and British challenges to the French in the area, but French control was firmly established by 1667.

During the next century there were substantial drainage and irrigation works established in the coastal area, and coffee and cocoa were grown on a substantial scale. Much of this development was under the supervision of Jesuit priests, and when the Jesuits were expelled in 1762 most of the agricultural enterprises which they had established declined and ultimately disappeared.

When the Indians retreated into the interior to escape slavery, the French brought in African slaves. During the French Revolution, slavery was abolished in 1794, but was soon afterwards reestablished by Napoleon. During this period, too, the first short-lived prison colony was established in the area.

After being captured by the British in 1809, French Guiana was restored to French sovereignty in 1817. Slavery was finally abolished by the Second French Republic in 1848, whereupon most of the ex-slaves abandoned the plantations and the surviving irrigation and drainage works, to become subsistence farmers or to live in Cayenne.

Under Napoleon III the prison colony at Devil's Island was established, in 1852. From then until 1939 some 70,000 prisoners were brought to Devil's Island. The prison colony was abolished in 1947.

The French Guianese economy which has developed since World War II is a peculiar one. Although about a quarter of the people are still engaged in shifting agriculture, most of the rest of them live in Cayenne and one or two other small towns. The country's only exports of any consequence are shrimp, which are processed by three U.S. companies, and some tropical wood, and they provide only about 5 percent of the income needed for the territory's imports. Rice, corn, manioc, bananas, and sugar are grown for internal consumption.

However, the largest part of the income of French Guiana comes from France. In 1979 it was estimated that 11,000 of the 18,000 employees in the territory were French civil servants who, whether from France or from French Guiana, receive a 40 percent overseas pay bonus on their basic salaries. About 950 local workers and 900 people from France are employed in the missile launching area at Kourou, established in the late 1960s by the de Gaulle government.

Since the French Revolution of 1848 all residents of French Guiana have been French citizens. Since 1877 French Guiana has been represented in the French parliament, and at the present time, the territory has one senator and one deputy in the French National Assembly. Since 1946 French Guiana has been an Overseas Department of France, with the same juridical status as a department in the metropolis.

There is a general council of the department, consisting of representatives of the sixteen cantons into which the territory is divided. It administers the budget drawn from local resources and some French government contributions. There is also a regional council which includes the members of the general council plus the department's deputy in the French National Assembly and a representative of the city of Cayenne. It decides on how the money from FIDOM, the French government's Fund for Investment in the Overseas Departments, should be invested in French Guiana. It also provides the input for the department to the French Government's economic plan.

Political parties in French Guiana have for the most part been branches of or associated with the parties in metropolitan France. Their strength in the territory to some degree has tended to reflect their strength in metropolitan France. These groups have taken differing positions on whether French Guiana should remain an Overseas Department as was decreed soon after World War II, or should be given a wide degree of autonomy. In recent years, there has appeared some support for the total independence of the territory, although it still represents only a minute part of the electorate.

The electoral turnout in French Guiana has been relatively low, compared with metropolitan France. This has been particularly the case in constitutional referendums; in that of 1972 it was as low as 27 percent. In presidential elections, the turnout has been higher, being 66 percent in 1965, but only 47 percent in 1969 and 58 percent in 1974. In legislative elections for members of the French parliament and the local general council, voter participation has run from 41 percent to 60 percent in postwar elections.

Bibliography

Personal contacts of the writer.

Gerard Brasseur. *La Guyane Française: Un Bilan de Trente Années.* Notes & Etudes Documentaires, 26, Dec. 1978.

Le Monde, Paris newspaper, various issues.

Political Parties

COMMUNISTS. There never has been organized in French Guiana a Communist Party, either as a federation of the French Communist Party or as an autonomous group. However, since World War II, the Union of Guyanese Workers (Union des Travailleurs Guyanais), which was affiliated until 1964 with the French General Confederation of Labor (CGT), the Communist-controlled central labor group, and has since then continued to have very close relations with the CGT, has been very active politically. It has backed candidates and functioned almost like a political party as well as a trade union organization. It has recently supported the idea of independence for the territory. However, in the 1978 election for the French Chamber of Deputies it backed the candidate supported by the Socialists and other Left groups.

FÉDERATION SOCIALISTE SFIO DE LA GUYANE FRANÇAISE. See SOCIALISTS.

GAULLISTS. One of the major tendencies in the politics of French Guiana since World War II has been that of the Gaullists, the supporters of General Charles de Gaulle. De Gaulle himself received an overwhelming majority in the 1958 election and won by more than two to one in French Guiana in that of 1965. In 1969, the voters supported de Gaulle's candidate, Georges Pompidou, by more than two to one; but in the second-round presidential election of 1974, the candidate of the heirs of de Gaulle, Valéry Giscard d'Estaing, defeated the Socialist François Mitterand by only 5410 votes to 4785 in the territory.

During most of de Gaulle's presidency his party, the Republican National Union (Union National Républicane—UNR) had a majority in the department. Robert Vignon, although originally a Socialist, represented this majority in the French Senate from 1962 to 1971.

Subsequent to de Gaulle's death, as in metropolitan France, the Gaullists in French Guiana split between the Neo-Gaullists of Jacques Chirac, in the Popular Republican Rally (Rassemblément Populaire Républicaine—RPR) and the supporters of Valéry Giscard d'Estaing, grouped in the Union for French Democracy (Union pour la Démocratie Française—UDF). Héctor Riviérez, the Gaullist deputy from French Guiana, headed the RPR there and has continued to win elections to the chamber since 1967.

In the 1978 parliamentary election, the forces of "the majority" as the French press refers to it, were divided. Claude Ho A. Chuck, president of the general council of the department and leader of the Movement for Guyanese Progress (Mouvement pour le Progrès Guyanais—MPG), ran against RPR candidate Héctor Riviérez, as the nominee of the UDF. The MPG is a moderate autonomist party, advocating that the territory have more right to determine its own economic policy. In 1978, the supporters of President Valéry Giscard d'Estaing had seven of the fifteen members of the general council of the department.

GUYANESE MOVEMENT FOR DECOLONIZATION (MOUVEMENT GUYANAIS DE DÉCOLONIZATION). The Guyanese Movement for Decolonization represents those in French Guiana who seek for it total independence from France. They remain a very small group, having received only 3.5 percent of the total vote in the parliamentary elections of 1973. They urged their supporters to abstain in the 1978 election.

GUYANESE POPULAR MOVEMENT (MOUVEMENT POPULAIRE GUYANAIS). See SOCIALISTS.

GUYANESE SOCIALIST PARTY (PARTI SOCIALISTE GUYANAIS). See SOCIALISTS.

MOUVEMENT GUYANAIS DE DÉCOLONIZATION. See GUYANESE MOVEMENT FOR DECOLONIZATION.

MOUVEMENT POPULAIRE GUYANAIS. See SOCIALISTS.

MOUVEMENT POUR LE PROGRÈS GUYANAIS. See GAULLISTS.

MOVEMENT FOR GUYANESE PROGRESS (MOUVEMENT POUR LE PROGRÈS GUYANAIS). See GAULLISTS.

PARTI RADICAL. See RADICAL PARTY.

PARTI SOCIALISTE GUYANAIS. See SOCIALISTS.

POPULAR REPUBLICAN RALLY (RASSEMBLÉMENT POPULAIRE RÉPUBLICAINE – RPR). See GAULLISTS.

RADICAL PARTY (PARTI RADICAL). Before World War II, the Radical Party was one of the two major parties with representation in French Guiana. However, as has been the case in metropolitan France, its influence has declined since then. The party in the department more or less closely associated with the metropolitan Radical Party is the Rally for the Defense of Guiana (Rassemblément pour la Défense de la Guyane). This party is a strong supporter of the continuation of the status of French Guiana as an Overseas Department. However, it is a weak party, without any representation either in the French parliament or the general council of the department.

RALLY FOR THE DEFENSE OF GUYANA (RASSEMBLEMENT POUR LA DÉFENSE DE LA GUYANE). See RADICAL PARTY.

RASSEMBLEMENT POPULAIRE REPUBLICAINE. See GAULLISTS.

RASSEMBLEMENT POUR LA DÉFENSE DE LA GUYANE. *See* RADICAL PARTY.

REPUBLICAN NATIONAL UNION (UNION NATIONALE RÉPUBLICAINE —UNR). *See* GAULLISTS.

SOCIALIST FEDERATION OF SFIO (FEDERATION SOCIALISTE SFIO DE LA GUYANE FRANÇAISE). *See* SOCIALISTS.

SOCIALISTS. Since before World War II, the Socialists have been one of the two major political currents in French Guiana. Until 1956 they were united in the Socialist Federation of SFIO (Federation Socialiste SFIO de la Guyane Française), part of the French Socialist Party. However, in that year the party's member of the French Chamber of Deputies, Justin Catayée, led a split in the group, which resulted in the formation of the separate Guyanese Socialist Party (Parti Socialiste Guyanais—PSG). The division was the result of a desire for autonomy from the French party by many of the Guianese socialists and personal rivalries among the leaders.

The PSG took most of the party members and voters with it. However, until the middle 1960s, at least, the SFIO federation still had eight members of the Cayenne city council, compared to the fourteen members of the PSG. More recently, the PSG has far surpassed its rival in strength.

In spite of the dissidence between the two Socialist groups, they sometimes cooperated. In the mid-1960s, they formed a coalition, the Democratic Front (Front Démocratique), together with a third party, the Guyanese Popular Movement (Mouvement Populaire Guyanais—MPG). The MPG was a party formed by a group of young professionals and students of socialist inclination, but unhappy with the two existing Socialist parties. It does not seem to have survived into the 1970s. In the French parliament, the members of the PSG have formed part of the caucus of the French Socialist Party.

Since 1971, the senator from French Guiana has been a member of the Parti Socialiste Guyanais. Until 1978, he was Léopold Héder, who was also president of the general council of the department from 1970 to 1973. Héder had succeeded Justin Catayée as member of the French Chamber of Deputies in 1960, when Catayée was killed in an airplane accident, but had been defeated by the Gaullist, Héctor Riviérez, in 1967 and had never regained his seat in the Chamber. In 1978 Héder was succeeded as senator by Henri Agarante, also a PSG member. At the end of 1978, the PSG had four of the fifteen members of the general council of French Guiana.

Both Socialist parties have supported an autonomous status for French Guiana.

UNION DES TRAVAILLEURS GUYANAIS. *See* COMMUNISTS.

UNION FOR FRENCH DEMOCRACY (UNION POUR LA DEMOCRATIE FRANÇAISE—UDF). *See* GAULLISTS.

UNION NATIONALE RÉPUBLICAINE. *See* GAULLISTS.

UNION OF GUYANESE WORKERS (UNION DES TRAVAILLEURS GUY-ANAIS). *See* COMMUNISTS.

UNION POUR LA DÉMOCRATIE FRANÇAISE. *See* GAULLISTS.

Robert J. Alexander

GRENADA

The southernmost island in the Windward chain of the Caribbean's Lesser Antilles, Grenada lies 90 miles north of Trinidad and 70 miles south of Saint Vincent. Grenada's 133 square miles is mainly steep and mountainous since the island is of volcanic origin. Over 100,000 people inhabit Grenada, giving the island a human population density of roughly 800 per square mile—the highest in the Leewards or Windwards. The state of Grenada, which achieved full political independence from Great Britain in February 1974, also includes two smaller islands of the Grenadine group to the north: Carriacou, with about 7,000 people; and tiny Petit-Martinique with a population of fewer than 1,000.

Grenada's populace is overwhelmingly of African descent, most Grenadians being either black or of "mixed" ancestry—a distinction with strong political overtones. A few descendants of indentured Indians and a tiny white minority also inhabit Grenada. The populace is principally rural and agricultural with many rural dwellers owning or leasing small landplots.

Columbus sighted Grenada on his third voyage in 1498, although the island was not settled permanently by Europeans until after the island Caribs, the original inhabitants, "ceded" Grenada to French settlers in 1650. Grenada came under the domination of the French Crown in 1674, and for the next century French planters imported slaves to cultivate tobacco, indigo, and some sugarcane. This early French colonization accounts for the ongoing persistence of Catholicism, the religion followed by most rural Grenadians, and the French-based patois spoken throughout the countryside. The British captured Grenada from France in 1763, and the two countries intermittently contested the island for three decades until British rule there was unequivocally established in 1796.

Shortly after British colonization in 1763, the Old Representative System of government modeled after the British parliament, was transferred to Grenada. In the first decades of parliamentary-style rule, legislative matters were often less important than the question of whether or not Roman Catholics (French planters) were to have political rights. Speaking very generally, most of the nineteenth century saw the colony governed by the Old Representative System: an executive branch, composed of the governor and nominated council, held power along with an elected legislative assembly which was responsible for taxation. The Old Representative System was abolished in 1875, and four years later Grenada became a Crown Colony. Thereafter, all of the legislative council, formerly elected by the island's white property holders, were nominated and served at the pleasure of the governor.

In the years between the British takeover of Grenada and the demise of parliamentary government there, slave emancipation (1838) released the black populace to establish a semblance of a highland peasantry subsisting on patches of land interspersed with larger estates. Thereafter, the white planter class, which had earlier depended on sugarcane supported by preferred British prices and cultivated by a captive labor force, found their position less and less tenable. The rescinding of West Indian price preferences in 1846 and the depression of the 1880s all but eliminated sugarcane from Grenada by the late nineteenth century. As cane disappeared so did many white planters, their estates often being purchased by persons of mixed blood. By the turn of the century, cacao and nutmeg had supplanted cane. Also during the nineteenth century, many of the black "lower classes" established their own economic independence by migrating to Trinidad for higher wages and then returning home, an adaptation their descendants have followed into the late twentieth century.

Politics in Grenada had been the exclusive domain of white property owners throughout the nineteenth century, domination that became the object of increasing unrest among the colored and black populace by the early twentieth century. In 1914, T. A. Marryshow, a colored Grenadian, organized the Representative Government Association and protested Crown Colony rule, arguing for elected members in the legislative council. The colonial office allowed four of the fourteen legislators to be elected after World War I, a concession roughly coincident with politically oriented demonstrations in Saint George's in 1920. Pan-Caribbean political consciousness, partially inspired by serious economic depression, was heightened during the next two decades. The number of elected legislators on Grenada was increased to seven in 1936, although property and income voting qualifications were maintained. In 1951 constitutional reform granted universal adult suffrage and called for a majority of elected legislators, although the colony's governor was still appointed by London. Political advances in Grenada had been achieved not least by tireless efforts by Marryshow who by this time had become a labor leader and spokesman for the laboring classes of the entire English-speaking Caribbean.

At the same time Grenada's people achieved voting rights, a flamboyant black political leader—Eric Matthew Gairy—emerged to become the central figure in Grenadian politics for the next three decades. Born in Grenada in 1922, Gairy was a political organizer first in Aruba among the migrant British West Indian refinery workers there in the 1940s. He returned to Grenada in 1949 and began to organize the Grenada People's Party which soon became the Grenada United Labour Party (GULP). In 1950 Gairy registered the Grenada Manual and Mental Workers' Union and made a series of wage demands upon the island's main employers. A general strike, marked by sporadic violence and arson, followed in 1951, which culminated in the granting of sizeable wage increases for workers and personal victory for Gairy.

Gairy's GULP party contested the general elections in 1951, 1954, 1957, 1961, and 1962 with mixed success, the most formidable competition coming from the Grenada National Party (GNP). The latter drew its support from the urban, colored, Anglican, middle-class voters in Saint George's, while Gairy's GULP supporters were mainly rural, black, Catholic, and members of the laboring class. Grenada was a member of the West Indian Federation from 1958 to 1962. During this time, the ministerial system of government was introduced to Grenada. GULP politician George Clyne became chief minister of Grenada in 1961. In 1962, amid charges that GULP and Gairy had misused government funds, the GNP won general elections, and Herbert A. Blaize of Carriacou became chief minister of the state.

Grenada achieved Associated Statehood with Britain in March 1967. Four months later, a general election returned seven GULP candidates to office versus three for the GNP. Gairy became the state's premier, then Grenada's prime minister as the island became independent in 1974. His actions were always tainted by accusations of financial impropriety, consorting with criminals, and bizarre occult beliefs. Gairy's political regime became increasingly repressive. The notorious "mongoose" gang, Gairy's local henchmen, occasionally intimidated rival politicians and looted shops of Gairy's nonsupporters. In March 1979, while Gairy was in New York at the United Nations, his government was terminated forcibly in a "revolution" that consisted of capturing key buildings and the radio station in Saint George's.

The leader of the coup was a political rival, Maurice Bishop, a London-educated lawyer. Bishop had in the decade of the 1970s emerged as the leader of the opposition New Jewel Movement and was briefly imprisoned at the time of independence. Bishop is now prime minister of Grenada's People's Revolutionary Government (PRG). During the first year of the PRG, Grenada embarked on a socialist path emphasizing economic improvement and an avowal to end the island's chronically high unemployment. A new airport near Saint George's is being built with Cuban aid. Regionally and internationally, Grenada's newly developed relationships with Cuba have caused American and British concern. Middle-class Grenadians, many of whom have left Grenada, have moreover expressed concern about Grenada's political future. Bishop has openly suggested that traditional Western elections may be "irrelevant" for Grenada and has postponed them indefinitely.

Bibliography

D. Sinclair DaBreo. *The Grenadian Revolution.* M.A.P.S. Castries, St. Lucia, 1979.

Patrick Emmanuel. *Crown Colony Politics in Grenada, 1917–1961.* Institute of Social and Economic Research, University of the West Indies, Cave Hill, Barbados, 1979.

A. S. Singham. *The Hero and the Crowd in a Colonial Polity.* Yale University Press, New Haven, 1968.

Political Parties

GRENADA NATIONAL PARTY (GNP). The GNP was organized in 1955 by a dental surgeon trained in the United States, Dr. John Watts. Watts was thereafter a political leader who never sought elected office himself. The GNP derives support from the colored middle classes of Saint George's and has therefore usually suffered a lack of broad-based patronage by the black workers of the Grenadian countryside. The most impressive GNP electoral showing — when the party won the general elections of 1962 — was partly because of the GULP's negative financial image. Also, GNP candidates campaigned hard in favor of potential political affiliation with Trinidad. This issue won the support of many of the Grenadian peasantry since a majority of them have relatives who have migrated to Trinidad.

Unlike its rival labor party, the GNP has a highly organized bureaucracy. The governing body of the party is the general council made up of party leaders and candidates, and party organization is composed of various types of membership. The GNP has occasionally offered specific plans for Grenada's economic improvement. A main goal of the GNP, as published in their official bulletin, is "The development of both the rich and the poor in Grenada."

The GNP has usually received strong support in Carriacou, the home of GNP candidate Herbert A. Blaize, who was Grenada's chief minister after the 1962 elections. Carriacouans consider themselves more sober and responsible than most Grenadians, and anti-Gairy sentiment was always strong in the smaller island.

GRENADA PEOPLE'S PARTY. *See* GRENADA UNITED LABOUR PARTY.

GRENADA UNITED LABOUR PARTY (GULP). The Grenada United Labour Party was formed in time for the 1951 general elections by Eric Gairy, and faced little organized opposition until the establishment of the Grenada National Party in 1955. From the outset the GULP was based on Gairy's charisma and his humble peasant origins. As head of the party as well as of the Grenada Manual and Mental Workers' Union, Gairy derived his support almost entirely from among the island's poorest black laborers and farmers. "Uncle Gairy" led crowds of angry protesters during the labor disturbances of 1950–1951, emerging as an articulate young hero who stood his ground against white planters and government officers.

Gairy held personal control over his party, relying on his own magnetism rather than organization to draw people together. Party supporters knew that a personal audience with Gairy was the surest way to get things done. Gairy's dual role as party leader and head of the trade unions moreover solidified his personal control; party and union dues therefore often served the same purposes. The hallmark of GULP political activities was a mass rally ("family" meetings), the highlight of which was an oration by Gairy.

Eric Gairy's personal control over the GULP was evident even during the years 1957–1961, when he was denied the vote and the right to hold public office for leading a steel band through an opponent's political meeting. Gairy then ran stand-in candidates for "his" seat in the legislative council, assuring his supporters that he would run the government regardless of who was elected.

NEW JEWEL MOVEMENT. The New Jewel Movement (Joint Endeavor for Welfare, Education, and Liberation) was formed in the early 1970s in opposition to Gairy's domination of Grenada. Cyclostyled *New Jewel* newspapers circulated throughout the countryside deploring "Gairyism," and calling for his overthrow. New Jewel candidates won six of fifteen contested legislative seats during the general election of 1976.

The "Jewel" acronym has now (1980) been dropped in favor of the People's Revolutionary Government (PRG) by the founder of the New Jewel Movement and Grenada's prime minister, Maurice Bishop. Bishop describes party philosophy as nationalist and socialist-leaning along the lines of Jamaica and Tanzania. Bishop, taking office as a result of the 1979 coup, accused Gairy of illegal financial dealings and collusion with Chile. Gairy replied that Bishop was a Communist. Since assuming office, Bishop has insisted that Grenada is nonaligned and that the island intends to follow her own independent path.

The New Jewel Movement or PRG is supported by an assortment of disenchanted intellectuals, the unemployed, and Grenadians opposed to Eric Gairy of whom there were many at the time of the coup. The forceful overthrow of the GULP regime was physically achieved by armed "youths," a point stressed in reporting of the event by the international news media.

Bonham C. Richardson